THE COMPLETE WORKS OF HARRIET TAYLOR MILL

INDIANA UNIVERSITY PRESS ◉ BLOOMINGTON AND INDIANAPOLIS

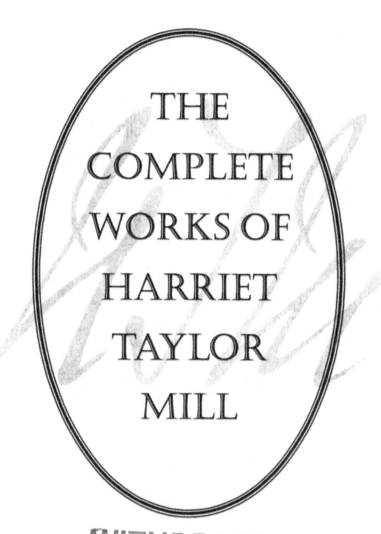

THE COMPLETE WORKS OF HARRIET TAYLOR MILL

Jo Ellen Jacobs, Editor

Paula Harms Payne, Assistant Editor

This book is a publication of

Indiana University Press
601 North Morton Street
Bloomington, IN 47404-3797 USA

http://www.indiana.edu/~iupress

Telephone orders 800-842-6796
Fax orders 812-855-7931
Orders by email iuporder@indiana.edu

Library of Congress Cataloging-in-Publication Data

Mill, Harriet Hardy Taylor, 1807-1858.
[Works. 1998]
The complete works of Harriet Taylor Mill / Jo Ellen Jacobs, editor,
Paula Harms Payne, assistant editor.
p.   cm.
Includes bibliographical references (p.   ) and index.
ISBN 0-253-33393-8 (cloth : alk. paper)
1. Women—History—19th century. 2. Women's rights. 3. Sex role—
Great Britain. 4. Domestic violence. 5. Mill, Harriet Hardy
Taylor, 1807-1858—Correspondence. 6. Mill, John Stuart,
1806-1873—Correspondence. 7. Philosophers—England—
Correspondence. I. Jacobs, Jo Ellen, date. II. Payne, Paula
Harms. III. Title.
HQ1154.M474 1998
305.42'09—dc21   97-50264

1 2 3 4 5   03 02 01 00 99 98

For the generations of women
in search of a history

especially those closest to us,
Cecil Staser, Patricia Workman
Frances Kramer Harms
Megan Elizabeth Jacobs and Emily Christine Jacobs

CONTENTS

Acknowledgments ix

Introduction xi

Textual Introduction xxxvii

Chronology xli

Section One: Writings on Women

1. EDUCATION OF WOMEN 3

2. MARRIAGE AND DIVORCE 15

3. WOMEN'S RIGHTS 27

4. VIOLENCE AND DOMESTIC VIOLENCE 75

Section Two: Writings on Other Issues

5. ETHICS 135

6. RELIGION 157

7. ARTS 165

8. MISCELLANEOUS 223

CONTENTS

Section Three: Letters

9. TO JOHN STUART MILL   319

10. TO FAMILY AND FRIENDS   379

11. TO JOHN TAYLOR   437

12. TO HELEN TAYLOR   507

Hardy Family Tree   589

References   591

General Index   595

Index of Documents   601

Acknowledgments

Millikin University helped provide the time and resources for the long work of transcription and editing in Illinois and London in the form of my appointment as Griswold Distinguished Professor of Philosophy. I will always appreciate that faith in my work. Millikin also made it possible to spend two hardworking but glorious summers with an extraordinary student, Amy Kuhl. Amy's talent at reading the nearly illegible handwriting of HTM, her research persistence, her careful proofreading, and her good cheer and enthusiasm made our association with this undergraduate researcher a joy. She also prepared the HTM motif for the title page.

The British Library of Political and Economic Sciences not only houses HTM's manuscripts in their archives, it also houses three dedicated librarians whose patience and willingness to bear the antics of the three Americans for weeks at a time was a blessing. Thank you, Angela Raspin, Sue Donnelly, and Emma Taverner. Librarians at the following institutions generously answered our questions, and many took extra care to find unindexed manuscripts: Eastern Illinois University; Millikin University; Yale University; Kings College, Cambridge; and the Mortlock Library of South Australiana. Special thanks to Prue McDonald in Australia for help locating the "History of the Hardy Family" and Hardy letters. We will always remember Ann Robson's graceful encouragement at the beginning of this project.

We are grateful to Mary Ellen Poole, Millikin University; Stephen Canfield, Eastern Illinois University; and Jean Guitton, Georgia College for their help in translating the French passages. Deciphering poor handwriting in a number of different languages is like playing a nightmarish word game. We value the help, but accept responsibility for any mistakes.

Appreciating secretaries is easy when they are as good as Tammie Powell at Millikin University. Thank you for adding to your already heavy workload!

We would also like to acknowledge the listserves we contacted, especially Victoria, whose members found some of the more obscure references. The Lincoln Lounge crew—Mary Ellen Poole, Edward Yonan, and Kevin Murphy—patiently listened to the ups and downs of this book while feeding Jo Ellen gyros. The summits sustained us!

Finally, life would not be as worthwhile nor work as enjoyable without Gary Jacobs and Stephen Payne. As they begin their own histories, Megan and Emily inspire us to look to the future as well as the past of brave, smart women.

Introduction

Virtually all that has been written about Harriet Taylor Mill focuses on her relationship with John Stuart Mill, and nearly all of these remarks have been vitriolic and uninsightful. S. E. Henshaw announced in 1874, "Men have been blinded by affection, and bewitched by womankind, . . . [but] John Stuart Mill out-Herods them all" (523). Biographers extend the view that John was "besotted," "bewitched," and "charmed" by Harriet, whom Thomas Carlyle called "a dangerous looking woman and engrossed with a dangerous passion" (quoted in Hayek 82). In a calmer voice, Alexander Bain claims JSM was in a "state of subjection" to HTM which "violates our sense of due proportion in the relationship of human beings" (171). Diana Trilling reveals part of the justification for these views of Harriet when she declares that HTM was "no woman, no real woman—the letters . . . show no touch of true femininity, no taint of the decent female" (119-120). Even less flattering, Ruth Borchard proclaims that Harriet's "morbid inclinations" resulted in an interest in domestic violence, and "this preoccupation with, and passionate railing against [domestic violence] denote that some primitive spring in Harriet herself was touched. A trace of masochism is part of a normal woman's psychology; it fits her for the job of childbirth. But Harriet's . . . hungry interest in sadistic treatment of women . . . point[s] to a deep-seated masochism unfitting her for normal physical love" (66-67). The portraits of Harriet as a frigid meddler in John's work do not represent ancient voices from the past, but continue to be presented, usually in slightly more disguised language, by JSM's biographers and historians of philosophy.

The reasons for this misevaluation and blindness are complicated.[1] After

---

1. See my "The Lot of Gifted Ladies is Hard: A Study of Harriet Taylor Mill Criticism." *Hypatia's Daughters*, ed. Linda Lopez McAlister (Bloomington: Indiana University Press, 1995),

reading more than 500 pages of her writing collected in this volume, readers will not replace the myth of "the overbearing shrew who bewitched poor dear John Stuart Mill" with a myth of "the martyr genius woman who was the source of all the important ideas John published as his own." The truth lies somewhere in the murky middle. Harriet Taylor Mill was a complex woman who composed a complicated life involving three children; an estranged husband, John Taylor; and a man she loved passionately and with whom she collaborated intellectually, John Stuart Mill. Finding a way to construct such a life took consummate skill in a society that disallowed divorce, prevented married women from maintaining financial independence, and discouraged women from obtaining a liberal arts education.

The difficulty in characterizing Harriet Taylor Mill begins with her name. In nearly all of history of philosophy scholarship in which she is mentioned, scholars refer to her as "Mrs. Taylor," "Mrs. Mill," or just "Harriet," while JSM is usually referred to simply as "Mill" (see, for example, Glassman, ch. 3). The appellation "Mrs. Mill" seems inappropriate, since both she and John were disgusted with the idea of marriage as ownership. JSM even wrote a formal renunciation of all legal rights marriage would offer him (*CW*: XXI, 97-99). Neither of the partners viewed Harriet as John's mistress in any sense of the term. The remaining names, Harriet Hardy and HTM, also seem limiting and inappropriate. Harriet Hardy was her mother's name as well as her own, and the initials HTM sound more like a corporation than a person. Using only her first name, "Harriet," hardly seems to present her as an important intellectual figure in the history of philosophy. Out of respect for her feminism, we have refused to use the title of "Mrs." and instead opt to use the initials HTM, or the informal "Harriet."[2] Neither of the designations seems to capture who she was, but perhaps the history of philosophy would be approached differently if students studied Immanuel, René, and Baruch instead of Kant, Descartes, and Spinoza. In any case, forgive us the oddity of appellations.

Harriet was born in 1807 and married John Taylor when she was eighteen. She gave birth to two children, Herbert and Algernon, within the first four years of her marriage. A few months after Algernon's birth, Harriet met John Stuart Mill. Their friendship quickly spiraled into love during Harriet's pregnancy with Helen, her third and final child, who was conceived when Algernon was less than nine months old. Harriet also

---

for all the sordid details of the history of opinions of HTM.

2. John Stuart Mill will likewise be referred to as "JSM" or "John." John Taylor will always be referred to by his full name or by his last name, so anytime "John" is used alone, the referent will be JSM.

began her publishing career during this pregnancy. She published poems, book reviews, and articles in the *Monthly Repository*. During this period she also drafted many of her essays and notes on women's education, marriage, divorce, ethics, religion, and the arts. All of this writing appears in Sections One and Two of this text.

When Helen was two years old, Harriet Taylor Mill completed a long article for the Society for the Diffusion of Useful Knowledge, an organization dedicated to dispersing educational materials to the working classes. The same year, after a brief separation from her husband, HTM organized living arrangements in order to provide for both the continuation of her intimate friendship with JSM and for her formal marriage with her husband. Helen lived full-time with her mother, while Algernon and Herbert visited when they were not in boarding school. John spent weekends and evenings with Harriet, and he traveled frequently with her during the following two decades. Yet her letters reveal that the first years of these new living arrangements were difficult ones as Harriet and John tried to negotiate the dimensions of their growing relationship. They also experienced recurrent health problems, and they faced constant gossip.

The next phase of Harriet's life included her closest collaboration with John. In the 1840s and early 1850s, Harriet co-authored a number of newspaper articles, despite a near-invalid condition caused by consumption and partial paralysis. During this same period, she completed one chapter of *Principles of Political Economy,* the "Enfranchisement of Women" for the *Westminster Review,* and a pamphlet on a domestic violence bill before parliament. Harriet and John shared ideas about women's rights which they wrote jointly. John Taylor died in 1849, and Harriet and John married in 1851. In the interval between Taylor's death and Harriet's remarriage, she and JSM collaborated on a number of newspaper articles on domestic violence. Harriet also worked with John on the manuscript that would become *On Liberty,* as well as his *Autobiography,* both published after her death in 1858.

Preliminary answers can be given to two important questions: What was the quality of her mind? and, What was the content of her character? First, the breadth of HTM's knowledge is admirable. She knew French, German, Italian, Greek, and Latin well enough to insert quotes and phrases in these languages into her informal notes to herself as well as her published works. In addition, Harriet's writing includes quotes from philosophers, poets, novelists, essayists, historians, and thinkers from a dozen different centuries and half a dozen countries. Harriet read voraciously everything from the daily newspapers to Renaissance histories of Venice to novels by Dickens and George Sand. Her knowledge of women's history is humbling. Yet there was nothing precious about her intellect. Harriet was practical enough to discern that the gold rush in California might require the kind of drugs John Taylor sold, and she could direct the extermination of a rat in their house that was plaguing JSM while she vacationed a continent away—a task he could not accomplish on his own. Her practicality was also political. HTM recognized the implications of Victorian sexual politics in her own life as well as in the lives of others. She wrote about women's suffrage, women's education, marriage, divorce, equality, and domestic violence because she wanted to understand the politics of being a woman. She also dared to publish some of those thoughts.

Sections One and Two consist of all her writing, from intimate scraps of papers, notes, and multiple drafts of poems and essays, as well as fully polished, published essays, chapters, and newspaper articles. The chapter titles of this volume comprise a list of the subjects she wrote about, including ethics, religion, arts, historical figures, political economy, and, of course, her extensive writing on women's issues. In nearly all of these categories, Harriet composed several pieces on each general topic. On domestic violence, for example, she wrote ten newspaper articles and a penny pamphlet. On the topic of the arts, Harriet created poems, penned book reviews, drafted essays on the unities of the arts, and jotted down travel journals listing and evaluating Italian Renaissance art in Florence, Venice, and northern Italy. She was a curious woman interested in a very broad collection of ideas.

Harriet Taylor Mill wrote like Henri Matisse painted—with large, passionate strokes. Her ideas were not neatly constructed and carefully articulated. HTM had big and sometimes messy thoughts. She was also very astute. For example, when JSM showed her Comte's letters, Harriet immediately saw the blatant sexism inherent in Comte's argument that women would be permanently subjected to men because of their physically smaller brains. Her response was not a carefully crafted criticism of each of Comte's ludicrous arguments, but ripe, open contempt for such a position (see pp. 31-32 and 337-338). Furthermore, twenty years or more before the ideas were published in John's name alone, Harriet notes the importance not only of the quantity but also the quality of pleasure when she writes to JSM that he must be the one to teach about "the higher . . . kind of enjoyment" (p. 24; see also pp. 7 and 12).

As early as 1831, Harriet also recognized that "every human being has a right to all personal freedom which does not interfere with the happiness of some other" (p. 19). The echo of this idea in *On Liberty* is unmistakable. Furthermore, Harriet proclaims that if by moral principles is meant those that an individual struggles to discern using her or his own intellect, "then eccentricity should be prima facie evidence for the existence of principle" (p. 138). The passage in *On Liberty* decrying the "tyranny of opinion" and claiming that "in order to break that tyranny . . . people should be eccentric" parallels Harriet's expression of the idea written a quarter century earlier. In HTM's personal notebooks, she regrets the general lack of moral reasoning, but claims that this conformity is because "there have not been experiments yet" in possible ways of life (p. 231). These words reverberate in *On Liberty*'s words, "so it is that there should be different experiments of living." HTM's phrase, "Truth has so many sides, one is always telling <u>one</u> side" (p. 232) is the core of chapter 2 of *On Liberty*. These central concepts in *On Liberty* first appear in the hasty writing of Harriet Taylor Mill.

The letters serve as proof that the life that Harriet and John led together was one filled with work on manuscripts and talk about political, philosophical, practical, and personal ideas. Anyone who has read all of Harriet Taylor Mill's writing would find that evidence for this conclusion abounds. However, the historians of philosophy who have written about Harriet conclude that either HTM forced JSM to have certain bad ideas (Hagberg, Himmelfarb) or HTM was completely ineffective in contributing any ideas to JSM's [*sic*] work (Loesberg, Stillinger, Pappe, Mineka). This collection of her writing demonstrates that HTM did not hold absolute sway over JSM's mind, nor was she uninfluential in his intellectual life.

Harriet's letters provide ample evidence of the intellectual exchanges of HTM and JSM which formed the core of their comradeship. In 1848, the infamous year of revolutions, Harriet had revolutionary ideas of her own. In one significant letter, Harriet expresses an opinion about the value of even failed revolutionary movements. This position differs somewhat from John's. Harriet asks John to defend his position while she offers evidence for her argument. She writes, "I am very glad you wrote that to Crowe. It is excellent & must do some good. I only disagree in the last sentence—but that does not much matter. How can you 'know' that a rising c^d. not succeed—and in my opinion if it did not succeed it might do good if it were a serious one, by exasperating & giving fire to the spirit of the people" (p. 339). This intellectual give-and-take seems to be the modus operandi of their life. John, like Harriet, is able to state openly when Harriet's arguments don't convince him. For example, in one letter he elucidates "the reason that the object [about] which you feel so strongly . . . did not completely decide the matter with me" (*CW: XIV*, 134). John does not accept each and every piece of advice Harriet offered. He was a big boy who could evaluate her reasoning, and Harriet must have assumed this in offering her counsel. Although they agreed on most issues in broad outline, they did not overlook the points on which they differed, and both were free to challenge the other's position or evidence.

Even when they agree on ideas, Harriet admits that John has a greater facility in written expression of ideas, even those ideas Harriet herself suggests. As she returns a manuscript to John, she writes, "I think the words which I have put the pencil through are better omitted—but they might with a little alteration be placed at the end? . . . The words I have added at the end do not go quite right but you will make them do so" (p. 364). Harriet contributes advice on the rhetorical aspects of John's writing (see p. 340), even outlining written responses she believed John might give. Harriet offers her ideas as suggestions only, as one honest person to another, recognizing John may or may not agree with her position. Listen to her advice about a man who had asked John for money: "W^d it be too base to say that you understand his note to mean—so & so—saying in the simplest truest expressions what you do think his note says—All this I only as the old man used to say 'throw out' for your approval" (p. 350). Some critics have identified Harriet as "passive-aggressive" in her attempts to manipulate John's ideas and relations with others, but nothing in these passages suggests anything other than a display of her candid reactions. Harriet recognized both that John wanted to hear her opinions and that he was free to accept or reject them.

Together, HTM and JSM develop an integrated writing process with each individual contribution based upon his or her strengths. Harriet's broad vision, her initiation of a line of argument, her general view form the clay that John refines into written text. The broad swipe requires articulation, just as the hand must write about some idea. That these two parts of writing might find their home not in one, but in two souls, seems obvious to those who have experienced it and impossible to those who have not. Harriet and John's collaborative writing begins in the mid-1840s in the form of newspaper articles and the chapter "On the Futurity of the Labouring Classes" for the *Principles of Political Economy*. John Taylor refers to "both authors" of *Principles of Political Economy* (XXVIII/180). After John Taylor's death in 1849, their letters provide even more evidence of their collaboration. Just days before Taylor dies, Harriet sends John her proposal for a newspaper article on domestic violence and includes a draft of the article that was later published (see p. 368 for this letter; pp. 77–100 for the article). Harriet's draft is the beginning of the final seven of the most important newspaper articles they write together. During the next couple of years, Harriet and John continue their collaboration on women's rights (see chapter 3). They also revised the *Principles of Political Economy* together (see pp. 291-315) and completed a pamphlet on domestic violence (see pp. 124-131). They also pore over the manuscript that would be published as *On Liberty* shortly after Harriet's death. John and Harriet work so closely together, John even asks her to help write a personal letter which he will send "when dearest one has made it right" (II/305).

Although HTM may not have been as skilled a writer as JSM, her oral contributions to their work were significant. Many of their conversations were about their feelings, as when at the end of a very angry letter, Harriet sighs, "How I long to walk by the sea with you & hear you tell me the whole truth about your feelings of this kind" (p. 333). Another example occurs after John Taylor's death, when Harriet longs for John's support as she writes, "Of feeling & thoughts there is far too much to be said in a note—I must see you soon" (p. 373). But many of their conversations were about political and philosophical ideas. After discussing in a seven-page letter the current arguments presented in the press for atheism (most of which she rejected), she notes Proudhon's public announcement of his atheism (which Harriet applauded) and concludes the paragraph with, "Adio caro carissimo till Sat^y when we shall talk over all these things" (p. 341). Her passion is not separated from their intellectual relationship; one feeds the other. Harriet believes that she has "so much to say to [John] that no one but [John] could understand" (p. 365, see also p. 368). The importance of this oral contribution is acknowledged by John in the *Autobiography,* when he says that the chapter "On the Probable Futurity of the Labouring Classes" was "wholly an exposition of her thoughts, often in words taken from her own lips" (173). HTM may not have been as adept at the pen as at oral communication, but her contribution was nonetheless significant. In fact, the glorification of written texts—at the expense of the collaborative, spoken give-and-take that shaped texts—is a broader issue within feminist scholarship.

Now turning to the second question posed earlier, what was the content of her character? Of one fact there can be no dispute: Harriet loved John wholly and completely. The letters are sprinkled with repeated terms of endearment and expressions of affection for JSM. "Dearest & kindest one," "my dearest love," "my delight," are perhaps standard salutations in love letters, while her "cher cher cher" seems the most heartfelt. Throughout their twenty-eight-year relationship, from first enchantment to married middle age, Harriet continued to express her love, as when she pleads, "If you have time to write <u>one</u> <u>word</u> do just say that you will keep me in your thoughts all the day to-morrow? as I shall every moment till I see you <u>darling</u>" (p. 334). Or when she opens her soul to him, saying, "But then thro' every moment of my life you are my one sole interest & object & I would at any instance give up all, were it ten thousand times as much, rather than have the chance of one iota of diminution of your love" (p. 332). These are but two examples of the many written announcements of Harriet's passion for John.

Although nearly every commentator on John's life concludes that he never experienced sexual intercourse with Harriet, the manuscripts do not explicitly resolve this question. Whatever their sexual relationship may have been, the letters clearly reveal the physical pleasure they derive from one another. Harriet murmurs, "When I think that I shall not hold your hand until Tuesday the time is so long & my hand so useless" (p. 335). Harriet often refers to their encounters with a zest that illuminates not a "masochistic" "aversion to sexual intercourse," as H. O. Pappe argues (29), but a soul full of intense desire. Harriet recounts with a smile, "Far from being unhappy or even <u>low</u> this morning, I feel as tho' you had never loved me half so well as last night—& I am in the happiest spirits & quite <u>quite</u> well . . . adieu darling How <u>very</u> nice next month will be. I am quite impatient for it" (p. 325). And, she beams,

> I have been quite well & quite happy since that delicious evening & I may perhaps see thee to-day, but if not I shall not be disappointed—as for <u>sad</u> I feel since that evening as tho' I never shall be that again.
> I am very well in all respects, but more especially in spirits.
> Bless thee—to-morrow will be delightful & I am looking to it as the very greatest treat. (pp. 323-324)

Whether Harriet's enthusiasm was met with an equal amount of energy on John's part is a question even Harriet recognized as a possible problem. Harriet responds to what must have been an expression of his own lack of will in a letter postmarked 6 September 1833, when she writes, "<u>Yes</u>—these circumstances <u>do</u> require greater strength than any other—the greatest—that which you have, & which if you had not I should never have loved you, I should not love you now" (p. 327). Whatever his qualms in the years just after Harriet's separation from her husband, the period in which this letter was penned, JSM expressed enough passion by the mid-1830s to elicit Harriet's passionate letters noted in the previous paragraphs and for Thomas Carlyle to declare that JSM had "fallen <u>desperately in love</u>" (quoted in Hayek 80). Harriet and John managed to remain devoted companions through nineteen years of her marriage to John Taylor (after JSM met HTM), through the two years of her widowhood, and throughout the eight years of their marriage.

Harriet was far from the heroine of a romance novel, clinging passionately and silently to her man. Harriet became angry with John on several occasions. One noteworthy rebuke occurs in two letters written after John complained that his relationship with her might result in lessening his impact in the social and political arena. She retorts,

> Good heaven have <u>you</u> at last arrived at fearing to be "<u>obscure & insignificant</u>'! What <u>can</u> I say to that but "by all means pursue your brilliant and important career'. Am <u>I</u> one to choose to be the cause that the person I love feels himself reduced to 'obscure & insignificant'! Good God what has the love of two equals to do with making obscure & insignificant if ever you <u>could</u> be obscure & insignificant you <u>are</u> so whatever happens & certainly a person who did not feel contempt at the very idea the words create is not one to brave the world. (pp. 332-333; see also pp. 330-332)

Having recently left her husband and relinquished the care of her two eldest children in order to sustain her relationship with John, Harriet can hardly be counted on for sympathy about John's career. When HTM cared for John Taylor during the final weeks of his illness, she once again expresses her annoyance with JSM when, for example, he suggests that she write "at some odd time when a change of subject of thought may be rather a relief than otherwise." To this proposal, Harriet counters, "<u>odd time</u>! indeed you must be ignorant profoundly of all that <u>friendship</u> or <u>anxiety</u> means when you can use such pitiful narrow hearted expressions" (p. 360). The following week, she records further irritation because "On Sunday I went down to you, sat down, stayed some time, & finally left the room in irrepressible indignation for you did <u>not once</u> during all the time you saw me ask how he was nor mention his name in any way! This fact and the feelings necessarily caused by it I can never forget as long as I live" (p. 360). Harriet's partnership with John encompasses her forthright expression of all of her feelings for him, including passion, affection, anxiety, irritation, and sarcasm.

Another part of Harriet's character which requires examination consists of her behavior toward her family. Living independently of her husband from her mid-twenties until her husband's death was not an easy task for a Victorian woman. If she were to prevent open scandal, Harriet must tread carefully. And that she did. She was quite conscious of the choices presented to her: to live openly with JSM and thereby humiliate her husband, abandon her children, and prevent JSM from becoming a social reformer, or to give up seeing JSM and return to the life of a dry salter's wife. Neither of these options would do, yet an alternative seems elusive. Harriet writes to JSM:

> I do not hesitate about the certainty of happiness—but I do hesitate about the rightfulness of, for my own pleasure, giving up my only earthly opportunity of 'usefulness'. You hesitate about your usefulness & that however greater in amount it may be, is certainly not like mine marked out as duty. I should spoil four lives & injure others. This is the only hesitation. When I am in health & spirits I see the possibilities of getting over this hesitation. When I am low & ill I see the improbabilities. Now I give pleasure around me, I make no one unhappy, & am happy tho' not happiest myself. I think any systematic middle plan between this & all impracticable. (p. 332)

Harriet did, however, manage a middle plan of maintaining enough of the outward forms of a family to protect her children and husband from the humiliation of abandonment, but satisfying enough of her need for John's companionship to make her happy.

Harriet had little help from her family in providing models or support in fashioning a life that would satisfy the demands of her heart and those of husband, children, and lover, because Harriet's family was, in a word, dysfunctional. Hardy family members seemed completely self-absorbed and ignorant of the emotional needs of others. Harriet's two eldest brothers died from tuberculosis as young men. Dr. Hardy, Harriet's father, sent the next two older brothers to Australia to prevent their deaths from the same disease. Arthur, Harriet's favorite sibling and the eldest to emigrate to Australia, at one time amassed a large sum of money and property while living in Adelaide. Unfortunately, he managed to lose nearly all of it before he died. Edward, Harriet's younger brother, dishonored the Hardys when he ran away with a family maid, a woman already married with a child. Harriet's sister, Caroline, married Arthur Ley, a philanderer and a thief, and probably a wife abuser (see pp. 448 and 449). In a sad description of her life, Caroline wrote to her sister:

> I did not go to the cricket meeting—much as I wished it. I had had some immensely disagreable [sic] fuss with A[rthur], about some of his family and had had one of the fits of excessive crying which are fits—& which I only have on very rare occasions and my face was so swollen and disfigured that I did not choose to go to be compared with other more successful women of whom he had one who follows him every where & who by insolence and boldfacedness carries him and everything else before her (XXVII/94).

Harriet reacts to her sister's situation with alternating pity and anger. And although there are moments of camaraderie with her parents recorded in personal missives (pp. 445–448) the emotions displayed in those letters contrast sharply with the usual grittiness of their relationship, as noted regularly in her communications with John Taylor. In one piece of writing, Harriet refers to a law suit between family members (p. 450), but the circumstances surrounding this legal matter are never clearly defined. Harriet's letters do supply evidence that Thomas Hardy refuses to speak to John Taylor for a number of years. This refusal of her parents to speak to her husband, and vice versa, may explain HTM's habit of vaguely referring to her parents merely as "he" or "she." Often Harriet refers to her father as "governor" when writing to John Taylor and her brother Arthur. When William Hardy died in Italy, Thomas Hardy refused to help his son's widow financially because of his stingy nature. Harriet's mother, Harriet Hardy, appears to have been a whining, often cruel woman, capable of complaining about the lack of attention she was afforded when her daughter's husband, John Taylor, lies on his death bed. Clearly, this family was not a happy one. Nonetheless, they never fell completely apart. Despite the anger, pettiness, and vengeance, they continued to visit and communicate, however grumpily, throughout Harriet's life.

Harriet maintained a cordial relationship with John Taylor after her separation from him. Her correspondence with him includes itineraries for her various trips, discussions of visits from their sons, and reviews of matters concerning her family. She always ends her correspondence with John Taylor by sending Helen's love and closing with "affectionately." Harriet rarely mentions JSM's name, but she doesn't avoid referring to him altogether. Harriet and John Taylor's affiliation seems marked with civility. Taylor's terminal cancer ultimately tests their bond. Harriet was initially nursing JSM for eye problems while the two were in France when Taylor first began to ask for her help. Shortly after Taylor's plea, she returned to England to discover the seriousness of his illness. John Taylor himself was probably unaware of his true state, since physicians during this period normally did not inform either patient or family that an ailment was terminal. The letters written by Harriet during the weeks of nursing John Taylor relentlessly question the medical professionals about possible cures and the need to secure the best physician available. Yet, she was also tempered by her recognition that her husband had different values from her own. Whereas she would wish to try experiments and to explore every medical option, Harriet fears that John Taylor will simply be unnerved by the very suggestion of a second opinion. In the end, she allows Taylor to die the way he wishes. HTM's continual nursing care of him during this painful event demonstrates her strength and her commitment to the man who acquiesced to her radical decisions governing the direction of her life.

Harriet Hardy, HTM's mother.

Thomas Hardy, HTM's father.

Caroline Hardy Ley, HTM's sister.

Arthur Hardy, HTM's brother.

John Taylor, HTM's first husband.

Herbert Taylor, HTM's son.

Algernon Taylor, HTM's son.

Helen Taylor, HTM's daughter.

John Stuart Mill, HTM's second husband.

Harriet's relationship with her sons suffers the most when she separated from her first husband. Algernon was three and a half and Herbert was six years old when Harriet began living apart from John Taylor. From that time forward, they remained in the custody of their father except for school holidays. Harriet was fond of the boys, enjoying her time with them on jaunts to southern England and on vacations in Europe, but she never bonded with them in the way she did with Helen. By the time Herbert was an adult, he corresponded infrequently with his mother. He even allowed himself to be used as the stumbling block to Harriet's quest to have Arthur Ley removed as trustee of the children's funds (see pp. 416–421). Algernon, better known as "Haji," remained closer to his mother. Harriet supported Haji on trips to Europe, and after she married JSM, he lived with them when he was in England.

Unlike the absentee mothering Harriet established with Herbert and Algernon, Helen was Harriet's companion, confidante, and pupil. Helen, like her mother, never attended school, but under her mother's direction she learned by reading widely, traveling extensively, and absorbing the various arts in England and Europe. Helen's reading tastes reflected those of her mother. As a teenager Helen studied Shakespeare, German philosophy, and histories of the locations she visited. As a fourteen-year-old she read Mary Wollstonecraft, and as a fifteen-year-old, during one week, she read Emerson and Fichte in the mornings and memorized Lady Macbeth's part in the afternoons.

In many ways the relation of mother and daughter matched the intensity HTM and JSM shared. Helen was devoted to her mother, and Harriet was equally dedicated to Helen. The letters Harriet wrote to Helen occur during their only separation, when Helen leaves home to become a professional actor in regional theaters. The extensive correspondence details the roller-coaster ride of emotions that afflict both mother and daughter as they attempt to achieve a balance of dependence and independence that fits their new situation. Helen sometimes begs for advice, only to be frustrated that her mother offers it. Harriet sometimes attempts to use guilt to influence her daughter's decisions. This struggle should sound familiar, because it offers a classic example of a child's move toward adulthood. On the whole, Harriet's maternal role is played with much love and support. It is often dangerous to extrapolate the quality of parenting from the character of a person, but Harriet's values seem reflected in Helen's life. Helen Taylor matured into an outspoken feminist, accomplished writer, and faithful supporter of JSM. The one person who knew Harriet most intimately, her daughter Helen, never abandoned her view of her mother as a wise and caring woman.

The Amberley Papers[3] record the clearest indication of Helen's adult view of her mother. Helen recalls being "allowed to read every book [I] wished, & [I] used to begin at one end of the shelf & go on straight through, often not understanding, but reading on. [I] read Berkeley at 11 & [my] father's[4] Logic at 14. [I] was never taught to believe anything but to judge for herself. All [my] mother used to say to [me] was: 'Be good & do what you know is right;' or 'I cannot love you if you are not good.' [My] mother used to say all that should be done was to awake the moral nature & leave the intellect & mind quite free." The journal continues, "once Miss Tayler was much inclined to R. Catholicism fr reading Th. à Kempis (which is still her favorite book) & her mother said nothing to dissuade her, but she got out of it alone" (372–373). Harriet's intellectual vigor and moral passion continued to live in her daughter.

A final note on this unusual woman's character concerns Harriet's extensive discussions of her health. Harriet's constant reference to the state of various ailments in herself and in others may appear to be whining to most twentieth-century readers. However, the context in which she wrote is critical in understanding this element of her personality. First, the state of Victorian medicine was crude, at best. The number of medications was limited, and their efficacy was questionable. Harriet's father was a physician and her husband, John Taylor, was a pharmacist, so she was quite aware of the limited success of medical intervention that was inevitable with the state of knowledge of diseases during the period. Life in the mid-1800s without aspirin, antihistamine, cough syrup, or any of the effective over-the-counter medications now available would have made every sinus headache, cold, and asthma attack excruciating. Also, the environmental hazards of living in a city choked with coal fires and industrial pollution caused a large percentage of the population to suffer from tuberculosis and lung diseases. Harriet's family history (which involved two of her brother's dying in their youth from tuberculosis, a terminal disease at the time), added to the scores of her friends and acquaintances who died of the same disease, sensitized Harriet to the most insignificant physical discomfort.

From 1841 Harriet suffered from a recurrent paralysis, numbness of extremities, face-aches, and other debilitating symptoms. On 15 June

---

3. Kate Amberley was Bertrand Russell's mother. JSM was chosen as Bertrand's "ungod"-father just before his death. Kate Amberley's journal records her meeting with Helen Taylor and John Mill on 20 February 1865.

4. The editor of the *Amberley Papers* added "[step-]" before this "father" to indicate that JSM was not Helen's father, but I have left the original, since it maintains Helen's sense of her relationship with John.

1841, Harriet writes her brother Arthur that she "had a severe illness with a sort of paralysis from which I have quite lost the power of moving my right leg, and very nearly that of the other" (PRG 101).[5] Although Harriet recovered to some extent, she continued to be plagued by ill health the rest of her short life. Symptoms included recurring inability to walk (1844, XXVIII/140; 1848, XXVIII/172, 175, 170, 207, 209, 213, 214, 222, 223; 1849, XVIII/221; 1857, LII/113), numbness in her hand (1857, LII/74, 116, 96, 100, 103, 108), coughing (1846, XXVIII/162; 1848, XXVIII/175, 204), face-aches (1847, XXVIII/173; 148, XXVIII/171, 174, 172, 178), headaches (1848, XXVIII/174, 216, 217; 1849, XXVIII/225; 1856, LI/29; 1857, LII/90, 117), broken blood vessels in the lungs (1853, XXVII/48; 1857, LII/71), and fevers (1850, XXVII/58; 1856, LI/5; 1857, LII/71). This chronic ill health culminated in her death at the age of fifty-one. These symptoms were recorded in letters to her family, most to John Taylor and Helen Taylor, but none in extant letters to JSM. Harriet took a number of tonics: tinct of bark, tinct of hops, quinine with sulfuric acid, laudanum, and Tuson's iodine treatment and cough medicine[6] in addition to the favorite Victorian treatment, baths.

Consumption, that quaint word for tuberculosis, the plague of the nineteenth century, probably accounted for the cough, and maybe the lung hemorrhages and fevers. However, the numbness in her legs or hands beginning in June 1841 remains a mystery. The traditional explanations are inadequate. Hayek reports that the paralysis is due to a carriage accident, citing as evidence Helen's diary of May 1842 (296). Aside from the discrepancy in dates, Hayek mistranscribed the diary entry, which actually says Helen's "gr[and] papa" and grandmother were in a carriage accident. Hayek apparently overlooked the critical "gr." Mazlish's declaration that "the paralysis in 1841 is clearly of psychological origin" (318) is doubtful.

Not only is it difficult to explain some of her symptoms, it is not apparent why she took some of the medications she did. Laudanum, bark, hops, and cough medicine were common, but an iodine/mercury treatment ("Tuson's iodine course") strong enough to loosen one's teeth (XXVIII/214) and quinine with sulfuric acid were serious treatments that were not prescribed for consumption.

One possible explanation for both the medication and the symptoms is that Harriet had syphilis. According to Herbert Mayo's *A Treatise on*

---

5. JSM reports the same incident to Sarah Austin in a letter of 4 October 1841 (*CW:* XIII, 485).

6. Each of these medications is discussed in more detail when one appears in the letters.

Syphilis, published in 1840, Mr. Tuson was noted for his treatment of syphilis based on his work in the Lock Hospital (for venereal diseases) in London (122). The recommended treatment of syphilis which manifested "bone involvement" was iodine with mercury (181) ("Tuson's Iodine course"), although bark, sulphate of quinine with diluted sulfuric acid, opium (laudanum) and baths[7] were also recommended. The therapies for syphilis exactly match those used by Harriet.

During this period, doctors identified the three main stages of syphilis. The primary stage usually involves small sores on the penis or vagina (these are often undetected by women); the secondary stage is a latency period during which the patient may occasionally suffer sore throats, sores, fevers, or other symptoms; and the tertiary stage often lasts as long as fifteen years after the initial infection. In the final phase the patient's joints are often inflamed & painful (Mayo 120) and, according to another treatise from the era, the nervous system is attacked, "manifest[ing] itself either by paralyses (hemiplegia, aphasia) or by epileptiform attacks" (Buret 220). It is during the tertiary period that iodine and mercury were generally prescribed (during the mid-nineteenth century). A diagnosis of syphilis seems to fit the numbness and paralysis of Harriet's limbs, which may have been temporarily relieved by the mercury and iodine treatment (helpful to some patients, just as arsenic helped Isak Dinesen in the post-mercury, pre-penicillin era).[8]

If Harriet had syphilis, she probably was infected by John Taylor, who became her husband when he was thirty and she was eighteen. Many middle-class men used prostitutes at this time. There may have been as many as 80,000 prostitutes in London alone (Pool, 189). Syphilis, an incurable disease at the time, was rampant among prostitutes and their clients. A man about to marry in the 1820s, when John Taylor married

---

7. Syphilis, like AIDS, does not always progress steadily, but has periods of remission. Doctors (correctly) realized that fresh air, a good diet, and the calm surroundings of a spa would often prolong a period of remission. Syphilis was also treated directly at the bath by having clients sit on a cane-bottomed chair under which was placed a steaming bowl of iodine or mercury infused water in an attempt to fumigate (!) the patient.

8. Five months after Harriet's death, John writes William E. Hickson to suggest Iodine combined with bromide of potassium as a remedy for paralysis (*CW:* XV, 602). He claims that Harriet took this treatment for "an injury to the spine, suffered in a carriage." It is possible that Harriet's condition was caused or exacerbated by traveling in a carriage, or John may have used this explanation to disguise his late wife's use of a popular medicine for treatment of syphilis. There is no other evidence for any accidental cause of HTM's paralysis, and this account contradicts the two accounts (HTM's to Arthur and JSM's to Sarah Austin) given at the time of her first attack that it occurred "out of the blue." It is also possible that she had a chronic disease like multiple sclerosis that was unidentified during this period.

Harriet, was advised incorrectly by his doctor that if the sores on his penis (the symptom of primary syphilis) were not oozing (a condition that usually only lasts a short period of time), he would not infect his soon-to-be wife. By mid-century the number of syphilitic middle-class women appearing in doctors' offices alerted physicians to the fact that middle-class men were infecting their virgin brides. This recognition may have been too late for Harriet.

Harriet's diagnosis of syphilis may have been determined at the time she discovered she was pregnant with her third child. Precisely at this point, she suddenly turned away from what had been a loving relationship with her husband. She met JSM within weeks of beginning the pregnancy,[9] and by the time Helen was delivered, Harriet was quite in love with John. The diagnosis would account for Harriet's refusal to have sexual intercourse with either John Taylor or John Mill from her mid-twenties through the rest of her life. It would elucidate John Taylor's much-praised "generosity" of feeling as well as money with his estranged wife. Minor occasional skin eruptions during the secondary phase of the disease might partially explain the secluded nature of her life beginning in early 1840s, a rather dramatic change from her style during the first ten years of her "affair" with John. Furthermore, her writing about the use of prostitutes by "3/4 of our adult male population" (see p. 13) and her comparison of middle-class women who barter themselves in marriage for respectability, food, and shelter (see pp. 21–23) with more obvious kinds of prostitution are both clarified by this diagnosis.

However, the convenience of the explanation does not verify the diagnosis. Since "syphilis is the great impersonator"[10] capable of presenting a wide variety of symptoms, an accurate diagnosis based on symptoms, especially without a physical exam, is difficult. For a proper confirmation of syphilis, one would need Harriet's doctor's report (which unfortunately does not exist) or an autopsy. Short of these checks, we are left with only an intriguing proposal that could radically change the way readers see HTM's life and work.

---

9. It is possible that she simply never mentioned her ailment in letters to JSM or that she was far more specific about her syphilis with him than with anyone else, and hence all references to her illness have been eliminated from her letters to him. (HTM's letters to JSM are obviously edited; parts of nearly every letter have been cut out.) JSM discusses his health with HTM regularly and in detail, so it seems odd that HTM never mentions hers.

10. David Christie, a retired professor of physiology from New Zealand who is interested in Victorian studies, remembered this phrase from his medical school training. One added difficulty in making such a diagnosis is that virtually no contemporary doctors see tertiary syphilis patients, since penicillin easily cures this disease.

Beyond the question of HTM's intellect and character, the most important question that must be addressed when considering a large collection of historical documents is how can scholarship advance by studying this woman? Throughout the critical studies of John Stuart Mill, Harriet Taylor Mill surfaces only in the shadows. Despite years of work building a canon of women's history, HTM still does not appear in the personal indices of the Bodleian Library or in the Fawcett Library, a library dedicated to women's history! So, the skeptic might conclude that this lack of attention on the part of historians of philosophy or world famous libraries indicates good reason to suppose HTM's work is unimportant. Even if all we had to publish at this point were the 250 pages of letters, this volume would be a significant contribution to knowledge because it is good gossip. Phyllis Rose explains the significance of gossip when she says:

> We tend to talk informally about other people's marriages and to disparage our own talk as gossip. But gossip may be the the the beginning of moral inquiry, the low end of the platonic ladder which leads to self-understanding. . . . If marriage is, as Mill suggested, a political experience, then discussion of it ought to be taken as seriously as talk about national elections. (9)

Harriet's letters provide insight into the alliance of two of the most important feminists of the nineteenth century. John's letters, for example, fail to record two important periods in their lives. There are only two letters extant from John prior to 1849. So the first eighteen years of their association would remain an enigma without Harriet's letters. Furthermore, no letters survive from JSM to HTM during her husband's terminal illness. The large numbers of letters from HTM provide the only window into this significant period. The knowledge gained about how Harriet fashioned her life with John will help us all gain wisdom into the struggles involved in sustaining a successful partnership, especially when it challenges socially and academically accepted standards.

This collection of letters is significant also because it uncovers the inner life of three generations of a Victorian family, presenting an interesting lens through which to see the world of nineteenth-century life. The correspondence discloses how they traveled, what they ate, and which hotels might provide good water closets. Harriet offers readers a glimpse of a Victorian woman's opinion of Renaissance art and architecture, theater costumes, and "watering places." Victorian attitudes toward both birth and death emerge in these epistles. What is said and what is left unsaid to each member of the family reveals the politics of this family and may reflect more general Victorian social patterns. Anyone interested in Victorian life will welcome this addition to the primary sources because of the extensive details it provides.

Most importantly, this volume contains more than just correspondence and offers more than gossip about the love life of JSM and HTM, as important as that is, or material on Victorian life. Harriet Taylor Mill's writings on women and the other subjects explore philosophical, historical, economic, and literary topics, as well as poems, book reviews, and newspaper articles. The quantity of Harriet Taylor Mill's writing (more than three hundred typewritten pages) meaningfully contributes to the history of women philosophers, and Harriet's total body of work is modest only when compared to John's collected works. HTM is not an undiscovered Kant, but her insights into a number of issues deserve careful study. Harriet's observations of the abuse of women and children are as pertinent today as they were 170 years ago. Harriet's writing on domestic violence preceded the sustained interest in the subject that began approximately twenty years later with Frances Power Cobbe's writing. Harriet Taylor Mill's recognition that public and private lives are intertwined and that both deserve the attention of a philosopher is a point that has often been overlooked in the history of philosophy. Her views of the damage inflicted by organized religion were controversial when they were written, and some readers may still find them offensive. Her defense of socialism is based on living examples as much as theoretical argument.

HTM's work on these topics must be added to her awareness of the importance of tolerance, eccentricity, the quality of pleasures, and the collaborative nature of the pursuit of truth. Students of *On Liberty* may be surprised to read these ideas in HTM's notes and essays twenty-five years before *On Liberty* was published: Helen claimed that readers could "see [Harriet's] mind & thoughts [in *Liberty*] for they were mostly her's—" (*Amberley Papers* 373). Harriet's flashes of understanding as well as her arguments should still serve as a springboard for contemplation, provoking readers to think more deeply about these ideas. Harriet's role as instigator and as passionate contributor to something greater than either she or John could have accomplished independently merits attention, perhaps even emulation. The coming-to-be of their work is as important as the final product. A comfortable lifestyle, psychological support and inspiration, intellectual challenges, provocative phrases, articulation of each other's ideas, revision, conversation—in short, all of the emotional and intellectual work that hides behind the dance called collaborative writing constitutes this coming-to-be.

HTM's own work as well as her collaborative work with John both deserve far more objective scrutiny than they have so far received. A fair evaluation of Harriet and John's joint philosophical inquiry must begin by reading all of her work, not simply his. An assessment of HTM's contribution to the history of philosophy must commence at the same point. We hope this collection provides the opportunity for scholars to take a much closer look at the fascinating writing that reveals the daring life and provocative thought of Harriet Taylor Mill.

Jo Ellen Jacobs
Griswold Distinguished Professor of Philosophy
Millikin University

Textual Introduction

Although approximately three hundred pages (typewritten) of Harriet's letters remain, these letters represent merely a fraction of the total number she actually wrote. Unfortunately, the bulk of her letters has been lost. The thirty-eight correspondences John penned to Harriet in just four months (December 1853 to April 1854) serve as a benchmark by which we can estimate the numbers of letters that Harriet wrote to John which have been destroyed purposefully or accidentally. Only one of Harriet's epistles from this period remains, despite the fact that each of JSM's missives refers to a letter he receives from HTM. Harriet guarded her letters carefully. When she was dying she even kept her writings under lock so that the servants would not see her correspondence. Some of her letters were probably destroyed at her request after she died.

Yet other papers as well may have been discarded when, years later, the accumulated papers of Harriet and John were quickly sorted, sold, and burned by friends of the Taylor family. This regrettable action took place after Helen Taylor, near her own death, was persuaded to leave the Avignon cottage which contained all of Harriet's papers. Even more of HTM's personal papers may have been lost before they arrived in the British Library of the London School of Political and Economic Sciences, in which they now reside. Thus this relatively small number of remaining letters and unknown percentage of her total writings must serve as the only direct source for understanding her life and work.[1]

We have attempted to display the manuscripts accurately, in a manner

---

1. The following is a list of files containing documents written by Harriet that are either illegible or too fragmentary for inclusion: Box III/88, 96, 139, 148, 202, and 205; and the back of letter XXVII/53.

which closely resembles the originals, since the documents are so fragile that future scholars may have little chance of re-transcribing these texts. We retained all the original spelling and punctuation, including HTM's use of superscripted letters, abbreviations, and quotation marks. A number of words are regularly misspelled, for example, "beleive," "dissapoint," and "disagreable." English spelling had not become completely standardized in the nineteenth century, which may account for the regularly "misspelled" words. The other inaccurately spelled words can be explained by understanding the context of writing habits and conditions of the period. Harriet wrote by lamplight; often in rooms that were a mere thirty-eight degrees; with messy pens; in moving carriages and on trains and ships. These conditions discouraged neatness and encouraged quick, informal writing. Many of these notes are analogous to e-mail messages of the late twentieth century—punctuation and spelling mistakes do not imply substandard intelligence, but rather errors made for the sake of time and convenience.

Any additions needed for clarification have been added in brackets, whether these additions are merely individual punctuation marks or descriptions of text placement. Especially in her personal notes, Harriet often wrote on a page in four different directions. It is unclear where the reader should begin and in what order the reader should continue. We have merely indicated that a particular text was perpendicular to or upside down when compared to another part of the manuscript. Any strikeovers that changed the text in any substantial way have been preserved in an attempt to retain a sense of Harriet's writing process. Even the spacing of dates, closings, and signatures have been preserved as accurately as possible. The only major change in the appearance of the texts is paragraph indentation. HTM rarely indented paragraphs. One can discern a paragraph only by a sentence which did not complete a line. Each time such a sentence occurs, we chose to indent the next line, so that readers would be able to detect Harriet's transition in thought.

In order to fully comprehend the context of the letters, the reader must be familiar with the nicknames of various family members. Harriet's eldest son, Herbert, is referred to as "Herby," and her second son, Algernon, is called "Haji." HTM's daughter, Helen, is always "Lily," except while Helen was on the stage and she disguised herself as "Miss Trevor." As he lay dying, John Taylor referred to HTM as "Hary." Caroline Hardy Ley is referred to as "Cary," "Carry," or just "Car." In each of the set of letters, the first appearance of the nickname will be footnoted, but will not be noted thereafter.

We have tried to date each piece of writing accurately. The justification for each dating is offered in a footnote at the beginning of the passage. Dating was determined by watermark on the paper, content of the letters, reference to published material, location of the sender or recipient, and by the obvious, a postmark or date on the envelope or letter. In a few cases, we have combined two drafts of substantially the same piece and merely noted differences in drafts in footnotes.

Determination of anonymous contributions for the *Monthly Repository* have been based on the key found in Francis Mineka's *The Dissidence of Dissent: "The Monthly Repository," 1806-1838.* Co-authored pieces were ascertained by referring to JSM's handwritten bibliography as published in *Bibliography of the Published Writings of John Stuart Mill,* MacMinn, Ney, J. R. Hainds, and James MacNab McCrimmon, editors.

Most of the unpublished documents included in this volume are housed in the Mill/Taylor Collection of the British Library of the London School of Political and Economic Sciences. One letter is housed in the Mortlock Library of South Australiana, State Library of South Australia. A note of HTM's included in a letter of JSM to William J. Fox is located in the Yale University Library. Four letters are located in King's College, Cambridge. The Mill/Taylor collection texts are designated by the appropriate volume or box number and individual file number—such as XXVIII/166, L/30, LIII(i)/8, and so on. All other pieces of writing are identified with a footnote.[2]

Three sources are cited regularly, and we use the following abbreviations: "*CW*" designates *The Collected Works of John Stuart Mill,* 33 vols. (Toronto: University of Toronto Press 1963-1991). Volume and page number follow the abbreviated title. "Hayek" refers to F. A. Hayek's *John Stuart Mill and Harriet Taylor: Their Friendship and Subsequent Marriage* (New York: Augustus M. Kelley, 1951). "Packe" designates Michael St. John Packe's *The Life of John Stuart Mill* (New York: The Macmillan Company, 1954). "Mineka and Lindley" refer to the "The Later Laters: 1849-1873" volumes of *The Collected Works of John Stuart Mill,* edited by Francis E. Mineka and Dwight N. Lindley.

---

2. The Mill/Taylor Collection has been microfilmed by Research Publications (1988); however, all penciled material is illegible on the microfilm, and unfortunately, HTM often wrote in pencil.

Chronology

1807	October 8	Harriet born	
1826	March 14	Marries John Taylor	|Drafts of Caxton article
	December	Pregnant with Herbert	
1827	September	Herbert born	
1828	July	Love letter to John Taylor	|Writing on ed. of women
			|Poems
1829	May	Pregnant with Algernon	
	July	With parents at Ryde	|Mermaid poem
1830	February	Algernon born	
	November	Pregnant with Helen	
		Meets JSM during fall/winter	
1831	January 28	Invitation to JSM for dinner	|Published Australia review
			|Writing on ed. of women
			|Writing on marriage/divorce
		Becomes intimate with JSM	|Writing on ethics
	July 27	Helen born	|Writing on religion
1832	April		|"Snow Drop" published
	June		|Reviews of Domestic
			Manners, German Prince,
			"Seasons," Plato Mirabeau,
			Hampden, French Revolution,
			|"Summer Wind"
	July	Small crisis with JSM	
	August	Resumes seeing JSM	
	September		|"Nature" published

	October	Taylors travel to Wales, move to Kent Ter.	Writing on Ed. of Women Writing on marriage/divorce Writing on ethics Writing on arts
1833	March		William Caxton published Review of Tale of Alroy
	Sept.–October	HTM, then JSM in Paris/ Crisis in marriage; separates from husband	
1834		HTM & JSM work together; troubled period	
	June	HTM moves to Keston Heath	Writing on arts
1835		Both HTM & JSM ill from this year on	
	January	Fox leaves his wife	
	March	JSM inadvertently burns Carlyle manuscript	
1836	June	James Mill dies	
	August	Trip with JSM, HTM's children, and two of JSM's brothers	
1837		Queen Victoria ascends Happy period for HTM and JSM	
1838	November	Arthur leaves for Australia	
1839		Trip from Dec. 1838–July 1839 through Europe	Travel journal
	August	HTM moves to Walton	
	September	Visits Birksgate first time	
1840	September	Visits Birksgate/break with Caroline, who has just married	
	November	William Hardy dies	
1841	June	Partial paralysis onset	
	July	Problems again with trustees for children's trust	
1842	August	John Taylor's mother dies.	Writing on ethics
1844	June–Aug.	Trip to Normandy	Comte letter controversy Writing on religion

1845			Collaboration on PPE
1846	February		Newspaper collaboration
	April	Herbert goes to U.S.	
	June		Newspaper collaboration
	June–July	Belgium/Rhine trip	
		Visit from Alfred	Collaboration on PPE
	October		Two newspaper collaborations
	November		Newspaper collaboration
	December		Newspaper collaboration
1847		Eliza Flower dies	Writing on women's rights
	April	Herbert returns from U.S.	Ch. of PPE/helped rewrite all
			Personal writing
1848			Writing on women's rights
	April	PPE published	
	May	Letter to Fox about PPE	
	August–Dec.	Ryde/Walton/Dover/Worthing	
		Beginning signs of John Taylor's illness	
	Christmas	Leaves for Pau	
1849	Jan.–April	Pau	
	May	HTM's father dies	
	May–July	HTM nurses John Taylor	Newspaper collaboration
	July 18	John Taylor dies	
1850	February		Newspaper collaboration
	March		Three newspaper collaborations
	May		Two newspaper collaborations
	June		Newspaper collaboration
1851	April	HTM and JSM marry	Writing on women's rights
	July	Fight with George Mill	"Enfranchisement" published
	August		Newspaper collaboration
1852			Revision of PPE
1853			Pamphlet on Fitzroy's Bill
1854			Request to reprint PPE chapter
1855	March	Renewed controversy about trusteeship	
	April–June	JSM to Greece	
	July	HTM and Helen to Switzerland	
	Sept.–Oct.	HTM and Helen in Ryde	

1856	November	Helen goes on the stage
1857	February	Harriet visits Helen in Glasgow; both ill, Helen quits stage
1858	October	Helen resumes stage career HTM and JSM leave for France
	November 3	HTM dies in Avignon, France

SECTION
ONE:
WRITINGS
ON
WOMEN

Few subjects can be of so vital importance and yet has been so little considered as that of the education of women. The importance of the subject is beyond calculation when we consider that in it is included that of their sons and their daughters and therefore of the whole community. Of all the influences to which children are exposed perhaps there is none at once so subtle and so imperceptible as that derived from the tone of thought and feeling of their mothers. It has been before remarked that were we to inquire with attention into the early history of most of the men who were in any way distinguished themselves in after life we should probably find their minds as much as their physical condition to have been derived from and modified by that of their mothers. But we have not need to refer to the lives of men to illustrate the truth of this position — we have only to look around us to see it exemplified in almost every instance in our acquaintance and friends.

In her early twenties, Harriet began cataloguing the many ramifications of the inadequate education of women.

EDUCATION OF WOMEN

1

In this group of seven drafts about the education of women, all written in the late 1820s or early 1830s, HTM deplores the lack of formal education for women, but more interestingly, she also recognizes that the restrictions on women's social experience constitute an equally disastrous restriction on their cultural education. Experience living and working with different elements of society leads to "self-knowledge" as well as insight regarding the dynamics of interpersonal relationships; lack of such experience stunts women's ability to achieve personal happiness and intellectual growth.

In the first essay, HTM compares the plight of the Victorian woman to that of Greek and Roman slaves. HTM recognizes the significant role that physical force plays in all oppression, and she concludes that as long as society tolerates the use of physical violence, women will be oppressed. This essay offers the reader the first sign of the interest in violence and domestic violence that will dominate her writing in the mid-1840s, when she uses newspaper articles and pamphlets on domestic violence to educate the public against the negative effects of physical force against women and children (see chapter 4, below).

In the second essay, HTM questions whether the purpose of women's education in nineteenth-century society is to achieve the greatest amount of happiness for women themselves or for the pleasure of men. Next HTM queries what kind of pleasure educating the gentle sex can afford either sex. Here, in the early 1830s, we can see HTM making the distinction between kinds of pleasures that will serve as the core of Utilitarianism in the 1860s.

The education of women is critical because of their special role as teachers of children and thus of the entire community. HTM makes this point in the third essay. She even suggests that women should study such subjects as mathematics for the same reason that men do: to improve their overall intelligence, not merely to solve mathematical problems.

In the fourth, fifth, and sixth essays, HTM outlines the typical education of a young girl (essays 4 and 5) and young boy (essay 6). In the fifth piece, HTM celebrates a young middle-class woman's abilities and spirit, but deplores her lack of sexual education, which results in her naively being married to someone she hardly knows and who is likely to destroy her spirit. The sixth essay analyses the unhealthy subversive power that a mother will exert over her children when she herself is trained to be tyrannical by being oppressed by her husband. A woman's education does not cease with her marriage.

The final essay begins with a critique of William Fox's article "Political and Social Anomaly,"[1] which appeared in the Monthly Repository. Fox points to the anomaly that the head of state is a woman, but most men continue to believe that women are not capable of the lowest form of civic participation, the vote. He also argues that "If {mind were} more generally cultivated in woman, {it} would render her aid to man tenfold more efficient, and her companionship tenfold more pleasurable." HTM's response is her most straightforward critique of the opinion that women should be trained for domestic duties. She argues that educating a woman merely to be a more effective aide to men amounts to being trained as a prostitute, since a young woman is directed to offer men pleasure for the price of a house and reputation. HTM states that three-fourths of the male population are accustomed to using prostitutes paid in cash, and marriage is only a more respectable version of the same kind of transaction. To be prepared for "domestic duties" will not result in the greatest happiness for the greatest number of people because it only results in men's happiness, not women's. One solution, which HTM suggests might "startle" the reader, is to eliminate the separation of males and females during their early education, hence not creating a mystery between the sexes.

---

1. William F. Fox, "A Political and Social Anomaly," *Monthly Repository* 1832, VI: 637–42.

1. [OPPRESSION OF WOMEN DUE TO LACK OF EDUCATION][2]

Much has been said and written, of late years about the proper influence of women, the proper rank of women in society, and so forth. But all this saying and writing, through all with a very good intent seems to me to be beside the mark. The extent of the false state in which women stand with regard to the rest of the community is in nothing more shown than in the mode by which they are defended. As the corrupt state of the unreformed House of Commons was shown by the fact, that members of it were not wanting to declare it altogether a pretty and well-working body. All that has yet been said respecting the social condition of women goes on the assumption of their inferiority. People do not complain of their state being degraded at all—they complain only that it is <u>too much</u> degraded. Now real lovers of justice will rather that their condition should get worse & worse rather than partially better—in as much as when a certain point of abuse is reached their comes from the nature of things a sweeping and large reform. Moderate reformation may be pleasant for the present time only, but on a wide calculation no reform unless a thorough one, will in a calculable time produce the best result. We hear nothing of the proper influence [of] men, the social rank of men—because that is established—but we hear of the proper degree of power which men should make over their own property and the proper influence of the national voice in the national interest—because these points are yet in an artificial and debatable state. It is <u>not</u> wonderful that ~~white~~ those men who beleive their own happiness to depend on other mens political degradation, should also hold the subserviency of women to be a needful ingredient in their creed of selfish and sensual enjoyment. But it is a lamentable instance of the strength of habits of opinion, that men who in their relation to all other men would be just even to generosity, yet in the case of women go on unthinkingly in the belief which their early associations of the natural inferiority of women.

To a person who wished for truth and justice I would say in regard to this supposed inferiority: that were women generally to show as much talent as men in the present state of society, I would argue, not equality but superiority—because they are entirely deprived of all those advantages of academical or university instruction emulation & example which are

---

2. Written on paper watermarked 1832. Box III/87. Harriet made additions and filled in blanks in pencil after completing a draft in ink. "AΦPOΔITH," the Greek for Aphrodite, was written in the margin.

open to all men: and what is much more important to the formation or development of individuality of character, the whole repute of their lives is made to depend on their utter exclusion from any source of knowledge or experience of the world—and the varieties of scene & of character which must be known and tried to give self knowledge, and decision of mind— and general information and useful ability. All this is entirely denied and a woman who has energy sufficient to choose and to act for herself—becomes a mark for the obloquy[3] of the great and little vulgar of both sexes—nor must it be thought strange that the great majority of women contribute much to their own debasement. Denied open power, they attain often an absolute power, by indirect and unworthy means—holding the condition of slaves they exercise retaliation by the vices of slaves, duplicity especially is a characteristic of women—yet who that knows any thing of a womans genuine nature but will declare frankness, generosity, to be peculiarly its attributes. Their extreme susceptibility[,] their fine nervous organization renders this almost a part of their physical nature—and in the old times of veils and cages, women were not deceitful because they we[re] so thoroughly[4]   as to see no wrong in the matter.

The Roman Helot

The born slave seldom complains, his mind is as degraded as his body by hopeless subjection. The Roman Helot and the modern Greek aware of better things, in the one case by violence in the other by deception, as suitable to their respective age, have kept in fear their taskmasters. Neither have seen that as free members of the community they might have been incalculably more useful to others and more happy themselves.

The 'Veil & Cage' era of womens condition has always been coeval with, the mere 'physical force' era of mens[.] a society once emancipated from either can never return to it. and the progress of this emancipation has always borne the same proportion, has evidently not been actually the same because in the first stage of physical force alone women were necessarily behind mans, & so must continue, as long as physical power exercises any influence over the moral power of a community. This is now fast ceasing to have a recognised existence, altho' it was not till quite late years that a man of a slight make was legally protected from the man of Hercules

---

3. Evil-speaking against a person; abuse.

4. Following blank space left by Harriet. Such spaces occur throughout these writings.

proportion—and even now, to their disgrace of the time bodily punishments are tolerated in the army, and in some schools—but this cannot last long. And every step in the recognition of the power of opinion is a guarantee for the improvement of women.

2. EDUCATION OF WOMEN[5]

Much has been said & written on this subject—and perhaps all that is to be said or written—but reiteration is the grand secret of popular impression. The saying being true in that connexion, that where ten steps will reach the goal, nine steps take us half way.

Our inquiring is not so much of how much they should learn, or how little they do learn—but of the prior question to what is it proposed they s^d learn at all? Is the end desired to make us better ministrants to the pleasures of men and if so to what description of pleasure are they to produce or increase[.] On the answer to these questions will depend the solution of the next—is the object of educating them the production of the greatest amount of happiness themselves of which they are capable

By what strange process is it that the end talked of is always happiness or pleasure to men—true that is one of the ends proposed—but only by implication in the theory that the greatest happiness of each being accords well with the greatest happiness of all. We hear nought of in disquisition on mens education of what sort of instruction will produce the greatest happiness [for] women. We hear of no profession of the act of making women happy, yet with the utmost gravity—this art appears as the ultimatum of [grace] and learned.

3. [THE EDUCATION OF MOTHERS][6]

Few subjects can be of so vital importance, and few have been so little considered as that of the education of women. The importance of the subject is beyond calculation when we consider that in their education is included that of their sons and their daughters and therefore of the whole

---

5. Written on paper watermarked 1832. Box III/87.

6. Written on paper watermarked 1828. Box III/81.

community for of all the influences to which children are exposed perhaps there is none at once so resistless and so imperceptable as that derived from the love of thought and feeling of their mothers. It has been before remarked that were we to examine with attention into the early history of most of the men who have in any way distinguished themselves in after life we should probably find their minds as much as their physical condition to have been derived from and modified by that of their mother, indeed we have not need to refer to the lives, of remarkable men to illustrate the truth of this position—we have only to look around us to see it exemplified in almost every instance in our acquaintance and friends.

[separate page]

again, it is said that the study of mathematics is neither necessary nor useful for a woman—nor is the reading of Euclid, abstractedly and for itself, useful to a man—it is for its results that it is good

4. A CHAPTER OF THE SOCIAL SYSTEM[7]

We will open our sketch of the incidents of a life, not at all singular in its incidents, but only in the organization and mental developement to which they were applied, by describing the effect, at the age of seventeen, of what is commonly supposed to be a sufficing and suitable education for the purposes of a woman's being. Helen Astley[8] was an only child. Her parents were rich, of gentle descent, and, as things have been, might be said to be persons of good education. They had sufficient taste to enjoy a life of comparative retirement among the groves and alleys of the provincial estate, and to cultivate literary occupations rather than the vapidities of what is called society. They were among the best specimens of what has been, until lately the best class of english, the higher middle rank. Bland in manner, exceedingly kindly in their intercourse with their neighbours and dependants, & of liberal political feeling: while in an inverse ratio to their capacity for forming opinions for themselves, was their tenacity in adherring to those they accidentaly adopted. It may be supposed that with

---

7. Box III/80. This appears to be the more final of two drafts of this essay.

8. It is possible Harriet was referring to the daughter or granddaughter of the founder of the famous Astley's Royal Amphitheatre, a popular circus-type equestrian show. Astley's is mentioned in the newspaper article Harriet and John wrote on Corporal Punishment (14 July 1849; see chapter 4, below), and John mentions having visited the show as a child in his journals for 1820 (*CW:* XXVI, 36).

such persons the care of an only child was looked upon as a matter of great interest, and her education as a charge of the utmost importance. In their own phrase they were determined that their daughter should become 'a throughly accomplished woman'. And accomplished she was, thanks to 'masters' & 'mistresses' of all kinds: but thanks to nature she was also something better. Nature had dower'd her with a heart and a soul. with mind and strength. These were cramped, but not extinguished . . .

[The remainder of this essay is written on the back of another draft.]

[S]he promised to honour a being, mentally & morally her inferior—to obey a lesser intellect & a temper uncurbed by responsibility and to love for ever more a person of whose existence they had been ignorant six months before, & for whom her affection was yet in the bud and so she became from that moment a dependant upon him for her daily food, which she was to purchase by personal concession of the & which on experience she abhored nature of which she was totally ignorant.[9]

5. WRITINGS OF A WOMAN IN THOUGHT & IN DEED[10]

Margaret Temple was born the first child, & unmarried the only child of one of the old English Squirarchy families—a race which blessed be the god of [?] is fast ceasing to have an existence. In the year 1800, the year of Margarets nativity that race still bore strong over the minds of the 'lower classes' & itself looked up in servile admiration succumbed to the next 'order' above it. The Lordship Curtis Temple was a fair specimen of average squire's intellect. He had imbibed somewhat of the dare-to-have-an-opinion spirit poured abroad by the french philosophy not but that he had the instinctive hatred of his order to all revolution & to the french revolution in particular—The spectacle filled his orderly mind with horror of a king brought to reckoning by the governed, of the 'distinction of institutions'—'institutions' being in his dim belief a certain abstract.

He was a Whig—but he never forgot that he was also an English gentleman—therefore he <u>disliked</u> tyranny on principle as the saying is to

9. A scrap of writing in Box III/97 includes the following passage: "and so Helen Astley died. and they wore mourning full six months afterwards." The passage is completely unrelated to the other content in that file.

10. Written on paper watermarked 1832. Box III/85.

have <u>hated</u> it to not have been in good taste. Strong feeling of any kind is decidedly vulgar—and Curtis Temple inherited the refinement of 12 generations of do-nothings—yet not all these generations contrived to embue him with any portion of that temperament wh is necessary for sensibility. his notions, not to call them opinions were liberal by the accident of his social circle; none of the thoughts which he believed he believed were his own property. his mind was the senseless wooden wheel constantly {working} & collecting what insight happen to come within {his} little orbit.

Strange that such a being sh^d have been the parent of   but the laws wh regulate physical conformation remains as yet totally unexplained while we regulate almost unerringly improve infinitely the race of all the lower animals the improvement of the human animal by means of regulating the hereditary pre-disposi{tions} is left utterly unconsidered in that no great improvement can be untill there come a complete sweeping away of any worn-out social institutions for that wh wholly distinguishes we're at heaven from earth, the passion of the human species from the instinct of the brute—is the presence of

{manuscript breaks off before the end of the page}

6. [EDUCATION OF AN ABUSIVE MOTHER][11]

Walter Denison was the second son[12] of parents holding a place in that class known[13] in Vernacular tongue by the name[14] <u>respectable</u>. They were persons who had never known what it was to have been dunned for a debt, nor to have done an act of generosity: they loved justice rather than mercy, and called sensitivity romantic.

[J.] Denison Esq, M.P. for his county,[15] & one of the representatives

---

11. Written on paper watermarked 1831. Box III/82.

12. It is important that HTM focused on second sons. Because of the inheritance laws giving all of an estate to the eldest son, the second son was treated very differently in society and in the family from the first son.

13. The word "designated" was written above "known," but neither had been penciled through.

14. The word "word" was written above the word "name," but neither had been penciled through.

15. HTM may have been referring to J. W. Denison, Esq. M.P. A pamphlet by W. Medley, "The Crisis: being a letter to J. W. Denison, Esq. M.P., on the present calamitous situation

(save the mark)[16] of the landed interest[,] had never doubted that it was by a mandate of nature that he set despotic power over the free-will, and actions of his mate, and vehemently agreeing to this in theory, she made herself amends for succumbing to one by constaining all the rest of her household—it was sufficient that any one [of] her children and servants manifested a strong inclination for any subject to cause her to feel a decidedly contrary wish[,] not that she did not like to give pleasure, but that she, like all ignorant people, enjoyed the consciousness of power of whatever kind & this petty social authority was all that her education had qualified her for, or that her condition in society allowed.[17]—She had too a pis[18] virtue which she called firmness, and this consisted in adhering, without benefit of reason, to an intention once adopted. Unfortunately, her son Walter, had from his very babyhood manifested the same characteristic, but in him this tendency his mother called obstinacy and almost from the day of his birth commenced the struggle between the him and his mother. Walter however had the advantage of unity of purpose, while firmness often shared the throne with a tribe of lesser motives, Walter's power was concentrated by opposition on the one parent of success—and union carried the day—accordingly at about 5 years old he was pronounced a boy of a very incorrigible disposition. Any relentings which he might have experienced on account of his mothers judgment of him, being prevented by seeing that his father had precisely the same opinion of her which she had of him. Still his young heart clung to her who he soon perceived to be the subject of injustice and it took him but few years to discover that the intellect of father & mother was much upon a par while her heart was sometimes softened to others from the effect of tyranny on herself, his by the exercise of unlimited power, without intellect.

In [?] it had become as hard as

[manuscript breaks off here]

---

of the country," published in 1822, recorded the author's anger about the banking crisis during this period.

16. Originally an archery phrase, "God save the mark" was used to emphasize an ironic statement.

17. The passage "not that . . . allowed" is included in another draft of this essay.

18. French word meaning "worse."

7. [EDUCATING WOMEN FOR MEN'S ENJOYMENT][19]

Notwithstanding the somewhat sarcastic tone, which we think in a measure marred the value, of the otherwise satisfactory & well-timed article, entitled a [']Political & social anomaly',[20] in the last <u>number</u> of this work it was calculated to do much good by fixing the attention of the unthinking on a fact & displaying in a manner which those interested in maintaining error could refuse to admit the injustice & absurdity which that fact implies.

So far is well—and would suffice, if the anomaly there set forth were the only one, or the greatest, in the social condition of women. But it is not so—their deprivation of a civil existence is only one page in the chapter of <u>womens</u>[21] degradation,—and that Chapter is the fullest & the first in the heavy vol. of social discontent and human unhappiness. Would that men saw how infallibly the mental frustration of the guide of his childhood[,] the companion of his manhood must re-act on their own condition the degradation of his mental & moral being & even to the diminution of those merely physical enjoyments which he falsely imagines to be purchased by her.

[M]uch has always been said by those among men & women too[,] who[,] sayers rather than thinkers[,] about educating women for their sphere, suiting them for domestic duties, & so forth—all which sayings are of most self-evident & undeniable truth—but which by those who use them are meant to <u>imply</u> much more than is said. The meaning in the mind of an ignorant person using the phrase educating women for domestic duties—is something of this.[22]

The very fact, indisputable as it is, that this description of enjoyment is in almost every instance a purchase is at once a proof & a result of the

---

19. Written on paper watermarked 1831. Box III/97.

20. This article was written by W. J. Fox, *Monthly Repository*, VI: 637–42. In it Fox points out the anomaly of a society that will not educate women as they do men, but who are now under the leadership of a queen.

21. It is unclear whether the word "womens" is underlined or struck out.

22. This paragraph was written on a separate page that included what appear to be reworkings of the opening paragraph and a passage which begins by repeating the last few words of the previous sentence and continues with this paragraph. It includes a less obvious reference to men's use of prostitutes and to the implication that all women are trained to be "purchased" with payment of a home, reputation, etc. than the following paragraph. It is not clear whether HTM intended to replace the next paragraph with this one or merely to insert this new paragraph as it is placed here. Also, "intended" is written over the word "meant."

of both sexes. Let me not be mis-understood when I speak of purchase—that is not less a purchase whose payment is a home, an establishment, a reputation even, than that for which money is counted out—nay
even to this last excess of degradation do 3/4 of our adult male population[.]²³

[A]las for the hopes of the regeneration of a community in which such
a state of things excites no disgust.

We w^d say[,] is the greatest [happiness] of the greatest no., the greatest
happiness of each consistent with the happiness of others[,] a desirable &
virtuo[u]s aim? this being granted[,] as who can deny—the next question
is[,] do women attain, in the position in which they now occupy in society
the fullest development of the mental & physical capabilities with which
nature has endowed them? We can imagine no obtusity equal to the notion
that they do so—if they do not then do they not attain their greatest
capability nor their greatest happiness, which we are already admitted to
be the most virtuo[u]s aim of a human[.]

[W]e²⁴ shall perhaps startle many people when we say that we thin[k]
the system of separating the sexes during childhood is a radically mistaken
one—it induces a mystery in the feeling of the sexes towards each other,
which being allowed, not by percept yet in practice free scope for its
solution in the boy, while by the girl so much of it as is natural to a woman
must not be mentioned not even thought of.

---

23. Whether HTM's statistics are correct or not, this kind of passionate denouncement would
certainly be expected of a twenty-four-year-old woman who had recently learned that she had
contracted syphilis from her husband.

24. It is not clear where this paragraph is meant to fit into the remainder of the essay.

According to HTM, the ability to divorce
is a necessary step in correcting
institutionalized inequality.

MARRIAGE AND DIVORCE

2

Early in their friendship, HTM and JSM decided to exchange essays on the topic of marriage.[1] Harriet apparently wrote several drafts of her essay (selections 1–3 below), and although they contained overlapping themes, each also contributed ideas that do not appear in the other drafts. The common topics include the need to keep the radical ideas about marriage private, the historical perspective on marriage, the lack of conscious choice for young women, and the view of marriage as ownership. Although there is no watermark or date to confirm when they were written, the fourth and fifth selections may date from a later period; these essays do, however, extend her ideas on marriage and divorce.

Harriet Taylor Mill worried that the ideas about marriage contained in the essay should not be made public, because most women were not properly prepared to implement the ideas. In the first essay HTM merely hints that the world is "not ready," but in the second she claims that these ideas could be applied only in an educated community. In the final essay in this series she specifies that women's oppression has resulted in their "timidity" and "dependence," and thus they would be taken advantage of by men if marriage laws were abandoned. Harriet recognizes that moral stands that might be theoretically correct when supported by those with courage and insight, might be dangerous for those made weak by centuries of oppression.

A second theme in these drafts is that several centuries from HTM's time, one of the most appalling ideas from the Victorian period will be

---

1. John's essay can be found in *CW*: XXI, 35–49.

marriage, or what she refers to as "the governmental regulation of affection." Harriet sees marriage in her era as laws primarily designed to assure the sexual satisfaction of men. The problem is not with sexuality as such, but with an inequality in marriage that results in male sexuality expressing itself without regard for female sensibilities or pleasures. In her first draft, HTM focuses on the "contemptible" nature of the males in marriage. She castigates men because they have "existed so degraded from all that is beautiful as to find the greatest pleasure of their existence in the lowest and blindest physical sensuality." Although this remark appears antisexual, she qualifies her sentiment. The next paragraph claims that while all pleasure begins with the senses, some pleasures act "on the mind thro' the sense" while others make "sense the sole object."

In the second essay, HTM clarifies the role of sex in marriage by suggesting, "No man of education more than any woman of education would derive pleasure from mere animal gratification—there must be some mind." The author's use of the word "mere" is important. Animal gratification is not bad in and of itself, but Harriet argues that pleasure which does not involve some intellectual companionship or connection along with the sex is probably the expression of a man's pleasure, not a woman's. HTM apparently would not have approved of a one-night stand—that hardly proves she is a prude. Indeed, in the final essay she wonders aloud whether the present differences between men, who appear to be "sensualists," and women, who appear to be "quite exempt from this trait," might not be merely the training of society and not an inherent difference. She does assert that "every pleasure would be infinitely heightened both in kind and degree by the perfect equality of the _sexes_." If (and perhaps only if?) women and men are equal, pleasure in sex would be heightened for both. HTM reiterates her celebration of sexuality in equality at the end of this essay, when she claims that "_Sex_ in its true and finest meaning, seems to be the way in which is manifested all that is highest best and beautiful in the nature of human beings." This, from the most infamous of "frigid" women in philosophical history!

A third common theme in these drafts concerns women's lack of conscious choice of marriage partner. If women must be chaste when they enter the marriage contract, Harriet reasons, they essentially enter this contract without knowing its "nature and terms." As long as women are not taught about the reality of marriage and hence continue to stumble into marriage, the law should make divorce relatively convenient, since "who on earth would wish another to remain with them against their inclination?" The author concludes that, in fact, if women had access to educa-

tion and were legally equal, they would control their own reproduction and there would be no need for marriage.

Finally, an idea that occurs in each essay in this section is that marriage amounts to ownership of one person by another. Women have used their sexual powers to buy protection and economic power for themselves and their children. Harriet rails against the reality of marriage as a kind of prostitution, whether for middle classes or lower. (This sentiment is fully comprehensible if Harriet is still reeling from her diagnosis of syphilis.)

The fourth essay on divorce argues a new point. (This essay may have been written much later than the first three, which are clearly drafts of the same essay.) HTM claims that divorce is needed for women because their inequality may result in domestic violence or, as she calls it here, the "power to tyrannise." Although she does not dwell on it here, this selection is a hint of her interest in domestic violence that will reoccur more fully in her newspaper writings and pamphlet on this issue in the mid-1840s (see chapter on violence and domestic violence, below).

In the final fragment in this group, HTM examines the importance of establishing equality of women in order to elevate the "lower classes." The connection between women's equality and class equality is an important one. Many of the liberals working on the campaign for universal male suffrage or the reform acts focused on class issues only. HTM argues that women's equality should be included in the political struggle for social justice. She also claims that marriage will continue to degrade women until two changes are made: economic equality for women and no-fault divorce.

Readers should note the number of times in these essays that HTM mentions ideas that reappear in Utilitarianism *or* On Liberty. *Phrases such as "higher" and "lower" pleasures; degree vs. kind of pleasures; and especially the phrase in the first essay, "No government has a right to interfere with the personal freedom," which was replaced with "Every human being has a right to all personal freedom which does not interfere with the happiness of some other": all appear twenty or more years later in work published under the name of John Stuart Mill.*

1. [THE NATURE OF THE MARRIAGE CONTRACT][2]

I do not know what the <u>means</u> of advancing my opinions about 'marriage' should be—nor how much of them might be advantageously said

---

2. Written on paper watermarked 1831. Box III/77.

to the world. nor If I could be allowed to be Providence to the world for a few years how I should commence the steps which should prepare its mind to receive the ultimate opinion that all restraint or interference whatever with affection or with any thing which might be or be supposed to be in demonstration of affection is perfectly unwarrantable. Nothing could be more mischievous than the promulgation of this belief, in the present condition of men—and the time when it might be held beneficially seems so distant that one is sometimes inclined to despair of it. But I do not despair. If one individual knows only one, much more if they know several who would be happier and cause more happiness to others by such a system, that is enough to warrant faith that the time <u>may</u> come. I should think that 500 years hence, there will be nothing among the whole mass of absurdity by which former ages will be remembered, which will so excite wonder and contempt as the fact of legislative interference with matters of feeling—yes there is one thing which will be then as astonishing and as contemptible that men should ever have existed so degraded from all that is beautiful as to find the greatest pleasure of their existence in the lowest and blindest physical sensuality.

Any one who would call this 'underline>sentimental</u>' nothing could be a greater mistake.[3] It is quite plain that all pleasure is 'from the outward to the inward brought'. That strictly all pleasures as well as all pains are of the senses. The difference between good and bad-tending pleasures of sense, seems to me to consist in that the one acts on the mind thro' the sense—so <u>directly</u> that the fact of the agency of the <u>sense</u> is unconscious—while the other makes sense the sole object.

There would be no objection to making sense the end instead of the means if it really gave any pleasure which could not be obtained by higher means and if it did not always stand in the way of improvement and the attainment of all that is universally regarded as good. But this it does: To find pleasure in mere sensualism is a proof of a very low state of being, and an obstacle to the perception of a better.

No institution that could possibly be devised[,] seems to be so entirely tending to encourage and create mere sensuality[,] as that of marriage.

In the first place it makes some mere animal inclination respectable and recognized in itself.

Then having encouraged this animal want to its utmost by the approval of opinion, it takes care to prevent all voluntariness, at least in the case of one party, by [sentence is incomplete]

---

3. This sentence is unclear.

It insists that this connection shall be merely animal by taking away at least in the case of one party all voluntariness.

It seems a necessary consequence of this institution—that what they call chastity is held in honour among women, as a virtue in itself. From which follows the immorality that women enter into an agreement to pass their whole life in at least the toleration of a <u>species</u> of immorality of which they are entirely ignorant. As it is the interest of the marriage institution to confound the ideas of affection, and of sensuality, and as it is the supposed interest of the married to keep up all the latter to himself, the next step is to limit the development of affection to one person, to the original bargainer.

Marriage is the only contract I ever heared of, of which a necessary condition in the contracting parties was, that one should be entirely ignorant of the nature and terms of the contract. For owing to the notion of chastity as the greatest virtue of women, the fact that a woman knew what she undertook would be considered just reason for preventing her undertaking it.

[upside down on same page]

By marriage I mean a legal obligation wh binds any person to live with, or be dependant on, another, against their inclination—wh makes the person of one human being the property of another.

~~No government has a right to interfere with the personal freedom~~ Every human being has a right to all <u>personal</u> freedom which does not interfere with the happiness of some other—

[on the opposite side of a folded page]

Many[4] of the best people—just & strong-minded people even, advocates for improvement, and who see the absurdity of [s]upposing that one state of society & age, can usefully legislate for another & a different state of society—are yet, from dread that evils may arise from any change—unwilling even to admit as a topic of discussion, the possibility of improving the institution of marriage

Yet none will admit that the institution in numberless instances works <u>its</u> [goods] <u>and it</u> is unworthy of any understanding to refuse to examine, it seems to imply a conscious weakness—we would 'try all things to the end that we may 'hold fast that wh is good'. To refuse to examine its grounds of usefulness can do honour to no cause.[']

---

4. All of this paragraph has been marked through to indicate that it is to be disregarded.

[upside down]
Wanderings of a Woman in thought[,] word & deed—I remember, well my first lesson of democratic feeling—who knew but that it was the foundation of all these wanderings wh I here record. 'Twas [a luxuriant] even^g was this

2. ["LEGISLATIVE INTERFERENCE IN MATTERS OF FEELING"][5]

If I could be allowed to be Providence to the world for a time, for the express object of raising the condition of women, I should come to you to know the <u>means</u>—the purpose would be to remove all interference with affection, or with any thing which is, or which might even be supposed to be, demonstrative of affection. To state this opinion <u>now</u>, without preparing men for it by raising their moral natures would no doubt be mischievous—and the time when it shall be universally held, and beneficially too, seems so distant when one sees what men now are, that I am sometimes inclined to despair of it—but I do not despair. If it is evident that all the best people one knows would be happier, and be the cause of more happiness to others (a necessary consequence of being themselves happy) by such a system[,] that is enough to keep alive the faith that such a time may come.

I should think that 500 years hence, among the whole mass of absurdity by which former ages like to be remembered, there will be nothing which will so excite wonder and contempt as the fact of legislative interference in matters of feeling—or rather in the expressions of feeling. It seems to me just as absurd that there should be legislation about marrying as about shaking hands. When once the law undertakes to say which demonstration of feeling shall be given to which, it seems to me quite inconsistent not to legislate for <u>all</u> demonstrations of feeling and say how many may be touched, how many seen, how many heared—the Turks is the only consistent mode.

When civilization was at so low a point as to make physical strength the foremost means of power I am surprised that men should have made any rules for their treatment of women. there was the master and there the slave—perhaps they <u>were</u> in all respects property until some notion of religion came—but I am still more surprised that in the chivalrous times women did not attain immense powers in all matters whatever;

---

5. Box III/79.

when they had attained as much consideration as they had then, I wonder they did not gain so much more by their power to gratify the sensuality of men, combined with the absence of sensuality in their own nature. In a low state of moral feeling such as the present there is such a tremendous power which the women are certainly not at all too elevated to use, if they felt what a power it might be, for they do, <u>now</u>, live by the power, only they are content to put forth only so much of it as gains them <u>bread</u>, or a <u>house</u>, or a <u>carriage</u>, or whatever they find sufficient for their desires. True, that they should know what a power this might be made is not desirable, because who would gain power by such means, is unfit for power; still as they <u>do</u> use this power for <u>paltry</u> advantages, I would rather if it must be used at all, that it were to gain some good purpose which should be a means to a better.

But that the attachments of persons of different sex should be left perfectly unshackled, is only desirable in an educated community—no man of education more than any woman of education would derive pleasure from mere animal gratifications—there must be some mind
[the manuscript ends abruptly]

3. ON MARRIAGE[6]

If I could be Providence to the world for a time, for the express purpose of raising the condition of women, I should come to you to know the <u>means</u>—the <u>purpose</u> would be to remove all interference with affection, or with any thing which is, or which even might be supposed to be, demonstrative of affection. In the present state of womens minds, perfectly uneducated, and with whatever of timidity and dependance is natural to them increased a thousand fold by their habits of utter dependance it would probably be mischievous to remove at once all restraints, they would buy themselves protectors at a dearer cost than even at present—but without raising their natures at all. it seems to me, that once give women the desire to raise their social condition, and they have a power which in the present state of civilization and of mens characters, might be made of tremendous effect. Whether nature made a difference in the nature of men and women or not, it seems now that all men, with the exception of a few lofty minded, are sensualists more or less. Women on the contrary are quite exempt from this trait, however it may appear otherwise in the cases

6. Written on paper watermarked 1832. Box III/79.

of some. It seems strange that it should be so, unless it was meant to be a source of power in demi-civilized states such as the present—or it may not be so—it may be only that the habits of freedom and low indulgence in which boys grow up and the contrary notion of what is called purity in girls may have produced the appearance of different natures in the two sexes. As certain it is that there is equality in nothing, now—all the pleasures such as there are being mens, and all the disagreables and pains being womens[,] as that every pleasure would be infinitely heightened both in kind and degree by the perfect equality of the <u>sexes</u>.

Women are educated for one single object, to gain their living by marrying—(some poor souls get it without the churchgoing in the same way—they do not seem to me a bit worse than their honoured sisters)—To be married is the object of their existence and that object being gained they do really cease to exist as to anything worth calling life or any useful purpose. One observes very few marriages where there is any real sympathy or enjoyment of companionship between the parties. The woman knows what her power is, and gains by it what she has been taught to consider 'proper' to her state. The woman who would gain power by such means is unfit for power, still they <u>do</u> use this power for paltry advantages and I am astonished it has never occurred to them to gain some large purpose: but their minds are degenerated by habits of dependance. I should think that 500 years hence none of the follies of their ancestors will so excite wonder and contempt as the fact of legislative restraint as to matters of feeling—or rather in the expressions of feelings. When once the law undertakes to say which demonstration of feeling shall be given to which, it seems quite inconsistent not to legislate for <u>all</u>, and say how many shall be seen, how many heared, and what kind and degree of feeling allows of shaking hands—the Turks is the only consistent mode.[7]

I have no doubt that when the whole community is really educated, tho' the present laws of marriage were to continue[,] they would be perfectly disregarded, because no one would marry. The widest and perhaps the quickest means to do away with its evils is to be found in promoting education—as it is the means of all good—but meanwhile it is hard that those who suffer most from its evils and who are always the best people, should be left without remedy. Would not the best plan be divorce which could be attained by <u>any, without any reason assigned</u>, and at small expence, but which could only be finally pronounced after a long period? not <u>less</u> time than two years should elapse between suing for

---

7. HTM refers to the Islamic custom of strict regulation of the types of physical contact allowed between men and women.

divorce and permission to contract again—but what the decision will be must be certain at the moment of asking for it—unless during that time the suit should be withdrawn.

(I feel like a lawyer in talking of it only! O how absurd and little it all is!)

In the present system of habits and opinions, girls enter into what is called a contract perfectly ignorant of the conditions of it, and that they should be so is considered absolutely essential to their fitness for it! But after all the one argument of the matter which I think might be said so as to strike both high and low natures is—Who would wish to have the person without the inclination? Whoever would take the benefit of a law of divorce must be those whose inclination is to separate and who on earth would wish another to remain with them against their inclination? I should think no one—people sophisticated about the matter now and will not believe that one "really would wish to go." Suppose instead of calling it a "law of divorce" it were to be called "Proof of affection." They would like it better then.

At this present time, in this state of civilization, what evil would be caused by, first placing women on the most entire equality with men, as to all rights and privileges, civil and political, and then doing away with all laws whatever relating to marriage? Then if a woman had children she must take the charge of them, women would not then have children without considering how to maintain them. Women would have no more reason to barter person for bread, or for any thing else, than men have—public offices being open to them alike, all occupations would be divided between the sexes in their natural arrangement. Fathers would provide for their daughters in the same manner as for their sons.

All the difficulties about divorce seem to be in the consideration for the children—but on this plan it would be the womans interest not to have children—now it is thought to be the woman's interest to have children as so many ties to the man who feeds her.

Sex in its true and finest meaning, seems to be the way in which is manifested all that is highest best and beautiful in the nature of human beings—none but poets have approached to the perception of the beauty of the material world—still less of the spiritual—and there never yet existed a poet, except by the inspiration of that feeling which is the perception of beauty in all for and by all the means which are given us, as well as by sight. are we not born with the five senses, merely as a foundation for others which we may make by them—and who extends and refines those material senses to the highest—into infinity—best fulfils the end of creation. That is only saying—Who enjoys most, is most virtuous. It is for <u>you</u>—the most worthy to be the apostle of all loftiest virtue—to teach, such as may be taught, that the higher the <u>kind</u> of enjoyment, the <u>greater</u> the <u>degree</u>—perhaps there is but one class to whom this <u>can</u> be <u>taught</u>—the poetic nature struggling with superstition: <u>you</u> are fitted to be the saviour of such—

4. RIGHTS OF WOMEN TO THE ELECTIVE FRANCHISE AND GENERAL CONSIDERATION ON THE RIGHTS OF WOMEN. BY AN ENGLISHWOMAN.[8]

Divorce more needed by women than men by all the difference between having <u>none</u> & having <u>all</u> the power. It is no answer to say that no man who is either a good man or a gentleman takes advantage of the unjust power the law gives him; what injustice is there which human beings will not commit when tempted by passion, even when they know they are wrong, how much more when law & custom tell them they are right! But even if it could be granted that no good man & no gentleman would take advantage of his power to tyrannise, how many men of any bodys acquaintance are in the christian sense good men or in any high sense gentlemen? But if they were both to depend on the forbearance of another is not a healthy or just state of human relations, nor one fitted to the best spirit of the time

—at a time of an effeto[9] religion, a religion effeto before its time, before it has yet fulfilled half the good which it is in its capacity & in its principles to fulfill, by the intellectual incapacity & still worse the absence of spiritual elevation, of any[,] in short[,] but the formal virtues which consist mainly in the absence of striking vices, of its ministers—

5. RIGHTS OF WOMEN[10]

It is in vain to work at small & selfish changes nothing will refine & elevate the lower classes but the elevation of women to perfect equality.

---

8. Box III/91.

9. Exhausted.

10. Folded in thirds to be enclosed in a letter—"Rights of Women" written on back. Box III/104.

It is just in proportion as women are practically tho' not legally treated as equals that men are refined & spiritualised; therefore the higher classes are the most so, altho their most defective education makes this advantage not tell for what it might in their circumstances. In the present state of the world & of opinion marriage as an institution can not fail to degrade & keep down the moral character of the people if it is subjected to two radical changes, namely, that it sh^d be made a <u>real contract</u> between equals—that the two persons sh^d each possess their own pecuniary means or earnings free from any power of the other—& that it sh^d be dissoluble upon either of the parties desiring it during a sufficiently long period.

Harriet ponders the effect of men's "ownership" of women throughout her writing.

WOMEN'S RIGHTS

3

All of the essays in this section concern the relations between women and men—current and historical, social and political, overt and subtle. The first is merely a short piece highlighting a concern that will recur in the longer piece (XLI) and in the published "Enfranchisement of Women": the danger of assuming that current gender or class differences are inherent instead of a result of socialization. The second short piece is a diatribe against books about women written by women who "apolog{ize} that women exist—apolog{ize} that they are women, which last is needless as it is easy to see they are so only in as much as they cannot help it." In the third selection, Harriet specifically condemns George Sand, whose novels she admired, for her lack of a political course.

The fourth selection is a combination of five shorter pieces that range from fairly complete essays to fragmentary notes. The reader will note immediately the change in "voice" between this group and all of the previous essays in this book. These essays and notes were co-authored by Harriet Taylor Mill and John Stuart Mill. The first piece is written completely in JSM's hand, although the title was added to the end of the text in HTM's hand. The second part is composed of small, cut pieces of paper scattered in a number of files in the Mill/Taylor Collection. At the end of one piece written in JSM's hand, HTM had written a circled "A." In her hand, on a separate page, was a passage that fit the context and began a sentence that was completed on another slip of paper in JSM's hand. This writing appears to have been a draft they worked on together, each adding directly to a text that they expected to put together as a whole later. However, each of the additions made in HTM's hand also appears in JSM's hand on a separate piece of paper. The only explanation that clarifies the duplication of passages is that HTM wrote addenda to insert at two separate points into the middle of a draft handwritten by JSM. (Her handwritten page contains sections marked "A" and "B.") They later cut the manuscript at the point where each insertion should be made, and then JSM recopied HTM's draft in his own handwriting on a small piece of paper so that they could insert it at the correct spot to avoid confusion. It appears that his written insertion was made after the original text was completed. HTM was not merely copying passages already written by JSM. The Robsons claim in the Collected Works of John Stuart Mill *(XXI, lxxiv) and again in* Sexual Equality: Writings by John Stuart Mill, Harriet Taylor Mill, and Helen Taylor *(161) that the remaining sections 3–5 are in JSM's hand. We disagree. There is a dramatic change in penmanship beginning with section 3 and it is our opinion that the remaining sections are in HTM's hand.*

Whoever's handwriting is on the paper, it is clear that these texts were written jointly. The first and most complete section of this group of drafts reiterates a history of progressive moves from oppression to freedom and notes that women's disability is one of birth—the type of disadvantage that modern Europe has most clearly tried to abandon. The disability Harriet and John focused on is the inability of women to participate in political activity: whether to vote, be on a jury, or be elected. As in On Liberty, *this essay is structured as a list of objections and Harriet and John's reply to the objections. To the objection to women's suffrage that nothing is lost in not having these powers, they respond, "Freedom, power, and hope, are the charms of existence." The freedom, power, and hope that come with voting are intrinsic goods. To a second objection to enfranchisement, that the proper sphere of women is domestic life, HTM and JSM ask their imagined audience to consider women writers and even the Queen; clearly, their domestic jobs do not prevent them from participating in other events. To the third objection raised, that women's vote would cause domestic squabbling, they retort, if this is so, it is a condemnation of that marriage. Marriage always includes differences, and they are often on far more personal issues than a disagreement on voting. Furthermore, HTM and JSM argue that if both partners in a marriage are interested in politics, there is a greater chance that neither will sink into apathy. This gain in political involvement is a much more real possibility than the unlikely possibility of domestic disharmony. The beneficial influence of women in public affairs is testified to by recalling that all the major social advancements—whether abolition of slavery, school improvement, or prison reform—have been the result of women inspiring men to improve the laws. Finally, they answer the objection "What is the use of giving women the vote?" by suggesting that the question should be, "What is the use of votes at all?" They assume the standard answer will be, "To protect one's own interests." Harriet and John assert that women have distinct interests from men (e.g., needing protection from domestic violence) and that those disparate concerns are precisely why women need the right to vote. HTM and JSM also promote voting as a means of fostering intelligence and moving women closer to an equal social position with men. Without the vote, they proclaim, women will remain inferior to men.*

In the subsection entitled "Women—'Rights of,'" the writing that is conglomerated from the "A" and "B" sections mentioned earlier, HTM and JSM again connect women's present oppressive treatment to the history of oppression. The authors claim that Victorian men thought that they should treat women kindly, as did masters of slaves in the past. But the important revolution will come when society realizes that treating women unequally is itself wrong. In part "B" HTM inserts the point that women are subjected to domestic violence both physical and psychological, yet another statement of her interest in this topic. Harriet and John reiterate that the difference between women's and men's occupations is probably due to education and socialization, but that even if this difference were "natural," it would not need to be legally enforced.

Subsection three of this collection begins with a kind of sentence outline of "The Rights of Women to the Elective Franchise and its Advantages," but the outline becomes complete paragraphs on a few points. The first important point is the need for women to have a critical liberal arts education so that they can learn to think for themselves. The co-authors ask, Why do commonplace women sneer at "Rights of Women"? The answer to this question, according to Harriet and John, is that religion reinforces their view of themselves as naturally subservient, and they are afraid of independence. Typically, a woman's entire talent goes into seducing a man without her realizing that the real evil for women is the necessity of dependence. The victim mentality of the Victorian woman seeks only a good master, not freedom from masters.

The fourth subsection in this group of writings is primarily a set of notes in answer to the title, "Why Women Are Entitled to the Suffrage." Harriet and John suggest that giving women the vote will help women be seen as citizens, not just as objects owned by men. The final subsection outlines political and social goals for women (e.g., no exclusion from suffrage; freedom of speech, religion, and association; marriage as partnership, and freedom for women to choose any occupation).

Between the long set of writings just outlined and "Enfranchisement of

Women" is inserted a one-paragraph snippet that echoes a theme seen throughout this section, namely that an age in which one person has the legal right to another is an age of barbarism.

The final selection, "Enfranchisement of Women," was published in the Westminster Review in 1851 and is the best known example of Harriet Taylor Mill's writing. Many of the ideas and themes found in the other writings in this section appear in this published paper: that the subjection of women is directly related to physical force, that women's history parallels the general history of oppression, and that inequality corrupts marriage. HTM begins the piece with an account of the recent women's suffrage convention in the United States. She wonders why the subjection of women has been a custom and concludes that oppression results because men like women to be subordinate. Because women are kept from the kind of education that would stimulate their complete development and because men have all the power in marriage, women learn deceptive ways to gain power. She answers four basic objections to women's involvement in political life: that enfranchisement is incompatible with rearing children, that it will create too much competition in the workforce, that it will "harden" the character of women, and that women themselves don't want emancipation. To the final objection HTM replies that "habits of submission" account for the refusal of most women to demand their just rights. According to her argument, Victorian women's complacency mirrors that of Asian women and other oppressed people around the world who do not recognize the injustice of their position. Even literary women still succeed only if they don't defy the men in power. The desire to flourish in a world run by men causes well-educated, articulate women, the very women who could and should be leaders in the fight for equality, to remain silent. The convention in the United States and some women's actions in the U.K., she argues, have begun to prove that many women do want emancipation and enfranchisement.

Any reader will be struck by HTM's knowledge of women's history in the enfranchisement essay (and throughout her writing). She mentions eleven different influential women from the 12th to the 18th century. After reading this essay, one cannot help but hear the heartfelt life she shared with John that informs sentences such as: "The mental companionship which is improving, is communion between active minds, not mere contact between an active mind and a passive. This inestimable advantage is even now enjoyed, when a strong-minded man and a strong-minded woman are, by a rare chance, united." The reader senses that sentences such as these grow out of her experience with JSM. Her own life is an example that "the highest order of durable and happy attachments would be *a hundred times more frequent than they are, if the affection which the two sexes sought from one another were that genuine friendship, which only exists between equals in privileges as in faculties."*

1. [COMMENT ON JSM'S CORRESPONDENCE
WITH AUGUSTE COMTE][1]

It appears to me that the idea which you[2] propose in the division of the functions of men in the general government proceeds on the supposition of the incapacity or unsuitableness of the same mind for work of active life & for work of reflection & combination: & that the same supposition is sufficient to account for the differences in the characters & apparent capacities of men & women considering that the differences of the occupations in life are just those which you say in the case of men must produce distinct characters (neither you nor Comte[3] seem to settle the other analogous question, whether original differences of character & capacities in men are to determine to which class of workers they are to belong.) & there is also to be taken into account the unknown extent of action on the physical & mental powers, of hereditary servitude.

I should like to begin the forming of a book or list of what in human beings must be individual & of in what they may classified.

I now & then find a generous defect in your mind or yr 'method'—such is your liability to take an over large measure of people—sauf having to draw in afterwards—a proceeding more needful than pleasant weak by excess of the moral or conscientious principle, seems to me to attain its finest expression only when in addition to a high developement of the powers of intellect, the moral qualities rise consciously above all—so that the being looks down on his own character with the very same feelings as on those of the rest of the world & so desiring the qualities he thinks

---

1. Written after Harriet saw John's correspondence with Comte (described below) in late 1843 or early 1844. Box III/103.

2. Apparently referring to John Stuart Mill.

3. In late 1843 or early 1844, after breaking off his correspondence with French Philosopher Auguste Comte, John showed copies of his letters and those from Comte to Harriet. The correspondence included a discussion of women. Comte argued that women's smaller brains condemned them to a permanent childishness and that their subordination in marriage and society at large was physiologically required. Here Harriet is taking issue with the concessions John had made in his replies to Comte's ideas.

elevated <u>for themselves</u> wholly unmoved by considerations proper to any <u>portion</u> of the race still less to himself.

"To do justly, to love mercy, (generosity) & to walk humbly before all men" is very fine for the age in wh it was produced, but why was it not '<u>before God</u>' rather than before <u>all men</u>? It make the sentiment seem rather Greek than Jewish.

2. [FRUSTRATION WITH WOMEN WRITERS WHO DO NOT SUPPORT WOMEN'S EQUALITY][4]

"The Lord <u>protect</u>[5] us from our friends![")] says the old proverb & truly of all instances might the saying be applied by women of the books about women written by women—The wolves in sheep's clothing[,] the Ellises [&] Jamesons[6]—they write as if their object was to bribe their masters into allowing a little, a very little freedom to their bodies by telling them that they have no idea how voluntarily servile their minds shall be—for the sentance . . . nothing could excuse the base servility & vulgar flattery but the supposition that the lady at the time of writing it was violently '<u>in Love</u>'—this fact can account for but not excuse the words. Ladies in love have no business to undertake to arrange what is right & wrong for other women & should be forced to keep their transports of flattery of the other sect for the ear of the 'one' alone who occasions them. We have heared this sentance quoted to men in the sly intention of making them look silly & it has always been received with immense laughter. As a goodnatured critic in the Qua[r]terly remarks the bathos is 'ludicrously absent between it & the statement that ces messieurs are much moved by the sight of a "favorite dish".' What solemn aldermanic creatures must these worthy old ladies be accustomed to. If disposed to sum up the whole subject pithily we might do so in these few words, men are great fools but women are greater—see the names at the head of this article—but say a few words seriously on the subject.

These writing it may truly say 'I am nothing if I am not apologetical'—

4. Box III/100.

5. The word "dafend" is written above "protect," but is not crossed out.

6. Harriet is probably referring to the "Mrs. Ellis" who wrote *The Mothers of England: Their influence & Responsibility* (London: Fisher, Son, & Co., 1843) and to Anna Browell Jameson, who wrote *Communion of Labour: A Second Lecture on the Social Employments of Women* (London: Longmans, et al., 1856), and many other works.

as far as they are individually concerned the[y] are indeed nothing beside. one long apology is all they have to say for themselves or for women. apology that women exist—apology that they are women, which last is needless as it is easy to see they are so only in as much as they cannot help it[.] then the tiresome repetition of the old woman's (& elderly "gentlemen's") phrase of their "lords" newspaper reporter & parvenue puristes[7]

3. [ON GEORGE SAND'S LETTER TO THE RÉFORME][8]

I am an old admirer of George Sand & was one of the first to give her honour public & private. When all other persons in England abused her as an immoral & indecent writer I & my circle of friends, persons not without influence, were the first to s'écrier[9] against the charges universally made 15 years ago against her writings & to appeal to all who condemned them, from their judgement then to the their judgement now, & the event has justified the appeal. How then can I express my astonishment, mortification & grief to find that when a great political crisis of the world has arrived, brought about by the noble[10]   of Paris, Mme G. Sand alone remains behind—not only takes no initiative, puts forth no principles, but in a manner worthy only of a timid & commonplace lady, repudiates the kindly flatteries made to her in your paper.

Her letter to the Réforme protesting against the use of her name in your paper is to me incomprehensible for its fatuity. I can only attribute it to a fear that her literary vanity may be compromised by the connexion of her established reputation with your unestablished—However this may be, the reply to her letter, in your paper, is as superior in dignity & disinterestedness to hers as her literary reputation to yours. I have only now to say for myself & for all women of strong mind & large heart I can only say I wish you all possible success in your undertaking & I only hope you will treat the disavowal of connexion with you by any woman whether

---

7. Upstart purists.

8. Unpublished letter to the editor of *Voix Des Femmes,* a feminist and socialist newspaper. Box XL/2. On 9 April 1848 George Sand had written to the newspaper objecting to attempts to draft her for the National Assembly. Although the manuscripts, both in French and English, are in JSM's hand, Harriet's familiarity with and admiration for Sand's fiction (see the references to Sand in chapter 8, below) make it plausible that this piece was co-authored.

9. To exclaim.

10. In the French version of this piece, the word "elan" appears here.

George Sand or any other with the silent pity which is the tribute one pays to weakness & timidity.

une anglaise.[11]

Sand is like one of our English writing women (I do not know how the case may be in France) who always commence by declaring that they do not intend to advocate the emancipation of women although to the partial emancipation of women gained by more generous spirits it is alone owing that they are able to make their voices heard & to take up that position in society & literary influence which they are afraid to compromise by any attempt to help on the same cause[.] English literary women have been hitherto particularly distinguished by their little basenesses caused by timidity.

I agree with you in your expression of admiration of her fine talent, beautiful stories & admirable style but I think you are making a great error & one most injurious to the cause of women in applying the term *philosophe* to her. If there be anything characteristic of Sand's writings it is the presence of imagination & feeling & the absence of thought.

She means to *écraser* them *du haut de sa supériorité*[12] which as a thinker or a practical person certainly does not exist. ~~I fear that contrary~~ Latterly however I have feared that she was destined, contrary to what I had hoped, to be no otherwise useful to the cause of women (from which the best interests of society can never be separated) than, in the manner in which all eminent women are so, by the mere fact of being women.

4. RIGHTS OF WOMEN — AND ESPECIALLY WITH REGARD TO THE ELECTIVE FRANCHISE — BY A WOMAN — DEDICATED TO QUEEN VICTORIA[13]

A great number of progressive changes are constantly going forward in human affairs and ideas, which escape the notice of unreflecting people,

---

11. An Englishwoman.

12. To bring them down from the height of their superiority.

13. This text is co-authored by HTM and JSM. XLI/2. The title and sections marked are in HTM's hand, while the remainder is in JSM's hand. Sections in JSM's hand have been altered by HTM and the passages in her hand are meant to fit into specific sections, even beginning sentences that were finished in JSM's hand; hence it is clear that the entire manuscript was a joint project.

because of their slowness. As each successive step requires a whole generation or several generations to effect it, and is then only one step, things in reality very changeable remain a sufficient length of time without perceptible progress, to be, by the majority of contemporaries, mistaken for things permanent and immovable and it is only by looking at a long series of generations that they are seen to be, in reality, always moving, and always in the same direction.

This is remarkably the case with respect to Privileges and Exclusions. In every generation, the bulk of mankind imagine that all privileges and all exclusions, then existing by law or usage, are natural, fit and proper, even necessary: ~~unless indeed some one~~ except such as happen to be, just at that time, in the very crisis of the struggle which puts an end to them—which rarely happens to more than one set or class of them at a time. But when we take all history into view we find that its whole course is a getting rid of privileges and exclusions. Anciently all was privilege and exclusion. There was not a person or class of persons who had not a line marked round them which they were in no case permitted to overstep. There was not a function or operation in society, sufficiently desirable to be thought worth guarding, which was not rigidly confined to a circumscribed class or body of persons. Some functions were confined to particular families—some to particular guilds, corporations, or societies. Whoever has any knowledge of ancient times knows that privilege and exclusion was not only the general rule in point of fact, but ~~was in entire~~[14] ~~was alone in~~[15] that nothing else was in accordance with the ideas of mankind. Whenever any action or occupation, private or public, was thought of, it seemed natural to everybody that there should be some persons who were allowed to do the action or follow the occupation, and others who were not. People never thought of inquiring why it should be so, or what there was in the nature of the particular case to require it. People seldom ask reasons for what is in accordance with the whole spirit of what they see round them, but only for what jars with that spirit. Even bodily freedom, the right to use one's own labour for one's own benefit, was once a privilege, and the great majority of mankind were excluded from it. This seems to the people of our day something monstrously unnatural: to people of former days it seemed the most natural of all things. It was very gradually that this was got rid of; through many intermediate stages, of serfage, villenage &c. Where this did not exist, the system of castes did: and that appears profoundly unnatural to us, but so profoundly natural to

---

14. In JSM's hand.

15. In HTM's hand, as is the final choice of phrase, "that nothing else was in."

Hindoos that they have not yet given it up. Among the early Romans fathers had the power of putting their sons to death, or selling them into slavery: this seemed perfectly natural to them, most unnatural to us. To hold land, in property, was throughout feudal Europe the privilege of a noble. This was only gradually relaxed and in Germany there is still much land which can only be so held. Up to the Reformation to teach religion was the exclusive privilege of a male separate class, even to read the Bible was a privilege: Those who lived at the time of the Reformation and who adopted it, ceased to recognize this case of privilege and exclusion, but did not therefore call in question any others. Throughout the Continent political office and military rank were exclusive privileges of a hereditary noblesse, till the French revolution destroyed these privileges. Trades and occupations have almost everywhere ceased to be privileges. Thus exclusion after exclusion has disappeared, until privilege has ceased to be the general rule, and tends more and more to become the exception: it now no longer seems a matter of course that there should be an exclusion, but it is conceded that freedom and admissibility ought to prevail, wherever there is not some special reason for limiting them. Whoever considers how immense a change this is from primitive opinions and feelings, will think it nothing less than the very most important advance which has hitherto been made in human society. It is nothing less than the beginning of the reign of justice, or the first dawn of it at least. It is the introduction of the principle that distinctions, and inequalities of rights, are not good things in themselves, and that none ought to exist for which there is not a special justification, grounded on the greatest good of the whole community, privileged and excluded taken together.

Considering how slowly this change has taken place and how very recent is its date, it would be surprising if many exclusions did not still exist, by no means fitted to stand the test which until lately no one ever thought of applying to them. The fact that any particular exclusion exists, and has existed hitherto, is in such a case no presumption whatever that it ought to exist. We may rather surmise that it is probably a remaining relic of that past state of things, in which privilege and exclusion were the general rule. That the opinions of mankind have not yet put an end to it is not even a presumption that they ought not, or that they will not hereafter do so.

We propose to examine how far this may be the case with one of the principal remaining cases of privilege, the privilege of sex: and to consider whether the civil and political disabilities of women have any better foundation in justice or the interest of society than any of the other exclusions which have successively disappeared.

In the first place it must be observed that the disabilities of women are exactly of the class which modern times most pride themselves on getting rid of—disabilities by birth. It is the boast of England that if some persons are privileged by birth, at least none are disqualified by it—that anybody may rise to be a peer, or a member of parliament, or a minister—that the path to distinction is not closed to the humblest. But it is closed irrevocably to women. A woman is born disqualified, and cannot by any exertion get rid of her disabilities. This makes her case an entirely peculiar one in modern Europe. It is like that of the negro in America, and worse than that of the roturier[16] formerly in Europe, for he might receive or perhaps buy a patent of nobility. Women's disqualifications are the only indelible ones.

It is also a peculiarity in the case, that the persons disqualified are of the same race, the same blood, the same parents, as the privileged, and have even been brought up and educated along with them. There are none of the excuses grounded on their belonging to a different class in society. The excluded, have the same advantages of breeding and social culture, as the admitted, and have or might have the same educational advantages of all sorts.

It is necessary to protest first of all against a mode of thought on the subject of political exclusions which though less common than it once was is still very common, viz. that a prohibition, an exclusion, a disability, is not an evil or a grievance in itself. This is the opinion of many grave, dignified people, who think that by uttering it they are shewing themselves to be sound, sage, and rational, superior to nonsense and sentimentality. Where is the grievance, they say, of not being allowed to be an elector? What good would it do you to be an elector? Why should you wish to be one? They always require you to point out some distinct loss or suffering, some positive inconvenience which befals you from anything you complain of. This class of persons are enemies of all sorts of liberty. They say to those who complain, Have you not liberty enough? What do you want to do more than you do at present? And what is strange is, that they think this is shewing peculiar good sense and sobriety. It is a doctrine however which they are not fond of applying to their own liberties. Suppose that a law were made forbidding them ever to go beyond the British isles, and that when they complained they were answered thus: Is not Great Britain large enough for you? Are not England, Scotland and Ireland fine countries? Is there not variety enough in them for any reasonable taste? Why do you want to go to foreign countries? Your proper place

---

16. Commoner.

is at home. Your duties are there. You have no duties to perform abroad: you are not a sailor, or a merchant, or an ambassador. Stay at home.— Would they not say—"My good friend, it is possible that I may never wish to go abroad at all; or that if I do wish, it may not be convenient: but that does not give you any right to say I <u>shall</u> not go abroad. It is an injustice and a hardship to be told that even if I do wish to go I shall not be permitted. I shall probably live all my life in this house, but that is a very different thing from being imprisoned in it."—What these people (who deem their notions wise because they are limited) think there is no harm in cutting off from the life of any body, except themselves, is precisely what makes the chief value of life. They think you lose nothing as long as you are not prevented from having what you have and doing what you do: now the value of life does not consist in what you have or do, but in what you may have and may do. Freedom, power, and hope, are the charms of existence. If you are outwardly comfortable they think it nothing to cut off hope, to close the region of possibilities, to say that you shall have no carrierè,[17] no excitement, that neither chance nor your own exertions shall ever make you anything more or other than you now are. This is essentially the doctrine of people legislating for others. Nobody legislates in this way for himself. When it comes home to them personally all feel that it is precisely the inconnu,[18] the indefinite, to be cut off from which would be unbearable. They know that it is not the thing they please to do, but the power of doing <u>as</u> they please that makes to them the difference between contentment and dissatisfaction. Everybody, for himself values his position just in proportion to the freedom of it: yet the same people think that freedom is the very thing which you may subtract from in the case of others, without doing them any wrong. The grievance they think is merely ideal: but they find in their own case that these ideal grievances are among the most real of any. "The proper sphere of women is domestic life." Putting aside the word "proper" which begs the question, what does this assertion mean? That no woman is qualified for any other social functions than those of domestic life? This will hardly be asserted, in opposition to the fact not only of the numerous women who have distinguished themselves as writers, but of the great number of eminent sovereigns who have been women—not only in Europe but in the East where they are shut up in zenanas. The assertion therefore can only be supposed to mean that a large proportion of mankind must devote themselves mainly to domestic management, the bringing up of children &c.

17. Career.

18. Unknown.

and that this kind of employment is one particularly suitable for women. Now, taking this for what it is worth, is it in other cases thought necessary to dedicate a multitude of people from their birth to one exclusive employment lest there should not be people enough, or people qualified enough, to fill it? It is necessary that there should be coalheavers, paviours, ploughmen, sailors, shoemakers, clerks and so forth, but is it therefore necessary that people should be <u>born</u> all these things, and not permitted to quit those particular occupations? Still more, is it necessary that because people are clerks or shoemakers they should have no thoughts or opinions beyond clerking or shoemaking? for that is the implication involved in denying them votes.

The occupations of men, however engrossing they may be considered, are not supposed to make them either less interested in the good management of public affairs, or less entitled to exercise their share of influence in those affairs by their votes. It is not supposed that nobody ought to have a vote except idle people. A shoemaker, a carpenter, a farmer have votes. Those who say that a scavenger or coalheaver should <u>not</u> have a vote, do not say so on account of his occupation but on account of his poverty or want of education. Let this ground of exclusion be admitted for one sex just as far as for the other. Whatever class of men are allowed the franchise, let the same class of women have it.

If a woman's habitual employment, whether chosen <u>for</u> or <u>by</u> her, is the management of a family, she will be no more withdrawn from that occupation by voting in an election than her neighbour will be withdrawn by it from his shop or his office.

The feeling, however, which expresses itself in such phrases as "The proper sphere of women is private life," "Women have nothing to do with politics" and the like, is, I believe, not so much any feeling regarding women as women, as a feeling against any new and unexpected claimants of political rights. In England especially there is always a grudging feeling towards all persons who unexpectedly profess an opinion in politics, or indeed in any matter not concerning their own speciality. There is always a disposition to say, What business is that of yours? When people hear that their tradespeople, or their workpeople, concern themselves about politics, there is almost always a feeling of dislike accompanying the remark. It seems as if people were vexed at finding more persons than they expected in a condition to give them trouble on that subject. Men have the same feelings about their sons unless the sons are mere echoes of their own opinions: and if their wives and daughters claimed the same privilege, their feeling would be that of having an additional disagreeable from a quarter they did not expect.

The truth is, everybody feels that whether in classes or individuals, having an opinion of their own makes them more troublesome and difficult to manage: and everybody is aware, in all cases but his own, that the intrinsic value of the opinion is very seldom much of an equivalent. But this is no more than the ministers of despotic monarchs feel with regard to popular opinion altogether. It is an exact picture of the state of mind of Metternich.[19] It is much more consistent in <u>him</u>. He says, or would say, Leave politics to those whose business it is. But these other people say, No: some whose business it is not peculiarly may and ought to have opinions on it, but others, workpeople for instance, and women, ought not. Constitutionalists and Liberals are right against Metternich only on grounds which prove them to be wrong against those whom they would exclude. Metternich is wrong because if none but those who make politics their business, had opinions and could give votes, all the rest would be delivered blindfolded into the hands of those professional politicians. This argument is good against excluding anybody, especially any class or kind of persons. It is a very great evil that any portion of the community should be left politically defenceless. To justify it in any case it must be shewn that still greater evils would arise from arming the class with opinions and votes. It may possibly admit of being maintained that this <u>would</u> be the result of giving votes to very ignorant or even in some cases to very poor people. But it is impossible to shew that any evils would arise from admitting women of the same social rank as the men who have votes.

Objection. "You would have perpetual domestic discussion." If people cannot differ in opinion on any important matter and remain capable of living together without quarrelling, there cannot be a more complete condemnation of marriage: for if so, two people cannot live together at all unless one of them is a mere cipher, abdicating all will and opinion into the hands of the other, and marriage can only be fit for tyrants and nobodies.

But the proposition is false. Do not married people live together in perfect harmony although they differ in opinions and even feelings on things which come much nearer home than politics do to most people? Does it not often happen for instance that they hold different opinions in religion? And have they not continually different opinions or wishes on innumerable private matters without quarrelling? People with whose comfort it is incompatible that the person they live with should think differently from them in politics or religion will if they marry at all generally marry a person who has either no opinions or the same sort of opinions with themselves. Besides, by discouraging political opinions in women, you

---

19. Prince Klemens von Metternich (1773-1859).

only prevent independent disinterested opinions. In a woman, to have no political opinions, practically means to have the political opinions which conduce to the pecuniary interest or social vanity of the family. If honest opinions on both sides would make dissension between married people, will there not be dissension between a man who has an opinion and a conscience in politics and a woman who sees what she thinks the interests of the family sacrificed to what seems to her a matter of indifference? except indeed that the man's public spirit is seldom strong enough to hold out long against the woman's opposition, especially if he really cares for her. Now when women and men really live together, and are each other's most intimate associates, (which in the ancient republics they were not) men never can or will be patriotic or public spirited unless women are so too. People cannot long maintain a higher tone of feeling than that of their favorite society. The wife is the incarnate spirit of family selfishness unless she has accustomed herself to cultivate feelings of a larger and more generous kind: while, when she has, her (in general) greater susceptibility of emotion and more delicate conscience makes her the great inspirer of those nobler feelings in the men with whom she habitually associates.

A part of the feeling which makes ma[n]y men dislike the idea of political women, is, I think, the idea that politics altogether are a necessary evil, a source of quarrelsome and unamiable feelings, and that their sphere of action should be restricted as much as possible, and especially that home, and social intercourse, should be kept free from them, and be retained as much as possible under influences counteractive of those of politics. One would imagine from this manner of looking at the subject, that the danger in modern times was that of too much political earnestness: that people generally felt so strongly about politics as to require a strong curb to prevent them from quarrelling about it when they meet. The fact however we know to be that people in general are quite lukewarm about politics, except where their personal interests or the social position of their class are at stake, and when that is the case women have already as strong political feelings as men have. And this wish to keep the greater interests of mankind from being thought of and dwelt on when people are brought together in private, does not really prevent ill feeling and ill blood in society, but only causes it to exist about things not worth it. Where is the benefit of hindering people from disliking each other on matters involving the liberty or the progress of mankind, only to make them hate each other from petty personal jealousies and piques? Active minds and susceptible feelings will and must interest themselves about something, and if you deny them all subjects of interest except personal ones, you reduce the personal interests to a petty scale, and make personal or social vanities the primum mobile of life: now personal rivalities are a much more fruitful source of hatred and malice than differences of political opinion.

How vain the idea that the way to make mankind amiable is to make them care for nothing except themselves and the individuals immediately surrounding them. Does not all experience shew that when people care only for themselves and their families then unless they are held down by despotism everyone's hand is against every one, and that only so far as they care about the public or about some abstract principle is there a basis for real social feeling of any sort? One reason why there is scarcely any social feeling in England, but every man, entrenched within his family, feels a kind of dislike and repugnance to every other, is because there is hardly any concern in England for great ideas and the larger interests of humanity. The moment you kindle any such concern, if it be only about negroes or prisoners in gaols, you not only elevate but soften individual character: because each begins to move in an element of sympathy, having a common ground, even if a narrow one, to sympathize on. And yet you would prevent the sympathetic[20] influence of women from exercising itself on the great interests. Observe, by the way, that almost all the popular movements towards any object of social improvement which have been successful in this country, have been those in which women have taken an active part, and have fraternized thoroughly with the men who were engaged about them: Slavery abolition, establishment of schools, improvement of prisons. In the last we know that a woman was one of the principal leaders,[21] and in all three the victory was chiefly due to the Quakers among whom women are in all points of public exertion as active as men. Probably none of these things would have been effected if women had not taken so strong an interest in them—if the men engaged had not found a constant stimulus in the feelings of the women connected with them, and a necessity for excusing themselves in the eyes of the women in every case of failure or shortcoming. And will any one say that the harmony of domestic life or of social intercourse was rendered less because women took interest in these subjects? It will be said, they were questions peculiarly concerning the sympathies and therefore suitable to women. But they were also subjects which concerned people's self interest and were therefore sources of antipathy as well as sympathy: and there have been few subjects on which there has been more party spirit and more vehement opposition

---

20. Their writing on the importance of "sympathy" as the motivation for social action seems to hint at the kind of position Martha Nussbaum outlines in "Compassion: The Basic Social Emotion," *Social Philosophy and Policy* 13, 1 (Winter 1996) 27-58.

21. Elizabeth Fry (1780-1845).

of political feeling, than on West India slavery and on the Bell and Lancaster schools?

"What is the use of giving women votes?" Before answering this question it may be well to put another: What is the use of votes at all? Whatever use there is in any case, there is in the case of women. Are votes given to protect the particular interests of the voters? Then women need votes, for the state of the law as to their property, their rights with regard to children, their right to their own person, together with the extreme maladministration of the courts of justice in cases of even the most atrocious violence when practised by men to their wives, contributes a mass of grievances greater than exists in the case of any other class or body of persons. Are votes given as a means of fostering the intelligence of the voters, and enlarging their feelings by directing them to a wider class of interests? This would be as beneficial to women as to men. Are votes given as a means of exalting voters in social position and estimation? and to avoid making, an offensive distinction to their disadvantage? This reason is strong in the case of women. And this reason would suffice in the absence of any other. Women should have votes because otherwise they are not the equals but the inferiors of men.

So clear is this, that any one who maintains that it is right in itself to exclude women from votes, can only do it for the express purpose of stamping on them the character of inferiors.

Women—(Rights of)[22]

The rights of women are no other than the rights of human beings. The phrase has come into use, and become necessary only because law and opinion, having been made chiefly by men, have refused to recognize in women the universal claims of humanity. When opinion on this subject shall be further advanced towards rectification, neither "rights of women" nor even "equality of women" will be terms in use, because neither of them fully expresses the real object to be aimed at, viz. the negation of all distinctions among persons, grounded on the accidental circumstance of sex.[23]

---

22. This manuscript is a combination of manuscripts often written on pieces cut from larger pages.

23. HTM has written a circled "A" at the end of the sentence. The paper on which JSM has written has been cut just under this sentence. On a separate page HTM has written two sections marked "A" and "B." The section labeled "A" appears at the beginning of the next paragraph. The "B" section is inserted later.

The present legal and moral subjection of women is the principal, and likely to be the latest remaining relic of the primitive condition of society, the tyranny of physical force. Society sets out from the state of lawlessness in which every one's hand is against every one, and each robs and slays a weaker than himself when he has any object to gain by it: the next stage is that in which the races and tribes which are vanquished in war are made slaves, the absolute property of their conquerors: this by degrees changes into serfdom or some other limited form of[24] dependence, and in the course of ages mankind pass through various decreasing stages of subjection on one side and privilege on the other, up to complete democracy which the advanced guard of the human species are now just reaching: so that the only arbitrary distinction among human beings, which the one or two most advanced nations do not now, at least in principle, repudiate, is that between women and men. And even this distinction although still essentially founded on despotism, has assumed a more mitigated form with each step in the general improvement of mankind, whether we compare age with age, people with people or class with class: which was also the case with all the other social tyrannies, in their progress towards extinction.

It deserves particular remark, that at every period in this gradual progress, the prevailing morality of the time (with or without the exception of a few individuals superior to their age) invariably consecrated all existing facts. It assumed every existing unjust power or privilege as right and proper, contenting itself with inculcating a mild and forbearing exercise of them: by which inculcation no doubt it did considerable good, but which it never failed to balance by enjoining on the sufferers an unresisting and uncomplaining submission to the power itself. Morality recommended kind treatment of slaves by their masters, and just rule by despots over their subjects, but it never justified or tolerated either slaves or subjects in throwing off the yoke, and wherever they have done so it has been by a plain violation of the then established morality. It is needless to point out how exactly the parallel holds in the case of women and men.

In the position of women as society has now made it, there are two distinct peculiarities. The first is, the domestic subjection of the larger portion of them. From this, unmarried women who are either in independent or in self-dependent pecuniary circumstances are exempt; so that by the admission of society itself, there is no inherent necessity for it; and the time cannot be far off when to hold any human being, who has past

---

24. End of inserted section written in HTM's hand. The text continues in JSM's hand.

the age which requires to be taken care of and educated by others, in a state of compulsory obedience to any other human being (except as the mere organ and minister of the law) will be acknowledged to be as monstrous an infraction of the rights and dignity of humanity, as slavery is at last, though tardily, among a small, comparatively advanced part of the human race, felt to be. Practically the evil varies, in the case of women,[25] (as it did in the case of slaves) from being slowly murdered by continued bodily torture, to being only subdued in spirit and thwarted of all those higher and finer developements of individual character of which personal liberty has in all ages been felt to be the indispensable condition.

The other point of the question relates to the numberless disabilities imposed on women by law or by custom equivalent to law; their exclusion from most public and from a great number[26] of private occupations, and the direction of all the forces of society towards educating them for, and confining them to, a small number of functions, on the plea that these are the most conformable to their nature and powers. It is impossible here to enter, with any detail, into this part of the subject. Three propositions however may be laid down as certain. First; that the alleged superior adaptation of women to certain occupations, and of men to certain others, does not even now, exist, to any thing like the extent that is pretended. Secondly; that so far as it does exist, a rational analysis of human character and circumstances tends more and more to shew, that the difference is principally if not wholly the effect of differences in education and in social circumstances, or of physical characteristics by no means peculiar to one or the other sex. Lastly; even if the alleged differences of aptitude did exist, it would be a reason why women and men would generally occupy themselves differently but no reason why they should be forced to do so. It is one of the aberrations of early and rude legislation to attempt to convert every supposed natural fitness into an imperative obligation. There was an apparent natural reason why the children should follow the occupation of their parents; they were often familiar with it from childhood, and had always peculiar facilities for being instructed in it; but this natural fitness, converted into a law, became the oppressive and enslaving system of Castes. Good laws, laws which pay any due regard to human liberty, will not class human beings according to mere general presumptions, nor require them to do one thing and to abstain from another on account of any supposed suitableness to their natural or acquired gifts, but will leave them to class themselves under the natural influence of those and of all

---

25. The insertion marked as "B," which is in HTM's hand, begins here.

26. "B" ends here.

the other peculiarities of their situation, which if left free they will not fail to do quite as well, not to say much better, than any inflexible laws made for them by pedantic legislators or conceited soi-disant philosophers are ever likely to do.

The Rights of Women to the Elective Franchise and its Advantages[27]

Statement of the Principle—perfect equality.

Although this requires no proof, necessary to consider the subject as usually treated and reply categorically to objections either to it as a principle or as a matter of practice.

Prevailing opinion is that some change is needed but not fundamental, only of degree—above all that the change shall not alter the principle of inequality, foundation of present condition.

Present state of opinion <u>divided into</u> the following:

Largest class, both men and women, composed of those who take things for granted because they are so and have always been so—have a natural fear of making any alteration in the relations on which they are accustomed to think the best things in life depend. We would prove to them that tho' the best things in life did depend on those relations as they are, the relation under its present conditions is worn out and no longer affords to either party a life either well or sufficiently filled for the spirit of the present time which requires more developement of the spiritual and less of the physical instead of the contrary. True, education is the great want of the time, but people have scarce begun to perceive in what <u>sense</u> of education—that which modern developement requires should be the desire, power and habit of using the person's own mind, instead of as almost all educationists seem to think <u>filling</u> the mind with an undigested mass from the minds of others, in consequence of which process the most educated people now are among the most ignorant—witness not only the (absurdly) called educated <u>classes</u> but preeminently the collegiate, legal, clerical, professional men. Placeman, clergyman, barrister, doctor, has each something to say on one subject—in the majority of cases this something is what he has heard from others and therefore comes from him deadborn[28]—

---

27. The remainder of this manuscript is in HTM's hand. This section consists of an outline that contains the sketch of arguments.

28. This may be an allusion to Socrates' view of education, in which the teacher is midwife of the student's idea.

if an active minded person, he is found to talk interestingly on his one subject, but let conversation be anything worthy the name of general, and the profound ignorance and inactivity of intellect presented by the educated classes in England is the only thing capable of exciting the mind in intercourse with them.

After all the objections that are made both by men and women have been considered, one may perhaps put it down as a fact that they are all based on the supposition that conceding equal political rights to women would be contrary to the interests of men. Some think it would be contrary to their real interests, some to their selfish interests. We think they would be not only in accordance with, but greatly advantageous to the interests of men with perhaps the sole exception of interests if such they can be called, as no man in the present day would venture to &c. It would probably put a stop to a sort of license of indulgence which everybody is now agreed in discountenancing.—

A great part of the feeling which resists the political equality of women is a feeling of the contrast it would make with their domestic servitude.

The evils of women's present condition all lie in the necessity of dependence: the just cause of complaint lies here and not elsewhere.

Objections made by common place women
   to freedom for women.
   by common place men
Historical parallel between men and women sovereigns.

The expression "Rights of Women," it is the fashion among women and among a certain vulgar class of men to affect to receive with a sneer and to endeavour to drown with ridicule. In neither case does this appear to be because they really regard it as meaningless for if the same people are asked why they receive it so, they invariably grow angry and this mode of reception perpetuates itself because the intense constitutional shyness of Englishmen makes them of all things fear ridicule and this phrase as well as the idea it includes has always hitherto been put down by ridicule. Commonplace women's aversion to it has more meaning. It contains the everlasting dread of the givers of the loaves and fishes— their lively imagination exaggerates the disagreables of having to work instead of being worked for, which their education having precluded all notions of public spirit or personal dignity, far from being revolted at the idea of dependence, elevates submission into a virtual per se. They enormously exaggerate both the talent and the labour required for the external details of life, unaware that they give as much labour and fritter away as much talent in executing badly those domestic details which they enlarge upon as arguments against women's emancipation, as would be sufficient to conduct both the public and private affairs of either an individual or a family. Is it not true that half the time of half the women in existence is passed in worthless and trashy work, of no benefit to any human being[?]

Objection. Well bred people never exercise the power which the law gives them. But all their conduct takes the bent which has been given to the two characters by the relation which the law establishes. The woman's whole talent goes into the inducing, persuading, coaxing, caressing, in reality the seducing, capacity. In what ever class in life, the woman gains her object by seducing the man. This makes her character quite unconsciously to herself, petty and paltry.

Why Women Are Entitled to the Suffrage[29]

1st. Because it is just

2nd. Because women have many serious practical grievances from the state of the law as it regards them.

3rd. Because the general condition of women, being one of dependence, is in itself a grievance which their exclusion from the suffrage stamps and perpetuates.

4th. Reply to objections.

The exclusion of women from the suffrage becomes a greater offence and degradation in proportion as the suffrage is opened widely to all men. When the only privileged class is the aristocracy of sex the slavery of the excluded sex is more marked and complete.

Notion that giving the suffrage does no good; a shallow fallacy. The greatest good that can be done for women and the preparation of all others is to recognize them as citizens—as substantive members of the community instead of mere things belonging to members of the community. One of the narrowness of modern times, in England, is that the indirect effects produced by the spirit of institutions are not recognized and therefore the immense influence on the whole life of a person produced by the fact of citizenship is not at all felt.

Even according to the most moderate reformers the suffrage should include clerks and other educated persons who are dependent on employers. These are not turned out of their employments for voting against their

---

29. Another set of notes written in HTM's hand.

employers, only because there is a point of honour on the subject. There ought to be the same between married people.

To suppose that one person's freedom of opinion must merge in that of the other and that they could not vote differently at an election without quarrelling is a satire on marriage and a reductio ad absurdum of it. All persons, men and women, in the present age, are entitled to ~~freedom of conscience~~ mental independence and marriage like other institutions must reconcile itself to this necessity.

The queen professes to live and act perfectly conscientiously: does she ask her husband's opinion and submit to it in all her acts as queen? is not this a case of married persons exercising their separate freedom of opinion and conduct?

The principle that all who are taxed should be represented, would give votes not only to single women but to married women whose property is settled.

Women should either not be allowed to have property or should have all which follows from the possession of property.

The man acquires the points of character that belong to one who is always having homage paid to the power vested in him; self-important, domineering, with more or less politeness of form according to his breeding; and more or less suavity according to his temper—the difference in the case of a well bred man being mainly this, that as he does not need to assert what never is disputed, so he does not do so, but contents himself with accepting the position which the law assigns and which the woman yields to him: it being a main point in the ways of well bred people that all occasions of bringing wills into active collision, are avoided, sometimes by a tacit compromise in which however the chief part always remains with the strongest, sometimes because that which knows itself to be the weakest makes a graceful retreat in time. In this as in other relations, good breeding does not so much affect the substance of conduct as the manner of it. When the man is ill bred the manner is coarse, tyrannical, brutal, either in a greater or in a less degree; there is superfluous self assertion, and of an offensive kind: well bred people's self assertion is only tacit, until their claims are in some way resisted, but they are not therefore less tenacious of all that the law or custom[30] gives them, and are often not less really inflated by self-worship caused by the ~~worship~~ deference they receive from dependents of every description.

---

30. "Or custom" has been added in Harriet's handwriting over the inked version.

Political[31]

No hereditary privileges whatever.

No exclusion from the suffrage, but an educational qualification (qu. what?).

Complete freedom of speech, printing, public meetings and associations, locomotion, and industry in all its branches.

No church establishments or paid clergy; but national schools and colleges without religion.

Social

All occupations to be alike open to men and women; and all kinds and departments of instruction.

Marriage to be like any other partnership, dissoluble at pleasure, and not merging any of the individual rights of either of the parties to the contract. All the interests arising out of marriage to be provided for by special agreement.

The property of intestates to belong to the state, which then undertakes the education, and setting out in life, of all descendants not otherwise provided for.

No one to acquire by gift or bequest more than a limited amount.

5. [NOTE ON WOMEN'S LEGAL SUBJUGATION][32]

The most remarkable thing about the present stage of mental developement of the times we live in is the extreme & marvelous barbarism of its moral notions—while science has advanced so greatly & the intellect also as an instrument on scientific matters—in morals we are scarcely one remove from the savage. At this time one human being has a legal right to the person of another without that other's consent!

---

31. This set of notes is also in HTM's hand.

32. XLI/2.

6. ENFRANCHISEMENT OF WOMEN[33]

Most of our readers will probably learn from these pages for the first time, that there has arisen in the United States, and in the most civilized and enlightened portion of them, an organized agitation on a new question—new, not to thinkers, nor to any one by whom the principles of free and popular government are felt as well as acknowledged, but new, and even unheard-of, as a subject for public meetings and practical political action. This question is, the enfranchisement of women; their admission, in law and in fact, to equality in all rights, political, civil, and social, with the male citizens of the community.

It will add to the surprise with which many will receive this intelligence, that the agitation which has commenced is not a pleading by male writers and orators for women, those who are professedly to be benefited remaining either indifferent or ostensibly hostile. It is a political movement, practical in its objects, carried on in a form which denotes an intention to persevere. And it is a movement not merely *for* women, but *by* them. Its first public manifestation appears to have been a Convention of Women, held in the State of Ohio, in the spring of 1850. Of this meeting we have seen no report. On the 23rd and 24th of October last, a succession of public meetings was held at Worcester in Massachusetts under the name of a "Women's Rights Convention," of which the president was a woman,[34] and nearly all the chief speakers women; numerously reinforced, however, by men, among whom were some of the most distinguished leaders in the kindred cause of negro emancipation. A general and four special committees were nominated, for the purpose of carrying on the undertaking until the next annual meeting.

According to the report in the *New York Tribune,* above a thousand persons were present throughout, and "if a larger place could have been had, many thousands more would have attended." The place was described as "crowded from the beginning with attentive and interested listeners."[35] In regard to the quality of the speaking, the proceedings bear an advantageous comparison with those of any popular movement with which we are acquainted, either in this country or in America. Very rarely in the oratory of public meetings is the part of the verbiage and declamation so small, that of calm good sense and reason so considerable. The result of

---

33. Published in the *Westminster Review,* 1851.

34. Paulina Kellogg Wright Davis (1813-76).

35. Jacob Gilbert Forman, *New York Daily Tribune,* 26 October 1850.

the Convention was in every respect encouraging to those by whom it was summoned: and it is probably destined to inaugurate one of the most important of the movements towards political and social reform, which are the best characteristics of the present age.

That the promoters of this new agitation take their stand on principles, and do not fear to declare these in their widest extent, without time-serving or compromise, will be seen from the resolutions adopted by the Convention, part of which we transcribe.

Resolved—That every human being, of full age, and resident for a proper length of time on the soil of the nation, who is required to obey the law, is entitled to a voice in its enactment; that every such person, whose property or labour is taxed for the support of the government, is entitled to a direct share in such government; therefore,

Resolved—That women are entitled to the right of suffrage, and to be considered eligible to office, . . . and that every party which claims to represent the humanity, the civilization, and the progress of the age, is bound to inscribe on its banner equality before the law, without distinction of sex or colour.

Resolved—That civil and political rights acknowledge no sex, and therefore the word "male" should be struck from every State Constitution.

Resolved—That, since the prospect of honourable and useful employment in after-life is the best stimulus to the use of educational advantages, and since the best education is that we give ourselves, in the struggles, employments, and discipline of life; therefore it is impossible that women should make full use of the instruction already accorded to them, or that their career should do justice to their faculties, until the avenues to the various civil and professional employments are thrown open to them.

Resolved—That every effort to educate women, without according to them their rights, and arousing their conscience by the weight of their responsibilities, is futile, and a waste of labour.

Resolved—That the laws of property, as affecting married persons, demand a thorough revisal, so that all rights be equal control over the property gained by their mutual toil and sacrifices, and be heir to her husband precisely to that extent that he is heir to her, and entitled at her death to dispose by will of the same share of the joint property as he is.

The following is a brief summary of the principal demands.

　　1. *Education* in primary and high schools, universities, medical, legal, and theological institutions.
　　2. *Partnership* in the labours and gains, risks and remunerations, of productive industry.
　　3. A *coequal share* in the formation and administration of laws—munic-

ipal, state, and national—through legislative assemblies, courts, and executive offices.

It would be difficult to put so much true, just, and reasonable meaning into a style so little calculated to recommend it as that of some of the resolutions. But whatever objection may be made to some of the expressions, none, in our opinion, can be made to the demands themselves. As a question of justice, the case seems to us too clear for dispute. As one of expediency, the more thoroughly it is examined the stronger it will appear.

That women have as good a claim as men have, in point of personal right, to the suffrage, or to a place in the jury-box, it would be difficult for any one to deny. It cannot certainly be denied by the United States of America, as a people or as a community. Their democratic institutions rest avowedly on the inherent right of every one to a voice in the government. Their Declaration of Independence, framed by the men who are still great constitutional authorities—that document which has been from the first, and is now, the acknowledged basis of their polity, commences with this express statement:

> We hold these truths to be self-evident: that all men are created equal; that they are endowed by their Creator with certain inalienable rights; that among these are life, liberty, and the pursuit of happiness; that to secure these rights, governments are instituted among men, deriving their just powers from the consent of the governed.

We do not imagine that any American democrat will evade the force of these expressions by the dishonest or ignorant subterfuge, that "men," in this memorable document, does not stand for human beings, but for one sex only; that "life, liberty, and the pursuit of happiness" are "inalienable rights" of only one moiety of the human species; and that "the governed," whose consent is affirmed to be the only source of just power, are meant for that half of mankind only, who, in relation to the other, have hitherto assumed the character of governors. The contradiction between principle and practice cannot be explained away. A like dereliction of the fundamental maxims of their political creed has been committed by the Americans in the flagrant instance of the negroes; of this they are learning to recognize the turpitude. After a struggle which, by many of its incidents, deserves the name of heroic, the abolitionists are now so strong in numbers and in influence that they hold the balance of parties in the United States. It was fitting that the men whose names will remain associated with the extirpation, for the democratic soil of America, of the aristocracy of colour, should be among the originators, for America and for the rest of the world, of the first collective protest against the aristocracy of sex; a distinction as accidental as that of colour, and fully as irrelevant to all questions of government.

Not only to the democracy of America, the claim of women to civil and political equality makes an irresistible appeal, but also to those Radicals and Chartists[36] in the British islands, and democrats on the continent, who claim what is called universal suffrage as an inherent right, unjustly and oppressively withheld from them. For with what truth or rationality could the suffrage be termed universal, while half the human species remained excluded from it? To declare that a voice in the government is the right of all, and demand it only for a part—the part, namely, to which the claimant himself belongs—is to renounce even the appearance of principle. The Chartist who denies the suffrage to women, is a Chartist only because he is not a lord: he is one of those levellers who would level only down to themselves.

Even those who do not look upon a voice in the government as a matter of personal right, nor profess principles which require that it should be extended to all, have usually traditional maxims of political justice with which it is impossible to reconcile the exclusion of all women from the common rights of citizenship. It is an axiom of English freedom that taxation and representation should be co-extensive. Even under the laws which give the wife's property to the husband, there are many unmarried women who pay taxes. It is one of the fundamental doctrines of the British Constitution, that all persons should be tried by their peers: yet women, whenever tried, are by male judges and a male jury. To foreigners the law accords the privilege of claiming that half the jury should be composed of themselves; not so to women. Apart from maxims of detail, which represent local and national rather than universal ideas; it is an acknowledged dictate of justice to make no degrading distinctions without necessity. In all things the presumption ought to be on the side of equality. A reason must be given why anything should be permitted to one person and interdicted to another. But when that which is interdicted includes nearly everything which those to whom it is permitted most prize, and to be deprived of which they feel to be most insulting; when not only political liberty but personal freedom of action is the prerogative of a caste; when even in the exercise of industry, almost all employments which task the higher faculties in an important field, which lead to distinction, riches, or even pecuniary independence, are fenced round as the exclusive domain of the predominant

---

36. Chartism was a working-class movement for parliamentary reform, including suffrage. The movement began in the 1830s.

section, scarcely any doors being left open to the dependent class, except such as all who can enter elsewhere disdainfully pass by; the miserable expediencies which are advanced as excuses for so grossly partial a dispensation, would not be sufficient, even if they were real, to render it other than a flagrant injustice. While, far from being expedent, we are firmly convinced that the division of mankind into two castes, one born to rule over the other, is in this case, as in all cases, an unqualified mischief; a source of perversion and demoralization, both to the favoured class and to those at whose expense they are favoured; producing none of the good which it is the custom to ascribe to it, and forming a bar, almost insuperable while it lasts, to any really vital improvement, either in the character or in the social condition of the human race.

These propositions it is now our purpose to maintain. But before entering on them, we would endeavour to dispel the preliminary objections which, in the minds of persons to whom the subject is new, are apt to prevent a real and conscientious examination of it. The chief of these obstacles is that most formidable one, custom. Women never have had equal rights with men. The claim in their behalf, of the common rights of mankind, is looked upon as barred by universal practice. This strongest of prejudices, the prejudice against what is new and unknown, has, indeed, in an age of changes like the present, lost much of its force; if it had not, there would be little hope of prevailing against it. Over three-fourths of the habitable world, even at this day, the answer, "it has always been so," closes all discussion. But it is the boast of modern Europeans, and of their American kindred, that they know and do many things which their forefathers neither knew nor did; and it is perhaps the most unquestionable point of superiority in the present above former ages, that habit is not now the tyrant it formerly was over opinions and modes of action, and that the worship of custom is a declining idolatry. An uncustomary thought, on a subject which touches the greater interests of life, still startles when first presented; but if it can be kept before the mind until the impression of strangeness wears off, it obtains a hearing, and as rational a consideration as the intellect of the hearer is accustomed to bestow on any other subject.

In the present case, the prejudice of custom is doubtless on the unjust side. Great thinkers, indeed, at different times, from Plato to Condorcet,[37] besides some of the most eminent names of the present age, have made emphatic protest in favour of the equality of women. And there have been voluntary societies, religious or secular, of which the Society of Friends is the most known, by whom that principle was recognised. But there has

---

37. Marie Jean Antoine Nicolas Caritat, Marquis de Condorcet (1743-94).

been no political community or nation in which, by laws and usage, women have not been in a state of political and civil inferiority. In the ancient world the same fact was alleged, with equal truth, in behalf of slavery. It might have been alleged in favour of the mitigated form of slavery, serfdom, all through the middle ages. It was urged against freedom of industry, freedom of conscience, freedom of the press; none of these liberties were thought compatible with a well-ordered state, until they had proved their possibility by actually existing as facts. That an institution or a practice is customary is no presumption of its goodness, when any other sufficient cause can be assigned for its existence. There is no difficulty in understanding why the subjection of women has been a custom. No other explanation is needed than physical force.

That those who were physically weaker should have been made legally inferior, is quite conformable to the mode in which the world has been governed. Until very lately, the rule of physical strength was the general law of human affairs. Throughout history, the nations, races, classes, which found themselves the strongest, either in muscles, in riches, or in military discipline, have conquered and held in subjection the rest. If, even in the most improved nations, the law of the sword is at last discountenanced as unworthy, it is only since the calumniated eighteenth century. Wars of conquest have only ceased since democratic revolutions began. The world is very young, and has but just begun to cast off injustice. It is only now getting rid of monarchial despotism. It is only now getting rid of hereditary feudal nobility. It is only now getting rid of disabilities on the ground of religion. It is only beginning to treat any men as citizens, except the rich and a favoured portion of the middle class. Can we wonder that it has not yet done as much for women? As society was constituted until the last few generations, inequality was its very basis; association grounded on equal rights scarcely existed; to be equals was to be enemies; two persons could hardly cooperate in anything, or meet in any amicable relation, without the law's appointing that one of them should be superior of the other. Mankind have outgrown this state, and all things now tend to substitute, as the general principle of human relations, a just equality, instead of the dominion of the strongest. But of all relations, that between men and women being the nearest and most intimate, and connected with the greatest number of strong emotions, was sure to be the last to throw off the old rule and receive the new: for in proportion to the strength of a feeling, is the tenacity with which it clings to the forms and circumstances with which it has even accidentally become associated.

When a prejudice, which has any hold on the feelings, finds itself reduced to the unpleasant necessity of assigning reasons, it thinks it had done enough when it has re-asserted the very point in dispute, in phrases which appeal to the pre-existing feeling. Thus, many persons think they have sufficiently justified the restrictions on women's field of action, when they have said that the pursuits from which women are excluded are *unfeminine,* and that the *proper sphere* of women is not politics or publicity, but private and domestic life.

We deny the right of any portion of the species to decide for another portion, or any individual for another individual, what is and what is not their "proper sphere." The proper sphere for all human beings is the largest and highest which they are able to attain to. What this is, cannot be ascertained, without complete liberty of choice. The speakers at the Convention in America have therefore done wisely and right, in refusing to entertain the question of the peculiar aptitudes either of women or of men, or the limits within this or that occupation may be supposed to be more adapted to the one or to the other. They justly maintain, that these questions can only be more adapted to the one or the other. They justly maintain, that these questions can only be satisfactorily answered by perfect freedom. Let every occupation be open to all, without favour or discouragement to any, and employments will fall into the hands of those men or women who are found by experience to be most capable of worthily exercising them. There need be no fear that women will take out of the hands of men any occupation which men perform better than they. Each individual will prove his or her capacities, in the only way in which capacities can be proved — by trial; and the world will have the benefit of the best faculties of all its inhabitants. But to interfere beforehand by an arbitrary limit, and declare that whatever be the genius, talent, energy, or force of mind of an individual of a certain sex or class, those faculties shall not be exerted, or shall be exerted only in some few of the many modes in which others are permitted to use theirs, is not only an injustice to the individual, and a detriment to society, which loses what it can ill spare, but is also the most effectual mode of providing that, in the sex or class so fettered, the qualities which are not permitted to be exercised shall not exist.

We shall follow the very proper example of the Convention, in not entering into the question of the alleged differences in physical or mental qualities between the sexes; not because we have nothing to say, but because we have too much; to discuss this one point tolerably would need all the space we have to bestow on the entire subject.[38] But if those who

---

38. An excellent passage on this part of the subject, from one of Sydney Smith's contributions to the Edinburgh Review, we will not refrain from quoting: "A great deal has been said of the

assert that the "proper sphere" for women is the domestic, mean by this that they have not shown themselves qualified for any other, the assertion evinces great ignorance of life and of history. Women have shown fitness for the highest social functions, exactly in proportion as they have been admitted to them. By a curious anomaly, though ineligible to even the lowest offices of State, they are in some countries admitted to the highest of all, the regal; and if there is any one function for which they have shown a decided vocation, it is that of reigning. Not to go back to ancient history, we look in vain for abler or firmer rulers than Elizabeth; than Isabella of Castile; than Maria Teresa; than Catherine of Russia; than Blanche, mother of Louis IX of France; than Jeanne d'Albret, mother of Henri Quatre.[39] There are few kings on record who contended with more difficult circumstances, or overcame them more triumphantly, than these. Even in semibarbarous Asia, princesses who have never been seen by men, other than those of their own family, or ever spoken with them unless from behind a curtain, have as regents, during the minority of their sons, exhibited many of the most brilliant examples of just and vigorous administration. In the middle ages, when the distance between the upper and lower ranks was greater than even between women and men, and the women of the privileged class, however subject to tyranny from the men of the same class, were at a less distance below them than any one else was, and often in their absence represented them in their functions and authority—a number of heroic châtelaines, like Jeanne de Montfort, or the great Countess of Derby as late even as the time of Charles I,[40] distinguished themselves not

---

original difference of capacity between men and women, as if women were more quick and men more judicious—as if women were more remarkable for delicacy of association, and men for stronger powers of attention. All this, we confess, appears to us very fanciful. That there is a difference in the understanding of the men and the women we every day meet with, everybody, we suppose, must perceive; but there is none surely which may not be accounted for by the difference of circumstances in which they have been placed, without referring to any conjectural difference of original conformation of mind. As long as boys and girls run about in the dirt, and trundle hoops together, they are both precisely alike. If you catch up one-half of these creatures, and train them to a particular set of actions and opinions, and the other half to a perfectly opposite set, of course their understanding will differ, as one or the other sort of occupations has called this or that talent into action. There is surely no occasion to go into any deeper or more abstruse reasoning, in order to explain so very simple a phenomenon." (*Sydney Smith's Works,* vol i, p. 200.) [HTM]

39. Elizabeth I of England (1533-1603); Isabella of Castile (1451-1504); Maria Teresa of Austria (1717-80); Catherine of Russia (1729-96); Louis IX of France, of Castile (1188-1252); and Jeanne d'Albret of France and Navarre (1273-1305).

40. Comtesse de Montfort, also known as Jeanne of Burgundy. She married Philip of Valois in 1313. After Philip became king in 1328, she became an important political advisor. Charlotte de la Tremoille Stanley (1599-1664); Charles I of England, 1600-49.

only by their political but their military capacity. In the centuries immediately before and after the Reformation, ladies of royal houses, as diplomatists, as governors of provinces, or as the confidential advisers of kings, equalled the first statement of their time: and the treaty of Cambray, which gave peace to Europe, was negotiated in conferences where no other person was present, by the aunt of the Emperor Charles the Fifth, and the mother of Francis the First.[41]

Concerning the fitness, then, of women for politics, there can be no question: but the dispute is more likely to turn upon the fitness of politics for women. When the reasons alleged for excluding women from active life in all its higher departments are stripped of their garb of declamatory phrases, and reduced to the simple expression of a meaning, they seem to be mainly three: first, the incompatibility of active life with maternity, and with the cares of a household; secondly, its alleged hardening effect on the character; and thirdly, the inexpediency of making an addition to the already excessive pressure of competition in every kind of professional or lucrative employment.

The first, the maternity argument, is usually laid most stress upon: although (it needs hardly be said) this reason, if it be one can apply only to mothers. It is neither necessary nor just to make imperative on women that they shall be either mothers or nothing; or that if they have been mothers once, they shall be nothing else during the whole remainder of their lives. Neither women nor men need any law to exclude them from an occupation, if they have undertaken another which is incompatible with it. No one proposes to exclude the male sex from Parliament because a man may be a soldier or sailor in active service, or a merchant whose business requires all his time and energies. Nine-tenths of the occupations of men exclude them *de facto* from public life, as effectually as if they were excluded by law; but that is no reason for making laws to exclude even the nine-tenths, much less the remaining tenth. The reason of the case is the same for women as for men. There is no need to make provision by law that a woman shall not carry on the active details of a household, or of the education of children, and at the same time practice a profession, or be elected to parliament. Where incompatibility is real, it will take care of itself: but there is gross injustice in making the incompatibility a pretence for the exclusion of those in whose case it does not exist. And these, if they were free to choose, would be a very large proportion. The maternity argument deserts its supporters in the case of single women, a

---

41. Margaret of Austria (1480-1530) and Louise of Savoy (1476-1531), respectively.

large and increasing class of the population; a fact which, it is not irrelevant to remark, by tending to diminish the excessive competition of numbers, is calculated to assist greatly the prosperity of all. There is no inherent reason or necessity that all women should voluntarily choose to devote their lives to one animal function and its consequences. Numbers of women are wives and mothers only because there is no other career open to them, no other occupation for their feelings or their activities. Every improvement in their education, and enlargement of their faculties, everything which renders them more qualified for any other mode of life, increases the number of those to whom it is an injury and an oppression to be denied the choice. To say that women must be excluded from active life because maternity disqualifies them for it, is in fact to say, that every other career should be forbidden them in order that maternity may be their only resource.

But secondly, it is urged, that to give the same freedom of occupation to women as to men, would be an injurious addition to the crowd of competitors, by whom the avenues to almost all kinds of employment are choked up, and its remuneration depressed. This argument, it is to be observed, does not reach the political question. It gives no excuse for withholding from women the right of citizenship. The suffrage, the jury-box, admission to the legislature and to office, it does not touch. It bears only on the industrial branch of the subject. Allowing it, then, in an economical point of view, its full force; assuming that to lay open to women the employments now monopolized by men, would tend, like the breaking down of other monopolies, to lower the rate of remuneration in those employments; let us consider what is the amount of the evil consequence, and what the compensation for it. The worst ever asserted, much worse than is at all likely to be realized, is that if women competed with men, a man and a woman could not together earn more than is now earned by the man alone. Let us make this supposition, the most unfavourable supposition possible: the joint income of the two would be the same as before, while the woman would be raised from the position of a servant to that of a partner. Even if every woman, as matters now stand, had a claim on some man for support, how infinitely preferable is it that part of the income should be of the woman's earning, even if the aggregate sum were but little increased by it, rather than that she should be compelled to stand aside in order that men may be the sole earners, and the sole dispensers of what is earned. Even under the present laws respecting the property of women, a woman who contributes materially to the support of the family, cannot be treated in the same contemptuously tyrannical manner as one who, however she may toil as a domestic drudge, is a dependent on the man for subsistence.[42] As for the depression of wages by increase of competition, remedies will be found for it in time. Pallatives might be applied immediately; for instance, a more rigid exclusion of children from industrial employment, during the years in which they ought to be working only to strengthen their bodies and minds for after-life. Children are necessarily dependent, and under the power of others; and their labour, being not for themselves but for the gain of the parents, is a proper subject for legislative regulation. With respect to the future, we neither believe that improvident multiplication, and the consequent excessive difficulty of gaining a subsistence, will always continue, nor that the division of mankind into capitalist and hired labourers, and the reg-ulation of the reward of the labourers mainly be demand and supply, will be for ever, or even much longer, the rule of the world. But so long as competition is the general law of human life, it is tyranny to shut out one-half of the competitors. All who have attained the age of self-govern-ment have an equal claim to be permitted to sell whatever kind of useful labour they are capable of, for the price which it will bring.

The third objection to the admission of women to political or profes-sional life, its alleged hardening tendency, belongs to an age not past, and is scarcely to be comprehended by people of the present time. There are still, however, persons who say that the world and its avocations render men selfish and unfeeling; that the struggles, rivalries, and collisions of business and of politics make them harsh and unamiable; that if half the species must unavoidably be given up to these things, it is the more necessary that the other half should be kept free from them; that to preserve women from the bad influences of the world, is the only chance of preventing men from being wholly given up to them.

There would have been plausibility in this argument when the world was still in the age of violence; when life was full of physical conflict, and every man had to redress his injuries or those of others, by the sword or by the strength of his arm. Women, like priests, by being exempted from such responsibilities, and from some part of the accompanying dangers, may have been enabled to exercise a beneficial influence. But in the present condition of human life, we do not know where those hardening influences are to be found, to which men are subject and from which women are at

---

42. The truly horrible effects of the present state of the law among the lowest of the working population, is exhibited in those cases of hideous maltreatment of their wives by working men, with which every newspaper, every police report, teems. Wretches unfit to have the smallest authority over any living thing, have a helpless woman for their household slave. These excesses could not exist if women both earned, and had the right to possess, a part of the income of the family. [HTM]

present exempt. Individuals now-a-days are seldom called upon to fight hand to hand, even with peaceful weapons; personal enmities and rivalities count for little in worldly transactions; the general pressure of circumstances, not the adverse will of individuals, is the obstacle men now have to make head against. That pressure, when excessive, breaks the spirit, and cramps and sours the feelings, but not less of women than of men, since they suffer certainly not less from its evils. There are still quarrels and dislikes, but the sources of them are changed. The feudal chief once found his bitterest enemy in his powerful neighbour, the minister or courtier in his rival for place: but opposition of interest in active life, as a cause of personal animosity, is out of date; the enmities of the present day arise not from great things but small, from what people say of one another, more than from what they do; and if there are hatred, malice, and all uncharitableness, they are to be found among women fully as much as among men. In the present state of civilization, the notion of guarding women from the hardening influences of the world, could only be realized by secluding them from society altogether. The common duties of common life, as at present constituted, are incompatible with any other softness in women than weakness. Surely weak minds in weak bodies must ere long cease to be even supposed to be either attractive or amiable.

But, in truth, none of these arguments and considerations touch the foundations of the subject. The real question is, whether it is right and expedient that one-half of the human race should pass through life in a state of forced subordination to the other half. If the best state of human society is that of being divided into two parts, one consisting of persons with a will and a substantive existence, the other of humble companions to these persons, attached, each of them to one, for the purpose of bringing up *his* children, and making *his* home pleasant to him; if this is the place assigned to women, it is but kindness to educate them for this; to make them believe that the greatest good fortune which can befal them, is to be chosen by some man for this purpose; and that every other career which the world deems happy or honourable, is closed to them by the law, not social institutions, but of nature and destiny.

When, however, we ask why the existence of one-half the species should be merely ancillary to that of the other—why each woman should be a mere appendage to a man, allowed to have no interest of her own, that there may be nothing to compete in her mind with his interests and his pleasure; the only reason which can be given is, that men like it. It is agreeable to them that men should live for their own sake, women for the sake of men: and the qualities and conduct in subjects which are agreeable to rulers, they succeed for a long time in making the subjects themselves consider as their appropriate virtues. Helvetius[43] has met with much obloquy for asserting, that persons usually mean by virtues the qualities which are useful or convenient to themselves. How truly this is said of mankind in general, and how wonderfully the ideas of virtue set afloat by the powerful, are caught and imbibed by those under the dominion, is exemplified by the manner in which the world were once persuaded that the supreme virtue of subjects was loyalty to kings, and are still persuaded that the paramount virtue of womanhood is loyalty to men. Under a nominal recognition of a moral code common to both, in practice self-will and self-assertion form the type of what are designated as manly virtues, while abnegation of self, patience, resignation, and submission to power, unless when resistance is commanded by other interests than their own, have been stamped by general consent as pre-eminently the duties and graces required of women. The meaning being merely, that power makes itself the centre of moral obligation, and that a man likes to have his own will, but does not like that his domestic companion should have a will different from his.

We are far from pretending that in modern and civilized times, no reciprocity of obligation is acknowledged on the part of the stronger. Such an assertion would be very wide of the truth. But even this reciprocity, which has disarmed tyranny, at least in the higher and middle classes, of its most revolting features, yet when combined with the original evil of the dependent condition of women, has introduced in its turn serious evils.

In the beginning, and among tribes which are still in a primitive condition, women were and are the slaves of men for purposes of toil. All the hard bodily labour devolves on them. The Australian savage is idle, while women painfully dig up the roots on which he lives. An American Indian, when he has killed a deer, leaves it, and sends a woman to carry it home. In a state somewhat more advanced, as in Asia, women were and are the slaves of men for purposes of sensuality. In Europe there early succeeded a third and milder dominion, secured not by blows, nor by locks and bars, but by sedulous inculcation on the mind; feelings also of kindness, and ideas of duty, such as a superior owes to inferiors under his protection, became more and more involved in the relation of companionship, even between unequals. The lives of the two persons were apart. The wife was part of the furniture of home—of the resting-place to which the man returned from business or pleasure. His

---

43. Claude Adrien Helvetius, *De L'esprit* (Paris: 1758), 53–55. (Cited in Robson, *Sexual Equality*, 192).

occupations were, as they still are, among men; his pleasures and excitements also were, for the most part, among men—among his equals. He was a patriarch and a despot within four walls, and irresponsible power had its effect, greater or less according to its disposition, in rendering him domineering, exacting, self-worshipping, when not capriciously or brutally tyrannical. But if the moral part of his nature suffered, it was not necessarily so, in the same degree, with the intellectual or the active portion. He might have as much vigor of mind and energy of character as his nature enabled him, and as the circumstances of his times allowed. He might write the *Paradise Lost,* or win the battle of Marengo. This was the condition of the Greeks and Romans, and of the moderns until a recent date. Their relations with their domestic subordinates occupied a mere corner, though a cherished one, of their lives. Their education as men, the formation of their character and faculties, depended mainly on a different class of influences.

It is otherwise now. The progress of improvement has imposed on all possessors of power, and of domestic power among the rest, an increased and increasing sense of correlative obligation. No man now thinks that this wife has no claim upon his actions but such as he may accord to her. All men of any conscience believe that their duty to their wives is one of the most binding of their obligations. Nor is it supposed to consist solely in protection, which, in the present state of civilization, women have almost ceased to need: it involves care for their happiness and consideration of their wishes, with a not unfrequent sacrifice of their own to them. The power of husbands has reached the stage which the power of kings had arrived at, when opinion did not yet question the rightfulness of arbitrary power, but in theory, and to a certain extent in practice, condemned the selfish use of it. This improvement in the moral sentiments of mankind, and increased sense of the consideration due by every man to those who have no one but himself to look to, has tended to make home more and more the centre of interest, and domestic circumstances and society a larger and larger part of life, and of its pursuits and pleasures. The tendency has been strengthened by the changes of tastes and manners which have so remarkably distinguished the last two or three generations. In days not far distant, men found their excitement and filled up their time in violent bodily exercises, noisy merriment, and intemperance. They have now, in all but the very poorest classes, lost their inclination for these things and for the coarser pleasures generally; they have now scarcely any tastes but those which they have in common with women, and, for the first time in the world, men and women are really companions. A most beneficial change, if the companionship were between equals; but being between unequals, it produces, what good observers have noticed, though without perceiving its cause, a progressive deterioration among men in what had hitherto been considered the masculine excellences. Those who are so careful that women should not become men, do not see that men are becoming, what they have decided that women should be—are falling into the feebleness which they have so long cultivated in their companions. Those who are associated in their lives, tend to become assimilated in character. In the present closeness of association between the sexes, men cannot retain manliness unless women acquire it.

There is hardly any situation more unfavorable to the maintenance of elevation of character or force of intellect, than to live in the society, and seek by preference the sympathy, of inferiors in mental endowments. Why is it that we constantly see in life so much of intellectual and moral promise followed by such inadequate performance, but because the aspirant has compared himself only with those below himself, and has not sought improvement or stimulus from measuring himself with his equals or superiors. In the present state of social life, this is becoming the general condition of men. They care less and less for any sympathies, and are less and less under any personal influences, but those of the domestic roof. Not to be misunderstood, it is necessary that we should distinctly disclaim the belief, that women are even now inferior in intellect to men. There are women who are the equals in intellect of any men who ever lived; and comparing ordinary women with ordinary men, the varied though petty details which compose the occupation of most women, call forth probably as much of mental ability, as the uniform routine of the pursuits which are the habitual occupation of a large majority of men. It is from nothing in the faculties themselves, but from the petty subjects and interests on which alone they are exercised, that the companionship of women, such as their present circumstances make them, so often exercises a dissolvent influence on high faculties and aspirations in men. If one of the two has no knowledge and no care about the great ideas and purposes which dignify life, or about any of its practical concerns save personal interests and personal vanities, her conscious, and still more her unconscious influence, will, except in rare cases, reduce to a secondary place in his mind, if not entirely extinguish, those interests which she cannot or does not share.

Our argument here brings us into collision with what may be termed the moderate reformers of the education of women; a sort of persons who cross the path of improvement on all great questions; those who would maintain the old bad principles, mitigating their consequences. These say, that women should be, not slaves, nor servants, but companions; and educated for that office (they do not say that men should be educated to be the companions of women). But since uncultivated women are not suitable companions for cultivated men, and a man who feels interest in things above and beyond the family circle wishes that his companion should sympathize with him in that interest; they therefore say, let women improve their understanding and taste, acquire general knowledge, cultivate poetry, art, even coquet with science, and some stretch their liberality so far as to say, inform themselves on politics; not as pursuits, but sufficiently to feel an interest in the subjects, and to be capable of holding a conversation on them with the husband, or at least of understanding and imbibing his wisdom. Very agreeable to him, no doubt, but unfortunately the reverse of improving. It is from having intellectual communion only with those to whom they can lay down the law, that so few men continue to advance in wisdom beyond the first stages. The most eminent men cease to improve, if they associate only with disciples. When they have overtopped those who immediately surround them, if they wish for further growth, they must seek for others of their own stature to consort with. The mental companionship which is improving, is communion between active minds, not mere contact between an active mind and a passive. This inestimable advantage is even now enjoyed, when a strong-minded man and a strong-minded woman are, by a rare chance, united: and would be had far oftener, if education took the same pains to form strong-minded women which it takes to prevent them from being formed. The modern, and what are regarded as the improved and enlightened modes of education of women, abjure, as far as words go, an education of mere show, and profess to aim at solid instruction, but mean by that expression, superficial information on solid subjects. Except accomplishments, which are now generally regarded as to be taught well if taught at all, nothing is taught to women thoroughly. Small portions only of what it is attempted to teach thoroughly to boys, are the whole of what it is intended or desired to teach to women. What makes intelligent beings is the power of thought: the stimuli which call forth that power are the interest and dignity of thought itself, and a field for its practical application. Both motives are cut off from those who are told from infancy that thought, and all its greater applications, are other people's business, while theirs is to make themselves agreeable to other people. High mental powers in women will be but an exceptional accident, until every career is open to them, and until they, as well as men, are educated for themselves and for the world—not one sex for the other.

In what we have said on the effect of the inferior position of women, combined with the present constitution of married life, we have thus far had in view only the most favourable cases, those in which there is some real approach to that union and blending of characters and of lives, which the theory of the relation contemplates as its ideal standard. But if we look to the great majority of cases, the effect of women's legal inferiority, on the character both of women, and of men, must be painted in far darker colours. We do not speak here of the grosser brutalities, not of the man's power to seize on the woman's earnings, or compel her to live with him against her will. We do not address ourselves to any one who requires to have it proved that these things should be remedied. We suppose average cases, in which there is neither complete union nor complete disunion of feelings and character; and we affirm that in such cases the influence of the dependence on the woman's side, is demoralizing to the character of both.

The common opinion is, that whatever may be the case with the intellectual, the moral influence of women over men is almost salutary. It is, we are often told, the great counteractive of selfishness. However the case may be as to personal influence, the influence of the position tends eminently to promote selfishness. The most insignificant of men, the man who can obtain influence or consideration nowhere else, finds one place where he is chief and head. There is one person, often greatly his superior in understanding, who is obliged to consult him, and whom he is not obliged to consult. He is judge, magistrate, ruler, over their joint concerns; arbiter of all differences between them. The justice or conscience to which her appeal must be made, is his justice and conscience: it is his to hold the balance and adjust the scales between his own claims or wishes and those of another. His is now the only tribunal, in civilized life, in which the same person is judge and party. A generous mind, in such a situation, makes the balance incline against his own side, and gives the other not less, but more, than a fair equality; and thus the weaker side may be enabled to turn the very fact of dependence into an instrument of power, and in default of justice, take an ungenerous advantage of generosity; rendering the unjust power, to those who make an unselfish use of it, a torment and a burthen. But how is it when average men are invested with this power, without reciprocity and without responsibility? Give such a man the idea that he is first in law and in opinion—that to will is his part, and hers to submit; it is absurd to suppose that this idea merely glides over his mind, without sinking into it, or having any effect on his feelings and practice. The propensity to make himself the first object of consideration, and others at most the second, is not so rare as to be wanting where everything seems purposely arranged for encouraging its indulgence. If there is any self-will in the man, he becomes either the conscious or unconscious despot of his household. The wife, indeed, often succeeds in gaining her objects, but it is by some of the many various forms of indirectness and management.

Thus the position is corrupting equally to both; in the one it produces the vices of power, in the other those of artifice. Women, in their present physical and moral state, having stronger impulses, would naturally be franker and more direct than men; yet all the old saws and traditions represent them as artful and dissembling. Why? Because their only way to their objects is by indirect paths. In all countries where women have strong wishes and active minds, this consequence is inevitable; and if it is less conspicuous in England than in some other places, it is because Englishwomen, saving occasional exceptions, have ceased to have either strong wishes or active minds.

We are not now speaking of cases in which there is anything deserving the name of strong affection on both sides. That, where it exists, is too powerful a principle not to modify greatly the bad influences of the situation; it seldom, however, destroys them entirely. Much oftener the bad influences are too strong for the affection, and destroy it. The highest order of durable and happy attachments would be a hundred times more frequent than they are, if the affection which the two sexes sought from one another were that genuine friendship, which only exists between equals in privileges as in faculties. But with regard to what is commonly called affection in married life—the habitual and almost mechanical feeling of kindliness, and pleasure in each other's society, which generally grows up between persons who constantly live together, unless there is actual dislike—there is nothing in this to contradict or qualify the mischievous influence of the unequal relation. Such feelings often exist between a sultan and his favourites, between a master and his servants; they are merely examples of the pliability of human nature, which accommodates itself in some degree even to the worst circumstances, and the commonest natures always the most easily.

With respect to the influence personally exercised by women over men, it, no doubt, renders them less harsh and brutal; in ruder times, it was often the only softening influence to which they were accessible. But the assertion, that the wife's influence renders the man less selfish, contains, as things now are, fully as much error as truth. Selfishness towards the wife herself, and towards those in whom she is interested, the children, though favoured by her dependence, the wife's influence, no doubt, tends to counteract. But the general effect on him of her character, so long as her interests are concentrated in the family, tends but to substitute for individual selfishness a family selfishness, wearing an amiable guise, and putting on the mask of duty. How rarely is the wife's influence on the side of public virtue; how rarely does it do otherwise that discourage any effort of principle by which the private interests or worldly vanities of the family can be expected to suffer. Public spirit, sense of duty towards the public good, is of all virtues, as women are now educated and situated, the most rarely to be found among them; they have seldom even, what in men is often a partial substitute for public spirit, a sense of personal honour connected with any public duty. Many a man, whom no money or personal flattery would have bought, has bartered his political opinions against a title or invitations for his wife; and a still greater number are made mere hunters after the puerile vanities of society, because their wives value them. As for opinions; in Catholic countries, the wife's influence is another name for that of the priest; he gives her, in hopes and emotions connected with a future life, a consolation for the sufferings and disappointments which are her ordinary lot in this. Elsewhere, her weight is thrown into the scale either of the most commonplace, or of the most outwardly prosperous opinions: either those by which censure will be escaped, or by which worldly advancement is likeliest to be procured. In England, the wife's influence is usually on the illiberal and anti-popular side: this is generally the gaining side for personal interest and vanity; and what to her is the democracy of liberalism in which she has no part—which leaves her the Pariah it found her? The man himself, when he marries, usually declines into Conservatism; begins to sympathize with the holders of power, more than with its victims, and thinks it his part to be on the side of authority. As to mental progress, except those vulgar attainments by which vanity or ambition are promoted, there is generally an end to it in a man who marries a woman mentally his inferior; unless, indeed, he is unhappy in marriage, or becomes indifferent. From a man of twenty-five or thirty, after he is married, an experienced observer seldom expects any further progress in mind or feelings. It is rare that the progress already made is maintained. Any spark of the *mens divinior*[44] which might otherwise have spread and become a flame, seldom survives for any length of time unextinguished. For a mind which learns to be satisfied with what it already is—which does not incessantly look forward to a degree of improvement not yet reached—becomes relaxed, self-indulgent, and loses the spring and the tension which maintain it even at the point already attained. And there is no fact in human nature to which experience bears more invariable testimony than to this—that all social or sympathetic influences which do not raise up, pull down; if they do not tend to stimulate and exalt the mind, they tend to vulgarize it.

For the interest, therefore, not only of women but of men, and of human improvement in which the modern world often boasts of having effected,

---

44. Inspired soul.

and for which credit is sometimes given to civilization, and sometimes to Christianity, cannot stop where it is. If it were either necessary or just that one portion of mankind should remain mentally and spiritually only half developed, the development of the other portion ought to have been made, as far as possible, independent of their influence. Instead of this, they have become the most intimate, and it may now be said, the only intimate associates of those to whom yet they are sedulously kept inferior; and have been raised just high enough to drag the others down to themselves.

We have left behind a host of vulgar objections either as not worthy of an answer, or as answered by the general course of our remarks. A few words, however, must be said on one plea, which in England is made much use of for giving an unselfish air to the upholding of selfish privileges, and which, with unobserving, unreflecting people, passes for much more than it is worth. Women, it is said, do not desire—do not seek, what is called their emancipation. On the contrary, they generally disown such claims when made in their behalf, and fall with *acharnement*[45] upon any one of themselves who identifies herself with their common cause.

Supposing the fact to be true in the fullest extent ever asserted, if it proves that European women ought to remain as they are, it proves exactly the same with respect to Asiatic women; for they too, instead of murmuring at their seclusion, and at the restraint imposed upon them, pride themselves on it, and are astonished at the effrontery of women who receive visits from male acquaintances, and are seen in the streets unveiled. Habits of submission make men as well as women servile-minded. The vast population of Asia do not desire or value, probably would not accept, political liberty, nor the savage of the forest, civilization; which does not prove that either of those things is undesirable for them, or that they will not, at some future time, enjoy it. Custom hardens human beings to any kind of degradation, by deadening the part of their nature which would resist it. And the case of women is, in this respect, even a peculiar one, for no other inferior caste that we have heard of have been taught to regard degradation as their honour. The argument, however, implies a secret consciousness that the alleged preference of women for their dependent state is merely apparent; and arises from their being allowed no choice; for if the preference be natural, there can be no necessity for enforcing it by law. To make laws compelling people to follow their inclination, had not hitherto been thought necessary by any legislator. The plea that women do not desire any change, is the same that has been urged, times out of mind, against the proposal of abolishing any social evil—"there is

---

45. Rancor.

no complaint"; which is generally not true, and when true, only so because there is not that hope of success, without which complaint seldom makes itself audible to unwilling ears. How does the objector know that women do not desire equality and freedom? He never knew a woman who did not, or would not, desire it for herself individually. It would be very simple to suppose, that if they do desire it they will say so. Their position is like that of the tenants or labourers who vote against their own political interest to please their landlords or employers; with the unique addition, that submission is inculcated on them from childhood, as the peculiar attention and grace of their character. They are taught to think, that to repel actively even an admitted injustice done to themselves, is somewhat unfeminine, and had better be left to some male friend or protector. To be accused of rebelling against anything which admits of being called an ordinance of society, they are taught to regard as an imputation of a serious offence, to say the least, against the proprieties of their sex. It requires unusual moral courage as well as disinterestedness in a woman, to express opinions favourable to women's enfranchisement, until, at least, there is some prospect of obtaining it. The comfort of her individual life, and her social consideration, usually depend on the good-will of those who hold the undue power, and to possessors of power any complaint, however bitter, of the misuse of it, is a less flagrant act of insubordination than to protest against the power itself. The professions of women in this matter remind us of the State offenders of old, who, on the point of execution, used to protest their love and devotion to the sovereign by whose unjust mandate they suffered. Griselda[46] herself might be matched from the speeches put by Shakespeare into the mouths of male victims of kingly caprice and tyranny: the Duke of Buckingham, for example, in *Henry the Eighth,* and even Wolsey. The literary class of women, especially in England, are ostentatious in disclaiming the desire for equality or citizenship, and proclaiming their complete satisfaction with the place which society assigns to them; exercising in this, as in many other respects, a most noxious influence over the feelings and opinions of men, who unsuspectingly accept the servilities of toadyism as concessions to the force of truth, not considering that it is the personal interest of these women to profess whatever opinions they expect will be agreeable to men. It is not among men of talent, sprung from the people, and patronized and flattered by the aristocracy, that we look for the leaders of a democratic movement. Successful literary women are just as unlikely to prefer the cause of women to their own social consideration. They depend on men's opinion for their

46. Heroine of Giovanni Boccaccio's *Decameron.*

literary as well as for their feminine successes; and such is their bad opinion of men, that they believe that it is not more than one in ten thousand who does not dislike and fear strength, sincerity, or high spirit in a woman. They are therefore anxious to earn pardon and toleration for whatever of these qualities their writings may exhibit on other subjects, by a studied display of submission on this: that they may give no occasion for vulgar men to say (what nothing will prevent vulgar men from saying), that learning makes women unfeminine, and that literary ladies are likely to be bad wives.

But enough of this; especially as the fact which affords the occasion for this notice, makes it impossible any longer to assert the universal acquiescence of women (saving individual exceptions) in their dependent condition. In the United States, at least, there are women, seemingly numerous, and now organized for action on the public mind, who demand equality in the fullest acceptation of the word, and demand it by a straightforward appeal to men's sense of justice, not plead for it with a timid deprecation of their displeasure.

Like other popular movements, however, this may be seriously retarded by the blunders of its adherents. Tried by the ordinary standard of public meetings, the speeches at the Convention are remarkable for the preponderance of the rational over the declamatory element; but there are some exceptions; and things to which it is impossible to attach any rational meaning, have found their way into the resolutions. Thus, the resolution which sets forth the claims made in behalf of women, after claiming equality in education, in industrial pursuits, and in political rights, enumerates as a fourth head of demand something under the name of "social and spiritual union," and "a medium of expressing the highest moral and spiritual views of justice," with other similar verbiage, serving only to mar the simplicity and rationality of the other demands; resembling those who would weakly attempt to combine nominal equality between men and women, with enforced distinctions in their privileges and functions. What is wanted for women is equal rights, equal admission to all social privileges; not a position apart, a sort of sentimental priesthood. To this, the only just and rational principle, both the resolutions and the speeches, for the most part, adhere. They contain so little which is akin to the nonsensical paragraph in question, that we suspect it not to be the work of the same hands as most of the other resolutions. The strength of the cause lies in the support of those who are influenced by reason and principle; and to attempt to recommend it by sentimentalities, absurd in reason, and inconsistent with the principle on which the movement is founded, is to place a good cause on a level with a bad one.

There are indications that the example of America will be followed on this side of the Atlantic; and the first step has been taken in that part of England where every serious movement in the direction of political progress has its commencement—the manufacturing districts of the North. On the 13th of February 1851, a petition of women, agreed to by a public meeting at Sheffield, and claiming the elective franchise, was presented to the House of Lords by the Earl of Carlisle.

We have on former occasions pointed out the defective state of the law and of its administration with respect to crimes of personal violence, and we have especially commented on the absence of protection for women and young persons, and for all those who are under the power of others, against domestic brutality. The case on which the Court of Queen's Bench pronounced judgment yesterday, exceptional as it is in some material respects—more particularly as regards the apparent absence of habitual or deliberate cruelty on the part of the defendant—recalls our attention to this very important subject; and we proceed to offer some further remarks on the general question of the social and legal wrongs affecting the most helpless portion of the community.

It is evident to all who take any pains to read the indications of the feelings of the populace, that they are impressed with the belief of their having a *right* to inflict almost any amount of corporal violence upon *their* wife or *their* children. That any one should claim to interfere with this supposed right, causes them unaffected surprise. Is it not *their* wife or child? Are they not entitled to do as they will with their own? These phrases are not, to their apprehension, metaphorical. The shoes on their feet, or the cudgel in their hand—the horse or ass that carries their burdens, and that dies a lingering death under their cruelties—the wife and children—all are "theirs," and all in the same sense. They have the same right, in their own opinion, over their human as over their inanimate property. Doubtless they are aware that they are not at liberty to inflict death; but when they actually do so, and find that they are to be tried for murder, they seem to receive the information with a kind of stolid astonishment; and it may well appear to them anomalous that a creature is given up to their power to be kicked or beaten, at the peril of life, as often as temper or intoxication may prompt—and yet that, on some one day when they have done no worse than they had done hundreds of times before, they are told that they are liable to be hanged. Not that they ever are hanged for these enormities, even though death ensue. If they are tried at all (which in general they are not), the jury are not convinced that they intended death, and they consequently escape with a verdict of manslaughter. This interpretation of the law had the sanction of Mr. Baron ALDERSON, in the recent case of ALEXANDER MOIR. If it be a correct interpretation, the law is, in this

HTM and JSM wrote many newspaper articles decrying domestic violence and suggesting legal and social reforms.

VIOLENCE AND
DOMESTIC VIOLENCE

4

All of the writing in this section was produced jointly by Harriet Taylor Mill and John Stuart Mill. Their collective work on violence in and outside of the home first appeared in the form of newspaper pieces and one pamphlet written for private distribution. The handwritten bibliography of JSM identifies these articles as "joint production—very little of which was mine" or by other similar designations, which clearly indicates that these news pieces were co-authored (MacMinn, 59ff). John was very careful to note various kinds of collaboration (see MacMinn, 9, 87, 90; CW: XII, 43, and CW: I, 265). JSM wrote about these topics on his own (CW: XXV, 406, 419), and in these cases, he did not designate the articles as co-authored. John scrupulously recorded when he did and did not write as a co-author.

All of these pieces can be grouped into two categories. The first includes the material written in 1846 and the second encompasses the material written from late 1849 to 1851. During the first period, Harriet and John were also collaborating on The Principles of Political Economy, *which was completed in 1848. In the early set of newspaper articles, they urge punishment for those who abuse those who are dependent upon them, as in the news accounts of Captain Johnstone and William Burn. However, Harriet and John publicly defend those individuals whom they believe innocent, as in their news articles involving Dr. Ellis and Private Matthewson. They also draw attention to the rights of single or widowed women to have custody of their children, as in the case of Sarah Brown and Mrs. North. The common argument throughout their news writing involves the ways violence degrades the victims and the refusal of the judicial system to educate the moral sensibilities of the public by consistently and effectively defending the rights of those who suffer abuse.*

The first article of the second group, in which Harriet and John speak out against the use of corporal punishment for property crimes, was written just days before Harriet's husband, John Taylor, died. There follows a series of short pieces on domestic violence, touching on the wife abuse of Susan Moir, assault laws, and wife murder. They do not stop with the domestic violence against wives, but also write on child abuse (Anne Bird and "Punishment of Children") and abuse of servants (on Mary Ann Parsons, I and II). In all but one, "Questionable Charity," HTM and JSM attempt to uncover the causes and effects of a variety of different types of domestic violence. The most general analysis of domestic violence can be found in the pieces of writing concerning the assault law and wife murder. Harriet and John conclude that common nineteenth-century language which promotes the idea that husbands own their wives may be one of the underlying causes of violence in the home. The final piece in this series was completed in August 1851, just after Harriet had published "Enfranchisement of Women" in the Westminster Review. *Harriet and John continued their campaign against domestic violence by issuing a pamphlet for private distribution on a bill introduced into Parliament by Henry Fitzroy. The bill was passed in 1853. We believe that the series of news articles written by Harriet Taylor and John Mill contributed to the public awareness that facilitated the passing of Fitzroy's bill.*

Throughout these articles Harriet and John actively attempted to alter the ongoing judicial proceedings upon which they reported. They called for judges to rule in favor of domestic violence victims, for new laws, for appeals to high court. Unlike newspaper reporting in the twentieth-century, they had no compunction against urging the public to alienate those whom the courts exonerated, as when they proclaimed that Robert and Sarah Bird "merited {the} designation of acquitted murderers" for the killing of Mary Ann Parsons. Here, too, they may have been effective in their intervention, since the Birds, acquitted of the murder of their servant Mary Ann Parsons, were later arrested and convicted of assault. In all their newspaper writings, Harriet and John sought to raise public awareness of the unfairness of laws concerning violence vs. laws concerning property. They aimed to educate the moral feelings of the public, not merely to inform about the facts of any given case.

NEWSPAPER WRITINGS

Morning Chronicle, 10 February 1846, p. 5, e-f
[Captain Johnstone]

George Johnstone, Captain of the ship Tory, was brought to trial for the murder of three sailors under his command on a voyage from China. As the result of the Captain's incompetence, the ship missed several ports, and hence food and water for the crew were scarce. After hearing rumors of the crew's complaints, Captain Johnstone ran his bayonet through two of the crew members. This article by Harriet and John follows two pieces which appeared in the Times on February 6 and 7. The first Times article contained nearly four columns of the trial transcript. The second article, quoted below, criticized the jury's leniency. The Times also carried more of the transcript from the trial on this date. In writing this article, Harriet and John connect the jury's verdict with jurors' inability to imagine a point of view that may be radically different from their own, an argument that may be a prelude to similar points made in On Liberty. *HTM and JSM also encourage the authorities to treat the defendant as a dangerous lunatic and not to set him free, despite the verdict of "not guilty."*

If the jury who have just acquitted the most atrocious criminal who has been brought to answer for his misdeeds at the bar of a court of justice for many years, had studied how they could bring the administration of justice most effectually into contempt—if they had meant to show what a wretched exhibition of human imbecility jury trial might be made, when carried on by men with neither heart nor intellect, and in whom maudlin weakness and moral poltroonery stand in the place of conscience—they could not have succeeded more completely. A man who has realized almost fabulous atrocities—who has made the metaphorical expression of "killing by inches" a physical fact—who, being placed in authority over a number of men, at a distance from all legal protection, after exhausting ordinary tyrannies, crowned a series of horrors by literally hewing in pieces two human beings, bound and unresisting—this man has been declared "not guilty," for no other cause whatever but the excess of his guilt, for it is not even pretended that he had shown any marks of insanity, or exhibited any of the characteristics of it, except the crimes which have been proved.

With regard to the wretched culprit himself, we have only now to look to the advisers of the Crown, and trust that he will be treated for the remainder of his life as the most dangerous kind of lunatic, and will not, at the easy price of a temporary confinement, be again let loose upon the world. But there is a lesson to be learnt from the verdict. The state of mind of the jurors is a specimen of the tendency of the humanity-mongering which has succeeded to the reckless brutality of our old laws, and which has brought us to such a pass, that every man is now to be presumed insane as soon as it is fully proved that he is a ruffian.

BURKE, long ago, spoke of the "credulous morality" of a certain kind of people, who, when a man acts like a villain, never have the courage to think him one. If jurors think every man insane whom they acquit as such, this credulous morality has made wonderful progress. The maxim so well expressed by our contemporary the *Times,* in an admirable article on Saturday, that a "crime without a motive is no crime at all," might now be inscribed over the door of every court of justice, as the creed of fools and the motto of juries. And a motive must be something which would be a motive to the juryman himself, or to people like himself—people who never framed a thought, had a feeling, or did an act different from everybody else. Time was when it was not thought incredible and miraculous not to be commonplace. But the modern type of civilization has so destroyed even the remembrance, even the idea, of individuality, that to the vulgar everything which shows character is a proof of madness. The conduct of the man JOHNSTONE did show character. It showed a man not exactly like all other people. It showed a ruffian, but it showed a man to whom custom was not the law of his life. This is as much as it is generally necessary to prove before a Commission of Lunacy. If the man had been as much better than other people as he was worse, and had shaped his life by his own inclinations, instead of by the doings and sayings of his neighbours, let the reader ask himself, if any one had an interest in proving him mad, how much chance he would have had of escaping a madhouse in the hands of such a jury?

The only murders which men need now expect to be punished for, are those which are committed for money, or from fear of exposure. These are motives, the reasonableness of which appears to be recognized. These inducements are considered by juries as capable of acting upon a sane man. They are, no doubt, the motives to most of the crimes of the age. The motives of great criminals—the vehement resentment, the bitter revenge, the determined self-will, the superstitious horror, the intense antipathy— are things which jurors have nothing corresponding with in themselves, and cannot recognize when before their eyes.

We have given the jurors the benefit of the supposition most favourable to them—that they are as great fools as they proclaim themselves. We have supposed that they really thought the man insane. If they did not think so, but were influenced by a mawkish dislike to having on their consciences the death of a man who had inflicted so many deaths, what are we to think of them? A morbid feebleness of conscience is in our time so common an accompaniment of other mental feebleness, that the supposition is by no means improbable. In the words of the *Times* "the contest lies between their judgement and their honour." We do not add, with our contemporary, "we will not suppose it to be the latter." We leave them to the alternative.

Morning Chronicle, 13 June 1846, p. 6, c–d
[Dr. Ellis]

Harriet and John argue in this piece that the poor state of medical science allows a reasonably educated doctor to misdiagnose upon occasion. They comment on the jury's decision in an inquest hearing to hold Dr. James Ellis over for trial for manslaughter because a patient died after he treated him with hydropathy. Harriet herself had "taken the waters" at various spas in England and on the continent and believed they could help various ailments (see her letters). She is also quite skeptical of "medical men" in general as evidenced by her persistent questioning of the doctors who attended John Taylor, whom she nursed through his final illness (again, see her letters to John Stuart Mill during this period). Harriet and John aim to influence the final outcome of the case. In the trial for manslaughter later in the month, Dr. Ellis was acquitted, so this article may have helped free Dr. Ellis.

Our paper, a day or two since, contained a report of proceedings before a coroner's jury, terminating in a verdict of manslaughter against Dr. ELLIS, the superintendent of the Hydropathic establishment at Sudbroke Park, Petersham, on account of the death of a patient, a Mr. RICHARD DRESSER, who died on Tuesday, having been under the care of Dr. ELLIS since the preceding Friday.

The case, in consequence of this verdict, will necessarily undergo investigation before a criminal tribunal; but to be put upon trial, even if acquitted, is so serious an injury and grievance to an innocent person, that it is worthy of deliberate consideration, both how far medical practitioners ought to be subject to such responsibility, and whether it has been judiciously applied to a case like the present.

The jury, of twelve, we dare say, respectable petty tradesmen, but not likely to be very enlightened critics of medical skill, have by this verdict pronounced a solemn opinion on two grave and difficult medical questions. They have decided that the patient died in consequence of Dr. ELLIS'S treatment, and that the error committed—assuming it to be an error—was of so culpable a kind as to constitute, in the eye of the law, a punishable offence.

They did not, of course, adopt these serious conclusions on their own knowledge, but on the faith of medical evidence. The professional witnesses in the case were two surgeons practising in partnership in the Kent-road—a circumstance not inconsistent with consummate medical skill, but which assuredly affords no guarantee of it. These surgeons had examined the body after death, by the desire of the family, but without the knowledge or presence, so far as appeared, of Dr. ELLIS, or of any one in his behalf. We hope, however, that it is still in his power to cause a re-examination of a more public kind, if he judges it desirable. Dr. ELLIS, not having examined the body, gave as his opinion that the death was occasioned by diseased liver. The surgeons, after examination, say that the liver was not diseased. They do not agree with each other on all points, one thinking the liver congested, while the other "hardly ever saw a healthier liver in his life." They both say, however, that the heart and lungs were congested, that they could find no other cause of death, and that this excessive congestion must have been produced by the very mild application of tepid (for it was not even cold) water which appears to have been used. They say besides, that if the liver had been diseased, the hydropathic treatment would have been extremely inappropriate; in which Dr. ELLIS concurs, since he said that if he had known the liver to be affected he would not have received the patient. The only ailment which the deceased complained of was rheumatism, or sciatica. An extraordinary circumstance is, that on the showing of the two surgeons there was nothing to account for death from so slight a cause. They were asked no questions about the patient's previous state of health; though one of them said that he had known and attended him for years. The only fact they stated was, that the action of the heart was feeble. But a feeble action of the heart is not enough to make a man die of suffocation from being fomented with tepid water. A man whom that would kill must have been at death's door first. Was it so unpardonable an oversight in Dr. ELLIS not to suspect such a condition in a man who complained of nothing worse than rheumatic pains? It must be remembered, too, that these professional men (we mean it not as an imputation, but as presumption, which justice requires to be taken into account) were in all human probability strongly prepossessed both against the irregular practice, and against the irregular practitioner; a sentiment, which the patient having quitted their care to place himself under Dr. ELLIS, was nowise calculated to mollify.

It is by no means a clear case, that in a free country medical men should *ever* be criminally responsible for the consequences of *bonâ fide* treatment; or that a person of full age and reasonable understanding, who, with his eyes open, places himself under the care of a practitioner, should not do it at his own risk. It is a question on both sides of which much still remains to be said. But there are weighty reasons to be urged for the responsibility in some other cases, which cannot be applicable to this. A quack may pretend to be acquainted with the whole medical art, and competent to apply all its expedients, each in its proper place. But Dr. ELLIS and his compeers profess nothing but hydropathy, practice nothing but hydropathy, do not pretend to judge of anything but hydropathy. Whoever submits himself to them does so because he believes in hydropathy. He knows what he is about, and acts not from faith in the doctor, but from faith in the treatment itself, and in its applicability to his case; and neither is hydropathy a thing of palpable fraud, the bare profession of which can be treated as an attempt to deceive. In its immense pretensions, or in those which have sometimes been made for it, we place no credence whatever; but its occasional efficacy is admitted by all, and the most scientific physicians often advise patients, in obstinate cases, to place themselves in one of these very establishments. All depends on judging rightly of the cases to which it is suited, and in that the most instructed physician may err, as well as the most ignorant.

The law of the case was fairly enough laid down by the coroner. He said that the jury had nothing to do with Dr. ELLIS'S being or not being a regularly licensed practitioner; that they had only to consider if there was proof of gross negligence or incompetence. But if thinking that a person has a liver complaint when he has not, is negligence or ignorance, deserving the penalties of manslaughter; thinking that a lady, whose lamentable case ought never to be forgotten, had *not* a liver complaint, when she was dying of it, does not seem to fall far short of the same criminality. Yet that was the mistake of one of the most instructed and really ablest men in the medical profession.[*]

The diagnostics of liver disease are proverbially uncertain; to say nothing of the general uncertainty and almost infant state of the medical art. And shall twelve Surrey tradesmen rush in where the best and most acknowl-

---

[*]The Queen's physician, Sir James Clark, had misdiagnosed a fatal liver disease in Lady Flora Elizabeth Hastings, a member of the royal court. (See *CW*: XXIV, 877, fn. 4, for more datails.)

edged authorities tread unsafely? Is it for them to take upon themselves the right of punishing the practitioners of the most fallible of all useful arts for not being infallible?

Morning Chronicle, 6 October 1846, p. 4, c–d
[Private Matthewson]

Private Thomas Matthewson was court-martialed for "abusive lan-guage." Harriet and John suggest that he is really being punished for his earlier testimony in a flogging case against his commanding officer. This article clearly aims to influence the final outcome of the case, since Matthewson has not been convicted, and the sentencing has yet to be deter-mined. Clearly the insinuation that there was insufficient evidence and that the commanding officer and prosecutor were biased aim to influence the one person who will determine the sentence, the Commander-in-Chief. (In this instance, their attempt was unsuccessful, since Matthewson was sentenced a few days later to six months in jail, including two months in solitary confinement (Times, 9 October 1846). As with many of their co-authored articles, they defend those who have attempted to reduce physical violence against dependents.

We think it very desirable that the Government and the public should keep their attention fixed on the case of Private THOMAS MATTHEW-SON, who was tried by court-martial at Hounslow, on Tuesday last, for abusive language to a non-commissioned officer. Whether he was found guilty by the court has not yet transpired, as the publication of the sentence does not take place until it has been confirmed by the Com-mander-in-Chief; but there is far more than enough apparent on the proceedings to require that the results should be watched.

This man MATTHEWSON, it may be remembered, was one of the witnesses in the case of death from flogging, which contributed so much to bring about the partial abolition of that punishment. His evidence was of a nature to be peculiarly disagreeable to his commanding officer, being one of those which imputed to him, in the most direct manner, neglect and want of feeling with regard to the sufferer. MATTHEW-SON, also, was the witness to whom menaces were said to have been indirectly held out as to the probable consequences to himself of the evidence he gave; and although this was not thought to have been substantiated, it was not denied that Colonel WHYTE publicly addressed him on parade, saying that he was as near as—(what type of nearness the colonel employed we do not think it necessary to repeat)— to having perjured himself. This gentle apostrophe, however merited it may in the colonel's opinion have been, neither betokened in the present, nor augured for the future, any amicable feelings on the part of the commanding officer towards Private MATTHEWSON. We are far from implying that because an officer has received what he thinks provocation from a private, he must necessarily become his unscrupulous enemy. But Private MATTHEWSON must have had far more than ordinary confidence in the magnanimity of his commanding officer, if he did not feel certain that, in some way or other, he would be made to smart severely for his evidence; that if a charge were not actually got up against him, an opportunity would be watched of exaggerating some trifling peccadillo into a grave offence; that, in short, he would be a marked man, and if not to the colonel himself, to some of those miserable waiters upon power, who, we may be sure, are not wanting in a regiment any more than in a court, and who might think that the ruin of one who had made himself obnoxious would be a satisfaction to those whom they wished to please, even if it were only the satisfaction derived from the fulfillment of a prophecy. If this surmise is not already verified by what has just taken place, there is a coincidence most unfortunate for all those upon whom any share of the suspicion can possible fall.

We will suppose that MATTHEWSON, after giving the evidence which reflected discredit upon Colonel WHYTE, was really guilty of a serious military offence. We should have expected that, considering what had happened, and the prejudice likely to exist against him, not only in his own regiment, but among any officers composing a court-martial (for the great majority of officers are supporters of corporal punishment, and it is no secret that the sympathies of officers are almost always with the officer against the soldier)—we should have expected, we say, that scrupulous care would have been taken to make it impossible for even the prisoner himself to deny that the most generous justice was done him. We should have expected that the testimony against him would have been sifted with the most jealous vigilance; that rather a greater amount of evidence than is deemed sufficient in ordinary cases would have been insisted on; and that the most studious and ostentatious attention would have been paid to giving him every facility, and to showing that every facility had been given, for the production of any evidence which he might think available to weaken, though it were only in a slight degree, the strength of the case against him.

Instead of this, what do we see? By a most unfortunate accident, if it be an accident, the trial takes place after MATTHEWSON'S own regiment has left the neighbourhood, and along with it the witnesses whom he could have called, either to points of the case itself, or to his general character. This obstacle, probably, was not insuperable; he might have "applied to the commanding officer" (Colonel WHYTE himself) to have the witnesses detained; and if he had done so, we will hope that the request would have been complied with. We, therefore, do not insist further on this point, which may be worse in appearance than in reality. But there is another feature in the case, which would be fatal to the prosecution—whether with a military tribunal we know not—but with any civil tribunal of decent impartiality. The man's alleged offence is the use of insulting words, and there is absolutely no evidence to the words he used, or to his having used insulting words at all, except that of Sergeant O'DONNELL, the very man alleged to have been insulted. There is no circumstantial evidence, and no corroborative testimony but that of Corporal ROUTH, who "was not sufficiently near to hear what took place," and could only affirm that "by his manner the prisoner appeared to be speaking disrespectfully to the sergeant." But it was not for disrespectfulness of *manner* that he was brought before the court. In the circumstance alleged there was nothing to explain or render probable the abusive expressions said to have been used, which are such as were only likely to be employed in the heat of passion, or as the consequence of a previous altercation. When policemen are declared to be in the habit of giving false evidence against innocent persons, is it too much to suspect an affronted sergeant of some exaggeration? Especially when the prisoner declares him to have been drunk at the time, and against the assertion of one of the two parties to a dispute it is not unfair to oppose the denial of the other.

We have argued the matter on the footings of simple justice, and the treatment due to every human being. If it were to be looked at on grounds of chivalrous or gentlemanly feeling, it would be much more concisely disposed of. Supposing such feelings to have had any voice in the matter, the commanding officer, one may presume, would rather have given up his commission than that Private MATTHEWSON, while under his command, should be in a position in which it would be felt that the one was inflicting, and the other undergoing vengeance for unacceptable evidence in a court of justice. There are means enough for ridding a regiment of a troublesome character, when his presence is no longer supportable. If MATTHEWSON was such a character, the consequences of giving him his discharge would have been (in the peculiar circumstances of this case) less prejudicial to discipline than the moral impression of his being made a victim—which, truly or not, he will be thought to be, if found guilty and sentenced on this inadequately supported charge.

The part of prosecutor was worthily filled by a Viscount ST. LAW-RENCE, who came armed with all the means which the books of the regiment and his own testimony could supply for crushing the already crushed man.

Morning Chronicle, 28 October 1846, p. 4, c–d
[Sarah Brown]

Harriet and John use the inquest into Sarah Brown's suicide as a means to discuss the lack of knowledge among women themselves and more shamefully among magistrates, about the law that directs the sole custody of illegitimate children to their mothers. Sarah Brown's two-year-old child had been taken from her by the illegitimate father. HTM and JSM argue that fathers have no right to custody of their illegitimate children since they have not taken legal responsibility for the child by marrying the mother. Despite this law, many judges operate under the assumption that the child should be shared by both parents, as witnessed by a recent case they discuss in this article. (On 19 October 1846, the Times reported a "novel and rather amusing case" of a child stolen by his father and whom the mother refused to marry because she feared he would abuse her.) Harriet and John claim that women "in the lower ranks of life" don't trust the legal system because of their experience with the leniency of domestic violence laws, so these women would fail to seek their legal rights when their children have been taken from them.

In a paragraph which has gone the round of the daily papers, it is stated that on Thursday last Mr. BEDFORD held an inquest, at the Star and Garter, St. Martin's-lane, on the body of SARAH BROWN, aged nineteen, who had drowned herself in the Thames. "Deceased, the daughter of respectable parents, was seduced by a gentleman two years ago, and had a child by him. Her seducer deprived her of her child." Several witnesses, it is added, "proved that since her child had been taken from her she had over and over again threatened to destroy herself." The verdict was temporary insanity.

The sad history of this poor girl might not have had so tragical a *denouement,* if there had been any one to inform her that the creature called "a gentleman," in tearing from her the last consolation and the last human interest which he had left her, acted as much in defiance of law as of the first elements of justice and feelings of humanity; that the father of an illegitimate child has absolutely no legal rights over the child; that he is, in the eye of the law, not related to it; and that its mother is its sole parent. But this piece of legal knowledge, though perfectly elementary, appears to be too recondite for some magistrates, judging from a case published in the police reports a short time since. In that case, as in this, the father had exerted the law of the strongest, and kept the child to himself. The mother had retaliated by the law of the cleverest, and had stolen it back. The man again seized on it, and the case ultimately came before a magistrate, who, according to the report, awarded that they should possess the child in alternate months. The magistrate, possibly, may have been guided to the adjudication by some indistinct reminiscence of the judgement of SOLOMON; but there was no similarity in the result, which was, that the disputants were no sooner out of court than they renewed their squabble, to determine which of the two should be entitled to the first month, a point which the magistrate, in his anxiety for equal partition, had forgotten to decide. The matter was at last amicably adjusted, and "ended happily"—for the most serious situation of life is equally capable of being the subject of a comedy or of a tragedy. But if the magistrate acted in any other capacity than as an adviser of the parties, and meant anything more than to suggest a compromise to be voluntarily adopted by them, he evidently violated the law. He had no right to compel the woman to give up one-half of her child. She paid dearly enough for it, and it was her's and her's it ought to be—most certainly no one's else. She had a legal and moral right to such comfort as it could afford her, and she had a right to any hold over the man, who had deserted her, that might be derived from the interest which it appears he had not ceased to feel in the child. If any limitation of her exclusive parental control could be allowable, it is not by or for the man, but by that which we should be glad to see exercised, not only in cases of this kind, but in many others—the tutelary intervention of a public authority, to see that the children of the miserable are not brought up to be miserable, or a source of misery to others.

In the case of lawful marriage, the law has thought fit to give to one only of the parents—that one being (need it be said?) the one who by himself or by his representatives *makes* the law—exclusive power over the children. The revolting excess of injustice, palpable even to the obtusest perceptions, which resulted from this provision of the law in certain extreme cases, induced the Legislature a few years back, on the proposition of Mr. Sergeant TALFOURD, slightly to relax in those extreme cases the rigour of the exclusive principle. How much more remains to be done in the same direction, before the state of the law can commend itself either to the reason or to the feelings of any one who views it not as an interested party, but as an impartial judge, we shall not at present discuss. The law, however, is not guilty of giving this excess of power, without annexing any conditions to it. Whatever the authority with which the law arms the father, it requires of him, as an essential preliminary, not only that he shall stand clear of having acquired his claim by the destruction of the social position, and in all probability the self-respect of a fellow-creature, but that he shall take upon himself all the obligations and responsibilities which, in the estimation of the law, ought to devolve upon one who, for his own purposes, presumes to call a human being into existence. He can claim none of the rights attaching to a position of which he does not fulfil the requirements. He cannot indulge himself in despotism as the patriarch of a family, and give himself a dispensation from extending to either the children or their other parent reciprocal (however unequal) rights over him.

If the father has not chosen to make himself liable *legally* to the obligations which, from the very nature of the case, belong *morally* to the parental condition, those obligations and responsibilities devolve undividedly upon the other parent, and along with them, as their inseparable accompaniment, those rights over the child's person and conduct, which have no legitimate ground of existence save as a means to the fulfilment of those obligations, or a reward and encouragement for fulfilling them conscientiously. And since this not only ought to be the law, but actually is so, it is wrong in any magistrate not to take every appropriate opportunity of making it known; for this end, among others, that one-half of the human species may occasionally have the satisfaction of believing that if the law is appealed to in their behalf it will do them justice.

At present it is very well known that women, in the lower ranks of life, do not expect justice from a bench or a jury of the male sex. They feel the most complete assurance that to the utmost limits of common decency, and often beyond, a tribunal of men will sympathize and take part with the man. And accordingly they die in protracted torture, from incessantly repeated brutality, without ever, except in the fewest and rarest instances, claiming the protection of law. If justice *is* invoked, it is generally by the outraged feelings of neighbours, and if the unhappy sufferer deviates into making her injuries known in a police court, at the next hearing she usually retracts everything; for who ever heard of a really severe punishment inflicted upon a man for any amount of brutal illtreatment of his wife? She knows well that if the case is too clear and strong to allow of dismissing the man with a reprimand, and the woman with a piece of kind advice to be gentle and submissive, the utmost he will have to undergo is a month or two of imprisonment, to be followed by a resumption of all his former power, and her imagination can well suggest with what consequences to her.

If such is the justice society deals out to those women, in the humbler classes, whom it calls respectable, what must the unfortunate creature like SARAH BROWN expect? And who can wonder, that driven to desperation by the cruellest wrong, though a wrong wholly unsanctioned by law, she seeks relief not from a magistrate but from suicide, without having had even a momentary thought that the law would do anything for her, or that the law *was* anything but one of the instruments by which society hunts down those who have violated its rules and incurred its displeasure?

Morning Chronicle, 17 November 1846, p. 4, b–c [William Burn]

Because of HTM's and JSM's high degree of sensitivity to the problems inherent in domestic violence, they use a case of animal abuse to draw attention to the plight of Victorian women. (It is interesting to note that there were many functioning Societies for the Prevention of Cruelty to Animals in England during this period, but the first Society for the Prevention of Cruelty to Women had yet to commence. Harriet and John want to connect these two types of abuse.) William Burn was convicted of beating his horse, but when the judge discovered that he had a large family he was not sentenced to the maximum fine. Instead of admiring the judge's compassion, Harriet and John prod the judge and readership of the Morning Chronicle *to consider that when a man beats his horse, he is also likely to beat his wife and children, therefore should not have been lightly sentenced. (The Lord Mayor referred to in the article was Sir George Carroll.)*

In a Mansion-house report of last week it is stated the one WILLIAM BURN was charged before the LORD MAYOR "with having most cruelly beaten one of the horses he was driving in a waggon. He had been sitting on the middle horse, which was without reins, and he struck one of the poor animals most desperately about the head with the butt-end of his whip. The horse fell, and the prisoner struck it even more brutally when down. The LORD MAYOR expressed great indignation at the conduct of the defendant, and was about to fine him to the utmost extent, when he suddenly learned that he had a large family," whereupon he said to him, "You deserve the highest punishment; but I cannot think of punishing your wife and children. The sentence of the court upon you is, that you pay a fine of ten shillings, or be confined in the House of Correction for fourteen days." The defendant "thanked his lordship, and paid the fine."

We regard this leniency, together with the reason assigned for it, as a match for the most unthinking and ill-judged exercises of magisterial discretion with which the London police-courts have lately favoured us. "A large family" has long been familiar as an excuse for begging, and a recommendation to the benevolent electors whose suffrages confer the responsible office of parish beadle. Hereafter, it seems, it is to be a license for violating the law, and, worse than that, for committing acts of savage brutality, which excite not merely regret but indignation that such a creature should have a wife and children in his power to treat in the same manner.

Let us look at the thing first on the general principles of the administration of justice. The LORD MAYOR thought the man deserved the full penalty, and was about to inflict it. He thought, therefore, that the highest fine which the law authorised, forty shillings, or in default of payment fourteen days in the House of Correction (for the law actually allows no longer term), would not have been more than enough to make some impression upon the man's obdurate nature, and induce him and others like him to put some restraint upon their brutality. And who will not agree with the LORD MAYOR in so thinking? Rather, who will not go far beyond him? Who does not see that the maximum penalty ought to be much higher; that it is ridiculously and lamentably inadequate; that it was fixed so low, not because it was thought sufficient, but because the promoters of the bill were too happy to get the consent of the Legislature to any penalty at all, in order at least to establish the fact that the law disapproves and stigmatises ferocious abuse of power against the helpless? This recognition, we suspect, is the chief part of the good which the Act against Cruelty to Animals has yet done; and even that, the insignificance of the penalties in a great measure neutralizes, for if those who commit the crime are now aware that their superiors think it wrong, they cannot suppose that it is thought to be anything very bad by people who are so very much more than gentle in their repression of it.

But to return to the LORD MAYOR. He thought, at any rate, that forty shillings, or imprisonment for fourteen days, was not more than sufficient severity to give the man a salutary lesson. If forty shillings were not more than enough, ten shillings are less than enough; and the man is let off with a penalty which the magistrate knows to be insufficient to correct his own vicious habits and to deter others. And this because the LORD MAYOR "cannot think of punishing" the wife and children. In the first place, the instantaneous payment of the ten shillings renders it more than probable that ample means existed for a fortnight's support. In the second place, did the law extend that the inconvenience which a man's wife and children may suffer, from penalties imposed on himself, should be a reason for not inflicting the punishment which he has merited by his misdeeds? Would the LORD MAYOR have given him the benefit of this excuse if he had stolen a handkerchief? No, truly; there would have been no thought then to hardship to the family, although in that case the offence might actually have been committed to relieve their hunger; and at any rate, the offender would not have been proved to be the kind of man from whom it would be a mercy to have separated them.

Real consideration for the wife and children would have spoken a very different language to the magistrate. It would have said something like this — A man capable of the act of which this man is found guilty, must be one of two things. He is either a wretch who wantonly ill-treats a helpless being, for the pleasure of tyranny, because it is in his power and cannot resist; or an irritable, violent creature, who on the smallest provocation (provocation from the unconscious dumb animal who slaves to death for his benefit!) flies into an uncontrollable rage, and cannot restrain himself from wreaking a savage vengeance. One of these two characters the man must be; and on either supposition we may infer what sort of a taskmaster he is to the unfortunate woman and the unfortunate children, who are as much in his power, and much more liable to rouse his ferocious passions than the animal over whom he tyrannised. It really seems to us, that they are more objects of pity for being compelled to live with such a man than they would have been for being deprived during a whole fortnight of his agreeable society, and that it would have been a greater kindness to them to have seized the opportunity of giving a severe lesson to one who had the power of making so many human creatures miserable. If he could have been made less brutal to his horses it would have made him less brutal to his human victims likewise. Disgusting enough it is that animals like these should have wives and children; and disgusting that, merely because they are of the male sex, they should have the whole existence of these dependants as much under their absolute control as slave masters in any modern slave country have that of their slaves; and without even the wretched compensation of supporting them — for in that rank the wife always, and the children by the time they are seven or eight years old, take part, to the full measure of their physical strength, in the labours for the support of the family. But as if all this was not enough, the man is told by a magistrate, that because he has a family to ill-use, he may indulge himself in ill-using any other creatures who come in his way, and may practise on them the amiable propensities of which his family are to reap the full enjoyment. We have no doubt the LORD MAYOR meant kindly; but the tender mercies of thoughtless people are cruel; and we wish that, instead of being thanked by the ruffian whom he let off, he had deserved that thanks of the public for a rigorous exercise of the most important moral power a magistrate possesses—that of putting down strongly and manfully, by word and deed, the brutal vices of the worst part of the populace.

Morning Chronicle, 29 December 1846, p. 4, b–c
[The North family]

As in the case of Sarah Brown, Harriet and John here argue for the rights of single mothers. In this case, the children have been taken by the paternal grandmother after their father's death. Here the writers focus attention on the court's unfairness when not awarding custody to mothers when a father dies. Harriet and John also suggest a religious bias against Roman Catholics exists in this case. As with all the newspaper articles, it actively aims to intervene in the ongoing case by influencing the judges who have not yet ruled, by encouraging Mrs. North to appeal the case if the court rules against her, and by shaming the in-laws into reconsidering their case. Mrs. North and her in-laws arrived at a mutual agreement and the case was withdrawn (see The Times, *12 January 1847, 8).*

The case of the NORTH family, heard last week before Vice-Chancellor KNIGHT BRUCE, and on which that judge has pronounced at least a temporary decision, suggests some queries on the state of the law respecting maternal rights, to which this judgment, if it represents the law correctly, gives anything but a satisfactory answer.

The parties to the cause are the widow of Lieut. DUDLEY NORTH on the one side, and his mother and sister on the other, and the contest is for the guardianship of the four children. The facts of the case are these:—The parents, originally members of the Church of England, had for some time before the father's death been in the habit of attending, along with two of their children, a Roman Catholic chapel, but had not publicly professed the Catholic religion. The father died from the effects of a coach accident, and on his death-bed refused to receive the Protestant clergyman who had been brought to the house by one of his relations. The widow soon after became an avowed Roman Catholic, as she asserts on oath that, according to her belief, her husband, but for his untimely decease, would have done. The husband's relations got possession of the children by a stratagem, and refused to restore them to their mother, placing them under the care of a maiden aunt. The mother sought legal redress; and the result is, that the Vice-Chancellor directs a reference to a Master, to appoint a guardian or guardians, and decides that in the meantime the children shall remain in the custody of their paternal relations, the mother "to have access to them for two hours daily," but only in the presence of one or more of the said relations.

We have attempted to discover, from the reported judgment, on what distinct principle this startling decision is founded. Vice-Chancellor KNIGHT BRUCE does not positively affirm any principle, but makes indistinct reference to two. He is very positive on one thing—that it is the duty of the court to have the children brought up in the religion of the Church of England. Sometimes it seems as if his reason was, that the father must be presumed to have intended it. But there are other sayings on which it is difficult to put any interpretation but that, even if the father intended otherwise, the court would not the less have thought it its duty to see the children brought up in the religious belief which this Vice-Chancellor sanctions by his approval.

It is a duty to society that a decision should be given by the highest authority on this question of law: Is, or is not, a widowed mother, in case of intestacy, the legal guardian of her children? The counsel for the widow asserts that she is. The judge, if we understand his meaning, decides that she is not; that there is no legal guardian; that it rests with the court to appoint one; that it is entirely at the court's discretion to appoint anybody, the mother, or any one else. If this is correct; if the mother, even when she is the sole parent, is in the eye of the law a stranger to her own children; if even when the father is silent the mother has no rights over the children, more than anybody has who chooses to claim them, and *can* have no rights unless the court thinks fit to confer them on her, as it is equally at liberty to do on any one else—if this is the law, it ought to be made universally known, in order that the common sense and sense of justice of the community may speedily put an end to so iniquitous an outrage on the most universally recognised and strongest tie of nature. Society is rigid in enforcing this tie *against* the mother; there are no bounds to its aversion and contempt for a mother who deserts her offspring; is it then entitled to arrogate to itself the power to deprive her of them for no presumed or alleged fault—nay, while saying, as in this case, that the mother's conduct is unimpeachable? The idea is monstrous, and repugnant to all feelings of justice. Again, if the widowed mother is not the legal guardian of the children, with what justice can she be bound to maintain them by her labour? In the case of mothers in the lower ranks, can the law, which acknowledges between them and their children no relationship, treat the mother as a parent for the sole purpose of forcing her to work for their maintenance?

But if the mother *is* the legal guardian of the children, unless the court for reasons assigned should appoint otherwise, what reasons appear in the Vice-Chancellor's statement which justify his setting aside her guardianship in this particular case? And here we cannot but express an opinion that the two reasons between which, as we before observed, the Vice-Chancellor halts, are each of them so bad, that we do not think he could have ventured to rest his decision upon the unassisted strength of either of them. He appears to intend to eke them out, one by another, under the idea that two bad reasons added together amount to a good one. In the first place, he argues at some length that the father, having never professed himself a Catholic, must be held to have died a Protestant, and to have intended therefore that the children should be brought up as Protestants. Now, if the mother has no rights, the father by his intestacy having abdicated his, it seems quite frivolous to discuss hypotheses about what the father may be presumed to have intended. The court, on this supposition, is the sole guardian, and ought to decide the matter on its own merits. But if the mother has rights, what can be more irrational than to supersede them on a presumption (not to say on a doubtful one) that the father desired something different? If he had desired anything different, he could have so provided by will; and his not doing so must be taken as complete evidence of his acquiescence in what, he had every reason to believe, would be the consequence of his intestacy—that the children would remain in the society and guardianship of their mother. Would the court have treated the question in this manner if it had been a question of property? A man dies possessed of an estate, which he could have bequeathed to whom he pleased; but he dies intestate, and it passes to the heir-at-law. Would the court receive evidence to prove that he disliked the heir-at-law, and would have preferred leaving the estate to some one else? The proposition is absurd, and would be so regarded. The deceased not having declared his intentions by will, the law would take its course, and the estate devolve on the person whom it had designated.

While, however, Vice-Chancellor BRUCE is willing to make all the use he can, in favour of his conclusion, of the imaginary intentions of the father, he intimates the right of the court to direct the children's religion, let the father's purpose be what it may:—"That it should view the religion of the children as a matter of indifference is of course quite out of the question. That no one can do. *That the religion of the children should depend on the mere will and pleasure of the person or persons who may happen to be guardian or guardians, ESPECIALLY when there is no testamentary guardian—* appears to me to be equally out of the case. As it is the duty of the court to superintend the education of infants in all cases where its powers are not excluded, so especially and most importantly it is the duty of the court to superintend that course of religious education in which the children ought, until they are of years of discretion, and able to think fit to choose for themselves, to be educated." Not only therefore when there is not, but when there is, a lawful guardian, the court will not permit the religion of the children to depend on the guardian's decision, but will make it depend on the court's pleasure. Nor is the maxim limited to cases in which there is no testamentary guardian. If Mr. NORTH had made a will appointing Mrs. NORTH guardian, or any one else guardian, and the person appointed had been supposed to intend to make the children Roman Catholics, the court would have set aside the will.

Hear this all parents who think that you have the power of confiding your children after your death to the relatives or friends on whose integrity, judgement, and affection you most rely. If the friend or relative be a Roman Catholic, he may be your choice, but some other person, perhaps one you have the greatest reason to despise and dislike, will be Sir J.K. BRUCE's. Nay, it is not certain that his interference will wait for your death. It is his duty, he says, to regulate the religious education of the children in all cases from which his powers "are not excluded;" and that they are not excluded from the cases of children whose father is alive, SHELLEY'S case and several other cases bear witness. For aught that appears, the children might have been taken out of the control of Mr. NORTH himself, if he had lived to declare himself a Roman Catholic, and the Protestant maiden lady who has them in custody might have been *in loco* of both their parents, as she now is of their widowed mother. If we could smile on so serious a subject, we should be moved to do so by the doctrine that a maiden aunt is as nearly related to children as their mother!

The case has two stages yet to go through. The Master has to report; and his report, when made, must receive the sanction of the court; from which, if the present temporary decision is made a permanent one, we sincerely hope the case will be carried by appeal to the LORD CHANCELLOR, and will not pass by without calling the attention of the public and of Parliament to the principles which it involves. It is they who should decide whether a mother is her child's nearest relation or no, and whether Sir J. K. BRUCE, under cover of his court's power as protector of infants, shall be permitted to commence, in the year 1846, a new form of religious persecution.

Daily News, 14 July 1849, p. 4, d-e
[Corporal Punishment]

Although this article begins with a discussion of the case of Alexander Smith, who may be punished by public whipping if he is unable to pay a fine of 17£, the real point of the article is to point to the discrepancy between punishments for property crimes and violent crimes, particularly domestic violence. Harriet and John suggest that if flogging were ever appropriate it would be against violent criminals, but even in those cases it would be better to dispense with corporal punishment. They argue that the "illegalising of corporal punishment, domestic as well as judicial, at any age" would do more to improve society than any number of other types of legislation. Recognizing the importance of nonviolent treatment of people in personal as well as public life is an important point in this essay.

While, in the popular discussions on criminal law, the idea of punishment is more and more sunk in that of reformatory discipline; while what were once deemed the main ends of penal infliction—retribution to the culprit, and the deterring of future offenders—are well-nigh sinking out of view, and prisons, in the opinion of many well-meaning persons, are regarded as little more than a sort of hospitals for the morally sick, where they are to be cured of their soul's diseases by mild alternatives; while this twist of the moral sentiment in the direction of shortsighted tenderness is increasingly manifest; in the actual administration of our criminal law, the tide is setting in the contrary direction, towards a revival of the brutal and barbarous practices of the middle ages and of the East. Amidst our talk of reformatory treatment we are returning to the most demoralising, the most brutalising, because the most degrading of punishments, the bastinado. There have been other instances lately of this, but none hitherto that comes up to what we extract from a Southwark police report of Friday last:

> *Alexander Smith,* described as a commission agent, was brought before Mr. Secker, charged with illegally pawning a gold watch, valued 20 guineas, the property of James Mills, the master of a West India trader.
>
> It appeared that the complainant formed a casual acquaintance with the prisoner, who prevailed upon him to accompany him to Astley's to witness the horsemanship. Previously, however, to their entering the theatre, the prisoner suggested the propriety of the complainant leaving a valuable gold watch in the hands of the landlord of a public-house adjacent, where they had partaken of refreshment, adding, that the article would be much safer there than at the theatre. The complainant at once assented to this suggestion, and the watch was accordingly left

with the landlord of the house. Before the performance was over, the prisoner made some frivolous excuse, and quitting the theatre proceeded to the public-house and got possession of the complainant's watch, which it was subsequently ascertained he had pledged at a pawnbroker's shop for 10£. Upon the discovery of the theft he promised to redeem the article, or pay the full value, neither of which he had since done; and the complainant, finding that there was no chance of obtaining restitution, gave the prisoner into custody on the charge of illegally pawning the watch.

The prisoner, a well-dressed middle-aged man, said that he had given the complainant his note of hand to pay at the rate of 10s. a week until the debt was paid.

Mr. Secker said that the mild term of "debt" could not be applied to such a fraudulent transaction. The prisoner had acted a most dishonest part in taking advantage of the absence of complainant to obtain possession of his watch.

The complainant admitted having taken a written guarantee from the prisoner, but said he did it for the purpose of strengthening the case against him.

The prisoner asserted that the watch was given him to pawn, which was flatly contradicted by the owner.

Mr. Secker denounced, in strong terms, the conduct of the prisoner, and sentenced him to pay a penalty of 5£. for illegally pawning the watch, besides 12£., the lowest value put upon the watch; and, in default of payment, to be committed for three months; and that, in addition to the above, if the prisoner omitted to pay the above sums within three days of the expiration of his imprisonment, he should be once publicly whipped within the precincts of the gaol.

The prisoner, who heard the latter part of the sentence with astonishment depicted on his countenance, was then removed from the bar.

Well might he be astonished; and his astonishment will be participated, we believe, by the majority of readers. We know that the office of police magistrate is one to which a man is appointed usually because he is fit for nothing else; because, being too stupid to fill any other appointment, he is thought good enough to be the dispenser of law, justice, and moral instruction to those who most need all these. But even a Mr. SECKER must, we suppose, have some law to bear him out in such a decision as this. What law? and how has such a law been smuggled through parliament? a law permitting the infliction of the bastinado for a pecuniary fraud—by which, if impartially enforced, half the bankrupts in England would be publicly flogged, and a London magistrate would become a Turkish Cadi. But there is another peculiarity in the case which must be wholly Mr. SECKER'S. The flogging, after all, is not to be inflicted for the offence. The punishment of that is a fine of 5£, added to another 12£, or, "in default of payment," to be committed for three months. But, after suffering the imprisonment, he is still "to pay the above sums within three days," and to be flogged if he "omits" to pay them. He is to be flogged therefore, not for the fraud, but for being unable to pay 17£. This is a person to be entrusted with the power of flogging!

But the pranks of police magistrates are not the worst of the political and social vices which this case illustrates. It exemplifies the total absence of true moral feeling which pervades our criminal legislation and all the functionaries who administer it, from the judges of the Court of Queen's Bench down to this Mr. SECKER. If a brutal punishment can ever be appropriate, it is in the case of ruffianly assaults, committed in the mere wantonness of brutality, against creatures whose sole offence is to be inferior in physical strength, oftenest of all against helpless children, or the slaves called wives, whose death, by a long continuance of personal torture, has of late been so frequently brought to light, and without a single exception so leniently passed over, that this has apparently become one of the safe ways of getting rid of those incumbrances. To such ruffians as these the degradation of corporal punishment would be very suitable. It does not make them brutes, it only stamps them as what they are. A coward who beats another because he is the stronger, would perhaps even be benefited by finding himself for once in the hands of a stronger than himself, and tasting of the degradation he has inflicted. But who ever hears of corporal punishment for assault? One or two months' imprisonment is all we hear of in the most atrocious cases; while, if property is in question—if pounds, shillings, and pence have been tampered with, years of imprisonment, with hard labour (not to mention transportation) are almost the smallest penalty. And this is not peculiarly the fault of the police magistrates, whose power of inflicting punishment for assault is very limited. It is the crime more especially of legislators and of the superior courts. They, it seems, have yet to learn that there is a thing infinitely more important than property— freedom and sacredness of human personality; that there is an immeasurable distance in point of moral enormity between any [of] the gravest offence which concerns property only, and an act of insulting and degrading violence perpetrated against a human being. Mankind could go on very well, have gone on in time past (as well as they have ever yet gone on), with property very insecure. But subject to blows, or the fear of blows, they can be no other than soulless, terror-stricken slaves, without virtue, without courage, without peace, with nothing they dare call their own. Yet because persons in the upper and middle ranks *are* not subject to personal outrage, and are subject to have their watches stolen, the punishment of blows is revived, not for those who are guilty of blows, but for middle-aged men who pawn watches. Is this to be endured?

A few weeks ago, the punishment of flogging, in the case of the young man who shot at the Queen, was omitted, it is said, at the special desire of the Queen herself. The forbearance was uncomplimentary to the legislatorial wisdom which had recently enacted that penalty as peculiarly fit for that particular offence: but no one can be surprised by an example of good sense, good taste, and good feeling, given by the Queen. The crime of HAMILTON was not of a degraded or brutal kind, though of a wicked and grave kind, deserving, in truth, and requiring, a server punishment than it received. To refuse so disgusting a tribute as the revival of a brutalising degradation as a punishment for offences against herself, was a worthy lesson to legislators and judges; and it was magnanimity, not like but most unlike a sovereign, to punish so serious an offence only as if it had been directed against the meanest subject. Would that her Majesty would take in hand this vast and vital question of the extinction of personal violence by the best and surest means—the illegalising of corporal punishment, domestic as well as judicial, at any age. We conscientiously believe that more large and lasting good, both present and future, to the moral and social character of the whole people, would be achieved by such an act of legislation, than fifty years of legislative efforts without it would be required to supply.

Daily News, 5 February 1850, p. 4, f
[Mary Ann Parsons]

Domestic violence in the nineteenth century went beyond wife and child abuse to abuse of servants. This article outlines the violence against a fifteen-year-old servant of a farmer and his wife that ended in her death. This article appears over six months after their previous co-authored newspaper pieces, and it is the first of several that they were to write in the following months.

We would earnestly call the attention of our readers to one of the most horrible cases of brutality which have ever disgraced the superficial civilisation of our time and country: we were going to call it the *most* horrible, but cases approaching to it in atrocity are so incessantly recurring in the police reports, that we hesitate to pronounce even this case unrivalled in those disgraceful annals.

MARY ANN PARSONS, a girl of fifteen, said by the master of the workhouse to have been "strong and healthy, although not particularly bright," was hired as a servant from the workhouse of the Bideford union, by a man and woman named BIRD, in September last. On the 5th January she died, of such an accumulation of wounds, mutilations, and other horrible injuries, that we will not repeat the sickening list as given in the examinations before the magistrates. On the Friday before Christmas-day, the evidence of a man named MORRISH shows that he saw her standing in the middle of the room where the prisoners and their four children were; that she was ordered "to go into the slee house, or back house," that as she "went across the kitchen" he "saw that her neck and shoulders were covered with blood, which appeared to have flowed just before" he "came in," that about ten minutes afterwards the man name BIRD "opened the slee door and ordered her to wash the blood off her neck." Another man named HOOPER saw her the day after Christmas day, when she "appeared to be very ill: she could not stand upright." He "heard her making a horrid noise after she got up stairs: she was crying, and making a 'wist' or 'moaning' noise as she was going up." This creature had seen her repeatedly flogged by both the man and woman, and neither he nor the former witness ever interfered even by a word of remonstrance. During the whole three months that she was in the service of these wretches, she appears to have been utterly friendless, uncared for, unenquired after. Her mother, who was an inhabitant of the same workhouse, never once saw her, and was ignorant of her fate until made aware of it by the ghastly spectacle which the body presented when in the coffin. The only person who seems to have said anything about the girl after she entered their service, was the master of the workhouse; this man, meeting the woman prisoner, who after a month's trial had told him that she was an "honest, good, industrious girl," and hearing on this occasion some complaint, gave his advice to "properly chastise" her. The instrument of torture is said in the report to have excited the horror of the spectators; it was "a strong stick of about a foot in length, to which were fastened eighteen stout sharp leather thongs, about a foot in length. This formidable cat was capable of inflicting the most cruel laceration, as bad as the army whip, and worse than the cowhide of the American slave owner." With this it was that the girl was reduced to the state in which her body appeared. The man SERMON, who gave the brutal recommendation to flog this girl of fifteen, and who admitted that he had "punished children in the workhouse," though he "never served a child anything like that," declared that in the army, where he had served, and had frequently seen sentence of flogging executed, the manner in which this poor victim had been treated would not have been considered fair flogging. With how much of this evidence before them does not appear, the coroner's jury, under the direction of the coroner, found that the girl died "from congestion of the brain, caused by external injuries, but how or by what means such injuries were caused there was no evidence to shew." Fortunately for justice, the "means," though mysterious to this "jury of respectable (!) yeomen," were apparent enough to others. An application having been made to a magistrate, the culprits have most properly been committed to take their trial for murder; and heartily were it to be wished that the wretch who counselled "chastisement," and the two base slaves who looked on calmly and saw—one of them the brutality itself—both of them its consequences—could be reached as accessories to the crime. From the report it would appear that justice might have been entirely defeated and the monsters might have escaped punishment, but for the clear, distinct, and manly evidence of the surgeon, Mr. TURNER. Too many of this gentleman's profession, in similar cases, give their evidence in softened terms, and profess doubt, from fear of injuring themselves with the lower class of their customers.

Our law, or at least its administration, takes abundant care of property, but the most atrocious personal violence it treats with a lenity amounting to actual license: even when death follows, the offence is generally pronounced to be manslaughter, and the criminal escapes with a year or two's imprisonment. Yet whether we look to the torments inflicted, or to the depravity indicated in the perpetrators, the crime against MARY ANN PARSONS is of far deeper atrocity than that of a RUSH, who fires a pistol at a man and kills him. RUSH intended death, but they intended torture, and inflicted death by torture. What the law is, and what its administrators thought of such crimes as this poor child has been the victim of, was shown in the case of the notorious Mrs. BROWNRIGG, who was hanged for murder, and has remained the traditional type of the worst and most odious species of murders. BROWNRIGG flogged two of her apprentices to death—exactly what these people have done to the unfortunate servant girl. The question in law was not whether she had premeditated their death: it was enough in law and justice that she had carried diabolical cruelty to the point which caused it.

Morning Chronicle, 13 March 1850, p. 5, d–e
[Anne Bird]

This important essay digs deeply into the issue of child abuse. Harriet and John explore not merely the case of Anne Bird's abuse of her two-year-

old, they disagree with the popular opinion that violence is on the decline because of the "progress of society." Pointing to police records of crimes, they argue that domestic violence, including wife abuse and child abuse, is far from unusual. They vividly describe the long tale of woe that often precedes death in cases of domestic violence. The authors point a finger at the unfairness of laws that punish property crimes severely, but treat violent crimes lightly, especially assault laws that fail to distinguish between a barroom brawl and the beating of women and children. More significantly, Harriet and John perceive the effect of domestic violence on those who live in its presence. It warps the sensibilities so that those who are abused are turned into abusers.

Much has been said and written, although as yet to very little purpose, on the effect which the progress of society in wealth, numbers, and education produces on the nature and amount of crime. Among many differences of opinion on this much-debated question, there is on one point a very general agreement. However it may be with offences against property, crimes of violence tend, it is generally believed, to diminution. There is nothing in which we seem to have so much the advantage over our fathers as in mildness of manners; and the delinquencies which prevail in the present generation are, according to common opinion, those which have their source in poverty or cupidity, but not in ferocity.

Though we do not deny the truth of this representation as it affects some classes of society and some offenses, yet, as a general fact, we are sorry to say that it is not borne out by that authentic register of the manners and habits of the populace—the Police Reports. Far from exhibiting any decrease in crimes of violence, hardly a day passes in which that record does not bear frightful witness to their unabated prevalence. And the crimes which thus abound are, in point of moral turpitude, the worst order of crimes of violence—not the outbursts of offended irascibility against an equal, but the habitual abuse of brute strength, and the indulgence of wanton cruelty. Women and children, or young persons, are usually the sufferers. Cases succeed one another with hardly any intermission, in which men are proved to have killed their wives by brutal maltreatment; every such death being the termination of a series of sufferings, extending through years, against which the vital principle was at last unable longer to bear up. For each such extreme case, we may be assured there are hundreds which stop just short of the infliction of death, or in which death is inflicted, but not ascribed to its true cause. In another very numerous class of cases, a man or a woman is found to have kept an unhappy child for weeks and months in some disgusting domestic dungeon, until it is nearly dead from cold, hunger, and neglect—or to have scourged it day after day, until it is brought into a state which strikes horror when at last exhibited, and from which in many cases the child never recovers. In other instances a parish apprentice, or a young person hired as a servant from the workhouse, is the miserable victim.

Whoever has sufficiently attended to the proceedings of the Police Courts to have observed the deplorable frequency of these cases, must have been no less forcibly struck with the scandalous impunity of the culprits. Often, even when the victim has died from their maltreatment, they are not sent to trial. If tried, they are, in a majority of cases, acquitted—sometimes in the face of the clearest evidence. Even if found guilty, it is only of manslaughter, and they get off with a year or two of imprisonment. Cases short of death are very seldom tried at all, but are disposed of summarily by the police magistrate. A recent instance at the Marylebone Police-office exemplifies the sort of justice usually administered. The case was one of peculiar enormity, the victim being a child two years old. The culprit, a woman named ANNE BIRD, was proved to have cruelly maltreated this infant with a whip. The magistrate did what magistrates in such cases usually do; he talked of the extreme atrocity of the case—as if strong words would do away with the effect of weak acts—and then sentenced the woman to the greatest penalty he could summarily inflict— a fine of five pounds, or, in default of payment, two months' imprisonment. If this woman, under the pressure of poverty, had stolen five shillings, the magistrate would not have failed to commit her for trial, and if found guilty she would probably have been transported. But her offence being brutal cruelty, practiced on a creature utterly helpless and unoffending, he did not deem it worth while to try whether a higher court would be of opinion that a case of extraordinary atrocity deserved greater punishment than two months' imprisonment. At the end of the two months the child, no doubt, will be given back to the torturer; unless before that time, as happened in a similar case not long ago, it dies of the injuries received.

The fault is partly in the Administration of the law, but chiefly in the law itself. The whole state of the law on the subject of offences against the person urgently requires revision. Toward offenders against property the law until very lately was ferocious, and even now does not err on the side of gentleness; but in case of personal violence, short of premeditated murder, it is chargeble with confounding together offenses the most widely separated, both in kind and degree of criminality, and with the most excessive and unwarrantable lenity towards all but the lightest. Legislators and judges have bestowed little consideration on the amount of guilt and suffering which lie disguised under the mild and euphonious designation of "common assault." That gentle phrase stands for nearly every sort of bodily maltreatment of which death or maiming is not obviously the result. There is but that one term to denote the whole range of acts of personal violence, from a quarrel between two strong and equally matched men, one of whom knocks the other down in a fair fight, to that habitual and wanton abuse of muscular strength against the weak and defenseless which makes life a martyrdom. Even if this confounding of the gravest moral distinctions were a mere matter of theory and classification, it would be very far from harmless in its effects on the popular mind; but, carried out as it is, to the full, in daily practice—some of the most detestable actions which one human being can perpetrate against another being punished, when punished at all, with about the amount of penalty which would be due to a simple breach of the peace—it would show a profound ignorance of the effect of moral agencies on the character not to perceive how deeply depraving must be the influence of such a lesson given from the seat of justice. It cannot be doubted that to this more than to any other single cause is to be attributed the frightful brutality which marks a very large proportion of the poorest class, and no small portion of a class much above the poorest.

Persons who are not conversant, either by their own knowledge or through the proceedings of courts of justice, with the breadth and depth of popular brutality, have very little idea of what is comprehended in the meaning of the words, "domestic tyranny." This is now the only kind of tyranny which, in the more improved countries of the world, still exists in full vigour. Even in the worst governed countries, of any tolerable degree of civilization, it is now but rarely that Kings or public functionaries have it in their power personally to maltreat any one. The barbarities of which history is full, and which in barbarous countries flourish as rankly as ever, very few persons in a civilized country now suffer from political authorities—millions are liable to them from domestic ones. The great majority of the inhabitants of this and of every country—including nearly the whole of one sex, and all the young of both—are, either by law or by circumstances stronger than the law, subject to some one man's arbitrary will. Every now and then the public are revolted by some disclosure of unspeakable atrocities committed against some of these helpless dependents—while, for every such case which excites notice, hundreds, most of them as bad, pass off in the police reports entirely unobserved; and for one that finds its way, even for that brief instant, into light, we may be assured that not hundreds but thousands are constantly going on in the safety of complete obscurity. If, through the accidental presence of some better-hearted person than these poor creatures are usually surrounded by, complaint is made to a magistrate, the neighbours—persons living in the same house—almost invariably testify, without either repentance or shame, that the same brutalities had gone on for years in their sight or hearing, without their stirring a finger to prevent them. The sufferers themselves are either unable to complain, from youth or ignorance, or they dare not. They know too surely the consequences of either failing or succeeding in a complaint, when the law, after inflicting just enough punishment to excite the thirst of vengeance, delivers back the victim to the tyrant.

As a matter either of justice or of humanity, these things speak so plain a language as ought to be in no need of commentary. What it is of more importance to insist upon, is their demoralizing effect. Attention has of late been much directed to the overcrowding of the labouring population as a source of moral evils. Let any one consider the degrading moral effect, in the midst of these crowded dwellings, of scenes of physical violence, repeated day after day—the debased, spirit-broken, down-trodden condition of the unfortunate woman, the most constant sufferer from domestic brutality in the poorer classes, unaffectedly believing herself to be out of the protection of the law—the children born and bred in this moral atmosphere—with the unchecked indulgence of the most odious passions, the tyranny of physical force in its coarsest manifestations, constantly exhibited as the most familiar facts of their daily life—can it be wondered if they grow up without any of the ideas and feelings which it is the purpose of moral education to infuse, without any sense of justice or affection, any conception of self-restraint—incapable in their turn of governing their children by any other means than blows? The law, whose utmost exertions would not be more than enough to withstand this mass of depraving influences, makes so little use of its powers and opportunities, measures out its reproofs and punishments by such a scale, that the culprits believe almost the worst of these brutalities to be venial, and all minor ones to be actually permitted—while the victims regard their suffering and debasement as the regular course of things, which the law sanctions and the world allows; and when not crushed entirely, they seek a wretched compensation by tyrannizing in their turn, when any hapless fellow-creature comes within their power.

Morning Chronicle, 26 March 1850, pp. 4, e-f; 5 a
[Mary Ann Parsons, Part 2]

In a follow-up to their article of 5 February, Harriet and John quote the disgusting details of the condition of the servant, Mary Ann Parsons, at the time of her death. The images of fingernails ripped from their append-

age so that the bone was exposed and the body covered with bruises and abesses recent and past are highlighted to excite pity and repulsion in the reader. Harriet and John plea for a change in law that would better protect victims of domestic violence, but also call into question the judgment of the magistrate who decided the case. They encourage the public to think of the perpetrators as "acquitted murderers." This angry essay is a powerful call for a review of the victims of domestic brutality who "cannot protect themselves."

The case of MARY ANN PARSONS, who died a cruel death from maltreatment, at Buckland, near Bideford, in January last, has terminated in a more complete frustration of public justice than, in our worst surmises, we had imagined possible. The criminals, ROBERT and SARAH BIRD, have *not* been convicted of murder—nor of manslaughter—nor even of a common assault. They have escaped totally unpunished—unpunished, except by public execration, which, it is to be hoped, will cling to them the more closely that they have not expiated their guilt by the retribution which the law appoints for such malefactors, but which in this instance, as in too many others, it has failed to inflict. Let any one who reads the report of the trial which appeared in our paper of yesterday, judge whether there can be the faintest shadow of doubt as the facts—whether the two prisoners will not carry to their graves the merited designation of acquitted murderers. The worst features of the case, as it appeared against them in the preliminary investigation, were all confirmed, and more than confirmed, by the evidence on the trial. Several witnesses swore to repeated acts of brutal maltreatment. Several others swore to admissions of such acts by the female prisoner, both as respected herself and her husband. The state in which the poor girl's body was found was sworn to by Mr. TURNER, the surgeon who made the post-mortem examination, in these clear and straightforward terms:—

"On the legs and thighs I saw several wounds, varying in extent, and evidently inflicted by some irregular or rough weapon. It struck me to have been by a birch. There was a bruise on the chest. The face was discoloured, and the forehead, and some abscesses were on the arms and fingers. The skin over the bowels was discoloured. On the left arm there was an abscess, and the skin immediately round it was discoloured, as if it had been bruised some time, perhaps a fortnight. The abscess had burst below the elbow. There was another abscess just forming. The nails of the little and fore finger were gone, apparently some time. The two middle finger nails were also gone, apparently more recently, and in one the bone protruded. On the right arm there was also an abscess that had also burst.

On the right hip there was a large slough. On the posterior part of the hips were several wounds, apparently inflicted some time. They were covered with plaster, and appeared to be old sores. Between the shoulders were two trivial bruises. There was also a mark on the face, from the temple down to the cheek. On removing the scalp I found another bruise on the back of the head, with considerable extravasation of blood diffused between the scalp and the skull." Then, after stating that he observed congestion of the membranes of the brain, and at the base of the brain extravasation of blood, and that he "found the cause of death in the head," Mr. TURNER continued:—"In my judgement, *death was the result of the external injuries*. I could not form a judgement how that violence had been inflicted. I don't think the injuries I saw in the head were produced from falls. The condition of the girl must have been extremely reduced before death, and the powers of life weakened. The injuries I observed would have produced an effect on the nervous system, which is connected with the brain." Another medical witness, Mr. EDGE, a surgeon to the hospital at Exeter, "conceives that Mr. TURNER is correct in the opinion that he formed, as to the time of death, and the cause."

After such evidence—unless the testimony was disbelieved, which it was not—it seems incredible that Judge (Mr. Justice TALFOURD) should have charged the jury for an acquittal. Every reader must be astonished at such a course, and must be anxious to know how so extraordinary a judgment came to be pronounced on such a state of facts. The explanation, however, is instructive, by the illustration which it affords of the state either of the law, or of the mind of this Judge—certainly not one of the worst of its administrators. Though there were statements and physical facts sufficient to convince the mind most recalcitrant to evidence, that the death of the girl was the work of the two prisoners, there was not, it seems *legal* evidence to bring it home to them. "The case," in the opinion of the judge, "had failed." But when we see in what points it was considered to have failed, we cease to wonder—or rather, our astonishment changes its object, and we wonder how there should *ever* be legal evidence of a murder committed in the manner in which these two culprits caused the death of their victim.

The grounds of acquittal were two; and which of them is the strangest it would not be easy to decide. The first was, that although there was superabundant evidence of brutality by the prisoners sufficient to cause the frightful state of the corpse, it was not proved that anybody struck the particular blow on the head to which the congestion of the brain, said to be the immediate cause of death, was thought to be more especially owing. The second reason was, that even if the blow had been struck by one of the prisoners, there was no evidence "to fix it upon one of these parties more than the other." But it is by no means clear that, in the opinion of the medical witnesses, the blow on the head was exclusively the fatal injury. Mr. TURNER, according to our report, "found the cause of death in the head"—meaning the congestion; but he distinctly said, "In my judgment death was the result of *the external injuries*." "The injuries I observed"—being those on the body generally—"would have produced an effect on the nervous system, which is connected with the brain." The other medical witness professed an unqualified agreement in Mr. TURNER's opinion. It would thus appear that neither of these gentlemen ascribed the cerebral congestion to any local injury to the head, but to general injuries, affecting the brain not directly, but indirectly through "the nervous system." Even assuming, however (what, it is fair to say, some of the reports of the trial appear to bear out), that death was more immediately caused by that particular injury, among the many of which the sufferer bore the hideous marks—that circumstance does not abate one iota from the moral certainty of the prisoners' guilt. They were proved to have been in the habit of inflicting, up to nearly the time of the girl's death, cruelties quite equal to the one assumed to have caused it. There was no direct proof that either of them struck that particular blow; but there was not the smallest evidence accounting for it in any other way. It was for them to rebut the presumption raised by their other brutalities. An adequate case had been shown for any result, however fatal, in their daily treatment of their victim. On them lay the burden of disproving the connection by proving the existence of some other cause for the catastrophe. If a man were found murdered on the highway, his body covered with wounds, some of which only were mortal, the assassins who were proved to have fallen upon him, and to have inflicted some of those wounds, would not be suffered to escape because no one could swear that the particular wounds inflicted by them were the mortal ones. It would be enough that they did wound him, that no other cause of death appeared, and that he died.

With respect to the very nice and scrupulous doubt—as to which of the two prisoners is answerable—it is easily disposed of. Both are answerable. The guilt rests on both, until one of them can get rid of it by throwing it exclusively on the other. If the atrocious acts—some one of all of which destroyed the victim—had been proved only against one of the prisoners, that one would justly have been made responsible for the catastrophe. But those acts were proved against both, and against both equally. Both, therefore, are accountable; just as is the case if a person is found with a gang of robbers at the commission of a crime—it is on himself that the burden rests of proving his non-participation in their guilt.

Under the jurisprudence of Mr. Justice TALFOURD, it is virtually proclaimed to such people as ROBERT and SARAH BIRD that there is impunity for murder, on condition of their adopting the commonest precautions. If the person to be murdered is an inmate of their house, and under their power, they must be dull indeed if they cannot effect their purpose without supplying those links of evidence for want of which the death of MARY ANN PARSONS goes unpunished. It matters not though the whole neighbourhood testifies to daily cruelties more than adequate to produce death. It matters not that the corpse excites universal horror by its glaring manifestations of those cruelties. They can surely contrive that no one shall be able to swear to the particular wound inflicted on a particular day, or to prove that *this* wound was give by one of the murderers, *that* by another—and the victim, who alone knew, is not alive to tell. This is not justice. If it be law, which, in opposition to a judge's dictum, we do not pretend to decide, it is law which cannot too soon be altered. When the law places any one—and that a person of inferior physical strength—under the power of another, who may be such a creature as these BIRDS, it exposes the individual to peculiar risks, and ought, therefore, to guard him by peculiar precautions. What is called the ordinary protection of the law is not sufficient. The ordinary protection of law is protection to those who can help themselves—who can in general keep themselves out of harm's way, or, at least, who can tell their own story. The victims of domestic brutality cannot protect themselves; and there is no protection for them, if, when death ensues, and violence is proved sufficient to cause death, the prosecutors are obliged to produce direct evidence connecting the death with the brutality. It is on the accused that the burden of exculpating themselves should in such cases rest. Death, and maltreatment sufficient to cause death, are the sole facts of which positive evidence ought to be required. Those to whom power over others is given, and who brutally misuse that power, should be thus far held responsible for the safety of those over whom they tyrannise. Otherwise there is no security even for the lives of any of those who have the wretched and disgracefully common lot of being in the power of a brute.

Morning Chronicle, 29 March 1850, p. 4, c–d
{On Susan Moir}

Just three days after their editorial about the Parsons murder, Harriet and John write again about domestic violence, this time in the form of wife murder. They again appeal to the public to be cognizant of the proceedings and urge the police and victim's family to not fail to pursue such cases in the future. The case was also reported in the Times *of the same day, but unlike Harriet and John's essay, the* Times *article offered only the transcript of the trial. Two new issues appear in this essay: the sexism of punishment and the sexism of all-male juries. This piece suggests that women who kill their husbands are readily convicted of murder, while men who kill their wives are not. They also point out the likely unfairness of juries composed only of men who are likely to sympathize with a husband's frustrations with a wife. In this case, Harriet and John's pleas may have been effective, since Alexander Moir was convicted of aggravated manslaughter and transported for life (The* Times, *10 May 1850, p. 7).*

Only three days have elapsed since we held up to public indignation the frightful details of the Bideford abominations, and the scandal of an acquittal, decisive of Mr. Justice TALFOURD'S calibre both as a judge and as a man. Already another case has presented itself, fully equal in its atrocious features, and in which, unless the public look well to it, similar impunity will probably be the result.

Our yesterday's paper contained the Coroner's inquest on SUSAN MOIR, wife of ALEXANDER MOIR, carrying on business as a baker at No. 24, Brydges-street, Covent-garden. "When the sheet," says our report, "with which the remains were covered was thrown aside, an expression of horror escaped all present, the body, from head to foot, being literally covered with bruises and contused wounds of old and recent date." The surgeon, Mr. WATKINS, deposed—"The integuments and muscles of the head were contused in a manner I never saw before—in fact they were a perfect jelly." The following are the statements of the other witnesses:

The first witness, MARY ANN BRYANT, as cousin of the deceased, said that she "called upon her on Saturday last, about half-past one o'clock, when deceased complained of having been very much ill-used by her husband. Deceased begged witness to ask him to allow her to go to bed, as she had been up all the previous night. She said to witness, 'You might say to him, let SUSAN go and lie down.' Witness did ask her husband, as requested, but he refused to allow her to go to bed, and said she must mind the shop. Witness remained with deceased until half-past three o'clock, and during that interval her husband frequently boxed her ears as hard as he could with his open hand, and once, when she got up to serve a customer in the shop, he kicked her behind with great force, because, as he said, she did not move quick enough. He requested witness to examine her head, remarking that he knew he had hurt her. Witness did so, and found her left ear and all that part of her head dreadfully bruised. There were also cuts upon the head, and the hair was matted with congealed blood that had issued from them. Witness told deceased's husband how much she was injured, but he did not appear to take notice of it." About six the same afternoon, on returning to the house, "he asked her whether she had supplied certain customers; and she replied that she had not; upon which he swore at her, and boxed her ears as hard as he could. He then directed her to put some bread in the shop-window; and while she was in the act of doing so she fell insensible on the shop-floor. Witness ran towards her, and saw that the blood was spiriting from a wound in her temple. Witness then called out, 'Oh, good God, uncle; cousin is in a fit—pick her up.' He replied that he would not. Deceased presently revived a little, and walked with witness into the back parlour. While doing so, she said, 'I am in a fit, and a very bad fit. Don't leave me, for God's sake—don't leave me, MARY ANN.' These were the last words she ever uttered. Witness wished to put her to bed, but her husband said she should never go into a bed of his again. Deceased was then standing over a sink; and presently her strength appeared to fail, and she sank down upon the floor with her head resting on the kitchen step." She never rallied, and died on the following Monday morning.

JOHN JOHNSON, a journeyman baker in this wretch's employment, said that on Tuesday night, soon after eleven o'clock, "he heard a great noise overhead, as of two persons quarrelling, and a cry of distress from the deceased woman. The noise was similar to that of one person dragging another across the room, and it continued up to three o'clock to such an extent that witness could not get any sleep. Witness did not hear any words distinctly, but he could tell that his master was speaking in a very ferocious manner. On the Saturday afternoon witness saw his master knock deceased about, and shortly afterwards she fell down insensible. Deceased's cousin asked witness to assist in raising her, but his master would not allow him. He said, 'D—n her, let her get up herself.'"

AMELIA MEREDES, who had lodged in the house for the last two months, "had frequently seen deceased with black eyes in that time; and on Saturday, about five o'clock, during a dreadful noise of quarrelling, she came down stairs into the passage, and while there heard deceased scream out and cry, 'Oh, oh! you'll kill me, you'll kill me!' Her husband replied, 'Yes, I will kill you. I'll murder you before I have done with you.' Witness also heard deceased's little boy call out at the same time, 'You'll kill my mother, father.'"

It was after such evidence as this that the Coroner's jury brought in a verdict of manslaughter! And were the ruffian to be tried (as he has been committed) on this verdict, and not on a bill of indictment sent before the grand jury, he would be tried for manslaughter only, and not for murder! We have, however, much satisfaction in perceiving, from the result of the examination which took place at Bow-street yesterday, that public justice will be spared this indescribably outrageous insult; and that, despite the enormous folly and heartlessness of the fifteen "highly respectable" jurymen, the prisoner will be put on his trial for the capital offence.

To prevent justice from being foiled in instances like these ought ever to be the primary object of all who have any power in the case. The parish officers, or any other public authority within whose competence it is to see that the most horrible crimes do not escape unpunished, are under a deep responsibility if they do not, when others fail in their duty, indict such culprits for murder. And when the case is not taken up by those who are most bound to do so, a public subscription ought to enable the relatives or friends of the unfortunate victim to take the proper means of invoking condign punishment on the murder.

It is necessary that it should be, once for all, understood by juries that to beat a human being to death is not manslaughter, but murder. If it were otherwise, the famous Mrs. BROWNRIGG was hanged contrary to law. What she was convicted of was a series of brutalities exactly resembling this, and the Bideford case. And she would most assuredly have been acquitted had she been tried before Mr. Justice TALFOURD. He would have said that there had been "chastisement of which he did not approve," but that there was no proof that the death of the victim was caused by the "chastisement."

In the Brydges-street case it is in evidence that the prisoner actually, and at the very time, *said* to the unhappy victim that he would murder her; and though this, or any other ruffianly speech under such circumstances, does not amount to proof that the speaker meant the full import of his words, experience shows what interpretation would have been put upon them if the case had been reversed, and if the woman had been charged with killing the man. If the husband had died in circumstances similar to the case of ANN MERRETT, and such a speech could have been proved to have been uttered by the wife—no matter under what circumstances of just exasperation—she would not have had a chance to escape a capital conviction.

Is it because juries are composed of husbands in a low rank of life, that men who kill their wives almost invariably escape—wives who kill their husbands, never? How long will such a state of things be permitted to continue?

Sunday Times, 19 May 1850, p. 2, e–f
["Questionable Charity"]

*Unlike all other joint newspaper articles, this piece is not about violence
in any form. Instead, it focuses on the economic impact of teaching poor
children needlework by actually having the children make dresses for their
patrons. In a previous week's paper (May 5), the* Sunday Times *had condemned such a practice because it would lead to unemployment among
women who make their living by needlework. Harriet and John argue
here that although there may be some worker displacement, that the capital saved in this charitable pursuit could be spent hiring other workers.
Thus the working classes in general would not suffer, and the good
gained by teaching real skills instead of "make work" is not offset by
harm to the working class as a whole. Their arguments are quickly followed by a counterargument against their "abstract principles" by the editors of the* Times.

"QUESTIONABLE CHARITY"

[The letter to the editor from Harriet and John was preceded by the
following paragraph.]

A correspondent, in the following letter, finds fault with our strictures,
under the above heading, upon an institution lately opened in Marylebone,
by certain charitable ladies, for the instruction of young friendless and
poor children, in needle work and other pursuits calculated to enable them
to procure a honest livelihood: —

"Mr. Editor, — Agreeing cordially with many of the sentiments expressed
in your journal of Sunday, May 5, and with much of the tone and spirit of
your paper generally, I regret to see one paragraph in which, as it appears
to me, you not only give blame where praise is deserved, but countenance
erroneous opinions on such important subjects as the direction of charity
and the employment of labour. The following is the passage: —

'In Marylebone, a society of ladies has formed a female school for the
purpose, as they state, of instructing the poor in such branches of useful
knowledge as are calculated to enable them, in after life, to gain a honest
livelihood. So far, excellent. The object is laudable, but is greatly defeated
by the very founders of this charitable institution, who, in order to save
the money which they should otherwise pay for the making of their
apparel, bring that apparel to the school, and get it made free of cost by

the children. Thus in the name, and under the guise of charity, they unintentionally inflict a gross injustice, rob honest industry of its fair reward, and drive to the workhouse or to prostitution the industrious and deserving female, who is willing to toil from the rising to the setting sun, and even half the night during the whole week, for a pittance scarcely sufficient to keep body and soul together.'

I know nothing of the facts, and assume them to be as here stated. What I object to is the doctrine that, whenever, in return for charitable assistance, the recipients are required to do anything useful, to perform any productive labour which any other persons might be paid to do, an injustice is done to those other persons, and a wrong to the world at large.

Your objection, if good at all, is good against every possible employment of labour. You cannot employ anybody without enabling it to be said that you prevent yourself from employing somebody else. If it is wrong to employ children, because of taking employment from needlewomen, by the same reasoning to employ one needlewoman, is taking employment from another. If it is wrong to employ children in needlework, instead of employing needlewomen, it must be wrong to teach the children needlework, for the express purpose of enabling them 'in after life to gain an honest livelihood' by practising needlework, and so competing with the needlewomen.

You will, perhaps, say that, at all events, the assistance so conferred is no longer charity, but an ordinary commercial transaction. I contend, on the contrary, that charity is much more charity, because much more useful when conferred in this way. The best kind of relief or assistance is that for which, as far as the case admits, a return is required to be made in useful labour. Especially in this case when the very object in view is to train up children to gain their living by labour. If they are to be taught needlework they must be made to do needlework, and would it be an improvement in their education that it should be *useless* needlework, as paupers have been employed to dig holes and fill them up again, for fear of displacing other labour?

But there is another aspect of the matter which is of still wider application. You seem to think that if you pay labourers to do nothing at all, or nothing useful, you do not take away employment from any one, but that you do so if you require a return in productive industry. The truth, I apprehend, is the very opposite. It is by what you *give* to one person that you diminish your means of employing others; not by the work you make him do in return; on the contrary, making him work in return is the only mode by which, while you give to him, you can still have undiminished means of employing others. If what you have given to a labourer comes back in value of that which he produces, or, what amounts to the same thing, in the saving of an equal sum of money, which you must otherwise have expended at a shop, you have conferred the benefit on him, and yet have as much money in your possession to make purchases, or employ labourers with, as if you had not given him anything. I do not mean to say that this money will find its way to the same shops, or the same labourers, but it will be spent at other shops, or on other labourers; if there is a disadvantage to some people, there is an advantage to others, and no detriment to the labouring class on the whole.

Objections are sometimes made, on similar erroneous grounds, to the introduction of useful labour into prisons—although useful labour is the only production of good prison discipline, and of the reformation of criminals—for want of considering, that since the prisoners must at any rate be supported, whatever they cause to be withdrawn from the support of honest labour is equally withdrawn, whether the prisoners work or not; while, by making them work, the value, or part of it, is got back, and may be used in giving employment to other labourers.

The subject, sir, will amply repay a more attentive consideration than, as it seems to me, the writer of the paragraph in your last Sunday's paper has yet given to it, and if what I have written should induce him to meditate further on things so closely connected with many of the important questions which come under the notice of journalists, I shall feel that I have been of some use."

"D."

[The following comments were added by the writer from the *Sunday Times*.]

The character, style, and tone of our correspondent's communication merit every respectful attention. Still we must at once declare our total and unqualified dissent from his opinions and principles concerning pauper and free labour. All his arguments contain abstract principles wrapped in sophistry. He must know that while abstract principles suit schools and colleges, they seldom can be brought to act upon practical life. The gist of his arguments resolves itself into this, that while we give employment, it is quite immaterial whom we employ or whether we pay them or not; and that the inmates of workhouses and gaols are as much entitled to employment as the artisan and mechanic outside those walls of improvidence, misery, and crime. The fallacy and injustice of such a proposition are strikingly obvious. Not only the several parochial authorities but government also were so convinced of the evil effects of workhouse and prison labour that they are doing all in their power to abolish it. They at first thought that it was an admirable plan to employ the male and female inmates of those places in the different branches of industry with which they were acquainted. What was the result? The honest hard-working tailor, shoemaker, and carpenter, and the equally indefatigable industrious needlewoman and milliner were deprived of work, and they and their families forced to the doors of our several unions, until they petitioned against the practice, and so unquestionably proved its evils, that the authorities in many instances totally, and in every case partially, prohibited workhouse paid labour. With regard to the charitable institution established by the Marylebone ladies, we again repeat our total condemnation of their practice of transferring to the objects of their benevolence that employment for which they would have to pay females who earn their livelihood by needlework.

It is a kind act for them to teach the children under their care useful pursuits; but it is an error of judgment to make them perform *gratis,* work for which they were in the habit of paying their milliners, dressmakers, and needlewomen. Can our correspondent attempt justifying this error of judgment? Those ladies instruct a number of young females in industrious and useful pursuits. What benefit will the instruction be, if ladies can get their millinery and their needlework done gratis? That is the way to view the question, and with that view of it, we leave our correspondent to solve the paradox that his opinions involve. Although most grateful for his kind feelings, we assure him that he never shall make converts of us to his abstract principles or his ideas of the laws of labour.

Morning Chronicle, 31 May 1850, p. 4, f; 5, a
{Assault Law}

This essay contains Harriet and John's most important summary of their views on domestic violence. Although this particular news article refers to a case before the courts involving Alexander Moir, this essay concentrates on a general investigation of the causes of domestic violence and a call for a declaratory Act of Parliament to clearly state that it is illegal. The authors focus on the common language used by men in the nineteenth-century which refers to wives and children as "mine." This language adds to the belief that the husband, the "owner," has the right to use or abuse his property as he sees fit. The general English population at this time accepted wife-beating as legal. Harriet and John suggest that like other unintended murders in common law (as set down by Blackstone), perpetrators of domestic violence should be tried for murder. Furthermore, if a man is convicted of abuse, the woman should not be required to live with

*the man. The husband thereby giving up conjugal rights would still
financially support his estranged wife. Without this provision, the authors
argue, women will never feel free to witness against an abusive spouse.*

We have on former occasions pointed out the defective state of the law
and of its administration with respect to crimes of personal violence, and
we have especially commented on the absence of protection for women
and young persons, and for all those who are under the power of others,
against domestic brutality. The case on which the Court of Queen's Bench
pronounced judgment yesterday, exceptional as it is in some material
respects—more particularly as regards the apparent absence of habitual or
deliberate cruelty on the part of the defendant—recalls our attention to
this very important subject; and we proceed to offer some further remarks
on the general question of the social and legal wrongs affecting the most
helpless portion of the community.

It is evident to all who take any pains to read the indications of the
feelings of the populace, that they are impressed with the belief of their
having a *right* to inflict almost any amount of corporal violence upon *their*
wife or *their* children. That any one should claim to interfere with this
supposed right, causes them unaffected surprise. Is it not *their* wife or
child? Are they not entitled to do as they will with their own? These
phrases are not, to their apprehension, metaphorical. The shoes on their
feet, or the cudgel in their hand—the horse or ass that carries their
burdens, and that dies a lingering death under their cruelties—the wife
and children—all are "theirs," and all in the same sense. They have the
same right, in their own opinion, over their human as over their inanimate
property. Doubtless they are aware that they are not at liberty to inflict
death; but when they actually do so, and find that they are to be tried for
murder, they seem to receive the information with a kind of stolid astonishment; and it may well appear to them anomalous that a creature is
given up to their power to be kicked or beaten, at the peril of life, as often
as temper or intoxication may prompt—and yet that, on some one day
when they have done no worse than they had done hundreds of times
before, they are told that they are liable to be hanged. Not that they ever
are hanged for these enormities, even though death ensue. If they are tried
at all (which in general they are not), the jury are not convinced that they
intended death, and they consequently escape with a verdict of manslaughter. This interpretation of the law had the sanction of Mr. Baron ALDER-
SON, in the recent case of ALEXANDER MOIR. If it be a correct
interpretation, the law is, in this matter, grossly inconsistent; for many
acts, venial in comparison with MOIR'S, are held by law to be murder

when death ensues as an unintended consequence. "If one intends," says BLACKSTONE, "to do another felony, and undesignedly kills a man, this is murder." If any one kills an officer of justice, or even a private person, who is endeavouring to suppress an affray or to apprehend a felon, it is murder. "It were endless," continues BLACKSTONE, "to go through all the cases of homicide which have been adjudged either expressly or impliedly malicious," and which are, therefore, legally regarded as murder. According to Mr. Baron ALDERSON, a wretch like MOIR is less criminal in the eye of the law than a person who, intending only to take the property of another, undesignedly causes death. But surely a man who, though he does not intend to kill, perpetrates such ruffian-like maltreatment that death is a natural consequence, commits an offence that is at least equal in depravity to most cases of murder.

Some good would be done, if, even in this extreme case, it were felt that there is no immunity for domestic ruffianism, and that the law has as much severity for the man who kills those whom he is peculiarly bound to protect, as it has for the one whose victim had no claims on him save those inherent in humanity. But, though even this would be some improvement, much more is required. It would be but a feeble restraint on habitual brutality to make the offender responsible for an extreme consequence which may or may not happen, and which may or may not be capable of being traced to its real cause. The arm of the law should be made to reach the tyranny of bodily strength in every instance in which it comes to light. The atrocious cases now summarily disposed of by magistrates with a forty-shilling fine or two months' imprisonment, should be tried with judicial solemnity in the courts which try other grave offenses, and should be visited with a just gradation of penalties, rising to the highest secondary punishment. Whatever additional legislation is required for this purpose should be provided. Legislation is also needed to disabuse the people of false notions of their legal rights. At present it is the universal belief of the labouring class, that the law permits them to beat their wives—and the wives themselves share the general error. We assume that it is an error. We take for granted, that the old saw, which most people have heard—if it ever was law in the savage times of our ancestors—has long been obsolete. If there be any doubt of this, there is the more reason why there should, without delay, be an authoritative termination to the doubt. There should be a declaratory Act, distinctly setting forth that it is *not* lawful for a man to strike his wife, any more than to strike his brother or his father. This would be merely doing what was done by the first settlers of New England. The seventeenth century was not remarkable for the mildness of its manners, nor were the Puritans by any means moderate in their notions of family discipline and authority. Their standard of social morals was taken from the Old Testament and the Patriarchs, not from CHRIST and the Sermon on the Mount. Yet the fundamental regulations of the first Puritan colonists in New England, as we read them in the latest published history of the United States, formally abrogated that provision, or reputed provision, of the common law of England, which permitted men to beat their wives. We hope that it is not too much to expect from the English Legislature now, the same amount of justice and humanity which was shown by its cast-out children two hundred years ago. It seems almost inconceivable that the smallest blow from a man to a man should be by law a criminal offence, and yet that it should not be—or should not be known to be—unlawful for a man to strike a woman.

There is yet another feature in the law and in its administration, connected with this subject, which, we would fain hope, need only be pointed out to be irrevocably condemned by public opinion. At present, no amount of brutal violence, nor even of deliberate cruelty, although judicially proved, has the legal effect of depriving the criminal of the power which he has misused. A man is convicted and imprisoned for the horrible maltreatment of his wife—and yet, when his imprisonment expires, the victim is again delivered into his hands, to suffer everything which brutality infuriated by revenge, or malignity made more cautious by detection, may inflict. Any words which might be used to characterize such a state of the law could hardly strengthen the impression which ought to be made by the simple knowledge of it. Apart from all that is revolting in the fact itself, and viewing the question in the coldest manner as one of mere legislative expediency, it is impossible to expect that these domestic atrocities should ever attain judicial publicity except by accident, when such are the consequences which the sufferers have to expect from complaining. According, these cases are hardly ever made known by the injured parties themselves; and if they happen to be brought before a magistrate or a criminal court by some one who casually becomes cognizant of them, the charge continually breaks down from the impossibility of inducing the trembling victim to speak the truth with sufficient plainness to procure a conviction, or to adhere to it when it has been spoken in the first instance.

It is a dictate of common sense—recognised and acted upon by the laws of almost all countries—that legal rights may be either suspended or forfeited for a certain amount of judicially proved misuse. If this is a reasonable and proper provision with regard to legal rights generally, it is so, above all, with respect to the powers which any one is allowed to exercise over the persons of human beings. The law confers every such power on the presumption (however fallacious) that it will be exerted for the good of those over whom it is given, and it cannot be justified except on that presumption. That there should be a slavery in civilized life, from which the most savage maltreatment, judicially proved, cannot liberate the victim, would be scarcely credible, if it were not notoriously true; and such a state of things cannot, we hope, be much longer tolerated, unless existing laws are deemed more sacred than the primary ends for which all laws profess to exist.

This evil might be removed without interfering with existing institutions on any other point, or raising discussion on any more general question. All that would be requisite is a short Act of Parliament, providing that judicial conviction of gross maltreatment should free the victim from the obligation of living with the oppressor, and from all compulsory subjection to his power—leaving him under the same legal obligation as before of affording the sufferer the means of support, if the circumstances of the case require it. We earnestly recommend this subject to the attention of those philanthropists who desire to signalize themselves by an eminently useful contribution to the work of mitigating the sufferings and raising the moral condition of the poor and the dependent.

Sunday Times, 2 June 1850, p. 2, b–c
{"Punishment of Children"}

Unlike the other newspaper writings in this series, this piece does not rely on the assumption that domestic violence is primarily or exclusively a matter involving the "lower classes." Here Harriet and John attack a judge for being conciliatory towards a barrister who had beaten his illegitimate six-year-old son. Although convicted, the prisoner was assured by the judge that "no serious stain would attach to {his} character." The authors wonder aloud whether the judge felt this way because the prisoner was middle class instead of working class. This awareness of class bias in judicial treatment adds to the sexism in the judicial system which Harriet and John had railed against throughout their joint newspaper writings.

PUNISHMENT OF CHILDREN

The case of Edward Kenealy, a man holding the rank of a barrister, who has been convicted by the Court of Queen's Bench of an assault on his illegitimate child, a boy six years old, cannot be allowed to pass without comment. The facts of the case, disgusting though they be, are such as we are accustomed to see in every day's newspaper, and no wonder, while, not police magistrates only, but a Chief Justice, like Lord Campbell in the present case, treats ferocious personal violence as if it were the merest peccadillo—a pardonable overstepping of the strict limits of the law, hardly deserving any moral blame. We shall first quote the evidence of the surgeon:—

> "I saw the child on the day after it was found. I found a mark round the front and sides of the neck, but not on the back part of the neck. On the front of the throat the skin had been removed by pressure. Scabbing had taken place in some portion. Others were undergoing suppuration, that had been produced by pressure, or some substance rubbing. The whole of the back, from the shoulders to the lower part of the posteriors, was covered with bruises. They were long in form; as if inflicted by castigation, and were in different states of inflammation. From the posteriors to the ankles there were marks of the same castigation. Great violence must have been used. From the shoulders to the hands there was evidence of the same kind of treatment, and apparently by the same instrument—by a rod or cane."

The following were Lord Campbell's remarks:—

> "There must be a verdict of guilty against the defendant. His chastisement of the child, for some unaccountable reason, had been infinitely beyond moderation. Though there was no doubt that a parent had a right to correct a child, and that the defendant here seemed to have had the welfare of the child in view, still, after the evidence of the surgeon, it was clear that he had done what the law did not justify. It was impossible to say that this was moderate chastisement of a child six years old."

It will hardly be believed, after such evidence, and after such an opinion given by himself on the evidence, that Lord Campbell, in his address to the jury, could say—

> "He rejoiced that the whole truth had come out, and that *no serious stain would attach to the character of Mr. Kenealy,* who appeared to have taken some care of this child, which was his illegitimate child, and to have bestowed pains upon it in giving it an education. Was not the charge here made out? The defendant, though not the legitimate father of the child, was its parent by the law of nature, and was entitled, under the circumstances of its living with him, to all the authority and rights of a father. Still, in exercising those rights in the way of punishment of

the child, he was bound to observe moderation. The jurors would declare whether, with a good conscience, they could say that he had done so; for if not, as immoderate punishment could not be justified in law, he must be found guilty."

Whether because the offender's station in life was nearer than usual to his own, or from a total absence of moral sense in the mind of the judge, we know not, but his address is almost an apology to the prisoner for convicting him; and he tells the offender—he, the guardian and vindicator of the law, declares to a man who, in his own showing, has broken the law, by such treatment of a child of tender years as the surgeon's evidence discloses, that "no serious stain would attach to his character," and this because the poor infant said in his evidence that the prisoner kissed and gave him playthings and toys, and taught him "to spell, and read, and say his prayers," as if the most brutal parents in anything like Mr. Kenealy's rank of life did not do such things as these! Lord Campbell would seem to have adopted the doctrine of Mr. Whately, the prisoner's counsel, who thought it "a thing to be applauded," in the defendant, "that he did not, like many other people, leave his illegitimate child to poverty and misery."

Why does not the unbrutal part of the public—the part which does not sympathise with cruelty, rouse itself and demand of the legislature how much longer the flogging of children shall be sanctioned by law? On the flogging of grown-up persons public opinion is made up. That practice, at last, by force of general feeling against the vehement remonstrances of those who had the power of inflicting the brutality, has been *almost* abolished. But it is assumed, and goes uncontradicted, that a punishment which is brutalising and degrading to grown men is quite fit and proper for helpless infancy; unfit to be inflicted, according to prescribed rules, by men called judges, after solemn inquiry and in the full light of publicity, but, "by the law of nature" (as Lord Campbell says), quite proper to be administered at discretion by men called fathers in the secrecy of their own houses, subject, when some peculiarly atrocious case accidentally comes to light, to a gentle admonition. It is only the other day that the House of Commons decided, after a long debate, that boys might be scourged at the discretion of two magistrates, but that men might not; the distinction, it appeared between men and boys being the difference between thirteen years and fourteen. It is as possible to govern children without the aid of the lash as grown persons. It is even much easier; their bad habits, if they have been allowed to acquire any, not being deeply rooted. A parent or teacher who cannot rule without the lash shows as much incapacity as brutality. There is no difference of nature between grown persons and boys, that what is most deeply degrading to the character of the one should not be so to the other. If the boy has no consciousness of his degradation the worse for him: it is a proof that his character is irreclaimably imbued with it. Mr. Whately said that they had all—judge, jury, and counsel—been flogged in their boyhood, and were much the better for it. This merely proves that Mr. Whately's sense of degradation depends, not on the fact, but on other people's opinion, and that nothing is revolting to him which is legal and customary. Take any naturally sensitive boy, who has been habitually flogged, and one who has never suffered that indignity, compare them, observe the difference in self-respect, and in all that depends on self-respect, which will mark those two human beings throughout life? On a boy of a dull, hard nature, its effect is to render him ten times harder than he would be without it—to qualify and prepare him for being a bully and a tyrant. He will feel none of that respect for the personality of other human beings which has not been shown towards his own. The object of his respect will be power. He will crouch to power in others, and will have nothing in his own nature to prevent him from trampling on those whom he has power over. If he does not do so, it will be from nothing better than fear of opinion or fear of punishment.

Morning Chronicle, 28 August 1851, p. 4, e-f
[Wife Murder]

Like the newspaper writing of 31 May 1850 on the assault laws, this article on wife murder is an important general discussion of the fundamental causes of wife abuse and a call for legislative action. This article, the first after their marriage in April of 1850,[1] pleads that the parliament educate the judges and general public by making clear laws that killing one's wife is as least as serious an offense as killing a stranger. The authors even chide the government for ignoring wife murder during the reign of Queen Victoria. In doing so, they invite Queen Victoria to personally step in and demand change in how these offenses are decided.

---

1. "A Recent Magisterial Decision," published in the *Morning Post,* 8 November 1854 (*CW,* XXV: 1197), is listed by the editors of *CW* as a collaboration between JSM and HTM. However, no textual evidence other than the subject matter connects this text with HTM. We have chosen to believe JSM when he says a text is co-authored. JSM did not designate this text as joint in his handwritten bibliography, as he did so many others both with HTM and others, and furthermore, unlike the other newspaper articles written together, this piece is signed "M." Therefore we do not attribute it to HTM.

In his recent charge to the grand jury at the opening of the Central Criminal Court, the Recorder said—

> "He was sorry that he could not congratulate them on the lightness of the calendar; for, although it did not contain any charge of murder, yet he was sorry to see that there were several charges of manslaughter, and also a great number of cases of personal violence; and it was very much to be regretted that, in a great majority of the cases, the violence was committed by men upon the persons of those whom they were bound to love and protect—namely, upon their wives."

It is well that Mr. WORTLEY should have said thus much—little though it was—on this disgraceful subject; and it is to be hoped that the feelings which dictated his brief remarks will still be in operation when, in the course of the next few days, it may become his duty to pass sentence on cases of this description. But he need not have confined his observation to the present sessions; for every sessions, every assizes, afford proof of the lamentable prevalence of this class of crimes, and of the impunity, or next to impunity, with which they are passed by. Within these few days we have recorded, almost simultaneously, four cases of men tried, or committed for trial, on the charge of killing their wives; and among these the case of EDMUND CURTIS stood conspicuous, both in atrocity and in the flagrant inadequacy of the punishment. The wife, an industrious woman, had passed the day in working as a charwoman, to earn money for the husband. In the evening, according to the testimony of the woman for whom she worked, he came to the house, and the wife "spoke to him, desiring him to come home. He refused. She said his place was at home, and he said, 'So is yours.' They then both left the room. He was sober. After they left the house—about three minutes after—I heard a violent shriek. I went out, and saw her lying across a low iron railing in my garden. He had hold of her over the left shoulder with his right hand, and was striking her on the head with his clenched fist. When I got out the shriek had ceased. I heard no noise after. I told him he would kill her, if he had not done so, and desired him to loose her. He did not do so. I called out WILLIAM KIRKLAND, who pulled him from her, and she fell on her left side on the ground, apparently lifeless. I told him he had killed her. I called assistance. She was lifted up and put in a chair. She fetched three sighs and died." These were the facts; and now for Mr. Baron MARTIN and his judgment. He said that nothing could justify a man in striking a woman; that the prisoner "indulged in a very violent degree of passion," but that he could "well believe" that he "did not mean to kill her;" and that "no doubt, when this result occurred," he was "sincerely

sorry for it;" and that, "considering all the circumstances," the "justice of
the case" would be satisfied by imprisoning him for six months with hard
labour! Such are the judgments which are to protect all the women of the
country against domestic ruffianism; and such is the caprice which presides
over the apportionment of penalties in English criminal justice. The day
afterwards, in a case not more atrocious, the culprit was sentenced by the
same judge to transportation for life. If CURTIS had killed, in any similar
manner, some other man's wife instead of his own—instead of the woman
whom, as Mr. WORTLEY said, he was bound to protect—there can be
little doubt that he would have been indicted for murder, and probably
hanged. The vow to protect thus confers a license to kill.

Two of the cases adverted to in the Recorder's charge have since come
on for trial before Mr. Justice WIGHTMAN. In one, the prisoner was
acquitted on the ground of insanity. In the case of ANDREW MACLEAN
also, the culprit was acquitted, to the disgrace both of the jury and of the
judge. The report says,

> "Early in the morning of the 4th of August, the persons lodging in the
> next room were disturbed by the cries of the prisoner's children, and
> their calling out, 'Oh, father, let mother down.' They got up in conse-
> quence, and went into the prisoner's room, where they found his wife
> hanging by the neck from the cupboard, and the prisoner was sitting
> upon the bed. The body of the unfortunate woman was quite suspended,
> and she was nearly black in the face. Upon the prisoner being told that
> he was a good-for-nothing villain for attempting to hang his wife, he
> replied that he would do it effectually the next time: and one of the
> witnesses answered that he would have done it effectually this time, if
> his wife had not been cut down. The prisoner was slightly intoxicated
> it appeared, at the time of the occurrence. The prisoner, in his defence,
> asserted that his wife had hanged herself."

The wife was not called as a witness, the reason of which appears from the
previous examination before the magistrate on which occasion the unfortunate creature, either from habitual fear or from the expectation that
she would be given back into his power, exculpated the man, stating that
she had spoken provokingly to him, and also that he had hanged her only
in jest. Her dread of appearing against him was not surprising: for what
would have been the consequence to her of having given strong evidence
against him, in the event of his acquittal? But her testimony was not
needed to show the state of the case, after proof of such facts as those
contained in the above extract. Yet "Mr. Justice WIGHTMAN, In sum-
ming up, said that the case was undoubtedly left in some obscurity by the

absence of the wife's testimony. If she had been called, she could have proved distinctly how the matter occurred; and in the face of the prisoner's declaration that his wife had hung herself, it was for the jury to say whether the other evidence was sufficient to justify them in convicting him of so serious an offence." On this encouragement the jury returned a verdict of not guilty; and consequently the woman is again given in to the power of the man, that he may, as he threatened "do it effectually the next time." We scarcely believe that there is an offence in the whole criminal code of which a prisoner would have been acquitted, in the face of such evidence, except that of an attempt at wife-murder.

In default of the judges, it is for the Legislature to apply vigorous measures of repression to this growing evil. The baser part of the populace think that when a legal power is given to them over a living creature— when a person, like a thing, is suffered to be spoken of as their own—as *their* wife, or *their* child, or *their* dog—they are allowed to do what they please with it; and in the eye of the law—if such judgments as the preceding are to be taken as its true interpretation—they are justified in supposing that the worst they can do will be accounted but as a case of slight assault. It is the duty of the Legislature to teach them the contrary. There ought to be severer penalties for killing or ill-treating a wife or child than for killing or ill-treating, in a similar manner, any other person. A greater severity is enjoined by all the motives which ought to regulate the adaptation of punishment to crime. The crime is greater; for it is a violation of more solemn obligations—it is doing the worst injury where there is the most binding duty to cherish and protect. It is also baser—for it is committed upon one who has trusted the culprit, who is in his power, and who is generally without sufficient bodily strength to resist or retaliate. Those who are exposed to these atrocities—the wives and children of the brutal part of the population—have not the means which all other persons possess of guarding themselves against the evil. Other people are but occasionally and rarely liable to ill-treatment; but these are exposed to it at every hour and every moment of their lives. Being thus far more in need than any other persons of the protection of the law, they ought to have it in fuller measure. The domestic tyrant can perpetrate his tyrannies with the utmost facility, and need never wait for an opportunity; and a stronger motive therefore is required, where the brutality exists, to deter from its indulgence. Finally, there is no crime in the whole catalogue of offences in which the single act which incurs the penalty of the law is an index to such an amount of undetected and unpunished wickedness, and to so vast a mass of horrible suffering. Such a spectacle as the final scene of the life of HESTER CURTIS is unspeakably revolting; but what is the suffering of a few minutes, to the prolonged death which in every such case must have been suffered for years previously, and to the pangs of thousands of women in the power of similar miscreants, who have enough of caution just to stop short of the point which terminates the existence of their victims? There is not to be imagined a position so degraded, or so hopelessly miserable, as that of the women thus at the mercy of ruffians; and it is a deep disgrace to our Government that, in the fifteenth year of the reign of a woman, nothing has yet been done for their relief.

REMARKS ON MR. FITZROY'S BILL FOR THE MORE EFFECTUAL PREVENTION OF ASSAULTS ON WOMEN AND CHILDREN

This pamphlet written by Harriet and John in 1853 was published anonymously and available only through private distribution. It responded to the bill {16 and 17 Victoria, c. 30 (1853)} introduced by Henry Fitzroy and subsequently passed. In the pamphlet Harriet and John argue that the bill needs to be strengthened by increasing the punishment of offenders to include an automatic sentence of hard labour when criminals were imprisoned. They also urge the inclusion of corporal punishment as a sentence in domestic violence cases. HTM and JSM acknowledge that they generally deplore corporal punishment, but they believe that in the case of wife abusers, only harsh punishment will sufficiently deter and provide proper moral education to these brutes who beat their wives. Harriet and John stress the law's role as a means of moral education especially of the "part of the population which is unreached by any other moralizing influences." Thus the authors, once again, reveal their class bias on the issue of domestic violence.

The Bill brought into Parliament by Mr. Fitzroy, as the organ of the Home Office, enlarging the powers of magistrates to inflict summary penalties for brutal assaults on women and children, is excellent in design; and if in execution it falls short of what is required to deal adequately with the enormity of the evil, the speech of the Mover indicated that he felt its imperfection, and had done as much as he thought it prudent to attempt without assurance of support. There have since been signs, both in and out of Parliament, that the Minister formed a lower estimate than necessary of what the public would receive at his hands, and that a measure far more likely to be efficacious would have been well received. The following remarks, on what the writer deems the shortcomings of the present Bill, are offered for the consideration of those who interest themselves in its success.

The speech of the Mover showed him to be strongly impressed with the horrible amount of domestic brutality which the law at present existing leaves unrepressed; and he made a selection of recent cases, exhibiting the disgraceful contrast which every reader of police reports is accustomed to see, between the flagrancy of the offence and the insignificance of the penalty. If any deficiency could be remarked in the statement, it is, that all the instances cited were cases of outrage against women, to the exclusion of the brutalities inflicted both by men and women on the still more helpless children. Without reckoning the frightful cases of flogging and starving which so often come to light, there have been two cases within the last few weeks in each of which a woman, entrusted with the care of an infant three or four years old, caused its death by burning with fire. In one of the cases the woman had forced the infant to grasp a red hot coal in its hand, and hold it there for some minutes; and being put on trial before the child had died, but when it was already certain that he would be a cripple for life, was sentenced, not by a police magistrate, but by the Central Criminal Court at the Old Bailey, to—a fortnight's imprisonment! Such cases prove that there is more amiss than an extension of the powers of the subordinate Courts will remedy; that there is not merely a want of power in the administrators of criminal justice to treat such culprits with a severity sufficient for example, but, in some cases at least, a want of will. Merely to authorize a greater amount of punishment for these offences, at the discretion of a judicial officer, is no guarantee against their continuing to be perpetrated with almost as near an approach of impunity as at present. To increase the penalty is an indication of intention on the part of the Legislature. To see that the intention be fulfilled ought to be the care of those with whom rests the choice of judges and of magistrates.

By the existing law, the utmost punishment which can be inflicted by summary sentence is five pounds fine, or two months' imprisonment. The Bill raises this limit to a fine of twenty pounds, or imprisonment of six months, *with or without hard labour*. With regard to the fine, when the prisoner cannot pay it, the power of fining is nugatory. When he can, it is revolting to the commonest sense of justice that any one should be able to buy the privilege of inflicting atrocious cruelty by paying twenty pounds. From the newspaper reports it appears to be the practice of police magistrates, not to pass sentence of imprisonment unless they have first ascertained that the prisoner cannot pay the fine. It is only because these criminals are usually of the most reckless and therefore the most needy portion of the labouring classes, that this power of compounding by payment of blood-money does not operate as an actual license to the offences intended to be repressed.

Remains the penalty of imprisonment, "with or without" the addition of labour. The remark is applicable to the question of secondary punishment in general, and peculiarly to these offences, that the alternative of imprisonment with or without labour is equivalent to that of conviction with or without punishment. Can it be supposed that any amount of imprisonment without labour (unless in the few jails in which the salutary rule of separation of prisoners has been made universal) has a deterring effect upon criminals of the class who come under the proposed enactment? What is a prison to them? A place where, probably, they are better fed, better clothed, better lodged, than in their own dwellings, with an abundance of society of their own description, while they are exempted from the hard work by which they earned their living until the justice of their country undertook to punish them. In return for this release from all the most disagreeable circumstances of their ordinary condition, they suffer the inconvenience of not being able to get gin and tobacco; that is, they are treated exactly as if they were in the union workhouse, except the hard labour. Even alms are not given to the able-bodied at the expense of the parish, though but for a day, without a day's work in exchange for it; and surely, now that attention has been awakened to these subjects, it must soon be recognized that when imprisonment is imposed as a punishment, even if only for a day, either solitude or hard labour (for those who are capable of it) ought invariably to be a part of the sentence. In the case of the poor, the addition of labour is not even a punishment. Their life when at large must be one of labour, and generally of a restraint even upon their power of locomotion, almost equal to that of imprisonment. With the addition of labour, imprisonment to the ordinary labourer scarcely amounts to a punishment; without labour it is a holiday.

But neither with labour nor without it, is imprisonment in any form a suitable or a sufficient penalty for crimes of brutality. For these nothing will be effectual but to retaliate upon the culprit some portion of the physical suffering which he has inflicted. The beneficial efficacy of the enactment now in contemplation will, it is safe to prophesy, depend on the adoption or not of Mr. Phinn's amendment, making corporal punishment a part of the penalty. The Mover himself did not disguise his conviction that nothing less than this would be adequate to the exigency; and it is earnestly to be hoped that the many adhesions which the suggestion has since received, including that of one of the most intelligent of the London police magistrates, will induce Mr. Fitzroy to incorporate it in the Bill.

Overwhelming as are the objections to corporal punishment except in cases of personal outrage, it is peculiarly fitted for such cases. The repulsiveness to standers by, and the degradation to the culprit, which make corporal maltreatment so justly odious as a punishment, would cease to adhere to it, if it were exclusively reserved as a retribution to those guilty of personal violence. It is probably the only punishment which they would feel. Those who presume on their consciousness of animal strength to brutally illtreat those who are physically weaker, should be made to know what it is to be in the hands of a physical strength as much greater than their own, as theirs than that of the subjects of their tyranny. It is the moral medicine needed for the domineering arrogance of brute power. After one or two cases of flogging for this description of crime, we should hear no more of outrages upon women or children for a long time to come. Probably such outrages would cease altogether, as soon as it became well known that the punishment of flogging, would be inflicted for them.

With this penalty in the Act, and a clear understanding on the part of the magistrates that it was not intended as a *brutum fulmen*,[2] nor to be reserved for those horrible cases for which, as a matter of moral retribution, hanging would scarcely be punishment enough; if the administration of the law were such that the ruffianly part of the population would know that they could not give loose to their brutal rage without imminent risk of incurring in fact, and not nominally, the only punishment which they would dread; the enactment would do more for the improvement of morality, and the relief of suffering, than any Act of Parliament passed in this century, not excepting, perhaps, the Act for the abolition of slavery. But this salutary impression can only be made by rendering punishment prompt and certain in infliction, as well as efficacious in kind; by avoiding, therefore, to let in, by the terms of the Act itself, certainty of delay, and probable chances of escape. This would, however, be an inevitable effect of adopting another amendment, of which notice has been given, allowing an appeal to the quarter sessions. An appeal is often a necessary evil, but in such a case as this, a palpably unnecessary one. These are not cases in which a magistrate, or two magistrates, are likely to err on the side of the inflicting too severe a sentence; there is abundant experience that the danger of error is all on the contrary side.

A government which should pass an act embodying these provisions, would confer a more immediate and a more certain benefit on the community, than it is often in the power of legislators to ensure by any enactment. The beneficial fruits of such a law are not to be measured by

---

2. "Senseless thunderbolt," as in "striking blindly."

the crime and suffering which it would directly prevent, though these would be sufficient to stamp it as one of the most beneficent acts yet done by Government for the improvement of our institutions. A measure such as this, is of wider scope, and still more extensive beneficence. It is a measure of moral education. All parties now acknowledge that it is the urgent duty of Government to provide that the people be educated, could they but discover how it is to be done; and the present Ministry made it one of their pledges, on coming into office, that they would do something effectual for education. But even if the measure they contemplate were far more considerable than they probably have it in their power to make it, what chance is there for education, if the schools teach one lesson, and the laws another contradictory to it? The administration of criminal justice is one of the chief instruments of moral education of the people. Its lessons of morality are of the utmost importance for good or for ill; for they take effect upon the part of the population which is unreached by any other moralizing influences, or on which others have been tried, and have failed of their effect. The lessons which the law teaches, it cannot fail of teaching impressively. The man who is brought, or who knows himself liable to be brought, to answer for his conduct at the bar of justice, cannot slight or despise the notions of right and wrong, the opinions and feelings respecting conduct and character, which he there finds prevailing. It is the one channel through which the sentiments of the well-conducted part of the community are made operative perforce on the vilest and worst. Yet, in this day of ragged schools, and model prisons, and plans for reformation of criminals, the most important instrument which society has for teaching the elements of morality to those who are most in need of such teaching, is scarcely used at all. So potent an engine must necessarily act in one way or another, and when it does not act for good, it acts for evil. Is there any system of moral instruction capable of being devised for the populace, which could stand against the lessons of a diametrically opposite tendency, daily given by the criminal courts? The law and the tribunals are terribly in earnest when they set about the protection of property. But violence to the person is treated as hardly deserving serious notice, unless it endangers life; and even then, unless premeditated intention is proved by such superfluity of evidence that neither ingenuity nor stupidity can escape from admitting it, the criminal generally gets off almost scot free. It is of little avail to talk of inculcating justice, or kindness, or self-control, while the judicial and police courts teach by actions, so much more efficacious than words, that the most atrocious excesses of ungovernable violence are, in the eyes of the authorities, something quite venial. The law has the forming of the character of the lowest classes in its own hands.

A tithe of the exertion and money now spent in attempting to reform criminals, if spent in reforming the minor criminal laws and their administration, would produce a real diminution of crime, instead of an imaginary reformation of criminals. But then, it must be allowed, it would not serve to fill so much of philanthropic gentlemen's time.

Not only is education by the course of justice the most efficacious, in its own province, of all kinds of popular education, but it is also one on which there needs be no difference of opinion. Churches and political parties may quarrel about the teaching of doctrines, but not about the punishment of crimes. There is diversity of opinion about what is morally good, but there ought to be none about what is atrociously wicked. Whatever else may be included in the education of the people, the very first essential of it is to unbrutalise them; and to this end, all kinds of personal brutality should be seen and felt to be things which the law is determined to put down. The Bill of Mr. Fitzroy is a step in the right direction; but, unless its provisions are strengthened, it will be rather an indication of the wish, than a substantial exercise of the power, to repress one of the most odious forms of human wickedness.

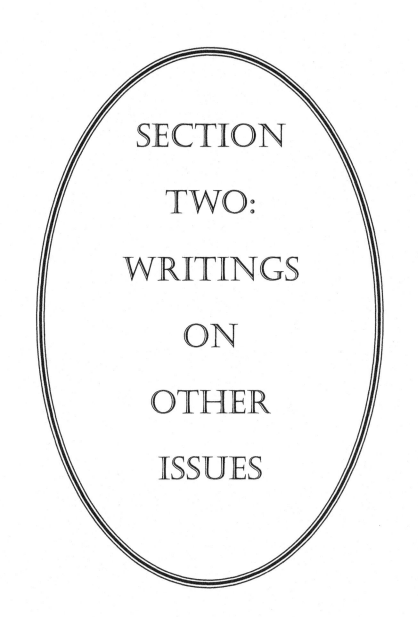

SECTION

TWO:

WRITINGS

ON

OTHER

ISSUES

Harriet wrote about the tension between moral and political obligations seven years before Thoreau's "Civil Disobedience."

ETHICS

5

The writings in this section can be neatly divided into two groups. The first group, 1–5, consists of five pieces, all written in 1831 or 1832, that examine tolerance and conformity to public opinion. The first selection in group one merely announces that toleration is a rare commodity in most nineteenth-century people's lives. Number 2 is Harriet Taylor Mill's study of the source of intolerance, namely conformity, and the corresponding need for self-reliance. Harriet claims that conformity is the opposite of acting on principle (defined as the "accordance of a person's conduct with self-formed opinion") and that eccentricity is prima facie evidence of principle. Many will, no doubt, recognize in this second essay elements foreshadowing the discussion of eccentricity in On Liberty, *written more than twenty years later. Most people, Harriet declares, are the slaves of someone else's principles; we must learn to think and act for ourselves, or at least not resent others who do. For Harriet, tolerance is the moral parallel to the recognition of the impossibility of any individual's comprehension of the whole of truth. Truth is not utterly relative; language, however, imposes barriers to conveying what we see of the truth. This frustration with language's ability to communicate truth appears in HTM's next two pieces on moral proverbs. Toleration is also linked to the ability or at least desire to know another person as completely as possible. Whereas science is advanced when rules become more exact, Harriet explains that moral knowledge advances by moving beyond rules. Tolerance is an approach toward others. When we are tolerant we approach with an admiring, not a critical, frame of mind. In selection 3, Harriet continues her assault on society's influence over our moral sentiments.*

In 4 and 5, also written in 1832, we have two different compilations of various bits of writing on a theme that occupied Harriet during this period. Because there are many different drafts of essays about "Laconicisms" or proverbs in Box III (86, 95, and 98), we can conclude that she took great care in working out her ideas. We may also surmise that much of her final writing is probably missing. Certainly Harriet Taylor Mill would not have produced six to eight drafts on this topic and then not completed a unified essay some time later. Number 4 is a compilation of several of these early drafts on proverbs. Because many sections are reiterated in more than one draft, we have tried to combine them into a coherent whole while noting overlaps and making observations about where the essays are patched together. Many passages also appear in essay two of group one, but in a different context. As noted in the text, we have marked all repeated passages at the beginning and end by superscripted symbols.

In the compiled version of Harriet Taylor's essay three on Laconicisms, Harriet proposes that proverbs are not good indicators of moral rules because words cannot contain anyone's whole insight. Words in the form of proverbs are used as a tool by those in power to control some less powerful group. Harriet's examples include proverbs on religion, loyalty, honour, and virtue—the word used by men to control women. HTM warns that these high sounding words are used to stir the passionate desire for the infinite, but we should not forget that what is seen as a virtue, for women in particular, furthers the interests of men.

Selection number 5 also combines drafts that appear in Box III, 86 and 95. Harriet again writes of the mischievous character of proverbs, which when read and accepted as truth often cause people to act without thinking. Although many words in these drafts have been smeared with ink, making them illegible in places, Harriet Taylor Mill's message is clear. This essay makes the point that moral knowledge must be gained through one's own experience and not by reading proverbs. Moral instruction can merely point the direction toward understanding. Since human existence is constantly changing, no textbook of moral knowledge offers complete comprehension of how we ought to live.

The material included in group two in this chapter, selections 6–8, covers a variety of ethical and political topics, including civil disobedience, Bentham's notion of self-interest, the connection between virtue and enjoyment, and blame. Selection 6 is on civil disobedience. Written seven years before Thoreau's essay on the same topic and probably included in a letter to John, Harriet writes that if we accept the penalty for civil disobedience, we are justified in violating unjust laws. However, she recognizes that when making these statements, she advocates a kind of social anarchy, since every law is opposed by some people. Laws work, HTM concludes, because most citizens are "unconscious and unconscientious." Harriet also responds to the argument that citizens should obey laws since laws are made by elected representatives. Essay 7 is a defense of Bentham's notion of self-interest. Harriet refutes the charge that Bentham's doctrine encourages a bald selfishness ("a doctrine worthy only of swine," à la Utilitarianism). Selection 8 is a comment on the notion of utility as distinguished from happiness. Number 9 defends the principle of utility, the view that "every thing but enjoyment is but a means to the attainment of that end." The final selection is a paragraph about the need for careful deliberation before assigning blame.

1. [PARAGRAPH ON TOLERANCE]

[I]t is said that people admire & talk more of the qualities they themselves are deficient in. This like most common sayings is true of the class of people of who use it—& toleration is in the latter the cardinal (not Cardinal's) virtue of fanatics & sectarians.[1]

2. [SOURCES OF CONFORMITY]

More than two hundred years ago, Cecil said 'Tenderness & sympathy are not enough cultivated by any of us; no one is kind enough, gentle enough, forbearing and forgiving enough.'[2] In this two centuries in how many ways have we advanced and improved, yet could the speaker of those words now 'revisit the glimpses of the moon', he would find us but at the point he left us on the ground of toleration: his lovely lament is to the full as applicable now, as it was in the days of the hard-visaged and cold-blooded Puritans. Our faults of uncharitableness have rather changed their objects than their degree. The root of all intolerance, the spirit of conformity, remains; and not until that is destroyed, will envy hatred and all uncharitableness, with their attendant hypocrisies, be destroyed too.

1. Written on paper watermarked 1831. Box III/98.

2. William Cecil (1520-98) managed the English government for Elizabeth I for forty years (1558-98). This selection appears in Box III/78 and was written on paper watermarked 1832.

Whether it be religious conformity, Political conformity, moral conformity or Social conformity, no matter which the species, the spirit is the same: all kinds agree in this one point, of hostility to individual character, and individual character if it exist at all, can rarely declare itself openly while there is, on all topics of importance a standard of conformity raised by the indolent minded many and guarded by a fasces[3] of opinion which, though composed individually of the weakest twigs, yet makes up collectively a mass which is not to be resisted with impunity.

What is called the opinion of Society is a phantom power,[4] †yet as is often the case with phantoms, of more force over the minds of the unthinking than all the flesh and blood arguments which can be brought to bear against it.† It is a combination of many weak, against the few strong; an association of the mentally listless to punish any manifestation of mental independance. The remedy is, to make all strong enough to stand alone; and whoever has once known the pleasure of self-dependance, will be in no danger of relapsing into subserviency. Let people once suspect that their leader is a phantom, the next step will be, to cease to be led altogether and each mind guide itself by the light of as much knowledge as it can acquire for itself by means of unbiased experience.

We have always been an aristocracy-ridden people, which may account for the fact of our being so peculiarly a propriety-ridden people. The aim of our life seems to be, not our own happiness, not the happiness of others unless it happens to come in as an accident of our great endeavour to attain some standard of right or duty erected by some or other of the sets into which society is divided like a net—to catch gudgeons.

Who are the people who talk most about doing their duty? always those who for their life could give no intelligible theory of duty? What are called people of principle, are often the most unprincipled people in the world, °if by principle is intended the only useful meaning of the word, accordance of the individual's conduct with the individual's self-formed opinion.° Grant this to be the definition of principle, then eccentricity should be prima facie evidence for the existence of principle. So far from this being the case, 'it is odd' therefore it is wrong is the feeling of society; while they whom it distinguishes par excellence as people of principle, are almost invariably the slaves of some dicta or other. They have been taught to think, and accustomed to think, so and so right—others think so and

---

3. In ancient Rome, an axe tied in a bundle of rods and carried by officials as a symbol of their authority.

4. Similar passages are found in selection 4 (Box III/86, "Laconicisms") at points marked by matching superscripted symbols.

so right—therefore it must be right. This is the logic of the world's good sort of people; and if, as is often the case their right should prove indisputable wrong, they can but plead those good intentions which make a most slippery and uneven pavement.[5]

To all such we would say, think for yourself, and act for yourself, but whether you have strength to do either the one or the other, attempt not to impede, much less to resent the genuine expression[6] of the others.

Were the spirit of toleration abroad, the name of toleration would be unknown.[7] It is[8] one of those strangely named qualities[,] a 'negative virtue'.[9]

It represents at best but the absence of vices, and under the shadow of whose respectable name many sins of omission pass. To tolerate is to abstain from unjust interference, a quality which will surely one day not need a place in any catalogue of virtues. Now, alas, its spirit is not even comprehended by many, 'The quality of mercy is strained', and by the education for its opposite which most of us receive becomes if ever it be attained, a praiseworthy faculty, instead of an unconscious and almost intuitive state.

'Evil-speaking, lying and slandering' as the catechism formulary has it, is accounted a bad thing by every one. Yet how many do not hesitate about the evil-speaking as long as they avoid the lying and slandering—making what they call Truth a mantle to cover a multitude of injuries. 'Truth must not be spoken at all times' is the vulgar maxim. We would

---

5. Another draft of this passage substitutes the following sentence for the sentence presented here: "People who think for themselves and act as they think will scarcely be found to use any of these general terms; for they can give if needful a specific reason for their conduct. While the followers of authority can at best but plead these good intentions which make a most slippery and uneven pavement" (Box III/86).

6. In this version of the essay there is a "+" at this point. Later, the following paragraph appears after a "+": "Toleration can not even rank with those strangely named qualities, a 'negative virtue' while we can be conscious that we tolerate there must remain some vestige of intolerance—not being virtuous it is possible also not to be vicious: not so in this—not to be charitable is to be uncharitable." This passage doesn't seem to fit the text at this point. Furthermore, in another version of this same section of the essay, the passage proceeds as it appears here (see Box III/86).

7. Added later in another color of ink: "~~as the existence of a sense can be known only by its exercise~~ the name implies the existence of its opposite. ~~it speaks of a province of the mind in wh there can be no neutral ground.~~"

8. Added later in another ink: "Toleration is."

9. Another draft inserts the following at this point in the text: "than which phrase a more complete contradiction in terms is not to be found" (Box III/86). In this version, this paragraph appears to be crossed out. But in another, less altered version of this passage, the section is included (see Box III/86). Harriet seems particularly uncertain about the ideas in this section.

have the Truth, and if possible all the Truth, certainly nothing but the Truth said and acted universally. But we would never lose sight of the important fact that what is truth to one mind is often not truth to another. That no human being ever did or ever will comprehend the whole mind of any other human being. It would perhaps not #be possible to find two minds accustomed to think for themselves whose thoughts on any identical subject should take in their expression the same form of words.# ~Who[10] shall say that the very same order of ideas is conveyed to another mind, by those words which to him perfectly represent his thought? It is probable that innumerable shades of variety, modify in each instance, the conception of every expression of thought; for which variety the imperfections of language offer no measure, and the differ- ences of organization no proof. To an honest mind what a lesson of tolerance is included in this knowledge. To such not a living heart and brain but is like the planet 'whose worth's unknown although his height <u>be</u> taken',[11] and feeling that 'one touch of nature makes the whole world kin'[12] finds something that is admirable in all, and something to interest and respect in each. In this view we comprehend that

> 'All thoughts, all creeds, all dreams are true,
> All visions wild and strange' — [13]

to those who believe them, for after all we must come to that fine saying of the poet-philosopher,

> 'Man is the measure of all Truth
> Unto himself'

of the same signification is that thought, as moral as profound, which has been often in different ways expressed, yet which the universal practice of the world disproves its comprehension of, 'Toute la moralité de nos actions est dans le jugement que nous en portons nousmeme'[14] — 'dangerous' may

---

10. The long section between this tilde and the next is only roughly equivalent to the section on pages 144–145.

11. From Shakespeare sonnet, "Let me not to the marriage of true minds."

12. From Shakespeare's *Trolius and Cressida*, 3.3.

13. The first stanza of the last of Alfred Lord Tennyson's *Poems, Chiefly Lyrical* (1830) reads: "All thoughts, all creeds, all dreams are true, / All visions wild and strange; / Man is the measure of all truth / Unto himself. All truth is change. / All men do walk in sleep, and all / Have faith in that they dream: / For all things are as they seem to all, / And all things flow like a stream."

14. "All the morality of our actions is in the judgment we pass on them ourselves."

exclaim the blind follower of that sort of conscience, which is the very opposite of consciousness: would but people give up that sort of conscience which depends on conforming they would find the judgement of an enlightened consciousness proved by its results the voice of God:

> 'Our acts our angels are, or good or ill,
> Our fatal shadows that walk by us still'[15]

and to make them pleasant companions we must get rid, not only of error, but of the moral sources from which it springs.~

As the study of the mind of others is the only way in which effectually to improve our own, the endeavour to approximate as nearly as possible towards a complete knowledge of, and sympathy with another mind, is the spring and the food of all fineness of heart and mind. There seems to be this great distinction between physical and moral science; That while the degree of perfection which the first has attained is marked by the progressive completeness and exactness of its rules, that of the latter is in the state most favourable to, and most showing healthfulness as it advances beyond all classification except on the widest and most universal principles. The science of morals should rather be called an art: to do something towards its improvement is in the power of every one, for every one may at least show truly their own page in the volume of human history, and be willing to allow that no two pages of it are alike.

Were everyone to seek only the beauty and the good which might be found in every object, and to pass by defect lightly where it could not but be evident, if evil would not cease to exist, it would surely be greatly mitigated, for half the force of outward ill may be destroyed by inward strength, and half the beauty of outward objects is shown by the light within. The admiring state of mind is like a refracting surface which while it receives the rays of light, and is illuminated by them gives back an added splendour; the critical state is the impassive medium which cannot help[16]

The sun's beams but can neither transmit nor increase them. It is indeed much easier to discern the errors and blemishes of things than their good, for the same reason that we observe more quickly privation than enjoyment. Suffering is the exception to the extensive rule of good, and so stands out distinctly and vividly. It should be remembered by the critically-minded, that the habit of noting deficiencies before we observe beauties, does really for themselves lessen the amount of the latter.

---

15. From "Epilogue to Beaumont and Fletcher's Honest Man's Fortune," probably cited from Emerson's use of this quote at the beginning of "Self-Reliance."

16. Long space left in text at this point.

Whoever notes a fault in the right spirit will surely find some beauty too. He who appreciates the one is the fittest judge of the other also. The capability of even serious error, proves the capacity for proportionate good, For if anything may be called a principle of nature this seems to be one, that force of any kind has an intuitive tendency towards good.

We believe that a child of good physical organization who were never to hear of evil, would not know from its own nature that evil existed in the mental or moral world. We would place before the minds of children no examples but of good and beautiful, and our strongest effort should be, to prevent individual emulation. The spirit of Emulation in childhood and of competition in manhood are the fruitful sources of selfishness and misery. They are a part of the conformity plan, making each persons ideas of goodness and happiness a thing of comparison with some received mode of being good and happy. But this is not the Creed of Society, for Society abhors individual character. It asks the sacrifice of body heart and mind. This is the summary of its cardinal virtues would that such virtues were as nearly extinct as the dignitaries who are their namesakes.

At this present time the subject of social morals is in a state of most lamentable neglect. It is a subject so deeply interesting to all, yet so beset by prejudice, that the mere approach to it is difficult, if not dangerous. Yet there are 'thunders heared afar' by quick senses, and we firmly beleive that many years will not pass before the clearest intellects of the time will expound, and the multitude have wisdom to receive reverently the exposition of the great moral paradoxes with which Society is hemmed in on all sides. Meanwhile they do something who in ever so small a circle or in ever so humble a guise, have the courage to declare the evil they see.

3. THE USAGES OF SOCIETY[17]

To disregard the forms of society in the opinion of a very large & probably very worthy portion of the community, nothing short of misprision of   , if it be not actual. And it is only not loss of caste whereby immense wealth [?] of nature or by an established character for oddity that such offences may escape with impunity.

Society like all tyrants, is an arrant coward. It bullies all who submit to be its subjects, but invariably succumbs before the quiet determination of earnest purpose & strong feeling Unfortunately its abstract sound has

---

17. Written on paper watermarked 1832. Box III/99.

had great weight with many merely because it is an abstraction. Many merely who c^d have stood like a rock to oppose any real & tangible have been cowed by the abstraction all whose force over them at least has been derived from the vividness of their own imagination. Now what is this name society, It is an aggregate amount of opinion which whether it be wise to be influenced by or not must depend on the value of the individual opinions wh make up this compound one. Now no honest dissent from the opinions & habits of what is called society rarely is found unsupported by the opinion of those whose interest & sympathy constitute the real world of the dissenter, this opinion will generally agree with that of those whom he respects in this man. Yet does he hesitate to adopt it for fear of the residue whose opinion he does not respect? we are now discussing this only as a moral question. As a [prudential]

[manuscript ends abruptly]

[crosshatched on first page]
one of course it must be always needful to [conciliate] ~~He~~ an overwhelming majorities

[crosshatched on opposite side of first page]
each ind^l feels it to be contempt for themselves. We forget who made the acute observation that in French Society the affectatives is to be natural in english to be artificial.

4. LACONICISMS[18]

There is scarcely any truth or any error, for which with good will to the task, might not be found the warrant of a proverb. And there is scarcely any proverb[19] which does not include both truth and falsehood. Proverbs have been called stepping-stones for the mind.[20] Truly they seem oftener

---

18. Written on paper watermarked 1832. Symbols refer to similar passages in section #4. Box III/86.

19. In this version the word "truth" appears where "proverb" is. I have replaced the word here since in the same sentence in two other versions, the word "proverb" appears in place of "truth." HTM may have miscopied the word, since "proverb" seems to make more sense in the context of the sentence.

20. An alternative sentence is found in another draft of this essay: "And truly those are oftentimes more convenient than profitable proverbs have been called stepping-stones for the mind."

stumbling-blocks; or if stepping-stones, at best slippery ones, leaving those who would take them on trust to the chances of a signal dis-comfiture.[21] It is a rule, to which few exceptions will be found, that maxim-mongers, of which species every ones experience will furnish at least an individual, are not thinkers. And the reason is evident. We should imagine it would scarcely #be possible to find two minds, accustom to think for themselves whose thoughts on any identical subject would take in their expression the same form of words.# No two human countenances were ever exactly alike in all their features and expressions, still less two human minds. According to each individual application of it, according to the peculiarities of each individual mind, will be to that mind the relative proportion of truth and error which any[22] contains. To him who resolves the genuine result of his personal experience into one of these short sayings, that identical combination of words, and no other, exactly represents one definite state of mind, to him it is wholly truth. But who that has, by experience and reflection made a proverb his own, but knows, that it is much more by what it implies, than by what it expresses that it is veritable. ˜Who shall say that the very same order of ideas is conveyed to another mind, by those words, which to him perfectly represent his thoughts? It is probable that innumerable shades of variety, modify in each instance, the conception of every expression of thought: for which variety the imperfections of language offer no measure, and the differences of organization no proof. To an honest and humble mind what a lesson of tolerance is included [in][23] this knowledge. he feels that 'one touch of nature makes the whole world kin'[24] & To such not a living human heart and brain but is like the planet 'Whose worth's unknown, although his height be taken',[25] not one that has not much that is admirable, not one that in some one or other of its phases is not worthy of his interest and respect. In this view we can comprehend that

---

21. The following passage appears at this point in another draft of this essay: "Nothing is more provoking than after one has perhaps with infinite trouble & pains hammered out some semblance of truth for oneself, to have, it replied to by the second-hand wisdom—& more provoking that perhaps there is no denying the 'saw' to be wisdom only its application may be imperfect but to convince the conceit of a maxim-monger that you have reason on your side is quite impossible & so you submit with the best grace you may. The spectators doubting not that you are, or ought to be convinced by so great an authority."

22. In this draft HTM leaves a small blank space at this point, but in another draft the next word follows directly.

23. Page torn.

24. From Shakespeare's *Trolius and Cressida*, 3.3.

25. From Shakespeare's sonnet, "Let me not to the marriage of true minds."

'all thoughts, all creeds, all dreams are true,
all visions wild and strange,'[26]

to those who believe them, for after all we must come to that fine saying of the poet-philosopher,

'Man is the measure of all truth
unto himself' —

In which term 'Man' we would have it to be borne in mind the duallism 'Woman' is also included.[27]

Of the same signification, is that thought, as moral as profound, which has been so often in different ways expressed, yet which the universal practice of the world disproves its comprehension of, 'Toute la moralité de nos actions est dans le jugement que nous en portons nous même'.[28]

Dangerous, exclaims the blind follower of that sort of conscience which is the very opposite of consciousness: would but people give up that conscience which consists only in conformity they would find the judgement of an enlightened consciousness proved by its results the voice of god.

'Our acts our angels are, or good or ill,
Our fatal shadows that walk by us still.'[29]

and to make them pleasant companions we must get rid not only of error, but of the moral sources from which it springs.~ Little has he observed who would say 'what's in a name' when speaking of the popular mind.[30]

---

26. See note 13, above.

27. HTM's meaning is much clearer in the sentence included here than in what may be a later draft, which states, "By which term man being intended the species, the sentence stands, a remarkable instance of a phrase, to all, and in all time, applicable."

28. See note 14, above.

29. From "Epilogue to Beaumont and Fletcher's Honest Man's Fortune," probably cited from Emerson's use of this quote at the beginning of "Self-Reliance."

30. In another draft the following passage is added: "To most people every thing is in a name. Names are things to them. What mischief has not that word of priestcraft, conscience, entailed. ~~What is~~ the real signification of the word? that conformity to exact rule—whose utility is taken upon trust."

Yet another draft (Box III/94) continues: "Little has he observed who would say 'whats in a name' when speaking of the popular mind. To most people every thing is in a name. To them names are things, status, every name which stands for a compound idea, however warped from its etymolgical meaning represents a host of associations it has at all times been the interest of some class to afix words of beautiful sound to the ideas they wish to make predominate in the minds over which their influence may have extended. For example their is no nation of the earth which own a priesthood in which that most beautiful name virtue does [not] find a every thing is in a name, since every name however warped from its use from its etymological meaning represents a map of associations which must be represented by some word.

Incalculable is the evil produced by this word 'conscience' on the common mind. †It signifies a phantom, yet a ghost whose power which is stronger than all the flesh and blood arguments of genuine morality.[31]† °In its largest sense it can be but consciousness of arguments or discordance between our actions and our principles.° Yet of all who familiarly employ the term how few are there who have[32] any definite principle of action, fewer still who have defined their principle for themselves. Indeed truly considered the phrases a 'good con[science]' a 'bad con.' so often on peoples lips, can designate either the one a right nor the other wrong moral state.

[C]onsciousness has reference not to the moral but to the intellectual condition: therefore can imply blame, only as all neglect of faculties is blameworthy—and vice versa. In proof of this let but each person who would employ the name 'conscience' [construct] for themselves any fixed principle or system or think it necessary to do so. They generally compose the class who glory in the name 'matter-of-fact-people' and who yet in this use of the word conscience as if it were some mysterious and innate and incomprehensible faculty, exercising incessant control over the whole life, transcend even German transcendentalism.

---

place: All revere it, or profess to do so—yet what different & opposed practices does it not stand. Where it stands for the individuals geniune feeling it will be found of much the same signification in all—But with the map Virtue is a thing of geographical position, it had only a local habitation & name in one latitude it is abstinence from animal food, & burning from 10 to 20 widows as the case may be—in another it consists in praying with the face towards the east, bathing every two hours, tumbling women in sacks in to the sea and impaling all who dissent from these views of views of morality with some it is in the number of human bones their prowess can affix to their girdle—with others the number of converts they can make to their sect, with some it is the domination of royalty & of the few—with others the equality of all—Some place it in hate—a few in Love—Some in passive submission to every wrong making it the utter exclusion of every mental moral or physical excitement others, the Athenian in Action as the birth 2nd or 3rd degree some in active resistance to internal emotions other in passive res[istance] to external injuries."

31. An alternative draft of this passage reads: "This very word 'conscience' in the sense authority would affix it to it, is a phantom. yet a ghost which by its early associations with the imagination, is often stronger than all the flesh and blood arguments of genuine morality." The following passage is added in another draft: "Morality is as bad, worse, it equally stands for definite injunction of some power person or   individual without the examination of reason
    could one suddenly induce people to change those words which have obtained an artificial and altogether imaginary signification, for other words more nearly representing the truth contained in in the" [sentence left incomplete].

32. The most complete draft ends at this point, but another draft (more incomplete in other ways) continues from here.

It has always been the interest of some class or other, to affix words of metaphysical vagueness to the notions of actual obligation by which they could profit.[33] Such is the word religion which all Priesthood has stood for the very comprehensible idea; pay. Such is the word loyalty which with all Statesmen has stood for   Such is the Honour of men of the world meaning immunity for the commision of any injury, if they are ready to shoot the injured on demand. Such the word Virtue which women too often believe to be consistent with even positive vice of a disposition & so long as is maintained one negative quality. All these words so debased in their use and so beautiful in themselves are the symbols of servitude or of freedom, according to the degree of mental vigour, and moral courage, which are brought to their interpretation. Power has always known the secret of the potency of words of majestic or beautiful sound, and whether as 'brother to the Moon and Lord of the Celestial Empire' as 'Successor to the Keys of St. Peter', or as 'Defendor of the Faith and most Christian King', with Brutus have said to the multitude 'lend me your ears', and like that wily person have known how to make usurious interest from the loan.

A euphonious, or spirit-stirring sentance, [even with little sense to recommend] it acts more than they might like to admit on both wise and vulgar: For ourselves we are not a wit ashamed of the proud swelling sensation which we always experience at that high sounding and to us quite incomprehensable line of Mrs Hemans beautiful ballad

'Tis the Cid   the Campeador![34]

The charm of partial mystery all have felt whether conscious of it or not; It has the same source whether it be conveyed by a ballad legend, or whether the boundless beauty of the infinite sea produces that state of the combination of all the senses into one other & higher sense which is called enthusiasm. It is the feeling connected with the very highest faculties of our nature. All make for themselves some hope or belief which is infinite and of however low a kind still the existence of some desire or idea which is in its nature

---

33. Added from III/89.2. Another version is "it has been the interest of some class or other at all times to affix words of beautiful sound to the ideas their wish to make predominate in the mind, over which their influence may have extended."

34. Here Harriet leaves a blank, but in another version she adds "Ruy Diez." Felicia Dorothea Hemans (1793-1835) was a popular poet during this period. Harriet is probably referring to a series of ballads called the *Songs of the Cid*. In "The Cid's Rising" the following line occurs: "That the Cid Ruy Diez, the Campeador." Harriet may have been trying to recall the poem from memory, thus slightly misquoting or leaving a blank in her manuscripts.

unattainable, and yet enduring, is the distinction of humanity.[35] The 'long-ing after immortality' is a logical reason for the 'hope which is us'.

Thus the word Virtue for how many different & opposite practices & thoughts has it stood—it has always answered the purposes of interested men to make it stand for this or that practice, but why has it always succeeded as a cover for interest because being in reality indifinite, and capable of infinite latitude of comprehension it has always stood for each persons standard of ideal perfection—for each human being has such a standard. however, how it may be placed, ~~this~~ fact is the destruction of humanity & this longing after the unattainable is the best reason for the hope which is in us.[36]

Endurance is another of these phantom virtues.[37] now what is endur-ance, it is bearing evils wh are remediless, this is a necessity, not a virtue in itself, but only an occasion for fortitude, which if it come is a strength & a dignity, but that is not the virtue of endurance—is it bearing evils which we might change, but will not? then our pseudo-virtue becomes matter of choice & so we may suppose of pleasure & there ends the virtue—or is it bearing lesser evil to avoid greater, that is a wise choice, but the credit then issue to the faculties of sagacity & clear-sightedness wh calculates the average justly—is it the sacrifice of our own happiness to the happiness of others this if wisely considered is heroism, not endur-ance, but that is an important one, for in nothing do people more decieve themselves than in the notion that they sacrifice their own happiness for that of others. it is the flattering unction wh they lay to the soul who are too feeble to make the struggle for individual will—true where the will does not, 'with the strong desire keep pace' we may reasonably beleive the strength of the desire to have been a fallacy, but these are the people who extol the virtue of endurance—wh in such cases, means either the absence of a strong feeling of the mental or moral courage—a person of principle is one who has maturely weighed & chosen his opinions & whose conduct agrees with his opinions.

people who really do things from principle will rarely use the words right & duty—for they can give a specific reason for each action & are not forced to have recourse to these general & indefinite terms [&] expressions

---

35. HTM added in pencil beneath this sentence, "All must clasp idols."

36. Another draft includes this passage.

37. Another passage on "phantom virtues" from III/98.

5. [MORAL KNOWLEDGE MUST BE GAINED THROUGH EXPERIENCE][38]

And for [the] reason [proverbs] are oftentimes more mischievous than profitable. The spirit of the vernacular mind may be distinguished by the maxims most in use, and these maxims, reversing the general order of things, are first effect, then cause—and this is the case with every opinion, and saying representing opinion, which is adopted, not discerned. That which people repeat, as a clever saying, without understanding, for if they understood it would no longer be repetition, ends by becoming the type as much of opinion as such persons are capable of exhibiting [smeared with ink]

It would be well if considering [this] by those in whose hands circumstances place the [smeared] mind were to reflect before they [become] the parents of   which may produce such obstinate offspring. The most they can do is to tell us that mental food is to be had, and to point in the direction of the road we must take to reach it. They cannot take us an inch on the road itself and the probability is that those who win profit by the direction would without such sign post, have found a path for themselves—and enjoyed the more from the fact while, all who never see any but its surface meaning would have been beter without possessing weapons which they know not how to handle. For these reasons we always dislike to see a vol. of Proverbs, Maxims, Pensées or by whatever name they may designate those vade mecum's for mental listlessness & unfounded assumption.

[39]A collection of veritable proverbs could never be perfected while there

---

38. Box III/86 and 95 (combined).

39. This section from Box III/95 seems to fit here, but unfortunately much of this file is missing: "And worse even than sentences speakers are those published manuals of ready digested wisdom those vade mecums for mental listlessness & unfounded assumption, maxim manuals & Proverbs & Phisical axioms are necessarily left out or they would be elements of science, and when we consider that scarcely on a single general proposition of moral truth will there be found no competent minds to fully agree it is not wonderful that they are unsatisfactory matters. For either we agree in the phrase rule or sentence in which case one is provoked at the bareness with which it stands, unchecked"

An alternative draft of this paragraph reads: "a collection of veritable proverbs could never be perfected while there remained any new situation in which humanity could be place[d]—every phasis of spiritual existence could not be delienated while there remained a living human heart.

Some approach to an Universal Textbook might be made were every one to inscribe a result of their Life were it but a single sentance, which they themselves had truly & earnestly felt. True many a human life might be like that of Thekla be concentrated in a single sentence. Yet what meaning there would be in those few words! Nay in the simple phrase Life & Death is implied a secret which the sum of human discernment mind has never yet fathomed—but tho the work would never be complete yet it would be always in advance of its contemporary mind—& be to it a sort of mute Areopagus" remained any new situation in which humanity could be placed every [phasis] of spiritual existence could not be ~~perfected~~ until the last human being should expire. When our volume would be but of little avail. Yet some approach to such an universal Text book might be made were every person to inscribe the result of their life were it but a single sentence, which they themselves had earnestly felt. The Biography of many a human life might be like that of Thekla[40] concentrated in a sentence. But what meaning there would be in those few words! were they but the magic-words Life & Death there would be implied in them more than the whole sum of, the whole journey, human mind has ever yet fathomed. yet what a vocabulary does not that phrase imply—enjoyment extasy—happiness—suffering—struggle—hopelessness! with the wide feilds on either side!—each being who has lived, for whatever the no. of years has that no. of years experience to profiit by, and to relate for others profit would but each relate it honestly.

6. [CIVIL DISOBEDIENCE][41]

<u>Please return me</u> this paper dear.

One of the most difficult questions for conscientious persons to settle with any thing like satisfaction to their own feelings is how far we are bound to conform to or to resist, or how far we are justified in conforming to or in resisting laws, or customs having the force of laws, with which we disagree. Are we justified in rectifying what we think in our individual case the defects of the laws & customs under which we live? It seems a clear case that if we are willing to endure the penalty we are justified in doing any thing which we ourselves think right.[42] But if we have knowingly incurred a penalty whether from law or custom are we, altho' prepared to accept it, justified in complaining of it? I think justification of the complaint against it is included in justification of the conduct. If what

---

40. Thekla is the daughter of the Duchess of Friedland, wife of Wallenstein. See Coleridge's poem "Death of Wallenstein."

41. Written on paper watermarked 1842. Box III/84. HTM has a line drawn through it all, indicating she is scrapping it. Paper is stationery size and has been folded in thirds and appears to have been sent in an envelope to someone, probably JSM.

42. In another draft of this essay she writes: "(This we say is to us a clear case—but we do not overlook the large class of dissidents who in accordance with the fashion of the time for weakness so it is but gregarious (on the principle that a thousand fools equal one wise man) place example among the highest moral considerations, [many] think that there are no rights but such as derive from duties. We mention such only to show that we are aware of the existence of this sort of people ~~otherwise w^d be likely to be [?]~~ end of note.)"

the law thinks right we think wrong we are justified in acting as we think right.[43] we should be prepared to accept the penalty & to protest against it. But according to this if every body were conscientious & acted according to their opinions there would be always an immense number of persons acting in opposition to the law because no law or scarcely any receives the assent of every body in the community—it is only because people in general are unconscious & unconscientious that each law does not create its own body of dissenters & society must have attained a perfection too distant to enter into present practical considerations before there can be anything like unanimity upon all the subjects on which the state of the law affects directly or indirectly the great & small interests of life.

on the whole we think that we are in many cases bound to protest, & in all cases justified in protesting, both[44] by speech & conduct[45] against laws or customs which we think wrong.

It is but adjourning the question of principle to say that all who have a vote for a representative must conform to whatever their representative has agreed to; their representative may be in the minority—& whether the representative is with the majority or otherwise does not affect our agreement in his opinion. Some must always disagree in the vote of the representative of many. In fact representation is a delusion.[46] A representative has only the choice of being a proxy or an approximation: practically two widely different things.

[bottom of same page]
If we beleive with Kotzebue[47] as we devoutly do that "The will of man in his heaven" we must rectify the laws of our society up to our own conscience & having made our own law, "act the law we live by without fear"

[written on back of folded sheet]
On Individual Collision with Law or Custom.

---

43. In another draft of this essay she adds: "If those who suffer penalties for breaking what they think an unjust law had not a right to protest against the penalty then heretics would not have right and reason to complain of being burnt!—and theirs is only an extreme case, not otherwise a peculiar one. We should be ready to admit (whenever we think it would be the truth) that the penalty is right from the point of view of those who inflict it; but this is a concession which need not affect the intensity of our protest."

44. The word "either" is written above "both," although neither is struck out.

45. The word "action" is written above "conduct," although neither is struck out.

46. In the alternative draft HTM uses "compromise" in place of "delusion."

47. August Kotzebue (1761-1819), a German playwright whom JSM had written about as early as 1824 (*CW:* I, 324).

[two thirds down the page]
This subject leads directly into cases of the duty of considering the public
interest in private conduct—as in population—
'My Mind to me a kingdom is'
'L'opinion est la reine du monde parce'qu la sottise & est la reine des sots'[48]
je regard &c.

Jean Paul

7. SOME USES OF THE WORD SELFISH SELFISHNESS & SENTIMENTALITY[49]

Both adherents and antagonists of Bentham's general principles are
accustomed to attribute to him the idea that all our notions are guided
by self interest in a sense in which we think he never intended it to be
taken or if he did which is by no means necessarily attached to it. Our
reason for thinking that he did not mean it is the sense usually given to
it as a statement & defence of selfishness are twofold. The one that his
most peculiar principle which he endeavoured to formulise in the phrase
'Greatest Happiness of the greatest number' is in its spirit in direct
contradiction to the idea of personal selfishness. The other that he did not
at all assume to take, moral philosophy still less the subtilties of metaphysical distinctions into account any further than absolutely necessary for
the purpose of forming a political philosophy at a time when the science
had scarcely begun to be recognized. According to this definition self-interest must be all the feelings one self has—a conclusion evidently absurd.

We must in considering people's interest take into account our own also—
on what possible ground but that of the most sentimental absurdity are we
to be interested for everybody <u>except</u> ourselves? Keeping ever so closely to
Bentham's rule or to any other we must still ourself be counted for <u>one</u>? we
have the strongest objection to this sentimental morality because it can make
& does make but two sorts of characters—good intentioned but hopelessly
weak people, since nature will prend le dessus[50] & if we have no interest in

---

48. Sébastien Chamfort (1741-1794), *Maxies et Pensées*, I: "Public opinion is the queen of the
world because foolishness is the queen of fools"; or "Public opinion rules the world because
foolishness rules fools."

49. Box III/92, written on paper watermarked 1832.

50. "Get the upper hand."

life but that of others we shall be wanting in all the strength which would enable us to do much good even to them, (& such are the characters which society has hitherto attempted & generally successfully to form in women). & thorough hypocrites or silent egotists[51] & these are generally to be found among men for the reason that society allowing to them a cage large enough for short flights [so] they do not wound their wings at every attempt to expand them as women do against their gilded bars.[52]

Sentimentality is made to fill the place in the mind & feeling which must be filled somehow either well or ill in everyperson who is not a mere dry stick or machine a mâchoir[e] otherwise occupied by poetry or religion. One does not wonder when one encounters persons in whom the finer instincts of the spiritual nature seem never to have existed or have never been awakened at the horror which persons of noble feelings feel who dare not look nature & facts fully in the face lest they should not be beautiful feel at the thought of yeilding up their finest susceptabilities & lofty aspirations generous impulses devoted affections to the coarse handling of the unformed hand & narrow natures who are always the readiest to imagine they understand all subjects because they see none but those narrow & low ones 'who runs may read'[53]

To make the practical business of life in which we include the external conduct of society in its largest sense to only rule & object of individual existence is to sacrifice the individual, & that is to say all individuals, to a confused idea of the whole.

8. [WHAT IS UTILITY AS DISTINGUISHED FROM HAPPINESS?][54]

What indeed is utility as distinguished from happiness? The mere negation of evil & [shailen][55] indeed must be the [intituled][56] the result

---

51. HTM has a single line indicating that the section beginning here and continuing until the next footnote is to be scratched.

52. End of crossed out section.

53. The phrase referred to comes from G. Babington, *Exposition of the Commandments* (1583), "O what a God serue we, that being able to set everie thought wee thinke visible in our foreheads in great letters, that everie one which runneth by, might reade them, yet most mercifully spare vs."

54. Paper watermarked 1831. Box III/127.

55. HTM's writing is nearly illegible here. She may be writing "shailen" used as a figure of speech to mean "to blunder." Or she may indicate "shadow," although this reading seems less likely.

56. Again, this word is very difficult to decipher. If the word is "intituled," she probably means

of whose experience can decide that ~~that~~ <u>such</u> is the only or the worthy result of human existence thus ~~they~~ bringing every <u>genuine</u> form of mind, that is to say every <u>individual</u> one, to the <u>crucifixion</u> of conformity to rules wh apply to <u>every</u> manifestation of mind, the measure wh is common to all minds. It is the custom to take the commonest & most marked results of those 5 senses & to make of them Procus's measure ~~to or~~ to wh minds wh do not fit—must be <u>made</u> to fit

9. THE VIRTUE OF ENJOYMENT AND THE ENJOYMENT OF VIRTUE,[57]

or a wrong end—which signifies weakness in choosing such an one—It is plain that each living beings real object must be his own happiness—in this desire he must be honest, and even the madman or the idiot comes under this necessity. it is a condition of sentient existence. And as all which truly tends to this end must be good. It is plain that an evil design must be a badly selected design for the object, happiness, desired—and therefore a mistaken aim, and therefore, in so far as it is mistaken, weak.[58] It is plain that were a wrong end, or a wrong means for attaining a right end is used—that cannot be an affect of intellect, however much the person may [opine] on other subject[s] and that in that [heart] of his subject he wants intellect—that is not intellect which has no tendency to produce enjoyment <u>somewhere</u>. Every thing but enjoyment is but a means to the attainment of that end, and the sternest [seetery[59]] the most rigid mortifier of the flesh that ever existed has in truth this much for his creed—yes quite as much those who (such there are who tell you that their notion of morality counts in the absence of enjoyment, since even such end by the

---

that utility is invested with an honorary function, or entitled.

57. Written on paper watermarked 1832. Box III/86.

58. The following passage echoes the thoughts found in Box III/86: "If happiness can only be produced by virtue, then wickedness must be inapplicability of means to ends and as far as this inapplicability exists shows a want of intellect rather than of heart, since all human kind make happiness their aim of whatever sort their heart as it is called may be."

59. The word in the original is unclear. It appears that Harriet may have made a noun out of the verb "seethe" or to boil. The root of seethe, according to the *Oxford English Dictionary,* is related to sacrifice and "boiled flesh." Seethe can be used to mean "to be boiled," and Harriet may have been using an example of a person who allows himself or herself to be boiled as an extreme instance of an ascetic.

phrase 'it is best for man' — To that now ill-assorted in the times are terms with opinions, and both with actions—From the injunction of the Archbishop, delivered with all the pomp of voice & words 'On the sabbath day ye shall do no manner of work ye nor your servants nor your horse nor your ass' while the sonorous voice is only interrupted by the impatient fawnings of his   asses do not suffice priests now. To the broad arch of the quaker's beaver more costly ample dimensions which for him is the Azrael's[60] bridge to the abodes of the blest.

10. [ASSIGNING MORAL BLAME][61]

Who is entitled to blame who? is one of the most important of all questions of morals. To award moral blame to another is about the utmost assumption & ought to be regarded as involving one of the utmost responsibilities that a human being can undertake. A truly conscientious person (we speak not of the innumerable pretenders to this fine character) thinks much & long & silently & is well assured that they have all the links in the chain of evidence complete[62] before they arrive at the conclusion that another is morally blameworthy, & then no one can for a moment deserve the high title of conscientious who declares this opinion except in order to attain by doing so some certain good. But so far is this the state of mind & conduct of people in general in this country at all events that everybody can in a moment call to mind fifty twaddles of their acquaintances the excitement of whose life seems to consist in passing judgments on the

almost all the actions which are matters deserving of moral reprobation if the reasons & motives are thoroughly examined into are found to proceed more from absence of good than from presence of bad qualities & then most often in the majority of cases from a good feeling carried to the excess which makes it a bad one.

---

60. The angel of death in Jewish and Islamic mythology.

61. Box III/145.

62. The text is marked with a "+" at this point, and the rest of the paragraph is added from a section on the back of the page, which is written upside down and also marked with a "+." However, this passage ends midsentence.

(2)

... the old religion has the monopoly of all the terms
expressive of & associated with spiritual & elevated ideas

———

Equality as a principle & feeling can only come from
the cultivation of spiritual ideas upon a different basis
from what are now called religious doctrines.

~~There are but two types of spiritual~~
There have existed, & appear to be, but two forms of spiritual
ideas — the Catholic, & the Protestant. Protestantism undertakes
the principle } to evolve all spirituality from the understanding as a basis
Catholicism, precisely opposed to this, wholly omits the understanding
from its means of spiritual elevation. It seems to me that
the two forms divide between them what should constitute
the true basis of religion

The object both of Catholicism & of Protestantism is the elevation
of the moral nature — Catholics succeed up to a certain point
in educating the moral through the hearted. Protestants
fail in teaching the moral through the understanding — I believe
because they attempt to commence where the Catholics leave
off, without passing through that elementary education which
the Catholics give.

35

HTM *argues that Christianity opposes equality.*
Her critique of religion joins that of Marx and
many others of the mid-nineteenth century.

RELIGION

6

Beginning in 1874 several biographers of John have decried Harriet's "infidelity and atheism" (Henshaw 1874, 522; see also Hagberg 1930, 196). Although the collection of her writing on religion is rather limited, the following five essays reveal her antagonism to both Protestantism and Catholicism, citing many of the same shortcomings Marx identified and popularized in the same century. The first piece, an unpublished co-authored letter to the editor of the Reasoner, *George Jacob Holyoake, rebukes the shoddiness of the arguments given for disbelief in God. Harriet and John go on to offer more worthy ones: the problem of evil, the wickedness of a God who creates sentient beings doomed to hell, the poverty of Christian morality. They suggest the need to focus on creating a healthier and juster set of ethical beliefs.*

In the first essay, Harriet shares her aesthetic sensitivity to the Gothic cathedral at Amiens, France, but she also deplores the Church, whose only remaining function is the "consolation of the victims of society," women and the poor. She wishes to have buildings dedicated to better ideas than the "old {religious} fables" and "old {religious} poetry," which she called obsolete. Further, she argues that the Catholic religion has been useful for the world, but now needs to be replaced by more "practical" and "elevated" ideas.

In the second essay, Harriet argues that equality will be promoted only by abandoning current religions, because neither Protestantism nor Catholicism elevate the moral nature sufficiently. Here HTM makes an interesting distinction when she observes that Catholics have succeeded in a limited way by teaching morality through the senses, but that the Protestants fail completely by attempting moral education through the understanding alone. The third essay comments snidely that Catholics have not succeeded in commerce in England because they have no inhibitions against lying. Protestantism has no better moral backbone, she says, but English Protestantism benefitted from the Puritan ethic that demanded trust, the core ethic required for commerce.

The final piece, on charlatanism, is difficult to follow. However, this essay offers the reader an interesting study of Harriet's writing process, so her strike-outs have been retained. Many times in this final essay on religion, HTM originally writes a strong, even aggressive idea, only to strike it out and replace it with a less offensive term. For example, she writes in her first draft, "opinionists agree," and then replaces "agree" with "seem to agree." A second example of her growing awareness of audience, which may have motivated her to soften her tone, involves her original phrase, "the era of political licentiousness" which she revised to read, "the era of dangerous innovation." Harriet concerns herself with the charlatanism which she believes has infected the Victorian Age with belief in "false appearances" that result from victims' fear.

ENLIGHTENED INFIDELITY[1]

Sir,—Observing that a subscription has been opened in aid of your publication, I send a small contribution towards it. I should much regret that the flag of avowed unbelief, unfurled by the *Reasoner* alone among English periodical writings, should be lowered for want of the support necessary to keep it flying. When you commenced writing, some courage was still required for the public profession and dissemination of infidel opinions, and although we may now hope that the time for legal persecution, such as that which you have undergone,[2] has passed away, the willingness to defy, in behalf of what is sincerely believed to be truth, even the idle talk of the multitude is unhappily sufficiently rare in all classes, to be entitled not only to honorable recognition, but to such positive assistance as the case admits of.

---

1. In a letter to John (L/8), Harriet writes about the "mixture of impudence . . . & imbecility" in the article by the editor of the *Reasoner* that sparked this unpublished letter. Although the manuscript (XL/4) is in John's hand, Harriet's letter suggests a "joint" answer. Box XL/4.

2. George Jacob Holyoake, editor of the *Reasoner,* had been jailed for blasphemy for six months in 1842.

It would however be a bad compliment to writers whom I am commending for speaking out their whole mind to the public, were I to be less free in expressing to them, my opinion of their performances. And I am compelled to say that my good will to the *Reasoner* does not arise from my thinking it at all an adequate representative of either the argumentative or the moral strength of enlightened infidelity. I give its writers credit for being partly aware of this, and I trust that they may become fully so, and may succeed in making the *Reasoner* a more valuable organ, than I think it has yet been, of the opinions it professes.

The strongest point of your writers is certainly the metaphysical argument on the existence of Deity, though even there they offer, I think, great hold to any dexterous adversary, and might learn, for example, from Hume's *Dialogues on Natural Religion,* far more conclusive modes of stating their argument. But this part of the subject, though it ought not be neglected, is neither the best suited for popular effect, nor in itself the most important. Whether the world has had a creator, is a matter of hypothesis and conjecture on which, in the absence of proof, people's judgment will vary according to the particular bias of their imagination: but the mischievous superstition consists in identifying this Creator, with the ideal of abstract perfection, and making him, as such, an object of adoration and imitation. Any one who considers the course of nature, without the usual predetermination to find all excellent, must see that it has been made, if made at all, by an extremely imperfect being; that it can be accounted for on no theory of a just ruler, unless that ruler is of extremely limited power, and hemmed in by obstacles which he is unable to overcome. Mankind can scarcely chuse to themselves a worse model of conduct than the author of nature. None but a very bad man ever manifested in his conduct such disregard not only of sufferings of sentient creatures, but of the commonest principles of justice in the treatment of them, as is manifested by the Creator of the World if we suppose him to be omnipotent.[3]

It is by treating such topics as these that infidel writers would strike the most effective blow at superstition while they would, by the same effort, plant something better in its place. On the subject of revealed religion there is room for a similar exposure; setting forth the essential wickedness of the character of the Deity, as Christian writers have been forced, often against their own better feelings, to conceive it: the atrocious

---

3. It is interesting to note the similarity of the arguments against the existence of the God of Christian Theism presented here and by JSM's "ungod" son, Bertrand Russell, in "Why I'm Not a Christian."

conception (for example) of a Being who creates on the one hand thousands of millions of sentient creatures foreknowing that they will be sinners, and on the other a hell to torture them eternally for being so. With regards to the question of Evidences, I am sorry to see that after all the light which has been thrown upon the origin and history of the Christian and other religions by many authors in the last and present age, your writers have not got beyond the crude guesses and fanciful theories which were current a century ago, when historical criticism, or any real sense of historical truth, had not yet come into the world.

On the subject of morals, I regret to observe that you do not even aim at any improvement of the common notions, but give in an apparently unqualified adhesion to them, exactly as they stand. This is a retrograde step on the part of infidel writers. Mankind have, as a race, hitherto grounded their morality mainly on religion, and if their religion is false it would be very extraordinary that their morality should be true. For my part I hold that the philosophy of morals is still in its infancy; that in its practical doctrines there is as much room for improvement, as in any other department of human thought; and that even now it is easy to lay down a far better, juster, nobler set of moral principles and rules than those generally received: the maxims of the Gospel though admirable in much of their spirit being both vague and most incomplete, while the attempts to supply their deficiencies by St. Paul and others amount, in my opinion, to very much worse than nothing.

2. [ON CATHOLICISM][4]

If against the tracery of the rose windows at Ameins is in the most flamboyant possible style & exceedingly beautiful. The inside dissapointed me, as in general the inside of of [*sic*] a Cathedral does after having looked long at the outside—one's feelings have been raised & under no roof is their vastness to satisfy them. It is however very fine—the altar & its accessories are wholly gilt & look more prosperous than usual with Catholic places, but in the whole beautiful building there is that confirmed air of thing & a system in a state of decadence which tho' in itself always causing a first impression to melancholy, is on reflexion as much a subject of satisfaction morally as it is a source of Artistic beauty. High mass was going on & the church was perhaps half filled by the usual attendants of such places, women

---

4. Box III/144.

& the poor. The function of the Catholic religion which remains suitable to the wants of this time is its character of consolation to the victims of society & those classes are accordingly its nearly sole supporters & attendants. How much I long to see noble buildings consecrated to nobler purposes than the repetition of old fables, whose old poetry does not make amends for the old coarseness gone by & mischievous moralities, nor the fine maxims of benevolent philosophy for its. Catholicism has done immensely much for the world but it must give way to ideas at once more practical & more elevated. Surely the unsuitability of any religion to its time is proved by the fact of its ministers not being the first people of their time, for the teachers & leaders should be the wisest & best & a body of persons set in places of authority would be piety sure to be recognised as the highest spiritually if they were so. The mass of the world appear to often have a mean jealousy of an individual superiority, but of large bodies occupying high places the tendency seems to be respect so long as their exists any however small claims to the feeling[.] Mankind are both loyal & rebellious & either feeling is worked on by its suitable means.

3. [ON CATHOLICISM AND PROTESTANTISM][5]

Now the old religion has the monopoly of all the terms repressive of & associated with spiritual & elevated ideas

----

Equality as a principle & feeling can only come from the cultivation of spiritual ideas upon a different basis from what are now called religious doctrines.

There have existed & appear to be, but two forms of spiritual ideas—the Catholic, & the Protestant. Protestantism undertakes to evolve all spirituality from the understanding as a basis. The principle of Catholicism, precisely opposed to this, wholly omits the understanding from its means of spiritual elevation. It seems to me that the two forms divide between them what should constitute the true basis of religion[.]

The object both of Catholicism & of Protestantism is the elevation of the moral nature. Catholics succeed up to a certain point in educating the moral through the sensual. Protestants fail in teaching the moral through the understanding. I believe because they attempt to commence where the

---

5. XLI/2.

Catholics leave off, without passing through that elementary education which the Catholics give.

4. [CHRISTIANITY AND ETHICS][6]

Perhaps much of the reason why catholic countries have never succeeded in commerce like Protestant—or especially like England—is that catholicism takes—scarcely any, if indeed any, account of speaking the truth. From this comes no feeling of dishonour in lying; England's great com[l] proof must be attributed to the system of credit & this rests very much upon personal sense of dishonour in untruth. England is the only country where it is universally felt to be an affront to doubt a person's word. I attribute this not so much to Protestantism wh for ought I know takes no particular note of this virtue, but to the accident of puritanism having adopted this fine principle, the purity & unselfishness of which suited well with the austerity of puritanism[.] It is one of the many invaluable lessons left by Chivalry—we do not find it among the recommendations of Christianity. Christianity avoided even by excess all the [public] virtues, probably because those held a high place in ancient ethics, while the benevolence was further inculcated by them & this virtue was most especially that of Christian character[.]

5. CHARLATANISM.[7]

The present, say the religionists, is the age of scepticism; ~~demagogues joy~~ now the governed delight in the word revolution which the governments declare means that the wheel stands still, while the philosophical fly sits on the axle & ~~coolly~~ observes with oligarchists, all the world over, 'tis 'what a dust I make'.[8] par excellance, the era of ~~political licentiousness~~ dangerous innovation; political economists see in its signs the greatest happiness 'in posse'[9] but the speedy manifestation of which principle they

---

6. Written on India House paper. Box III/157.

7. Written on paper watermarked 1831. Box III/90.

8. English proverb on vanity: "The fly sat upon the axeltree of the chariot-wheel and said, what a dust do I raise!"

9. Might exist.

would somewhat paradoxically produce through[10] the least happiness 'in esse';[11] the conservatives abuse the pulling down system, which say the ~~liberals~~ radicals is a necessary ~~process~~ preliminary to building up[12] — 'to renounce' must take precedence of 'to reverance' says the philosopher, & every third form boy knows by practice if not by theory that ~~the dynamical comes before the synthetical, that is to say intangible creations of a speculative brain~~ that he proceeds from the known to the unknown. ~~as well in the most exact sources as in the most~~ all opinionists ~~agree~~ seem to agree, each in a different sense, that it is an age of transition. The searcher after the origin of the sublime and beautiful weept over the departure of the age of chivalry. Had he lived a few years later he might have hailed the dawn of as prolific an age, that of charlatanerie: of which indeed he ~~himself was well fitted to be the~~ might have made a worthy leader;

if our material senses are no longer haunted by 'shapes [in] the air' our moral & mental perceptions suffer an equal martydom from 'false appearances', and an essay on 'the Distaste of Principle' would be to the full as 'instructive as on 'the Principles of Taste'[.] The generic characteristics of charlatanism, are pretty uniform, — those of its various species differ as widely as the character & circumstances of individuals — in the pseudo-religious instance most means of deportment, & as in influence rarely extends above the most fatuous minds it reigns by negative properties & influences its victims through their fears.

of this class the main-spring of all their mental operations is objective, & in accordance with the 'body of the time'[.]the march of their intellects is always on a <u>rail</u>-road. There favorite verb is to aim, (not <u>aime</u>[13]), & truly like sharp-shooters they always fire <u>low</u>.

let ~~their~~ his phrase be as it oftenest is, the elite of technical precision, & a ~~talk as they well as they may to them the planet~~ subsisty of logical sophistication which slips snake-like from conviction[.] we do not less feel, & know that is like a planet "whose worth's unknown, although his height be taken".[14] & whose nature he understands best who feels it most —

---

10. "By" is written below "through" and neither is crossed out.

11. Existing.

12. "Reconstructing" is written under "building up" and neither is crossed out.

13. French "aimer," "to love."

14. From Shakespeare's sonnet, "Let me not to the marriage of true minds."

HTM appreciated the arts deeply and struggled to give voice to her own creative urges.

ARTS

7

Harriet Taylor Mill's work on the arts, all written in the 1830s, includes theoretical comments about the arts, personal observations of individual art works, and published and unpublished book reviews and poetry. She comments on theater, music, painting, architecture, and literature, thus demonstrating her wide interest in the arts. The first three pieces consist of theoretical and personal reflections on these topics. The next group of writings contains one unpublished and seven published book reviews. HTM's poems and an article entitled "The Seasons," written for the Monthly Repository, *comprise the final set of writings on art.*

The first selection concerns the unity of the arts, which Harriet Taylor Mill addressed to an unnamed person whom she heard speak on this topic. Harriet argues that drama is decidedly different from novel reading because drama needs more literal resemblance to the physical world than fiction and because drama requires a condensation of time. Selection 2 is HTM's diatribe against "art" in England, which she declares to be a "dead word." She also claims that there is an incompatibility between the scientific and artistic habits of mind. The third piece is Harriet's travel diary written on a trip from Italy to Germany in the late spring of 1839. The diary contains Harriet's observations of geography, travel details, and her comments on galleries, paintings, sculptures, and architecture. Also included in this travel journal are the author's opinions on the art of Northern Italy, as well as an interesting historical account of travel in the 1830s. (Her disdain for Baedeker's travel guides as she wanders through the streets of Florence will bring to mind E. M. Forster's A Room with a View *for many twentieth-century readers.)*

Writings on Other Issues

*Next follow Harriet's book reviews. All but the first were published in
the* Monthly Repository, *a very liberal literary and political magazine
that included original articles, poems, and book reviews. It was edited at
the time by W. J. Fox, the close friend of Harriet who had introduced her
to John. HTM's review of* The Wondrous Tale of Alroy, *written by
Benjamin Disraeli, remains unpublished, although Harriet worked on
more than one draft of the article. The review of Disraeli's book was written in 1833, a year after her published reviews. She concludes that the author did not have an "analytical habit of mind" and demonstrated no
"fixed theory of moral principles." However, later in the same review, Harriet praises Disraeli for painting rather than describing the exotic scenes in
the novel. This is not only the sole review that was not published, it is
also the only novel she reviewed. Harriet either chose to write about travel,
political, historical, or philosophical books because of her interest in these
subjects, or perhaps the editor assigned her these projects because he recognized her experience and willingness to contribute reviews on these topics.*

*The second review centers on a book on Australia. Here Harriet comple-
ments the author's sensitive descriptions of geography and applauds the
author's views that the aboriginal people of Australia only become violent
if provoked by the white colonists. In the third review, HTM takes a
rather different approach when commenting on a German author who describes his reactions to England and English society. The piece of writing is
particularly interesting since it was translated by Sarah Austin, a dear
friend of John's and soon to be (unconsummated) lover of the author, Prince
Puckler-Muskau.*[1] *Harriet dislikes the author's "unbounded coxcombry"
and "unconsciousness," but praises the translator. The fourth review offers
Harriet's negative evaluation of an Englishwoman's travel observations of
the United States. Harriet calls the author "spiteful" and an "imbecile,"
and HTM points out the contradictions in the author's narrative, although HTM later reports that she doesn't want to judge the author differently because she is a woman. Ending this fourth review with a
comparison of the appreciative as opposed to the critical faculties, Harriet
echoes the same distinction she made in selection 2 in the previous chapter.*

*Harriet Taylor Mill's fifth book review shifts from travel narratives to
historical and political writing. In the review of Hampden's life, Harriet
encourages others to write biographies instead of novels because biographies
are more morally edifying. She also restates the events that lead from the*

---

1. Muskau's "affair" with Sarah Austin is recorded in Lotte and Joseph Hamburger's *Contemplating Adultery: The Secret Life of a Victorian Woman* (New York: Fawcett Columbine, 1991).
See especially pages 80–81 for a description of Sarah Austin's role in translating and finding
an English publisher for the book.

transition from Catholicism to Protestantism in England, concluding that any combination of state and religion is wrong. In addition, the reviewer explains that religious skepticism resulted from the way in which Protestantism was imposed on the English people. This critical evaluation of religion, Harriet suggests, may cause the kind of necessary moral doubt that precedes the constructing of a more stable moral foundation for society. The sixth review also concerns the relation between church and state. HTM's evaluation of Mirabeau's letters reconstructs his argument for the right of the state to intervene in the bequests of people who leave money to a church body. Although generally negative, Harriet acknowledges the touches of humor in some of Mirabeau's aphorisms. One sentence of note in this review may reveal Harriet's view of the importance of healthy intellectual partnerships, "The more the mind, either of man or woman, is enriched by acquirement and reflection, the more does it fit its possessor to give and to receive the highest species of enjoyment, social usefulness, and sympathy." The seventh review praises the author's attempt to distinguish Plato's idea of logos and the Christian notion of God, but HTM regrets that the book has no "soul." Harriet ends this series of book reviews by connecting the French Revolution with the current reform movement in England.

The penultimate section in Harriet's writings on the arts is an unusual essay on the aesthetics of the seasons written for the Monthly Repository. *Harriet describes the joys of the sensual pleasures of each season and argues that such enjoyment results from the engagement of a receptive mind and body with nature and is unavailable to a "frigid heart." Her essay is sprinkled with quotes from an impressive number and variety of sources.*

Harriet Taylor Mill's poems, both unpublished and published, constitute the final section of her writings on the arts. Because her earliest poems are on paper watermarked 1827, we speculate she wrote this poetry while her children were still babies. Her only published poems are from 1832. Several of the others remain undated. The first set of six drafts of "Daybreak" reveals the care and work that Harriet devoted to writing poetry. The drafts were composed around the same time that her first child, Herbert, was born, 24 September 1827, when Harriet was only twenty years old. The second poem in the series describes an infant sleeping. Like many mothers, Harriet broods about the "rough" realities that will touch the innocence of her child. Her worry about the inevitability of "wild excitements joys, / And maddening pleasures syren song; / To the dark gulf of guilt and pain; / With the full tide he's borne along—" may reveal that Harriet's fears for her child are a reflection of some unhappiness of her own. The next two poems, each titled "Song," continue the same motif—the fleeting quality of life's happiness.

The following year, 1829, just after discovering she is pregnant with her second child, and after receiving a letter from her husband, John Taylor, filled with anxious chastisements about the wisdom of her bathing in the sea, Harriet writes "Mermaid's Song" on the envelope flap which enclosed John Taylor's letter. Isolated from its context, this poem hardly appears a song of rebellion, but if we notice that the poem is written on the back of an envelope that contains a letter pleading with her not to indulge in the sea, the poem takes on a strikingly different tone from her other poetic work.

Although there is no date on the "Autumn" poem, it is grouped with her published poems, "The Snow-drop," "To the Summer Wind," and "Nature." These seem to invoke the sensuality of the seasons, also reflected in the essay entitled "Seasons." The poems as well as the essay appeared in the Monthly Repository *in 1832. The last three poems are all undated. Two of the poems reflect Harriet's passion for travel. She gathered much intellectual stimulation from visiting European and British cities and countrysides. Her poems, like her travel diary, brim with her enthusiasm for the light, air, and art of other lands. The last poem is an assertion of will: "I hold the future in my own control / A god unto myself—because of stedfast will." HTM's will had been "gained by long struggle from the storm." What storm? The trial of her separation from her husband would be an obvious answer, but whether it is* the *answer remains unclear.*

1. [THE UNITY OF THE ARTS][2]

I have been much interested by your remarks on the Unities. but will you excuse my saying that with some of them I do not find myself able to agree without some modification. Of course I quite concur with you as to the error of excluding from the province of art many subjects admirably adapted for it, tho' not capable of being brought within the Unities. I also admit that ideal & not material imitation is the object of Art, & that resemblance to the mere material circumstances is not to be attended to as a means of producing effect, but only as far as to avoid any clashing or shock to the imagination which might interfere with the legitimate & designed effect of the <u>ideal</u> likeness. All this is indisputable: but what I

---

2. Written on paper watermarked 1834. Box III/102.

cannot quite go with you in, is the opinion (substantially that of Johnson[3] in his preface to Shakspeare) that there is no <u>specific</u> illusion in the case of a drama more than in a novel. This I have never found to accord with my own personal experience. <u>Reading</u> a play no doubt is like reading a novel; the imagination makes any jump wh is required of it, without the slightest shock; but why? Because in reading[,] the imatation is avowedly <u>ideal</u> <u>only</u>, & as there is no pretence of material resemblance, there can be no feeling of any deficiency in such resemblance: but when a play is acted, there <u>is</u> an attempt at material <u>resemblance</u> <u>as</u> <u>well</u> <u>as</u> ideal. The endeavour is that the <u>external</u> sensations of the spectator shall be as nearly as possible the same as if he were actually witnessing the events: & <u>because</u> complete material resem^{ce} is attempted & to a great degree attained, therefore any great <u>absence</u> of material resemblance, in certain particulars while it is preserved in others is felt as a shock.

As an analogous instance—sculpture, not aiming at <u>colour,</u> is eminently beautiful; but <u>paint</u> the statue, & the slightest variance in the colour from that of life, w^d be absolutely disgusting. In seeing Shakspeare—King John for instance, I can scarcely express to you what a shock it was to me to find embassing[4] going & returning, battles fought &c in the mere trifling of a scene. In <u>reading</u> the play I do not feel that.

Speaking from personal experience I sh^d say that the unity of <u>place</u> is of no importance at all. I find the imagination accommodates itself at once to the shifting of the scene: The unity of <u>time</u> I find absolutely necessary—only I think it is commonly misunderstood: the sh^k to the imagⁿ I always feel to consist, <u>not</u> in passing over a lapse of time, but in supposing ev[e]nts to take place in a single instant wh manifestly require days & hours. According to my notion of the unity in Wallenstein[5] the action <u>all</u> takes place on the stage, none behind the scenes & strikes me that a play acted, differs from a novel or a play read, as painting differs from poetry. In painting the material imitation is professed (in addition to the idea) & being professed ought to be accomplished. We are offended by deviations in points not connected with the [artistic?] effect; but even trifles must be covered in a painting, not bec^e any thing depends on them, but bec^e if not r^t they are nic^{ly} <u>wrong</u> & therefore offend. When we see a play we do not look on it as a reality, it is

---

3. Dr. Samuel Johnson's preface to his edition of Shakespeare is still considered one of his best works.

4. Sending of ambassadors.

5. Albrecht von Wallenstein, Prince Mecklenburg (1583-1634). Harriet is probably referring to either Johann Christoph Friedrich Schiller's dramatic trilogy on Wallenstein's life, or Samuel Taylor Coleridge's "Death of Wallenstein."

true, but nether do we look on it wholly as a mental <u>conception</u>. We reg^d & feel it as a <u>picture</u> (of a pec^{ly} vivid kind) & any[t]hing wh reminds us that it is <u>but</u> a picture, such as change of scene, does not shock us, but any thing wh w^d be a defect in it even <u>as</u> a picture, does.

2. [The Arts in England]⁶

—in short in what department of art have the English as a people other than the narrowest & lowest conception In England Art in any high signification is a dead word. & not least is this true of the learned: when a speaker the other day on the Education board question said he wished the board to be composed of men not only liberal but learned he was paying himself with words—what was in his mind w^d have been better expressed by saying <u>not</u> learned but liberal[.] in England certainly & the remark applies in some measure everywhere the qualities wh make an academician are now as they ever have been the reverse of those which make a man 'liberal' & this not unnaturally or unreasonably—the scientific faculties & the steady application of them to scientific purposes must almost infallibly stand in the way of the various experience & the catholic habits of mind which original organization are the elemental qualities of an artistic character We say an artistic character advisedly the faculties which make a youth an artist are such as will absolutely prevent his becoming scientific. he may attain an artistic character which we [h]old to be a as [*sic*] far more admirible thing <u>per se</u>⁷

    [Shelley]⁸ was an artist

    Goethe had an artistic character (formed for himself)

3. [Italian Travel Journal]⁹

HTM traveled through Italy during the spring of 1839. During the trip she kept a small journal in which she recorded her impressions in pencil. The notebook included many blank pages headed only by a city name. The

---

6. Box III/105.

7. HTM drew two lines through the text beginning with "artistic" and ending at "per se."

8. Percy Bysshe Shelley, English poet (1792–1822).

9. Box II/63.

first page begins "Padua May 12ᵗʰ 1839," followed by pages for each of the following cities: Genoa, Cornice, Spezzia, Riviera, Pisa, Volterra, Road to Rome, Naples, Naples to Rome, Albano Tivoli, Rome, Terni, and Perugia. Writing begins on the page with "Florence" at the top.

Florence

quite worthy its reputation for beauty—the valley so exactly the right size to frame the city, which from whatever point one sees it is very beautiful. The best view is from the bank of the Arno opposite the Cascini, in the eveng. The Appenines are less beautifully shaped here than at any point at which I have seen them. I think the view of Florence from Fiesole the least pretty, as I think Fiesole the least pretty suburb of Florence. it quite agre[e]s with continental notions of country going that even the plague shᵈ drive Boccacio's company no further than Fiesole. Florence is the most indeed the only middle age looking place in Italy

The Gallery—the beautiful old Tuscan paintings—the badness of putting paintings & sculptures on gilded pedestals side by side, or within sight of each other.

The Bacchus & fawn.
The Tribune, the Niobe Venus

Bologna Ferrara.

the Pitti Palace[10]
The Boboli garden
The Cascini
The Palazzo Vecchio
The Quays
The bridges
The Churches & Music

Paduas.

Anecdote of Cardinal Albani (canaille)[11] of
Brindley the engineer of canals[12] of Michel Angelo & the Prior
History of Venice Daru's not so good

---

10. This list is of places in Florence which Harriet must have visited.

11. Scoundrel.

12. James Brindley (1716-1772), a pioneer English canal builder, built 360 miles of canals.

as Sismondi[13]

Horace's [Sorates][14]

Parva Domus, Magna Quies.[15]

thro' the whole day in Italy one is invited either to give or to take 'qualche
  cosa'[16]

Character of Maximilian

Bavaria &c representation

governments = Prussia

& Austria undertake to adjudicate between the princes & parliaments
  when they differ & of course always decide for the former.

The word Waldensee evidently Saxon & not derived from the Latin as
the stupid red book[17] says

Tyrolise braces.

Lafontaines saying of the regions below.

Danube the most famous river in history.

Stuttgart: 'si on ne cueillir pas les raisins la ville irait se noyer dans le
  vin.'[18]

from Florence to Bologna the road is extremely beautiful—saw the fire on
a mountain near Pietra Mala, it is on a small table-land at the top of a
little hill & near the base of the mountain overhanging Pietramala. The
fire which burns always covers a space of about fifteen feet. it is no doubt
some gas which takes fire when it touches common air.

Poggioli is a very pretty place. The inn is most beautifully situated it
is almost at the end of the hilly country.

Bologna is one of the finest Italian towns I have seen. The Gallery is
delightful. a Guido, & the crucifixion, the finest thing there, a large altar
piece of Guido & a Samson! a very fine Pietro Perugino & a Francia quantities

---

13. Pierre-Antoine Daru (1767-1829) published a seven volume *Histoire de la République de
Venise* in 1819. Simonde de Sismondi (1773-1842) published a sixteen-volume *Histoire des
républiques italiennes du moyen âge*, 1809-1818.

14. 65 BCE to 8 BCE. HTM may be referring to Horace's *Satires*, but the word in parenthesis
appears as is in the manuscript.

15. "Little house, great resting-place."

16. Something.

17. Baedecker's travel guides.

18. "If we don't pick the grapes the city will drown in wine."

of the Carracci Ludovico Annibale Agostino Domenichino Guido Guercino Albani[19] &c all of the Bolognese school. The Pelleguino a very good inn.

[empty page with "Ferrara. Padua." written at the top]

Ferrara somebody calls it uno vasto e bello Solitudine[20] — the cathedral a strange looking building Italian gothic & rather fine. I did not think the aspect of the town at all fine crossed the Po. Rovigo. Montselice. Abano with its inscription

Euganean hills. Shelley.
Petrarch[21]
Padua fine in the manner of Bologna but inferior
The Duomo (St Antonio)
St. Ginstina the strangest mosque like looking buildings. from Padua to
    Mestre this a very pretty excessively green & rich country. from Mestic
    to Venice two hours. Venice quite realises my idea of it & Canalletto's
    pictures.
Venetian school Titian
Paulo Veronese, Paris Bordone
Tintoretto, Bassano,
Giovanni Bellini,[22] a very fine collection in the Pallaggo Manferino

The Scoula delle Belle Arts[23] the most beautiful rooms in the world containing a splendid collection. This building was formerly a convent & the room which was the refectory has a most splendid golden & pictured roof & mosaic floor. here are very fine pictures of all the venetian school — a very fine assumption of Titian seeming to me to combine the amazing

---

19. Perugino (c. 1450-1523) was an Italian painter; Francia was the surname of an Italian family of painters and goldsmiths, 15th-16th centuries. The Carracci family of Renaissance artists included Ludovico (1555-1619), Annibale (1560-1609), and Agostino (1557-1602). Domenichino (1581-1641) and Guercino (1591-1666) were Renaissance painters. The other artists mentioned: Guido da Siena (1262?-127?) and Francesco Albani (1578-1660).

20. "A vast and beautiful place of solitude."

21. Percy Bysshe Shelley, English poet (1792-1822) who lived in exile in Italy; Petrarch (1304-74) Italian renaissance poet.

22. Italian Renaissance painters, as follows: Canaletto (1697-1768), famous for his scenes of Venice; Titian (c. 1485-1576); Veronese (1528-88); Bordone (1500-71); Jacopo Tintoretto (1519-94); Bassano, a family of early 16th- to early 17th-century painters; and Bellini (1431-1516).

23. School of Fine Arts.

quantity of colour of Raphael,[24] with the deep & strongly marked shadows which are characteristic of the Venetian school.

The collection in the Doge's[25] palace contains some fine things among a great number, in very fine rooms—but generally this collection is less fine than the others. a Europa of Paolo Veronese & a Bacchus & Ariadne of Tintoretto pleased me most. here also is a Paradise of Tintoret[to] the largest picture on canvas in Europe—the size is enormous. round the same hall are pictures of the Doges in the order they reigned: the character & expression & even physical complexion are singularly alike[.] the space for Marino fabrics is occupied by a blk painted curtain on which are the words: Hiec est locus Mar. Falic decapitati pro criminibus[26] by the way not particularly good latin

The churches have old names there is a St. Moses, St. Job, St. Zachariah

The churches of Santa Maria di Salute has three Luca Giordano's[27] containing the three facts in the life of the Virgin, a Giovanni Bellini &c a descent of the Holy Ghost by Titian at 64 the church is very fine & rich. as are all the Venetian churches St Giorgio Maggiore St Salvatore &c St Marks

from Venice to Mestic with four rowers two hours. in the midst of the lagune the boat is aborde by another which runs along side & thrusts in at the door the long pole & purse Judas like like that in the Chiesa del Arena at Padua, to quote for the Madonna del Mar whose little oratory is elevated on a pole close by—the customs officers invite a fee in lieu of examining ones effetti:[28] not a bad way of getting an average duty. From Mestic to Bassano posts, thro' the most verdant country. Bassano the loveliest situation possible—here the mountainous country begins but there is not a hill worth mentioning on the road all the way to Trent except a long descent into Trent. from Bassano to the lovely village Borgo di Val Sugano 4 posts & thence to Trent 2 ½. Trent on the Adige most beautiful & imposing as we approached it from Borgo. a very fine town with German spaciousness cleaness & <u>pleasant eatables</u>. delightful to find oneself in Germany again. At Borgo the inn people spoke german & there was german frankness niceness simplicity & hon-

24. Italian renaissance painter (1483-1520).

25. Elected chief magistrate of Venice.

26. "Here lies Mar. Falic, decapitated for his crimes."

27. The most celebrated painter in Naples in the late seventeenth century, Giordano lived from 1632 until 1705.

28. Belongings.

est charges. and from an opposite house, for the first time for six months the great pleasure of hearing the sound of german music played with ~~the~~ german touch on a german piano-forte. certainly the Italians have no taste for music.

From Trent to Brixen 8 ½ posts took us 12 hours. The inn at Brixen looked very large. stayed the night 25th at Brixen. inn[,] The Elephant, not good but tolerable. Brixen to Steinach 4 posts, took 8 hours inn the Post & not good but tolerable. Steinach to Innspruck 2 posts 4 hours Inns the Sun good & dear & the Golden Adler, the house in which Hofer,[29] lived, plain not very good & dear from Innspruck to Mittenwald posts took us   hours—the inn the post a decent country inn they took off half their charge on attempting to impose upon us Mittenwald to Munich posts took 13 hours—the road the most beautiful of the whole route—especially the Waldensee

Munich contrasts strangely & not unagreably with Italian cities—it looks so very new, so dear & spacious—200 years hence it will be fine. the Gly_____[30] is a fine gallery injured by the same bad poste as at Florence, the mixing gilding with sculpture. The finest things are the torso.

The loveliest thing imaginable; the Faun the Ceres & a bas relief of Hercules slaying Lycas[31]

Pinco   a fine gallery the cabinets very pleasant but the light coming from the side not good in such very small rooms. The most remarkable things are the Rembrandts & together the Rubens, wh raise ones estimation of Rubens, especially a very nice Virgin & child & several beautiful Murillo's.[32]

Altogether Munich is a most cheerful happy looking place & if as dissipated as people say presents an argument for dissipation.

---

29. Andreas Hofer (1767-1810), Tirolese patriot and popular hero.

30. A space is left in the text here. Harriet is probably referring to the Glyptothek, an art museum designed by Leo von Klenze (1784-1864) and built between 1816 and 1830.

31. HTM may be referring to Canova's sculpture *Hercules and Lychas* (also spelled "Lichas"), 1802, or to the Red-figured Kylix in the style of Douris which depicts Hercules slaying *Linus* and which is owned by the State Collection of Classical Art and Glyptotek in Munich. Neither, however, fits her description of a bas-relief.

32. Rembrandt Harmensz. van Rijn (1606-69); Peter Paul Rubens (1577-1640); Bartolome Murillo (1617-1682).

4. BOOK REVIEWS

a. The Wondrous Tale of Alroy[33]

This new work of the author of Vivian Grey and Contarini Fleming[34] is of a quite different class to either of its predecessors as the title indicates it is a story of by gone times and in so much appears to be a more suitable feild for the author's talent than the delineation of character or the construction of physological autobiography. There is shown in those works an absence of both the contemplative and analytical habit of mind which are needful to the comprehension of any emotion which has not actually formed part of the individual experience, and of any fixed theory of moral principles, with an evident, almost ostentatious display of carelessness on such points. In the Tale of Alroy the author paints rather than describes — and this is his province. He appears to have a most vivid enjoyment of physical and inanimate beauty, and the taste which is innate in persons of acute sensations. This is the temperament for improvisitation: and the carelessness of the style might lead to the supposition that the whole was improvised within a very short time. It is often poetry in posse:[35] least so however where occasionally we stumble upon two or three pages or sentances which rhyme, and which have an odd enough effect — as tho what was intended to be the poetical portion of the book had been mosaic-worked into the prose from some other work. The real poetry is in the completeness with which it wraps the senses in the scenes and objects it describes or suggests. as we read we are unconscious of receiving any impression from the white paper and printers ink. The space between the eye and the book glitters with gems. We are environed by gorgeous eastern sights and sounds — sunshine & perfumes & beauty & triumph. The very type, bold and untroublesome, 'meandering like a river of print through an oceean of margin,' savours of Oriental ease, and each page contains a picture. The melodramatic effect is perfect. There needs neither scene nor actor — as by the Arabian nights a spectacle is presented to the mind of each reader, varying in colouring and grouping as the fancy and the imagination vary. There should have been no story, or a better. It is a heap of eastern images

---

33. Written on paper watermarked 1832. Box III/83. *The Wondrous Tale of Alroy* was published in 1833.

34. Benjamin Disraeli.

35. Temporarily.

with little order or connection, yet all Orient pearls, though at random strung: words of beauty are clustered upon each other—reiterated, in language soft and glowing, like a dreamy chorus.[36] It is beautiful enough to bring back our Childish Arabian nights pleasures so beautiful is it that as in the case of so many other beautiful things it makes us sad that where so much is done, so much remains undone. There is a story but object it has none, and unless the plot be wholly historical, which we do not conceive to be the case, there seems no reason why the plot might not have had a good moral as easily as a bad one (or none at all) unless indeed the authors experience leaves him without faith in any consistent or enduring purity of purpose or moral energy. The attempt to delineate noble mindedness seems an effort or mere occasion for pompous language. The character infallibly breaks down sooner or later.

[37]Here is a strain, worthy to be chanted by Babylon's waters—the feast of the New Moon is one of the most important of the Hebrew festivals. "She comes not yet! her cheerful form not yet it sparkles in our mournful sky! She comes not yet! The shadowy stars seem sad and lustreless without their Queen. She comes not yet!"

> "We are the watchers of the
> Moon and live in loneliness
> to herald light."

"She comes not yet! her sacred form, not yet it summons to our holy feast. She comes not yet! our brethren far wait mute and motionless the saintly beam.
She comes not yet!"

> "We are the watchers of the
> Moon, and live in loneliness
> to herald light."

"She comes, she comes! her beauteous form sails with soft splendour in the glittering air. She comes, she comes! The beacons fire, and tell the nations that the month begins! She comes, She comes!"

> "We are the watchers of the
> Moon, to tell the nations
> that the month begins."

---

36. Another draft is the same until this point, but adds the following passage.

37. The original text continues from this point without a paragraph indentation.

Instantly the holy watchers fired the beacons on the mountain top, and anon a thousand flames blaze round the land. From Caucasus to Lebanon, on every peak a crown of light!

b. ART IX.-*The Present State of Australia; a Description of the Country, its Advantages and Prospects with reference to Emigration, and a particular Account of the Manners, Customs, and Condition of its Aboriginal Inhabitants.*
By Robert Dawson, Esq.,
late Chief Agent to the Australian Agricultural Company.[38]

The next thing to the personal enjoyment of the cloudless skies and sunny prospects of a southern climate, is to read of them in such a book as this of Mr. Dawson's where, without being convicts, we may enjoy in fancy all the charms of that paradise of evil-doers, New South Wales.

The author's pursuits led him repeatedly into the wildest paths of this unfrequented region. The whole country presents the appearance of a vast forest, occasionally broken into glades and vistas of great beauty.

"The hills are every where clothed with wood to their summits, with eternal verdure beneath them, in their natural state, unaccompanied by brush or underwood, so that we are often reminded of gentlemen's pleasure grounds seen from a distance." — "I could discern, to a considerable distance, the bendings of the stream, which was marked by a fringe of casurino and mimosa plants. The sun was just receding behind the western ranges, which on that side bounded this comparatively extensive plain. The beautiful effect of its departing rays, as reflected from the opposite hills and broken ranges in the distance, formed a magnificent picture. The stillness of the scene was only interrupted by the chirping of grasshoppers, and the grazing of the horses upon the luxuriant herbage at a short distance from the tent." —Pp. 52, 190. Alone, with the exception of a few attendants, he met the native savages, of whom we have heard so formidable a description; and here we have, perhaps, the most interesting portion of the work, an impartial and picturesque account of the aborigines of the country:

"The natives are a mild and harmless race of savages; and when any mischief has been done by them, the cause has generally arisen, I believe, in bad treatment by their white neighbours. They have usually been treated

---

38. *Monthly Repository*, 1831: V, 58-59.

in distant parts of the colony as if they had been dogs, and shot by convict servants, at a distance from society, for the most trifling causes. The natives complained to me frequently that 'white pellow' shot their relations and friends, and shewed me many orphans whose parents had fallen by the hands of white men near this spot. They pointed out one white man, who they said had killed ten; and the wretch did not deny it, but said he would kill them whenever he could." — "Their painted bodies, white teeth, shock heads of hair; their wild and savage appearance, with the reflection of the fire in a dark night, would have formed a terrific spectacle to any person coming suddenly and unexpectedly upon them. They are, however, one of the best-natured people in the world, and would never hurt a white man if treated with civility and kindness." — Pp. 57, 68.

Most of this gentleman's attention appears to have been given to the observation of the capabilities of the climate and soil of the colony for rearing sheep for the production of wool; and the result, in his opinion, is, that the fleeces of New South Wales might, under good management, compete with the finest productions of Europe.

Our limits will not allow us to do justice, by longer extracts, to this interesting volume, which we recommend to our readers as by much the most full and clear account which has yet appeared of New South Wales, and of the objects to be kept in view by persons proposing to settle there.

c. Review of *Tour of a German Prince.* Vols. III and IV. E. Wilson.[39]

Our faith in the identity of the 'German Prince' is not lessened by this his re-appearance in an English dress, although with such perfect tact and skill is this garb managed, that, but for the often-recurring evidence of a very un-English, Catholic spirit, both in feeling and in the mode of viewing things, we might have been led into the mistake of believing otherwise. Few works of its pretension have been more criticised, and often with a severity which would be unaccountable, but for the fact that in this land of 'caste' he avows his sympathy with the *paria,* — and that he does not hesitate to speak his mind of religious intolerance and religious extortion, — these are the unpardonable sins of Prince Puckler Muskau's authorship. His unbounded coxcombry is rather amusing than offensive, and if unconsciousness be the sign of health, he is sound indeed. Too much

39. *Monthly Repository,* 1832: VI, 353-54.

praise cannot be awarded to the translator,[40] though we must regret that such a complete facility in rendering this language, so rich and full of meaning, should not be more worthily employed—lamentable is it, that there should be place for a doubt of the reception which the works of Goethe, of Richter, and a host of others, would meet in this country. Surely the time indicated in the translator's preface, is not distant,—'Whenever I find that the English public are likely to receive, with any degree of favour, such a German work as it would be my greatest pride and pleasure to render into my native tongue to the best of my ability, I shall be too happy to share with the illustrious and humanizing poets and philosophers of Germany any censure, as I should feel it the highest honour to partake in the minutest portion of their glory. Hitherto I have found no encouragement to hope that any such work as I should care to identify myself with would find readers.'

d. Review of *Domestic Manners of the Americans.* 2 vols. Mrs. Trollope.[41]

AMERICA—the nursery of civil freedom; the growing and vigorous disproof of the theory of the necessity of leavening the reason and the demands of the present age, by an anomalous admixture with the opinions and institutions which were wisdom to our fore-fathers, but for the present state of society are worse than foolishness;—that gigantic territory which lay unknown for ages, ripening for the dominion of civilized man, and which less than three centuries has sufficed to transform, from an unbroken forest, to the home of twelve millions of human beings, speaking the language of, and acknowledging their derivation from, an island, which, had we the desiderated lever of Archimedes, might be set down in one of its unoccupied prairie-meadows, without displacing a living thing—this country, as vast and as important in its moral as in its physical aspect, presents to every intelligent mind a subject of contemplation and curiosity which constantly demand materials and knowledge. As yet this demand has been but scantily answered. It has unfortunately chanced that, with few exceptions, the descriptions of the United States have been those of persons either of small intellect, and incapable, with their best efforts, of judging between that which is essential and that which is accidental, as

---

40. Sarah Austin.

41. *Monthly Repository*, 1832: VI, 401-6.

instance Basil Hall; or, worse, those whose prejudices make their principles, and whose long-formed habits of subserviency make them fancy
servility refinement, and its absence coarseness: and of this latter class is
the author before us. We are always sorry to see any species of talent
wasted; and it was with this feeling we laid down the two volumes of Mrs.
Trollope. The descriptions are spirited, and the style so easy and pleasant,
that she would seem to possess every mechanical facility for recording,
amusingly, any and all the adventures which fate or her own good pleasure
may induce her to try. But here ends all of praise which can be accorded
to this book. It abounds in misrepresentations, which we cannot but think
wilful, and the deductions from which are as spiteful as they are imbecile.
To cover the rancour of her dislike to republicanism, the author makes a
sort of confession that she had herself a leaning to what she wittily calls
sedition, before she saw in America the lamentable effects of freedom and
competence; which bad effect she makes to consist in certain coarsenesses
of manner among the middle and lower classes, which, as they do not
happen to be of precisely the same sort as those of the corresponding rank
here, excite the good lady's spleen to the utmost; but which, after all, were
the habits and manners of those good old times, of which Mrs. Trollope
is, doubtless, an especial admirer. She admits that the best society in
America equals, in refinement of manner, even that of the 'old countrie';
while in no class is to be found the empty-headedness, which forms the
grand characteristic of our sleek-mannered aristocracy.

'The total and universal want of manners, both in males and females,
is so remarkable, that I was constantly endeavouring to account for it. It
certainly does not proceed from want of intellect. I have listened to much
dull and heavy conversation in America, but rarely to any that I could
strictly call silly.' 'They appear to me to have clear heads and active
intellects; are more ignorant on subjects that are only of conventional value
than on such as are of intrinsic importance.'—(Vol. i., p. 63.)

This seems scarcely consistent with the continual reiteration of the utter
nothingness of the women: 'in America, where women are guarded by a
seven-fold shield of habitual insignificance,'—p. 96; an odd sort of shield
that; again:—'It is obvious, that the ladies who are brought up amongst
them cannot have leisure for any development of the mind: it is, in fact,
out of the question; and, remembering this, it is more surprising that some
among them should be very pleasing, than that none should be highly
instructed.'—(p. 81.)

Presently, forgetting, we suppose, all she had said about the neglect of
the women's minds, the good lady attempts to be very satirical on the
extent of the education they receive.

'I attended the annual public exhibition at this school, and perceived, with some surprise, that the higher branches of science were among the studies of the pretty creatures I saw assembled there. One lovely girl of sixteen *took her degree* in mathematics, and another was examined in moral philosophy. They blushed so sweetly, and looked so beautifully puzzled and confounded, that it might have been difficult for an abler judge than I was to decide how far they merited the diploma they received. This method of letting young ladies graduate, and granting them diplomas on quitting the establishment, was quite new to me.'—(p. 114.)

Here the ridicule is intended to fall on the words,—'pretty creatures, lovely girl,' &c.: if there is no absurdity in the fact stated, we cannot perceive that it makes any difference whether the pupils were pretty creatures or ugly creatures, boys or girls; but it was an opportunity of blame, and that is Mrs. Trollope's object; in fact, towards the end of her book she distinctly declares her dislike to every thing American.

'I do not like them, I do not like their principles, I do not like their manners, I do not like their opinions; both as a woman, and as a stranger, it might be unseemly for me to say that I do not like their government, and therefore I will not say so.'

This is about as logical as the old rhyme,—

> 'I do not like you, Dr. Fell,
> The reason why I cannot tell,
> Only this I know full well,
> I do not like you, Dr. Fell!'

Only that 'the reason why,' we doubt not our author *could* tell, if she would.

'The immense superiority of the American to the British navy was a constant theme, and to this I always listened, as nearly as possible, in silence. But the favourite, the constant, the universal sneer that met me every where, was on our old-fashioned attachments to things obsolete. It is amusing to observe how soothing the idea seems, that they are more modern, more advanced, than England. Our classic literature, our princely dignities, our noble institutions, are all gone-by relics of the dark ages. This, and the vastness of their naked territory, make up the flattering unction which is laid upon the soul, as an antidote to the little misgivings which from time to time arise, lest their large country be not of quite 'so much importance among the nations, as a certain paltry, old-fashioned little place that they wot of.'—(p. 225.)

'I took some pains to ascertain what they meant by their glorious institutions; and it is with no affectation of ignorance that I profess I never could comprehend the meaning of the phrase, which is, however, on the lip of every American, when he talks of his country.'—(p. 227.)

'Their unequalled freedom, I think, I understand better. Their code of common law is built upon ours; and the difference between us is this,—in England the laws are acted upon, in America they are not.'—(p. 228.)

In discussing questions relating to their government, and its effects on the social and moral condition of the people, Mrs. Trollope resorts to the old expedient of taking benefit of sanctuary, and deprecating criticism, on the plea of sex; now, if she understand the subjects upon which she attempts to write, there surely needs no apology for stating her opinion; if she were conscious that she did not understand them, it would have been wise to have left them untouched. The old custom of making gentle critiques for gentle authors is, we hope, falling fast to disuse; and women, as well as men, must be content that their works, and not themselves, form the subject of judgment. Let both one and the other write only of what they feel and understand; the time is passed for the toleration of crudeness and vapidity under shelter of either sex or rank.

Here is one of those sweeping decisions in which our author loves to indulge; its severity somewhat mitigated by the saving clause of which we have spoken:—

'All the freedom enjoyed in America, beyond what is enjoyed in England, is enjoyed solely by the disorderly, at the expense of the orderly; and were I a stout knight, either of the sword or of the pen, I would fearlessly throw down my gauntlet, and challenge the whole Republic to prove the contrary; but being, as I am, a feeble looker on, with a needle for my spear, and "I talk," for my device, I must be contented with the power of stating the fact, perfectly certain that I shall be contradicted by one loud shout from Maine to Georgia.' (p. 148.)

As an amusing instance of the determination to find fault, of pretended humility, and of inconsequent conclusion, take the following remarks:

'If I mistake not, every debate I listened to in the American Congress was upon one and the same subject; namely, the entire independence of each individual state, with regard to the federal government. The jealousy on this point appeared to me to be the strongest political feeling that ever got possession of the mind of man. I do not pretend to judge the merits of the question. I speak solely of the very singular effect of seeing man after man start eagerly to his feet, to declare that the greatest injury, the basest injustice, the most obnoxious tyranny, that could be practised against the state of which he was a member, would be a vote of a few millions of dollars, for the purpose of making their roads or canals, or for drainage, or, in short, for any purpose of improvement whatsoever.

'One great boast of the country is, that they have no national debt, or that they shall have none in two years. This seems not very wonderful, considering their productive tariff, and that the income paid to their president is 6000£ per annum, other salaries being in proportion, and internal improvements, at the expense of the government treasury, being voted unconstitutional.' (p. 21.)

'This seems not very wonderful, considering'—but the wonder consists in the consideration that this immense country is governed, to the entire satisfaction of all its inhabitants, at a cost of a trifling part of the sum paid for the misgovernment of the 'old fashioned little place.' But the lady thinks an enormous taxation an advantage, which, to be duly appreciated, needs but to be lost.

'The low rate of taxation, too, unquestionably permits a more rapid accumulation of individual wealth than with us; but till I had travelled through America, I had no idea how much of the money collected in taxes returns among the people, not only in the purchase of what their industry furnishes, but in the actual enjoyment of what is furnished. Were I an English legislator, instead of sending sedition to the Tower, I would send her to make a tour of the United States.'

Our author, after making a comparison between London or Paris, and the larger cities of the Union, of course greatly to the disadvantage of the latter, makes this very candid acknowledgement: 'Now God forbid that any reasonable American (of whom there are so many millions) should ever come to ask me what I mean; I should find it very difficult, nay, perhaps, utterly impossible to explain myself.'

Mrs. Trollope pays her tribute of high admiration to the talents of the star of the west, Dr. Channing.

'As a preacher he has, perhaps, hardly a rival anywhere. This gentleman is an Unitarian, and I was informed by several persons well acquainted with the literary characters of the country, that nearly all their distinguished men were of this persuasion.' (p. 156.)

She is, and most justly, disgusted with their cant about religious matters, with hypocrisy of the teachers, and the imbecile credulity of the taught. But before we can allow this to be a national trait of the Americans only, we must find our own sectarians wonderfully altered.

It has been said; that absence strengthens strong feelings, and weakens weak ones: travel has an analogous effect in increasing prejudice, where it already exists, or in enlarging the knowledge of those who are capable of loving truth for itself: in this class, we fear, the author of these volumes cannot yet be placed. She can see but one side of a question; and that, unfortunately, is not the fairest or the happiest side. The world might be divided into those whose eye rests first on the good and the beautiful in every object, moral or physical, which can be presented to it; and with whom to see evil, is to bend their minds to its removal: or, the larger number, those who would hide, rather than eradicate abuse; with whom ignorance is, if not bliss, at least content, and whose capacity of admiring stands always on the defensive, while their critical faculties are more readily roused to irritation, than their admiring ones to imitation of any good, national or individual, which they do not themselves posses. But these also, like every thing else, may do good in their generation. And so we hope Mrs. Trollope's lucubrations may become useful, by calling attention to subjects which cannot be too much canvassed, though we cannot but express a wish that her next performance may be on a subject, which, not calling for the expression of her political antipathies, may allow us unreservedly to admire her power of facile and graceful composition.

e. Review of *Hampden: Some Memorials of John Hampden, his Party and his Times.* By Lord Nugent. 2 vols. 8 vo. London: Murray. 1832.[42]

'To form, according to the best evidence within our reach, our conclusions as to the sincerity of his objects, their tendency, and extent,—as to the exigencies which may have justified, and the wisdom and moderation with which he pursued them,—is what surely may be undertaken, if not with a mind altogether uninfluenced by preconceived impressions, at least in a spirit not to be betrayed by them into injustice. Nor is it an occupation uninteresting, to such as have any desire to deal truly with the memory of a person who acted a great part in one of the greatest events that ever befell England.' Such Lord Nugent declares to have been his object in the composition and publication of this work, which will connect his name in the literature of his country with that of one of her worthiest children. Much novelty we did not expect to find. Hampden's was a race which, though short, was too glorious, and too much placed before the eyes of all men, not to have made it necessary that we should, long ere this, have known all that could be known concerning his history, his thoughts and his opinions. Accordingly, with the exception of a few letters which passed between him and his tried friend, Sir John Eliot, during that illegal imprisonment of the latter, which ended in consigning his worn-out frame to

42. *Monthly Repository,* 1832: VI, 443-50.

the grave, and his cowardly oppressor to the block he so justly merited, we have no new light thrown upon it here; but that which we had before to gather, from the often contradictory authorities of Clarendon, Denham, Hume, or Godwin, is sifted and arranged with impartiality and elegance. Lord Nugent's book will take its place among English classics. Would that the men of fortune of the present day, who share in the general and increasing taste for literature, would profit by his example, and employ their time on biography, that inexhaustible and always interesting subject, rather than on such ephemera as are most modern novels and even 'Personal Narratives!'—To collect materials, internal and external, to qualify for the editorship of a good biography, is an undertaking which requires much time and fortune; and in no way could those advantages be more usefully employed. What work of fiction can ever interest our sympathies so deeply as the adventures of those who, in good truth, have voluntarily suffered for the benefit of their fellow-creatures?—the names of Hampden, of Pym, of Sidney, of Vane, are indissolubly linked with our first boyish instinct of love of liberty: we pity him for whom those names do not awaken a host of associations and bring back youthful dreams of high daring, and lofty purpose, and chivalrous honour, and constancy unto the death.—There is a charm in these things which we never lose, because it has its origin in the principle, eternally fixed in humanity, of opposition to wrong. We love to look back to the old picturesque times of feudal domination, and popular discontent, while sincerely do we hope they may never again return: we look to them for lights on the motives and workings of the human mind;— we see resolved in them the problem of the effect of actions and passions, which effect the men who acted and felt could only surmise and doubtingly hope; we are interested in them as in an important chapter in the chronicle of the world's history. And they were, for their purpose, fine and grand times, those, when the need of protection gave a species of devotion to the loyalty of the lowly, and the proud consciousness of protecting invested with a factitious nobility the grossness of self-interest. Then, as since, liberty and religion were banner-words, and perhaps by the mass have been in all times equally little understood. But, since those high and palmy feudal days, a great moral change has been steadily taking place. One of tyranny's strongest defences is founded in that blind belief of the many in the sacredness of whatever is in any way superior to them, arising from the principle of reverence, innate in every human mind, and which, if it be enlightened, is the noblest, and if servile, the meanest, of human emotions. When John's victorious barons established an oligarchy more hateful than the tyranny which it curbed, because more intimately and securely interwoven with what was denominated law, the numbers saw, with stupid vacancy, or with unthinking admiration, the liberty of the subject emblazoned on their bearings. Their boasted charter partook more of the nature of a patent of nobility, than of a popular defence. Yet so omnipotent have names ever been found with the multitude, that it was not until four centuries after the establishment of that charter, that the people discovered that they had been cheated by a shadow in the name of a reality.

The pampered and greedy selfishness of Henry the Eighth, intent only on the gratification of his degraded passions, was the cause of the overthrow of the Catholic faith as a state form, and thereby of the commencement of an important revolution in the habits and education of the English people. In abandoning their ancient worship, they also dared to question the authority for the doctrine of passive submission which marked the whole band of the ministers of the court of Rome. Not but that every religion, suffering under the baneful influence of union with the state, will almost necessarily hold the same tone; it has always been so, whatever the faith protected, but that fact was not yet felt. Luther, and his brother reformers of the church, were amply disposed to reform the state also, could they have found the power; and, as in the case of all new institutions, the first apostles of Protestantism sought popularity by a show of moderation. True, both Henry and his successors attempted, and often with some success, to unite the old awe of the spiritual, with that of their temporal authority, but it never again bound the minds of men in that entire and willing thraldom which had done. The sacredness of mystery was gone. Men had been reared in belief of the immutability of that spiritual power, and of its superiority to all kings, princes, and powers; and when the insolent tyrant dared, unpunished, to question its tenets, supplant its authority, and appropriate its wealth, the charm of habitual reverence, while it left the church, was not transferred to the throne. There sprung up in its place the small beginnings of those habits of inquiry, which, step by step, have led, in our time, to universal doubt. This doubt even, we think to be promising of good—to be a transition to purified belief. To construct a stable foundation we must first clear the ground. It is not less needful in moral than in mental progression that analysis should precede synthesis. And the wisest and loftiest of our time see cause of hope in its signs. But the first effect of men's change of faith was to leave them more free for the consideration of their political condition. The quick tact of Elizabeth saw the bent of the popular mind: with consummate skill and energy she discerned the points on which she must inevitably yield, she made her concessions before the people had become aware of their power:

so that they received from her as acts of grace, what she only had the foresight to see she would have been obliged to concede as pure right. Thus she not only prevented further demands, but in the very fact of so doing won the hearts of her subjects. But less than her talent could not have effected the same result. The weak-minded egotist who succeeded her, invited contempt for his person and for his office; but it remained for the blind pertinacity of his son to put the finish to the work. The English have always been proverbial for their sensitiveness where their purses are concerned; and though they might have borne, for a time, even greater political humiliation, they were not disposed both to bear it and to pay for it. The political feelings of the people were roused into action by pecuniary injustice. But among the men, whose distinction, though not their ability, was born of the tyrannous exactions of the first Charles, were some of the first spirits of any time. They dared openly to proclaim the nullity of law when opposed to justice and reason. Hampden, especially, was a man not of this or that time only, but whose mind was prepared to expand indefinitely. He appeared in parliament at the age of twenty-seven, and was even then distinguished. After serving in two parliaments he retired, in 1628, to his house in Buckinghamshire. There he passed the next eleven years, in the quiet and reflection, which are the only efficient preparatives for useful exertion. There are at any one time in the world few such men as Hampden. It is one of the most remarkable and admirable traits of his character, that, with the ability to guide others and to meet the most unlooked-for emergencies, he was not only content, he preferred, living within the little world of his affections and of his own high thoughts. The finest combination of human character is that of calm and trusting simplicity of manner and habits, with the strength of purpose which uncontrollably produces that which it has maturely willed:—such was Hampden's. During this period he could have been but of little use in public. It was passed in a series of the most flagrant acts of tyranny and injustice on the part of the king, and on that of the people in an untired opposition. Imprisoned, branded, fined, and executed, their determination seemed to grow more firm by defeat; their detestation and forbearance arrived at its height. Hampden watched the spirit of the time: he saw the hour and the occasion when united resistance must succeed. He took upon himself the danger. He was the first to refuse payment of the illegal tax, which though it fell lightly upon himself individually, would, had the people then succumbed, have been the means of riveting the disgraceful bonds, which were offered them. He announced his intention to try in the courts of law the great question which involved the right of one man to unlimited control over the persons and property of every inhabitant of the kingdom. Clarendon, whose leaning to the court interest hinges most of his conclusions, is forced to yield admiring testimony to his hearing during this arduous period. He says, 'till this time he was rather of reputation in his own country, than of public discourse or fame in kingdom; but then he grew the argument of all tongues, every man inquiring who and what he was that durst, at his own charge, support the liberty and prosperity of the kingdom. His carriage throughout that agitation, was with that rare temper and modesty, that they who watched him narrowly to find some advantage against his person, to make him less resolute in his cause, were compelled to give him a just testimony!' As might have been expected, the venial court decided for its patron. The King then set his agents at work to endeavour by bribery or intimidation to secure the connivance or the silence of the man whose talents he estimated sufficiently to dread; but he had not in this attempt estimated the force of the principles which he had to encounter. Having refused both bribes and submission, the leaders of the popular party, among which Hampden was now perhaps the first, felt themselves no longer safe while within reach of the despotic usurpation which they could not yet crush. They determined for a time to leave England. It was by a remarkable and fortunate want of policy that John Hampden and Oliver Cromwell, his cousin, were arrested by an order from the king on board the ship in which they had taken their passage for North America. Thus did Charles, by illegal force, retain in England the man by whose masterly councils the war was carried on, which ended in the forfeit of his life, and the man who was to succeed to his throne.

After a lapse of eight years, during which the king had resorted to every expedient which he could contrive, to prop up his tottering authority, without a meeting of Parliament, in November, 1640, was held the first meeting of what is emphatically called the Long Parliament: Hampden's place was by all accorded to him among the most influential, and with just self-knowledge he ranged himself foremost in the patriot ranks. Clarendon well describes the influence of his character at this time. 'When this Parliament began, the eyes of all men were fixed upon him, as their *patriœ pater,* and the pilot that must steer the vessel through the tempests and rocks which threatened it. And I am persuaded his power and interest at that time were greater to do good or hurt than any man's in the kingdom, or than any man of his rank hath had in any time; for his reputation of honesty was universal, and his affections seemed so publicly guided, that no corrupt or private ends could bias them. He was of an industry and vigilance not to be tired out or wearied by the most laborious, and of parts not to be imposed upon by the most subtle and sharp.' At this time the natural progress of affairs was once more checked, and a last chance given to the king by the ascendancy which the moderate party suddenly acquired in the House of Commons: men felt themselves on the eve of a convulsion, fearful in its progress and the end of which was most uncertain; all the horrors of civil wars were before them and they made, in the famous 'Remonstrance,' an appeal, which, had Charles not been utterly infatuated, must have been accepted by him with eagerness. They were willing to pass over in silence his manifold acts of treachery, cruelty, and falsehood: they offered him, unquestioned, all the power and wealth which the law had ever allotted for the support of the dignity, office, or pleasure of the crown; but the man was wholly blinded by selfishness to the real position in which he stood with regard to the country, and in the sword which was suspended as by a hair above his head, he fancied he could discern an instrument with which to enforce the slavery of millions. The answer to the 'respectful' remonstrance of his faithful Commons, was an order, in violation of every law on the subject for the arrest and impeachment of the principal leaders of the opposition: this was in the month of January, 1642, and this may well be considered as the commencement of the war between Charles Stuart and the English people, and it was also the era of the Hampden's short but brilliant course of active exertion. Accepting a command in the army, he enlisted his tenants and friends into his little band: wearing the colours of his family, the green, which betokens hope, and carrying at their head their leader's motto, 'Vestigia Nulla Retrorsum,'[43] they followed him to the field where he fought and died for the good cause of human amelioration. He met his death in a manner worthy of him, not in an act of technical duty but in one of generous choice. 'Some of his friends would have dissuaded him from adventuring his person with the cavalry, on a service which did not properly belong to him, wishing him rather to leave it to those officers of lesser note, under whose immediate command the picquets were. But wherever danger was, and hope of service to the cause, there Hampden ever felt that his duty lay.'—p. 431. He put himself at the head of the attack, and in the first charge he received his death-wounds. 'His head bending down, and his hands resting on his horse's neck, he was seen riding off the field before the action was done, a thing says Clarendon, "he never used to do, and from which it was concluded he was hurt." It is a tradition, that he was seen first moving in the direction of his father-in-

---

43. "There are no backward footsteps." Similar to the phrase "He has burned his bridges."

law's house at Pyrton; there he had in youth married the first wife of his love, and with her he would have gone to die. But Rupert's cavalry were covering the plain between. Turning his horse's head, therefore, he rode back across the grounds of Hazeley in his way to Thame. At the brook which divides the parishes; he paused awhile; but it being impossible for him in his wounded state to remount, if he had alighted to turn his horse over, he suddenly summoned his strength, clapped spurs and cleared the leap. In great pain and almost fainting, he reached Thame, and was conducted to the house of one Ezekiel Brown, where, his wounds being dressed, the surgeon would, for a while, have given him hopes of life. But he felt that his hurt was mortal; and, indulging no weak expectations of recovery, he occupied the few days that remained to him in despatching letters of counsel to the Parliament, in prosecution of his favourite plan.' — p. 435. His last words were a prayer for his country; and the news of his loss was the signal for universal sorrow. 'All the troops that could be spared from the quarters round joined to escort the honoured corpse to its last resting-place, once his beloved abode among the hills and woods of the Chilterns. They followed him to his grave in the parish church close adjoining his mansion, their arms reversed, their drums, and ensigns muffled, and their heads uncovered. Thus they marched, singing the 90th psalm as they proceeded to the funeral, and 43d as they returned.' — p. 440. And thus died Hampden. It is impossible to read this simple detail without being strongly affected. The cause for which he had perilled his all, seemed, at the time of his death, to be on the point of succumbing less before the vigour of its opponents than the weakness of its own counsellors. It must have been bitter to die at the moment when he must have been conscious that his were the talents most efficient for his beloved cause, and when his clear judgment had already discerned the deficiencies of its leaders. We, who know as matter of long-past history, that result which his earnest gaze could only dimly and doubtingly see shadowed forth in the future, may feel a melancholy gratification in the fact, that he was spared the sight of the unworthiness of some of those on whom his hopes were placed, and the eventual recall of the dynasty by means of which he and his country had so deeply suffered. But his sacrifice, and that of the numbers of brave and honourable men who fell in the same conflict, was not in vain, did it achieve no more than afford a pattern and precedent for succeeding years. Who shall say what extremes tyranny might have dared, or to what excess of subjection men might have believed themselves forced to submit, had not the example of the conduct of Hampden and his compatriots, and of the death of Charles, been alive in the world's memory? Wherever, since, men have armed themselves with courage to beard usurpation or oppression, the English Commons of the 17th century have been quoted for an example of right, and for a ground of hope: instructing each individual to do his best for the prevalence of his own honest notions of right, secure that in the end right must prevail.

Over the bust of Hampden in the Temple of British Worthies, is this inscription: "With great courage and consummate abilities, he began a noble opposition to an arbitrary court in defence of the liberties of his country, supported them in Parliament, and died for them in the field: Let us revere his memory!"

f. Review of *Mirabeau's Letters, —During His Residence in England*[44]

This is a very tempting title, but a very disappointing book. We know no distinguished person of late times, whose character was so likely to have been thoroughly displayed in his correspondence, as that of Mirabeau. All that was good, as well as all that was bad in him, was matter of impulse. Without either superstition on the one hand, or reflection on the other, he was wanting in fixed principles of action. But with a strong, though vague, feeling of attachment to the cause of freedom, wrought almost into passion by reiterated attacks upon his own; with acute perceptions, and a woman's talent of observation, we should have expected his really confidential correspondence to have been exceedingly curious and amusing. The translator

---

44. an insignificant occurrence,—I happened one day to quote in her hearing a sentence from Kant's writings:—"There are two objects, which the more I contemplate them, the more they fill my mind with astonishment,—the starry heaven above me, and the moral law within me." *"Ah! que cela est beau,"* she exclaimed *"il faut que je l'ecris* [*sic*];" [Oh! how beautiful that is . . . I must write it down]—and she was instantly at her *tablettes*. Some years afterwards I was amused by reading in Corinne—*"Car, comme un philosophe Allemand a tres bien dit, pour les coeurs sensibles il y'a deux choses,"* [For, as a German philosopher has said very well, for tender hearts there are two things] & c. Thus Kant,—one of the profoundest thinkers, but at the same time, one of the coolest and most unimpassioned of men, on account of the expression of a thought wise but not recondite, which places in juxta-position the two greatest phenomena, the one of the natural, and the other of the moral world,—becomes a *tender heart*! No wonder that a person so incurably French should have some repulsive qualities in the eyes of such thorough Germans as Goethe and Schiller. On the other hand, old Wieland was quite fascinated by her. But then Wieland was more French in his tastes that any other eminent German in his day. One evening after a display of great eloquence on the part of our hostess, Wieland turned to me, and folding his hands and looking upwards, with a sort of pious sentimentality exclaimed, "Ach Gott! dass ich bis in meinem vier und siebzigsten Jahr leben sollte, um solch ein Geschöpf guschen,—Oh that I should live into my seventy-fourth year in order to see such a creature!" [HTM]

Monthly Repository, 1832: VI, 604-8. [Ed.]

of these two volumes of letters, tells us, that there exist some hundreds of others of not inferior interest. We cannot but fancy that with respect to those here given any change would have been for the better. The Notice of the Life, Character, Conduct, and Writings of the Author, prefixed to them, forms a sort a 'scandalosum supplementum' to Dumont's amusing memoir. And surely the conservative spleen of the wickedest of Quarterly reviewers could not have made out a stronger case against a condemned radical author, than does, we suppose unconsciously, this pseudo-'graphical delineator' of poor much-abused and much bepraised Mirabeau. The best part of the book is that which relates to the politics of the time. Mirabeau was an enthusiast of the measures and character of Chatham, whose opinions and those of his celebrated son were on many subjects the opposite of each other; and on none did they differ more widely than those of religious toleration and ecclesiastical property. The latter question was then beginning to be actively mooted in France, as it is now in our own country.

Mirabeau saw, very clearly, the evils of the commonly received notion of the inviolability of foundations, whatever their object, or however unsuitable they might have become to the use or the intelligence of the time. He saw that a government, meaning always by government the true representation of the national will, must inherently possess the right to alter, to abrogate, to suppress the distribution of its own pecuniary and physical means, as well as to change the spirit of its legislation, or the mode of its executive. And this fact all see plainly enough, while it only is made to bear on a single law, or a slight change. No one thinks of disputing the right of one parliament to alter the acts of a former. It is not supposed that the legacy of opinion left by one set of men is to exercise any other influence over their successors than such as its inherent truth makes necessary; but there still remain an immense number of persons who are filled with a superstitious dread at the thought of making the best use of the property of a community because that property once belonged to individuals holding certain notions of usefulness: so that with such, improvement is a question not of principles of justice, or of expediency even, but a problem of the least change which can be made to satisfy the demand for reformation. How impossible that any man, or set of men, could judge the mode of employing their wealth most advantageously for the uses of a community, which should exist some six or eight centuries after their death! Had a conscientious catholic of Mary's time bequeathed the income of a large estate to raise the piles which then periodically blazed in Smithfield, the vile intention would long since have been scouted. The most determined defender of the sacredness of the designs of a founder would smile at such an instance. Yet the instance is a possible one and if there exist a single indefensible case, the principle is virtually accorded, and the adhesion to the spirit of wills must become, as it should be in every individual instance, a question of general utility. The license allowed in the testamentary distribution of property is continually producing the most mischievous effects. Many years will not pass, we think, before this subject will be one of general consideration. Neither in the material, nor in the moral constitution of things does there exist anything which is not in its nature liable to change.

We have no power to realise by our imagination the idea, changeless. It is a term which can only be justly used in a comparative sense. How unwise then is the attempt to set bounds to the progress of after times, by willing that the application of any portion of property shall be change-less. A nation must always retain the right to dispose of its own possessions for its own benefit; and this benefit is subverted by the existence of any corporation which, constantly increasing in wealth and portionably in influence, has an interest in the state, directly opposed to that of the rest of the community. Great indeed must be the virtue which, in these circumstances, can resist the temptation to become an instrument of mischief. Mirabeau, desirous to avoid the necessity of making the clergy *ex officio* proprietors, yet anxious that none should be reduced to the miserable condition of being passing rich with forty pounds a-year, brought into the National Assembly a bill to fix the salaries of ministers of the established church, at a minimum of about 500£ sterling per annum. It was carried by a large majority: — 1st. 'That all ecclesiastical property belongs to the nation, with the charge of providing in a proper manner for the expenses of worship, the support of its ministers, and the relief of the poor, under the inspection and instruction of the provinces;' and 2nd. 'That, in the dispositions to be made to provide for the ministers of religion, no curate shall receive less than 1200 livres per annum, exclusively for houses, garden, and dependencies.' The remark which applied forty years since, becomes every day more true, that numbers, nay, we shall not be far wrong if we say the larger portion of those who are supported by the wealth of the church, neither practise its injunctions, nor believe in its doctrines. Large as is the number of persons holding what are called deistical opinions, we believe, if it could be made matter of proof, it would appear, that a considerable proportion of such belong to that state church. In one of the letters is this passage: 'Socinus has a great many followers, both amongst the clergy of the church of England, and the Puritans. The Freethinkers, or, as the Sorbonne classes them, the Theists and Deists, have given a new extent to the spirit of toleration, to which the political atheist is declared enemy. This spirit, which was the chief foundation of the grandeur of the Romans, is at present the source of that of England and Holland. From these two countries arose its first apostles. To this spirit the Roman Catholics are indebted for the peace and quietness they enjoy under both these governments. Indeed every one, regarding his country-men who are out of the pale of the church, as damned, should wish them rather to damn themselves as Freethinkers, without joining any persecut-ing sect, than as untolerating sectaries. It may with truth be observed, that freethinking is, in a free state, an asylum open to those who, in other countries, are obliged to have recourse to the mask of hypocrisy. And with regard to public morals, the consequences of this freethinking are less dangerous than those of hypocrisy,'—p. 22. Church reform, however, like all other reforms, must come. And the signs of the times seem to point to this as the first. To enter into the wide question of church property would exceed our present design. Suffice it to record the opinions of this, on all political questions, most sagacious observer. To those who would examine the subject for themselves, we would recommend the perusal of two pamphlets, which together pretty nearly exhaust the moral and legal arguments on the question.[45] We shall need no apology for citing from one of them the following forcible sentences:—'The existing church has now a weak side which it had not forty years ago. Within that period a co-partnership has been formed with the Irish church, in which it is said the abuses are still more flagrant than here. Some reforms must be made in Ireland; and they will be much stronger precedents for reform in England than if the two churches had remained distinct. I never could understand the advantage accruing to the English church from that union; yet the measure, when proposed in the English parliament, passed without an observation of any kind. Not a word uttered either to approve or disapprove. The laity seemed to think that the measure did not concern them in any way; while, no doubt, the bishop felt pleased at the approach-ing extension of their corporation to the sister island. For this worldly conduct, however, the English church bids fair to be severely punished; and deservedly, as she has been instrumental in perpetuating the clerical abuses in Ireland. Had the English church never taken that of Ireland into partnership, the latter would have undergone a change long ago. But since the association, the failings of the Irish church have to be accounted for by the English church also; it being the universal law of partnership, that the acts of some of a firm are considered as being done in the name of the whole. Thus will the consequences of the Irish errors be made to fall upon

---

45. Church Reform: Effingham Wilson.—A Legal Argument on Tythes, & c. Effingham Wilson. [HTM]

those who have lent a hand to uphold them; thereby confirming the justice of that law of nature, which ordains that vices should carry their own chastisements in their train.'

We have somewhat dilated upon what, to us, was the most interesting topic of these letters. But they contain much lively gossip and are not without scattered touches of humour and wit. Some of Mirabeau's apophthegms run thus:—'Nobility, say the aristocracy, is the intermedium between the king and the people: true, just as a sporting dog is the intermedium between the sportsman and the hare.'

'The man possessed of superior mental qualifications is often little suited to society. You do not go to market, with ingots, but with small change.'

This is true only where the person of superior mind is placed in society unworthy of him; such as artificial or uneducated society. The more the mind, either of man or woman, is enriched by acquirement and reflection, the more does it fit its possessor to give and to receive the highest species of enjoyment, social usefulness, and sympathy.

We fear there are too many who, like the Abbé de Languerne, can enjoy nothing which has not the evidence for its immediate utility stamped upon its front. 'The Abbé de Languerne was an extremely learned man, but had not the slightest taste for poetry; like the geometrician before whom a high eulogium was passed on the tragedy of Iphigenia: such lofty praises excited his curiosity; he requested the person to lend him the tragedy, but, having read some scenes, he returned it, saying, "For my part, I cannot imagine what you find so beautiful in the work; it proves nothing." The Abbé equally despised the grandeur of Corneille and the elegance of Racine; he had, he said, banished all the poets from his library.'

That 'vices are more frequently habits than passions,' is a reflection as just in its observation of nature, as benevolent and useful in application. It would be easy to find many equally good things; and the book is, on the whole, an amusing one, though not of the kind we had been led to expect.

g. Review of *The Mysticism of Plato, or Sincerity rested upon Reality.* Hunter. 1832.[46]

No truly great or fine mind was ever yet utterly lost to the world;—nay more,—no mind containing within itself the capacity for any kind of greatness, has ever been so far the slave of circumstances as to be com-

---

pletely smothered by them; force of any kind, mental or physical, must expend itself, otherwise it is not force, but weakness. And thus it has always happened, that when there has been no place found for its evident and external operation, it has yet, by turning inwards its mental vision, found ample room and verge enough, in exploring the recesses of its own nature, its origin, and its hopes. To trace, through generation after generation, and age after age, the superstructure raised by time upon one such mental substratum, might be the study of a life; and it was in the expectation of finding some steps hewn towards the attainment of this extended view, that we eagerly took up the 'Mysticism of Plato.' But to those, who, attracted by the volume contained in this title, look to find some, if it were only the small coin, of the riches of imagination, or the treasures of heart-wisdom, it will prove a disappointment. Such is not here. We find ourselves suddenly in the midst of scholastic criticism, couched, it is true, in most nervous and eloquent sentences, on the old subject of the λογος. The body of Plato is there, but, alas! the soul is afar off.

Yet this criticism has its use in these days of dogmatical controversy, and rarely is it touched in so philosophical a spirit. The author shows 'that orthodoxy was borrowed from Platonism; yet, that in transferring the idea, as well as the word, what was abstract in Platonism was made personal in orthodoxy; what was mystical was made real; and, in one word, a Platonic mysticism was converted into an orthodox reality.' (p. 34) In the comprehensive spirit of his master's doctrine, 'the founder of an universal religion, that is, of a religion which was to supersede all other religions, and into which every other religion was to be absorbed, as rivers flow into the sea,' the evangelist identified him with the Platonic λογος, and it was only in after times that the word was personified, and the mystic doctrine literalized, and vulgarized, misrepresenting alike the apostle and the philosopher, and fabricating from the language of metaphysical truth, common to them both, a preposterous creed, to be enforced by persecution.

The name of Plato made us expect more and other matter. Doubtless at this time but a faint semblance can be had of that unfathomable and majestic mind, and that little only to be grasped by those who have an ardent love and search after that truth and beauty which is immutable, and of which, were there the desire for it, some portion might be seen by all, as it rests not in things, but in the mind of the searcher. Still, for this work, if he did no more, the author must rank high among those who have done good in their generation; with an ardent, yet acute and calm intellect, he has boldly stepped over the little mud entrenchments, and innumerable hillocks which are error's favourite abiding places; and though he has not passed on to the high mountains, yet his is not the mind to be discouraged that still higher and higher the bright peaks arise beyond him, nor because that the distance is to our sight lost in clouds; he will go on his way rejoicing in each inch of ground gained to the good cause; and with heart and soul we say, God speed him. Will the realist smile, and the cold-hearted scoff? Surely,—for is not the power of each being to approach the source of all good, limited by the imperfections of its own character? So it was from the beginning, and ever will be. But if when the fulness of time shall have come, and the mists shall have cleared, and the sun shine out fully, better spirits shall predominate, then will they bow their hearts to the few, who, through doubt and thick darkness, kept alive a hopeful faith in higher things.

h. Sarrans on the French Revolution of 1830.[47]

The events of July, 1830, were charged with consequences not only to France, but to all Europe. Nevertheless, the change in the French government which was then effected is less entitled to be called a revolution than that which, within the last few months, has given a new impulse to our own country. It may be true that there exist in France many patriotic and thinking men, who see great evils in the constitution of their government, and who have, in their own minds, thoroughly digested the ideas upon which their hope for France relies. That there is such a party cannot be doubted, nor that it existed with the same opinions, the same wishes and hopes, at the time when the change in the person of the chief magistrate of France took place. To these men, most of whom are in some manner connected with the public press, may be fairly ascribed the praise of having incited the population of Paris to resistance to the 'Ordinances.' The people of Paris rose, as one man, to oppose that actual and definite attack upon the very foundation of the social compact. But, as towards the great mass of the men who fought in the contest of the three days, the injury was exact and obvious, so was their remedy. We believe that the political feeling which actuated the majority of the Parisian mob was simply,—'we have for our king, a man without a sense of public justice and obligation;

---

47. "Lafayette, Louis-Philippe, and the Revolution of 1830. By B. Sarrans, jun. 2 vols. 8 vo. Eff. Wilson." There is another translation of this work in circulation, published by Messrs. Colburn and Bentley. We have not compared the two; and, comparison will scarcely be thought necessary by those who are aware that Mr. Wilson's is by the accomplished pen of the translator of the 'Tour of a German Prince.' [HTM].

The *Tour of a German Prince,* also reviewed by HTM, was translated by Sarah Austin, but Harriet incorrectly attributes the translation of Sarrans' work to her.

we know him to be of the race of incurables; let us expel him from the office for which he has proved himself to be unfit, and place there a more suitable person.' The men of genius had higher hopes and aims; they believed that, in addition to a weak and selfish monarch, they had faulty institutions. They thought that the latter tended mainly to induce the former evil; and they desired, in changing the one, to reconstruct the other also. It is in this that they were mistaken: they over-estimated the political education of the body of the French people, and, as it afterwards proved, the political honesty of many of their most trusted representatives. The nation was not, in July, 1830, prepared unanimously to desire a change in their form of government. They hoped to amalgamate popular government with the respectability of the monarchial name. How far the efforts of Carlists and Philippists[48] may now have induced them to alter their opinion, remains to be proved. They may have reaped the knowledge of experience,—applicable alike to political and social arrangements,—that anomalous means are not likely to produce unity of effect. The fact of so great a change as that of the ruling dynasty, wholly unforeseen by all but a numerically inconsiderable portion of the people, having been effected in three days, might be sufficient to warrant the presumption, that the plans, so hastily adopted, would be insufficient to the emergency. The very fact of its being a revolution of three days may account for its proving so useless a revolution.

Between the publication of the obnoxious decrees, which took place on the 26th of July, and the general uprising of the city, there intervened but a few hours. Measures of resistance were conceived; men were called to think and to act without premeditation,—insecure of the strength of feeling of those to whom they had to look for support, and knowing that upon them rested the onus of recommencing a state of internal feud in France, not yet recovered from the storms of the conclusion of the eighteenth century;—weary after that terrible disorganization which yet had thrown off a vast mass of political disease, she was willing to endure much, rather than again evoke a power which had once been so tremendous.

The moral character evinced by the actors of those three days was a glorious one; and the choice of the individual to place upon the vacant throne was the grand mistake. The haste in which their election was made seems the only explanation of how such men as the leaders of July could,

---

48. Carlism was a Spanish political movement beginning in the 1820s that opposed liberalism and the succession of Isabella to her father's throne. By "Philippists," Harriet is probably referring to those who brought Louis-Philippe to power in the July Revolution of 1830.

for a moment, have consented to admit as their leader such a man as the Duke of Orleans.

We believe almost all parties agree in thinking France to be in a worse condition than during the administration of Charles X.; and why is this? Because, though the mass of people may have desired no revolution of institutions, yet they did desire a change in the character of their ruler; as it is, they have only changed one king for another, who is, as far as he dare show himself, of the same make and mould as his predecessor. May he speedily follow on the same road!

It is now seventeen years since the Bourbons returned to France — France, weary of turmoil, yearning for tranquillity, and prepared to welcome them, if not certainly with enthusiasm, yet with content and hope. In such a complexion of things, how little might have sufficed to have awakened the gratitude of a generous and enthusiastic people. That little was withheld, in conformity with the short-sightedness which seems to become inherent in hereditary rulers.

The first measures of a restored dynasty, which might well have considered that it held the throne on sufferance, were either avowedly or in secret, to vitiate some of the most popular clauses of the newly-obtained charter. Then came that insult to every free country — the invasion of Spain. From the period, positive dislike took the place of indifference in the public mind towards Louis, but which fell yet more strongly on the intriguer Villèle. Accordingly, it was seen needful to change the administration; and Charles may be said to have begun his reign with all the chances of popularity in his favour. The people, with renewed hope, sent their Parliament popular members; and, showing towards the king affection and gratitude for this so small concession, ventured to believe him sincere.

But, as of old, it may still be said 'Put not your trust in princes.' The liberal ministry found itself looked upon with suspicious eyes, and their measures, though rather those of conciliation and time-serving, than of effective remedy, were found to be neutralized by the secret machinations of the court and its advisers. This was in 1829, and the month of August saw an 'extrême droit' ministry, with Polignac[49] for its head, preparing to wield the sceptre of France.

For all who had watched the progress of events, the names composing this cabinet afforded ample foresight of the measures to be expected. An association was formed for the purpose, if needed, of resisting the payment of taxes. The press performed its duty of warning, counselling, and en-

---

49. "Extrême droit": Extreme right. Auguste-Jules-Armand-Marie de Polignac (1780–1847) conspired against Napoleon in 1804.

couraging. The Tory ministers, intimidated for a time, endeavoured, without effect, to veil the designs of their government. All was distrust and dissatisfaction on the part of the people, and on that of the ministry blind determination, when, in May, was convened the last parliament Charles X. was destined to meet. The royal address was peremptory; the reply of the liberal members anxious and supplicatory, yet firm. The refractory Chamber was speedily dismissed, with a view to corrupt the new elections. But, spite of all the arts and the influence which the government could bring to bear on the returns of the electoral colleges, an immense majority for the popular cause appeared on the list of deputies. No sooner was the fact of this majority decided, than were issued the 'Ordinances;' the first of which pronounces the Chamber dissolved before it had yet assembled; the second annulled the existing electoral laws, by which the Chamber had been appointed,—decreed the reduction of the number of representatives from 430 to 250, leaving to certain colleges, which had hitherto the privilege of electing, only that of recommending candidates, and abolished the vote by ballot; the third appointed the time for the meeting of the new assembly; the fourth abrogated the law which guaranteed the liberty of the press. Such were the famous Ordinances of the 26th of July. On the evening of the 27th, an attack was made by the royal troops on various groups which had assembled in the streets, but which had as yet manifested no intention of resorting to force. By this attack the resolution of all Paris was determined. At the time of the appearance of the Ordinances, Lafayette was at some leagues distance from Paris. On receiving the intelligence, he hesitated not a moment in taking post; and in the evening of the 27th, put himself at the head of the insurgents. On the morning of the 28th, the people, led by bands of the Polytechnic students, assembled in the principal avenues of the city, at each point met by detachments of troops. At noon the Hotel de Ville was in the hands of the people, with whom, at the close of the day, it remained, after having been three times taken and retaken. While this scene was transacting without, a meeting of editors of journals, by whom it had been convened, and of influential liberal deputies, was held, at which Lafayette opposed the hesitating counsels of the timid, and declared his resolution, whatever might be the result, to give the people the whole weight of his name and his experience.

During the night of the 28th not less than one hundred thousand men were employed in active preparation for the struggle of the morrow. The result of the next day was the complete triumph of the popular force over the royal troops, and the virtual dethronement of the elder branch of the Bourbon family. At this time it would appear that neither the Duke of Orleans, who remained quietly at Neuilly, nor the people who had effected the revolution, had any idea of his succeeding to the throne. There, however, existed a party, with M. Lafitte[50] for its leader, who had long kept this object in view. This party planned its measures quickly and well. The body of the people hesitated between the desire to place the crown on the head of Lafayette and the policy of appointing a regency in the name either of the young Napoleon or in that of Henry the Fifth. These regencies were both repeatedly offered to Lafayette, but this consistent republican steadily refused to compromise the principles of his life. The event was the offer, first of Lieutenant Generalship, and then of the crown, to the head of the younger branch of the old dynasty.

After the immediate excitement of this great effort had somewhat subsided, the men of the 'Movement' party began to look for the altered system, which alone could make the revolution valuable. The most evident display of the spirit of the new government was to consist in its external policy. With regard to this policy two courses presented themselves—the one was to cast aside the web of the old system of diplomacy, with all its entanglements, its hollowness, and its legitimacies, and in its stead to make all arrangements and relations of France correspond with the spirit of the revolution of 1830. As respects the moralities of faith of treaties, it is plain that equity could not bind France to alliances made for, but not by, her—alliances, the whole tendency of which was opposed to her present condition and principles. Were precedent to constitute a ground for disregarding them, there was sufficient example in the manner in which those of Amiens, of Presburg, and of Vienna had been violated by the very parties who now so loudly appealed to 'the conscience of the king.'

The non-intervention system had also its honest adherents, and, in the then state of France, had much to recommend it to deliberate men; that is to say, a true, and not a sham, non-intervention principle. The word, in its government acceptation, has hitherto stood for non-intervention where any popular cause stood in need of it: it will be found to have been but little remembered when to forget it might promote the ascendancy of might over right. In adopting neutrality for herself, France was called upon in consistency, wherever she had the power to maintain, and if needful to force, the neutrality of the governments which opposed themselves to her principles. In this, the only just application of the principle of neutrality, the monarchy of July professed its concurrence; yet have we but to look to Italy, to Poland, or even to Belgium, to see in each instance its practical abandonment.

The Lafitte ministry, with all its virtues of moderation, could never be

---

50. Jacques Lafitte (1767-1844), French banker and politician prominent from the end of the Napoleonic era to the July Monarchy.

brought to answer the purposes of either Louis-Philippe or of the people. From the time that Louis-Philippe felt himself secure on the throne of his family, his whole bearing has displayed the strongest partiality towards, so called, legitimate measures; but, as nothing short of absolute madness would be implied in the attempt to carry out such principles in revolutionized France, he has contended himself with heading the timid and sophisticating party of the *doctrinaires;* a party which, however respectable as to talent,—at least if talent can be respectable without honesty,—yet, by their timidity, rest in that sort of good intentions with which it has been said hell is paved, and allow their fears to be a rational ground for the hopes of regalists of all degree. The ministry, which may be called the 'Guizot ministry,' since M. Guizot, both by his literary reputation and his political bigotry, is the most prominent character therein, took office with the declared intention of making the organization of 1814 combine with the circumstances of 1830. The lamentable absence of clear-sightedness, as to the requirements and the strength of popular feeling, which distinguishes this party and its leaders, MM. Guizot, Thiers, and Royer Collard,[51] were amply evinced in the discussion on the question of hereditary peerage. All thought that in an hereditary order was involved the very essence, the existence of the government. 'With the hereditary principle (said one of them) perishes the peerage; with the peerage the hereditary royalty; and in the commonwealth itself the principle of stability, dignity, and duration.'

Much of the same calibre were the prophetic wailings of the English conservatives on the social anarchy and destruction which were to follow our very innocent Reform Bill. Both measures were successful; we have but to hope that their effects may be as wide-spread, though of a quite different sort, as those which interested alarmists have in both countries predicted. Doctrines formed without the consideration of circumstances, and then blindly opposed to them, are as much, and no more, likely to stand than would be the chain-pier, if placed at the Land's End, to stem the vast sweep of the Atlantic.

There can be no doubt that the state of things in France is again slowly tending towards a great moral or physical revolution. That the former may suffice, all friends of humanity must desire; but, should that force of itself be insufficient to produce agreement between the spirit of the government and the spirit of the time, they will be no true friends of humanity who

51. François Pierre Guillaume Guizot (1787-1874), a French political figure and Ambassador to England in 1840; Adolphe Thiers (1797-1877), French statesman and liberal rival of Guizot; Pierre-Paul Royer-Collard (1763-1845), French statesman and philosopher.

shall not welcome any power which, by means of some evil, may work the regeneration of the people who lead the political education of Europe. As needful is it to be kept in mind by nations, as by individuals, *Aide toi, le ciel t'aidera.*[52]

5. The Seasons[53]

SUMMER is gone—winter is come. Which is the most enjoyable of the seasons? is a common question. Unimpressible by the beauty of any must he be who feels not that it is in the state which he receives each that its power of pleasure lies. The kind of mind, and the state of mind, make spring of December, or of highest summer, winter. Autumn, the destroyer, has swept into eternity many a blossom both of flower and heart: its rich suns have set on the wrecks which its gales had made; and its ripe harvest moon has lighted much both of animate and inanimate nature to 'the bourne from whence no traveller returns.'[54] But those setting suns and waning moons may also have been the signal for many a hope's spring, over which the howling blasts of the external world's wilderness pass unheeded, having no power but to say or sing 'soul take thy rest.'[55] And 'tis a fit time for the body, too, to take its rest in winter. Those curtains, with their heavy falling folds of purple drapery, whose graceful lines erst harmonized so lovelily with the young, blooming green of drooping acacias, and the scarlet bells of the pendant fucia, the lady of the flowers, and by the moral effect of the entire satisfaction they gave to the sense of form and colour, showed forth the utility of beauty,—now reversing the order, make us glory in the beauty of utility, as, drawn closely to exclude the breath of evening, fold upon fold, they meet the downy carpet.

Yet would we rather be without bread than without flowers in the dreariest days of old December weather. Now that Cassiopeia, bright and beautiful, has taken herself away, chair and all; and Bootes, outdoing the

---

52. "Heaven helps those who help themselves."

53. *Monthly Repository,* 1832: VI, 825-28.

54. *Hamlet,* 3.1 79-80. "The undiscover'd country from whose bourn / No traveller returns."

55. This phrase occurs in James Chamberlayne's *A Sacred Poem* (London: Robert Clavell, 1680). "And said unto his Soul, 'Soul take thy rest, / For I have laid me up a lasting Store / Of Wealth & Honour, which the World adore." The poem refers to Luke 12:19, which reads, "And I will say to my soul, Soul, thou hast much goods laid up for many years; take thine ease, eat, drink, and be merry."

seven-leaguers of our redoubtable friend Jack the Giant Killer, has strode towards some other planet; and the Snake, with its eyes of light, has 'trailed its slow length along,'[56] and vanished in 'the dim obscure;'[57] and were the sky ever so clear, and the stars ever so bright, with their wakeful prying eyes, it is too cold to stay to look at them; have we not laurestinus, white and pure as snow, but not as cold; and holly, with its blood-red drops and crown of thorns like the occasion it commemorates; and the passion-flower, with its exhausted colour and exaggerated form, fit emblem of its name; and chrysanthemum, star-like, with the addition of fragrance, and with its shadows (which it is a pity stars have not—only the moral is good, that light has no shadow) moving fantastically over the rose-tinted wall, as the fitful gleams of our beloved firelight shoot up and fall as good as summer lightnings or northern meteors? Firelight! We would match firelight against twilight for any number of pleasant sensations. We never could perceive the supereminent charm of English twilight; it has always seemed to us but another name for darkness, and that not 'aiding intellectual light;'[58] besides that it implies both cold and dampness, two things the most opposed to our notions of enjoyment.

Like that of the ancient magi is the worship we pay to the bright element, in return for the content which it gives to our senses, and the faculties which it unlocks in our souls. It is climate and companion too-increasing tenfold the charm of the society of those who we love, the only kind of society worthy the name.

It is sweet in the still night-air 'to discourse eloquent music'[59] under that deep everlasting roof; and the noblest of earth's emotions fill the soul to overflowing in the silent presence of the infinite sea. But these, 'like angels' visits, few and far between,'[60] are scattered sparingly over life's way; while every day in every winter month may bring the pleasures of friendship and the heart's home.

Talk of suicide in November! they must be fit for nothing else who can be moved thereto by bad weather. Much more natural would it be to leave

---

56. HTM is probably referring to Alexander Pope's line in "Essay in Criticism": "That like a wounded Snake, drags its slow Length along" (II.357).

57. Sophocles, *Oedipus Rex,* Part I.

58. "Thus, Darkness aiding intellectual light, / And sacred Silence whispering truths Divine" are lines in Edward Young's *Night Thoughts on Life, Death and Immortality,* Night IX "The Consolation," 2 "A Night Address to the Deity," line 2411.

59. *Hamlet,* 3.2, 366-67. "Give it breath with your mouth, and it will discourse most eloquent music."

60. Robert Blair, *The Grave* (1743), 589. "Its Visits Like those of Angels short, and far between."

the world when it is too beautiful to be endured. In the bad there is something to resist—and resistance is the principle of life, say the learned. One may imagine some suicidal impulse in spring time, if it were but in impatience of the Mephistophelian mockery of so much beauty and life, and enjoyment and hope.

All the enjoyments of winter are of the kind which can the most easily be brought within the compass of the individual will. If they are in their nature less spiritual than those of spring and autumn, they admit of being made the most perfect of their kind. A thousand checks of custom or convenience may and do arise to prevent our having, in the right mood and with the right society, the breath of morning, newly alighted on a heaven-kissing hill; whence, in the devout stillness of the blue and dewy air, we might look down on 'the kingdoms of the world and the glory thereof;'[61] intense admiration of 'the world,'[62] which 'is all before us,' making it hard to bear that it is not for us 'to choose where.' But in winter the eye is 'satisfied with seeing and the ear with hearing,'[63] when for the one there is a bright fire, and for the other a voice we love.

All objects take the impress of the mind which receives them; and if 'tout devient sentiment dans un cœur sensible,'[64] not less does all become vulgarized by a merely external eye. No more than the flower constitutes fragrance without the corresponding sense, does the unstored mind or frigid heart constitute a sentient being: he whom no 'spirits teach in breeze-born melodies,'[65] would perchance find such breezes but 'an ill wind that blows nobody good'[66]—

> 'The better vision will not come unsought,
> Though to the worshipper 'tis ever nigh.

After the night, the day—and after winter spring comes again, with its bubbling sounds and sparkling, odorous air, its beamy skies and rapid life;

---

61. Matthew 4:8.

62. John Milton, *Paradise Lost,* Book 12. "The world was all before them, where to choose / Their place of rest."

63. Ecclesiastes, 1:8.

64. "Everything turns into feeling in a tender heart."

65. From the Corn-Law poet Ebenezer Elliott, "The Primrose." "Surely that man is pure in thought and deed, / Whom spirits teach in breeze-borne melodies; / For he find tongue in every flower and weed / And admonition in mute harmonies; / Erect he moves, by truth and beauty led. . . ."

66. William Congreve, *The Old Batchelour"* (1693), 2.1 "'Tis an ill Wind that blows no body good."

and not the less do we enjoy it that we have made the most of its surly predecessor. Happiness is the true transmuter for which science has always sought in vain—the fuser of circumstances, the Ithuriel's spear—'exalting the valleys, making low the hills, and the rough places plain,' of the journey of life: it alone can produce the miracle of 'figs on thorns and grapes on brambles:' it is the golden sun which gilds all, 'the blue sky bending over all.'[67]

Spring-time and flowers! each day brings forth a new class in its progress towards perfection. 'Stars of the fields, the hills, the groves!' Who loves not flowers? Be he who he may, he loves not friend or mistress, his species nor his country; nay, truly loves not himself, for all these are included in self. As to the more graceful sex, they may see in flowers types of their own nature, often emblems of their own fate.

Flowers are utilitarians in the largest sense. Their very life is supported by administering to the life of others—producers and distributors, but consumers only what, unused, would be noxious. Ornaments in happiness, companions in solitude, soothing 'the unrest of the soul.'[68] Hear what says the classic Roland—'La vûe d'une fleur caresse mon imagination, et flatte mes sens à une point inexprimable; elle réveille, avec volupté le sentiment de mon existence. Sous le tranquil abri du toît paternel, j'étois heureuse des enfance avec des fleurs et des livres; dans l'étroite enceinte d'une prison, au milieu des fers imposés par la tyrannie la plus revoltante, j'oublie l'injustice des hommes, leurs sottises, et mes maux, avec des livres, et des fleurs.'[69] As impossible as to find two human countenances alike in all their features and expression, is it to discover duplicate flowers. Who shall say how much of consciousness they may be endued with? It will not be hastily decided that they are without it, by any who has watched and tended them; who has seen in the morning their whole form bend towards light and the cheerful sun; who knows at evening to give the long deep draught of the element they love, and has seen the delicate fibers fill, and

---

67. Allusions are as follows: Ithuriel refers to "Ithuriel with his spear," in John Milton's *Paradise Lost,* 4:810; "exalting . . . plain," Isaiah 40:4; "figs . . . brambles" refers to Matthew 7:16 ("Do men gather grapes of thorns, or figs of thistles"); and the "blue sky" is from Samuel Taylor Coleridge's *Christabel,* 331 ("For the blue sky bends over all").

68. Jones Very, *Soul-Sickness:* "Some unrest of the soul, some secret pain."

69. "The sight of a flower caresses my imagination, and delights my senses to an inexpressible degree; it voluptuously reawakens my life's emotion. Under the tranquil shelter of my father's roof, I was happy with my flowers and my books from childhood onward. In the narrow confines of a prison, in chains imposed by the most revolting tyranny, I forget the injustice of men, their follies and my pains, with books and flowers" *Mémoires de Madame Roland* (Paris: Henri Plon, 1864), 7.

the colours brighten, and the stalks expand, and the leaves rise, and, by one consent, do obeisance like the sheaves of the Syrian boy's dream. And those which here we speak of are but the favourites of civilization, which, like their human prototypes, by their too abundant training, lose in strength what they gain in richness, which, after all, is but a bad exchange for the graces of nature and freedom. It is to those which 'dwell in fields and lead ambrosial lives' that we must look for the perfection of their beauty. 'Nor use can tire, nor custom stale *their* infinite variety.'[70]

And when Spring's dancing hours have paved her path, they usher in the stately splendour of voluptuous summer—gorgeous in beauty like an Eastern queen. Gray's notion of felicity was to lie on a sofa and read new novels:—our sofa should be the blooming turf, and our book the untiring novel of earth, sea, and sky; while summer airs, heavy with fragrance, float languidly by, mingled 'keen knowledges of deep embowered eld' with high presages of happy future days. 'Oh, it is pleasant, with a heart at ease,' to revel in the beauty of lurid-eyed summer, while every motion, odour, beam, and tone,

> 'With that deep music is in unison,
> Which is a soul within the soul!'[71]

Spring promises, summer performs, and then comes autumn, weaving together flowers and fruits like the garland of an Ipsariote girl. Its 'green old age' soon changes to decay, and a grave beneath 'the moist rich smell of the rotting leaves:' and so the year dies. Peace to its manes! Its life and its death are too closely united for us to perceive the parting; and of its seasons, 'each hiding some delight,' we would say and feel 'how happy could I be with either!'[72]

---

70. Edward Young, "The complaint; or, night-thoughts on life, death and immortality," III, 124. "Queen lilies! and ye painted populace! Who dwell in fields, and lead ambrosial lives." Shakespeare, *Antony and Cleopatra*, 2.2, 236-37. "Age cannot wither her, nor custom stale / Her infinite variety."

71. "Keen . . . eld": Alfred Lord Tennyson, *Poems*, 99 ("Keen knowledges of low-embowerèd eld"). "Oh . . . ease": the opening lines of Coleridge's "Fancy in Nubibus or The Poet in the Clouds." "With that . . . soul!": Percy Bysshe Shelley, *Epipsychidion*, 454-455.

72. "Ipsariote," i.e., from the Aegean island Ipsara. "Green old age" is from Oliver Goldsmith, *The Vicar of Wakefield*, xiv: "His green old age seemed to be the result of health and bene- volence." The "rotting leaves" are Tennyson's, from "A spirit haunts the year's last hours": "my whole soul grieves / At the moist rich smell of the rotting leaves, / And the breath / Of the fading edges of box beneath." "Each hiding some delight" is from Shelley's *Epipsychidion*, 472, and "how happy could I be with either!" appears in John Gay's *Beggar's Opera*, Air xxxv.

6. Poems

DRAFTS OF "WRITTEN AT DAYBREAK"

A.

The heralds of the Sun announce the Morn[73]
First dew in sober grey.[74]
Then slowly stepping on with solemn pace
More gorgeous still they come,
In purple, orange, crimson, gold;
Till all as[75] morning clouds dissolve away
Before the coming of the day.[76]

B. WRITTEN AT DAYBREAK[77]

Hushed are all sounds, the sons of toil & pain,
The poor & wealthy, all are one again—
Sleep closes ov'r the high & lowly head
And makes the living fellow with the dead.
The clouds of night role sullenly away
Mutely obedient to the approach of day—
The fragrant flowers unfold their heads
The birds with gladness leave their leafy beds—
Now unperceived at first the orb of day,
Sending alone a faint and trembling ray;
At last he comes majestically slow
Pouring bright radiance on the world below
And springing upwards from the embrace of night
Guilding the heav'ns with beams of orient light—

C.

Hushed are all sounds—the sons of toil & pain[78]
The poor and wealthy all are one again;

---

73. Box III/189.

74. The word "white" has been struck out and replaced with "grey."

75. The word "like" has been replaced with "as."

76. The word "perfect" preceded "day," but has been struck out.

77. Box III/204. Two other less complete versions are included in this folder.

78. Box III/205.

Sleep[79] closes o'er the high & lowly head,
And makes the living fellows with the dead—

But unperceived at first the approach of day
Sending alone a faint & trembling ray
The fragrant flowers unfold their scented heads
The birds with gladness leave their leafy beds—
At last he comes majestically slow
Pouring[80] bright radiance on the world below
And springing upwards from the embrace of night
Gilding the heav'ns with beams of orient lights
O beauteous hour to minds of feeling giv'n
Filling the heart with thoughts & hopes of heav'n.
Lofty with purposes airs arise
Giving the soul communion with the skies
To Natures God and highest hopes ascend
The bounding heart paints joys which cannot end
Oh if to mortals it were[81] ever given
To choose the path the spirit takes to heav'n
On such a morn as this hour should be
To spurn the earth & let the spirit free
The   streaming with floods of gold
The   clouds a thousand fires unfold
And they whose love illumes this world of care
Would thou the joys forever willing there

D.   WRITTEN AT DAYBREAK[82]
Hushed are all sounds, the sons of toil and pain,
The poor and wealthy are all one again;
Sleep closes o'er the high and lowly head,
And makes the living fellows with the dead.
The clouds of night roll sullenly away,
Humbly[83] obedient to th' approach of day;

---

79. "Night" was replaced by "Sleep."

80. "Coming" was replaced by "Pouring."

81. "Could" was replaced by "were."

82. Box III/207. Except for the last few lines this draft is the same as Box III/206.

83. "Humbly" was replaced by "Mutely."

The fragrant flowers unfold their scented heads,
The birds with gladness leave their leafy beds—
But unperceived at first the orb of day,
Sending alone a faint and trembling ray;
The glowing east, streaming with floods of gold
The fleeing clouds a thousand hues unfold.
At last he comes majestically slow
Pouring bright radiance on the world below,
[S]pringing[84] upwards from th' embrace of night
Gilding the heavn's with beams of orient light—
O beauteous hour to minds of feeling giv'n
Filling the heart with thoughts and hopes of heav'n.
Lofty and noblest purposes arise
Giving the soul communion with the skies; & give
To Nature's God our highest hopes ascend
The bounding heart paints joys which cannot end—
Oh, if to mortals it could e'er be given,
To chuse the path the spirit takes to Heav'n;
Guided by him, from whom my doating heart
Not opening heav'n itself could tempt to part,
Mine should ascend, on such a morn as this
On wings of glorious light to realms of bliss
And he whose love illumes this world of care
Would they double all the bliss forever welling there.[85]

Now—Then
And

But imperceptably the orb of day[86]
Pierces the darkness with a trembling ray

E.   WRITTEN AT DAYBREAK[87]
Hushed are all sounds, the sons of toil and pain,
The poor and wealthy all are one again;

---

84. "And" preceded "springing," but was struck out.

85. "Which waits me there" was replaced by "forever dwelling there."

86. These last two lines are included as lines 5 and 6 of the final draft, Box III/208.

87. Box III/206. Except for the last two lines, this draft is the same as Box III/207.

Sleep closes o'er the high and lowly head,
And makes the living fellows with the dead.
The clouds of night roll sullenly away,
Humbly obedient to th' approach of day;
The fragrant flowers unfold their scented heads,
The birds with gladness leave their leafy beds —
But unperceived at first the orb of day,
Sending alone a faint and trembling ray;
The glowing east, streaming with floods of gold
The fleeing clouds a thousand hues unfold.
At last he comes majestically slow
Pouring bright radiance on the world below,
And springing upwards from th' embrace of night
Gilding the heavn's with beams of orient light —
O beauteous hour to minds of feeling giv'n
Filling the heart with thoughts and hopes of heav'n.
Lofty and noble purposes arise
Giving the soul communion with the skies;
To Nature's God our highest hopes ascend
The bounding heart paints joys which cannot end —
Oh, if to mortals it could e'er be given,
To chuse the path the spirit takes to Heav'n;
Guided by him, from whom my doating heart
Not opening heav'n itself could tempt to part,
Mine should ascend, on such a morn as this
On wings of glorious light to realms of bliss
And he whose love illumes this world of care
~~Would double all the joys which wait/awaiting us there~~
Should dwell with me in endless transports there.

F.   DAYBREAK[88]   1828

Hushed are all sounds, the sons of toil and pain,
The poor and wealthy are all one again;
Sleep closes o'er the high and lowly head,
And makes the living fellows with the dead.
How imperceptably the orb of day
Peirces the darkness with a trembling ray

---

88. Box III/208.

And clouds of night roll sullenly away,
The fragrant flowers unfold their scented heads,
The birds with gladness leave their leafy beds —
At last he comes majestically slow
Pouring bright radiance on the word below
The glowing east is streaked with waves of gold
A thousand hues the parting clouds unfold
Then springing upwards from the embrace of night
He guilds the heavens with beams of orient light
O beauteous hour to minds of feeling giv'n
Filling the heart with thoughts and hopes of heav'n.
Lofty and noble purposes arise
And give the soul communion with the skies;
To nature's God our highest hopes ascend
The bounding heart paints joys which cannot end —
Oh if to mortals it were ever giv'n
To chuse the path the spirit takes to Heav'n

On such a morn as this the hour should be
To spurn the earth and let the spirit free

2.

1

How beautiful an infants sleep — [89]
The rounded cheek the fair high brow!
Pity that sorrow ere should break
Upon a mind so cloudless now; [90]

2

But come it will those dimpled cheeks,
With graceful limb, and
That open brow, that guileless mind,
Will eager join the busy world,

---

89. Box III/208, p 2. This poem is written on a sheet folded to form four sides. The "Written at Daybreak" dated 1828 is on the first page. This and the next two poems form the remainder of the four sides.

90. Harriet added the following words in pencil around the "2" separating the stanzas: "ah too soon that that fair boy   cherish'd boys."

Where joys unmix'd he thinks to find—

3

Soon will realities rough touch,
Efface the sketch which hope had made—
And quick, dispelling one by one,
All the bright tints of fancy fade;

4

And then come wild excitements joys,
And maddening pleasures syren song;
To the dark gulf of guilt and pain;
With the full tide he's borne along—

5

But still one spark of light remains,
Like the slight spray on yonder river,
More bright for the dark gloom around
And[91] not like it to sink for ever!

6

No! That bright flame immortal is!
Still pointing to the peaceful skies,
And bursting thro' the clouds of life
A glorious Sun, to heav'n shall rise!

3. SONG[92]

Oh what can we wish for in life's little day
But to bask in the sunshine & then drop away
Like that beautiful flower which gladdens our eyes
For an hour, and then sickens, withers, & dies.

For this life is composed of hopes and of fears
Let us sip the bright hopes in youth's sunny years
And before the dark winter of age comes around us
Sink peacefully down while gay visions surround us.

---

91. "But" was replaced by "And."

92. Box III/208, page 3. The first page of this folded sheet of paper is dated 1828.

A fragrant plant of eastern clime
A mighty conqueror's name
Season of hope & joy & love That which o'erlooks both Nile and Thames
A man of holy fame

When shepherds only rov'd[93] the land
Which Grecian heroes since have trod
And Delphin groves and Athens stand

4. SONG[94]

1

How beautiful at eve,
Is yonder rippling river,
The sun-beam tumbling on the wave
As it glides away for ever!

2

Just like that sunbeams ray,
On the waves of that sweet river,
The joys of life tho' bright today,
To-morrow fade for ever!

5. MERMAID'S SONG[95]

In chrystal caves of ocean's deep
I made my pearly home
The rocking surges sooth my sleep
With wild & plaintive moan.

---

93. "Trod" was replaced by "rov'd."

94. Box III/208, p. 4. The first page of the folded sheet of paper is dated 1828. The page is headed by a few bars of musical composition.

95. On back of envelope of letter (28/144) from John Taylor to HTM. The letter, dated 14 July 1829, reads in part: "Papa told me that sea bathing will suit you on a warm day if you feel quite disposed for it, & if you only just dip in & out again; you must on no account remain in longer than just time enough to get one dip, & if you feel the least cooler in shivering afterwards you must not repeat the bath.—Attend to all this dearest & you have your husband's full permission to bathe." John Taylor's reference to "Papa" identifies HTM's father, a "man-midwife."

Sometimes I roam where glist'ning sands
Reflect bright Hesper's ray
Or bend to distant sunny lands
My happy cheerful way

Say how is Memory fresh, is she a creature young [?] beautiful as summer
flowers after refreshing storms, glittering & bounding in the pride of
beauty. No this is [strife] or present pleasure, gay & fit companion of all
thats young and beautiful & joyous—But Memory eh ah—how shall I
draw her—she's ushered in by sighs, her face seems beautiful through the
dim veil caused by the vapour of unnumbered tears—& then she's very
various & uncertain—now she'll be young & fair—and then ere we have
caught one certain glance she's changed to aged woe-begone & then the
frightful & malicious then she will not be disdained, for if we try to fly
she'll face us whensoe'r we turn, & laughs in scorn to [see] us writhe. &
sorrowful & turn where we will she'll face us still yet still we love her
under every form.

6. "Autumn"[96]

Autumn's Past sun has shone,
On the wrecks of the summer's prime;
Its murmuring airs are gone,
To their home in some Southern clime;
Even the infinite sea,
No longer the same shall be.
But its calm majesty,
Change for wild anarchy,
And the pride of restless sway—
The hollow winds arise,
Sweeping their haughty way
O'er the once beaming skies—
All the buds and blossoms gay,
All that made glad the golden day
Now prostrate lies
And nature dies—

---

96. Box III/212.

But spring again will bound
And the valleys and the hills
Echo the rich sound
Of the laughing tumbling rills—
The torrents and the streams
And the many coloured beams
Of the young exalting Sun,
Its warm life just begun,
    Make new the Earth,
    As at its birth.
'Soul take thy rest'—for thee shall bring
Another sun, another spring

"AUTUMN"[97]

Autumn is gone—her last Sun has shone
On the wreck of summer's prime:
The murmuring airs are gone
To their home in some bright southern clime—
infinite[98] sea
No more the same shall be;
But its calm majesty
Changed for wild anarchy
and the pride of resistless sway—
Bleak winds arise,
Sweeping their haughty way
O'er the once beaming skies—
All blossoms gay,
All that made glad the golden day,
Now prostrate lies
And nature dies

But Spring again will bound
And the valleys and the hills
Echoing the rich sound
Of the laughing rumbling rills:

---

97. Box III/212 (second version).

98. Harriet struck out "Even the," which preceded "infinite."

The torrents and the stream
Of the young exalting Sun[99]
make new the earth
As at its birth
When creation's work was done.
Of brighter future days.
Soul take thy rest—for thee shall bring[100]
Another Spring—another Sun

7. THE SNOW-DROP.[101]

Welcome, once more, Flower of the pale cold bell,
Sure it some spirit is! so chaste and pure
Its pendant head, as it would ring the knell
Of hoary Winter in his dying hour—
And well one sigh from things so fair might lure[102]
The frozen stream back to his wither'd heart,
And warm the hand of Death!
Constant and true it is, it will not part
From its accustom'd haunt—and when the breath
Of wanton Zephyrus would touch its cheek,
Congeals it into snow. A tale there goes,
That once a gentle girl, tender and meek,
Died for the love of the bright God of Day—
When straight her Spirit to this flow'ret rose—
And now he vainly courts her with his ray.

8. TO THE SUMMER WIND.[103]

Whence comest thou, sweet wind?
Didst take thy phantom form

---

99. The line following this line, "Its warm Life just begun," was struck out by Harriet.

100. "Come" was replaced by "bring."

101. *Monthly Repository* (new series) VI, 266. Signed "H T. March 1832."

102. A draft of the poem in Box III/187 replaces this line and the following with these words: "And well one sigh from things so fair and graceful, / Might thaw the crust about his wither'd heart."

103. *Monthly Repository* (new series) VI, 617.

'Mid the depth of forest trees?
   Or spring, new born,
   Of the fragrant morn,
'Mong the far-off Indian seas?

Where speedest thou, sweet wind?
Thou little heedest, I trow—
Dost thou sigh for some glancing star?
   Or cool the brow
   Of the dying now,
As they pass to their home afar?

What mission is thine, O wind?
Say for what thou yearnest—
That, like the wayward mind,
   Earth thou spurnest,
   Heaven-ward turnest,
And rest canst nowhere find!

9. NATURE.[104]

Manifold cords, invisible or seen,
Present or past, or only hoped for, bind
All to our mother earth.—No step-dame she,
Coz'ning with forced fondness, but a fount,
Rightly pursued, of never-failing love.—
True, that too oft we lose ourselves 'mong thorns
That tear and wound.—But why impatient haste
From the smooth path our fairest mother drew?
'Tis man, not nature, works the general ill,
By folly piled on folly, till the heap
Hides every natural feeling, save alone
Grey Discontent, upraised to ominous height,
And keeping drowsy watch o'er buried wishes.

---

104. *Monthly Repository* (new series) Vol. VI, September 1832.

10.

Beautiful Rhine! Beautiful Rhine![105]
Girt like a God with the deep-blooming vine;
Or Cybele thou, crown'd with turrets and towers,[106]
Here cloud-meeting crags, there green-mantled bowers,
Beautiful Rhine! that it were mine,
To pass on thy bosom the fast fleeting hours—

O the blue Rhine! the clear blue Rhine!
Softly, she sleeps while the yellow moon-shine,
Gazes, enamoured of creature so bright,
And curtains her beauty, with shadows of night

11. BEAUTIFUL FABLES OF POETIC GREECE![107]

How many hearts have felt, how many [choirs] have sung
Thy [witcheries] power! whether ye trace[108]
with light & graceful touch the scenes luxuriant
which laughing nature sheds abundant,
On thy delicious land
Skies redolent of brightness, seas whose gentle swell
and sportive waves come softly murmuring
To say this curled head below the gazer's foot
On low yet deep sing in melodious numbers[109]
The boundless torrent of resistless passion,
Which swan-like burst from dying Sappho's breast
As[110] with firmer nerve and manlier strain
Recite the glorious list of Athen's heroes

---

105. Box III/186.

106. Over the "e" in "towers" and "bowers" in the next line HTM has written an apostrophe, but she has not struck out the "e," so apparently she had not decided whether to change the spelling or not.

107. Box III/203.

108. "Touch" was replaced by "trace."

109. "Strike the full chord" was replaced by "in melodious numbers."

110. "Perhaps" was replaced by "As."

[W]ho[111] with front undaunted stood to meet
The Persians countless myriads
As the young eaglet plums his wing
And soars to meet the Sun.

Unconsciously ye rise
And like own[112] Parthena
Spring unexpected & mature to birth[113]
Whate'r the[114] moody mind would turn to grave or tender
Sad or bright still cherish'd stories[115] of our boyhoods

And the lovely vallies and embowering woods
Peopled with young bewitching dieties

12.

I hold the future in my own control,[116]
A god unto myself—because of stedfast will.
That neither[117] Time nor circumstance may change
For that the[118] soul of virtuous Life
Of useful acts, and lofty purposes
Is voluntariness—with mind & heart
To wish, & therefore will,
And so achieve, is the main secret
of the growth of good—
Therefore let those who have it hold it firm
As the wreck'd mariner the stedfast rock.
~~After long struggle with the storm~~
of vantage, gained by long struggle from the storm.[119]

---

111. "How" was replaced by "who."

112. "Thy" was replaced by "own."

113. This line replaces the line "And spring fullarmed to birth."

114. "Our" was replaced by "the."

115. "Fables" was replaced by "stories."

116. Box III/188.

117. These first two words replace the words "unchanged by," which were struck out by HTM.

118. HTM inadvertently repeats "the" here.

119. This line was written sideways on the page.

Popular Fallacies.

That the chief object of women's life is love.

                    + enjoyment.

That the chief objects in life of mankind are &
should be the legalised propagation of the
   species & the education of their young.

That that is useful & beautiful in the religious
feeling is necessarily connected with any
traditions on the subject — either Jewish or
Christian or any other.

religion is a name for that one enshrined is high qualities of
intellect & heart. Beauty & integrity. these are to be found in
that there must always be poor.

                       Corollaries

That the exercise of the sexual functions
is in any degree a necessity.
          (It is a matter of education)
That the non exercise of them is necessarily
a deprivation. (& &c)

That sensuality is in itself unworthy.
(It takes its colour chiefly from the individual)
That chastity is in itself a virtue,

   (It is neither virtuous nor vicious.)

+ superstition in persons who have been brought up in disbelief
of religion & in others who have been brought up in the most
entire belief and reverence for religion but who have
given it up on examination. the persons of the highest
moral principle, both sides dissolute & in fidelity of

MISCELLANEOUS

8

This section consists of three different types of writing. "Personal writing" is a collection of very scattered, highly interesting, personal, and even intimate scraps of writing. The "The Life of William Caxton" was published as a chapter in a book sponsored by the Society for the Diffusion of Useful Knowledge. "On the Probable Futurity of the Labouring Classes" is a chapter from Principles of Political Economy. *Each piece is distinct and will be introduced more as it appears.*

The personal writings require the most background. They consist of a conglomeration of scraps from Box III of the Mill/Taylor Collection in the British Library of the London School of Political and Economic Sciences. Despite the scattered and incomplete state of these manuscripts, we see here more than anywhere the inner life of Harriet Taylor Mill. The first fragment of writing is a recitation of popular sayings which HTM sees as fallacies—for example, "That the great object of women's life is love." Harriet also lists a set of corollaries and then expresses her ridicule of each in a short commentary on each. For example, about women's need and desire for sex, the corollary for the fallacy just mentioned, she writes "That chastity is in itself a virtue (It is neither virtuous nor vicious)." Harriet expresses her strong anti-religious sentiments. Listed as a popular fallacy, with Harriet's editorial following, is the claim "That the Bible is Holy. (It is in the highest degree immoral & indecent, cruel & unjust.)" Harriet even asserts that it is a fallacy "that there must always be poor" and disagrees as well with its corollary, "That money is a low & unworthy object," claiming, "It is a necessity for all improvement and enjoyment." The second bit of personal writing is best remembered for its *reference to the connection between morality and enjoyment. Harriet claims the two "sh*^{d}* be one."*

The largest amount of personal writing is found in Box III/101. This file contains six pieces of paper folded in half to form four writing surfaces. Harriet did not write in a linear fashion on these sheets, but often seemed to have used them as a form of written conversation. Clearly she was asking and responding to questions someone else must have been writing on separate paper. One can imagine carrying on such a "dialogue," for example, during a concert or even a lecture. Usually it is impossible to identify who the intended audience is, yet the person reading these intimate notes must surely have been John Stuart Mill or Helen as an adult. (At least one of them must be dated later than 1847, since it refers to Sand's novel written that year.) These notes are filled with expressions of emotion (anger, irritation, sensuality, fury, arrogance) as well as Harriet's most closely held judgments of ideas and character (William Fox, Carlyle, and others). Harriet offers ideas about progress, breeding, democracy, fashion, truth ("Truth has so many sides, one is always telling one *side"), and books (Sand, Hahn Hahn, Dickens, Anderson, etc.). Her most anguished writing is found in the fifth and sixth selections, when she discusses the advantages of an unnamed woman leaving an abusive relationship. To whom Harriet is referring and to whom she is addressing this communication remain unclear. On the first page of the fifth selection, Harriet begins with a comment about Mr. (William J.) Fox having behaved badly. On the same page is the comment, "*How *much I suffered from losing her I* could not *tell." Harriet had been extremely close to Eliza Flower, the woman who would become Fox's live-in lover while his invalid wife continued to live in the same house. One interpretation of her writing throughout this section may be a response to Eliza Flower's relationship to William Fox.*[1] *Another possible referent for the passages may be Harriet's sister, Caroline, who may have been physically abused by her husband, Arthur Ley.*

In the middle of the final selection from Box III/101, Harriet switches from the discussion of the abused woman to an entirely different topic, the sensuality and superiority of Italians. Her story of having her hand kissed by a Venetian rower reveals that she is anything but insensitive.

Box III/106 is equally ambiguous and intriguing. This tirade is written about an unnamed man. Does Harriet refer to JSM, Carlyle, Comte or some other? Her strong condemnation of him ("if I were God, he

---

1. Eliza Flower's death in 1847 may have prompted this outpouring of anger. See Harriet's letters to John Taylor about Eliza (28/136 and 28/163).

*would be tortured"), her sarcasm about his inability to love because of his
overintellectualization, and her reference to his inability to love men make
speculation about the identity of this person inevitable. Box III/138 and
Box III/147 are as enticing as they are short. Were these open statements
meant to be completely private, or were they written, as so much else in
this section is clearly meant to be, as part of a dialogue with some unnamed person? The next to last selection is about the propriety of her
sister's gift of a single shilling, and the final piece of writing is about
young people's reaction to Thomas Carlyle's writing.*

PERSONAL WRITING

I.

POPULAR FALLACIES[2]

That the great object of women's life is love.

That the cheif objects & enjoyments in life of Mankind are & should
be the legalised propagation of the species & the education of their young.

That what is useful & beautiful in the religious feeling is necessarily
connected with any traditions on the subject—either Jewish or Christian
or any other.[3]

That there must always be poor.

Religion is a name for what are recognized as high qualities of the
head & heart. Poetry & integrity. These are to be found in +perfection
in persons who have been brought up in disbelief of 'religion' & in others
who have been brought up in the most entire beleif and reverence for
religion but who have given it up on examination. The persons of the
highest moral principles, embodying rigidest integrity & most ardent
admiration of the beauties of nature & the keenest curiosity & deepest
interest in the unknown powers & mysteries of the universe & the highest
appreciation & acutest judgment of acts are & have been to my knowledge

---

2. Box III/107.

3. The expansion on the theme of religion begins before the next fallacy, but because HTM
added so much to this section, it seemed more appropriate to include the final fallacy before
the added material.

entire disbelievers. Serious calm conscientious erudite warm hearted cool headed ~~unbeleivers men & women~~ unbeleivers.

COROLLARIES

That the exercise of the sexual functions is in any degree a necessity.
(It is a matter of education)
That the non-exercise of them is necessarily a deprivation. (&c &c)
That sensuality is in itself unworthy. (It takes its colour wholly from the individual)
That chastity is in itself a virtue.
(It is neither virtuous nor vicious)
That money is a low & unworthy object. It is a necessity for all improvement & enjoyment
That those are richest who have fewest wants. (Those are richest who have most capacity for enjoyments and most means of obtaining enjoyment.)
That money will not give happiness. (It will give happiness to those we love, why not then to ourselves)
That money will not procure affection. (The happier people are the more they are inclined to love—if we can make people happier they will love us more.)
That the Bible is Holy.
 (It is in the highest degree immoral & indecent, cruel & unjust.)
That Christianity is a Philosophy.
(It is the inculcation of one single virtue—Benevolence.)

2.

Endurance & Courage[4]
Beauty & Utility
Toleration & Subserviency
Enjoyment & Morality
we put enjoy^t first because the end sought is a finer thing than the means by wh we seek & these two sh^d be one, in that some mental Medea w^d [transmute] the old morality into the youth's enjoyment & give it immortality in the minds & manners of we

---

4. Box III/128.

[right hand side of page]
how one might go on to—except that you might thus know better than I do
rest assured
Ernst [in das leid leben][5] so.
so so. tis
tis tis
tis
Than the Man
you may
which
things
Those of
of
of mine
mine
I think yet.

[written perpendicular to first two sections]
*they will be only dependent upon a dependance which equal & worthy—
unavoidable evil, they will bear ~~manfully or~~

[on back of page]
apparently [instinctive] state
<u>conscious</u> error or weakness in the mental world, has a horror of codes, as
in the moral of principles & in the political of constitutions—so law is
subservient to precedent feeling to sensation & national character, to
diplomacy—& individual character to the caprice of Society

[perpendicular to above]
Subserviency
What is it
Toleration
What it is
What sh^d be

———
5. "To live seriously in pain/sorrow/grief."

3.

A.

The extreme & radical difference between our modes of viewing things[6]—
different standards different tests cause a feeling of emptyness if not even
of falseness in our intercourse—if we <u>do</u> by a rare chance think the same
thing right it nearly always proves to be for the most opposite & <u>opposed</u>
reasons. our very <u>sanctions</u> turn their backs to each other! Tis true as I said
to you, you choose to look only on the sunny side of things, I generally
see the shady, (perhaps because I look from the sunny) might I be permitted to say that I think your philosophy is to deny the existence in nature
& life of those things you dislike—mine to a necessity to begin by looking
the worst in the face, in order the sooner & the surer to combat & get rid
of it, whether in generals or particulars—I cannot go on my own road &
leave evil behind me. I must <u>destroy it</u>, not for my own sake but that it
may no longer exist. I cannot blind myself to evils & then think & act as
if they did not exist. Then the <u>motif</u> of my life is <u>progress</u>. to do what I
can for "progress of the species"—as Carlyle in his foggy—supercilious
way, says—

    Sureness & progress—
Immutability is my personal taste
Progress my enthusiasm

[upside down on page]
This is what I mean when I say you have not sympathy.
    I said I had my throat swelled <u>now</u> from nervousness.
You answered was it owing to those two days—
        (tho I had said <u>now</u>)
then I said O no, it has only just come—
Then you began again to say you wondered what caused it.
It never occurred to you that it was caused by seeing that <u>you</u>
looked nervous—
yet you <u>should</u> have guessed that & understood it
Bless you.

[another page]
Arguments answered by metaphor & similes

---

6. Box III/101.

Died of a Rose in Aromatic Pains,
Surrounded by a crowd of disciples, very ordinary people, whose only claim
to superiority consists in wishing to be extraordinary.

[another page]
Lily might—if it happened to be convenient—
    perhaps—
Have you an order

----

*

You have grown in the most remarkable manner like her[.] I never saw
such a likeness in the eyes
    You <u>had</u> always a stronger interest than yourself—now you will not
have

[upside down at *]
Your love of beauty is quite as great. The difference is you have not gone
through so much <u>personal</u> feeling before—

B.

There are such <u>radical</u> differences between us
    I do not think Poetry is the staff of life.

When ordinary people emancipate themselves from the ordinary rules of
conduct you never know what badnesses they may commit in their relations with others. The rules they make for themselves are pliable to their
occasions under temptation.
    The use of high breeding seems to be to make common natures act, in
their relations to others, like fine natures.
    That need not be aristocratic—
I am heart & soul <u>democrat</u>[7]—but high breeding is found in the lowest
of fine natures.
In the world as it is the protection of high breeding is indispensable. It
is nature to the <u>fine</u> & improvement & good for the coarse

[back of page]

---

7. Underlined four times.

at all events that only shows the good nervous organization—

But the best & finest natures are often the wickedest people—
development is <u>as</u> important as nature—perhaps more—
but the finer the being the more naturally selfish—unless the ardent
desire for enjoyment is ruled by the <u>cultivated</u> will, intellect
Unconscious fine natures are intensely egoist—at first unknowingly—
I refer to their relations to others.

C.

How long have you given up the beautiful why you used to put up your
hair? I miss it so
You used to put it up in the Greek Knot with a few scattered curls
coming out from comb the shortning the head, The rounding it, by this
manner, loses the <u>length</u>
<u>No</u>—you are <u>just</u> what you were—only now you neglect your beauty
so do I when I am quite alone
I think they sh^d do as they are inclined—but I like what you discribe—
a look of carefulness
I used somewhat to try—but now I detest every thing, but simplicity
in that respect
How frightful is anything worn which suggest money!

but I am disgusted even with them[,] from seeing them on "Miss this &
that" The person enters with meaning & prettyness in every thing but the
face & person!
I do not think you can form any judgment from the dress[.] The better
the person[,] the more it is accidental but dress is so unsimple now that
accidentally things dont come well together. This is a bad state[.] so many
of the bourgeois ladies dress in perfectly beautiful things—all is right
except the bearer—who is nothing & worse & this disgusts with wearing
those things

[different page]
The best they can be without cultivated intellect. We have that dynasty
yet to come The poor natured mother teaches the poor natured daughter
to <u>act</u> as she was taught to act—she does not think about it

[perpendicular to above]
good everything I think—remember how ignorant they are—I think the

advantages of birth very impartially distributed[.] there have not been experiments yet[8] She simply teaches as she was taught grace, courtesy, gentle manner, or proud manner, calmness, apparent care for others &c.

[upside down]
I think the poor breed as many aristocratic natures as the rest

D.

+Keep it altogether—it is not however much worth having—he is very little. a german Mr Fox
    always simple+[9]
yes, but if people wish for sympathy from every body that is the consequence—
Timidity—Vanity—Shyness—
    underbreeding again.

[upside down on page]
I know one often can smile on all sorts of people from mere quiet good natured & bland sensation—
    This is not false—it is true—

[back of page]
only it is so troublesome

[written perpendicular]
    base

[back of previous page]
    I agree too, I think, with Lily who says dress does not matter but attend to person.
    The putting hair in the most suitable way—

[upside down on page]
I never had that satisfaction, of feeling harmoniously dressed
It requires thought & trouble, & I dont give enough of either

---

8. Note the similarity to chapter 3 of *On Liberty*.

9. Lines beginning and ending with "+" have a single diagonal line indicating a scratchout.

[perpendicular to both of above]
The difference between the Aristocracy & the middle classes is that the
first all <u>act as if they were fine natures</u>—this is the <u>traditional education</u>
of the class—give the same education to an ordinary person & you have
the same result
     Fine blood finds it out for itself

[across the folded page]
    I dont know. Truth has so many sides, one is always telling <u>one</u> side[10]—
    I did not mean to say you despised or neglected neatness—I meant you
despise care for looking your best—
    It is a healthy action on oneself & others—
    I preach this all the more that I know I neglect it myself
    & Lily too despises it—
    so I am always preaching it

[on back of this page & upside down]
Yet I prefer even the [first] to the Howitt?[11] sentimentality
    but I dislike Dickens[12] as much
~~Did you~~ read the Improvisatore[13]?
        It is pretty—
Do you read Sand
    or Hahn Hahn
as usual it has only some rare glimpses of truth—but it has some. & is
very interesting as showing what german women are doing
    read Sands
    Lucresia Floriani
but have you read her Lelia?[14]

---

10. Note similarity to chapter 2 of *On Liberty*.

11. Harriet may be referring to Mary Botham Howitt, who wrote *Ballads and other Poems* (1847) and *The Childhood of Mary Leeson* (1848).

12. Dickens wrote *Martin Chuzzlewit* (1843-44), *A Christmas Carol* (1843), *Dombey and Son* (1846-48), *David Copperfield* (1849-50), and *Bleak House* (1852-53) during the period to which Harriet may be referring.

13. By Hans Christian Anderson, 1845.

14. George Sand published both *Consuelo* and *LeDiable a Paris* in 1845. Ida Grafin Hahn Hahn published *Grafin Faustine* (1841), *Ilda Schonholm* (1845), and *Sigismund Forster* (1845). She visited London in 1846 and was all the rage that summer (See Alethea Hayter, *A Sultry Month: Scenes of London Literary Life in 1846* (London: Faber and Faber Ltd., 1965). Harriet misspells *Lucrezia Floriani,* which was published in 1847; thus, this note must have been written some time after its publication. *Lelia* was published in 1833.

Have you the 2^d vol of Richter?[15]
if you like to keep it you had better have the 1st

E.

+Mr. Fox has behaved ill surely?
I do not know
I do not like a divided feeling when I meet a person—
but one often has—
you know how inexpressive I am
I let things go—+[16]
surely you are wrong to pay him money
It is absurd—if one would think of such
thing it is he who is indebted!

[perpendicular to above]
How much I suffered from losing her I could not tell—I tried so hard to
stay

[perpendicular the opposite side of page]
It is ten years since I have known either

[next page]
my steady opinion that they sh^d separate
    separated her & me

[upside down on page]
I think he would—She has said to me so much severer things of him than
you have
Why not say strongly what she feels strongly—if one trusts the discretion
of the person—
I feel now that I do not know how to feel to [him]—that is I do not know
how he has behaved

---

15. Harriet may have been referring to Karl Ernst Richter's *Nordamerikanisches Volksleben*,
published in 1852. Or she may be referring to Johann Paul Friedrich Richter, better known
as "Jean Paul." Jean Paul is quoted elsewhere in HTM's writing, but it is odd that she would
not use his pseudonym. If the Richter referred to is Karl, Harriet's notes must be dated after
1852, but since we cannot be certain that this is the work referred to in the text, we can only
date the note as after publication of the Sand piece in 1847, which is referred to by name.

16. HTM drew three lines through text indicated by "+."

[I,] as far as I have known him, always
[missing line]
not making ~~the~~ separation when he felt separation—all those years of slow suffering would have been exchanged for a sharp suffering supported by indignation

[opposite page]
early. She w^d have found another life
When people of common natures emancipate themselves[17]

F.

then (if that could be desired!) he would have got up all the old desire ~~for~~ communication—oh if she would but have left him—
  boldly clearly—
  he would after some year or years have become a beggar for the crumbs that fell from her table—
  (if that would have gratified her)
I should advise you not to give him up

----

he enjoys wit more than he possesses it

----

respect for the possession of that in others which he desires to possess himself

----

  & to <u>equal</u> high respect for oneself & others—
  That is my democracy
  you must go there some day
  all is harmonious & beautiful in human nature there
  To the <u>mere</u> outward eye Italy must dissapoint, <u>perhaps</u> not at first. They dissapoint—you must grow into it. it is the <u>people</u> that are the charm of Italy—as they are the curse of England
  I never saw but in one head of Titian an <u>ideal</u> Christ except my boatman on Como. One cannot choose but look for a moment at that head—the man understands in a moment ones true feeling—its meaning & amount—

---

17. This line is marked through vertically four times.

as he passes to reach an oar he takes ones hand to his lips for an instant—in
<u>fullest</u> view of everybody—a half gentle smile—then passes on never again
looks or shows any thing but the never ceasing   intense respect
  The English men look so shy & funny in such occasions

yes—but that proves nothing of qualities
  If you did but see the roads in Italy—you are rowed by a <u>god</u>—a
fisherman to whose <u>his</u> head is little
you never speak to man or woman that you do not find the <u>highest</u>[18]
breeding possible & <u>always</u> high intellect

[upside down]
In the Pontine Marshes <u>you</u> come out
  no one c^d tell her from you—she was like all Italians of the lower class,
a perfect high bred <u>lady</u>—<u>Annunziata</u>

4.

He[19] has tried to make something of what he calls ~~love~~[20] & been
dissapointed for two reasons—first that as things are there are scarcely any
~~women~~ worth loving to a person of intellect—and secondly that is physical
& so his spiritual constitution is eminently 'scottish' he is incapable of
strong sympathy, only <u>seeing</u> its beauty with his mind—<u>therefore</u> he has
never <u>loved</u> men, for his feelings are not strong enough & he may well
place very near together the words nausea & love for the animal instinct
he talks of w^d be disgusting in & to such a person as he—
  He has been ~~thrown~~ much in the Society of extremely commonplace
people & has

[back of sheet]
  at sometime been [even] <u>wounded</u> by assumption—
  He is selfih quite without imagination and soured—of a poor physical

---

18. Underlined twice.

19. The person HTM refers to is unknown; he could be JSM, Carlyle, Comte, or someone else.
Her strong condemnation (if I were God, he would suffer) and her sarcasm about his inability
to love make speculation about the identity of this person inevitable. The letter is in Box
III/106.

20. This word has been scratched out in an uncharacteristically forceful way. Unlike her usual
single strikeover, she has attempted to scribble out this word.

constitution except 'in re' a certain intellectual force wh has produced honesty of purpose <u>not</u> possibly magnanimous but eagerly desiring to be so & his selfish admiration irritated at the dim perception that it is impossible to him.

—Spite of what <u>he</u> says If I were providence he (c) sh^d <u>suffer</u> acutely— with some tremendous physical evils—How thoroughly he mistakes—he thinks he has healthy <u>vigour</u>—'tis morbid instability he'll end devotee

[sideways across previous page[21]]

has he been brought up in very poor circumstances—he has never felt luxury.

5.

Whatever shall be made of Mr Mills.[22]

6.

Strength, efficiently to act what he has intelligence wisely to will. The noblest heart and the wisest head in the world.[23]

7.

the money she possesses as much in proportion as do the poor still I felt that the shilling was not in proportion—I felt that she had a contracted heart—that had she had the impulse to benefit 5 shillings w^d have been as unfelt by her as the one—that is our relative position it was not a suitable gift—that in fact she gave it by rote & without feeling— therefore

---

21. It is unclear where this passage belongs. It follows the train of thought that ends the first page, although it repeats the "has" that ends the first page. However, the second page also seems to follow naturally from the end of the first page. HTM was in the habit in her letters of writing to the end, then returning to the first page to finish either by writing around the margins or cross-hatch across the page. She may have simply added this as an addendum after she had finished the second page.

22. Box III/138.

23. Box III/147.

I thanked her only by rote—I felt that her superiority over me was only in the artificial advantages of life—that I was as much her superior spiritually as she mine in these advantages & so I got into a charitable mood & ceased to despise her & was willing to recognize her as a sister.[24]

8.

Young people feel about Carlyles writing as they regard the clouds which to hide paradise—& to our feelings while the illusion lasts they create the paradise which they seem to hide[25]

LIFE OF WILLIAM CAXTON

The second piece of miscellaneous writing is the "Life of William Caxton," a chapter from a book published by the Society for the Diffusion of Useful Knowledge. This group of liberal writers and thinkers included James Mill and John Taylor and was formed to find ways of educating those in the working classes who did not have the advantage of formal education. Their publications contained what the society's members saw as "useful knowledge" about science, history, geography, art, and so on. Harriet's chapter is about the history of the inscription of language, including a history of paper, pens, manuscripts, and finally printing. In this historical framework she includes the biography of William Caxton, the man credited with bringing printing to England. Harriet's wide range of knowledge, as exemplified in this essay, is impressive when one considers that she did not benefit from any formal education and was a teenager at the time.

A few draft passages of this piece are found in Box III/113. The paper is watermarked 1826, the year that Harriet married John Taylor, and scraps of the writing are written in both HTM's and John Taylor's handwriting. This indication of early collaboration with John Taylor indicates the intellectual curiosity of Harriet as an eighteen-year-old writer. Since neither person's drafts very closely imitate the final draft, much work remained before the piece was published in 1833. Clearly Harriet's

---

24. Box III/150.

25. Box III/154.

*interest in writing, as well her commitment to liberal politics, began be-
fore she met John Stuart Mill. Like George Eliot's Dorothea, Harriet
may have begun her marriage believing that her Mr. Casaubon, John
Taylor, would open doors for her intellectual development, only to discover
that her husband's intellect did not match her own.*

LIFE OF WILLIAM CAXTON,[26]
WITH
AN ACCOUNT OF THE INVENTION OF PRINTING, AND OF THE MODES AND MATERIALS USED FOR TRANSMITTING KNOWLEDGE BEFORE THAT TOOK PLACE

*The ease which we now find in providing and dispersing, what
number of copies of books we please, by the opportunity of the press,
makes us apt to imagine, without considering the matter, that the
publication of books was the same easy affair in all former times as
in the present. But the case was quite different. From when there
were no books in the world, but what were written out by hand,
with great labour and expense, the method of publishing them was
necessarily very slow, and the price very dear; so that the rich only
and curious would be disposed or able to purchase them; and to such
also it was often difficult to procure them, or to know even where
they were to be bought.* —Middleton's Free Enquiry, p. 198.

CHAPTER I

*Introductory—Different kinds of Biography—Kind to which that of Caxton
belongs—Principal object in selecting it—Nature and arrangement of the subjects
necessary to be touched upon in order to attain that object.*

The lives of some men supply scanty materials for private and personal
biography; whereas the materials that connect them with the advancement
of the human race in knowledge, civilization, and happiness, are, in no
common degree, rich and interesting. Such is the case with the life of
William Caxton. Very few of the events of his life are known; and it is

<hr/>

26. *Lives of Eminent Persons* (London: Baldwin & Cradock, Paternoster-Row, 1833), 1-32.

highly probable that, if we had them in minute detail, they would have presented nothing very curious or very instructive,—nothing that would have justified us in selecting his life, on account either of the insight it afforded into the formation of the human mind and character, or of the impressive and practical lesson it taught, that, in moral conduct, as certainly as in the material world, like causes will always produce like effects. Such lives as give this insight, and teach by powerful and repeated examples this most important, but too often neglected truth, are certainly of the highest utility as well as interest: they give biography a just claim to be ranked above all other studies, in so far as it teaches, most emphatically, that close attention, and persevering and zealous industry, are absolutely necessary for the acquisition of knowledge; and that these qualities, united with probity, are equally necessary to our success in the world, and to our usefulness and respectability in society.

The biography of those men, however, whose lives have contributed to the improvement of the human race, even though they have displayed no superior talent, ought, by no means, to be neglected.[27] Such lives must always command interest, and they may be so written as to convey useful information. On these accounts we have chosen the life of William Caxton. Through his zeal, industry, and perseverance, the art of printing was introduced into England, and firmly established here. It is a trite remark, that we know very little of the value, or even of the real nature of those advantages which have been familiar to us from our infancy, which we see all around us, the want of which never entered into our imagination, but of which, in times not very remote, our ancestors were utterly ignorant, and which are still unknown to the great majority of mankind.

At present, in our country, there could not, most probably, be found a single hovel in the most lonely and remote district, in which some books would not be found—not treasured as a great rarity and of high value, but, on the contrary, accessible to all. The art of printing has done this. Before it was found out, few books were to be seen except in monasteries, universities, and the libraries of those who were very fond of literature, or very rich. They were preserved by such as had them with the utmost care; guarded

---

27. A draft of a similar passage written in Harriet's hand appears in Box III/113: "It gives us great pleasures to see that [they] do not confine themselves to the biography of ~~splendid~~ brilliant characters whose splendour dazzles the mind & ~~prevents hides~~ throws a light even on their faults and vices that in a publication intended for all ranks we are presented with the history of those who have been useful rather than brilliant—of those whom the humblest may fairly endeavour to ~~imitate~~ emulate & the imitation of whom w^d do honour to all.—In doing this they are really benefiting mankind & may they proceed in the course they have so well begun unmoved by the snears of the cynic or the. . . ." The manuscript breaks off abruptly at this point.

against loss equally with their most precious jewels; and never lent except with the utmost precaution and the best security for their return.

Now, when we wish to purchase a book we go into a bookseller's shop, pay its price, and, without delay or formality, it is our own. *Then,* if the manuscript were rare and costly, the transfer by purchase was often conducted in manner as circumspect, and guarded by as strict and legal evidence, as were necessary in the sale and purchase of an estate. *Now,* very little labour or time is requisite to ascertain where the scarcest books are to be procured. *Then,* as Dr. Middleton remarks, it was not only often difficult to procure them, but even to know where they were to be bought. Now, a small portion of the week's wages of a labouring man is sufficient to purchase books, which, while only existing in manuscript, could not be obtained except at the cost of a sum equal to his whole year's earnings: and for the manuscripts of many works, sums were *then* given equivalent (taking the value of money at those periods into the account) to the income of most persons in the middle ranks of life at present, and to what would now purchase a whole library suited to their station and adequate to their desires.

Then, not only did all books exist solely in manuscript, but, in many instances, there were few copies of those manuscripts; in some cases, perhaps not a dozen. Their destruction, therefore, at all times and under all circumstances, must have been no improbable event; and in those days of almost uninterrupted warfare and devastation, it very frequently occurred. Some were absolutely destroyed, no copies remained, others were mutilated and rendered imperfect, and their imperfections could not be removed. Others were lost by negligence, or too much care for their preservation during scenes of rapine and warfare, and in the midst of the plunder of ignorant and barbarian soldiers; and thus withdrawn, for ever, or for a long period, from the perusal and instruction of mankind. *Now,* since the invention of printing, the utter destruction, or the irreparable mutilation of a book, cannot scarcely occur, at least after it has once passed from the printing—office into the shops of booksellers: if such an event could take place even then, the dispersion of an usual edition of seven hundred or one thousand copies among purchasers in every part of the kingdom, renders it perfectly secure from destruction or loss.

In the days of manuscript books, what expense and labour must have been submitted to, what a length of time must have elapsed, before an author could have conveyed his discoveries, or reasoning, or instructions, what would benefit or bless human life, to one thousandth part of the number of readers to whom the art of printing enables him to convey the fruits of his study or imagination with infinitely less expense and labour, and in an infinitely shorter space of time! What would our ancestors, who lived before printing was discovered, have said, had they after having been present in the House of Commons till two or three o'clock in the morning, read at their breakfast table a detailed account of speeches, which had occupied nearly twelve hours in the delivery, and learnt not one or two, but many thousand copies were, at that time, circulating?

Such is a very general representation of the state and means of literary communication before printing was discovered: whoever reflects on it will not be surprised that the progress of mankind, in every thing useful and valuable, was extremely slow and difficult. Individuals and uncommunicated knowledge cannot purify itself from error; and, till printing was discovered, how much knowledge must necessarily have been individual and uncommunicated! The greater the number of minds that are brought to bear on any topic of research, experiment or thought, the sooner will its truth be ascertained and established. But when "there were no books in the world but what were written out by hand, with great labour and expense, the method of publishing them was necessarily very slow, and the price very dear, so that the rich only and curious would be disposed and able to purchase them." In these circumstances, error gained strength; important and valuable truths died at their very birth, or struggled useless and unproductive till the art of printing nourished them to maturity, and enabled them to strike their roots deeply and widely, and to produce their natural and genuine fruit of practical good to the human race.

But no general picture, however strongly and accurately it may be drawn, can speak so emphatically, either to the understanding or the imagination, as a picture, the outlines of which are filled up with strokes, minute but characteristic. No general contrast can exhibit a difference so clearly and powerfully as a contrast that enters into detail, and sets the individual circumstances directly in array against one another.

The facts already stated may enable and dispose our readers to prize, with some degree of justice, the advantages derived from the art of printing, and to form a vague and imperfect notion of what the state and amount of knowledge must have been, when all the books in the world were written out by hand. But we think we shall render these feelings and impressions much more vivid, distinct and permanent—we shall set the inestimable advantages derived from the art of printing in clearer and more powerful light—we shall impress the contrast between our own means of improvement and those possessed by our ancestors, and even by the enlightened philosophers of Greece and Rome, in the very noon-tide of their intellectual vigour and glory, more deeply—if, before we give a sketch of the invention of printing, and of the life of Caxton, by whom the infant art was introduced into this country, and established here—we devote two chapters to a detail—first, of the modes and materials employed for the communication and transmission of knowledge among the Greeks and Romans, and during the dark and middle ages; and secondly, of the writing and company of manuscripts—where it was executed, and by whom—their rarity and value—destruction—loss and recovery. We shall take care that the facts detailed in these chapters are well established—that they are curious and interesting, and, above all, that they bear directly and powerfully on the grand object we have in view,—to draw the deliberate attention and the well-grounded belief of our readers to this important truth, that the press has bestowed, is at present bestowing, and cannot cease to bestow, on mankind greater blessings than any other art has done or can do; since, without it, knowledge, and consequently, all the benefits derived from knowledge, must have crept on with slow and feeble steps, whereas, with it, knowledge must proceed at a steady, onward pace, and with a vigour that will tread down or remove every obstacle.

CHAPTER II

A Description of the Modes and Materials for communicating and transmitting Knowledge before the Invention of Printing.

The few and simple laws, necessary in the very earliest stages of society, seem, at first, among the Greeks, to have been set to music, and chanted or sung. Afterwards they were engraved on a hard and solid substance, as stone, metal or wood. According to some authors the laws of Solon were engraved on tablets of wood, so constructed that they might be turned round in wooden cases. Some of his laws, however, were certainly engraved on stone. The laws of the Twelve Tables among the Romans were engraved on the oaken planks, ivory tables, or brass; most probably on the last. In order to give the Athenians an opportunity of judging deliberately on a proposed law, it was engraved on a tablet, which was hung up for some days at the Statue of the Heroes, the most public and frequented place in the city of Athens. And that no man might plead ignorance of his duty, the laws, when passed, were engraven on the walls of the royal portico; and persons were appointed to transcribe such as were worn or defaced and to enter the new ones. The Arundelian Marbles, preserved in the University of Oxford, sufficiently prove for what a variety of purposes inscriptions on stone were used among the ancients. Some of the inscriptions on them record treaties, others the victories or good qualities and deeds of distinguished persons, others miscellaneous events: most of them, however, are sepulchral. By far the most important and celebrated is the Parian Chronicle, which, when entire, contained a chronology of Greece, particularly of Athens, for a period of 1318 years, viz. from the reign of Cecrops, A. C. 1582, to the archonship of Diognetus, A. C. 264. The Romans engraved on brass, even so late as the reign of the Emperors, in general, their code (plebiscita), contracts, conventions, and public records. The landmarks of estates were engraven on the same metal. The Roman soldiers were allowed, in the field of battle, to write their wills on their bucklers or scabbards; and in many cabinets are preserved the discharges of soldiers, written on copper plates. Lead was employed as well as brass for preserving treaties and laws. And Pausanias informs us that he had seen, in the Temple of the Muses, the Works and Days of Hesiod, inscribed on leaden tables. In the year 1699 Montfauçon purchased, at Rome, a book of eight leaden leaves, (including two which formed the cover,) four inches long and three inches wide. Leaden rings were fastened on the back, through which a small leaden rod ran, to keep the leaves together.

Wood, however, was most generally used, both for public and private purposes, in various forms and modes. The inscription of laws on it has been already mentioned. Even in the 4th century the laws of the Emperors were published on wooden tables, painted with white lead; and formerly the Swedes inscribed or engraved their laws on wood: hence their term Balkar (laws), from *balkan,* a balk or beam. Wooden boards, either plain or covered with wax, were used long before the age of Homer; the former were called Schedæ, whence our word *schedule.* At first, the bare wood was engraved with an iron style: the overlaying them with wax was a subsequent invention. The styles used in both cases were of metal, ivory, or bone; one end pointed, the other smooth, for the purpose of erasing: hence our word *style,* used metaphorically, to signify the choice and arrangement of words employed by an author to express his thoughts. These tablets, or thin slices of wood, when fastened together, formed a book, *Codex,* so called from its resemblance to the trunk of a tree cut into planks. Hence our word *code.* When the Romans wrote letters on their tablets, they fastened them together with thread, and put a seal upon the knot. Table-books continued in use so late as the fourteenth century, and even later, as Chaucer evidently describes one in the Sumpner's Tale.[28] They were then formed into a book by means of parchment bands glued to the backs of the leaves. The Roman boys used them at school; and in the middle ages, young men learning the sciences had table-books, and psalms for meditation were written on them.

---

28. His felaw had a staf tipped with horn,
    A pair of tables, all of ivory,
    And a pointel (style) ypolished fetisly (neatly),
    And wrote always the names, as he stood,
    Of all folk that yave bem any good. (v. 33-37.) [HTM]

The expenses of Philip le Bel, written on the tables of wax, may be seen in the library of St. Victor, at Paris; and in the archives of the town-hall of Hanover, are twelve wooden boards, covered with wax, on which are inscribed the names of the owners of houses in the city. There is reason to believe that this enumeration was made at the beginning of the fifteenth century. The ancients generally used box and citron wood; in the middle ages beech was principally employed. The rich Romans used thin pieces of ivory, instead of wooden tablets. The edicts of the senate, the proceedings of the Roman magistrates, the principal transactions of the emperors, and the affairs of the princes, were recorded on ivory leaves or tablets. These were deposited in the magnificent library founded by Trajan at Rome.

The employment of leaves for the transmission of ideas is of great antiquity; and it is still common in different parts of the east. Hence the word *folio,* (from the Latin folium, a leaf,) and the meaning of *leaf,* when applied to a book. This mode of writing on leaves seems to have been superseded by the use of the bark—a material employed in every age and quarter of the globe. The outer bark was seldom used, being too coarse and rough. The inner bark was preferred, especially that of the line tree. This bark the Romans called *liber*—hence *Liber,* the Latin name for a book. In order that these bark books might be conveniently carried they were rolled up; and in this form called *volumen;* this name was afterwards applied to rolls of paper and parchment—hence the origin of the word *volume,* applied to modern books, though of a different shape. Ancient manuscripts in bark are very scarce; but the use of bark for books still prevails in the east, especially among the Birmans. The custom of making books from bark prevailed among our Scandinavian and Saxon ancestors: the bark of the beech tree was most commonly used. The primitive meaning of the Anglo-Saxon word *boc* is the beech tree; its secondary meaning, a book— and hence our word *book.* There are still extant some letters, and even love-letters, written by the ancient Scandinavians on pieces of bark. A very curious library of the kind was discovered some time ago among the Calmucs; the books were very long and narrow; their leaves of thick bark, varnished over; the writing white on a black ground.

Linen cloth, on which letters were drawn or painted with pencils, was employed by the Egyptians when, it is supposed, they wished to transmit such things as they designed to last very long. In the British Museum there is a piece of writing of this nature, taken out of a mummy. The Romans likewise employed linen (*librilintei*) not merely for what related to private subjects and persons, but also to enter the names of magistrates, treaties, and other public documents.

The employment of the skins of animals, rudely prepared, is stated by

Herodotus to have originated with the Ionians, as a substitute for the papyrus, when it could not be procured without much difficulty and expense; those of sheep, goats, and asses were preferred. Several of these books are in the Vatican, the Royal Library of Paris, and some other libraries. The poems of Homer were written on the intestines of a serpent in letters of gold: this roll was first deposited in the library of Ptolemy Philadelphus, and afterwards taken to the great library of Constantinople, where it was destroyed by fire in the sixth century: it was 120 feet long.

Leather, or skins prepared in the present manner, seems to have been often used by the Jews, on which to write the Law, Pentateuch, and other parts of their Sacred Scriptures. Dr. Buchanan informs us, that in the coffer of the synagogue of the Black Jews, in Malayala, there is an ancient copy of the Law, written on a roll of leather; it is about fifteen feet long; the skins are sewed together. A copy of the Pentateuch, written beautifully in Hebrew characters, (without vowel points,) large, and of a square form, belonged formerly to M. Santander. It occupied fifty-seven skins, which were fastened together with the same material.

The Egyptian papyrus was applied to the purpose of writing upon before the preparation of parchment and its application to the same use were known. But in order to notice in connexion all the subjects employed by the ancients, which have been entirely superseded (except in very few instances) by the use of paper, we shall postpone our account of the papyrus, till we have stated a few particulars regarding the ancient use of parchments.

The common opinion, derived from the authority of Varro and Pliny, that the preparation of parchment from skins owes its origin to a dispute between Eumenes, King of Pergamus, and one of the Ptolemies, concerning their respective libraries, in consequence of which the Egyptian king prohibited the exportation of papyrus, and Eumenes invented parchment, is certainly unfounded. Its manufacture and use are mentioned by Josephus, Diodrus Siculus, and other authors, as having been known long before the age of the Ptolemies: the name given to it by the ancients, however, Charta Pergamena, (paper of Pergamus,) renders it highly probable that its mode of preparation was improved, or its manufacture and use more general there, than in other places. Most of the ancient manuscripts now extant are written on parchment. From their appearance, the parchment has evidently been polished: according to ancient authors, by the pumice stone. They used three kinds—that of the natural colour; the yellow, bicolor membrana of Persius, which seems to have been so called because one side of the leaf was white, the other yellow and the purple; the parchment being tinged with colour, when silver or golden letters were to be used. It sometimes happened that parchment of the very finest kind was extremely scarce; about the year 1120, "one Martin Hugh, being appointed by the convent of St. Edmundbury to write and illuminate a grand copy of the Bible, for their library, could procure no parchment for this purpose in England."

Vellum, a finer kind of parchment, made from the skins of very young calves, was also prepared and used by the ancients, and in the dark and middle ages, for writing upon. There is one manuscript of vellum, of a violet colour, all the letters of which are of silver, except the initials, which are of gold,—which we particularly notice, for two reasons: first, it is the only specimen extant of the parent tongue, from which our own language, and the languages of Sweden, Denmark, Iceland, Norway, the Netherlands, and Germany, are derived; and, secondly, it was long supposed by many to exhibit a very near approach to printing, nearly 1000 years before the art was invented—we allude to the Gothic translation of the Gospels, by Ulphilas, in the fourth century. An imperfect copy of it is preserved in the library of Upsal. It is called the 'Codex Argenteus,' or silver book. The letters appear, and were generally judged, to have been stamped or imprinted, singly, on the vellum, with hot metal types, in the same manner as book-binders at present letter the backs of books. We are not aware that this opinion was called in question, till Mr. Coxe minutely and closely examined the MS., when he convinced himself that each letter was painted, or drawn in the same manner as the initial letters in several of the finest missals. He seems also doubtful, whether to call the leaves vellum, parchment or papyrus.

We come now to paper. The most ancient kind was made from the *papyrus,* whence the word *paper* is derived. This is a species of rush, which the ancients procured exclusively on the banks of the Nile. The particular species, till lately, was not known; but it is now ascertained to be the cyperus papyrus of Linnæus, growing on the banks of different rivers in the east, and likewise, we believe, in the Trinidad. The term *biblos,* originally applied by the Greeks to the inner bark of trees, and equivalent to the liber of the Romans, was afterwards more usually applied to the papyrus. Thence the term was transferred to books in general; and now it is confined by us to the scripture, as *the* book.

It is not known when the papyrus was first manufactured into paper; but there were certainly at a very early period, at least three hundred years before Alexander, manufactories of it at Memphis. Afterwards, and at the time of the conquest of Egypt, by the Romans, it was made chiefly at Alexandria. Till this conquest, however, the paper was of inferior quality. The Roman artists paid great attention to its improvement, and at length made it of considerable thickness, perfectly white and smooth. Even in this state, however, it was so friable and weak, that, when great durability was requisite, leaves of parchment were intermixed with those of papyrus. "Thus the firmness of the one substance defended the brittleness of the other, and great numbers of books, so constituted, have resisted the accidents and decays of twelve centuries."

The papyrus was highly useful to the ancient Egyptians, on many accounts, besides that of supplying them with paper: from the pith they extracted a sweet and nutritive juice; from the harder and lower parts they formed cups, &c.; staves, and ribs of boats, from the upper and more flexible part; and the fibrous part was manufactured into cloth, sails, ropes, strings, shoes, wicks for lamps, and paper. Pliny gives a full description of the manner in which it was made by the ancients; and Bruce, who succeeded in making it, both in Abyssinia and Egypt, has offered several very curious observations on the natural history of the papyrus, in the seventh vol. of his Travels, 8vo. edition, page 117, &c. In one point he differs from the account given by Pliny, of the mode of manufacturing paper from it. According to the latter, one layer of the fibrous coats of the plant was laid across another layer, on a table; they were then connected together by the muddy water of the Nile. Mr. Bruce affirms, that the water of the Nile is no degree glutinous, and that the strips of papyrus adhere together solely by means of the saccharine matter, with which the juice of the plant is abundantly impregnated. He adds, that the Nile water must have been used simply to dissolve this saccharine matter, perfectly and equally. The cemented fibers were pressed, dried, beat with a mallet, and polished with a tooth, shell, or other smooth and solid substance. The Roman artists, in Alexandria, paid great attention to the operations of washing, beating, glueing, sizing, and polishing. It was sized in the same manner as paper from rags is at present. After the first sizing, it was beat with a hammer; sized the second time, pressed, and then polished. It was then cut into various sizes, — never more, however, according to Pliny, than thirteen inches wide. The same author mentions a great variety of kinds, to each of which a specific name was given.

For at least three hundred years before Christ, this article was exported in large quantities from Egypt. Of the extent and value of the manufactures, in Alexandria, and of the wealth derived from them, we may form some idea from an anecdote of Firmus. This person, the friend and ally of Zenobia, queen of Palmyra, a wealthy merchant, or rather manufacturer of paper and glue, in Alexandria, broke into the city in the middle of the third century, at the head of a furious multitude, "assumed the imperial purple, coined money, published edicts, and raised an army, which he boasted he could maintain from the sole profits of his manufactures." The time when the manufacture of this paper was lost, or superseded, is not known. The possession of Egypt by the Saracens certainly interrupted and diminished its manufacture and export; and it is generally supposed that few, if any, manuscripts on papyrus are of a later date than the eight or ninth century. About this period, cotton paper was first made: according to some, in Bucharia; according to others, it had been known long before in China and Persia. There is no doubt, however, that the Arabs, have gained a knowledge of the process, established a manufactory at Ceuta, and afterwards in Spain; and thus introduced it into Europe, about the twelfth century. In the next century this paper was in common use in the eastern empire, and in Sicily. At first it was made of raw cotton; then of old worn-out cotton cloth. While the paper manufactories of Spain were possessed by the Arabians, this article was of a very coarse and inferior quality, in consequence of their employing only mortars, and hand or horse-mills, to reduce the wool or cloth to a pulp; but as soon as their Christian labourers got possession of the paper mills of Toledo and Valencia, they worked them to more advantage, by the use of water-mills, an improved method of grinding and stamping, and by the invention or adoption of moulds. The use of cotton paper became general only in the thirteenth century; and about the middle of the fourteenth, it was almost entirely superseded by paper from linen rags, such as is at present made and used in Europe, and wherever Europeans have settled or colonised. There is much uncertainty respecting the exact time when linen paper was invented, and in what country. It is probable that at first a mixture of cotton and linen rags was employed, especially in those countries, where flax was much and easily cultivated, and where cotton was an article of import, and consequently scarce and dear. Montfauçon, who, on these subjects, is great authority on account of the diligence and extent of his researches, could find no books, either in France or Italy, made of linen paper, before the year 1270. A specimen a little earlier, however, in 1239, has been discovered by De Vaines. In the fourteenth century, the use of this kind of paper became general. Italy seems to have had paper manufacture[d], for exportation, at this time. In 1380, part of the cargo of a ship, from Genoa to Sluys, in Flanders, which was driven ashore on the coast of England, consisted of twenty-two bales of writing paper. The oldest German paper-mill was erected at Nuremberg, in 1390. There are English manuscripts, on linen paper, so early as 1340 and 1342; but the manufacture was not introduced, according to the general opinion, into this country, till the year 1588. At that time a German named Spielman, jeweler to Queen Elizabeth, erected a paper-mill at Dartford, in Kent. This opinion, however, has been controverted on good grounds; as the paper used by Wynkyn de Worde (who may justly be considered as Caxton's real successor) for Bartholomeus, *de proprietatibus rerum*—described by Mr. Dibdin, "as one of the most splendid typographical productions of the early British press," was made at Hertford by John Tate, junior, who may therefore be deemed the earliest paper-maker in England.[29] Our principal supply of fine paper, for printing and writing, was from the Continent—(Holland and France chiefly)—till about one hundred years since. At this period two-thirds of the paper used was home made; at present, besides manufacturing sufficient for our own use, we export it to a considerable amount.

The instruments employed to write with, by the ancients, and in the dark and middle ages, of course varied according to the nature of materials on which they wrote. They may be divided into two kinds: those which acted by the assistance of fluids; of the first kind were the wedges and chisel, for inscriptions on stone, wood, and metal; and the style for wax tablets. The last has been already mentioned and described; the others need no description. As the style was too sharp for writing on parchment and Egyptian paper, and moreover, was not adapted for holding or conveying a fluid, a species of reed was employed. The Egyptian reeds were preferred, but many others were also used. They were cut in the form of our modern pens, and split in the points; when they became blunt, they were sharpened either with a knife, or on a rough stone. Persons of rank and fortune often wrote with a calamus of silver—something probably like our silver pens. However carefully made or mended, the strokes made by the reed-pens were in general coarse and uneven. Both the styles and the reeds were carefully kept in cases. From ancient authors, as well as from the figures in manuscripts, we learn that they used a sponge to cleanse the reed, and to rub out such letters as were written by mistake; a knife for mending the reed; pumice, for a similar purpose, or to smooth the parchment; compasses for measuring the distance of the lines; scissars, for cutting the paper; a puncher, to point out the beginning and end of each line; a rule, to draw lines, and divide the sheets into columns; a glass, containing sand, and another glass filled with water, probably to mix with the ink.

Neither the particular species of calamus, used as pens by the ancients, nor the manner in which they prepared them for this purpose, is known. This is remarkable, since all the places, where these reeds grow wild, have

---

29. John Tate, the younger—
   Which late hath in England do make this paper thynne,
   That now in our English, this boke is printed inne.
   Proemium to Bartholomeus, about 1494. [HTM]

been ascertained, and explored by botanists: with so little success, however, that after a variety of learned as well as scientific conjectures, the calamus of the ancients has not yet found a place in the botanical system of Linneus.

This is yet more remarkable, as reeds are still employed by many eastern nations to write with. Ranwolf, who travelled in the sixteenth century, informs us that canes for pens were sold in the shops of Turkey, small, hollow within, smooth without, and of a brownish colour. Tavernier, Chardin, Tournefort, and other travellers, give a similar account, adding, that the reeds are about the size of large swan quills, and are cut and split in the same manner that we do quills, except that their nib is much larger. The best grow near the Persian Gulph. It is highly probable, that, of whatever species these are, they are of the same as those employed by the ancients; and that the mode of preparing them, still practised in the east, was followed by the ancients. They are put for some months in a dunghill; this gives them a dark yellow colour, a fine polish, and the requisite hardness.

Reeds continued to be used even so late as the eighth century, though there can be no doubt that quill pens were known in the middle of the seventh. The earliest author who uses the word *penna* for a writing pen, is Isidorus, who lived in that century, a Latin sonnet to a pen was written by an Anglo-Saxon author. There is, indeed, in the Medicean Library, a MS. of Virgil, written in the beginning of the 5th century, evidently, from the gradual and regular fineness of the hair strokes, by some instrument as elastic as a quill; but there is no proof that it was really written with a quill. Considering that pens from quills were certainly known in the seventh century, they must have come into a general use very slowly; for in 1433, a present of a bundle of quills was sent from Venice by a monk, with a letter, in which he says, "Shew the bundle to Brother Nicholas, *that he may choose a quill*."

The composition and the colours of the ink used by the ancients were various. Lamp-black, or the black taken from burnt ivory, and soot from furnaces and baths, according to Pliny and other writers, formed the basis of it: the black liquor of the cuttle fish is also said to have been used as ink, principally on the authority of a metaphorical expression of the poet Persius. But of whatever ingredients it was made, it is certain, from chemical analysis, from the solidity and blackness in the most ancient manuscripts, and from an ink-stand found at Herculaneum, in which the ink appears like a thick oil, that the ink then made was much more opaque as well as encaustic than that used at present. Inks, red, purple and blue, and also silver and gold inks, were much employed by the ancients; the red was made from vermilion, cinnabar, and carmine; the purple from the *murex;*

one kind of this coloured ink, called the sacred encauster, was set apart for the sole use of the emperors. The subscription at the end of most Greek manuscripts, containing the name of the copyist, and the year, month, day, and sometimes hour, when he finished his labour, were generally written, in the period of the Lower Empire, in purple ink. Golden ink was used by the Greeks much more than by the Romans. The manufacture both of it and silver ink was a distinct and extensive, as well as a lucrative business in the middle ages; and another distinct business was that of inscribing the titles, capitals or emphatic words, in coloured and gold or silver inks.

CHAPTER III.

Manuscript Books — where written and copied, and by whom — Causes of their Destruction or Loss — their Rarity and high price — Libraries — Schools.

The foregoing chapter proves very strongly and clearly the obstacles and impediments in the way of the communication and transmission of knowledge among the ancients, and in the dark and middle ages, in so far as the nature of the materials employed for those purposes is concerned. Masses of stone or marble, metal, or blocks or planks of wood, were too heavy and cumbrous to circulate: in order to learn what the inscriptions on them related to, it was necessary that they should be consulted on the spot. Even after better materials were used, such as tablets, parchment, and the papyrus paper, the difficulties and disadvantages were great. Wax tablets might answer for notes, letters, or very short treaties, but scarcely for writings of any great length. Besides it appears that they were chiefly intended and applied for private use, and never circulated. Parchment never could have been abundant and cheap; and being at least during the Greek and Roman period manufactured exclusively or principally, in one place, other parts of the world must have been dependant for their supply upon it. Papyrus paper was cheaper, and in much greater abundance; but for a supply of it, the world was indebted to Egypt alone; and we have seen how this supply was cut off or much diminished when the Saracens obtained possession of that country.

The invention of paper from linen rags succeeded. Dr. Robertson re-marks that "it preceded the first dawning of letters and improvement in knowledge towards the close of the eleventh century, and that by means of it, not only the number of manuscripts increased, but the study of the sciences was wonderfully facilitated." So far, indeed, as respects *material,* after this period, the European world was nearly as well off for the means of circulating and transmitting knowledge, as we of the present day are. But we must never lose sight of this fact, that all books were manuscript, written by the hand. How this was accomplished, by whom, and where, form part of the inquiries answered in the present chapter.

If we look at the voluminous works of some of the ancient Fathers or schoolmen, we must be struck with astonishment, when we reflect that copies of them were made by the pen alone, and that their circulation, which seems to have been extensive, could not proceed unless the pen supplied copies. From this single fact, we shall be prepared to expect that the copyist of books must, at all times before the invention of printing, have been very numerous; following a regular business, that afforded full employment, and required experience and skill, as well as legible and expeditious writing.

This was indeed the case in Greece, Rome, Alexandria, and other places before the Christian era; and after its establishment, in the monasteries, universities, and many other places. At Athens copyists by profession were numerous, and gained a steady and considerable livelihood, as, notwithstanding their number and labours, books were seldom very common. The booksellers of Athens employed them principally to copy books of amusement, most of which were exported to the adjoining countries on the shores of the Mediterranean, and sometimes even to the Greek colonies on the Euxine. In many of these places the business of copying was carried on, and libraries formed. Individuals also employed themselves, occasionally, in copying; and there are instances recorded of some forming their own libraries by copying every book they wished to put into them. Not long after the death of Alexander, the love of sciences and literature passed from Athens and Greece generally, to Alexandria, where, patronised by the Ptolemies, they flourished vigorously, and for a considerable period seemed to have concentrated themselves. Under the same roof with the celebrated library there, (which is said to have contained at one time 700,000 volumes,) were extensive offices, regularly and completely fitted up for the business of transcribing books: and it was the practice of foreign princes, who wished for copies of books, to maintain copyists in this city. Some of the libraries of Rome, having been destroyed by fire, the Emperor Domitian sent copyists to Alexandria, that they might be able to replace them. This practice continued for some centuries after Domitian, probably till the conquest of Egypt by the Saracens in the middle of the seventh century. The supposed invention of parchment by a king of Pergamus has already been mentioned. This is doubtful; but it is certain that there were extensive manufactories of that article there, almost entirely for the use of the copyists, who were attached to the royal library; this is said to have contained 200,000 books.

We are ignorant of the class of people in ancient Greece, by whom the business of copying was chiefly followed, and of the education they received. But we know, that, in Rome, the copyists were usually slaves who had received a liberal education. Sometimes they were freedmen, especially those employed by private individuals. The Romans, of rank and consequences, seldom wrote their works, speeches, or even letters themselves; — it was customary for them to dictate to such of their slaves or freedmen, as had been liberally educated, who wrote the MS. in a kind of short hand, or rather in contractions and signs which stood for words and syllables. If the work was intended for publication, it was sent to the booksellers who employed people to copy it fairly in the ordinary characters. This kind of short hand is said to have been invented by Xenophon: it was certainly much extended and improved by the Romans. Tyro, Cicero's freedman, in copying the speeches of Cato, first regulated the method of taking down public harangues — hence their *notæ* to his name, *Notæ Tyroniana;* they were in use in the tenth and eleventh centuries. Many of the speeches of Cicero and other distinguished statesmen and orators, in the senate or at the forum, were taken down by short-hand writers stationed there. Extreme rapidity of writing was absolutely necessary: this led them to contract words more and more, and to multiply the number of contractions. In many cases, either for the sake of greater expedition, or of secrecy, "signs or marks which could be currently made with one dash or scratch of the *style,* and without lifting or turning it, came to be employed, instead of those letters which were themselves abbreviations of words. This mode of dictation, and of rapid and abbreviated writing, continued to be practised, at least as late as the fourth century."

This, itself, must have occasioned many errors; but the chief source of errors in MSS. of the ancients arose from the transcribers employed by the booksellers; these were often ignorant and careless; and complaints on that score are made against them, at a very early period, by Lucilius, in one of his satires, and afterwards by Cicero, Strabo, Martial, and other authors. Strabo informs us that in his time the copyists were so careless that they neglected to compare what they wrote with the exemplar: this, he adds, has been the case in many works copied for sale, at Rome and Alexandria. Individuals seldom copied books for their own use at Rome. Plutarch, indeed, mentions, that Cato the Censor, out of his great anxiety for the education of his son, wrote out, for his use, with his own hand, in large letters, such historical works as he wished him to read; but this is evidently noticed as an extraordinary and unusual action. When a person, from the absence of his scribe or other cause, wrote his letters himself, the extreme rapidity to which he had been accustomed while dictating unavoidably produced rapid and illegible writing. Cicero, in reply to the complaint of his brother Quintus, that he could not read his letters, tells him that when he wrote himself, he wrote with whatever pen he took up, whether good or bad.[30]

When the seat of the Roman Empire was transferred to Constantinople, that city, for upwards of one thousand years, became the chief seat of literature, and source of books. The liberality and munificence of the emperors in purchasing books, and having them copied, are repeatedly noticed, especially by the Byzantine historians. The manuscripts executed in that city are, in general, beautifully written, and sometimes most splendidly decorated. Though the number of books, and the demand for them in ancient times, were, comparatively, extremely limited, yet, in consequences of the frequent destruction of manuscripts, by common accidents and casualties, the business of copyists must have been very extensive. When the Roman empire began to decline, their destruction was extended and increased in the midst of turbulence and rapine of the civil contests for the imperial throne. Christianity, properly understood, and exercising its due influence on the understanding and character, must be a warm friend of knowledge and literature: but the spurious Christianity, believed and acted upon in the dark ages, was hostile to some of the noblest productions of the human mind. The temples of the Heathens, with the public libraries they contained, were the objects of vengeance and destruction. The classics were represented as sinful books. In addition to these causes, the capture of Rome in the fifth century,—the devastations committed by Alaric, Genseric, and Attila—and the plunder of Milan, which next to Rome, was the principal repository for books in Italy—greatly reduced the number of manuscripts, or contributed to their mutilation.

Soon after monachism was regularly formed in the sixth century, the monks, especially those under the rules of St. Benedict, which did not prohibit the reading of the classics, turned their attention to procuring and copying manuscripts. Most of these indeed were worthless; but truth obliges us to add, that many of the abbots, and even monks, employed themselves in procuring or copying the choicest works of Greece and Rome.[31] Cassiodorus, to use the words of Gibbon, "after passing thirty

---

30. Quintilian informs us that wax tablets were preferred to paper, when it was necessary or desirable to write with rapidity, as the pen required to be frequently raised from the paper, to be dipped in the ink—an intermission and delay not required when writing with a style on tablets. [HTM]

31. Some of the early fathers employed much of their time in dictating their works. Eusebius gives a curious picture of Origen's mode of composition: he had seven *notarii,* or short-hand writers, who succeeded each other, as they became weary with writing: he had also a regular establishment of men and young women, who wrote beautifully, to copy his works. [HTM]

years in the honours of the world, was blessed with an equal term of repose in the devout and studious solitude of Squillace." To this place, the monastery of Monte Cassino, in Calabria, he carried his own extensive library, which he greatly enlarged by manuscripts bought at a considerable expense in various parts of Italy. His fondness for literature spread among the monks; he encouraged them to copy manuscripts; and even wrote a treatise giving minute directions for copying with correctness and facility. What he did there seems to have been imitated in the other monasteries of that part of Italy; for fifty religious houses there are mentioned, which afterwards principally supplied the libraries of Rome, Venice, Florence, and Milan, with manuscripts. The north of Italy had also similar establishments in monasteries for copying. The monastery of Benedictines at Bobbio, according to Tiraboschi, was celebrated for its cultivation of literature. The same author fixes the systematic commencement of the copying of the classics in the sixth century. The monasteries of the Morea, and of the islands of Eubea and Crete, but more especially the numerous religious houses which covered the heights and sides of Mount Athos, had always some of their inhabitants employed in the transcription of books.

It was a fixed rule in religious houses that all their inmates should devote a portion of the day to labour. Such as were unable to work at employments requiring toil and strength, or particular skill, discharged their duty by copying manuscripts; and as it was another rule, that every vacancy should be filled up, as soon as ever it took place, there was always a considerable number of copyists. In every great abbey, an apartment, called the *scriptorium,* was expressly fitted up, as a writing-room. That of St. Alban's abbey was built about 1080, by a Norman, who ordered many volumes to be written there; the exemplars were furnished by Archbishop Lanfranc. Estates and legacies were often bequeathed for the support of the scriptorium, and tithes appropriated for the express purpose of copying books. The transcription of the service books, for the choir was intrusted to boys and novices; but the missals and Bibles were ordered to be written by monks of mature age and discretion. Persons qualified by experience and superior learning were appointed to revise every manuscript that came from the scriptorium. The copying of books was executed in other places besides monasteries; sometimes by individuals, from their attachment of literature; but generally by persons who made it their professed employment. Richard of Bury, bishop of Durham, in the thirteenth century, is highly celebrated for his love and encouragement of literature. Besides his libraries, which were numerous in all his palaces, and the books which covered the floor of his common apartments, so that it was no easy matter to approach him, he had a great number of copyists, illuminators, and binders, in his pay. While

Chancellor and Treasurer of England, he preferred receiving the usual perquisties of his office in books, instead of the usual new year's gifts and presents. Copyists were found in all the great towns; but were most numerous in such as had universities. It is said that more than six thousand persons at Paris subsisted by copying and illuminating manuscripts, at the time when printing was introduced into that city: they held their privilege under the University. We know little certain of the rate at which copyists were paid; one fact, however, mentioned by Stow, in his 'Survey of London,' may be given: In 1433, 66£ 13*s.* 4*d.* was paid for transcribing a copy of the works of Nicholas de Lyra, in two volumes, to be chained in the library of the Grey Friars. The usual price of wheat at this time was 5*s.* 4*d.* the quarter. The wages of a ploughman were one penny a day; of a sawyer, four-pence; and of a stone-cutter, the same.[32]

The Jews practised the business of copying, and greatly excelled in fine and regular writing. But they confined their labours chiefly to the Old Testament, and their own religious books. In some of the Hebrew manuscripts, executed by them, the letters are so equal, that they seem to have been printed. Even at present, as Mr. Butler remarks, "those who have not seen the rolls used in synagogues, can have no conception of the exquisite beauty, correctness, and equality, of the writing."

The ancients most commonly wrote only on one side of the parchment or paper, joining the sheets together till their work was entirely written.[33] The manuscript was then rolled on a cylinder, and called volumen. More than one book was seldom included in a volume. Thus the fifteen books of Ovid's Metamorphoses, were in fifteen volumes. The volume being formed, a ball of wood, bone, ivory, &c., was fastened to it on the outside, for ornament and security. This was the most ancient mode of binding

---

32. It must be noticed, however, that the illuminations, as well as the ornaments, are probably included in the sum; if not the materials used, at least the workmanship. The works of Nicholas de Lyra seem to have been in high repute, and much honoured. John Whethamstede, abbot of St. Alban's highly celebrated for his studious employment and love of literature, began, during his abbacy, a grand transcript of the Postilla of De Lyra; the ornaments and handwriting were most splendid. The monk, who mentions it, and who lived after him, when it was still unfinished, exclaims, "God grant that this work may receive, in our days a happy consummation." [HTM]

33. Pasting the leaves together was a distinct and regular business, carried on by persons called glutinatores. In parchment there appeared to have been ruled lines to direct the writing; whereas, when writing on paper, which in general was very fine, and almost transparent, a leaf of ruled paper was put beneath. The double paper, mentioned by Pliny, on both sides of which the ancients wrote, was made by pasting two leaves together, in such a manner that the grain of the paper was crossed. The blank side of the manuscript, written on single paper, was sometimes used for rough drafts, or given to children for copy-books—hence the Latin term, *adversaria,*—a note-book, loose papers. [HTM]

books, if so it may be called; and it was followed long after the time of Augustus. The square form, it is said, was first given to books by one of the kings of Pergamus; and it is certain that Julius Cæsar introduced the custom of dividing his letters to the senate, and folding them like our books. Previously to his time, when the consuls wrote to the senate, their letters were rolled up in a *volume*. When books were exposed to sale, they were covered with skins, which were rendered smooth by pumice-stone. There was one particular street in Rome, or rather a part of one street, in which the booksellers chiefly lived. In the middle ages books were usually bound by monks. There were also trading binders, called ligatores, and persons whose sole business it was to sell covers. White sheep-skin, pasted on a wooden board, sometimes overlapping the leaves, and fastened with a metal cross, was the most common kind of binding. It was deemed the duty of the sacrists in particular to bind and clasp the books. There is a curious charter of Charlemagne's, in 790, to the abbots and monks of Sithin, by which he grants them unlimited right of hunting, on condition that the skins of the deer they killed should be used in making them gloves and girdles, and *cover for their books.*

We know little about booksellers in the early part of the dark ages; it is probable, indeed, that for many centuries there was no mode of procuring a copy of a book but by borrowing it, and employing a copyist, to transcribe it. Books, however, as well as other articles, were occasionally sold in the porches of the churches—a place where law meetings were held, and money paid, in order that its payment might be attested, if necessary, by some of the persons there assembled. We may suppose that, for the same reason, books were sold there. This custom seems to have been adopted from a similar one which prevailed in the porticoes of the Greek and Roman temples; for in them goods were sold, and business transacted. We may also trace to the schools which were established there, for the children even of the highest rank,—the custom mentioned by Shakspeare, of parish schools being held in the porch, or in a room above the church.

Mr. Hallam says booksellers appear in the latter part of the twelfth century; and quotes of Peter of Blois, who mentions a law book which he had bought from a public seller of books. The Jews of Spain about this period were much devoted to literature: Leo Africanus alludes to one Jewish philosopher of Cordova who, having fallen in love, turned poet: his verses, he adds, were publicly sold in a street in that city, which he calls the Bookseller's-Street; this was about the year 1220. The Greek and Roman authors adopted rather a singular custom, either to make their works sell after they were actually published, or, more probably, to create a disposition to purchase them when they should come into the hands of the booksellers. We learn from Theophrastus, Juvenal, Pliny, and Tacitus (particularly from the last,) that a person who wished to bring his writings into notice, hired or borrowed a house, fitted up a room in it, hired forms, and circulated prospectuses, and read his productions before an audience, there and thus collected. Giraldus Cambrensis did the same in the middle ages, in order to make his works known.

Having thus given an account of the manner in which manuscripts were copied and increased in monasteries, &c. we shall now state the causes of their destruction and loss. Till the establishment of Monachism, Christianity, or rather its blind and bigoted professors, were hostile to the classics;—the monasteries in a great degree made up for this by the care they took and the copies they made of them. But one of the causes of their destruction arose, even in the monasteries. The high price of parchment at all times, and its firm and tough texture, tempted and enabled the ancients to erase what had been written on it, (especially, we may suppose, when the contents were of little moment,) in order to use it again for writing upon. A manuscript of this kind was called a Palimpsest. Cicero's self-love took the alarm when his friend Tribatius wrote a letter to him on such parchment. After praising him for his parsimony, he expresses his wonder what he had erased to write such a letter, except it were his law notes; "for I cannot think that you would efface my letter to substitute your own." This practice, in the dark and middle ages, became so prevalent, and was productive of such serious consequences, the most important documents often being destroyed to make way for trash, that the emperors of Germany, in their patents of nobility, with power to create imperial notaries, inserted a clause to the following effect: "On condition that they should not make use of old or erased parchment, but that it should be quite new." The parchment was generally creased: but the monks had also a practice of taking out the writing by a chemical process; and sometimes they peeled off the surface of the parchment. They had recourse to these destructive practices, not only when they wished to add to their stock of religious works, but also when they wanted to raise a sum of money. In this case, they erased the old writing—paying little regard to its value or rarity— wrote a legend or a psalter, and sold it to the common people. Though it had been long known that the writings of classical authors lay concealed and nearly obliterated beneath the literary rubbish of the monks—and this in numerous cases—for Montfauçon affirms that the greater part of the MSS, he had examined were of this description; yet no steps were taken to recover the original and more valuable writings, till Angelo Mai undertook the task: he has succeeded in recovering several works, the most important of which is a considerable portion of Cicero's de Republica that had been erased, and replaced by St. Augustine's Commentary on the Psalms.

The conquest of Egypt by the Saracens, which rendered it almost impracticable to procure papyrus paper, and the consequent high price of parchment, and temptation to erasure, were injurious to literature, not only in this respect, but by the alarm it gave to Europe. This event, their subsequent conquest of Spain, the Norman invasion of France, and the wars by which various parts of Europe were so long and dreadfully afflicted, afforded opportunities and pretexts for plundering the convents and cities, and thus created the destruction and loss of a great number of valuable manuscripts.

We have already alluded, generally, to the facility with which books can be procured now, and the extreme difficulty even of ascertaining where they were to be found before the invention of printing; when that was ascertained, of gaining access to them, or a loan of them; and the high price at which they were then sold. We shall now give several instances of the truth of this general statement, for, in no other manner, can we so clearly point out and prove the very great advantages that literature and science have derived from the art of printing. The materials employed formerly to write upon—the cumbersome or perishable nature of some— the dearness of others—the length of time necessarily taken up, in writing books with the hand—the few places in which they were accumulated— the difficulty of access to them—their liability to destruction,—and the practice of the monks' erasing the writing,—have prepared our readers to anticipate their great rarity and value. We must premise, however, that though the facts we shall state will sufficiently prove the high price of manuscript books, yet we cannot gain a precise notion of the subject, because, in many cases, that arose in a great measure from the splendour of their illuminations, and cost of outward workmanship—and, setting aside this consideration, because it is not possible to ascertain exactly the comparative value of money in those ages, and in the present times. Where we have dates, we shall add the price of wheat, and the wages of labour— perhaps the best criteria for ascertaining the purchasing power of money. We shall begin with instances of the rarity of manuscripts, as it is shown in the anxiety to borrow them, and the conditions on which they were lent. We have already mentioned Richard of Bury. In his Philobiblion he devotes one entire chapter expressly to an enumeration of the conditions on which books were to be lent to strangers. In 1299, the Bishop of Winchester borrowed a Bible in two volumes folio, for a convent in that city, giving a bond drawn up in a most formal and solemn manner, for its due return. This Bible had been given to the convent by a former bishop, and in consideration of this gift, and 100 marks, the monks founded a daily mass for the soul of the donor. In the same century several Latin Bibles were given to the University of Oxford, on condition that the students who read them should deposit a cautionary pledge. And even after manuscripts were multiplied by the invention of linen paper, it was enacted by the statutes of St. Mary's College, at Oxford, in 1446, that "no scholar shall occupy a book in the library above one hour, or two hours at most, lest others should be hindered from the use of the same." Money was often lent on the deposit of a book; and there were public chests in the universities, and other places in which the books so deposited were kept. They were often particularly named and described in wills—generally left to a relation or friend, in fee, and for the term of his life, and afterwards to the library of some religious house. "When a book was bought,"observes Mr. Warton, "the affair was of so much importance, that it was customary to assemble persons of consequence and character, and to make a formal record that they were present on the occasion." The same author adds, "Even so late as the year 1471, when Louis XI. of France borrowed the works of the Arabian physician Rhasis, from the faculty of medicine at Paris, he not only deposited, by way of pledge, a quantity of valuable plate, but was obliged to procure a nobleman to join with him as surety in a deed, by which he bound himself to return it under a considerable forfeiture." Long and violent altercations, and even lawsuits, sometimes took place in consequence of the disputed property of a book.

Books were so scarce in Spain in the tenth century, that several monasteries had among them only one copy of the Bible, of Jerome's Epistles, and of several other religious books; and monasteries had frequently only one missal. There are some curious instances given by Lupus, abbot of Ferrieris, of the extreme scarcity of *classical* manuscripts in the middle of the ninth century: he was much devoted to literature; and, from his letters, appears to have been indefatigable in his endeavours to find out such manuscripts, in order to borrow and copy them. In a letter to the Pope he earnestly requests of him a copy of Quintilian, and of a treatise of Cicero; for, he adds, though we have some fragments of them, a complete copy is not to be found in France. In two other of his letters, he requests of a brother abbot the loan of several manuscripts, which he assures him shall be copied and returned as soon as possible by a faithful messenger. Another time he sent a special messenger to borrow a manuscript, promising that he would take very great care of it, and return it by a safe opportunity, and requesting the person who lent it to him, if he were asked to whom he had lent it, to reply, to some near relations of his own, who had been very urgent to borrow it. Another manuscript, which he seems to have prized much, and a loan of which had been so frequently requested, that he thought of *banishing* it somewhere that it might not be destroyed or lost, he tells a friend he may perhaps lend him, when he comes to see him, but that he will not trust it to the messenger who had been sent for it, though a monk, and trustworthy, because he was traveling on foot. We shall extract only one more instance of the scarcity of manuscripts from the letters of Lupus: he requests a friend to apply in his own name to an abbot of a monastery, to have a copy made of Suetonius; "for," he adds, "in this part of the world, the work is no where to be found."

We possess few facts respecting the price of manuscript books among the ancients. Plato, who seems to have spared no trouble or money in order to enrich his library, especially with philosophical works, paid a hundred minæ, equal to 375£, for three small treatises by Philolaus, the Pythagorean; and after the death of Speusippus, Plato's disciple, his books were purchased by Aristotle; they were few in number; he paid for them three talents, about 675£. It is said that St. Jerome nearly ruined himself by the purchase of religious works alone. And, though, at this period, we have no specific prices of works, yet, from the account already given of their rarity, of the difficulty of ascertaining even where they were to be found, and of the extreme reluctance, in many instances, even to lend, them, we may easily credit the general fact, that persons of a moderate fortune could not afford to purchase them, and that, by the rich even, they could seldom be procured without the payment of sums that required the sacrifice of some luxuries. The mere money paid for them, in the dark ages, whenever a person distinguished himself for his love of literature, was seldom the sole or the principal expense. It was often necessary to send to a great distance; to spend much time in finding out where they were. In the ninth century, an English bishop was obliged to make five journies to Rome, principally in order to purchase books; for one of his books thus procured, Alfred gave him an estate of eight hides of land, or as much land as eight ploughs could till. About the period of the invention of cotton paper, 1174, the homilies of St. Bede and St. Augustine's Psalter, were bought by a prior in Winchester, from the monks of Dorchester, in Oxfordshire, for twelve measures of barley, and a pall richly embroidered in silver. Stow informs us, that in 1274, a Bible, in nine volumes, fairly written, with a gloss or comment, sold for fifty marks, at 6s. 8d.; about this time the price of wheat averaged about 3s. 4d. a quarter; a labourer's wages were 1 1/2d. a day; a harvest man's, 2d. In a blank page of Comestor's Scholastic History, deposited in the British Museum, it is stated, that this MS. was taken from the King of France, at the battle of Poictiers: it was afterwards purchased by the Earl of Salisbury for a hundred marks, and directed, by the last will of his Countess, to be sold for forty livres. One hundred marks were equivalent to 66£ 13*s.* 4*d.* This sum was exactly the pay of Henry Percy, keeper of Berwick Castle, in 1359; at this time the king's surgeon's pay was 5£ 13*s.* 4*d.* per annum, and one shilling a day beside. Master carpenters had four-pence a day, their servants two-pence; the price of wheat about 6*s.* 8*d.* a quarter. At the beginning of the century, some books were bequeathed to Merton College, Oxford, of which the following are the names and valuation: A Scholastic History, 20*s.*; a Concordantia, 10*s.*; the four greater Prophets, with glosses, 5*s.*; a Psalter, with glosses, 10*s.*, St. Austin, on Genesis, 10*s.* About the year 1400, a copy of the Roman de la Rou was sold before the palace gate at Paris, for forty crowns, or 33£ 6*s.* 6*d.* The Countess of Anjou paid for a copy of the Homilies of Bishop Haiman, two hundred sheep, five quarters of wheat, five quarters of barley, and five quarters of millet. On the conquest of Paris, in 1425, the Duke of Bedford sent the royal library to England: it consisted of only eight hundred and fifty-three volumes, but it was valued at two thousand two hundred and twenty-three livres, rather more than the same number of pounds sterling. At this time the price of a cow was about 8*s.*, of a horse about 20*s.* And the pension paid by the English Government to the Earl of Wallachia, who had been driven out of his territories by the Turks, was 26£ 13*s.* 4*d.* per annum. This library is thought to have formed the foundation of the celebrated library of Humphrey Duke of Gloucester. This nobleman was one of the most zealous and liberal patrons of literature and learned men of his age; he invited learned foreigners into England, whom he retained in his service, employing them in copying and translating from Greek into Latin; and he had constantly persons in his pay collecting valuable manuscripts for him. He gave to the University of Oxford, about the year 1440, six hundred volumes, one hundred and twenty of which alone were valued at more than 1000£. Wheat about this period might be exported, when not above 6*s.* 8*d.* a quarter. In the middle of this century, a nobleman of Bologne, a desirous of purchasing a copy of Livy, which had been transcribed by the celebrated Poggio, was obliged to sell an estate for this purpose, and with the purchase money, Poggio bought another estate, near Florence. Archbishop Usher tells us, from the Register of William Alnwick, Bishop of Norwich, that in 1429, the price of one of Wickliffe's English New Testaments was four marks and forty pence, or 2£ 6*s.* 8*d.*, which, the Archbishop observed, "is as much as will now (about 1630) buy forty new Testaments." Afterwards copies were multiplied so much, in consequence of the increase of Wickliffe's disciples, that the price fell to 20*s.*, when the price of a Porteus of breviary was six marks. In 1468, 1£ 6s. 8*d.* was lent on the security of a MS. of Petrus

Comestor (a work already mentioned), deposited as a pledge. Wheat at this time was 6s. 8d. a quarter; beef, 10s. the carcase; mutton, 1s. 4d.; veal, 2s. 6d.; pork, 2s.; ale, 1¼d., a gallon. When Faust sold his Bibles at Paris (about 1460), the price of parchment copy was reduced from four to five hundred to sixty, fifty, and forty crowns.[34] Other instances might be given of the extreme rarity and enormous price of books, in every country, and at all periods, previous to the invention of printing: but these are amply sufficient to prove the facilities which that discovery has given to the spread of literature and science, by removing this most serious and formidable impediment.

Had not sovereigns and rich individuals formed libraries to which men of learning had access, knowledge could not have advanced, even in the very slow manner in which it did; as they, in general, were too poor to purchase books, and had not sufficient leisure to be met with. The most celebrated libraries in ancient times, which may fairly be regarded as having contained a very large portion of the books then existing, were, 1. The Alexandrian Library founded by Ptolemy Soter, who reigned about 300 B.C. His successors enlarged it; one of them seized all books imported into Egypt, giving copies of them, made by his orders, and at his expense, to the proprietors: in a similar manner he got from the Athenians, the originals of Æschylus, Sophocles, and Euripides, returning them only copies, and giving them fifteen talents in exchange, upwards of £3000. This library suffered much during the first Alexandrine war; and was afterwards totally destroyed by the Calif Omar in A. D. 642. 2. The library founded by Pisistratus at Athens. This and the other libraries of this city, continued to flourish till after the time of Justinian. 3. Julius Cæsar projected a library at Rome, which was to be, strictly speaking, public; but his assassination frustrated the design: and the first public library was erected by Asinius Pollio, in the reign of Augustus. This emperor also founded two public libraries, the Octavian and the Palatine—the latter survived till the time of Gregory the Great, about the end of the sixth century. 4. But the most extensive and splendid of the libraries at Rome, was the Ulpian, founded by Trajan: it is believed that, at the suggestion of Pliny the younger, this emperor commanded all the books that were found in the conquered cities to be placed in this library. Most of the

34. The supplying of books for divine service—Missal—parishioner, or Breviary-Manual, &c. originally fell upon the rector; as they were all written, and some of them beautifully illuminated, it was a very expensive duty. On the institution of vicars, the parishioners agreed to supply some of the books: Among them were the Antiphoners, two of which, in 1424, cost twenty-six marks, or 17£ 6s. 8d. The vicars were at the expense of binding and preserving the books; also of finding the Porteus; the price of this was about five or six marks. [HTM]

principal cities throughout the Roman empire, at this time, had public libraries. The desolation of the western empire by the barbarians destroyed or dispersed most of the books in them, so that, in this part of the world, after this period, and during the dark ages, monasteries almost exclusively possessed libraries. In the eastern empire it was different: both Constantinople and Alexandria preserved theirs, till the Turks obtained possession of these cities. The library of the former was founded by Constantine, and enlarged by succeeding emperors, especially by Julian and Theodosius the younger.

Dr. Henry, after mentioning Alfred's purchase of one book, for an estate of eight hides of land, observes—"At this rate none but kings, bishops, and abbots, could be possessed of any books: which is the reason that there were then no schools but in kings' palaces, bishops, sees, or monasteries!" It is generally believed that there were no public schools in Rome till three hundred years after its foundation; parents teaching their children the little they knew. Even after the establishment of schools, private education at home was common. The teachers were generally slaves or freed men; and a slave always accompanied the boys of rank to school, carrying a box, containing books, paper, tablets, and instruments for writing. In learning their letters they were instructed by another boy, or usher.[35] Homer was taught to the Greek boys, and Virgil to the Roman. They were moved to different schools, according to their proficiency: being taught to read and write in one, and arithmetic, by *calculi* or counters, in a separate school. The porticoes of temples were common places for schools. In an ancient bas-relief, published by Winkelman, the education of two children of rank is represented; one about twelve years old holds a double tablet, long, and fastened by a hinge. The master, half naked, like the ancient philosopher, holds a roll (volumen), and is addressing the child. Some of the table-books must have been large; for, in Plautus, a school-boy, seventeen years old, is represented as breaking his master's head with one. From the origin of monasteries till the close of the tenth century, there were no schools in Europe, except those belonging to monasteries or episcopal churches. At the beginning of the eleventh century, they were opened in most of the cities of Italy and France, by qualified persons among both the laity and clergy. But though their general introduction and establishment must be assigned to this period, yet it is certain that Charlemagne founded several in his dominions; and long before his reign St. Augustin was an usher in a school. His business was to preside over the dress, morals, gait, &c., of

---

35. See Dodwell's Greece, for further proof of a system of education in ancient Greece, similar to that of Bell and Lancaster. (Vol. ii. p. 37.) [HTM]

his pupils, and to sit with them in a kind of anti-school, separated from the principal school by a curtain. Here they said their lessons to the usher, before they went to the master; when the curtain was drawn back. In the middle ages, there were distinct schools for clerks, for laymen, and for girls; and two hundred children at a time are represented as learning their letters. Itinerant schoolmasters were also common. The whole of the education, however, even of those of the highest ranks, seldom went beyond reading and writing, and the more simple rules of arithmetic. Parochial grammar schools, in villages, were established in the fifteenth century. The following account of their origin is given by Mr. Fosbroke: "To prevent the growth of Wickliffism, it had been made penal to put children to private teachers; and the consequent incessant influx to only a few schools, rendered, in 1447, grammar learning so low, that several clergymen in London petitioned parliament for leave to set up schools in their respective churches, in order to check seminaries, conducted by illiterate men. Thus commenced grammar schools, properly so called."[36]

CHAPTER IV

Restorers of Literature, and Discoverers of Manuscripts, in the Middle Ages—First steps towards the Art of Printing—Invention of that Art—Early History—Introduction of it into the Kingdoms of Continental Europe.

It is generally the fate of discoveries that are made prematurely, and under unfavorable circumstances, either to be strangled in their birth, or to struggle through a very short and useless existence. Had the art of printing been invented during the deepest ignorance and gloom of the dark ages, its value and importance would not have been appreciated, and it might gradually have sunk into neglect and total oblivion. Books were indeed excessively rare and dear; but very few sought for them, for few had the curiosity or ability to read, and fewer the money to purchase them. After the tenth century, literature began to revive; paper from linen rags was invented; a tendency to commerce appeared. This caused a gradual accumulation of capital, and rendered necessary some attention to learning. Then succeeded the agitation of men's minds, which preceded the Reformation, and which could not be set at rest but by reading and inquiry. The monks themselves, so far as they contributed to the perusal

---

36. "It was not till the reign of Henry IV (1399-1413) that villeins, farmers, and mechanics, were permitted, by law to put their children to school (7 Henry IV. chap. 17;) and long after that they dared not to educate a son for the church, without a license from their lord."—(Henry's England, book v. chap. 4. sect 1). [HTM]

of legends and miraculous stories, were the unconscious instruments of that spreading desire for knowledge, which ushered in the invention of printing and which issued in the Reformation itself.

We have already named several individuals who, even in the darkest ages, spent much of their time or money, in endeavoring to discover and procure manuscripts. Long before the fall of Constantinople, the love of classical literature had been gradually reviving;—that event increased it, by compelling a great number of learned Greeks to seek a shelter in Italy. But it could not be gratified, till the manuscripts, which lay buried and neglected, were brought to light. As the labours of those who may justly be called the restorers of classical literature, were mainly instrumental in producing that state of things, which turned men's minds towards the invention of printing, and nourished it to maturity, when invented, we shall give a short account of the most celebrated of them, before we proceed to the invention itself.

Silvester II., before he became pope, which was in the last year of the tenth century, had been indefatigable in acquiring and communicating learning, and these qualities distinguished him during his whole life. In order to obtain a knowledge of the sciences and manuscripts, he visited Spain, and caused Italy, and the countries beyond the Alps, to be diligently explored. The Crusades interrupted the spread of literature; but in the fourteenth century, Petrarch roused his countrymen from their slumber—inspired a general love of literature—nourished and rewarded it by his own productions; and rescued the classics from the dungeons, where they had been hitherto shut up from the light and instruction of mankind. "He never passed an old convent, without searching its library, or knew of a friend travelling into those quarters, where he supposed books to be concealed, without entreaties to procure for him some classical manuscripts." Had not such a man appeared at this time, it is probable that most of the classical manuscripts would have been totally lost; so that in this case, he might have excited among his countrymen the love of literature, without being able to gratify or nourish it. Boccaccio, who shares with Petrarch the glory of having enriched the Italian language with its most perfect beauties, at the very moment when it may be said to have begun to exist, shares also with him the glory of being a zealous and successful restorer of classical manuscripts and literature. No man, during the first half of the fifteenth century, devoted himself with so much industry to this search, or made so good a use of them, when discovered, as Poggio. No difficulty, no want or assistance, no expense or labour discouraged him. His youth was spent in travelling to attain what seemed to be the sole object of his life; and when he became secretary to the Popes, eight of whom employed him in succession, he used the influence and opportunities his situation gave him, for the promotion of literature and the collecting of manuscripts at Rome. To these names we shall add only those of the Medici family; Emanuel Chrysolas, who was one of the first who introduced a knowledge of the Greek language and literature into Italy; and Theodore Gaza.

Europe seemed now ripe for the art of printing, and to require it. Persons of high rank felt a more general and powerful love of literature than they had ever experienced before. The minds of the great mass of the people too were now beginning to work; but materials were wanting on which they might work and by which they might work. At this important crisis, the art of printing was discovered, and an impulse given to knowledge which now no power, no conceivable combination of circumstances can possible destroy.

Playing-cards, which were known and used in Germany at the very beginning of the fourteenth century, were first painted; but towards the end of that century a method of printing them by blocks was discovered. This was the first step towards the art of printing. The manufacturers of playing-cards naturally turned this discovery of printing from blocks to advantage and profit by engraving the images of saints—for which there was a regular and great demand—on wood. This may be considered as the second step. Books of Images were of two kinds: those without any text, and those with text; but even in the first words and sentences are interspersed. A wood cut of St. Christopher, the oldest known of the first kind, is now in the collection of Earl Spencer: at the foot of it are three short sentences, engraved and printed together with the figure, with the date 1423. The most celebrated of the books of images without text is the Biblia Pauperum. It consists of forty plates of figures and images, with sentences relating to them, the whole engraven on wood on one side of the paper. It seems to be a kind of catechism of the Bible, and was sold at a low price to young persons and the common people; it has no date. Another work, a system of artificial memory, engraven on wood, in the same manner as the Biblia Pauperum, has the text separate from the figures; fifteen plates of each. The characters are very large, resembling those on ancient monuments. But, "of all the ancient books of images," observes Mr. Horne, "which preceded the invention of printing, the Speculum Salutis is confessedly the most perfect both in its design and execution." It is a collection of historical passages from the Scriptures, with a few from profane history. It was very popular, frequently reprinted, and translated into German, Flemish, and other languages.

The change and improvement from the manner in which these books of images were executed to moveable wooden characters, seems obvious and not difficult; but there is no evidence that these were ever used, except in the capital letters of some early printed books. It has been, indeed, contended strenuously by several antiquarians, that Lewis Coster, of Haarlem, invented and used them; that he, therefore, was the original inventor of the art of printing, and that Haarlem was the place where the invention was first put into practice. But it is now proved, that this opinion is without foundation; that wooden types were never used; that the claims of Coster of Haarlem cannot stand the test of accurate investigation; and that the art of printing, as at present practised, with moveable metal types, was discovered by John Guthenberg, of Mayence, about the year 1438.

Three years before this, Guthenberg entered into a partnership with three citizens of Strasburg, binding himself to disclose a secret which would enrich them all. One of the partners dying, and some of the most important implements having been stolen from the workshop, a lawsuit took place. In the course of this lawsuit, five witnesses, among whom was Guthenberg's confidential servant, proved that he (Guthenberg) was the first who practised the art of printing with moveable types. The result was a dissolution of partnership. The whole proceedings on this trial are in existence, and have been published in the original German.

After this, Guthenberg returned, poor and disappointed, but not dispirited, to his native city, Mayence. It is doubtful whether he had hitherto really printed any thing. Heinecken, who has investigated this subject with great diligence and labour, is of opinion that he had ruined both himself and his partners, without being able to produce a single clean and legible leaf. However that may be, in 1450, he entered into partnership at Mayence, with John Fust; they seem at first to have gone back to wooden blocks, and then to have tried moveable wooden letters and moveable metal ones, formed with a knife: all without effect. This partnership was also unfortunate; for, in consequence of the great expense incurred by Fust (who supplied the capital), in printing a Latin Bible, he commenced a suit against Guthenberg; the latter was obliged to give up his apparatus to Fust. It is not certain whether, during their partnership, they found out the art of casting characters in metal, which they had previously been obliged to cut with the hand; or whether this great improvement was made by Schoeffer, an ingenious man, who assisted them at this time, and was afterwards taken into partnership by Fust. The general opinion is, that the idea of punches and matrices for casting metal types originated with Schoeffer. He certainly improved this method, by rendering it more certain, easy, and expeditious.

Guthenberg, not discouraged by this second misfortune, established a new printing office, until 1465, when he obtained a situation, with a good salary, under the Elector Adolphus. In the mean time, Fust, in conjunction with Schoeffer, continued printing. In August, 1457, they published a beautiful edition of the Psalms; one of the earliest books yet discovered which has the name of the place and printers, with the date annexed. In 1462, the city of Mayence was taken by the Elector Adolphus, when the partners suffered much; and their workmen dispersing themselves, the art of printing was thus spread over Europe. Their masters, however, still carried on the business in Mayence. Fust's name appears to a Treatise of Cicero printed in 1466; all subsequent books have Schoeffer's name alone; he continued to print till his death in 1502, when he was succeeded by his son.[37]

The date and cause of the dispersion of Fust and Schoeffer's workmen, and the consequent spreading of the art of printing over the continent of Europe, have been already stated. The respective periods of its first intro-

---

37. In order to give a clearer idea of the progress of the art in its infancy, we shall subjoin short notices of some of the works executed by Guthenberg and his partners. The two earliest works are supposed to be an alphabet, engraved on a plate for the use of schools, and some doctrinal tracts. Then followed two editions of Donatus on the parts of speech: the first from wooden blocks, which are still in the Royal Libraries of Paris; the second with moveable types on vellum. The celebrated first edition of the Bible from metal types; remarkable for the texture of the paper, excellence of execution, and blackness and lustre of the ink; supposed to have been printed in 1455. The expense of printing it gave rise to the lawsuit between Guthenberg and Fust. Like all other very ancient printed books, it has no title or paging, and many of the initial letters are printed by illumination. In 1456, Guthenberg printed an almanack, the first ever printed, and the very first book with a certain date. In 1457, Fust and Schoeffer printed their celebrated Psalter. In a colophon, (the sentence frequently added at the conclusion of a work by the early printers) the invention of the art of printing is announced to the public in boasting, though by no means unreasonable or unwarranted terms. This Psalter is printed on vellum; the psalms in larger letters than the hymns, all uncommonly black. The capital letters are cut in wood the largest of these, which are black, red, and blue, it is supposed must have passed three times through the press. Not more than six or seven copies are known to be in existence. The first edition of the Latin Bible, with a date, at Mayence, by Fust and Schoeffer, in 1462. Fust sold by himself, or by his agents, copies of this Bible at Paris, as manuscript, and supplied them so regularly and abundantly as to lower the price. From the facility with which he supplied them, and the uniformity of the copies, he was taken up as a necromancer; hence arose the story of the Devil and Dr. Faustus. The books were seized either on this occasion, or afterwards, in virtue of the *droit d'aubaine*, on the death of his agent, but they were restored by order of Louis XI. In 1465 Fust and Schoeffer published an edition of Cicero's Offices, "the first tribute of the new art to polite literature." After the death of Fust, about 1466, Schoeffer carried on the printing business alone for thirty-five or thirty-six years, in the course of which period he executed a great many works. By far the most important of these was an edition of Justinian's Institutes, the date is not known. In 1484 he printed an Herbal in 4to., with figures of plants; and in 1485, a folio edition of it. In 1490 he printed a third edition of the Mentz Psalter. In the preceding editions the full chant was written, in this it is printed. Schoeffer terminated his labours by a fourth edition of the Psalter in 1502. [HTM]

duction into the principal continental kingdoms, together with some interesting anecdotes, we shall now mention. The first book printed at Rome was Cicero's Letters to his friend, in 1457. The printers were Conrad Sweynheim, and Arnold Pannartz. They left Germany for Italy in 1465, having served their apprenticeship to Fust and his partner. At first they settled at the monastery of Lubeaco, in the neighbourhood of Rome, where the printed the works of Lactantius, being encouraged and assisted by the monks, who were Benedictines, and very rich and learned. On their removal to Rome they were equally patronised by John Andreas the Pope's librarian. He not only supplied them with the most valuable manuscripts from the Vatican, but prepared the copy, the proofs, prefixed dedications, prefaces, &c. Notwithstanding the encouragement they met with, they were obliged to petition the Pope for relief and assistance in 1472, having printed during the seven previous years, twenty-eight different works, some of them very large and expensive, the impressions of which amounted to 12,475 volumes. In this petition, after stating that they were the first who introduced this art into his holiness' territories, and the number of volumes printed by them, they added that their house was full of books in quires, but destitute of the necessaries of life. As they contrived to print for some time afterwards, it is supposed that assistance was granted them.

The first book printed at Venice was also Cicero's Epistles; the printer, John de Spira, the date 1469. He and his brother, also a printer, natives of Germany, surpassed all their predecessors in the beauty of their types and the elegance of their impressions; they employed two very learned men as correctors of their press. The Spiras were the first who applied the art on a regular and extensive scale to the publication of the classics. By an order of the senate, 1469, the exclusive privilege of printing the letters of Cicero and Pliny was granted to them for five years, in consequence of the beauty of their impressions. Venice became celebrated for its types, and supplied the printer of Rome with them. One of the best printers of the fifteenth century was settled at Nuremberg, his name was Coburger; he was styled by his contemporaries the prince of booksellers and printers: he employed daily twenty-four presses and one hundred men, besides furnishing work to the printers of Basle, Paris, and Lyons. His books, which relate chiefly to the cannon law and theology, are distinguished for the blackness of the ink, and the squareness and fineness of the type, as well as the good quality of paper, and the excellence of the press-work.

The first work from the Paris press is dated 1470; the printers were three Germans from Colmar. On the establishment of their office, the copyists, finding their business much injured, presented a memorial to the parliament; but Lewis XI. interfered in their behalf.

Lewis, who, amidst all his faults, was an encourager of literature, is said to have sent Nicolas Jenson, a native of France, to Mayence, to learn the art of printing, in 1470. But, owing to civil dissensions in his kingdom, Jenson settled at Venice, where he printed from 1470-1480. He introduced great improvements; planning and reducing to their present proportions the characters called *roman,* so that his works are justly deemed very highly finished in every respect.

The first book printed at Naples, was in 1471. Two years afterwards, printing was introduced into Buda, in Hungary. The first work printed at Basle, in Switzerland, is dated 1474. The same year appeared a book, printed by the monks of a convent in Rhingau. They were of the Augustine order, and by their rules, they were obliged to copy the works of the Fathers and ecclesiastical writers as part of their regular duty, and likewise as their chief means of subsistence. The discovery of printing having deprived them of these means, they immediately applied themselves to learn and practise that art, and were thus enabled at the same time to support themselves and fulfill the spirit of their rule.

The first work printed in Bohemia is dated 1476, but the printer's name is not known. John Snell, a German printer, invited into Sweden by the administrator Stein Sture, printed the first book in that kingdom in 1483. John Mathison, a Swede, who was patronised by the Bishop of Holun in Iceland, introduced the art of printing into that remote and desolate island, in the year 1531. The first book printed in Portugal is dated 1489; it is a commentary on the Pentateuch in Hebrew, and from the printers' names, they appear to have been Jews.

In 1493 the art was introduced into Denmark, when a grammatical treatise was published. This first treatise relating to commerce seems to have been published at Provins, 1496. Three years afterwards the Catholicon was printed in Bretagne, or Breton, French, and Latin.

The first work printed in Moravia, is dated 1500: it is a treatise against the Waldenses. In 1560, a Russian merchant, having bought a quantity of types, printing press, &c., introduced the art into Moscow. The mob, however, at the instigation, it is supposed, of the priests, destroyed the office, press, and types.

The most early printed books were principally of the folio and quarto size. In 1465 the old Gothic character was changed for a kind of semi-Gothic, in the Lactantius, printed at Lubeaco. The roman type was first used at Rome in 1467, and soon afterwards brought to perfection by Nicolas Jenson. The celebrated printer, Aldus Manutius, introduced towards the end of the fifteenth century, the *italic*. Aldus was extremely careful in correcting his proofs, so that he never printed more than two sheets a week. He printed a great number of Latin and Italian books in 8vo., which are executed with great elegance and correctness. In the edition of Cicero, printed at Mayence, 1465, a few sentences in Greek type are given. The same year, Sweynheim and Pannartz, having produced a very small quantity of Greek types, began to print the Lactantius, already mentioned; before the work was completed, however, they seem to have procured a further supply, for in the first part of the work a blank is left wherever a long sentence occurs, whereas, after the middle of the work, all the Greek quotations are printed. The first book, entirely Greek, is supposed to be the Greek grammar of Lascaris, printed at Milan in 1476. Aldus, in addition to his other merits, is justly celebrated for having first produced beautiful and correct editions of Greek works. Printing in Hebrew was first executed by Soncino, in Milan, in 1482. The Pentateuch was printed there this year. The first Polyglott bible, in Hebrew, Arabic, Chaldee, Greek, and Latin, was printed at Genoa in 1516, by Pormo. Aldus seems to have planned, and even to have begun to execute, a Polyglott bible, in Hebrew, Greek, and Latin. There is one specimen page, in folio, preserved in Royal Library at Paris.

Till 1476 or 1480, the titles of books were printed on separate leaves. In the infancy of the art, blanks were left for initial letters, which were afterwards filled up by the illuminators; but this trade did not long survive the invention of printing. Divisions into sentences were seldom made; the orthography varied much; punctuation was confined to the colon, period, and an oblique stroke. This is supposed to have arisen from a desire to imitate manuscripts as near as possible. Aldus added the semicolon; notes of interrogation and admiration were not used till long afterwards. The paper was very thick and solid; this, and the frequent use of vellum, were the result of the desire to imitate manuscripts. It is known, besides, that at that period the disproportion between the price of paper and vellum was not nearly so great as at present. Very early printed books are also distinguished by their numerous and difficult abbreviations, by the absence of signatures and catch-words, and of the printer's name, place, and date; when inserted, they are at the end of the book. Signatures, however, were used in 1472 and 1474; and catch-words, which appear in manuscripts of the eleventh century, were first used in printing, by Spira, at Venice, about the same time. They are at present little used, either on the continent or in Britain.

CHAPTER V

Life of WILLIAM CAXTON

WILLIAM CAXTON was born in the Weald of Kent, as he himself tells us; in what part of it, and in what year, is not known, but it is supposed about the year 1412. Of the rank or employment of his parents we are entirely ignorant. His father came to London, and resided with his son, in Westminster, at the time of his greatest fame, as a printer. There he died at a very advanced age, in 1480. It may be presumed that his parents were in good circumstances from the education they gave him, and the business to which they put him. At this period learning of all kinds was at a much lower ebb in England than in most of the continental states of Europe; in consequence, principally, of the civil wars in which the nation was embroiled, the habits of restlessness thus produced, and the constant pre-occupation of men's time and thoughts in promoting the cause they espoused, and in protecting their lives and property. Under these circumstances the most plain and common education was often neglected. Caxton's parents, however, performed their duty to him: "I am bounden," he says, "to pray for my father and mother's souls, that, in my youth, sent me to school, by which, by the sufferance of God, I get my living, I hope truly." When he was about fifteen or sixteen, he was put apprentice to William Large, a considerable mercer, of the city of London, and afterwards sheriff and mayor. The name, *mercer,* was given at this time to general merchants, trading in all kinds of goods. After he had served his apprenticeship, Caxton took up his freedom in the Mercer's Company, and became a citizen of London. That he conducted himself, while an apprentice, to the satisfaction of his master, may be presumed from the circumstances, that he was left in his will, in 1441, a legacy of twenty marks, or 3£ 6s. 8d., a considerable sum in those days, when the usual price of wheat was 5s. 4d. a quarter; malt, 4s. the quarter; and a pair of plough oxen could be purchased for about 1£ 3s.

In what manner he employed himself from the expiration of his apprenticeship, till he went abroad, is not known; but that he did not go abroad till some years afterwards, a comparison of dates will render apparent. He was born about 1412; he could not have been more than sixteen when put apprentice; so that his apprenticeship of seven years must have expired in the year 1435. The opinion, therefore, that he went to the Low Countries on the termination of his apprenticeship is not correct, as he did not leave England till 1442, the year after he received the legacy.

In what capacity or for what purpose he left England, we are ignorant;—probably as a merchant, either on his own account, or as agent for some other merchant. He informs us that he continued for the most part in the countries of Brabant, Flanders, Holland, and Zealand,—all at this time belonging to the Duke of Burgundy, one of the most powerful princes in this part of Europe, whose friendship and alliance were anxiously sought for by the kings of France and England.

In the year 1464, he was appointed by Edward IV, ambassador, along with Richard Whetenhall, "to continue and confirm a treaty of commerce with Philip, Duke of Burgundy, or, if necessary, to inform a new treaty." In the commission, which is given in Rymer's Foedera, they are styled ambassadors and special deputies; and full powers to treat are given to either, or both of them. The Low Countries were at this period the great mart of Europe, in which were to be purchased, at all times, and in great abundance, the produce and manufacturers of most parts of the world. Treaties of commerce between England and them were frequently made and broken; and it required not only considerable knowledge in commercial affairs, and in the relative commercial wants and advantages of the two countries, but also a sound judgement, and much circumspection and prudence, to make or renew them. Merchants seem to have been generally employed on these occasions; and we may reasonably conjecture that Caxton's character and experience, as a merchant, and his long residence in the Netherlands, pointed him out as a fit person for this embassy.

Philip, Duke of Burgundy, was the most magnificent prince of his age: his court, one of the most polished; and his fondness for the expiring customs of chivalry, and for literature, equally great and influential. In the prologue to a book of the whole life of Jason, translated under the protection of King Edward, Caxton thus describes the chamber of this prince, in his castle of Hesdein, in Artois. It ought to be premised, that Philip had instituted the order of the Knights of the Golden Fleece. "But well wote, I that the noble Duke Philip, first founder of this said order, did do maken a chamber in the castle of Hesdein, wherein was craftily and curiously depainted, the conquest of the Golden Fleece, by the said Jason; in which chamber I have been, and seen the said history so depainted; and in remembrance of Medea, and of her cunning and science, he had do make in the said chamber, by subtil engine, that, when he would, it should seem that it lightened, and after, thunder, snow, and rain, and all within the said chamber, as oftimes, and when it should please him, which was all made for his singular pleasure."

During his residence in the Low Countries he acquired or perfected his knowledge of the French language, gained some acquaintance with the Flemish or Dutch (as appears by his translation of Reynard the Fox from the latter); imbibed his taste for literature, and passion for romance, and made himself master of the art of printing, "at great charge and dispense," as he informs us. His passion for romance he most probably derived from his intimacy with Raoul le Fevre, chaplain to the Duke of Burgundy, and with Henry Boulonger, canon of Lausanne. The former of these persons was the author of the Romance of Jason, and of the Recueill of the Histories of Troy, both of which were afterwards translated and printed by Caxton; and at the instance of the latter he translated, compiled, and printed, 'The History and Lyf of the most Noble and Christian Prince Charles the Great, Kyng of Vienna and Emperor of Rome.'

In June, 1467, Philip Duke of Burgundy died, and was succeeded by his son, Charles. A treaty of marriage between this prince and Margaret, sister to Edward IV., was at this time negotiating but was interrupted by the sudden death of Philip: the marriage, however, took place a year afterwards, on the 3d of June, 1468. Caxton was appointed to a situation in the household of the duchess, soon after her arrival in the Netherlands; but in what capacity, or with what salary, is not known. He seems, however, to have been on familiar terms with Margaret, and not to have been much occupied. For he informs us, that in 1469 he began translating the Histories of Troy, of his friend Raoul le Fevre, in Bruges, continued it at Ghent, and finished it at Cologne; he, however, laid the translation aside for some time. "In 1469," he says, "having no great charge or occupation, and wishing to eschew sloth and idleness—which is mother and nourisher of vices—having good leisure, being at Cologne, I set about finishing the translation. When, however, I remembered my simpleness and imperfections in French and English, I fell in despair of my works, and after I had written 5 or 6 quairs, purposed no more to have continued therein; and the quairs laid apart; and in two years after laboured no more in this work: till in a time it fortuned Lady Margaret sent for me to speak with her good Grace of divers matters, among the which I let her have knowledge of the foresaid beginning." "The Duchess," he adds, "found default in myne English, which she commanded me to amend, and to continue and make an end of the residue which command I durst not disobey." The Duchess rewarded him liberally for his labour. In his prologue and epilogue to this work, he mentions that his eyes are dimmed with over much looking on the white paper; that his courage was not so prone and ready to labour as it has been; and that age was creeping on him daily, and enfeebling all his body;—that he had learnt and practised at great charge and dispense to ordain the said book in print; and not written with pen and ink, as other books be.

The translation of the Recueill was published at Cologne in 1471; but he had printed there, at least, two works before that; the original of the

Recueill—a work unknown to German bibliographers—in 1464-7; and the oration of John Russel, on Charles, Duke of Burgundy, being created a knight of the garter in 1469. The existence of this was unknown till the year 1807, when it was discovered at the sale of Mr. Brand's books. No other book printed by Caxton at Cologne has been discovered; but that he printed there Bartholomeus de Proprietatibus Rerum, is plain from Wynkyn de Worde. This successor of Caxton printed, in 1494, Trevisa's translation of Bartholomeus; and in his proeme he requests his readers "to remember the soul of William Caxton, first printer of this boke in Latin tongue at Cologne;" this is the only instance of Caxton's having printed a Latin work, and would seem to imply some knowledge of that language.

It is supposed, that he returned to England about the year 1472, and brought with him the unsold copies of the translation of the Recueill. His first patron was Thomas Milling, Bishop of Hereford, who held the abbotship of St. Peter's, Westminster, *in commendam*. Caxton took up his residence and established his printing-office, either in the immediate neighbourhood of the abbey, or in one of the chapels attached to it.

That Caxton introduced the art of printing into England, and first practised it here, was never doubted till the year 1642: a dispute arose, at this time, between the Company of Stationers and some person, respecting a patent for printing; the case was formally argued; and in the course of the pleadings, Caxton was proved, incontestably, to have been the first printer in England. Soon after the Restoration, a book was discovered in the public library at Cambridge, the date of which was Oxford, 1468. The probability is, however, that the date of this book is incorrect, and that it should have been 1478, not 1468; this is inferred from its being printed with separate fusile metal types, very neat and beautiful, from the regularity of the page and the appearance of signatures; and moreover, from the fact, that no other production issued from the Oxford press till eleven years after 1468, it being highly improbable that a press connected with a university should have continued so long unemployed. But, even granting that the date is accurate, and that the book was printed in 1468, six years before the execution of any work by Caxton, the merit of Caxton, and the obligations of this country to him, are but little lessened by this circumstance.

Frequent and unprofitable disputes have arisen, at different times, and on various occasions, respecting original discoveries and inventions. He, who first unfolds and demonstrates a grand and important principle, or, by his skill, penetration, and labour, succeeds in applying a known power to new purposes of benefit to mankind, may excite our admiration for his genius or his knowledge; but if, from the circumstances of the times, and men's minds not being ripe and prepared, or from a combination of untoward and unfavourable events, or from any other cause, dependent on himself or not, his discovery or invention, of whatever nature it may be, dies with him, or is barren and unproductive, without shedding its light or influence on his contemporaries and future ages, we must withhold from him our gratitude and sense of obligation, and reserve them for the man to whom we can trace the benefits we enjoy.

The common opinion is, that the 'Game of Chess' was the first book printed by Caxton at Westminster: Mr. Dibdin, however, thinks its more probable that the Romance of Jason was the earliest specimen of his press in England. These are supposed to have been printed in 1474; this date is, indeed, specified in the 'Game of Chess,' but is doubtful whether it signifies the year when it was written, or that in which it was printed. This book was dedicated to George Duke of Clarence, the oldest surviving brother of King Edward. Caxton enjoyed the patronage of Henry VII., and his son, Prince Arthur, as well as of Edward and his brother; some of the nobility also encouraged him. Whether their patronage and encouragement displayed themselves in a substantial and profitable manner, we do not learn, but he himself was indefatigable in cultivating this new art. Besides the labour necessarily attached to his press, he translated not fewer than five thousand closely printed folio pages, though well stricken in years. From the colophon of Wynkyn de Worde's edition of the Vitas Patrum, 1495, it appears that this book was translated out of French into English by William Caxton, of Westminster, late dead, and that he finished it "at the last day of his life." The productions of his press amount to sixty-four. Of the most interesting of these works, either from the anecdotes connected with them, from the insight they give into his life and character, or into the manner of the times, or from the specimens they afford his talents and information, we shall give a short account, arranging them in chronological order.

1477 'Dictes and Sayings of the Philosophers.' This is the first book printed by Caxton with the year and place specified. It was translated from the French by Antony Woodville, Earl of Rivers. This nobleman had left out some strictures on women, which were in the original French; these Caxton translated and added as an appendix in three additional leaves; of his reasons for doing so, he gives the following statement. Lord Rivers had desired him to look over the translation, and to correct it. Caxton observed that the Dictes of Socrates on Women were not there, and indulged in many conjectures respecting the reason of their omission. He supposed that some fair lady had used her influence with his lordship, or that he was courting some fair lady at the time, or that he thought Socrates said more than what was true, or that these Dictes were not in his lordship's copy: "or else peradventure that the wind had blown over the leaf at the time of the translation." As, however, his lordship had given him permission to correct the translation, Caxton thought he should not be going beyond due limits if he added these Dictes. But, he tells us, "I did not presume to put and set them in my said lord's book, but in the end apart, in the rehearsal of the works, that Lord Rivers, or any other person, if they be not pleased, may with a pen erase it, or else rend the leaf out of the book, humble beseeching my said lord to take no displeasure on me presuming." He then requests the reader to lay the blame on Socrates, not on him.[38] From his insertion of these strictures on women, which are not the most courtly, it has been inferred that he was a womanhater; but that he was not so, appears from some of his prologues, especially from that to the 'Knight of the Tower.' This work he was requested to translate and print by "a noble lady, who had brought forth many noble and fair daughters, which were virtuously nourished and learned."

1478 'The Moral Proverbs of Christina, of Pisa.' The same year Caxton began to print a work called 'Cordyael,' but did not finish printing it, or at least is was not published till 1480. It does not appear that any other work came from his press during this interval. These two books were also translations from the French, by Caxton's patron, Lord Rivers. Of the political life of this accomplished and amiable nobleman, who was one of the very few who, in that age, promoted the cause of literature in this country,—this is not the place to speak: his dreadful catastrophe is well known.

> "Rivers, Vaughan, and Gray,
> Ere this, lie shorter by the head at Pomfret."

Caxton gives the following account of him and his works. "The noble and virtuous Lord Anthoine, Earl Rivers, Lord Scales and of the Isle of Wight, under governor to my Lord Prince of Wales, notwithstanding the great labour and charge that he hath had in the service of the King and of the said Lord Prince, as well in Wales as in England, which hath be to him no little thought and business both in sprite and body, as the fruit thereof experimentely sheweth; yet, over that, t' enrich his virtuous disposicion, he hath put him in devoyr, at all times, when he might have a leisure, which was but startmele, to translate divers works out of French

---

38. A manuscript of Lord Rivers' translation of this work, with an illumination representing him introducing Caxton to Edward IV., his queen, and the prince, is preserved in the Archbishop of Canterbury's Library, at Lambeth Palace. [HTM]

to English. Among other passed through myn hand, the book of the Wise Sayings or Dictes of Philosophers, and the wise holsom Proverbs of Christine of Pisa, set in metre. Over that, he hath made divers balads agenst the seven dedly synnes. Furthermore, he took upon him the translating of this present work, named Cordyale, trusting that both the reders and the hearers thereof should know themself hereafter the better, and amend their lyving." These ballads are supposed to be lost; but John Rouse, of Warwick, a contemporary historian has preserved a short poem of the Earl. Rouse seems to have copied it from his handwriting; it was written during his confinement in Pomfret Castle, a short time before his death in 1483; and, as Dr. Percy justly remarks, "gives us a fine picture of the composure and steadiness with which this stout Earl beheld his approaching fate."[39]

In this year (1480) also, Caxton printed his Chronicle, and his Description of Britain which is usually subjoined to it. These were very popular, having been reprinted four times *in this century,* (twice, however, without the Description;) and seven times *in the sixteenth century.*

1481 'The Mirror of the World,' 'Reynard the Fox,' from the Dutch, 'Tully on Old Age,' 'Tully on Friendship,' and 'Godfrey of Boulogne,' appeared this year. The two Treatises of Tully were translated by John Tiptoft, Earl of Worcester.[40]

1482 This year Caxton published the 'Polychronicon,' from the English version of John of Trevisa, who translated it from the Latin of Higden. It is a large volume, and seems to have been intended by Caxton as a helpmate to his Chronicle. The printing must have occupied him the

---

39. It is printed in Percy's Reiques of Ancient English Poetry, vol. ii, p. 44; and in Ritson's Ancient Songs, p. 87. [HTM]

40. This nobleman possessed great talents, received an excellent education, and devoted his purse and leisure time to the purchase of books, and the promotion and encouragement of literature. Horace Walpole remarks, that whatever disputes there may be about his titles in the state, there is no doubt but he was anciently at the head of literature, and so masterly an orator, that he drew tears from the eyes of Pope Pius II. (the celebrated Eneas Sylvius) when he visited Rome, through a curiosity of seeing the Vatican Library. (On his return to England, he presented books to the Library at Oxford, which had cost him 500 mark, upwards of 330l.—a large sum at this period.) His fondness for literature, and perhaps his political opinions, both being zealous Yorkists, brought him acquainted with Caxton. When Edward IV. was obliged to abandon his kingdom in order to save his life, in October, 1470, the Earl of Worcester was taken and beheaded on Tower Hill, on the 15th of that month. Caxton speaks in warm and affectionate language of him. "In his time," he says, "he flowered in vertue and cunning, and to whom he knew none lyke among the Lords of the Temporalty in science and moral vertue." Again: "O, good blessed Lord God! what grete loss was it of that noble, vertuous, and well-disposed lord; and what worship had he at Rome in the presence of our holy fader, the Pope; and so in all other places unto his deth; at which deth every man that was there might lern to die, and take his deth patientlye." [HTM]

whole year, as no other publication came from his press in 1482. Besides printing it, however, he added an eighth book, bringing the history down from 1357 to 1460; "because," he says, "men, whiles in this time ben oblivious and lightly forgotten, many things deygne to be put in memory; and also there cannot be founden in these days but few that wryte in their regysters such things as daily happen and fall." He was also obliged to take trouble of altering many parts of Trevisa's language; for, though only 124 years had elapsed, many works were quite obsolete and unintelligible. This, Caxton particularly notices in the 'Polychronicon;' and at greater length in the following curious passage in the preface of his 'Eneid,' a work from his press, that will be afterwards noticed.

"After divers works, made, translated, and atchieved, having no work in hand, I, sitting in my study, where as lay many divers pamphlets and books, it happened that to my hand came a little book, in French, which late was translated out of Latin, by some noble clerk of France, which book is named 'Eneid,' as made in Latin by that noble person and great clerk, Virgil, which book I saw over, and read therein. (He then describes the contents.) In which book I had great pleasure by cause of the fair and honest terms, and words, in French, which I never say tofore like, ne none so pleasant nor so well ordered: which book as me seemed should be much requisite to noble men to see, as well for the eloquence as histories; and when I had advised me in this said book, I deliberated, and concluded to translate it into English, and forthwith took a pen and ink, and wrote a leaf or twain, which I oversaw again, to correct it; and when I saw the fair and strange terms therein, I doubted that it should not please some gentlemen, which late blamed me, saying that in my translation, I had over curious terms, which could not be understand of common people; and desired me to use old and homely terms in my translation; and fain would I satisfy every man, and so to do, took an old book, and read therein; and certainly the English was so rude and broad, that I could not well understand it; and also, my Lord Abbot of Westminster, did do shew to me late certain evidence, written in old English, for to reduce it into our English, now used; and certainly it was written in such wise, that was more like to Dutch than to English. I could not reduce, nor bring it to be understanden."

Again: "Certainly the language now used varieth far from that which was used and spoken when I was born; for we, Englishmen, been borne under the dominacion of the moone, which is never stedfaste, but ever wavering." In his time, the inhabitants of one country hardly understood those of another: "The most quantity of the people understand not Latin nor French, in this royaume of England." The intermixture of French words and idioms, of course, was most prevalent in the capital. "That common English, that is spoken in one shyre varyeth from another—in so much that in may dayes happened, that certain merchants were in a ship, in Thamys, for to have sailed over the sea to Zealand; and, for lack of wind, they tarried at Forland, and went to land for to refresh them; and one of them, named Sheffield, a mercer, came into an hous, and axed for mete, and especially he axed after egges; and the good wyfe answerde, that she could speke no Frenche, and the merchant was angry, for he also could speke no Frenche, but would have had egges, and she understood him not. And then at last another sayd, that he would have eyrun. Then the good wyfe sayd, that she understood him well."[41] Caxton seems to have been a good deal puzzled and perplexed about the language he should use in his translations; for, while some advised him to use old and homely terms: "Some honest and great clerks," he adds, "have been with me, and desired me to write the most curious terms that I could finde—and thus, betwixt plain, rude, and curious, I stand abashed." There can be no doubt, however, that either by following the advice of those honest and great clerks, or from his long residence abroad—in his translations, as Dr. Johnson observes, "the original is so scrupulously followed, that they afford us little knowledge of our own language; though the words are English, the phrase is foreign."

1483 Caxton printed more books this year, than in any other. Seven bear this date. Among them were 'Gawin's Confessio Amantis;' and the 'Golden Legend.' A very full and particular account of the former is given by Mr. Dibdin, in his 'Typographical Antiquities,' vol. i., p. 177-185. Caxton informs us, that the printing of the 'Golden Legend' made him "half desperate to have left it, and to have laid it apart;" but he took courage, and went on, when the Earl of Arundel promised to take a number of copies, and to send him "a buck in summer, and a doe in winter."

1484 He printed four books, of which two were 'Æsop;' and the 'Order of Chivalry.' Mr. Dibdin, who has seen and examined more early editions of Æsop, in different languages, than most people, considers Caxton's edition, on the whole, as the rarest of all those in the fifteenth century. His Majesty's copy of it, he adds, is the only perfect one known. In the 'Order of Chivalry,' which he translated out of French, he gives a curious picture of the manners of his age; and at the same time laments, in strong and feeling language, the decline of chivalry: "O! ye knights of England,

---

41. If Caxton is correct in this story, the language of this part of Kent (in the weald of which, where he was born, he acknowledges English is spoken broad and rude) must have borrowed the word of egg from the Teutonic, and not from the Anglo-Saxon; æg, being the Anglo-Saxon, an ei the German, for an egg. [HTM]

where is the custom and usage of noble chivalry that was used in those days. What do you now, but go the baynes (baths,) and play at dyse; and some, not well advysed, use not honest and good rule again all order of knighthode. Leve this—leve it! and read the noble volumes of St. Graal, of Lancelot, of Galaad, of Trystram, of Perseforest, of Percival, of Gavaine, and many more. There shall ye see manhode, curtsys, and gentleness. And look in latter days of the noble actes sith the Conquest; as in King Richard dayes, Cuer de Lion; Edward I. and III., and his noble sones; Syr Robert Knowles, &c. Rede Froissart. Also, behold that noble and victorious King Hary the Fifthe. I would demand a question, if I should not displese: How many knyghtes, be ther now in England, that have th' use and th' exercise of a knyghte. That is to wit, that he knoweth his horse, and his horse him. I suppose, an a due serche sholde be made, there sholde be many founden that lacke. The more pyte is. I would it pleased our soverayne lord, that twyse or thryce a year, or as the lest ones, he wold do cry justes of pies, to th' ende, that every knyghte sholde have hors and harneys, and also the use and craft of a knyghte; and also to tornay one against one, or two against two, and the best to have a prys—a diamond or jewels, such as should plese the prynce."

Caxton, probably, like most other persons when they become old, regarded the manners of youth as much worse than they were in his early days. We must make allowances for his failing, in reading his Picture of London, and its youthful inhabitants. "I have known it in my young age much more wealthy, prosperous and richer, than it is at this day; and the cause is, that there is almost that intendeth to the commonweal, but only every man for his singular profit." And, in another place, "I see that the children that ben borne within the said citye encrease and proufitte not like their faders and olders: but for moste parte, after that they ben coming to their perfite years of discretion and ripeness of age, how well that their faders have left to them grete quantity of goods, yet scarcely amonge ten, two thryve. O blessed Lord, when I remember this I am all abashed; I cannot juge the cause; but fayrer, ne wiser, ne bet bespoken children in theyre youth ben no wher then ther ben in London; but at their full ryping there is not carnel, no good corn founden, but chaffe for the most parte."

In 1485, his press was entirely occupied with romances. The first was 'Morte Arthur the Liff of King Arthur of the Noble Knyghts of the Round Table, and in the end the dolorous Deth of them all.' This had been translated from the French, by Sir Thomas Mallery, knight; and Caxton printed it from the MS. It is a magnificent volume, and is supposed to have occupied him seven months. 2. The History of Charlemagne, already mentioned, as having been compiled and translated from two French books, by the advice of his friend Henry Boulonger, cannon of Lausanne. Only one more was printed by him this year—'The Storye of the right noble, right valiant, and worthy Knight Parys;' this also he translated from the French. In the year 1486, his press seems to have been idle; at least none of his works bear this date: and in 1487, only one book appeared, entitled, 'The Book of Good Manners.' The original French, from which he translated it, he informs us, was given to him by a special friend of his, a mercer of London.[42] In 1488 no books appeared. In 1489 Caxton published four, of which 'The Fait of Armes and Chivalry' was one. "This was delivered to me, William Caxton, by the most Chrystin King and redoubted Prince, my natural and sovereign lord, Kyng Henry the 7th, Kyng of England and of France, in his palace of Westmestie, the 23 day of Janyure, the 4th yere of his regne; and desired and willed by to translate this said boke, and reduce it into our English and natural tongue, and to put it in imprynte." It is a compilation by Christine of Pisa, from the Military Treatises of Vegetius Frontinus, and the Arbre des Battailles. Another book printed this year was the 'Eneidos,' translated from the French; it is a mere compilation in prose of the principal events recorded in Virgil's poem, and has no pretension to an imitation of that poet, in any one respect. It does not, therefore, deserve the contemptuous and sarcastic notice taken of it, by Gawin Douglas, in the preface to his Scotch translation of Virgil. Caxton's work was dedicated to Arthur, eldest son of Henry VII. He represents himself as at all time well stricken in years: and if the date usually assigned to his birth (1412) be accurate, he must have been seventy-seven years old. The 'Doctrinne of Sapience,' also published in 1489, is the last that bears a date, if we except his edition of the Statues: a perfect set of these, passed in the reign of Henry VII. till the death of Caxton (1490-1) have very recently been discovered. Twenty-eight of his known publications are without dates. Some of these have been already noticed; a few of the remainder will supply some interesting matter. Caxton printed Chaucer's Canterbury Tales twice; each edition is without date, but the first is supposed to have been one of the earliest productions of his press. Mr. Warton regards it as much more to his honour, than it can be to his discredit, that he printed them very incorrectly. "He probably took the first manuscript that he could procure to print from, and it happened unluckily to be one of the worst in all respects that he could

---

42. The mercers of London seem to have been great encouragers of literature. Prefixed to Wynkyn de Worde's reprint of Caxton's 'Polichronicon' in 1495, there are a few poetical stanzas, in which one Roger Thoornye, a mercer, is praised for ordering and encouraging the printer to undertake so laborious a performance. [HTM]

possibly have met with." As soon, however, as he found out these imperfections and errors, he began a second edition "for to satisfy the author, whereas tofore, by ignorance, I had erred in hurting and defamying his boke." Caxton's extreme and conscientious desire to fulfil one of the most important duties of an editor and printer, (and he acted as both,) by giving the works as the author himself wrote them, as well as his candour and ingenuousness, are depicted in a clear and interesting manner, in the preface to his second edition.[43]

He seems to have had a veneration for the memory of this poet, and to have formed, with sound judgment and good taste, a most correct and precise estimate of the peculiar merits of his poetry. As a proof of the former, we may mention, that Caxton, at his own expense, procured a long epitaph to be written in honour of Chaucer. This was inscribed on a tablet, hung on a pillar near the poet's grave in the south aisle of Westminster Abbey. The following remarks will amply justify what we have stated respecting Caxton's ability, fully to understand, and thoroughly to relish, the merits and beauties of Chaucer's poetry. "We ought to give a singular laud unto that noble and great philosopher, Geoffrey Chaucer, the which, for his ornate writings in our tong, may well have the name of a laureate poet. For, to fore that he embellished and ornated and made fair our English, in this royaume was had rude speech and incongrue, as yet it appeareth by old books, which, at this day, ought not to have place, ne be compared among unto his beauteous volumes and ornate writings, of whom he made many books and treatises of many a noble history, as well in metre as in rhyme and prose: and the so craftily made, *that he comprehended his matters in short, quick, and high sentences, eschewing perplexity; casting away the chaff of superfluity, and shewing the picked grain of sentence, uttered by crafty and sugared eloquence.*"

And speaking of Chaucer's 'Book of Fame,' which he also printed, he says, "Which work, as me seemeth, is craftily made and digne to be written and known; for he toucheth in it right great wisdom and subtle understanding; *and so in all his works he excelleth, in mine opinion, all other writers in our English, for he writeth no void words, but all his matter is full of*

---

43. The following draft of a similar passage appears in Harriet's handwriting (Box III, 113): "But it is a mistake to imagine that W. Caxton was merely either a translator or editor. his observations on the works on which he employed his press proves him ingenious & persevering but a quick discrimination of refined taste—No critique on his favorite Chaucer can surpass the following, speaking of Chaucer's Book of Fame page 29. 'Which work'—to 'and writing"—.'

Harriet must be referring to page 29 of another draft, although the quote referred to does appear on page 29 of the published manuscript.

high and quick sentence, to whom ought to be given laud and praise for his noble making and writing."

Chaucer's translation of Boethius was also printed by Caxton, without date. It is alternately in Latin and English, but the former is not given entire; a few verses of a period in Latin being succeeded by the whole of the corresponding period in English, and so through the whole volume: the Latin type is large compared with the English.

A curious volume was printed by Caxton, about the period when the French, which had hitherto been spoken almost exclusively at court, was giving place to the English language; it is entitled the 'Book of Travellers.' It contains the corresponding terms in both languages, for those things most commonly talked of at court, especially such as related to dress.

We have already stated that he continued his labours as a printer to the very last; he seems also to have taken an active part in the affairs of the parish of St. Margaret, Westminster, in which he lived and died; since, for some years before his death, his name appears to the churchwardens' accounts, as one of the parishioners who had undertaken to examine their details. He died in 1490-1, was buried in St. Margaret's, and left some books to that church.

His character may be collected from the account we have given of his labours, and the extracts we have made from his prefaces; he was possessed of good sense and sound judgment; steady, persevering, active, zealous and liberal in his services for that important art which he introduced into his kingdom; labouring not only as a printer, but as translator and editor. It has been objected that he was too much given to admire and print romances; but in this he only partook of the spirit of the age; perhaps, indeed, it survived in him longer and with more power, than in most of his contemporaries; but that his love of romance did not blunt his judgment and taste for real talent is evident by his printing Chaucer's works, and his criticisms on them. It should be recollected, also, that in the selection of works for the press he was necessarily guided by public opinion, and by the probability that what he did print would repay him for his labour and expense. The remarks of Gibbon on this point are sensible and candid. "In the choice of his authors, that liberal and industrious artist was reduced to comply with the vicious taste of his readers, to gratify the nobles with treatises of heraldry, hawking, and the game of chess, and to amuse the popular credulity with romances of fabulous knights, and legends of more fabulous saints. The father of printing expresses a laudable desire to elucidate the history of his country, but instead of publishing the Latin Chronicle of Ralph Higden, he could only venture on the English version by John de Trevisa; and his complaint of the difficulty of finding materials for his own continuation of that work, sufficiently attests, that even the writers which we now possess of the fourteenth and fifteenth centuries, had not yet emerged from the darkness of the cloister." If we reflect, too, on the state of England at this period, that he established his press soon after the murder of Henry VI., and that he carried on his works during the remainder of the reign of Edward IV., and the reigns of Edward V. and Richard III., when the minds of those most likely and able to encourage him were seldom free from alarm for their own safety, their time much occupied, and their means necessarily reduced by the distracted and wasted state of the country; and when little attention or money could be spared for literature; we must give Caxton great credit for having done so much; for having in the midst of confusion persevered in his labours, and succeeded in establishing the art of printing in his native land. That England at this period was much behind France in literature, is proved by the fact that Caxton was obliged to have recourse to the French language for most of the works which he printed. He thus, it may be supposed, employed his press profitably to himself, and certainly with advantage to our literature; for, as Mr. Warton truly observes, "had not the French furnished him those materials, it is not likely that Virgil, Ovid, Cicero, and many other good writers, would, by means of his press, have been circulated in the English tongue, so early as the close of the fifteenth century."

There was, perhaps, at this time, no man in England, whose talents, habits, and character, were so well fitted to introduce and establish the art of printing as those of William Caxton: to have succeeded in this enterprise, the benefits of which, in a national point of view, we may even now be enjoying, is praise enough; for it is the praise of having been a useful citizen of the state and member of society,—the highest that man can bestow or receive.

Caxton's printing is inferior, in many respects, to the printing executed on the continent during the same period. The types employed in the latter have a squareness, fineness, and brilliancy not in those of Caxton; the paper and press-work are much superior; the order and symmetry of the press-work are qualities which appear in very few of his productions. He seems not to have been able to procure, or to have rejected, the roman letter, even after it had been employed with excellent effect by the continental printers. On the other hand, as Mr. Didbin remarks, "whenever we meet with good copies of his books, his type has a bold and rich effect, which renders their perusal less painful than that of many foreign productions, where the angular sharpness of the letters somewhat dazzles and hurts the eye." His ink is of an inferior quality; his paper is fine and good, resembling the thin

vellum on which MSS. were then generally written; his letter is a mixture
of secretary and Gothic, also resembling that used in MSS. at that period;
his leaves are seldom numbered, his pages never. When the impression was
finished, Caxton revised a single copy, and corrected the faults with red ink;
the copy thus corrected was then given to a proper person to correct the
whole impression; as he was extremely exact, this operation occasioned him
much troublesome and minute labour.

CHAPTER VI

*Notices of some other Printers in England, contemporary with Caxton, or im-
mediately after him—Printing introduced into Oxford, Cambridge, St. Alban's,
York, Southwark, Tavistock, Ipswich, &c.—into Scotland and Ireland.*

PRINTING-PRESSES were set up in England by some foreigners and
natives, before Caxton's death. In 1480 and 1481, John Lettou, a foreigner,
printed in London. He is said to have come over to this country on
Caxton's invitation. This, however, is not likely, as his unskilfulness is such
that Caxton would scarcely have invited or encouraged such a bad workman. The types he employed in the only two books he is known to have
printed himself, are rude and broken. After he had published them, he
was taken into the printing-office of William de Machlinia—first, it is
supposed as a journeyman, and afterwards as a partner. Machlinia also was
a foreigner; the only celebrity that can attach to the names of these
partners, arises from their having printed the first edition of 'Littleton's
Tenures,' in a small folio, without date. Their printing-office was near
All-Hallows church; their letter, a coarse Gothic one. The partnership was
of very short continuance; for, in 1483, Machlinia's name alone appears.
Wynkyn de Worde was a man of very superior talents and skill. He was
a native of Lorraine, and came into England either along with Caxton, or
was afterwards invited by him; he was employed as Caxton's assistant till
his death. He continued in his office, as his successor, till between the
years 1500 and 1502; when he removed his printing-office to the sign of
the Sun, in the parish of St. Bride's where he died in 1534. Soon after he
began business for himself, he greatly improved the art by cutting his own
punches, which he sunk into matrices, and casting his own letters. His
books are remarkable for their neatness and elegance. Four hundred and
eight are known to have been printed by him. His edition of the 'Polychronicon' is deemed uncommonly well executed. Dr. Dibdin calls it "one
of the most beautiful folio volumes of that skilful artist:" its date is 1495.
Several grammarians of repute, Stanbridge, Garlandea, Whittinton, Holt,
and Lilye, lived at the period of the introduction of printing into England;

and Wynkyn de Worde, who appears to have been a man of good education as well as talent, printed some of their works. He printed the 'Accidence' of Stanbridge, "in Caxton's house, at Westminster." The date unknown. His 'Vocabulary,' in 1500. This De Worde continued to republish till 1532. The 'Multorum Vocabulorum Equivocorum Interpretatio,' by Garlandea, was printed in 1500, by De Worde, and at least as late as 1517. He also printed repeatedly the grammatical works of Whittinton. Holt's 'Lac Puerorum, or Milk for Children,' was printed by him in 4to, without date. No impression of the grammar of Lilye (but which, in reality, was drawn up by several persons,) by De Worde, or in Lilye's lifetime, has been discovered. The first Greek letters used in England are found in a Grammatical Treatise of Whittinton, by De Worde, in 1519: they are cut out of wood. We have gone into this detailed mention of those works chiefly in order to show the assistance which the press was already giving, in its earliest days, to elementary education. 'Accidences,' 'Lucidaries,' 'Orchards of Words,' 'Promptuaries for Little Children,' were published in great numbers.

Richard Pynson, a Norman by birth, was in Caxton's office. He carried on his business from 1493 to 1531. His known productions are two hundred and ten. He styled himself King's Printer; but it is doubtful whether he had any patent. He introduced the Roman letter into this country. His types are clear and good; but his press-work is hardly equal to that of De Worde. Most of the works he printed are of a higher character for merit and usefulness than those either of Caxton or De Worde. The first treatise on arithmetic, published in this country, was printed by Pynson, in 1522, 4to, 'Libri 4 de arte Supputandi.' It was written by Cuthbert Tonstall, Bishop of London, one of the best mathematicians, as well as general scholars, of his age. In 1499, the first edition of the 'Promptorius Puerorum' came from Pynson's press. He was a voluminous printer of early statutes; and in his time began the publication of what are still called 'Year Books.' Soon after Caxton's death he printed an edition of the 'Canterbury Tales,' and in 1526, reprinted them with a collection of some other pieces of Chaucer. William Jaques was contemporary with Pynson, and printed in conjunction with him the acts passed in 1503. He used a new cut English letter, "equalling, if not excelling, in beauty, any produced by modern foundries." In 1530, the first French and English Dictionary ('Eclaircissemens de la Langue Françoise') was published by John Hawkins. No other work from his press is known.

On the death of Pynson, Thomas Berthelet was appointed King's Printer, by a patent, the earliest that has been found. He dwelt at the sign of Lucretia Romana, Fleet-street. Thomas Godfray was a printer at the same time. These printers embarked in the same concern. From their press came (1532), a complete edition of all that had then come to light of the works of Chaucer. It is on fine paper, and the types and press-work are remarkably neat and elegant. This edition was superintended, and published, under the patronage of William Thynne. To one of this family—perhaps to the same person—Caxton had been indebted for the manuscripts, which enabled him to publish his second and much improved edition of the 'Canterbury Tales.'

If the title of the book (already noticed) purporting to be printed at Oxford, in 1468, be erroneous, as there is strong reason to suspect it to be, then the establishment of printing in this city must have been in 1478. The first known printers there, however, were Theodore Rood, a German, and Thomas Hunt, and Englishman; and their first production Herbert assigns to the year 1485. It is not known in what year printing was introduced into Cambridge. It certainly was very shortly after Caxton established his press in Westminster. The types of the earliest known work which issued from Cambridge, very much resembled Caxton's largest. The first printer at Cambridge, whose name is known, was John Sibert, who is supposed to have been born at Lyons. A few Greek words are interspersed in his edition of Linacre's translation of one of Galen's treatises. This is the earliest appearance of Greek *metal* types.

In 1480, a printing-press was established in the Benedictine Monastery at St. Albans, of which William Wallingford was at that time prior. Wynkyn de Worde informs us that the printer was "sometime a school-master," and he probably was a monk. The types of the book, which is a Treatise on Rhetoric, in Latin, are very rude. Printing was introduced into York, in 1509, by Hugh Goes, supposed to have been the son of a printer at Antwerp. His first production was the *Pica* of the Cathedral of that city; he afterwards removed to Beverley, and then to London. Peter de Triers, probably a native of that city, printed in 1514, the first book in Southwark; it was the 'Moral Distichs of Cato,' with Erasmus's 'Scholia,' in Latin, 1525, Tavistock. Here was an exempt monastery, celebrated for its lectures on the Saxon language, which were discontinued about the period of the Reformation. Several of its abbots were learned men; and the encouragement in literature is evident by the establishment of a printing-press a few years after the introduction of printing into England. The first printed book was John Walton's Translation of Boethius de Consolatione, in 4to; the printer's name was Thomas Rychard, monk of that monastery. A book, called the 'Long Grammar,' was printed at Tavistock, but no copy of it has been found. A printing-office was first established in Canterbury about 1525; but no name or date is in the book supposed to have been the first printed there. Cardinal Wolsey, on his visit to do honour to his native city, established or patronised a printing-office at Ipswich in 1538; the printer was John Oswen, who removed to Worcester in 1548, where he published a folio and quarto edition of the New Testament. The art was introduced into Norwich about 1570, by Anthony Solen, one of the many foreigners from the Low Countries who introduced all sorts of woollen manufactures into that city.

Between the year 1471, when Caxton began to print, and the year 1540, the English press, though conducted by industrious, and some of them learned printers, produced very few classics. 'Boethius de Consolatione,' in Latin and English, three editions of 'Æsop,' 'Terence,' the 'Bucolics' of Virgil twice, and 'Tully's Offices,' were the only classics printed. From Cambridge no classical work appeared; and the University of Oxford produced only the first book of 'Cicero's Epistles,' and that at the expense of Wolsey.

The most ancient specimen of Scotch printing known, is a collection entitled 'The Porteus of Nobleness,' Edinburgh, 1508. A patent had been granted by James IV. to Walter Chapman, a merchant of that city, and Andrew Mollar, a workman, for establishing a press there in 1507. Very few works, however, appear to have issued from this or from any other Scotch press for the next thirty years. In 1554, one of Knox's Theological Treatises was printed at Kalykow, or Kelso. Hamilton's, Archbishop of St. Andrews, Catechism, and Treatise on the 'Seven Sacraments.' 4to, was the first book printed at St. Andrews, 1552. It was nearly a century after this, before Aberdeen, the seat of another University, could boast of a press. Edward Raban, who published a poem on the death of Bishop Forbes, in 1635, styles himself "Master Printer,—the first in Aberdeen." Ireland was the last European country, except Russia, (and this, in the sixteenth century, could scarcely be reckoned European,) that received the art of printing. The earliest book known is the Common Prayer, printed in Dublin, 1551, by Humphrey Powell. The Library of Trinity College, in that city, contains but one book printed there, even so early as 1633. The first book in the Irish character, was a Liturgy, 1566, for the use of the Scotch Highlanders.

The advantages which have been derived from the invention of printing, and from the perseverance and ingenuity of those by whom it was established, among whom we may place William Caxton, are vast and important; but they are too obvious to require, in this place, an elaborate detail. The productions of men of genius and learning; the records of literature and of science; of whatever is either brilliant in imagination or profound in thought; whatever may either adorn or improve the human mind,—thenceforth became imperishable. The light of knowledge cannot again be quenched—it is free, and open, and accessible as the air we breathe. The future history of the world may, indeed, disclose enough both of misery and of vice; but it cannot again present an universal blank, or be disgraced by another age of utter and cheerless ignorance.

FROM PRINCIPLES OF POLITICAL ECONOMY, BOOK IV
CHAPTER VII
ON THE PROBABLE FUTURITY OF THE LABOURING CLASSES

The final piece of miscellaneous writing is a very different sort of collaboration from that of the William Caxton article, and with a different co-author—John Stuart Mill. Harriet contributed this chapter to Principles of Political Economy, *first published in 1848. In his* Autobiography, *John writes:*

The first of my books in which [Harriet's] share was conspicuous was the 'Principles of Political Economy.' . . . The chapter of the Political Economy which has had a greater influence on opinion than all the rest, that on 'the Probable Future of the Labouring Classes,' is entirely due to her: in the first draft of the book, that chapter did not exist. She pointed out the need of such a chapter, and the extreme imperfection of the book without it: she was the cause of my writing it; and the more general part of the chapter, the statement and discussion of the two opposite theories respecting the proper condition of the labouring classes, was wholly an exposition of her thoughts, often in words taken from her own lips. (173)

The first edition of the book was to have contained a dedication to Harriet Taylor, but John Taylor was infuriated at the idea,[44] so the following dedication was merely pasted in a few gift copies to friends:

To
Mrs John Taylor,
as the most eminently qualified
of all persons known to the author
either to originate or to appreciate
speculations on social improvement,
this attempt to explain and diffuse ideas

---

44. Harriet's letter appears on p. 472. John Taylor's response appears on pp. 472–473.

many of which were first learned from herself,
is
with the highest respect and regard,
dedicated

The chapter was revised extensively as part of the complete revision of the book in 1852. Since this third edition was the last completed in Harriet's lifetime, was the most extensive revision either before or after her death, and was one of the first pieces Harriet and John worked on after their marriage in 1851, the 1852 edition is the one most likely to have received Harriet's closest attention and is the one reprinted below.[45]

The letters John sent to Harriet during her stay in Pau in 1849 and Hyères in 1854 offer insight into the depth of their collaboration on all of the Principles of Political Economy *as well as revision of this chapter. John was approached in 1854 by the Christian Socialists with a request to reprint Harriet's chapter as a separate pamphlet. Although never published in this form, the request demonstrates the importance of this chapter as a distinct feature of this nearly one-thousand-page-book. Those Mill scholars who are not fond of the "socialist" leanings in Mill tend to contribute ideas such as those found in this chapter to Harriet alone. For example, in her review of the volumes of the* Collected Works *devoted to the* Principles, *Gertrude Himmelfarb says that John understated Harriet's contribution to this chapter and that John had "succumbed" to Harriet's dumb ideas* (The New Leader, *10 May 1965, 29*). *Readers may evaluate the value of the ideas contained in the following passage.*

In chapter 6 of Book IV, the chapter Harriet refers to in her opening paragraph, John writes about the ideal of a progressive economic state. Most economists predicted that as long as the total GNP kept increasing, a society would be fine, but that at some point in the future, because they would run out of new markets, the richest countries would reach an economic stability that would be disastrous. John argues that the goal was not overall economic expansion, but rather a controlled population and better distribution of wealth that would supply means for each to develop one's gifts. He suggests a "limitation of the sum which any one person may acquire by gift or inheritance" as a way of helping redistribute wealth more fairly. John reminds the reader that population control is critical not merely for its economic consequences, but for the sake of the environment and the need of humans for solitude.

---

45. For a complete elaboration of changes made to this chapter in each of the editions, see *CW: III, 758–96.*

§ 1. The observations in the preceding chapter had for their principal object to deprecate a false ideal of human society. Their applicability to the practical purposes of present times, consists in moderating the inordinate importance attached to the mere increase of production, and fixing attention upon improved distribution, and a large remuneration of labour, as the true desiderata. Whether the aggregate produce increases absolutely or not, is a thing in which, after a certain amount has been obtained, neither the legislator nor the philanthropist need feel any strong interest: but, that it should increase relatively to the number of those who share in it, is of the utmost possible importance; and this, (whether the wealth of mankind be stationary, or increasing at the most rapid rate ever known in an old country,) must depend on the opinions and habits of the most numerous class, the class of manual labourers.

When I speak, either in this place or elsewhere, of "the labouring classes," or of labourers as a "class," I use those phrases in compliance with custom, and as descriptive of an existing, but by no means a necessary or permanent, state of social relations. I do not recognise as either just or salutary, a state of society in which there is any "class" which is not labouring; any human beings, exempt from bearing their share of the necessary labours of human life, except those unable to labour, or who have fairly earned rest by previous toil. So long, however, as the great social evil exists of a non-labouring class, labourers also constitute a class, and may be spoken of, though only provisionally, in that character.

Considered in its moral and social aspect, the state of the labouring people has latterly been a subject of much more speculation and discussion than formerly; and the opinion, that it is not now what it ought to be, has become very general. The suggestions which have been promulgated, and the controversies which have been excited, on detached points rather than on the foundations of the subject, have put in evidence the existence of two conflicting theories, respecting the social position desirable for manual labourers. The one may be called the theory of dependence and protection, the other that of self-dependence.

According to the former theory, the lot of the poor, in all things which affect them collectively, should be regulated *for* them, not *by* them. They should not be required or encouraged to think for themselves, or give to their own reflection or forecast an influential voice in the determination of their destiny. It is supposed to be the duty of the higher classes to think for them, and to take the responsibility of their lot, as the commander and officers of any army take that of the soldiers composing it. This function, it is contended, the higher classes should prepare themselves to perform conscientiously, and their whole demeanour should impress the poor with a reliance on it, in order that, while yielding passive and active obedience to the rules prescribed for them, they may resign themselves in all other respects to a trustful *insouciance,* and repose under the shadow of their protectors. The relation between rich and poor, according to this theory (a theory also applied to the relation between men and women)[46] should be only partly authorative; it should be amiable, moral, and sentimental: affectionate tutelage on the one side, respectful and grateful deference on the other. The rich should be *in loco parentis* to the poor, guiding and restraining them like children. Of spontaneous action on their part there should be no need. They should be called on for nothing but to do their day's work, and to be moral and religious. Their morality and religion should be provided for them by their superiors, who should see them properly taught it, and should do all that is necessary to ensure their being, in return for labour and attachment, properly fed, clothed, housed, spiritually edified, and innocently amused.

This is the ideal of the future, in the minds of those whose dissatisfaction with the Present assumes the form of affection and regret towards the Past. Like other ideals, it exercises an unconscious influence on the opinions and sentiments of numbers who never consciously guide themselves by any ideal. It has also this in common with other ideals, that it has never been historically realized. It makes its appeal to our imaginative sympathies in the character of a restoration of the good times of our forefathers. But no times can be pointed out in which the higher classes of this or any other country performed a part even distantly resembling the one assigned to them in this theory. It is an idealization, grounded on the conduct and character of here and there an individual. All privileged and powerful classes, as such, have used their power in the interest of their own selfishness, and have indulged their self-importance in despising, and not in lovingly caring for, those who were, in their estimation, degraded, by being under the necessity of working for their benefit. I do not affirm that what has always been must always be, or that human improvement has no tendency to correct the intensely selfish feelings engendered by power; but though the evil may be lessened, it cannot be eradicated, until the power itself is withdrawn. This, at least, seems to me undeniable, that long before the superior classes could be sufficiently improved to govern in the tutelary manner supposed, the inferior classes would be too much improved to be so governed.

I am quite sensible of all that is seductive in the picture of society which this theory presents. Though the facts of it have no prototype in the past,

---

46. The phrase in parentheses was added in the 1852 edition.

the feelings have. In them lies all that there is of reality in the conception. As the idea is essentially repulsive of a society only held together by the relations and feelings arising out of pecuniary interests, so there is something naturally attractive in a form of society abounding in strong personal attachments and disinterested self-devotion. Of such feelings it must be admitted that the relation of protector and protected has hitherto been the richest source. The strongest attachments of human beings in general, are towards the things or the persons that stand between them and some dreaded evil. Hence, in an age of lawless violence and insecurity, and general hardness and roughness of manners, in which life is beset with dangers and sufferings at every step, to those who have neither a commanding position of their own, nor a claim on the protection of some one who has—a generous giving of protection, and a grateful receiving of it, are the strongest ties which connect human beings; the feelings arising from that relation are their warmest feelings; all the enthusiasm and tenderness of the most sensitive natures gather round it; loyalty on the one part and chivalry on the other are principles exalted into passions. I do not desire to depreciate these qualities. The error lies in not perceiving, that these virtues and sentiments, like the clanship and the hospitality of the wandering Arab, belong emphatically to a rude and imperfect state of the social union, and that the feelings between protector and protected whether between kings and subjects, rich and poor, or men and women,[47] can no longer have this beautiful and endearing character where there are no longer any serious dangers from which to protect. What is there in the present state of society to make it natural that human beings, of ordinary strength and courage, should glow with the warmest gratitude and devotion in return for protection? The laws protect them, wherever the laws do not criminally fail in their duty. To be under the power of some one, instead of being as formerly the sole condition of safety, is now, speaking generally, the only situation which exposes to grievous wrong. The so-called protectors are now the only persons against whom, in any ordinary circumstances, protection is needed. The brutality and tyranny with which every police report is filled, are those of husbands to wives, of parents to children. That the law does not prevent these atrocities, that it scarcely attempts, except nominally, to repress and punish them, is no matter of necessity, but the deep disgrace of those by whom the laws are made and administered. No man or woman who either possesses or is able to earn an independent livelihood, requires any other protection than that which the law could and ought to give. This being the case, it argues great

---

47. The phrase beginning with "whether" and ending here was added in the 1852 edition.

ignorance of human nature to continue taking for granted the relations founded on protection must always subsist, and not to see that the assumption of the part of protector, and of the power which belongs to it, without any of the necessities which justify it, must engender feelings opposite to loyalty.

Of the working men, at least in the more advanced countries of Europe, it may be pronounced certain, that the patriarchal or paternal system of government is one to which they will not again be subject. That question was decided, when they were taught to read, and allowed access to newspapers and political tracts; when dissenting preachers were suffered to go among them, and appeal to their faculties and feelings in opposition to the creeds professed and countenanced by their superiors; when they were brought together in numbers, to work socially under the same roof; when railways enabled them to shift from place to place, and change their patrons and employers as easily as their coats; above all, when they were encouraged to seek a share in the government by means of the electoral franchise. The working classes have taken their interests into their own hands, and are perpetually showing that they think the interest of their employers not identical with their own but opposite of them. Some among the higher classes flatter themselves that these tendencies may be counteracted by moral and religious education; but they have let the time go by for giving an education which can serve their purpose. The principles of the Reformation have reached as low down in society as reading and writing, and the poor will no longer accept morals and religion of other people's prescribing. I speak more particularly of this country, especially the town population, and the districts of the most scientific agriculture and highest wages, Scotland and the north of England. Among the more inert and less modernized agricultural population of the southern counties, it might be possible for the gentry to retain for some time longer something of the ancient deference and submission of the poor, by bribing them with high wages and constant employment; by ensuring them support, and never requiring them to do anything which they do not like. But these are two conditions which never have been combined, and never can be, for long together. A guarantee of subsistence can only be practically kept up, when work is enforced, and superfluous multiplication restrained, by at least a moral compulsion. It is then, that the would-be revivers of old times which they do not understand, would feel practically in how hopeless a task they were engaged. The whole fabric of patriarchal or seignorial influence, attempted to be raised on the foundation of caressing the poor, would be shattered against the necessity of enforcing a stringent Poor-law.

§ 2. It is on a far other basis that the well-being and well-doing of the labouring people must henceforth rest. The poor have come out of leading strings, and cannot any longer be governed or treated like children. To their own qualities must now be commended the care of their destiny. Modern nations will have to learn the lesson, that the well-being of a people must exist by means of the justice and self-government, the δικαιοσύνη and σωφροσύνη,[48] of the individual citizens. The theory of dependence attempts to dispense with the necessity of these qualities in the dependent classes. But now, when even in position they are becoming less and less dependent, and their minds less and less acquiescent in the degree and dependence which remains, the virtues of independence are those which they stand in need of. Whatever advice, exhortation, or guidance is held out to the labouring classes, must henceforth be tendered to them as equals, and accepted with their eyes open. The prospect of the future depends on the degree in which they can be made rational beings.

There is no reason to believe that prospect other than hopeful. The progress indeed has hitherto been, and still is, slow. But there is a spontaneous education going on in the minds of the multitude, which may be greatly accelerated and improved by artificial aids. The instruction obtained from newspapers and political tracts may not be the best sort of instruction, but it is vastly superior to none at all.[49] The institutions for lectures and discussion, the collective deliberations on questions of common interest, the trades unions, the political agitation, all serve to awaken public spirit, to diffuse [a] variety of ideas among the mass, and to excite thought and reflection in the more intelligent. Although the too early attainment of political franchises by the least educated class might retard, instead of promoting, their improvement, there can be little doubt that it is greatly stimulated by the attempt to acquire them. In the meantime, the working classes are now part of the public; in all discussions on matters of general interest they, or a portion of them, are now partakers; all who use the press as an instrument may, if it so chances, have them for an audience; the avenues of instruction through which the middle classes acquire such ideas as they have, are accessible to, at least, the operatives in the towns. With these resources, it cannot be doubted that they will increase in intelligence, even by their own unaided efforts; while there is reason to hope that great improvements both in the quality and quantity

---

48. Justice and Self-government.

49. Beginning with her writing for the Society for the Diffusion of Useful Knowledge in the 1830s (her "Life of William Caxton") and continuing with the newspaper articles of the 1840s, Harriet had already tried to implement this idea.

of school education will be effected by the exertions either of government or of individuals, and that the progress of the mass of the people in mental cultivation, and in the virtues which are dependent on it, will take place more rapidly, and with fewer intermittences and aberrations, than if left to itself.

From the increase of intelligence, several effects may be confidently anticipated. First: that they will become even less willing than at present to be led and governed, and directed into the way they should go, by the mere authority and *prestige* of superiors. If they have not now, still less will they have hereafter, any deferential awe, or religious principle of obedience, holding them in mental subjection to a class above them. The theory of dependence and protection will be more and more intolerable to them, and they will require that their conduct and condition shall be essentially self-governed. It is, at the same time, quite possible that they may demand, in many cases, the intervention of the legislature in their affairs, and the regulation by law of various things which concern them, often under very mistaken ideas of their interest. Still, it is their own will, their own ideas and suggestions, to which they will demand that effect should be given, and not rules laid down for them by other people. It is quite consistent with this, that they should feel respect for superiority of intellect and knowledge, and defer much to the opinions, on any subject, of those whom they think well acquainted with it. Such deference is deeply grounded in human nature; but they will judge for themselves of the persons who are and are not entitled to it.

§ 3. It appears to me impossible but that the increase of intelligence, of education, and of the love of independence among the working classes, must be attended with corresponding growth of the good sense which manifests itself in provident habits of conduct, and that population, therefore, will bear a gradually diminishing ratio to capital and employment. This most desirable result would be much accelerated by another change, which lies in direct line of the best tendencies of the time; the opening of industrial occupations freely to both sexes. The same reasons which make it no longer necessary that the poor should depend on the rich, make it equally unnecessary that women should depend on men, and the least which justice requires is that law and custom should not enforce dependence (when the correlative protection has become superfluous) by ordaining that a woman, who does not happen to have a provision by inheritance, shall have scarcely any means open to her of gaining a livelihood, except as a wife and mother. Let women who prefer that occupation, adopt it; but that there should be no option, no other *carrière* possible for the great majority of women, except in the humbler departments of life, is a flagrant social injustice. The ideas and institutions by which the accident of sex is made the groundwork of an inequality of legal rights, and a forced dissimilarity of social functions, must ere long be recognised as the greatest hindrance to moral, social, and even intellectual improvement.[50] On the present occasion I shall only indicate, among the probable consequences of the industrial and social independence of women, a great diminution of the evil of over-population. It is by devoting one-half of the human species to that exclusive function, by making it fill the entire life of one sex, and interweave itself with almost all the objects of the other, that the animal[51] instinct in question is nursed into the disproportionate preponderance which it has hitherto exercised in human life.

§ 4. The political consequences of the increasing power and importance of the operative classes, and of the growing ascendancy of numbers, which even in England and under the present institutions, is rapidly giving to the will of the majority at least a negative voice in the acts of government, are too wide a subject to be discussed in this place. But, confining ourselves to economical considerations, and notwithstanding the effect which improved intelligence in the working classes, together with just laws, many have in altering the distribution of the produce to their advantage, I cannot think that they will be permanently contented with the condition of labouring for wages as their ultimate state. They may be willing to pass through the class of servants on their way to that of employers; but not to remain in it all their lives. To begin as hired labourers, then after a few years to work on their own account, and finally employ others, is the normal condition of labourers in a new country, rapidly increasing in wealth and population, like America or Australia. But in an old and fully peopled country, those who begin life as labourers for hire, as a general rule, continue such to the end, unless they sink into the still lower grade of recipients of public charity. In the present stage of human progress, when ideas of equality are daily spreading more widely among the poorer classes, and can no longer be checked by any thing short of the entire

---

50. It is truly disgraceful that in a woman's reign, not one step has been made by law towards removing even the smallest portion of the existing injustice to women. The brutal part of the populace can still maltreat, not to say kill, their wives, with the next thing to impunity; and as to civil and social *status,* in framing a new reform bill for the extension of the elective franchise, the opportunity was not taken for so small a recognition of something like equality of rights, as would have been made by admitting to the suffrage, women of the same class and the same householding and tax-paying qualifications as the men who already possess it. [HTM]

51. This word was added in the 1852 edition.

suppression of printed discussion and even of freedom of speech, it is not to be expected that the division of the human race into two hereditary classes, employers and employed, can be permanently maintained. The relation is nearly as unsatisfactory to the payer of wages as to the receiver. If the rich regard the poor as, by a kind of natural law, their servants and dependants, the rich in their turn are regarded as a mere prey and pasture for the poor; the subject of demands and expectations wholly indefinite, increasing in extent with every concession made to them, while the return given in the shape of service is sought to be reduced to the lowest minimum. It will sooner or later become insupportable to the employing classes to live in close and hourly contact with persons whose interests and feelings are in hostility to them. Capitalists are almost as much interested as labourers, in placing the operations of industry on such a footing, that those who labour may feel the same interest in the work they perform, which is felt by those who labour for themselves.

The opinion expressed in a former part of this treatise respecting small landed properties and peasant proprietors, may have made the reader anticipate that a wide diffusion of property in land is the resource on which I rely for exempting at least the agricultural labourers from exclusive dependence on labour for hire. Such, however, is not my opinion. I indeed deem that form of agricultural economy to be most groundlessly decried, and to be greatly preferable, in its aggregate effects on human happiness, to hired labour in any form in which it exists at present; because the prudential check to population acts more directly, and is shown by experience to be more efficacious; and because, in point of security, of independence, of exercise for any other than the animal faculties, the state of a peasant proprietor is far superior to that of an agricultural labourer in this or any other old country. Where the former system already exists, and works on the whole satisfactorily, I should regret, in the present state of human intelligence, to see it abolished in order to make way for the other, under a pedantic notion of agricultural improvement as a thing necessarily the same in every diversity of circumstances. In a backward state of industrial improvement, as in Ireland, I should urge its introduction, in preference to an exclusive system of hired labour; as a more powerful instrument for raising a population from semi-savage listlessness and recklessness, to persevering industry and prudent calculation.

But a people who have once adopted the large system of production, either in manufactures or in agriculture, are not likely to recede from it; and when population is kept in due proportion to the means of support, it is not desirable that they should. Labour is unquestionably more productive on the system of large industrial enterprises; the produce, if not greater absolutely, is greater in proportion to the labour employed: the same number of persons can be supported equally well with less toil and greater leisure; which will be wholly an advantage, as soon as civilization and improvement have so far advanced, that what is a benefit to the whole shall be a benefit to each individual composing it. And in the moral aspect of the question, which is still more important than the economical, something better should be aimed at as the goal of industrial improvement, than to disperse mankind over the earth in single families, each ruled internally, as families now are, by a patriarchal despot, and having scarcely any community of interest, or necessary mental communion, with other human beings. The domination of the head of the family over the other members, in this state of things, is supreme; while in the chief, its tendency is towards concentration of all interests in the family, considered as an expansion of self, and absorption of all passions in that of exclusive possession, of all cares in those of preservation and acquisition. As a step out of the merely animal state into the human, out of reckless abandonment to brute instincts into prudential foresight and self-government, this moral condition may be seen without displeasure. But if public spirit, generous sentiments, or even justice and equality are desired, association, not isolation, of interests, is the school in which these excellences are nurtured. The aim of improvement should be not solely to place human beings in a condition in which they will be able to do without one another, but to enable them to work with or for one another in relations not involving dependence. Hitherto there has been no alternative for those who lived by their labour, but that of labouring either each for himself alone, or for a master. But the civilizing and improving influences of association, and the efficiency and economy of production on a large scale, may be obtained without dividing the producers into two parties with hostile interests and feelings, the many who do the work being mere servants under the command of the one who supplies the funds, and having no interest of their own in the enterprise except to earn their wages with as little labour as possible. The speculations and discussions of the last fifty years, and the events of the last five, are abundantly conclusive on this point. Unless the military despotism now triumphant on the Continent should succeed in its nefarious attempts to throw back the human mind, there can be little doubt that the *status* of hired labourers will gradually tend to confine itself to the description of workpeople whose low moral qualities render them unfit for anything more independent: and that the relation of masters and workpeople will be gradually superseded by partnership in one of two forms: temporarily and in some cases, association of the labourers with the capitalist; in other cases, and finally in all, association of labourers among themselves.

§ 5. The first of these forms of association has long been practised, not indeed as a rule but as an exception. In several departments of industry there are already cases in which every one who contributes to the work, either by labour or by pecuniary resources, has a partner's interest in it, proportional to the value of his contribution. It is already a common practice to remunerate those in whom peculiar trust is reposed, by means of a percentage of the profits: and cases exist in which the principle is, with the most excellent success, carried down to the class of mere manual labourers.

In the American ships trading to China, it has long been the custom for every sailor to have an interest in the profits of the voyage; and to this has been ascribed the general good conduct of those seamen, and the extreme rarity of any collision between them and the government or people of the country. An instance in England, not so well known as it deserves to be, is that of the Cornish miners. "In Cornwall the mines are worked strictly on the system of joint adventure; gangs of miners contracting with the agent, who represents the owner of the mine, to execute a certain portion of a vein, and fit the ore for the market, at the price of so much in the pound of the sum for which the ore is sold. These contracts are put up at certain regular periods, generally every two months, and taken by a voluntary partnership of men accustomed to the mine. This system has its disadvantages, in consequence of the uncertainty and irregularity of the earnings, and consequent necessity of living for long periods on credit; but it has advantages which more than counterbalance these drawbacks. It produces a degree of intelligence, independence, and moral elevation, which raise the condition and character of the Cornish miner far above that of the generality of the labouring class. We are told by Dr. Barham, that 'they are not only, as a class, intelligent for labourers, but men of considerable knowledge.' Also, that 'they have a character of independence, something American, the system by which the contracts are let giving the takers entire freedom to make arrangements among themselves; so that each man feels, as a partner in his little firm, that he meets his employers on nearly equal terms.'. . . With this basis of intelligence and independence in their character, we are not surprised when we hear that 'a very great number of miners are now located on possessions of their own, leased for three lives or ninety-nine years, on which they have built houses;' or that '281,541£ are deposited in saving banks in Cornwall, of which two-thirds are estimated to belong to miners.'"[52]

---

52. This passage is from the Prize Essay on the Causes and Remedies of National Distress, by Mr. Samuel Laing. The extracts which it includes are from the Appendix to the Report of the Children's Employment commission. [HTM]

Mr. Babbage, who also gives an account of this system, observes that the payment to the crews of whaling ships is governed by a similar principle; and that "the profits arising from fishing with nets on the south coast of England are thus divided: one-half the produce belongs to the owner of the boat and the net; the other half is divided in equal portions between the persons using it, who are also bound to assist in repairing the net when required." Mr. Babbage has the great merit of having pointed out the practicability, and the advantage, of extending the principle to manufacturing industry generally.[53]

Some attention has been excited by an experiment of this nature, commenced about ten years ago by a Paris tradesman, a house-painter, M. Leclaire;[54] and described by him in a pamphlet published in the year 1842. M. Leclaire, according to his statement, employs on an average two hundred workmen, whom he pays in the usual manner, by fixed wages or salaries. He assigns to himself, besides interest for his capital, a fixed allowance for his labour and responsibility as manager. At the end of the year, the surplus profits are divided among the body, himself included, in the proportion of their salaries.[55] The reasons by which M. Leclair was led to adopt this system are highly instructive. Finding the conduct of his workmen unsatisfactory, he first tried the effect of giving higher wages, and by this he managed to obtain a body of excellent workmen, who would not quit his service for any other. "Having thus succeeded" (I quote from an abstract of the pamphlet in Chambers' Journal,[56]) "in producing some sort of stability in the arrangements of his establishment, M. Leclaire expected, he says, to enjoy greater peace of mind. In this, however, he was disappointed. So long as he was able to superintend everything himself, from the general concerns of his business down to its minutest details, he did enjoy a certain satisfaction; but from the moment that, owing to the increase of his business, he found that he could be nothing more than the centre from which orders were issued, and to which reports were brought in, his former anxiety and discomfort returned upon him." He speaks

---

53. *Economy of Machinery and Manufactures*, 3rd edition, chap. 26. [HTM]

54. His establishment is (or was) 11, Rue Saint Georges. [HTM]

55. It appears, however, that the workmen whom M. Leclaire had admitted to this participation of profits, were only a portion (rather less than half) of the whole number whom he employed. This is explained by another part of his system. M. Leclaire pays the full market rate of wages to all his workmen. The share of profit assigned to them is, therefore, a clear addition to the ordinary gains of their class, which he very laudably uses as an instrument of improvement, by making it the reward of desert, or the recompense for peculiar trust. [HTM]

56. For September 27, 1845. [HTM]

lightly of the other sources of anxiety to which a tradesman is subject, but describes as an incessant cause of vexation the losses arising from the misconduct of workmen. An employer "will find workmen whose indifference to his interests is such that they do not perform two-thirds of the amount of work which they are capable of; hence the continual fretting of masters, who, seeing their interests neglected, believe themselves entitled to suppose that workmen are constantly conspiring to ruin those from whom they derive their livelihood. If the journeyman were sure of constant employment, his position would in some respects be more enviable than that of the master, because he is assured of a certain amount of day's wages, which he will get whether he works much or little. He runs no risk, and has no other motive to stimulate him to do his best that his own sense of duty. The master, on the other hand, depends greatly on chance for his returns: his position is one of continual irritation and anxiety. This would no longer be the case to the same extent, if the interests of the master and those of the workmen were bound up with each other, connected by some bond of mutual security, such as that which would be obtained by the plan of a yearly division of profits."

Even in the first year during which M. Leclaire's experiment was in complete operation, the success was remarkable. Not one of his journeymen who worked as many as three hundred days, earned in that year less than 1500 francs, and some considerably more. His highest rate of daily wages being four francs, or 1200 francs for 300 days, the remaining 300 francs, or 12£, must have been the smallest amount which any journeyman, who worked that number of days, obtained as his proportion of the surplus profit. M. Leclaire describes in strong terms the improvement which was already manifest in the habits and demeanour of his workmen, not merely when at work, and in their relations with their employer, but at other times and in other relations, showing increased respect both for others and for themselves. The system was still in operation in 1848; and we learn from M. Chevalier that the increased zeal of the workpeople continued to be a full compensation to M. Leclaire, even in a pecuniary sense, for the share of profit which he renounced in their favour.[57]

---

57. "Je tiens de M. Leclaire que chez lui l'advantage du zèle extrême dont sont animés les ouvriers, depuis qu'il a adopté le système de la participation, fait plus que compenser le sacrifice représenté par la somme des parts qu'on leur alloue." Lettres sur l'Organisation du Travail, par Michel Chevalier, (1848,) lettre xiv. [HTM]

"I agree with M. Leclaire that in his home country the advantage of the extreme zeal by which workers are driven, since he adopted the participatory system, more than compensates for the sacrifice represented by the sum of the parts allotted to them. Letters on the organization of work, by Michel Chevalier, letter 14."

§ 6. The form of association, however, which if mankind contrive[58] to improve, must be expected in the end to predominate, is not that which can exist between a capitalist as chief, and workpeople without a voice in the management, but the association of the labourers themselves on terms of equality, collectively owning the capital with which they carry on their operations, and working under managers elected and removable by themselves. So long as this idea remained in a state of theory, in the writings of Owen or of Louis Blanc, it may have appeared, to the common modes of judgment, incapable of being realized, and not likely to be tried unless by seizing on the existing capital, and confiscating it for the benefit of the labourers; which is even now imagined by many persons, and pretended by more, both in England and on the Continent, to be the meaning and purpose of Socialism. But there is a capacity of exertion and self-denial in the masses of mankind, which is never known but on the rare occasions on which it is appealed to in the name of some great idea or elevated sentiment. Such an appeal was made by the French Revolution of 1848. For the first time it then seemed to the intelligent and generous of the working classes of a great nation, that they had obtained a government who sincerely desired the freedom and dignity of the many, and who did not look upon it as their natural and legitimate state to be instruments of production, worked for the benefit of the possessors of capital. Under this encouragement, the ideas sown by the Socialist writers, of an emancipation of labour to be effected by means of association, throve and fructified; and many working people came to the resolution, not only that they would work for one another, instead of working for a master trades- man or manufacturer, but that they would also free themselves, at what- ever cost of labour or privation, from the necessity of paying, out of the produce of their industry, a heavy tribute for the use of capital; that they would extinguish this tax, not by robbing the capitalists of what they or their predecessors had acquired by labour and preserved by economy, but by honestly acquiring capital for themselves. If only a few operatives had attempted this arduous task, or if, while many attempted it, a few only had succeeded, their success might have been deemed to furnish no argu- ment for their system as a permanent mode to industrial organization. But, excluding all the instances of failure, there exist, or existed a few months ago, upwards of a hundred successful, and many eminently pros- perous, associations of operatives in Paris alone, besides a considerable number in the departments. An instructive sketch of their history and

---

58. The printer may have erred in the 1852 edition since the word was corrected in subsequent editions to read "continue."

principles has been published, under the title of "L'Association Ouvrière Industrielle et Agricole, par H. Feugueray:"[59] and as it is frequently affirmed in English newspapers that the associations at Paris have failed, by writers who appear to mistake the predictions of their enemies at their first formation for the testimonies of subsequent experience, I think it important to show by quotations from M. Feugueray's volume that these representations are not only wide of truth, but the extreme contrary of it.

The capital of most of the associations was originally confined to the few tools belonging to the founders, and the small sums which could be collected from their savings, or which were lent to them by other work-people as poor as themselves. In some cases, however, loans of capital were made to them by the republican government: but the associations which obtained these advances, or at least which obtained them before they had already achieved success, are, it appears, in general by no means the most prosperous. The most striking instances of prosperity are in the case of those who have had nothing to rely on but their own slender means and the small loans of fellow-workmen, and who lived on bread and water while they devoted the whole surplus of their gains to the formation of a capital. "Souvent," says M. Feugueray,[60] "la caisse était tout-à-fait vide, et il n'y avait pas de salaire du tout. Et puis la vente ne marchait pas, les rentrées se faisaient attendre, les valeurs ne s'escomptaient pas, le magasin des matières premières était vide; et il fallait se priver, se restreindre dans toutes ses dépenses, se réduire quelquefois au pain et à l'eau . . . . C'est au prix de ces angoisses et de ces misères, c'est par cette voie douloureuse, que des hommes sans presque aucune autre ressource au début que leur bonne volonté et leurs bras, sont parvenus à se former une clientèle, à acquérir un crédit, à se créer enfin un capital social, et à fonder ainsi des associations dont l'avenir aujourd'hui semble assuré."[61]

---

59. "Industrial and Agricultural Workers' Association, by H. Feugueray."

60. P. 112. [HTM]

61. ["Often, the till was completely empty, and there was no salary at all. And when sales were not going well, we were waiting for income, securities could not be counted on, the warehouse was empty of raw materials; and it was necessary to deprive ourselves, cut back on all expenses, sometimes reducing ourselves to bread and water. . . . It was at the cost of these anxieties and these miseries, by this painful path, that men with hardly any resources other than their good will and their arms succeeded in building a clientele, acquiring credit, and finally creating a social capital, thus founding those associations whose future today seems assured."—Ed.]

I will quote at length the remarkable history of one of these associations.[62]

"La nécessité d'un puissant capital pour l'établissement d'une fabrique de pianos était si bien reconnue dans la corporation, qu'en 1848 les délégués de plusieurs centaines d'ouvriers, qui s'étaient réunis pour la formation d'une grande association, demandèrent en son nom au gouvernement une subvention de 300,000 fr., c'est-à-dire la dixième partie du fonds total voté par l'Assemblée constituante. Je me souviens d'avoir fait, en qualité de membre de la commission chargée de distribuer ces fonds, des efforts inutiles pour convaincre les deux délégués avec qui la commission était en rapport, que leur demande était exorbitante. Toutes mes instances restèrent sans succès; je prolongeai vainement la conférence pendant près de deux heures. Les deux délégués me répondirent imperturbablement que leur industrie était dans une condition spéciale; que l'association ne pouvait s'y établir avec chance de réussite que sur une très grande échelle et avec un capital considérable, et que la somme de 300,000 fr. était un minimum au-dessous duquel ils ne pouvaient descendre; bref, qu'ils ne pouvaient pas réduire leur demande d'un sou. La commission refusa.

---

62. Pp. 113-6. [HTM]
A translation of the text quoted by HTM follows:

The need for strong capital for the establishment of a piano factory was so well recognized in the corporation, that in 1848 the delegates of several hundred workers, who had united for the formation of a large association, required in its name a subsidy of 300,000 francs from the government—that is, one tenth of the total funds voted for by the Constituent Assembly. I remember having made, in my capacity as a member of the commission charged with distributing these funds, futile efforts to convince the two delegates with whom the commission had dealings that their request was exorbitant. All my entreaties remained unsuccessful; in vain I prolonged the meeting for almost two hours. Unperturbed, the two delegates answered that their industry operated under special conditions: that the association could not establish itself there with any chance of success except on a very large scale and with considerable capital, and that they would not go below a minimum of 300,000 francs. In short, they could not reduce their request by a single cent. The commission refused.

However here is what happened after this refusal, when the project of the great association was abandoned: fourteen workers (and it is rather curious that one of the two delegates should be among them) resolved among themselves to found an association for the piano factory. To say the least, the plan was reckless on the part of men having neither money nor credit, but faith does not reason, it acts.

Our fourteen men set to work, then, and here is the story of their first attempts, which I borrow from an article in the National, very well written by M. Cochut, to whose exactitude I am pleased to attest.

Several among them who had been self-employed brought, as much in tools as in materials, a value of around 2000 francs. In addition, working capital was necessary. Each member made, not without difficulty, a deposit of 10 francs. A certain number of workers, not interested in the society, made a gesture of membership, bringing small contributions. In short, on 10 March 1849, a sum of 229 francs 50 centimes having been realized, the association was declared established.

"Or, après ce refus, et le projet de la grande association étant abandonné, voici ce qui arriva: c'est que quatorze ouvriers, et il est assez singulier que parmi eux se soit trouvé l'un des deux délégués, se résolurent à fonder entre eux une association pour la fabrique des pianos. Le projet était au moins téméraire de la part d'hommes qui n'avaient ni argent ni crédit; mais la foi ne raisonne pas, elle agit.

"Nos quatorze hommes se mirent donc à l'oeuvre, et voici le récit de leurs premiers travaux, que j'emprunte à un article du *National,* très bien rédigé par M. Cochut, et dont je me plais à attester l'exactitude.

"Quelques uns d'entre eux, qui avaient travaillé à leur propre compte, apportèrent, tant en outils qu'en matériaux, une valeur d'environ 2000 fr. Il fallait, en outre, un fond de roulement. Chacun des sociétaires opéra, non sans peine, un versement de 10 fr. Un certain nombre d'ouvriers, non intéressés dans la société, firent acte d'adhésion, en apportant de faibles offrandes. Bref, le 10 mars 1849, une somme de 229 fr. 50 cent. ayant été réalisée, l'association fut déclarée constituée.

"Ce fonds social n'était pas même suffisant pour l'installation, et pour

---

This social fund was not even sufficient to set up shop, nor for the various small expenses which the maintenance of a workshop incur daily. With nothing remaining for the salaries, almost two months passed without the workers earning a centime. How did they live during this crisis? As workers live during unemployment, by sharing the ration of the comrade who works, by selling or pawning the few things one owns, piece by piece.

They had done several jobs, and they reaped the benefits on 4 May 1849. For the association, that day was like a victory at the beginning of a military campaign, therefore they wanted to celebrate. All outstanding debts having been paid, each member's dividend amount rose to 6 frances 61 centimes. They agreed to give each a bonus of 5 francs of his salary, and to dedicate the surplus to a fraternal meal. The fourteen members, most of whom had not drunk wine in a year, met with their wives and children. They spent 32 sous per household. They still talk about that day in the workshops, with an emotion it is difficult not to share.

For one more month it was necessary to be content with a paycheck of 5 francs per week. During the month of June, a baker—a music-lover or speculator?—offered to buy a piano payable with bread. They negotiated a price of 480 francs. This was a stroke of fortune for the association. At least they had the indispensable thing. They did not want to figure the bread into their salaries. Each ate according to his appetite, or to put it better, according to his family's appetite; the married members were authorized to take bread home to their wives and children.

Nevertheless, the association, composed of excellent workers, overcame little by little the obstacles and deprivations which had hindered their debut. Their account books are the best testimony to the progress that their instruments have made in the estimation of buyers. Since August 1849, they saw their weekly share rise to ten, to fifteen, to twenty francs; but that last sum does not represent all the benefits, and each associate has left in the kitty much more than he has taken.

In fact, it is not through the sum which the member receives each week that his situation must be appreciated, but through his share in the property acquired by an already considerable establishment. Here is the financial statement as I have taken it from the inventory of 30 December 1850.

les menues dépenses qu'entraîne au jour le jour le service d'un atelier. Rien ne restant pour les salaires, il se passa près de deux mois sans que les travailleurs touchassent un centime. Comment vécurent-ils pendant cette crise? Comme vivent les ouvriers pendant le chômage, en partageant la ration du camarade qui travaille, en vendant ou en engageant pièce à pièce le peu d'effets qu'on possède.

"On avait exécuté quelques travaux. On en toucha le prix le 4 mai 1849. Ce jour fut pour l'association ce qu'est une victoire à l'entrée d'une campagne: aussi voulut-on le célébrer. Toutes les dettes exigibles étant payées, le dividende de chaque sociétaire s'élevait à 6 fr. 61 cent. On convint d'attribuer à chacun 5 fr. à valoir sur son salaire, et de consacrer le surplus à un repas fraternel. Les quatorze sociétaires, dont la plupart n'avaient pas bu de vin depuis un an, se réunirent, avec leurs femmes et leurs enfants. On dépensa 32 sous par ménage. On parle encore de cette journée, dans les ateliers, avec une émotion qu'il est difficile de ne pas partager.

"Pendant un mois encore, il fallut se contenter d'une paie de 5 fr. par semaine. Dans le courant de juin, un boulanger, mélomane ou spéculateur, offrit d'acheter un piano payable en pain. On fit marché au prix de 480 fr. Ce fut une bonne fortune pour l'association. On eut du moins l'indispensable. On ne voulut pas èvaluer le pain dans le compte des salaires. Chacun mangea selon son appétit, ou pour mieux dire, selon l'appétit de sa famille; car les sociétaries mariés furent autorisés à emporter du pain pour leurs femmes et leurs enfants.

"Cependant l'association, composée d'ouvriers excellents, surmontait peu

---

At that time, the associates numbered thirty-two. Huge workshops or warehouses, rented for 2000 francs, no longer sufficed.

	Francs	Centimes
Independent of equipment, valued at	5,922	60
In merchandise, and particularly in raw materials, they possess a value of	22,972	28
They have in cash	1,021	10
Their securities and portfolios go up to	3,540	
Debts owed them total	5,861	90
The society's assets therefore come to	39,317	88
Of this total, only 4,737 fr. 86 c. are due to creditors, and 1,650 fr. to		
80 members; in all	6,387	86
Remainder	32,930	2

form the real assets, including the joint capital and the reserve capital of the members. At that time, the association had seventy-six pianos under construction, and could not fill all their orders.

à peu les obstacles et les privations qui avaient entravé ses débuts. Ses livres de caisse offrent les meilleurs témoignages des progrès que ses instruments ont faits [*sic*] dans l'estime des acheteurs. A partir du mois d'août 1849, on voit le contingent hebdomadaire s'élever à 10, à 15, à 20 fr. par semaine; mais cette dernière somme ne représente pas tous les bénéfices, et chaque associé a laissé à la masse beaucoup plus qu'il n'a touché.

"Ce n'est pas, en effet, par la somme que touche chaque semaine le sociétaire, qu'il faut apprécier sa situation, mais par la part de propriété acquise dans un établissement déjà considérable. Voici l'état de situation de l'association, tel que je l'ai relevé sur l'inventaire du 30 décembre 1850.

"A cette époque, les associés sont au nombre de trente-deux. De vastes ateliers ou magasins, loués 2000 fr. ne leur suffisent plus.

	Francs	Centimes
Indépendamment de l'outillage, évalué à	5,922	60
Ils possèdent en marchandises, et surtout en matières premières, une valeur de	22,972	28
Ils ont en caisse	1,021	10
Leurs effets en portefeuille montent à	3,540	
Le compte des débiteurs s'élève à[63]	5,861	90
L'actif social est donc en totalité de	39,317	88
Sur ce total, il n'est dû que 4,737 fr. 86 c à des créanciers, et 1,650 fr. à quatre-vingts adhérents;[64] ensemble	6,387	86
Restent	32,930	2

formant l'actif réel, comprenant le capital indivisible et le capital de réserve des sociétaires. L'association, à la même époque, avait soixante-seize pianos en construction, et ne pouvait fournir à toutes les demandes."

The same admirable qualities by which the associations were carried through their early struggles, maintained them in their increasing prosperity. Their rules of discipline, instead of being more lax, are stricter that those

---

63. "Ces deux derniers articles ne comprennent que de très bonnes valeurs, qui, presque toutes, ont été soldées depuis." [HTM] ["These last two articles only include very good securities, which since then have almost all been paid off." —Ed.]

64. "Ces adhérents sont des ouvriers du métier qui ont commandité l'association dans ses débuts: une partie d'entre eux a été remboursée dépuis le commencement de 1851. Le compte des créanciers a aussi beaucoup diminué, au 23 Avril, il ne s'élevait qu'à 1,113 fr. 59 c." [HTM] ["These members are the expert workers who led the association in its early years: some of them had been reimbursed since the beginning of 1851. The creditors' account had also diminished greatly; on 23 April it amounted to only 1,113 francs 59 centimes." —Ed.]

of ordinary workshops; but being rules self-imposed, for the manifest good of the community, and not for the convenience of an employer regarded as having an opposite interest, they are far more scrupulously obeyed, and the voluntary obedience carries with it a sense of personal worth and dignity. With wonderful rapidity the associated workpeople have learnt to correct those of the ideas they set out with, which are in opposition to the teaching of reason and experience. Almost all the associations, at first, excluded piecework, and gave equal wages whether the work done was more or less. Almost all have abandoned this system, and after allowing to every one a fixed minimum, sufficient for subsistence, they apportion all future remuneration according to the work done: most of them even dividing the profits at the end of the year, in same proportion as the earnings.[65]

It is the declared principle of most of these associations, that they do not exist for the mere private benefit of the individual members, but for the promotion of the cooperative cause. With every extension, therefore, of their business, they take in additional members, not to receive wages from them as hired labourers, but to enter at once into the full benefits of the association, without being required to bring anything in, except their labour: the only condition imposed is that of receiving during a few years a smaller share in the annual division of profits, as some equivalent for the sacrifices of the founders. When members quit the association, which they are always at liberty to do, they carry none of the capital with them: it remains an indivisible property, of which the members for the time being have the use, but not the arbitrary disposal: by the stipulations of most of the contracts, even if the association breaks up, the capital cannot be divided, but must be devoted entire to some work of beneficence or of public utility. A fixed, and generally a considerable proportion of the annual profits, is not shared among the members, but added to the capital of the association, or devoted to the repayment of the advances previously

---

65. Even the association founded by M. Louis Blanc, that of the tailors of Clichy, after eighteen months trial of his system, adopted piece-work. One of the reasons given by them for abandoning the original system is well worth extracting. "En outre des vices dont j'ai parlé, les tailleurs lui reprochaient d'engendrer sans cesse des discussions, des querelles, à cause de l'intérêt que chacun avait à faire travailler ses voisins. La surveillance mutuelle de l'atelier dégénérait ainsi en un esclavage véritable, qui ne laissait à personne la liberté de son temps et de ses actions. Ces dissensions ont disparu par l'introduction du travail aux pièces." Feugueray, p. 88 [HTM]

["Besides the vices of which I have spoken, the tailors blamed him for unceasingly instigating arguments and quarrels, because everyone has an interest in making his neighbors work. The mutual supervision of the workshop thus degenerated into a veritable slavery, which left no one with the freedom of his time or his actions. This dissent disappeared with the introduction of piecework."—Ed.]

made to it: another portion is set aside to provide for the sick and the disabled, and another to form a fund for extending the practice of association, or aiding other associations in their need. The managers are paid, like other members, for the time which is occupied in management, usually at the rate of the highest paid labour: but the rule is adhered to, that the exercise of power shall never be an occasion of profit.

It is painful to think that these bodies, formed by the heroism and maintained by the public spirit and good sense of the working people of Paris, are in danger of being involved in the same ruin with everything free, popular, or tending to improvement in French institutions. The unprincipled adventurer who has for the present succeeded in reducing France to the political condition of Russia, knows that two or three persons cannot meet together to discuss, though it be only the affairs of a workshop, without danger to his power. He has therefore already suppressed most of the provincial associations, and many of those of Paris, and the remainder, instead of waiting to be dissolved by despotism, are, it is said, preparing to emigrate. Before this calamity overtook France, the associations could be spoken of not with the hope merely, but with positive evidence, of their being able to compete successfully with individual capitalists. "Les associations," says M. Feugueray, "qui ont été fondées depuis deux années, avaient bien des obstacles à vaincre; la plupart manquaient presque absolument de capital; toutes marchaient dans une voie encore inexplorée; elles bravaient les périls qui menacent toujours les novateurs et les débutants. Et néanmoins, dans beaucoup d'industries où elles se sont établies, elles constituent déjà pour les anciennes maisons une rivalité redoutable, qui suscite même des plaintes nombreuses dans une partie de la bourgeoisie, non pas seulement chez les traiteurs, les limonadiers et les coiffeurs, c'est-à-dire dans les industries où la nature des produits permet aux associations de compter sur la clientèle démocratique, mais dans d'autres industries où elles n'ont pas les mêmes avantages. On n'a qu'à consulter par exemple les fabricants de fauteuils, de chaises, de limes, et l'on saura d'eux si les établissements les plus importants en leurs genres de fabrication ne sont pas les établissements des associés."[66]

---

66. Pp. 37-8. [HTM] ["The associations founded in the last two years really had many obstacles to overcome. Most absolutely lacked capital, all were taking a path still unexplored, and they braved the perils which always threaten innovators and beginners. And nonetheless, in many industries where they were established, they already constituted a formidable rivalry for the old companies, arousing numerous complaints in one part of the bourgeoisie: not only the caterers, the café owners and the hairdressers (where the nature of the products permits associations to depend on a democratic clientele), but in other industries without the same advantages. One only has to consult, for example, makers of armchairs, chairs, and files, and one will see that the most important establishments in these kinds of manufacturing are not establishments of the associates." —Ed.]

Though the existing associations may be dissolved, or driven to expatriate, their experience will not be lost. They have existed long enough to furnish the type of future improvement: they have exemplified the process for bringing about a change in society, which would combine the freedom and independence of the individual, with the moral, intellectual, and economical advantages of aggregate production; and which without violence or spoliation, or even any sudden disturbance of existing habits and expectations, would realize, at least in the industrial department, the best aspirations of the democratic spirit, by putting an end to the division of society into the industrious and the idle, and effacing all social distinctions but those fairly earned by personal services and exertions. Associations like those which we have described, by the very process of their success, are a course of education in those moral and active qualities by which alone success can be either deserved or attained. As associations multiplied, they would tend more and more to absorb all work-people, except those of an inferior class in capacity and in true morality. As this change proceeded, owners of capital would gradually find it to their advantage, instead of maintaining the struggle of the old system with workpeople of only the worst description, to lend their capital to the associations; to do this at a diminishing rate of interest, and at last, perhaps, even to exchange their capital for terminable annuities. In this or some such mode, the existing accumulations of capital might honestly, and by a kind of spontaneous process, become in the end the joint property of all who participate in their productive employment: a transformation which, thus effected, (and assuming of course that both sexes participate equally in the rights and in the government of the association) would be the nearest approach to social justice, and the most beneficial ordering of industrial affairs for the universal good, which it is possible at present to foresee.

§ 7. I agree, then, with the Socialist writers in their conception of the form which industrial operations tend to assume in the advance of improvement; and I entirely share their opinion that the time is ripe for commencing this transformation, and that it should by all just and effectual means be aided and encouraged. But while I agree and sympathize with Socialists in this practical portion of their aims, I utterly dissent from the most conspicuous and vehement part of their teaching, their declamations against competition. With moral conceptions in many respects far ahead of the existing arrangements of society, they have in general very confused and erroneous notions of its actual working; and one of their greatest errors, as I conceive, is to charge upon competition all the economical evils which at present exist. They forget that wherever competition is not, monopoly is; and that monopoly in all its forms, is the taxation of the industrious for the support of indolence, if not of rapacity. They forget, too, that with the exception of competition among labourers, all other competition is for the benefit of the labourers, by cheapening the articles they consume; that competition even in the labour market is a source not of low but of high wages, wherever the competition *for* labour exceeds the competition *of* labour, as in America, in the colonies, and in the skilled trades; and never could be a cause of low wages, save by the overstocking of the labour market; while, if the supply of labour is excessive, not even Socialism can prevent its remuneration from being low. Besides, if association was universal, there would be no competition between labourer and labourer; and that between association and association would be for the benefit of the consumers, that is, of the associations; of the industrious classes generally.

I do not pretend that there are no inconveniences in competition, or that the moral objections urged against it by Socialist writers, as a source of jealousy and hostility among those engaged in the same occupation, are altogether groundless. But if competition has its evils, it prevents greater evils. As M. Feugueray well says,[67] "La racine la plus profonde des maux et des iniquités qui couvrent le monde industriel n'est pas la concurrence, mais bien l'exploitation du travail par le capital, et la part énorme que les possesseurs des instruments de travail prélèvent sur les produits. . . . Si la concurrence a beaucoup de puissance pour le mal, elle n'a pas moins de fécondité pour le bien, surtout en ce qui concerne le développement des facultés individuelles, et le succès des innovations."[68] It is the common error of Socialists to overlook the natural indolence of mankind; their tendency to be passive, to be the slaves of habit, to persist indefinitely in a course once chosen. Let them once attain any state of existence which they consider tolerable, and the danger to be apprehended is that they will thenceforth stagnate; will not exert themselves to improve, and by letting their faculties rust, will lose even the energy required to preserve them from deterioration. Competition may not be the best conceivable stimulus, but it is at present a necessary one, and no one can foresee the time when it will not be indispensable to progress. Even confining ourselves to the industrial department, in which, more than in any other, the majority may

---

67. P. 90. [HTM]

68. ["The deepest root of the evils and inequities in the industrial world is not competition, but really the exploitation of labor by capital, and the enormous part that the possessors of the instruments of labor levy on products. . . . If competition has much power for evil, it is not less fruitful for good, above all in that which concerns the development of individual faculties, and the success of innovations." — Ed.]

be supposed to be competent judges of improvements; it would be difficult to induce the general assembly of an association to submit to the trouble and inconvience of altering their habits by adopting some new and promising invention, unless their knowledge of the existence of rival associations made them apprehend that what they would not consent to do, others would, and that they would be left behind in the race.

Instead of looking upon competition as the baneful and anti-social principle which it is held to be by the generality of Socialists, I conceive that, even in the present state of society and industry, every restriction of it is an evil, and every extension of it, even if for the time injuriously affecting some class of labourers, is always an ultimate good. To be protected against competition is to be protected in idleness, in mental dulness; to be saved the necessity of being as active and as intelligent as other people; and if it is also to be protected against being underbid for employment by a less paid class of labourers, this is only where old custom or local and partial monopoly has placed some particular class of artisans in a privileged position as compared with all the rest; and the time has come when the interest of universal improvement is no longer promoted by prolonging the privileges of a few. If the slopsellers and others, so unjustly and illiberally railed at—as if they were one iota worse in their motives or practices than other people, in the existing state of society— have lowered the wages of tailors, and some other artisans, by making them an affair of competition instead of custom, so much the better in the end. What is now required is not to bolster up old customs, whereby limited classes of labouring people obtain partial gains which interest them in keeping up the present organization of society, but to introduce new general practices beneficial to all; and there is reason to rejoice at whatever makes the privileged classes of skilled artisans feel, that they have the same interests, and depend for their remuneration on the same general causes, and must resort for the improvement of their condition to the same remedies, as the less fortunately circumstanced and comparatively helpless multitude.

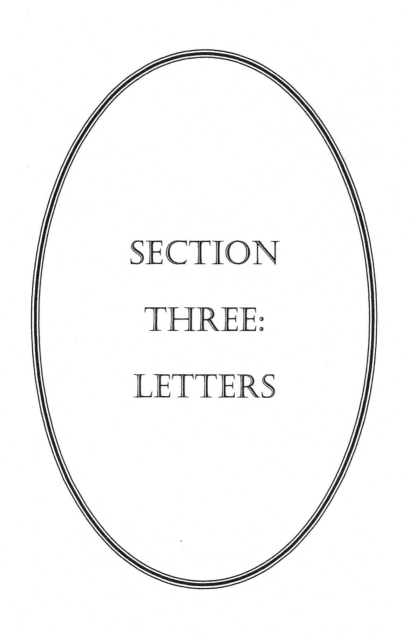

SECTION

THREE:

LETTERS

yes dear I will meet
you, in the chaise, some
where between this and
Southend — the hour
will depend on what
your note says to morrow.
(that is supposing the
chaise is to be that of
which there is very
little doubt.)

but you dearest! I did
not write yesterday. I
wish I had for you
seem to have expected
it. I have been quite

703

HTM's letters to JSM
reflect her passions.

TO JOHN STUART MILL

9

Harriet Taylor Mill's letters to John Stuart Mill are the most emotionally volatile of her correspondence. None contains a greeting to John Stuart Mill indicating his name, although some are addressed to "Dearest" or "Dear one." Since most of these missives move directly into the text, some scholars have tentatively mislabeled some of these letters as being sent by Harriet Mill, JSM's mother.[1] Dating the letters is also difficult, since almost none contain a date. The justification for the dates we have assigned appears at the beginning of each letter. Some dates are based on watermarks which appear on the stationery, combined with independent knowledge of specific individuals mentioned in the text, the location of these individuals in London, or current events Harriet describes. Even though some of these personal correspondences can only be dated within a one- or two-year time span, this chronology offers a contextual coherence which will make reading this intimate communication between Harriet Taylor Mill and John Stuart Mill easier to follow.

These surviving letters probably date back to the late fall or early winter of 1830, about the time she became pregnant with her daughter Helen. The first correspondence in this group is a formal invitation and a follow-up letter mentioning M. Desainteville, a Frenchman known to have been living in London during that period. As John Stuart Mill became acquainted with Harriet Taylor during the winter of 1830–31,

---

1. Letters II/313–325 are labeled "[Mill(?)] from [Harriet Mill (?)]" in *John Stuart Mill: The Economic, Political and Feminist Papers: A Listing and Guide to the Research Publications Microfilm Collection* (Woodbridge, CT: Research Publications Ltd., 1988), 18.

she became more and more obviously pregnant with Helen, born on 27 July 1831. From that winter until 1833, no communication between Harriet and John survives. However, the next four letters in this collection reveal the development of a very intimate relationship that included clandestine meetings. In 1832 Harriet busily wrote and published most of her contributions to the Monthly Repository. *About this time, Harriet and John apparently had a minor crisis in their relationship. In a letter that has not survived, Harriet apparently forbids John to see her again, since his letter to her, forwarding flowers he had collected for her, acquiesces to her request. However, the separation did not last long. They were writing margin notes together on Browning's poem "Pauline" before the end of the year.*

In 1833 a major crisis plagued their relationship. John Taylor asked that Harriet separate herself from both men in her life, John Taylor and John Stuart Mill, so that she could evaluate the marriage clear-headedly. However, from letters that John Stuart Mill wrote to William Fox from this period, we know that shortly after Harriet left (supposedly for a secluded stay in Paris), JSM joined her; they spent several weeks together. At the conclusion of Harriet's visit to France, she refused to renounce her friendship with John Stuart Mill. After this significant turning point in her marriage to John Taylor, she lived apart from her husband, although he continued to provide her financial support. Although Harriet apparently was not unfriendly to John Taylor, they probably never cohabited as husband and wife again. She wrote three long letters to JSM in the middle of this emotional turbulence (II/323, II/321, L/4), rebuking him for his apparent reticence regarding his feelings for her. The emotional openness that Harriet requested from JSM was not something that came naturally to him. After their tryst in Paris and clarification of Harriet's relation to John Taylor, one might have assumed that the partnership between John Stuart Mill and Harriet Taylor Mill would be closer. The letters L/5, XXVIII/235, L/7, and L/6 prove otherwise. Unlike George Sand, who departed France with Alfred de Musset in late 1833, and unlike Eliza Flower, who began acting as William Fox's common-law wife in 1834, Harriet refused to live openly with John. Harriet constructed a strategy for living that maintained a private association with John Stuart Mill without the scandal of adultery that would dishonor her husband and children. Harriet moved out of her husband's house and parented her sons in absentia. She secured temporary housing outside of London and traveled abroad frequently, which she explained to family and friends as a required accommodation of her health problems. Her youngest child, Helen, lived with her, and Harriet served as her tutor as well as her mother. Most importantly, Harriet never discussed with outsiders her relationship with JSM, hiding her feelings for him from her parents, siblings, and friends. The letters she penned between 1834 and 1835 reveal the high physical and emotional price she paid because of this delicate balancing act.

The years 1837 and 1838 seem to highlight the most happy period of her life. The letters from this period (XXVIII/238, II/319, 11/318, 11/314, XXVIII/234, II/330, XXVIII/233, and XXVIII/239) bubble with passion and joy. Especially enjoyable for Harriet, from Christmas 1838 to July 1839, was her travel throughout Italy and Germany with Helen and JSM.[2]

Harriet writes the next group of letters from 1841 to 1848. We learn that she suffered from partial paralysis in 1841, and one particular letter (II/313) describes her inability to stand. The next letter (II/325) skips to summer 1844, when Harriet and Helen vacationed in Normandy. The correspondence which took place from 1844 to 1848 (II/327, II/315, L/8, and II/322) reveals Harriet's interest in political events and her self-confidence in offering her opinions on philosophical ideas, practical matters, current events, and the French revolution. During this time, Harriet worked diligently on her chapter of the Principles of Political Economy, *"On the Probable Futurity of the Labouring Classes." She also began to collaborate with John Stuart Mill on writing newspaper articles, and she wrote the papers on women's rights that would be the source of her "Enfranchisement of Women," published in 1851 (see chapter 3, on "Women and Women's Rights").*

Harriet left England after Christmas 1848 to visit the Basque town of Pau. After a restful winter in Pau with Helen, she returned to England in May to nurse her husband through his final illness. The largest group of surviving correspondence to JSM (L/9 to L/37) was written during the six weeks before John Taylor's death on 18 July 1849. These poignant letters disclose Harriet's intelligence in wanting to understand the medical cause of her husband's malady,[3] her struggle to respect John Taylor's unwillingness to seek further medical opinions, her growing acceptance of his impending death, and the emotional exhaustion caused by her around-the-clock nursing.

Harriet and John Stuart Mill married in 1851, two years after John Taylor's death. Her remaining letters were composed from 1854 until her

---

2. Harriet's notebook in chapter 7 was written during this trip.

3. HTM's persistence in questioning the diagnosis may be the result of her suspicion that John Taylor was dying of syphilis, not cancer.

death in 1858. They reveal the intimacy of collaborative work on John's autobiography and the plans for future work. Harriet and her second husband wrote constantly to one another when they were apart; thus, these missives reflect their shared gossip and interest in Harriet's daughter, who began an acting career in 1856. The letters are full of concern and bring to life the comfortable state of their relationship at this point in their lives.

The reader must remember that these letters to JSM represent only a small fraction of the total number of letters Harriet wrote John during their twenty-eight years together. John wrote approximately 250 typewritten pages of letters in the six months between December 1854 and June 1855. In nearly all of these he refers to letters he had received from Harriet. Yet in this period, only one letter of Harriet's (XXVIII/236) remains. An obvious question persists: what happened to the hundreds of missing letters that Harriet wrote to John during their long association? Just before her death, Harriet left a note, LIII/(i)/30, for Helen referring to the papers she locked in a chest so the servants could not have access to them. Based on this evidence and other concerns about privacy expressed in her correspondence, we can assume that Harriet took great pains to control what papers would remain after she died and who would have access them. John may have destroyed many of the letters she had written to him, anticipating any attempt to discredit Harriet and disparage John for befriending her, marrying her, and collaborating with her. In addition, the majority of the manuscripts of letters from HTM to JSM have been edited by having been cut. Pieces of many letters have been purposefully removed. There is no evidence of who, when, or for what purpose these alterations took place. Further destruction of the letter collection probably occurred when, as Helen was dying, friends of the family cleared out her house in Avignon, the house Harriet had died in and to which John Stuart Mill and Helen had returned regularly after Harriet's death. During the visit to the Avignon cottage after Helen had returned to England, the friends of Mary Taylor, Helen's niece and executor, did "the work of three months in three weeks. Half a ton of letters {had} to be sorted" (cited in Hayek, CW: XII, xix). Working quickly, with a mission to preserve John Stuart Mill's reputation but not necessarily Harriet Taylor Mill's, they no doubt left behind or deliberately destroyed many letters.

Thus, only these few scraps of letters remain, from which we must reconstruct the inner life of Harriet Taylor Mill and her complex relationship with John Stuart Mill. One cannot read the entire collection without recognizing the intensity of their emotional involvement. Harriet's fiery passion warmed John's heart and led him to emotional depths he did not eagerly embrace, but which he recognized as valuable for his existence as a complete human being. Their nearly thirty-year love affair was, at times, raw as well as tender; piercing as well as soothing. During most of these years, they had no binding marital contract. They were held together only by their mutual commitment, despite the pain they sometime gave one another—as when Harriet accuses John of being an emotional coward or John attacks Harriet's pettishness. The mutual care and warm affection they displayed for one another shines throughout their correspondence. It was not a perfect relationship, but most of us would be happy to achieve the tenderness and intimacy this famous couple shared.

Mr and Mrs Taylor request the pleasure of Mr. Mills' company at dinner on Tuesday next at 5 o'clock when they expect to see Mr. Fox and some friends of M. Desainteville.[4]

Finsburg Sq.
January 28th

Friday Morning[5]

My dear Sir

You may imagine how much we were afflicted by this sad story of our poor friend M. Desainteville the <u>first</u> intelligence of which I got from your <u>two</u> notes which I received <u>together</u> yesterday: how unkind and neglectful we must have appeared? Pray express to him my sympathy and best wishes. Mr. Taylor has seen him and found him better than he expected: what a terrible state of emotion he must have suffered to have so reduced him.

in haste yours very truly
H. Taylor

Yes dear I will meet you, in the chaise, some where between this and Southend—the hour will depend on what your note says to-morrow (that is supposing the chaise is to be had of which there is very little doubt.)

bless you dearest! I did not write yesterday. I wish I had for you seem to have expected it. I have been quite well & quite happy since that delicious eveng & I may perhaps see thee to-day, but if not I shall not be disappointed—as for <u>sad</u> I feel since that eveng as tho' I never shall be that again.

4. 1831? B. E. Desainteville was a Frenchman living in London from 1830-48. John and Harriet often invited political exiles and immigrants to their home. II/300.

5. The paper is watermarked 1828. L/3. This letter was probably written in 1830 or 1831, what may have been the year of their first meeting. The letter is addressed to John Mill Esq.

I am very well in all respects, but more especially in spirits.

Bless thee—to-morrow will be delightful & I am looking to it as the very greatest treat

so dear—if you do not meet me on your road from Southend you will know that I could not have the chaise

Friday[6]

How are you my own darling? be sure you tell me just how you are, if you are well & happy I shall be too. yet I never felt an absence more, & but that I am perfectly happy in the very deepest of my heart, I should be low rather to think of the enormous length of time that has to be passed before I am again to see the light of my life, my most admired my most beloved—the only inclination I have, not being able to see you, is to write such words as those—<u>darling</u> <u>sweetest</u> <u>dearest</u>

but dear love much as I long to have these two day I feel how much wisest it is not <u>to</u>[7]

No one ever loved as you love me nor made their love <u>one</u> half quarter so happy. I <u>am</u> perfectly happy & my blessed one what a letter this is of yours!

[on reverse]
but not[8]

yesterday I went to town intending to go to King's Way but finding that no stage passes nearer than 1 ½ I did not think it worth while

In the beautiful stillness of his lovely country—and with the fresh feeling of all the enjoyment it has been to him—and so soon after that which to him is such a quick-passing pleasure—he is perhaps feeling again, what he only once said to me, that 'the less human the more lovely' I seemed to him. do you remember that my love? <u>I</u> have, because I felt that whatever such a feeling was, it was not love—and since how perfectly he has denied it—or that may not be exactly the feeling, but only his old 'vanity of vanities' may have come back? neither one nor the other

---

6. No date or watermark is on the letter. II/317.

7. The manuscript breaks off at this point. No date is indicated on the manuscript. II/320.

8. The remainder of this line is unreadable. This undated manuscript has been deliberately cut, so that only this section remains. Box III/155.

would grieve <u>me</u>, but for his own dear sake—for me I <u>am</u> loved as I desire to be—heart & soul take their rest in the peace of ample satisfaction after how much calm & care which of that kind at least have passed forever—o this sureness of an everlasting spiritual home is itself the blessedness of the blessed—& to that being added—or rather that being brought by, this exquisiteness which is & has been each instant since, & seems as if with no fresh food it would be enough for a long lifes enjoyment. O my own love, whatever it may be or not be to you, you need never regret for a moment what has already brought such increase of happiness and can in no possible way increase evil. If it is right to change the "smallest chance" into a '<u>distant certainty</u>' it w^d surely show want of intellect rather than use of it, to[9]

Far from being unhappy or even <u>low</u> this morng, I feel as tho' you had never loved me half so well as last night—& I am in the happiest spirits & quite <u>quite</u> well part of which is owing to that nice sight this morng. I am taking as much care of your robin as if it were your own sweet self. If I do not succeed in making <u>this</u> live I shall think it is not possible to tame a full grown one. It is very well now but so was the other for two days.

{sideways on page}
& so I shall do adieu darling How <u>very</u> nice next month will be. I am quite impatient for it.[10]

This is one thing so perfectly admirable to me, that you[,] never in any mood, doubt the worth of enjoyment or the need of happiness—one less fine w^d undervalue what he had not reached. does not this <u>prove</u> that you have the poetic principle? for me my hope is so living and healthy that it is not possible to me to doubt that it will increase more & more until it assumes some new and higher form—going on towards perfection

Those words yesterday were <u>cold</u> and distancing, <u>very</u>, at <u>first</u>—Do you not know what it is to receive, with an <u>impulse</u> of thankfulness and joy and comfort, the packet which proves at first sight only a collection of <u>minerals</u>—one feels somewhat like a <u>mineral</u>—but this comes & must come from the uncongenial circumstances—The circumstances wh. <u>tend</u>

9. The letter ends midsentence about four-fifths of the way down a page. Written on paper watermarked 1831. Box II/324.

10. Dated in *CW* index as summer 1833, but there is no indication on the letter to confirm this date. II/316.

to elate or to despond do not come at the same time to both—and tho' such things in no degree <u>alter</u> ones mind, they <u>have</u> their effect in deciding which state of the mind shall be for the time uppermost—and always will have as long as it pleases Heaven to endow us with a body and senses.

<u>Yes</u>—dearest friend—things as they are now, bring to me, beside <u>moments</u> of quite complete happiness, a <u>life</u> & how infinitely to be preferred before all I ever knew! I never for an instant could wish that this had never been on my own account, and only on yours if you c^d think so—but why do I say <u>mine</u> & <u>yours</u>, what is good for the one must be so for the other & will be so always—<u>you</u> say so—& whatever of sadness there may sometimes be, is only the proof of how much happiness there is by proving the capacity for so much more.

You say that what you think virtue, "the wise & good" who have long known and respected you, wont think vice—How can you think people wise, with such opposite notions? You say too that when those who profess different principles to the vulger, <u>act</u> their principles, they make all worse whom they do not make better & I understand you to believe that they would make many worse & few better in your case—Is not this then the 'thinking with the wise, & acting with the vulgar' principle? And does not this imply compromise & insincerity? <u>You</u> cannot mean that, for that is both base & weak—if made a rule, & not an occasional hard necessity.

[written in crosshatch]
I was not <u>quite</u> wrong in thinking you feared opinions.—I never supposed you dreaded the opinion of fools but only of those who are otherwise wise & good but have not your opinions about Moralities[11]

I on the contrary never did either 'write or speak or look as I felt at the instant' to you. I have always suffered an instinctive dread that mine might be a foreign language to you. But the future must amend this, as well as many other things.[12]

I am glad that you have said it—I am <u>happy</u> that you have—no one with any fineness or beauty of character but must feel compelled to say <u>all</u>, to the being they really <u>love</u>, or rather with any <u>permanent</u> reservation

---

11. No date is indicated. II/323.

12. No indication of date on manuscript. *CW* index lists as September 1833, but no evidence for this date is found on the letter. II/321.

it is not love,—while there is reservation, however little of it, the love is just so much imperfect. There has never, yet, been entire confidence between/ what a bad frame of expression around us. The difference between you and me in that respect is, that I have always yearned to have your confidence with an intensity of wish which has often, for a time, swallowed up the naturally stronger feeling. The affection itself—you have not given it, not that you wished to reserve—but that you did not need to give—but not having that need of course you had no perception of that I had & so you have discouraged confidence from me 'till the habit of checking first thoughts has become so strong that when in your presence timidity has become almost a disease of the nerves. It would be absurd only it is so painful to notice in myself that every word I ever speak to you is detained a second before it is said 'till I'm quite sure I am not by implication asking for your confidence. It is but that the only being who has ever called forth all my faculties of affection is the only in whose presence I ever felt constraint. At times when that has been strongly felt I too have doubted whether there was not possibility of dissapointment— that doubt will never return. You can scarcely conceive dearest what satisfaction this note of yours is to me for I have been depressed by the fear that what I w^d most wish altered in you, you thought quite well of, perhaps thought the best of your character. I am quite sure that want of energy is a defect, would be a defect if it belonged to the character, but that thank Heaven I am sure it does not. It is such an opposite to the sort of character.

Yes—these circumstances do require greater strength than any other—the greatest—that which you have, & which if you had not I should never have loved you, I should not love you now. In this, as in all the most important matters there is no medium between the greatest, all, and none—anything less than all being insufficient[.] there might be just as well none.

If I did not know them to be false, how heartily I should scorn such expressions, "I have ceased to will"! then to wish? for does not wish with the power to fulfill constitute will? It is false that your "strength is not equal to the circumstance in wh you have placed" yourself.—It is quite another thing to be guided by a judgment on which you can rely & which is better placed for judgment than yourself.

Would you let yourself "drift with the tide whether it flow or ebb" if in one case every wave took you further from me? Would you not put what strength you have into resisting it? Would you not wish to resist it, would you not will to resist? Tell me—for if you would not, how happens it that you will to love me or any most dear!

However—since you tell me the evil & I believe the evil, I may surely beleive the good—and if all the good you have written in the last two or three notes be <u>firm</u> <u>truth</u>, there is <u>good</u> <u>enough</u>, even for me. The most horrible feeling I ever know is when for moments the fear comes over me that <u>nothing</u> which you say of yourself [is to be] absolutely relied on. That you are not <u>sure</u> even of your strongest feelings. Tell me again that this is <u>not</u>.

[perpendicular to rest of text on page]

If it were certain that "whatever one thinks best the other will think best" it is plain there <u>could</u> be no unhappiness—if that were certain want of energy could not be <u>felt</u>, could not be an evil, unless both wanted energy—the <u>only</u> evil there can be for me is that you should <u>not</u> think my best your best—or should not agree in <u>my</u> opinion of my best.

[across edge of p. 5]

<u>dearest</u> I have but five minutes in wh to writ this or I should say more— but I was <u>obliged</u> to say something before to-morrow. t'was so long to wait <u>dearest</u>.[13]

To William J. Fox and Eliza Flower[14]

I had written to you dearest friends both,—as you are—but now that I have seen that letter of y^{rs}, I cannot send mine. It is sad to be misunderstood by you—as I have been before—but it will not be always so—my own dear friends. O what a [letter] was that! but my head & soul bless you both.

He tells you quite truly our state—all at least wh he attempts to tell—but there is so much more might be said—there has been so much more pain than I thought I was capable of, but also O how much more happiness. O this being seeming as tho God had willed to show the type of the possible elevation of humanity. To be with him wholly is my ideal of the noblest fate for all states of mind and feeling which are lofty & large & fine, he is the companion spirit & heart desire—we are not alike in trifles only because I have so much more frivolity than he. why do you not write to me my dearest Lizzie? (I never wrote that name before) if you w^d say on the merest scrap what you are talking about what the next sermon is about where you walked to, & such like, how glad I should be!

---

13. L/4. Postmarked 6 September 1833, to John Mill Esq: India House.

14. HTM enclosed this note in a letter of JSM's to William J. Fox on the fifth or sixth of November 1833, while John was staying with Harriet in Paris after her estrangement from her husband. The note is directed to Eliza (Lizzie) Flower, William Fox's lover. Yale University Library.

You must come here—it is a most beautiful paradise. O how happy we might all be in it. You will see it with me, <u>bless</u> you! won't you?

<u>Happiness</u> has become to me a word without meaning—or rather the meaning of the word has no existence in my beleif. I mean by Happiness the state wh I can remember to have been in when I consciously used the word—a state of <u>satisfaction</u>, by satisfaction meaning not <u>only</u> the <u>mind made up</u>, not only having <u>conviction</u> of some sort on every large subject, but <u>cheerful</u> hopeful <u>faith</u> about all wh I could contemplate & not understand & this along with great & conscious enjoyment from my own emotions & sensations—that Happiness I had often a year ago—I believe that if the world were as well directed as human beings might direct it, & may be expected to direct it, that all might be <u>Happy</u>, in proportion to their capacity for Happiness & that those with <u>great</u> capacity might be <u>actually</u> happy—live in a <u>satisfied</u> state, without <u>need</u> of more but with, for their <u>forward</u> view, a placid contemplation of the probability of still greater capacity in some other state of existence. I do not believe I shall ever again feel that—the <u>most</u> this world can do for me is to give present enjoyment sufficient to make me forget that there is nothing else worth seeking—for the great mass of people I think wisdom would be to make the utmost of sensation while they are young enough & then die—for the very few who seem to have an innate incomprehensible capacity of emotion, more enjoyable than any sensation but [consistent] with & adding to all pleasurable sensation for <u>such</u> <u>if</u> such there be wh I greatly doubt, <u>their</u> wisdom like the others is to <u>live</u> <u>out</u> their pleasures & die—<u>now</u> I believe that such beings w^d not c^d not live out those enjoyments but that I think is because they come to them late, thro' struggle & suffering generally, wh gives an artificial depth & tenacity to their feeling, for those who come to such feelings at all are those of the most imagination—& so hold them firmest. I do not believe <u>affection</u> to be natural to human beings—it <u>is</u> an instinct of the lower animals for their young—but in humans it is a made up combination of feelings & associations wh will cease to exist when artificiality ceases to exist: only passion is natural that is temporary affection—but what we call affection will continue as long as their is dependance.[15]

---

15. A typed envelope indicates the date of 20 February 1834, but there is no indication of a date on the manuscript. The envelope was probably typed by Mary Taylor, Harriet's grand-niece, in the early twentieth century and may be unreliable. L/5.

I don't know why I was so low when you went this morning. I was <u>so</u> low— I could not bear your going my darling one; yet I should be well enough accustomed to it by now. O you dear one! dear one!

They are not coming to-day nor at all at present, & I am not sorry for it. I shall get on very well, I have no doubt, untill Thursday comes & you[.] I wish to-morrow were Thursday, but I do not wish you were coming before Thursday because I know it would be so much harder to bear afterwards.

If I knew where at Sevenoaks L & Sallie are I would go in the chaise & see them. but that will do any time.

be well & happy dearest—but <u>well</u> before everything. dearest I cannot express the sort of dégout[16] I feel whenever there comes one of these sudden cessation of life—my only spiritual life—being much with you— but never mind—it is all well & right & very happy as it is. only I long unspeakably for Saturday. This place is very lovely but it both looks & feels to me quite lifeless. farewell darling mine.[17]

Tuesday eveng.[18]

Dearest—You do not know me—or perhaps more truly you do not know the best of me—I am not one to 'create chimeras about nothing'—you should know enough of the effects of petty annoyances to know that they are wearing & depressing not only to body but to mind—these, on account of our relation, I have & you have not—& these make me morbid—but I can say most clearly & surely that I am <u>never</u> so without being perfectly conscious of being so—that I always know that in a better state of health all those morbid & weakly feelings & views & thoughts would go. So far from your two instances being like this—those women took the life with the men they loved at once as a desperate throw[19] without knowing anything of those men's characters—if I had done that do you think that I should not have been blindly devoted? of course I should—in such a case the woman has absolutely nothing to make life of but blind implicit devotion. It is not true that my character is 'the extreme of anxiety and uneasiness' if my circumstances do not account to you for all or more of anxiety & uneasiness which I show to you, why there is nothing to be said about that—you do not know the natural

---

16. "Dégoût": Disgust, distaste, or loathing.

17. Harriet is probably referring to Eliza and Sarah Flower, whom she often called "Lizzie" and "Sallie." Paper is watermarked 1833. XXVIII/235.

18. The watermark on the paper is 1835. L/7.

19. Harriet may have been alluding to the cliché "throw of the dice."

effect of those circumstances.²⁰ If it is true that so long you concealed your feelings from me for fear of paining me, I can only say I am sorry for it because I know you too well not to know that no real feelings of yours would ever pain me. Then as to your inquiry of how I should like that you sh^d go for a walk without me I can only say that I am not a fool—& I should laugh at, or very much dislike the thought, that you sh^d make your 'life obscure insignificant & useless' pour les beaux yeux²¹ & I cannot think it was consistent with love to be able to think or wish that. If it is true, & I suppose you know yourself, that then 'you would never speak a true word again' never 'express natural liking' never 'dare to be silent or tired' why I can but say that if you would take such a life as that you must be mad. That one <u>might</u> never be wholly satisfied with the finite is possible but I do not believe that I sh^d ever show that—I think it would & must be true of persons of intellect & cultivation without acute feelings—but I have always observed where there is strong feeling the interests of feeling are always paramount & it seems to me that personal feeling has more of infinity in it than any other part of character—no ones <u>mind</u> is <u>ever</u> satisfied, nor their imagination nor their ambition—nor anything else of that class—but feeling <u>satisfies</u>—All the qualities on earth never give happiness without personal feeling—personal feeling always gives happiness with or without any other character. The desire to give & to receive feeling is almost the whole of my character.

With the calmest, coldest view I beleive that my feeling to you would be enough for my whole life—but of course only if I were conscious of having as good a feeling.

I have always seen & balanced in my mind all these considerations that you write about therefore they do not either vex or pain me. I know <u>all about</u> all these chances—but I know too what you do not, but what I have always told you, that once having accepted that life I should make the very best of it. I used long ago to think that in that case I should have occasional fits of deepest depression, but that they would not affect our happiness, as I should not let you see them—for long now I have been past thinking that. I shall always show you & tell you <u>all</u> that I feel. I always do. & the fact that I do so proves to me that I should have but little that was painful to show. as to the rash & blind faith & devotion of those women you instance look at the result to them! & that is the natural result of such an engagement entered into in that way. If when first I knew

---

20. HTM may be referring generally to her estrangement from her husband or specifically to her life with syphilis.

21. "For my beautiful eyes."

you I had given up all other life to be with you I sh^d gradually have found if not that you did not love me as I thought at least that you were [different?] to what I had thought & so been dissapointed—there would never be dissapointment now. I do not know if 'such a life never succeeds' I feel quite sure that it would succeed in our case. You may be quite sure that if I once take that life it will be for good.

With not only all that you write—but more all that can be said, fully before me I should without hesitation say 'let it be', I do not hesitate about the certainty of happiness—but I do hesitate about the rightfulness of, for my own pleasure, giving up my only earthly opportunity of 'usefulness'. You hesitate about your usefulness & that however greater in amount it may be, is certainly not like mine marked out as duty. I should spoil four lives & injure others. This is the only hesitation. When I am in health & spirits I see the possibilities of getting over this hesitation. When I am low & ill I see the improbabilities. Now I give pleasure around me, I make no one unhappy, & am happy tho' not happiest myself. I think any systematic middle plan between this & all impracticable. I am much happier not seeing you continually here, because then I have habitually enough to make me able to always be wishing for more, when I have that more rarely it is in itself an object & a satisfaction.

I think you have got more interest in all social interests than you used to have, & I think you can be satisfied, as I can at present perhaps with occasional meeting—but then thro' every moment of my life you are my one sole interest & object & I would at any instance give up all, were it ten thousand times as much, rather than have the chance of one iota of diminution of your love.

This scrawled literally in the greatest haste—because you said write— but in the morng I shall see you. mine.

Wednesday[22]

Dear one—if the feeling of this letter of yours were your general or even often state it would be very unfortunate for—may I say us—for me at all events. Nothing I beleive would make me love you less but certainly I should not admire one who could feel in this way except from mood. Good heaven have you at last arrived at fearing to be "obscure & insignificant'! What can I say to that but "by all means pursue your brilliant and important career'. Am I one to choose to be the cause that the person I love feels himself reduced to 'obscure & insignificant'! Good God what

---

22. The paper is watermarked 1835. L/6.

has the love of two equals to do with making obscure & insignificant if ever you <u>could</u> be obscure & insignificant you <u>are</u> so whatever happens & certainly a person who did not feel contempt at the very idea the words create is not one to brave the world. I never before (for years) knew you to have a mesquin[23] feeling. It is a horrible want of unanimity between us. I know what the world is, I have not the least desire either to brave it or to court it—in no possible circumstances sh[d] I ever do either—those imply some <u>fellow-feeling</u> with it & that I have only in case I could do it or any individual of it any good turn—then I should be happy for the time to be at one with it—but it is to me as tho' it did not exist as to any ability to hurt me—it could not, & I never could feel at variance with it. how I long to walk by the sea with you & hear you tell me the whole truth about your feelings of this kind. There seems a touch of Common Place vanity in that dread of being obscure & insignificant—you will never be that—& still more surely <u>I</u> am not a person who in any event could give you cause to feel that <u>I</u> had made you so Whatever you may think <u>I</u> could never be either of those words.

I am not either <u>exceedingly</u> hurt by your saying that I am of an anxious and uneasy character. I know it is false & I shall pity you[24]

I went this morning there in hopes of your word my delight & there it was. believe all I ever say when I tell you how happy I am, that is, how happy you make me.

This sweet letter has been with me at every moment since I had it & it keeps me <u>so</u> well <u>so</u> happy <u>so</u> in spirits—but I cannot tell thee how happy it made me when first I read it on the highest point of the nice common with those glorious breezes blowing. It has been like an equinoctial tempest here ever since you left. Mama and C[25] are here—I like it & it does me good—in the absence of the only good I ever wish for.

Thank God however the promised summer which was to be so much is come & will be all it was to be—has been already so much. I am to see you on Saturday. indeed I could not get on without.

I can not write better to-day—tho' I never <u>felt</u> better or more.

Adieu my only & most precious—till Saturday—dear Saturday[26]

---

23. Sordid.

24. Manuscript breaks off at this point.

25. Caroline Ley, Harriet's sister.

26. The paper is watermarked 1837. XXVIII/238.

bless you, dearest—dearest   I cannot write a word worth having for I am feeling nothing in the world but the immense angst this absence is going to be. I know there is no remedy for it, & so, it must, but I shall feel it more than usual for I do so already.

If you have time to write <u>one</u> <u>word</u> do just say that you will keep me in your thoughts all the day to-morrow? as I shall every moment till I see you <u>darling</u>[27]

I do hope <u>dearest</u> that you knew the reason I did not write yesterday. I went so very early to that place that I had not a moment to write, but the fear that you might expect a word kept me uneasy all the day.[28]

a thousand thanks my kindest for that note on Thursday—it was a great happiness to me & kept me well & in spirits ever since it came. all that Mondays adventure is the most delightful possible to think of, has been & will be always.

I long to hear from you again dear. do[29]

Saturday morning[30]
I am so perfectly well & so happy that I <u>must</u> tell you dearest & <u>beg</u> you again & again to be well & in spirits—it would seem sparking[31] that I should be <u>so</u> happy—that you should make me so happy & not be so your own dear self I cannot write half that I feel & want to say these children are making such a tassage[32]—so dearest only know that I am & shall be the happiest creature in this world & thank God Monday will come at last.

You will want to know how she is before you go shall you not dear—so I write—I want so much to hear how you got on last night that you were not tired or uncomfortable in that, I should think, very tiresome expedition? I did so hate your leaving me—yet that little visit made me very happy—perhaps that is the reason I am better as I am this morng—not

---

27. Written on paper watermarked 1837. II/319.

28. The letter has been torn so that the rest of this page and the end of the next page (which begins with the following paragraph) are both missing.

29. The manuscript breaks off at this point. II/318. Written on paper watermarked 1837.

30. The paper is watermarked 1837. II/314.

31. One of the definitions of "sparking" is courting or wooing.

32. Ramming or crowding an opponent in boxing.

very much but really <u>somewhat</u> better & that <u>is</u> much. I do not think I shall see you before Tuesday—that is a <u>terrible</u> long time, but it does not feel to me longer than Monday. It is your going away that makes it feel so long but that cannot be avoided. Only do <u>you</u> my darling be well & happy & I shall be well as I am happy, the <u>happiest</u> possible—(<u>no</u> not <u>possible</u>—there <u>is</u> a happier possibility always)—but I am perfectly happy. I do not see exactly how to manage going to the sea—so I give it up at present.

When I think that I shall not hold your hand untill Tuesday the time is so long & my hand so useless. Adieu my delight

je baise tes jolis pattes[33]

<u>cher cher cher</u>[34]

that I am sure you must believe what is so true at all times how I feel the immensity of your love—& how true & noble & in all things admirable you have been <u>love</u> for me.[35]

a thousand thousand thanks & blessings dearest & kindest one. What a deal of trouble I have made you take—but you think nothing trouble for me <u>beloved</u>!

I think I had best not hope to see you to-day <u>dearest dearest</u> because Arthur is coming & will be here at the time you would come—but to-morrow <u>certainly</u> for I <u>could</u> <u>not</u> be longer without. I will get the stupid ticket & we will go for an hour & see our old friend Rhino—will you dear come here & take me to-morrow about five?

Yesterday I walked to Norfolk St—they were not there & then Haji and I went to mama at the old place—she was very busy & I helped her all day untill ten at night, when I came home—so you see dear all the fatigue that had gone before was little compared to this last—& if I had known what it would be I sh^d not have gone there it was a great deal too much—but I am so perfectly & entirely happy, without one single cloud, that I shall soon get over this merely physical fatigue.

I shall hear from Herby[36] soon & on that will depend if I go to that place again. If he is going on well I shall not go 'till next week to bring

---

33. "I kiss your pretty paws [or sideburns]." "Pattes" is most often used as slang for "paws," but can also mean "sideburns" (and JSM had fashionably large ones).

34. "<u>Cher cher cher</u>": beloved. The paper is watermarked 1838. XXVIII/234.

35. This fragment has been cut at the top and bottom. The reverse bears a postmark, "[?]u 30/38," which probably indicates 30 June 1838. II/330.

36. Harriet's son, Herbert Taylor. "Haji" is Algernon, her younger son.

them up. So we can have Sunday if we please love & we will talk of it to-morrow.

Adieu & bless you my perfect one.[37]

<u>My Beauty</u>—[38]

What a nice walk that was! I am quite thoroughly enjoying the thought of this journey. I write this word only to say, do not dear take that thing I told you of in Regent Street. do not, for I would rather very much that you would not—when that day comes you shall do whatever you like if you happen to remember it you <u>darling</u>—

I shall hear this evening from thee all about our nice to-morrow—

Adieu—<u>caro</u>

Saturday eveg[39]

They keep me here yet—indeed I could not stand when I tried to get up—but 'tis only cold—except that I am nervous & feverish a little but know I shall be well—You did not come today. Mr. Fox said he would write but I told him not that he has just been here, & I am so tired—that I could sleep—I have told them to wake me in the morning early & then I can say a word more to you

We started my friend Ernest & I accompanied by the <u>puer ingenuno</u>[40] Louis by the Southampton Railroad, intending to make a hasty tour thro some parts of Normandy & principally with a view to examine the fine specimens of Gothic architecture with which it is said to abound previous to sitting in to six months of winter & study.

It has always seemed to me that the Gothic & Grecian architecture like the classic & romantic in literature, exemplify the fundamental differences between modern & ancient poets—between modern & ancient, that is Grecian art. The latter evidently spring from a finite conception & fulfilling that

---

37. No watermark or postmark. XXVIII/233. Arthur Hardy emigrated to Australia in late 1838, so this letter was probably written earlier that year.

38. No watermark or other indication of date. XXVIII/239.

39. No date is indicated on the manuscript, but Harriet was quite ill in June of 1841, so the note may have been written about this time. II/313.

40. Harriet may have been making a play on the German "Ernst" to refer to her own "seriousness." See Box III/128 (p. 226, above). "Puer ingenuno": young innocent boy. Louis is probably Louis Ley, her nephew.

conception completely, which modern art in all its manifestations exhibiting aspirations far beyond the mere material & sensuous however perfected in their passage thro' the poetic imagination—like the religions of those different periods in the world's history—The one beautiful sensual defined—the other seeking in the super-sensuous & unknown that element of infinity which constitutes, along with its other great & modern characteristic the abasement of the merely animal nature. The Divine spirit of Christianity.[41]

These have greatly surprised & dissapointed me, & also they have pleased me, all this regarding only your part in them. Comte's[42] is what I expected—the usual partial & prejudiced view of a subject which he has little considered & on which it is probable that he is in the same state that Mr. Fox is about religion. If the truth is on the side we I defend I imagine C. would rather not see it. Comte is essentially French, in the sense in which we think French mind less admirable than English—Anti-Catholic—Anti-Cosmopolite.

I am surprised in your letters to find your opinion undetermined where I had thought it made up—I am dissapointed at a tone more than half apologetic with which you state your opinions. & I am charmed with the exceeding nicety elegance & finesse of your last letter. Do not think that I wish you had said more on the subject, I only wish that what was said was in the tone of conviction, not of suggestion.

This dry sort of man is not a worthy coadjutor scarcely a worthy opponent. with your gifts of intellect of conscience & of impartiality is it probable, or is there any ground for supposing, that there exists any man more competent to judge that question than you are?

You are in advance of your age in culture of the intellectual faculties, you would be the most remarkable man of your age if you had no other claim to be so than your perfect impartiality & your fixed love of justice. These are the two qualities of different orders which I believe to be the rarest & most difficult to human nature.

---

41. The following passage is written in pencil on the next page. The page is merely the other half of a folded paper, so it seems unlikely that the penciled section is a draft: "Like the religions of those different periods in this world's history, the one beautiful sensual defined the other seeking in the super-sensuous & unknown that element of infinity which constitutes, along with its other great & modern principle the Divine spirit of Christianity[.]" This letter seems to reflect the same kind of thinking as the essay on Amiens cathedral in chapter 7 and was probably written during Harriet and Helen's trip to Normandy in 1844. II/325.

42. Auguste Comte (1798-1857) corresponded with John from 1841-43. John presented copies of his letters and Comte's letters to Harriet. The letters include Comte's view that because their brains are smaller than men's, women will be permanently in a childlike condition. This is her response to John.

Human nature [is] essentially weak, for when it is not weak by defect of intellect it is almost inevitably weak by excess of the moral or conscientious principle, seems to me to attain its finest expression only when in addition to a high development of the powers of intellect, the moral qualities rise consciously above all—so that the being looks down on his own character with the very same feelings as on those of the rest of the world, & so desiring the qualities he thinks elevated for <u>themselves</u> wholly unmoved by considerations proper to any <u>portion</u> of the race, still less so to himself. "To do justly, to love mercy, (generosity) & to walk humbly before all men" is very fine for the age in which it was produced, but why was it not 'before God' rather than before <u>all men</u>?

It makes the sentiment seem rather Greek than Jewish.

It appears to me that the idea which you propose in the division of the functions of men in the general Government proceeds on the supposition of the incapacity or unsuitableness of the same mind for work of active life & for work of reflection & combination: & that the same supposition is sufficient to account for the differences in the characters & apparent capacities of men & women considering that the differences of the occupations in life are just those which you say in the case of men must produce distinct characters (neither you nor Comte seem to settle the other analogous question, whether original differences of character & capacities in men are to determine to which class of workers they are to belong) & there is also to be taken into account the unknown extent of action on the physical & mental powers, of hereditary servitude.

I should like to begin the forming of a book or list of what in human beings must be individual & of in what they may be classified.

I now & then find a generous defect in your mind of yr 'method'—such is your liability to take an over large <u>measure</u> of people—sauf having to draw in afterwards—a proceeding more needful than pleasant.[43]

Not with you—you very dear it was not with you:—I <u>had</u> been annoyed—or displ[i]rited a minute before—but was from no word or look of yours, only I seemed just then more especially to cling to, and linger after you & could have shouted through the shut door again do let me hear from you before a day or two and so she did & it was so precious to have them & bless her. shall I tell you how it was yesterday'—I first went to the Richardsons,[44] & had some biscuit, & wine <u>very</u> much, & Robert went

---

43. The Comte letters were probably shown to HTM in 1844. II/327 and Box III/103.

44. Harriet may be referring to her aunt, Ann Hardy Richardson.

with me to St. Paul's (Kit won't let me write she rubs her head against the pen then get down) and then I took coach to King Street.

Sally was lying down, suffering from headache & [Bolton] says she has gone back in the last week & promises more regular hours, while she promises not to walk about so much with Miss Michelle—

Still it was disheartning to see her in the old way as bad as ever after all—Well, I staid till they dined & then wended slowly along & all the way did I walk to the flowerpot! There was no coach, but instead, a little, little person a waiting for me—wasn't it funny—regular destiny—presently came a Hackney stage, wh took us to the church, & we had to walk the rest of the way—only a little worse & I should have taken him up & carried him—but to-day he is none the worser—weve been a tiny walk— how pretty it is hereabouts—do make haste & be quite strong & free—now O how sweet you would think & say these flowers are—& love to sit & watch them brighten and flutter as the gleam[,] the wind passes their benediction on them—I slept so sweetly & was up [betimes] this mo[r]n[g] and determined to make such a good day of it, but nothing's come for on going to the cupboard for the ink bottle Der [Freitz][45] (the whole opera in German given in years since & all I never could quite make out) trembles down, & so I thought I[']d first look at it, & that looking 'a begin at the begins,' & a finish with the last note just took up from 9, till[46]

It seems to me that you[47] are the only man with a mind & feeling living in this country—certainly in public life there is none possessing the first named requisite. Only think of Fox[48] saying that he "entirely approved & w[d] do all in his power to enable the ministers to carry the bill the earliest possible"![49] Is this place hunting or John Bullism—

I am very glad you wrote that to Crowe.[50] It is excellent & must do some good. I only disagree in the last sentence—but that does not much

---

45. This may be HTM's shorthand for *Der Freischütz,* first produced in Berlin in 1821.

46. No date is indicated on the manuscript, but Sarah (Sally) Flower Adams visits Harriet in April and dies later in the year of 1847. II/315.

47. The letter is postmarked 25 July 1848 and is addressed to J. S. Mill Esq., East India House, Leadenhall Street, London. L/8.

48. William Fox was a Unitarian minister and friend of HTM and JSM.

49. According to Hayek (298), the *Daily News,* 24 July 1848, reported W. J. Fox as saying the following during a debate in the House of Commons on the suspension of the Habeas Corpus Act in Ireland "that the sooner the bill was passed into law the better. [Fox] would do all in his power to aid the government in carrying it at once."

50. Eire Evens Crowe was the editor of the *Daily News* during this period.

matter. How can you "know" that a rising c^d. not succeed—and in my opinion if it did not succeed it might do good if it were a serious one, by exasperating & giving fire to the spirit of the people. The Irish w^d I sh^d hope not be frightened but urged on by some loss of life. However that is entre nous[51] & is not the thing to say to these dowdies—the more that it might not prove true. I suppose it is <u>impossible</u> that Ireland c^d. eventually succeed & if so you are right. I am disgusted with the mixture of impudence (in his note & marked passages) & imbecility in the article which he sends of the Reasoner[52] of this <u>foolish</u> creature Holyoake. I suppose he must too be answered. What do you think of the ci joint notion of an answer? I should like to see your answer to him before it goes if quite convenient.[53]

I fancy I sh^d say that the morality of the reasoner appears to me as far as <u>any</u> meaning can be picked out of the mass of verbiage in which its opinions on morality are always enveloped to be as intolerant slavish & selfish as that of the religion it attacks, and the arguments used in the reasoner against religion are even if possible more foolish & weak than those of its opponents. None of the marked quotations against people who are afraid to acknowledge their opinions touch me, in the slightest degree I am ready to stand by my opinions but not to hear them travestied, & mixed up with what appear to me opinions founded on no principles & arguments so weak that I should dread for the furtherance of my anti religious opinions the imputation that they do not admit of being better defended.

In the very number you send me of "<u>The</u> <u>Reasoner</u>" a vulgar epithet of abuse is applied to the French for having imagined <u>Reason</u> as a ~~Goddess~~ their head! You say your "atheism does not '<u>negative</u>' (I suppose this means in English <u>deny</u>) the worship of a God to set up reason instead?' The sentence has & admits no other meaning.

The fool ought to be sharply set down by <u>reasons</u>—but he is such an <u>excessive</u> fool & so lost in self sufficiency that he will cavil & prate say what you will. But as I suppose he must have an answer the only plan is to strike hard without laying yourself open. I am glad of the quarrel with him as I am glad not to have your name and influence degraded by such a connection.

The sentence I copied above runs thus—"our atheism is not the" &c "for it does not negative the worship of God to set up the worship of a harlot"

What does the fellow mean except by a sideblow to crush those who practise illegally what he practises legally. If he had any <u>principles</u> of

---

51. "Between us."

52. G. J. Holyoake edited *The Reasoner: A Weekly Journal, Utilitarian, Republican and Communist.*

53. The "answer" was never published, but appears in chapter 6, above.

morality he c^d not use such an expression. The fact is his irreligion like Fox's liberalism is a trade.

Will you please dear keep this note as I have put down my notions about this man.

I am as you see utterly disgusted with the adhesion to Russell[54] of Fox & that is the cause that I can for the first time in my life speak of him without the title of respect. The tame & stupid servility of saying he "would do all in his power to make Russell to carry it—says 'come and buy me' as plainly as words can speak for what c^d. be, or be supposed to be, in his power beyond his vote! It was the roast pig[']s 'come eat me.[']"}

I was excessively amused by the top paragraph in the Daily News[55] from Paris saying that Prudhon[56] moved that the fiction of the acknowledgement of being of a God sh^d be erased. It does one good to find one man who dares to open his mouth & say what he thinks on that subject. It did me good, & I need something for the spirits, as did also your note to Crowe—The reading that base selfish & imbecile animal Trench[57] has made my spirits faint. But the 2^d vol. is the corpus delicti. Adio caro carissimo[58] till Sat^y when we shall talk over all these things.

Among other trash did you observe Hume[59] said—'To interfere with the labour of others and to attempt to establish community of property is a direct violation of the fundamental laws of society'. What a text this would be for an article which however no paper would publish. Is not the Ten Hours' Bill an 'interference &c &c'? Is not the 'interference' with their personal freedom by this Suspension Bill a 'violation' &c, what is the meaning of 'fundamental laws of society' the very point in debate on the subject, communism, on which he professed to be speaking.

Oh English men!
English intellect!

---

54. Lord John Russell (1792-1861), prime minister of Great Britain 1846-52 and 1865-1866. He led the fight for passage of the Reform Bill of 1832.

55. According to Hayek (298), the Paris correspondent of The Daily News on 24 July 1848 reported: "The only event which signalized the day was the effrontery of M. Proudhon, who moved a resolution in the 4th bureau, that the fiction, as he regards it, of the acknowledgement of the existence of God, with which the preamble opens, should be erased."

56. Pierre-Joseph Proudhon (1809-65) a French socialist and journalist whose ideas support anarchism.

57. Probably referring to the Archbishop of Dublin, Richard Chenevix Trench (1807-86).

58. "Goodbye with my love."

59. Joseph Hume (1777-1855) was a British radical politician who worked to bring about several important social reforms, including a campaign against the law forbidding trade unions.

& also might it not be said that if they are justified in interfering with personal liberty (a fundamental law if there is any) would they not be equally justified in enacting a law that all Irish landlords whatsoever must instantly repair to Ireland? This w^d be in accordance with their professed principles of noble & propertied government in exchange for benefits, of duties accompanying rights—but no; troops & force—but not interference with the liberty of the propertied or extra constitutional measures for them!

I am so disgusted with the French Assembly & also with the Daily News that it makes me sick to think of defending the one or helping the other. Surely the intense & disgusting vulgarity of the Daily news might be noticed somehow. Did you observe its Paris correspondants notice of Flocon's speech.[60] Progress of liberty forsooth advocated by a paper which applauds the Suspension of the Habeas Corpus—that is to say the suspension of the boasted freedom of the english constitution the moment any people endeavour to profit by it. & applauds the exclusion by law of women from clubs! This last is so monstrous a fact & involves so completely the whole principle of personal liberty or slavery for women that it seems to me a case of conscience & principle to write—specially on it. Certainly I cannot conceive publishing this[61] or any article in defence of the French revolution unless accompanied by one specially on the subject of this act of the chamber by such an article you would also have the means of saying out fully to the readers of the Daily News that in principle women ought to have votes &c This would be in some degree pledging the Daily News still more it w^d teach many timid young or poor reformers that such an opinion is not ridiculous. It [is] this last that makes the low dread to advocate it. Look at that disgusting sentence in their Paris correspondants letter.

The French article I return with some few pencil marks attached. If you follow it by one on this vote of the Assembly & on the true & JUST meaning of Universal Suffrage—on the propriety of keeping that title as best expressive of the true & just principle instead of as some low-minded reformers have done merging the principle in the vulgar selfishness of

---

60. Hayek cites the Paris correspondent of the *Daily News,* who reports on 24 July 1848 (third edition, p. 3) concerning a debate about the Law of the Clubs: "Much amusement was produced by the ardour with which M. Flocon assailed the clause of the measure which interdicted the presence or participation of females in the debates" (Hayek 298).

61. The article referred to here and in the next paragraph as the "French article" is probably that published by John, 9 August 1848, in the *Daily News.* See Hayek 298.

manhood suffrage which I perceive is quite the fashion among the active low reformers.

I confess I prefer an aristocracy of men & women together to an aristocracy of men only—for I think the last is far more sure to last—but all this we have often said. I sh^d be sorry this really excellent article on French affairs sh^d go unless it is to be followed by an attack on the assembly. If you think this can be done & were to do it before Sat^y we could talk it over together but you will scarcely have time—

The note to Holyoake I think very good   bring me the draft again will you? Perhaps you will think it better to leave out about Md^e D'arusmont[62] yet I long to give the rascal that retort.

[sideways on page] The pencil marks on the article are meant only as hints.[63]

[across the edge of page one] I wholly disagree that the influence of Ireland on the english mind is now anti-revolutionary.[64]

K.T. Tuesday 5 oclk[65]

You will have wondered not to get a word from me before, but I have not been able to get a moment in which to write—& now it is in the midst of Arthur's[66] disquisition &c

I got through the crossing & the custom house much better than I expected—I think I sh^d not have been ill at all but for the enormous crowd of people on the steamboat.

I got here at about ½ past 11. The same time that you did, as I know by your kindest sending of the note on Sunday which arrived at that hour

---

62. Frances d'Arusmont, a Scotswoman, who, according to Hayek, helped start the women's movement in America and objected to Holyoake's unsanctioned printing of her lecture in the *Reasoner* during her visit to England in 1847 (Hayek 298-99).

63. Hayek designated this letter as written from Ryde and adds a final sentence. Neither Hayek's reference to the location of the writer or additional sentence are contained in the original as it now exists.

64. Newspaper reference dates this letter to July 1848. II/322.

65. Letter is postmarked 16 May 1849. L/9.

66. Harriet may be referring to Arthur Ley and the investigation of his embezzlement of money (XXVII/48), or she may have been referring to her brother Arthur Hardy, who had a financial squabble with their father just before his death in early May of the year this letter was written (XXVIII/224, XXVIII/227, XXVIII/228).

& very fortunately—for he[67] w^d have been made even worse if he had been left in uncertainty—& the smallest irritation or anxiety might be fatal.

I was extremely shocked to find that his account of his state was altogether short of the facts.[68] He is very ill indeed, but my coming he says has given him a better day than he has had for many. he is ordered to take Morphia and Opium incessantly & does take immense doses His sisters who come every day are of opinion & tell me privately that he is in the greatest danger in fact that they give him up but I do not at all—I have great hope that by care he may get over this bad state—but I see that all depends on keeping up his spirits & nothing does this but my constant presence—& cheerful talk—and as there are constant people calling, things wanted &c (as you know one cannot describe a sick room) I am very tired—& have not been able to find a moment before in which to write

I will write more at length this even^g or to-morrow—& say then when we shall meet which must be soon. I want to know how you are exceedingly. I am well considering all the fatigue both of body & spirits. He is very good & patient & keeps up his spirits excellently tho' he thinks himself in danger

Adio con tutti amor[69]

Wednesday night[70]

All I can think of to say to Geo is that in Clarks[71] opinion he w^d be better in England for the summer—& also that it w^d of course be useless for you to attempt getting an appointment if it is uncertain whether he is prepared to accept it.

This is all I can think of on this subject because my whole time & thoughts are engrossed here. I thought him very ill from the moment I arrived & heared the symptoms & yesterday saw his state but I did not see any reason for thinking there was danger—but today I have seen the Dr. Power[72] who has been attending him all along & I cannot feel <u>quite</u>

---

67. John Taylor.

68. This letter marks the first indication of John's terminal illness, which would end in his death in July of the same year.

69. "Goodbye with all love."

70. Written during John Taylor's final illness, summer 1849, probably Wednesday, May 16, since on May 17 Harriet refers to a letter written earlier about George. L/10.

71. George Mill, JSM's youngest brother. Clark is probably James Clark (1788-1870), who wrote treatises on consumption and was an important physician during this period. See John's letter to Harriet concerning Clark's treatise and various other doctors (*CW*: XIV, 198-99).

72. One of two primary physicians who diagnosed and treated John Taylor during his final

sure whether his evading & altogether positively avoiding to say anything like a yes to my plain question—if he does not get worse do you not expect that he will recover? whether this was the over caution of a very slow man. I do not know—he would not say yes to this question—in any shape—& ever since I have been dreadfully anxious & depressed—he is so good so courageous & considerate & it seems so very hard, that it seems to me as if I could not bear it—all my time is now taken up in trying to amuse him—which succeeds for he is not at all impatient but quite amusable. There is not so much of extreme pain but only once in an hour or so, extreme writhing. They give no medicines, but opium incessantly, & as they tell him in any quantity. They talk of relying wholly on "preventing exhaustion." from all this I greatly fear that they expect mortification[.] I professed to Power another opinion & he said he thought nothing more c^d be done but if it w^d be any satisfaction he sh^d be happy &c & mentioned Ferguson as the opinion he thought highest—but why not Brodie? Tell me what surgical opinion is now thought highest of? It is it seems wholly a surgical case (at least in this Powers & Travers'[73] opinion) & faintness after eating anything & nothing retained all this is bad & I can write about nothing else. Take care of your-self pray—

On looking over G's letter again it occurs to me that you might well suggest the unnecessity of a horse at all—he says in his childish way that as a horse costs others more therefore it is very cheap for him at such & such a price—but as he is fat & well & strong & can walk it is perfectly absurd his having a horse at all. Then as to the price wh he calls so cheap, it is ~~excessively~~ dear. Your only mode of curing this foolish extravagance will be by keeping to precision in money matters & exact accounts. He never seems to know or care what he has got. Might you not also suggest the possibility & hope for the probability of his return to the I.H.[74] This mode of writing is like a youth with a large fortune For the ~~present~~ next few days at all events I am as much reparativ[e] as if I were still at Pau. —&

---

illness. Of all the doctors mentioned in the following letters, HTM had the least respect for him, and he is the only physician referred to in these letters who is not mentioned in *The Dictionary of National Biography* of Great Britain or *Monk's Roll,* a list of doctors of the Royal College of Physicians of London.

73. Robert Ferguson (1799-1865), a physician who wrote on women's illnesses, became Queen Victoria's doctor; Sir Benjamin Collins Brodie (1783-1862) was sergeant-surgeon to the queen; and Benjamin Travers (1783-1858) published several books, including one on intestinal injuries, and was appointed one of the Queen's "surgeons extraordinary" and eventually "sergeant-surgeon."

74. India House.

it must be so—& is best so for untill some favorable change takes place I can neither speak nor think of anything but doing all I can towards it. Adieu & a thousand thanks & blessings.[75]

Thursday Eveng[76]

Thanks for this note, it is a great comfort. He says & I can see that my coming has made a great change for the better in his spirits. He has been better each day than the last since the worst days which were in the middle of last week & the ten days before. And each day now he is certainly better considerably as to all the symptoms manifestations of disease, but of this improvement Power (who evidently is the echo of Travers) appears to think nothing.[77] I sh^d be quite in spirits as to his chances of recovery but for the manner of this man, who certainly positively evaded saying yes when I pousse[78] about by his determined silence) said "well but if he continues to get better he will in time get well?" To this he w^d not reply—& this prevents my keeping in any spirits for long together—as I fear they expect some dangerous crisis—

He is in good spirits & to-day almost free from any pain. The Opium must be right as Travers orders him to take it incessantly in almost any quantity, & tho' heretofore he could not take any opium without headache now he takes it all day without any apparent effect not even sleepiness, therefore it must be right. From the day Travers saw him he stopped all medicine & he takes none whatever. so this does not look like mistaking the case—in fact I am quite persuaded they know exactly what it is & that it is one which depends on favorable chances from nature. They reiterate that everything may depend on keeping up the spirits & preventing exhaustion. His spirits are excellent now & he eats with great pleasure yet he seems to get weaker & thinner. However to-day he is certainly a very good day following an excellent night.

I wrote you a wretched letter & in the course of to-day thought of

---

75. The letter was probably written in mid-May 1849. The evidence for this dating is the discussion of George Mill's health. See Letters L/10 and L/11 in this volume. L/13.

76. Postmarked 18 May 1849. Written on stationery with black edges, signifying mourning. Harriet's father had died earlier in May. L/11.

77. According to W. F. Bynum's *Science and the Practice of Medicine in the Nineteenth Century* (Cambridge: Cambridge University Press, 1994), 211, doctors were in the habit of keeping patients and family unaware of the terminal nature of a disease until the end was near. This practice may help to explain the difficulty Harriet has in persuading the doctors to be open with her about her husband's condition.

78. Push(ed).

several things which might have been well to say to Geo but no doubt your letter is gone & you can write more next time.

I will write a few words often. I fear [Gravin's] case was of a different organ

Adieu dearest

Monday[79]

I had for the first time an interview with Travers <u>alone</u> to-day—Hitherto I have heared from Power only disjointed expressions for he is a man who wont or cant speak plain. T[ravers] said the disease is called in the medical Profession 'schirrous rectum' he added 'There is a tumour too in the thigh' but whether this last was meant to be more than a mode of finishing his speech by dropping down the subject I do not know. <u>Otherwise</u> it seems to strange to mention at the same time, & as if as important, <u>a tumour</u> as the former I suppose frightful disease under this name is there any account to be found of the disease in that book of Watson's?[80] I still feel even more perplexed as to what is best for him with regard to seeing another man. If any I sh^d certainly have Brodie—I think Travers the best & there can be only Brodie comparable or more <u>in reputo</u>,[81] & this consideration would weigh much with him—I mean I think he himself w^d think more of B[rodie]'s opinion than of any other except T[ravers]'s—<u>But</u>, & this is my difficulty Travers sees as I do that everything may depend on keeping up his spirits—he is occasionally <u>fidgetted</u> about his state & asks me questions, but his mind is soon turned from alarm & he does not <u>now</u> think, or at least show, nearly so much idea that it <u>may</u> be dangerous as he did ten days ago. He is made nervous by illness & morphia & I think the shock would go near to kill him if he now thought himself in real danger. I hope to God he may be able to get through it, but T[ravers]'s opinion is apparently bad—he does not say <u>exactly</u> what it is because I do not ask him to do so, feeling that I could scarcely bear to hear a very bad reply— but I fear it w^d be given. sometimes I hope that the bad impression both T[ravers] & Power give is their way—It does seem strange that it can be

---

79. Probably written Monday, 28 May 1849, since Harriet had not seen the written diagnosis yet. L/20.

80. Sir Thomas Watson (1792-1882), physician and professor of clinical medicine at University College from 1828-31 and professor of medicine at King's College London thereafter. In 1843 he published his famous *Lectures on the Principles and Practice of Physic,* which continued for thirty years as the primary English textbook on medicine.

81. To account, reckon, or calculate.

so bad while he is in all other respects than the local pain & discomfort, so well, so himself 'tis true much of this bearing up is because he <u>will</u>, he is very brave & enduring & never complains still the <u>pain</u> is itself is shortlived Tho' severe & when not in pain, & that is the greater part of the day he reads a vol or two a day & the papers, dictates letters, & speaks in his usual quick cheerful way. Then another good symptom is that notwithstanding the incessant morphia the appetite is quite as good & he eats as much or more than in health—all this I mentioned to T[ravers] who agreed that they were good (signs he w^d not say) but good as enabling him to bear up. T[ravers] thought the morphia agreed wonderfully with the stomach & head causing <u>no</u> disturbance in either being as he said <u>unusual</u>—this then is good.

Power is his long prosy talkings <u>lets drop</u> rather than says things—the words I mentioned to you in my last note were in this way <u>disjointed</u> but to me very frightful—T[ravers] you see made no use of the word cancer at all.

Yesterday he had a terribly painful distressing morning from daybreak to 10 o'clk one constant <u>distress</u>—He w^d not take more Morphia, the dose of which had been diminished. The last few days, untill he saw Power who came at noon & immediately ordered it—On talking of the cause of this distress Power said 'It is the ulceration &c &c (all Power says is mixed in a sea of low murmuring words) now this word I had not heared before—so that I do not feel that I now know <u>anything</u> clearly the nature of the disease—so many expressions you see have been used between them & one w^d think <u>all</u> these terms can scarcely express one disease. for instance what has ulceration to do with tumour in the thigh & so many other terms.

If it were you or I we both prefer <u>experiments</u> in disease & sh^d do so certainly if the case was of a kind not admitting of any medical or surgical treatment as it appears this in their opinion does not—he has taken nothing but the Morphia at night & occasionally for many weeks—but one cannot experiment on others without saying will you try desperate remedies & then I know none. I <u>myself for myself</u> or for one who I said leave it <u>entirely</u> to you, sh^d try Tuson[82]—here it seems impossible—Yet I am sure Tuson told me that he had being trying experi^{ts} upon Cancer & thought he sh^d succeed in finding a cure for it in some form of Zinc—I just <u>tried</u> Power about Zinc & he smiled pityingly & said 'That c^d do

---

82. Dr. Edward William Tuson (1802-65). See letters from John referring to Dr. Tuson in *CW*: XIV, 223, 226, 231, 233, and 305. HTM seems to know Tuson personally. Mr. Tuson is mentioned for his work in Lock Hospital, a famous London hospital for the treatment of venereal disease, in Hebert Mayo's *A Treatise on Siphilis* (London: Henry Renshaw, 1840), 122.

nothing but mischief' I have some idea Tuson says something about this in his book about the spine wh is at Walton—Have you an opportunity of looking at this at Highley's to see if he does so? Perhaps you can hear (from the name I gave the disease, of some book or authority on the subject—Symes[83] is a mere popular sketch & too short to enter into his subjects. If you c^d find me that great book if it contains anything I sh^d be glad but do not send it by parcel—I will send Haji to ask you for a parcel for me & if you have it will you give it him enveloped—If not tell him only To say 'it is not ready yet' I do not wish the young ones to get hold of medical books nor therefore to see them read.

Herbert got to Liverpool this morn^g & is to be here to-night say for me all the rest that I would say to you.

4   Monday[84]

I fear, if you have not yet answered him I must have caused you inconvenience about Holyoake[85]—& now when I find a few minutes to write I cannot put my hand on his letter. I do not think I returned it—but I will seek for it & enclose it you soon. I ~~agreed with you~~ think it duty when you tell him you will subscribe ~~to his~~ as he requests to tell him some of your opinion on the very false & vicious sort of note it is—I think it is impossible you can agree with the humbug (even when translated into honest expressions it is humbug) that hearing men lecture at the London or any other University is a means of improvement of knowledge of ~~learning~~ being 'learned'. as he so boastfully & vulgarly calls it such as can never be equalled by reading—That lecturers & lecturers such as exist at present are means of improvement superior to all reading—Then his hypocritical cant about "violating austere incorruptibility" either the words are a useless & therefore insincere braggadocia, or the man is 'violating &c' by his letter.

The whole thing in an honest man's language amounts to this I want to get a degree or some other University honour in order to try to get on in the world are you disposed to help me with a little money?

This is the whole—while his note is like all his a heap of boastful conceited vulgar insincerity & I wish that he sh^d see or feel that you are not humbugged by him. And this only because it feels to me im moral

---

83. James Syme (1799-1870), a surgeon, was recognized as the greatest living authority in surgery. He wrote many books, including *On Diseases of the Rectum*.

84. Postmarked 22 May 1849 and written on mourning stationary. The 4 must be referring to 4 o'clock on Monday, 21 May 1849. L/12.

85. George Jacob Holyoake, founder of the Rochdale Pioneers, reprinted *Principles of Political Economy* as a serial, while adding an introduction that cast JSM as a militant atheist.

to let falseness think itself more successful than honesty w^d be with true & intelligent people. W^d it be too base to say that ~~as for~~ you understand his note to mean—so & so—saying in the simplest truest ~~most~~ expressions what you <u>do</u> think his note says—

All this I only as the old man used to say 'throw out' for your approval.

Monday night[86]

I have not written partly because I have not a moment unoccupied in trying to ease his suffering or to divert his thoughts from it & still more because I have had nothing good to tell. I feel dreadfully anxious I fear it is a most dangerous disease. I saw Travers to-day for the first time—He said "It is a serious case, it would be wrong to conceal from you that it is a serious case, but I may say that I think his state somewhat better to-day than when last I saw him". The manner was worse than the words—& I fear he is much worse the last 24 hours—Altogether I am dreadfully depressed about him—& so do not be surprised if I do not write untill I have something better to say of his state. I will return Holyoakes[87] letter—I would give but not unaccompanied with a suitable lesson on his vain & senseless affectation—besides the <u>sense</u> of what he says is fundamentally false & wrong—so he sh^d be told so—but perhaps this can wait.

Wednesday[88]

Many thanks for your note & the sympathy which is a comfort. The excitement of excessive anxiety has kept me able to go through an <u>immense</u> deal of fatigue hitherto but I am beginning to get worn out—yet if I could have some hope, or rather if this man Power did not either stupidly or intentionally give an impression each day afresh of hopelessness while nothing will make him speak out, I could still keep up strength & energy ~~as long as~~ & indeed I do so for surely nature must be able to do something in a case in which <u>all</u> is left to nature & yet which both these men <u>say</u> they perfectly understand. I put the question in the most formal

---

86. Probably written Monday night, May 21. On June 12 Harriet writes to John about the Holyoake controversy she had written to him about three weeks before. Since this letter and the previous letter (also probably written the same day) refer to Holyoake's letter, I conclude that they were written on the same day, May 21. L/18.

87. George Jacob Holyoake. See letters L/12 and L/17.

88. Written on mourning paper, probably on Wednesday, May 23, since Monday, May 21 had been a day of great pain (see L/18), and this was written after an easing of the pain "yesterday & to-day." L/14.

way to <u>both</u> of them separately 'Is it a case of a not uncommon kind & which is perfectly understood, or is there the slightest doubt as to what it is, or what the treatment should be' both said the same, Traver's words were "These ~~is~~ are unfortunately not at all ~~an~~ uncommon cases & there is no possibility of doubt about it—they are always very serious cases & it w^d be wrong to conceal from you that this is a very serious case but I can say that I find him him [*sic*] better to day, easier, than the last time I saw him" you will observe the word <u>easier</u> which is <u>invariably</u> inserted whenever I try to force Power to allow that he is better to-day—The emphasis too in this <u>speech</u> (as in manner it was) was all laid on the word <u>find</u> as if he w^d not say <u>is</u>.

How I wish I knew if there is anything more c^d be done. The whole time I have been here he has taken nothing but morphia. The dose of which now allow^g of being somewhat diminished—(a few drops of Sal Volatile & Tinct of Hops[89] are added to the morphine) & this taken each night at ten is all in the way of remedy of any kind. He eats with appetite more than when in health & has not been at all low till to-day (a little) Sunday & Monday were most distressing days owing to pain, not so much extreme as incessantly recurring. Yesterday & to-day he has scarcely any pain & is quite comfortable. I have scarcely evr left him till yesterday & to-day a little—his spirits have been very good & his spirit is admirably brave & patient. He said to that dull hearted sluggish Haji, who of course had thought of nothing "my dear boy why <u>dont</u> you bring checks for me to sign I mayn't be able to sign to-morrow' & to Power the D^r who is a careful attentive nullity following servility Travers—'<u>Its all my eye</u> not taking more morphia it never does any harm—and this morn^g we could scarcely help a fit of laughing in spite of care & anxiety by the funny way he said 'there's a <u>new</u> dodge' about some change I do not know, & I do not know how people find out, the stupid etiquettes of what the fools call their profession. I sh^d exceedingly like a quite <u>fresh</u> opinion, but I suppose any new man called in w^d only be in consultation with these two—So that one sh^d never know in what they agreed or disagreed. Do you know the custom on this subject? I sh^d like (which I suppose to be impossible or to involve sending away one or both these two) Bright[90] to see him. He is the only man I can think of. This Power is strong in recommending Ferguson, <u>not</u> the Physician but <u>M^r</u> Ferguson Surgeon. I wonder if he is any authority—I see the Irishman ~~wants~~ recommends him, if any, tho' he

---

89. Typical nineteenth-century medicines, which are basically smelling salts and beer, respectively.

90. Richard Bright (1789-1858), physician extraordinary to Queen Victoria, wrote several works on medicine, including a paper on "Abdominal Tumours."

says none is wanted because he is a private acquaintance &c. I cannot help fearing that they expect mortification—Why else do they <u>do</u> nothing yet refuse to give any hope? I cannot get this Power to give any account of <u>what</u> the disease is—I shall <u>try</u> from Travers tomorrow. It can hardly be <u>stricture</u>[91] (he says they call it disease of the Rectum) for that case there would be more pain—& It appears they early declared it was <u>not</u> fistula.[92]

His sisters fancy that he saw a surgeon too late—I asked this of Power who said "not at all, don't torment yourself about that, this has been coming on for eighteen months or two years"

I think Power a very commonplace creature but <u>unless</u> the case is a hopeless one he must be a thorough fool as he has given that impression by determinedly avoiding either to give a precise opinion or to assent to my often repeated do you not think him better to-day? To this he <u>always</u> says 'well he is easier' Tell me what you think about hiring anyone else—& if you think of any way of making them give an opinion—Tho' unless the opinion were hopeful it is better not to have it unless one c^d think of new means of relief. <u>Still</u> one <u>ought</u> to be told the <u>truth</u>—as if it were bad one might <u>try</u> some one else.

This Power is too much Irishman to be capable of telling the truth I beleive—let alone that I dont think he has confidence enough in himself to feel sure that he [knows][93]

Friday[94]

Symes book he had had—I do not see any reason to think anyone could understand the case better than Travers. He tells me that it is a case about which there can be no doubt. <u>If</u> he is as good an authority as any, still more if he is <u>the</u> <u>best</u>, it would be uselessly disturbing & alarming him to see any other man.

Travers appears to me a man of strong sense & decision, & speaks to me as to the same. But this Power who is always present when I see Travers, with his incessant slow stream of small talk prevents my seeing as much of T[ravers] as I should like.

However I have heared from Travers what shows his opinion to be the

---

91. Stricture is an abnormal narrowing of a passage or canal.

92. A fistula is an abnormal hollow passage from an abscess.

93. Harriet writes "in knowe," but clearly means "knows."

94. Written on mourning stationery, probably Friday May 25, 1849, or the following Friday, June 1. L/15.

worst almost that is possible yet still I cannot but hope that nature may make this one of the <u>very</u> rare cases which do not prove the worst.

<u>After</u> Travers had told me his opinion yesterday, this Power told me his to-day which he w^d not have done but in imitation of T[ravers]. He gave no exact name to the disease but called it 'cancerous schirrous'—whether this is curable ever becomes chronic or dies away without killing the patient I do not know but this is my hope. Poor fellow! he is so good & patient, tho' I fear he is beginning to get a little depressed—& to prevent this, to keep up his spirits is the best chance as both the medical men agree with me in saying. My feeling is that I w^d not call in a third man to teaze & alarm him unless with hope of a new opinion—This T[ravers] says is impossible—If it were my call I w^d get Tuson's opinion but these men w^d doubtless not meet him & besides <u>he</u> himself w^d not wish it[,] having full confidence in Travers. In such a case what would you do—If I acted as for myself I sh^d see others—Against this is to be set that he does not wish it, & it might disturb him uselessly—

Symes does not mention the case of the words Power used about the disease—but in any case it must be bad yet I hope.

Wednesday[95]

I wrote to you on Monday but did not send it & I now enclose it to show how your note yesterday was a comfort as it gave me some hope that other surgeons might do something more. I will now tell you the exact state at present.

After the bad morn^g of Sunday, he went on tolerably easy & well till yesterday at noon when he had a sudden fit of pain of the most sudden acute & violent kind we ran for brandy & a few drops poured into his mouth seemed to keep him from fainting—at this moment fortunately Power came in & added 25 drops of Morphia w/ the brandy which in a short time gave him ease—at 4 o'clk (he having eaten a little rice & had a glass of port wine) We gave him 25 drops Morphia—at ten (he having had about 1 ½ hour sleep) 60 drops—at ½ past 2 this morn^g 25—This plan is to be kept up & Power says "give him a little more each time'—Now <u>this</u> seems to me unnecessary & therefore not good practise? is it? but on the other side perhaps Power fears worse attacks of pain & wishes to prevent them—indeed if his & Travers opinion of the case is true it is the kindest & best thing to do. Power has just left—I will write down the things he said—I

---

95. Written on mourning stationery, probably Wednesday, May 30, since Harriet has not been given the written diagnosis which she received 5 June. L/26.

said—do you call this <u>cancer</u> <u>exactly</u>? he said "I am afraid I must say so, the schirrous stage has passed into the cancerous" &c I said—Is it possible if anything more had been done than has been done in an earlier stage of his complaint that a better result might by even a chance have been hoped for? He said "I think it is impossible that anything could or can do more tha[n] alleviate & for a short time ~~arrest~~ defer the progress of the disease" I said 'Are such cases never cured?' He said 'Never' I said 'do they ever get better & live on for years?' He said Never[.] I mentioned Ld Metcalfe[96]—he said he knew the whole case well, that <u>that</u> was only <u>local</u> cancer, affecting only the <u>skin</u>, & he thought was often eradicated by the knife but that Brodie's prided himself on ~~curing~~ treating cancer without the knife & so he thought had operated too late on L^d M's case & so lost him—but that that sort of cancer & this are of two <u>wholly</u> different kinds ~~that~~ (tho' he himself thinks that cancer even when operated on always breaks out elsewhere sooner or later) but that this is wholly different, not to be got at, has disorganised all the surrounding parts so that if it c^d be cut out it would be useless (This I dont beleive but it has nothing to do with the practical question). That the <u>tumour</u> is not as I hope an external abcess which might relieve the disease but a secondary (something I forget what words he joined to <u>secondary</u>) that this disease is glandular—he used the words ulceration & disorganisation often—This is the result of my conversation this morn^g & I instantly that he is gone set down to tell you <u>exactly</u> his words that you may think what you would do for yourself & <u>also</u> what <u>in the circumstances</u> which are that he is not <u>really</u> aware that he is in <u>any</u> danger—now & then when feeling very ill & low, he says poor dear as he takes my hand 'do you know dear Hary sometimes I think I shall never get over this" but this 'low spirits' as he thinks it is immediately dispelled by me 'oh it will never do to get out of spirits' & the first hour or day he is at ease again he evidently thinks quite the contrary as he said this morn^g that yesterday's pain, he saw now, was not the disease but simply that the Aperient[97] was too strong—(which is in fact next to none) I want to hear from you what you think of all these indications? Have you Salmon's[98] book & can you compare the symptoms & can you compare the symptoms here mentioned

---

96. Charles Theophilus Metcalfe (1785-1846).

97. Laxative.

98. William Salmon (1644-1713) authored a number of important books on medicine, including *A New method of curing the French-pox* [a veneral disease]; *Pharmacopoeia Londinensis: or, the New London Dispensatory; Ars chirurgica: a compendium of the theory and practice of chirurgery in seven books*; and *Latrica, seu, Praxis medendi: the practice of curing, being a medicinal history of many famous observations in the cure of diseases performed by the author.*

with anything he says—I mentioned Salmon to Power who said this book did not describe this case—

Can you lend me Salmon? If so enclose it to me here by Parcels Company—

Whatever I said in the enclosed former note about sending take no notice of I forgot what it was—It feels to me ages since I wrote it—I only send that note as it is ready & says what Travers said—Travers is coming tomorrow—will you think what question I could ask him & let me hear directly?

My idea is now to induce him to see Brodie as what Power said about him is in favor of seeing him—but I want your opinion about this, which is kindest to dispel the really pleasant after all state in which the greater part of his time is passed by alarming him—or sacrifice that for the chance of B's suggesting something—

I put this question to Power who said "It is impossible he can suggest anything but by all means try"

All goes on as it has done for the last three weeks—to my feelings they might be months or year—

I am nearly knocked up & have a really bad cough but the excitement of doing all that is possible for him has kept me up in a sort of fever & I hope will continue to enable me to go on. My whole object now is that he should not have the slightest contrariety but that every moment shall be made as easy as possible, with the most of soothing & pleasurable & the least pain that unceasing attention & affection can give him & in all this I have been able to succeed—The house & every one in it is kept perfectly noiseless so that all day a mouse might be heared from one end to the other of it—& this extreme quiet has succeeded in keeping his nerves quiet, & the Morphia driving away pain as soon as it begins he has on the whole any thing but intolerable days—as is shown by his being in good spirits & talking cheerfully always. For me the consideration that I am able to keep him in this easy comfortable state of nerves & spirits is the only feeling to set against extreme sadness & the constant acute sense of being in an utterly false position—It is now that I feel in this most serious affair of his life the terrible consequences of the different milieu[99] All his relations & he himself have no idea beyond entire submission to whatever happens to you so long as you are in the regular path—Therefore because he has two regular Doctors they all open their eyes in pitying as

99. Harriet is probably referring to the awkwardness of her being in love with JSM while remaining John Taylor's wife.

to his lament at my 'enthusiasm' in wishing for more opinions—& as no one but myself will agree in wishing to see any other it is only I who can occasionally make a <u>little</u> suggestion of the kind. I dare not do more lest I upset the tranquil placid state of nerves he is now in. If I felt <u>much</u>, instead of as I do next to no chance of his seeing Brodie being of use I would run the risk of depressing him by <u>urging</u> it—but it is so out of his & all the people he has to do with notions to do anything <u>strong</u> that I am sure to <u>urge</u> it would if not half kill him yet make all peace of mind go & then there w^d be only pain.

I have now been here three weeks—during this time I think that week by week he is worse, tho from day to day he varies, having now about 3 bad days, consisting of extreme unrest which w^d be pain but for Morphia, which changes the waking pain into long uneasy dozing, varied by occasionally a very deep sleep with convulsive twitchings. Then he wakes after from 12 to 24 hours of this state, unaware of any thing peculiar in his sleep thinking himself much better & that the sleep is a very good sign, & then follow 2 or 3 days of comfort & only occasional short sharp pains. He grows weaker yet sometimes I think he is not weaker—

I have at last got from the dilatory fool Power a written statement of the case I kept it some hours before I could take courage to read it so frightful I dreaded it would be. It does not to an inexperienced person read so bad as I feared. I will copy it & enclose it that you may tell me if it in any degree alters your opinion of the possible good of consulting Brodie.

Also, tell me, if it seems best to show this paper to Brodie in the first place is it possible that he will give any opinion without himself examining? In the 2nd place <u>how</u> had I best show it Brodie? By letter? This does not seem a good plan. By Herbert taking it, & this he wishes to do? but he is quite ignorant of medical language & quite incompetent to <u>judge</u> from signs a man's half expressed thought. To go myself w^d be best, but I cannot be away from him at the only hours I sh^d be likely to find Brodie without him asking where I am. besides I am not strong enough for so nervous an interview except it were at my own house & that ~~I suppose~~ c^d not be ~~as it w^d be~~

However tell me what you think of the statement and also if anything occurs to you.

The being in the midst of such a solemn and terrible fact surrounded entirely by people destitute of all ~~strength~~ ideas will or tolerance but for strict commonplace makes me feel like a caged lion sometimes when I feel that I cannot do more for him. They are all however perfectly kind & considerate only they take it as a matter of course that what the Doctors say is & must be all & <u>look</u> <u>so</u> <u>coolly</u> <u>to</u> <u>the</u> <u>result</u>.

I have thus you see given you my only confident & comfort a sketch of

357 @ TO JOHN STUART MILL

all that I am in the midst of but it is written so hastily & I am so constantly weary in body & spirits that you will not be surprised at its incompleteness. I should like to have the book Walshe[100] you mention if you can send it by Parcels Company.

Will you be so kind as to get us those old pills from Godfreys or send me the prescription for I have it not. I will send Haji to you to ask for them on Thursday.

Statement of Case
a scirrhous Tumour forming a hard ridge across the posterior surface of the rectum, about three inches above the sphincter—an ulcer on the upper edge of the ridge, extending above & behind it about the size of a Crown piece. The tumour and ulceration was first detected in the beginning of Octobe[r] 1848. The usual symptoms are nearly all present, and well marked.

June 1849[101]

When I first sent[102] your letter I agreed with you that that statement of Powers was a meagre one & that more ought to be done or attempted. But I suppose you have not looked at that book you sent me? Walshe appears to me to agree precisely with those mens idea of the case he gives but a short chapter to the particular form of the disease which these men say this is for the terrible reason that he dismisses this form of it as hopeless. They call it malignant scirrhus—& say it is absolutely incurable They say scirrhus remains simultaneously with the ulceration not that it is an earlier stage, but that the one extends afresh in one part as it changes into ulceration at another that the secondary tumour is only a sign that the diseased flesh has spread to those glands & that no relief is to be expected from that tumour. up to Friday, tho daily worse he had not suffered unbearably—but since then it is beginning to be not only constant suffering but this interspersed often & oftener each 12 hours with agony. how this is to be borne I know not, for the strength tho utterly exhausted several times a day yet hopes[103] again at each temporary diminution only to be again tortured horribly. To say the spirits which heretofore were so good have quite sunk.

I have taken half an hour to write this being the first thing I have done of any kind for a week except wait upon him

---

100. W. H. Walshe (1812-92), a Paris-trained doctor who practiced in London.

101. Written during the third week of her nursing John Taylor, probably 5 June 1849. L/19.

102. "Saw" is written above "sent" and neither is crossed out.

103. The word "arises?" is written over hopes, but neither is marked through.

Do not write anything which it would be disagreable to lose. please to put w/ correspondance on your notes that I may see I have them all—~~the~~

Adieu now—I hope you are well—though this you said pretty well—I w^d write a word often but I know you like nothing but <u>long</u> letters when I cannot now give you[104]

Monday[105]

I should be anxious about your health dearest if I felt time to be anxious or to think of anything but to try to relieve him—which thank (I was going to say <u>God</u> but can not use that form so repugnant more than ever to my present feelings) We do manage to keep him as yet tolerably easy except yesterday—This morn^g there was to have been the usual surgical examination by Travers—He passed a very good night after that dreadful day & was almost comfortable this morn^g. When Power came I described the tremendous pain he was seized with yesterday on trying to put his coat on to get up about 2 o'clk. Power looked grave at the account & when Tra^s came they went up & came down instantly saying that a large swelling had made its appearance (Power said it was what he had been fearing and endeavouring to avert the breaking of some membrane) and so they c^d make no examination, but the tumour is to be kept fomented & poultriced 'till Wednesday morn^g when Travers is to come again. from all this I fear worse suffering may come. To-day however he is easier & has a little revived again. I see Walshe thinks very badly of the sort of case, but even in the worst cases, he appears to <u>try</u> some curative measures. both these men say that <u>any</u> medicine is impossible or w^d only add to the suffering. They <u>seem</u> to understand what they are about judging by the <u>decision</u> of their manner & speech. It is extraordinary the hard work both I & L[ily] have gone through & still take each day but I have lost almost all count of the days & know not when it is the beginning or end of a week—the whole time passed in soothing the pain by words of sympathy or diverting it by inventing talk or actively engaged in all the incessant operation for releif. He is most patient & firm & endures with the utmost strength & courage—but <u>why</u> sh^d he have these torments to endure! what good to any body is <u>all</u> this—He never hurt or harmed a creature on earth. If they want the life why cant they take it—what useless torture is all this! & he is so sorry & hurt to give so much labour to me—he feels that I am the greatest good to him & the feeling that no servant

---

104. Probably written 7 June 1849, since Harriet had received the book she requested from John in letter L/19. L/21.

105. Probably written Monday, June 11, since by the next Monday Harriet was quite angry with John (see 28/241). L/16.

could do what I do for him enables me to keep up. He said 2 days since 'well if I ever do recover it will be entirely owing to you' How cruel to feel that his chance is so slight—alas I feel as if he besides you is the only life I value in this wretched world. He is so thoroughly true direct honest strong & with all the realities of nice feelings, as I constantly see now. What a contrast is such a man to the vapid sentimental egotists Stirling, Carlyle[106] &c who let inflated conceit of their own assumed superiority run away with all true strength & humility.

[sidways on margin, page 1]
this great pleasure comfort is quiet & the house is kept so still with all doors & windows open that it is all day as if uninhabited except for knocks of people enquiring

[across the margin, p. 4]
I knew you were not heartless—& your letter & sympathy is a great comfort but I feel & know all the time that I have it all

[across the margin, p. 6]
I had written to you before but the note did not go so I have written again. I will soon write again to say how he goes on.

As to Holyoake,[107] I think your note should certainly have omitted from it the sentence I have put my pencil through—and I doubt whether it w^d not be best to also omit the second part of the first paragraph—I think that second part good but the whole note is bold & cold & rough if not insolent he or any body will think it so. The note would do with only the first 3 & last 14 lines—I sh^d have liked a better note sent containing the same sense, but said without hardness but as this cannot be I think it had best go in on[e] of the two ways I mention as to the sum I have not the least idea what you intend or intended when you told me 3 wks ago that you were disposed to subscribe but as to that part of the subject you are by far the best & only judge.

If Mrs King[108] wants money I sh^d think you had best tell your mother

---

106. John Sterling (1806-44); Thomas Carlyle (1795-1881).

107. George Jacob Holyoake (1817-1905). Probably written during the second week in June 1849, since Harriet refers to a letter about giving Holyoake money three weeks prior. A letter (L/12) refering to the request for money is dated 22 May 1849. L/17.

108. Wilhelmina Mill King, John's eldest sister (1808-61).

that you should like to send her 25 towards her present expenses & so let them mention it to her

You talk of my writing to you "at some odd time when a change of subject of thought may be rather a relief than otherwise"! odd time! indeed you must be ignorant profoundly of all that <u>friendship</u> or <u>anxiety</u> means when you can use such pitiful narrow hearted expressions. The sentence appears to have come from the pen of one of the Miss Taylors. It is the puerility of thought & feeling of any utterly headless & heartless pattern of propriety old maid.

As to "odd time" I <u>told</u> you that I have not a moment unfilled by things to be done when not actually standing by the bedside or supporting the invalid—& as to "change of subject of thought a relief"! Good God sh^d you think it a relief to think of somebody else some acquaintance or what not while <u>I</u> was dying? If so—but I will say no more about this—only after such a mode of feeling on your part I feel it sacrilegious to enter into any account of what I feel & suffer in this most dreadful & most melancholy & most piteous case—my heart is wrung with indignation & grief

Kent Terrace
June 19[109]

For ten days of the most horrible sufferings I have scarcely left his room nor seen any one of the many anxious enquiries about his dreadful state except for a few moments his sisters—

On Sunday I went down to you, sat down, stayed some time, & finally left the room in irrepressible indignation for you did <u>not once</u> during all the time you saw me ask how he was nor mention his name in any way! This fact and the feelings necessarily caused by it I can never forget as long as I live.

In answer to your note—he now suffers comparatively little but lies in almost a hopeless state. If I am to lose him I shall lose the best & most dearly loved friend, and one of the most upright generous true and good men that ever lived.

H. T.

Friday[110]
I feel now at some moments some gleams of hope that either these men

---

109. The content of the letter indicates the year as 1849, the year of John Taylor's death. XXVIII/241.

110. Letter postmarked 22 June 1849. L/23.

may have been in some degree mistaken, or that it may be an exceptional case. To this later supposition they however continue to shake their heads. It is certain that their opinion of the <u>state</u> of the case at the end of last week & the beginning of this has not been realised.

The great change from that atrocious suffering to all but complete freedom from pain took place last Friday—Then they talked of sloughing and said effusion had taken place into the cavity of the abdomen & Travers took leave on Sat^y as if he thought he should not be wanted again—since then he has been each day better in all respect—while yesterday & to-day both strength & ability to eat seem returning He has been up to have the bed made (the first time for 13 days) been shaved & reads the papers with interest. Certainly they had no idea of the possibility of such a resurrection some days ago. Is it <u>likely</u> they have made any mistake?

We still continue to sit up all night & never to leave him a moment which I mention to account to you for my not writing—Tho' the terrible anxiety & passion of pity which I feeling at every moment before is in some degree less active the various requirements of severe illness & total helplessness continue, & as we do <u>every thing</u> for him ourselves, he having over & over again expressed even in his worst moment to the medical men the great comfort & consolation it is to him to be served so perfectly & by his own family only we still choose to keep it up & this you may suppose implies great fatigue & unceasing petits soins[111] I am scarcely ever away from his room except when I am so tired that I go for a short time for change & <u>then</u> I can hardly get my thoughts together or take the labour of writing. But I think you will not doubt the comfort the thought of your sympathy is to me altho I do not attempt to write it. The fact is in a great crisis the feeling of its actual living existence & truth is too complete & ever present a consolation for it not to feel even unnatural to <u>be required</u> to write it.

In haste—always the same.

Monday[112]

He continues easy and to all appearance better—but on my saying this these men shake their heads. Power explains to me to-day that he expected last Sat^y week that the ulceration would break into the cavity of the peritoneum (at the time he said it <u>had</u> done so) but that it having broken outwardly the whole state has been temporarily relieved by the discharge—which he calls

---

111. To fuss over or to wait hand and foot on.

112. Probably written Monday, June 25, since John Taylor appeared to have been in less pain during the previous week (see L/23). L/22.

sloughing—& that the part ulcerated is now looking in their medical language "clean & healthy"—Yet for all this neither he nor Travers will allow
that there is hope, except indeed when I say but there is no limit to the efforts
nature sometimes makes—They reply in a way which is equivalent to saying
'no doubt there <u>are</u> miracles & for this disease to cease or even for any length
of time to cease to run its usual course would be one'—But then Power adds,
as tho' there could be any comfort in that that by continuing every means
by keeping up nourishment & morphia there is no saying how long life may
be supported—This he says with a sort of self-gratulatory esprit de corps as
a medicine man. as tho' the 'patient' was interesting as the means of their
cleverness. I like Power however as a medecin[113] better than at first—he is
really anxious zealous & in his business capable. But what a melancholy
prospect is this! And I have to try to keep up his spirits by hopes of this
improvement leading to better & better! It again seems strange to me that
no medicines are tried in this interval—Both these men scout the idea of
doing any thing but "palliating" It appears like a far worse form of consumption—He lies here too weak to move even to take food, yet with the mind
quite intact & all the senses too—growing the more weary the better he gets
& for all I can make out they contemplate his lying thus for as they say "an
indefinite period" It is strange to me that he himself does not wish for more
opinions—But I scarcely can think it right or best to harass him on the
subject while these people's opinion is so entirely decided—Then again when
I feel that their opinion is a condemnation it fevers me to 'let alone'.[114]

Thursday[115]

I had said nothing more about those letters lately because I understood
from your note a fortnight ago that it was all decided, that you meant to
leave out all mention of yourself in them & also to withdraw all letters
addressed to you. I supposed that this had been done & that the thing was

---

113. French "médicine," doctor.

114. The rest of the page has been scribbled out completely.

115. L/27. There are three extant letters concerning publication of the correspondence of John
Stuart Mill and John Sterling (L/25, L/27 and L/29). L/25 is the only dated letter. It is
postmarked Saturday, June 30. L/29 is clearly written close to John Taylor's death (on July
18) and was probably written on July 8. The dating of this letter is the least certain. The letter
refers to correspondence concerning Sterling's letters a fortnight ago. If the June 30 letter was
the first on the subject, the L/25 was written on July 12 and is the last in the series. But
emotionally that doesn't fit the other content of the letter in which Harriet is still debating
the advisability of seeking further consultation from doctors. By July 12 it was obvious to
everyone that John Taylor was about to die. So, I place the letter on June 28 and assume she
is referring to correspondence about Sterling that has not been preserved.

settled. I am quite sure that it ought to be done both in justice & honour and as to the difficulty you find in doing it, that does not seem to me great even if, what is not the case, your usual ways were exactly like those of ordinary people. In a matter of taste & one wholly concerning yourself that you should change your mind is certainly not fatally odd. I heard that you called yesterday—do not call again for some time—not for a week.

With what is said in that book of Walshes fresh in my recollection I do not agree with you in thinking these people to have been mistaken, or that it is more like ordinary abcess. Walshes insists often on the fact that it is a chronic disease, and from the first Travers said to me that tho' the cure was absolutely hopeless yet there was no saying how long life might be prolonged by good management. This he said the first day I saw him—I entirely agree with you in the wretchedness & melancholy of the state of having ones life staved up as it were by the clever management of these people, for a few weeks or months of suffering & only at last to end fatally—but like the sort of people they have very little sympathy in this feeling, being, as Power is, always occupied in congratulating himself & me on the success of some nice adaption of a happily timed dose, or mechanical operation, or lotion or gargle, or ingenious mode of getting him to swallow. Then rubbing his hands with satisfaction as he says "There now that has succeeded & I do think we shall get a good night" He comes twice each day & Travers every other day—When through all these contrivances to keep life going I say "but the result Dr Power do you think him better or that this will make him better eventually? To this he always replies 'There is no man of character in London who will tell you that this is ever other than a fatal disease, but we may keep him up & hope shall be enabled to do so for a long while." Meanwhile he is weaker every day & about every third or fourth day seems to take a step worse, generally, tho' it is difficult to define in what the deterioration consists. Does it not appear that they must be right both as to its character & in their treatment when in spite of all that can be done to sustain he always gets weaker? They say any medicines would disagree with the stomach & increase suffering. Power says Brodie's sole means of acting for cancer is cautery. This I dont beleive & therefore think he does not know Brodies mode. I think he cannot have been cauterising Lord Metcalf's[116] face all the three years he according to Power's account kept him alive—Power never fails to add "but you see with all his professed treating cancer without the knife he only kept him alive three years" and then he says that cutaneous cancer is next thing to another disease to this which they call malignant

116. Charles Theophilus Metcalfe (1785-1846). His treatment for cancer was also mentioned in L/26.

scirhus Then it appears to me that Walshes account of the symptoms agree altogether with this & Walshe does not profess to think the disease curable.

I am wretched when I sometimes think there might have been the least chance of a cure by other men if it had been attempted earlier. But more often I beleive in the dreadful truth of their account of it. It is so dreadful to feel sure as I do that at some not distant time some specific for it will be discovered. But <u>now</u> it seems to me out of the question seeing any other surgeon. First because it seems entirely impossible that Travers who has written on the subject & is one of Walshes often quoted authorities can be so utterly & blamably mistaken as it would be to declare that any mistake as to the nature or treatment of the case is impossible. Then if at a former time it might have been of some use or satisfaction to see another[.] do you think it could be so now when he seems almost at the last stage of weakness & when to ask his consent would be quite to[o] much for his nerves which can bear only the most gentle something? The mere question would flush the poor wan face scarlet. And do you think that in this stage any medecines could do good?

I think the words which I have put the pencil through are better omitted—but they might with a little alteration be placed at the end?

The <u>reason</u> I should give to Capt S.^117 if a reason is asked, is that the way in which you are mentioned in the letters is calculated to give an errone[o]us impression of you This is the simple truth. The words I have added at the end do not go quite right but you will make them do so. It is ~~in fact~~ if possible ~~even more~~ as desirable to get those passages omitted than your own letters. Therefore something of the kind (like the words I have added) should be said.

I am in such haste that I cannot stay to choose words but you will see what I mean I suppose. Please not to call again till I ask you. Yesterday & the day before he was worse—To day seems better. I much fear that I shall knock up[.] I am so exhausted—but I shall do the very utmost not to.^118

in haste

This disease seems to combine the evils of consumption with those of acute distress—all the pains of exhaustion by slow wasting away with terrible local

---

117. Anthony Sterling (1805–71), John Sterling's brother, had requested that he be permitted to include John's letters to John Sterling in a collection of letters he was preparing after his brother's death.

118. Postmarked 30 June 1849. L/25.

characteristics of its own. So terrible & frightful is this disease that it is something to be glad of that he remains free from pain—only those who have watched with the deep sympathy of true affection & pity can fully estimate the infinite distinction there is between freedom from pain & freedom from suffering. I am sure almost any pain is less bad (tho' not perhaps less <u>hard</u>) to bear than this which he poor poor dear calls so truly dying by inches.

However he has hours of comparative pleasure now—& himself & those who dont hear the medical opinions seem to flatter themselves he may be going on well—but they say that tho' it is a wonderfully easy case of the kind, that others suffer so very much more than he (the truth of which is that no one I sh^d think was ever so well nursed) Yet that the result will be the same. For me after two days of feeling ill & knocked up I have now recovered again. I am now feeling scarcely tired. The certainty of being really of the greatest use & quite indispensable to him (or to any one) gives me a quantity of strength & life—so that I feel sure how my health will not suffer—unless indeed the disease is contagious which I dare say it is not—if it were we three who do all for him w^d be sure of it. However never mention this idea to them.

His sisters who come to see him & others say no one w^d think there was illness in his room it is so fresh & gay—& this freshness & cheerfulness I am sure have much to do with his ease & comfort & almost complete freedom from nervous depression. Neither window nor door have been shut either night or day for a month, & the sight & scent of fresh flowers & christal iced water & all sorts of nice looking things beguile him into a feeling of pleasure & cheat the low spirits.

So all this incessant attention & effort to keep up his spirits, & also the long time it now is since I heared the dreadful truth, has combined to sink the deep grief & indignation I feel below the surface—but I have so much to say to you which no one but you could understand.

What a duping is life & what fools are men who seem bent upon playing into the hands of the mischievous demons! One comfort & hope lies in the fact that the worst they suffer is from their own bad qualities—but the good suffer with the bad.

I shall write a few words every few days—Perhaps you will enclose George's letter for H[119] to me. Tell me how you are? Take care of yourself for the worlds sake.

I cannot think how you can have been silent all this while about the Roman <u>heroism</u>—never equalled—& the French utter baseness. I have

---

119. Haji, Algernon Taylor.

been longing to write myself[.] The only person who seems to feel it as strongly as I do is Landor[120] & he seems half mad.[121]

Since last Sunday in time it seems a moment but in feeling a life. I have wished to write to you but have never had a moment not either fearfully occupied or too worn out bodily & too sad to write. On Sunday last the fearful agony of this poor poor patient martyr commenced. He <u>tried</u> for the last time to get up from the bed and oh the piteous spectacle to see the poor wasted limbs & haggard pain-worn face after an hour of miserable suffering in slowly achieving the getting on of the clothes as he then at last fell face forward on the bed with a sharp cutting agony & so had to lie half an hour before he could endure to be touched sufficiently to get into the bed again—From that time till Mid day yesterday his suffering has been more such as one hears of the tortures inflicted by demons than anything else. Often I have thought, what would crucifixtion be compared to this—<u>mercy</u>—his patience firmness & courage are & have been infinite. He has never uttered a complaint of the slightest kind. Three days & most of the nights he lay with the mouth wide open & eyes turned up or rolling round as if asking for some mercy & all that time paroxysms, as he said, 'the tortures of the damned' coming on about each two hours. Yesterday morn^g I thought & he thought he was at the last gasp—he took my hand & that of Haji & Lily to say the most affecting adieu—I kept up my countenance & tried to cheer him & succeeded at once, as every thing I do or say he agrees to—in half an hour from that time the pain had entirely left him—so that his cheerful sanguine spirit all rose again & he said 'ah if I ever recover how can I ever thank you' & all the rest of the day Thank God (the good one who must abhor this wicked work of the demons as much as I do) he was absolutely free from all pain only wanting the parched lips often moistened & he dropt off into sleeps which lasted about an hour each & at each waking he said with a fullness of meaning & depth of comfort which is indescribably "I am in heaven"— Power came & said it was that <u>sloughing</u> had commenced. The same ease lasted thro' the night & to-day too it is peace compared with that raging storm of the infernal deities & battle between life & death of those four days but alas alas the powers of death are to conquer—he is growing heated & restless & the remains of power to resist seem gradually fading

---

120. Walter Savage Landor (1775-1864).

121. Postmarked 6 July 1849. L/28.

away. And this is the beautiful order of nature! Such order as demons &
tyrant make . . . ever kind to him & about you.[122]

Sunday Eveng

He has again had an easy day—of course the term <u>easy</u> is comparative—on Friday & part of yesterday it was <u>absolute</u> ease, by the sensation
of relief from what had gone before. Pain itself has ceased but extreme
weakness more than equals all ordinary pains. To-day too the spirits have
somewhat sunk. Now there seems a gradual fading away. My heart &
feelings have been so wrung & for so long a time now that acute sorrow
comes only at intervals, it is deadened too by bodily fatigue—but the
deepest & truest grief pity & indignation at the fate of one of the best &
truest & kindest & most upright natures that ever lived will remain with
me as long as I live.

I have had but a few moments in which to look at those extracts from
S's letters. I cannot at all <u>understand,</u> & I mean this wholly <u>sincerely</u> and
not at all ironically, how you could ever see with complacency or even
with indifference such a quantity of misapprehension of your character to
be published. I know that you place great vanity in not being vain but
with me love of truth as well as vanity w^d make repugnant to me the
myself giving to the world an appreciation of me made by an <u>evident</u>
inferior who makes it with all the air of judging from a height which is
conceivable. a second thing which hurts me intensely tho' it does not
surprise me is your perfect readiness to put your own hand & seal to the
mention of your name & character soi-disant[123] appreciatingly by a man
who you perceive was weak & foolish enough to be in agreement with his
correspondent in <u>judging</u> yr relations with some unknown woman in
unknown circumstances. Of course the old bugbear words 'married woman' were at the bottom of this unanimity of fear & sorrow which these
men honoured (or disgraced selon moi[124]) you with. Nowadays I sh^d have
thought that with our opinion we must thoroughly despise men who have
not got out of that baby morality & intellect. That you c^d be willing to
have these things printed hurts me more deeply than any thing else I think
c^d do. It has disturbed my mind & feelings even amidst these trying days
& nights. but if you have engaged yourself about them I suppose some of
them must stand.[125]

---

122. The edge of the page on which HTM continues this sentence was glued over when the
letter was placed in the library volume.

123. Supposedly or ostensibly.

124. "In my opinion."

125. Probably written 8 July, since it was written on a Sunday evening near John Taylor's

Will you send any Mags or Revs you have, for him—if you have any that is.

He has got, for July, the New Monthly & the Quarterly—

Especially I want the Edinburgh[126] at the earliest possible.

Don't call again.

You have no notion what a mistake you make in saying that it could be no more contagious than a fractured skull—Any one who saw & watched this & thought so must have already got a fractured skull. I have very little doubt that this is as often contagious as Typhus or plague—It seems very like the latter—probably all are contagious in circumstances—& to persons predisposing or predisposed. However I cannot now give my reasons for this opinion.

I have so very much to say which must wait.

What an iron despotism we live under, & who can wonder that men are bad while they take the government of this world for their model. I am glad to hear that the timid upper classes think the Romans fine—if indeed they do so—but Grote always paints his fine acquaintance couleur de rose.[127]

That they dislike & condemn the French proceedings I have no doubt.

Tocqueville is a notable specimen of the class which includes all such people as the Stirlings Romillys Carlyles Austins[128]—the gentility class—weak in moral narrow in intellect timid, infinitely conceited, & gossiping. There are very few men in this country who can seem other than more or less respectable puppets to us.[129]

The enclosed paper marked A[130] I wrote one Sunday some weeks ago but did not send it feeling that I had so ill expressed the fullness of my meaning. However another case which I will enclose gives so admirable an occasion for an article in the Daily News on the subject—against legalising corporal punishment anywhere public or private—that I think it ought to be written.

Mark this case—how there was no pretence of brutality or violence in the offence that it sh^d be punished by brutal degradation (you sh^d take

death on 18 July. L/29.

126. *Edinburgh Review.*

127. George Grote. "Couleur de rose": Rosy colored.

128. Alexis de Tocqueville (1805-59); probably Anthony and John Sterling; Sir John Romilly; Thomas and Jane Carlyle; and John and Sarah Austin.

129. Postmarked 9 July 1849. L/30.

130. During this period Harriet and John were collaborating on newspaper articles on domestic violence. See chapter 4, 77-100 above.

care to copy in the report the words <u>middleaged</u> man for tho' it adds nothing to <u>our</u> feeling it strengthens the case as against the magistrates immensely with the commonalty). Then <u>do</u> hit police magistrates in general & Secker in particular as hard as possible—all the ~~rest of~~[131] the subject you will at once see as strongly & clearly as I.

How the most brutal attacks of personal violence are sentenced to <u>imprisonment</u> only—how you never see a case of that kind met by personal violence i.e. by corporal punishment—how bad & disgusting as corporal punishment is ever—if used it ought to be only for personal violence.

Sunday Even^g.

A

My eye fell just now on the Examiner as it lay open with an account of the trial of the young man who shot at the Queen.

I see it said that the newly revived barbarous & degrading punishment of flogging which ever since the offence the Newspapers, especially the Examiner, have been gloating over with disgusting toadying satisfaction is said to have been omitted by especial desire of the Queen—now whether this is so or not w^d it not be an excellent opportunity to treat the statement as true: to compliment her ~~or any body~~ for refusing so unworthy & disgusting a tribute as the revival of a brutal degradation as punishment for offences against her. Pointing out that the offence was not of a Degraded or brutal kind but of a wicked & grave kind, and that flogging is no more fit for it than it w^d be for murder. Admiring too the <u>unsovereignlike</u> magnanimity of punishing such a serious offence only as if it had been directed against the meanest subject. In fact the punishment is not severe enough.[132]

Monday.[133]

I have exceedingly wanted to write about many things, but cannot find a moment.

Yesterday & to-day this sad sad tragedy seems drawing to a close in the most piteous yet most patient & calm way.

Alas poor thing what a mocking has life been to him! ending by this fierce contest in which death gains inch by inch!

The sadness & the horror of Nature's daily doings exceed a million fold

---

131. The phrase "~~rest of~~" may be "<u>rest of</u>," but her underlining in the remainder of the letter seems to indicate a strike-out instead of underlining.

132. A sentence is lost here because it was glued over when the letter was placed in the library volume. Postmarked 10 July [1849]. L/31.

133. Probably written on Monday, 16 July 1849, the Monday closest to John's death on Wednesday, 18 July. L/32.

all the attempts of Poets! There is nothing on earth I would not do for
him & there is nothing in earth which <u>can</u> be done
    do not write[134]

I cannot express how deeply and sadly I have felt through all this, & while
this dear good creature places all his hope & all his reliance on me, how
wretched it is to have quite different modes of seeing & feeling & taking
life & mankind. If my way had been his all the advice & opinions of medical
people who could have given the least chance would have been tried—
    And what a cheat is life! With a fatal painful hopeless tragedy at all
moments hanging over the head of every creature & sure to descend at
last—And what weak selfish fools are men that instead of all joining heart
& hand to oppose the common enemies chance & death they call it religion
to praise it all, punish suicide, & pray to be delivered from sudden death!
Tell me if, at almost the last as it now appears (it <u>may</u> not be so but I fear
alas it is) you should still think it desirable to see any other man?[135]

You will describe the impression of my dear John's countenance & state
when you call it sweet & happy—& this is the only consolation I feel for
all his suffering & his most untimely death. To the last he had the same
~~happy~~ affectionate manner & cheerful tone of voice & what I had so much
feared—pain at the end—he was altogether ~~spared~~ without. He spoke half
an hour before the last moment in his unusal gentle affectionate way & at
the last there was not the slightest[136] suffering of any kind. ~~I am constantly
obliged to dwell upon this~~
he was sleeping, when for half an hour I perceived that the breathing was
rather quicker than usual.[137]

Wednesday.[138]
    I cannot write much now not on account of the sorrow & distress for
that has been as great for weeks—but I find I am quite physically exhausted
& faint after two nights & a day of most anxious and sad watching ended

---

134. This last sentence is scribbled on the back of the page.

135. Probably written 17 July 1849, the day before John Taylor's death. L/33.

136. HTM has written "no" above "slightest."

137. Written in 1849, after John Taylor's death. This note is not addressed and may have
been a draft of a letter either to JSM or her brother Arthur. See her description of John Taylor's
death in XXVII/45 in the next chapter. XXVIII/126.

138. Postmarked 18 July [1849]. L/34.

by his gently breathing the last without a sigh or pang at 3oclk this morning.—I must defer saying anything till this next week has passed—To me a very painful one—feeling has to remain in abeyance while the many absolutely necessary mechanical details are ordered & attended to all by me who never saw anything of the kind before & having no person <u>whatever</u> but the three children to advise with it is the most trying time.

I do not know <u>where</u> he should be laid—having no connection with any place—I have thought of either Kensal Green or Hampstead as not too far? Tell me what you think! Write to me ~~under cover~~ enclosed to Herbert at Cross Street.

There is a person here who is medisance personified & just now I w^d not have a shadow of {t}he kind—so for a few days write to me only thus.

Thursday.[139]

I want your opinion which is right & best—about coming to the funeral next Wednesday. I have no doubt your first impulse is like mine, to say, <u>of course</u>, yes—The grounds of all I wish done at this time are twofold— what the world thinks most respectful to him, & what he would have wished. But the latter <u>in this case</u> is I think pretty much included in the former, which is the reason I think at all of the former. I wish every thing done which can be honourable & respectful to him being the last testimony of of [*sic*] the affection I felt & feel for him & of the true & strong respect he has added too so much during this illness—& in all this I know you most truly sympathise. My <u>first</u> impression about your coming was a feeling of 'better not' grounded on the sort of distance which of late existed. But now on much consideration it seems to me in the first place that coming is certainly thought a mark of respect? Is it not? and that therefore your not doing so will be a <u>manque</u>[140] of that. Then again the public in some degree & <u>his</u> public too have heared or are sure to hear (through Arthur[141] if no other way) of the Dedication—of our intimacy— & on the side of his relations, nor that I know of on mine, there does not appear to be any medisance. (Indeed the kindness & attention to me of all his relations is as marked as the neglect of these by mine.)

Thus all who know or care to hear anything on the subject must hear

139. Probably written on July 19, based on the reference to Thursday and the context of the week of John Taylor's death. L/36.

140. Lack.

141. Arthur Hardy, Harriet's brother, had received one of the copies of *Principles of Political Economy* containing the dedication to Harriet.

of great intimacy[.] does not therefore <u>absence</u> seem much more noticeable than coming? On the other side nothing is more true of common world than 'out of sight out of mind' & the thought about it may never occur to any one as they are principally relations or daily associates who will come. I fancy Herbert has like him a sort of Ostrich instinct, like morally timid people, always <u>not</u> <u>to</u> <u>do</u>—while my instinct is always to <u>do</u>.

Tell me by a note addressed here what you think or feel about this.

My first impulse was against—my present is <u>for</u>—but the reasons are so nearly balanced that an opinion of yours would turn the scale.

Write soon—I will write again too—soon—I have decided for Kensal Green. Tell me if there is <u>choice</u> as to situation there? I mean as to <u>niceness</u>, I know we can <u>choose</u>.

Do you know Gilbert Elliot? The clergyman? Is he not incumbent somewhere near here? At Kensal Green I beleive one has to find ones own clergyman? Do you know? And w^d it be a suitable thing to ask him?

Every detail without exception I have to order as there is no one here but the three children. Herbert does the speaking to the people. [He]¹⁴² is gone to business to-day. I thought the inserting it so soon in the Papers very ugly & unpleasant but Herbert so insisted upon it on account of his having to reply to so many enquiries, that I gave way—which I repent. Tell me if it <u>struck</u> you as indecent haste?¹⁴³

Sunday¹⁴⁴

I fear you will have been dissapointed at not hearing from me yesterday. I was not well & very much over done—untill it was too late to write.

I feel uneasy at not being sure of being right about your coming on Wednesday. The consideration which determined me, so far as it is deter-mined against, (it can still be if we think it best) was the remark you made that no one w^d notice your absence—This is certainly true, for few if any who will be there have probably heared of you in any way to make them either expect to see you or the contrary. There are now asked only the few relations & two or three others, each for a special reason.

---

142. The paper is torn at the spot, but "He" seems to fit the remaining handwriting and the context.

143. Postmarked "pm 19 July 1849." L/35.

144. Postmarked Monday, 23 July 1849, written the previous Sunday, 22 July. L/37.

Do you know if it is considered de rigeur[145] to ask <u>both</u> the medical men? I have to judge for myself of every thing. There is not & has not been a person in the house but Haji & Lily. The old Uncle called to-day but I excused myself from seeing him. If you come I should have <u>Cooper</u> asked because he has taken much interest & wishes to come as do several other of his friends, but to whom Herbert has said that the invited are to be only relations or near connexions, I think it best to have none but such if you do not come, as thus you are only excluded with other friends who wish to come.

I was so anxious to have a good situation at Kensal Green that I got up very early on Friday & went & chose a place—It was raining fast so that I did not perhaps see all there was to see but that I chose seemed to me the best situation where all things considered—but it does not as you say command a road. It has however a nice view & is I think as pretty as any part of Pere La Chaise.[146] I got my feet very wet & took a rather bad cold which has made me feel ill, combined with sadness & something of anxiety to have every thing done well. However nothing can possibly be better managed than every thing is by the very sensible man to whom by a fortunate thought I sent—so that there is nothing to be done but that which is absolutely inseparable from being the only directing person.

Of feeling & thoughts there is far too much to be said in a note—I must see you soon—it occurs to me that it might be well to go down to Walton to spend next Sunday & that in that case you might come down for the Sunday. As there is no one there but old Mrs Delarne it w^d not do for any one to sleep there but me & Lily as she is too old to do anything— but even a day would be much after such an interval.

14 and 15 February[147]
I do not think you at all fidgetty about your illness dear, and I never should think you too much so. I never feel objections to any thing you do but when I think it tends to increase an ailment. I think (you may be sure) that you were quite right to go to C.[lark][148] about that bleeding, but I cannot help believing that the practise of looking at the expectoration in the morning, is itself in a great measure the cause of there being any

---

145. Proper act.

146. Père Lachaise is a famous old cemetery in Paris.

147. This letter was written in 1854; Harriet refers to a newspaper article from the same month of that year. L(ii)/40.

148. James Clark (1788-1870), John's doctor; see *CW*: XIV, 160, for the complaint that prompted Harriet's reply.

expectoration at all. I cannot but think that if you tried as earnestly as I have done since Octr to avoid <u>any</u> expectoration that you could lose the habit altogether. as I have done. I am far more anxious about your health than about my own, and the more because I do not think a continental life would suit you. You would soon miss the stimulus and excitement of the daily intercourse with other men to which you are accustomed. However you must be the only judge on that subject & you are not likely to have to decide it at present at least. I hope you have not taken severe cold again—here after a cold east wind last Friday and Sat, on Monday the bright sky suddenly darkened and a snow storm more violent than we have them in England covered the whole town & country with deep snow in about an hour. Last night it froze hard & they express great fear for the olives. To-day the sun has melted the snow, tho' not in shady places, and it continues very cold. I do not feel at all worse for the cold, but it is true it has not lasted long as yet. They say here that March is a cold windy month. After the bad days I had last week, I have been something better again, as I see I always am after an unusually bad week.

About the Essays dear[,] would not Religion[,] the Utility of Religion[,] be one of the subjects you would have most to say on.[149] There is to account for the existence nearly universal of some religion (superstition) by the instincts of fear hope & mystery &c and throwing over all doctrines & theories, called religions, as devices for power, to show how religion & poetry fill the same want, the craving after higher objects, the consolation of suffering, the hope of heaven for the selfish, love of God for the tender and grateful—how all this must be superseded by morality deriving its power from sympathies & benevolence & its rewards from the approbation of those we respect.

---

149. In a letter of 7 February 1854 (*CW*: XIV, 152), John had written: "I am quite puzzled what to attempt next—I will just copy the list of subjects we made out in the confused order in which we put them down. Differences of character (nation, race, age, sex, temperament). Love. Education of tastes. Religion de l'Avenir. Plato. Slander. Foundation of morals. Utility of religion. Socialism. Liberty. Doctrine that causation is will. To these I have now added from your letter: Family, & Conventional. It will be a tolerable two years work to finish all that? Perhaps the first of them is the one I could do most to by myself, at least of those equally important."

I will paraphrase Packe's (368-69) list of the contributions in the respective topics:
The utility of religion: *Three Essays on Religion*, 1874
Liberty and convention: *On Liberty*, 1859
Socialism: *Chapters on Socialism*, unfinished
Causation is will: *Examination of Sir Wm. Hamilton's Philosophy*, 1865
Religion of money: *Auguste Comte and Positivism*, 1865; *Utilitariansim*, 1861
Foundation of morals, education of tastes: *Utilitarianism*, 1861
National differences of character: *Representative Government*, 1861
Plato: Article "Plato," *Edinburgh Review*, April 1866
Family: *Subjection of Women*, 1869; *On Liberty*, 1859

There[,] what a long winded sentance, which you would say ten times as well in words half the length. I feel sure dear that the Life[150] is not half written & that half that is written will not do. Should there not be a summary of <u>our</u> relationship from its commencement in 1830—I mean given in a dozen lines—so as to preclude other and different versions of our lives at Kes[n] and Wal[n151]—our summer excursions &c This ought to be done in its genuine truth and simplicity—strong affection, intimacy of friendship, & no impropriety: It seems to me an edifying picture for those poor wretches who cannot conceive friendship but in sex—nor beleive that expediency and the consideration for feelings of others can conquer sensuality. But of course this is not my reason for wishing it done. It is that every ground should be occupied by ourselves on our own subject.

I thought so exactly as you did about that trash in the Ex[r] about the Russell letters[152]—she was an amiable woman as there are [hardly?] a good deal spoilt, hardened by puritanism[,] who was excessively in love with her husband (tho' she did not admire him much.)

Will you observe dear before paying Sharpers if the Bill deli[d153] you have is dated? He never has sent a bill, but I suppose if the Bill deli[d] is dated Christmas 1853 that is sufficient. Will you tell Haji on his birthday (21)[154] that I asked you to wish him many happy returns of it for me. The garden will soon want crops put in but I will write about it next time. I am very glad Kate continues satisfied & well conducted.

Adieu with all love to my kindest & dearest.

It gives me much pleasure to have a few words from you. I thought that long ere this I sh[d] have written you a ~~dozen~~ half a dozen long letters—but l'homme propose & le temps[155] I cannot too much thank you for your kind hospitality to my dear girl & all the help & advice & trouble you have taken for her—<u>She</u> is pleased & with her choice, so I can be & must

---

150. John's *Autobiography*.

151. Places referred to appear to be Kensington and Walton, where JSM and HTM had lived most of the previous twenty years.

152. Lady Rachel Russell's (1636-1723) letters had been reviewed in the *Examiner* (4 February 1854). John had written about the "ludicrous" "deification" of these letters in his letter to Harriet (*CW*: XIV, 152).

153. Delivered.

154. Haji turned 23 on 21 February 1854.

155. Could be a play on "l'homme propose et Dieu dispose" (Man proposes, God disposes). Harriet writes "man proposes and time" disposes.

be—It really is best for all of us that she sh^d have her preference out—
Then if she still prefers that life, well & if not, <u>well</u> also.¹⁵⁶

Blackpool
Saturday¹⁵⁷

Dearest love

We got on well to Fleetwood (luggage & all) but it is a strange place, or
rather a place <u>meant to be</u> but not built. It is like a beginning of Herne
Bay—roads planned but no houses—only a great staring Inn called Euston
Hotel adding to the deserted look of the place—no lodgings fit to go
to—so this morning we have driven over here (nine miles) & I write while
we wait a few minutes which will account for a hurried note. This place
is as they call it a little Brighton—a poor copy thereof except in the crowds
of people so that it reminds me of your account of Southend. It is therefore
not tempting at all, & as Lily has a great inclination to go to Lemington
I decide to do, so & to go on to-day. I shall order your letter to be sent
on from Fleetwood but hope you will write to Post Office Lemington as
soon as you get this, that I may soon know where to direct to you dear. I
am so pleased at its being such a lovely day for Helvellyn that it makes
me quite in spirits. my heart is with you all the time so do dearest enjoy
the climbing and take good care not to slip.

I will write again to morrow Adieu now

in haste ever yrs
H M

Monday Even^g¹⁵⁸

I was quite in spirits all yesterday because you had such a nice day for the
journey dearest. This morning I got your account of your day which shows
that all went well. It is pleasant to hear that Wallock turns out better than
we expected. To-day has been very hot, tho without bright sun & looks this
evening as tho' there would be rain in the night, & already one has begun
to wish for more rain. The air is so close & sultry. Among the hills no doubt

---

156. No watermark or postmark. The content may refer to Helen's acting career, which began
in late 1856. XXVIII/242.

157. No watermark indicates date; written between 13 and 16 September 1857 as a response
to John's letter, (*CW:* XV, 535). 28/240.

158. Written on paper watermarked 1855, this letter was written in July 1858, since it refers
to the Bulwer case, which appeared in the London press during that time, and is in response
to John's letter (*CW,* XV. 565). XXVIII/236.

you will not find it too hot. I <u>am</u> so pleased it is fine. As the people at the Inn are disagreable you must leave it. I hope you have already, for it would much lessen the good walking may do if you are uncomfortable in the house. The Times has not yet come, but I have the Telegraph. I need not tell you the things in it which will be in the Times, as you will see that, but it has a very long account of Bulwers[159] wife being seized & sent to a madhouse, which seems a <u>most</u> nefarious affair. It ought to lead to Bulwer being turned out of the ministry. I hope it will, such an incarnation of vanity & dishonesty as the man is—he could not face the ridicule of his wife talking against him on the husting.[160] But it is a disgrace to the law that <u>any body</u> can be made prisoner & carried off on the certificate of two medical men!

If the expedition proves pleasanter than you expected, & seems to be doing good, I do hope you will stay into next week—It will be excessively painful to me if you come back sooner than you need, on account of what I said, or on any account. Adieu dearest[.] if this sh[d] get lost it certainly will be no prize to the finder!

Tuesday morning[161]

I have just got your dear letter & shall send this & my last nights scrap to Bakewell.[162] I hope you will get among wilder country—Matlock seems fitter for an excursion together at some future time. I was very poorly yesterday partly the sudden heat was very exhausting. To day is cool & pleasant tho' no sun. It look as if there would be rain, but I hope you will have fine weather throughout as there has been so much less rain in Derbyshire than here. I am so glad to hear you have had no need or thought of fires—& that you have got some plants—Oh, I do so hope you will have pleasant scrambles & stay out as <u>long as possible</u> & then come home perceptibly better for the change & fresh air.

Your note to M[r] Bumpus[163] went yesterday & the good little book came this morn[g]. Adieu my dearest love & just as I say so comes out the bright sun as if to say yes to it all.

---

159. Lady Rosina Doyle Wheeler Bulwer-Lytton (1804–82) was confined against her will by her husband Edward Bulwer-Lytton on 22 June 1858. John wrote about the case in a newspaper article, "The Law of Lunacy," published in the *Daily News* 31 July 1858, p. 4 (*CW*: XXV, 1198–99).

160. "Husting" is the term for political stumping or politicking.

161. No watermark. Letter was written just after the previous one, during July 1858. See John's letters (*CW*: XV, 565–67). XXVIII/237.

162. Bakewell and Matlock are two small towns in the Peak District of Derbyshire.

163. A bookseller.

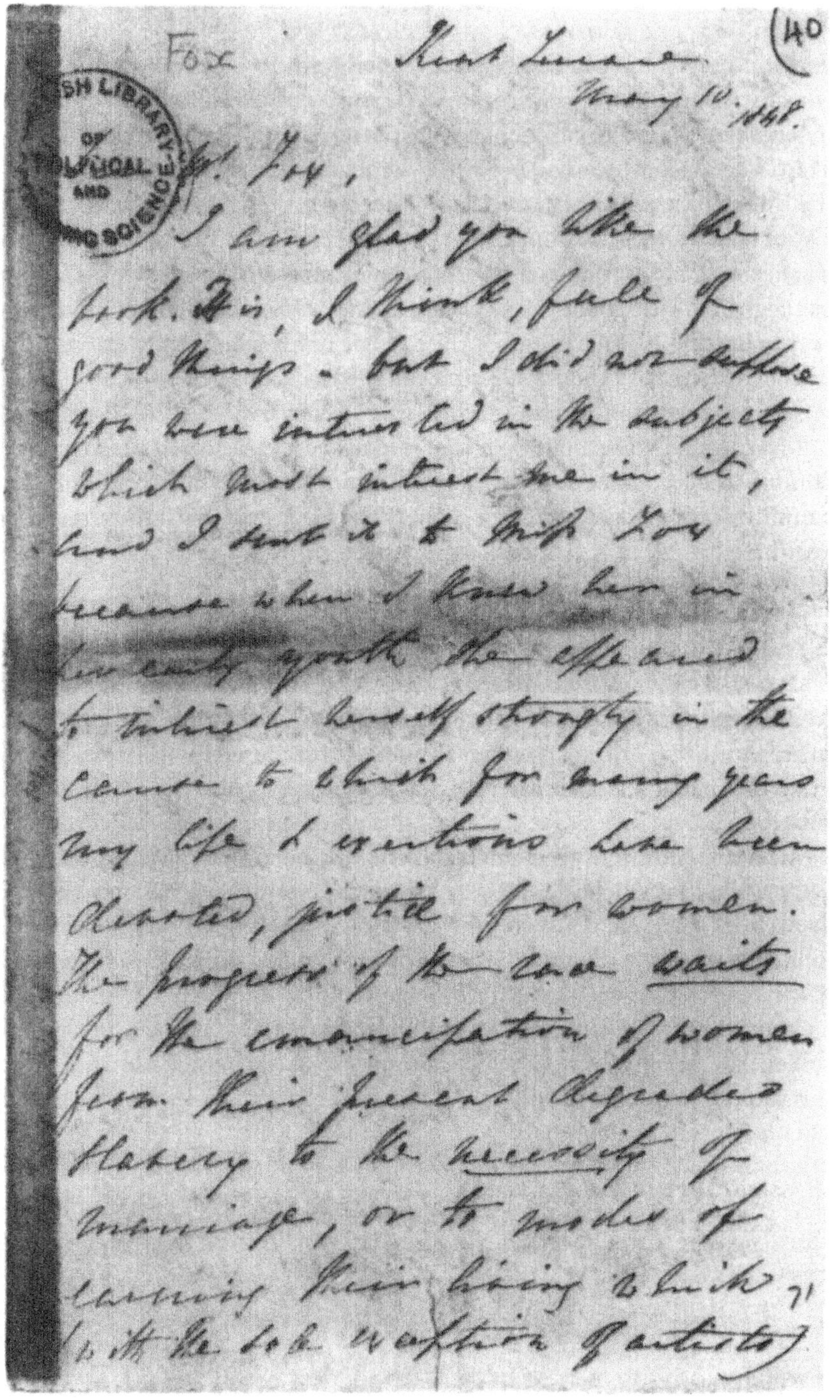
Fox

140

Kent Terrace
May 10th 1848.

Mr. Fox,

I am glad you like the book. It is, I think, full of good things — but I did not suppose you were interested in the subjects which most interest me in it, and I sent it to Miss Fox because when I knew her in her early youth she appeared to interest herself strongly in the cause to which for many years my life & exertions have been devoted, justice for women. The progress of the race waits for the emancipation of women from their present degraded slavery to the necessity of marriage, or to modes of earning their living which (with the sole exception of artists)

Harriet's letters to William J. Fox express her pride in Principles of Economy *and her commitment to women's rights.*

TO FAMILY AND FRIENDS

10

These letters reveal the troubled relationships Harriet Taylor Mill experienced with her mother, Harriet Hardy; her father, Thomas Hardy; her brother-in-law, Arthur Ley; her sister, Caroline Ley; and her son Herbert Hardy. In addition, this correspondence offers knowledge about the affectionate bond she shared with her sister-in-law Emilia (widow of Harriet's brother William), her youngest son, Algernon Hardy, and her brother Arthur Hardy. As with many families, the jealousies, backbiting, and reprimands are as evident in these communications as the concern and affection.

Harriet's father, Thomas Hardy, a surgeon and "man-midwife," was often an unpleasant man. Harriet's brother, Edward Hardy, described him as "occasionally half cranky" when he quarrelled with John Taylor and then refused to speak to John, even in the public domain of their Club.[1] The dispute which initiated the estrangement between John Taylor and his father-in-law is not divulged in the letters, but the argument must have intensified in late 1840, after William Hardy's death.

The summer before her brother William's death in November of 1840, Harriet spent the summer in Brighton. From there she writes an affectionate note to her friend Eliza Flower about Thomas Carlyle's lectures. Harriet also displays affection for Emilia in letter XXVII/54, probably written in the early fall of 1840, after Harriet's return from Brighton. In November, after learning of his son's death, Thomas Hardy refused to pay William's small debts or financially support his widow, Emilia.

---

1. See PRG 101 and *History of Hardy Family*, Mortlock Library of South Australiana.

Harriet pleads with her father to assist Emilia in the most emotionally wrenching way. Thomas Hardy ignores his daughter's request. Harriet's last letter to her father beseeches him to reconcile with Emilia "in the presence of the one only great event of life—death." A letter to her brother Arthur in Australia (PRG 101), exposes Thomas Hardy's vindictive, niggardly responses to his daughter's petitions on Emilia's behalf.

Of the next collection of letters, composed between 1848 and 1849, all but the first two were written to Harriet's son, Algernon, better known in the family as "Haji." The first two letters, penned to William Fox in May 1848, are responses to Fox's praise of Principles of Political Economy, *a book which appeared that year and to which Harriet had contributed a chapter entitled "On the Futurity of the Labouring Classes." This year marked a period of revolt throughout Europe, and Harriet's frustration with the lack of attention that women's oppression was attracting within the revolutionary movements emerges in her correspondence with William Fox and Haji. Harriet complains about the Chartists in Great Britain, "who with their one idea of universal suffrage are too purblind to perceive or too poltron[2] to proclaim that half the race are excluded" (XXVII/101). Harriet believed the Chartists acted selfishly by not considering the cause of women in their reform package.*

To her eighteen-year-old son she writes a series of notes full of motherly affection and spiced with references to current political issues, including the Hampden controversy (XXVII/103), the affairs of journalists who immigrated to Australia (XXVII/109), and Brougham's pamphlet about the Revolution of February (XXVII/110). Harriet also sends Haji vivid descriptions of her travel to Pau the winter of 1848–49 (XXVII/108, XXVII/109, and XXVII/110). Although John Taylor was ill during the winter of 1848–49, Harriet was unaware of the seriousness of his illness until she returned to England in May to find him dying of cancer. What may appear as insensitivity toward her husband is probably the result of the nineteenth-century habit of keeping patients and their families uninformed about the terminal nature of illnesses. John Taylor himself was long unaware of the seriousness of his malady.

A series of letters Harriet writes to her mother, Harriet Hardy, begins just two days before John Taylor's death on 18 July 1849 and characterizes the complex link between them. After six weeks of twenty-four-hour-a-day care for her dying husband, and out of sheer exhaustion, Harriet asks that her mother not visit them. After John's death, Harriet's mother writes, but rather than supplying her daughter with sympathy and sup-

---

2. Cowardly.

port during this period of grief, she harshly rebukes Harriet for not having properly notified her of John's death. Harriet responds with righteous indignation (XXVII/56). Mrs. Hardy fails to acknowledge her daughter's exhaustion, frustration, depression, and sense of loss when John Taylor dies, and HTM feels outrage at her mother's lack of empathy (XXVII/57). Somehow mother and daughter apparently settle their quarrel, because in January of 1850, Harriet sends her mother advice regarding an awkward request for money from another relative (XXVII/58). Although they never broke completely, Mrs. Hardy's hypersensitivity and lack of warmth for another's pain and discomfort made a close relationship between them impossible.

After Harriet's marriage to John Stuart Mill, her relation to her mother continued its bumpy path. Six letters from 1855 plead for her mother to return the letters she had mailed over the years. A note from Mrs. Hardy (XXVII/76) indicates that she had sent the package, but Harriet doubts her mother's word. And as late as December of the following year, 1856, mother and daughter are still squabbling over whether Mrs. Hardy actually returned the letters (XXVII/83 and XXVII/80). More evidence of the misunderstanding recurs in XXVII/67. The touchy Mrs. Hardy goes into a dither because of an innocent comment by Harriet: "I know these particulars will not interest you but I have nothing more amusing to write about." Since Harriet's letter is filled with nothing more exciting than her concern over her children's health, Harriet may have believed her comment to be justified, and she was merely recognizing that her letter was indeed dull. Mrs. Hardy, however, takes the remark as an insult (XXVII/70). This reaction indicates the ongoing problems Harriet experienced when trying to communicate with her mother.

This collection of family letters is also filled with the petty sibling rivalry that afflicts many families. Harriet's subtle sarcasm regarding her mother's attention to her sister's children is obvious in the following passage from XXVII/80: "I am very glad to hear you have so much satisfaction in Caroline's children & that Louis improves so much. That Annie is making not only a pleasant but an improving visit is indeed fortunate." The "I-got-to-see-it-but-you-didn't" childishness of mentioning to her mother that she had seen a photograph of Arthur Hardy's children — and returned it without showing it to her mother — demonstrates that Harriet is not above peevishness herself. By her last letter, a Christmas missive(!), Harriet is flat-out calling her mother a liar as she writes, "In yours of Nov 22ᵈ you repeat what you said in a former letter that my having written to you last February is a delusion. Now I hold in my hand your answer, dated March 1st 1856 which begins with these words. . . ." *Obviously, these mother-daughter correspondences are not filled with sympathy or grace. Mrs. Hardy's poor mothering skills may have resulted in Harriet's overprotection of Helen. The thin-skinned quality of Harriet's relation to Helen is more understandable in light of Mrs. Hardy's behavior. Certainly Harriet's letters to Helen reveal that she strives for a far more loving relationship to her daughter than she experienced with her own mother and father.*

Harriet's main concern in her letters to her brother Arthur Hardy, involves her squabble with her brother-in-law, Arthur Ley, over the trusteeship of a marriage settlement for her children. Beginning in 1842, Harriet wrote to Thomas Carlyle (XXVII/2) asking him to replace John Taylor's brother-in-law, who served as one of the trustees and who was about to leave England. Harriet was concerned that Arthur Ley would abscond with the money from her marriage settlement to John Taylor. In August 1849 Herbert Taylor writes Arthur (it is unclear whether it is Arthur Ley or Arthur Hardy) saying the trust should be left in the hands of the acting trustee, John Ingram Tavers. A week later Arthur Hardy writes to Arthur Ley (with a copy to Herbert) saying that he got a letter from the other trustee asking whether Arthur Ley intended to continue as trustee. Ley writes to Arthur Hardy in Australia (who Ley knew was on a multi-month voyage to England) to ask what "Mrs. Taylor's" wishes are! The connection between Arthur Ley and Harriet was so strained by 1851 that Harriet refused to accept a wedding gift from Arthur, and merely hoped that she could bear to submit "to have half an hours conversation with you again before you finally leave London" (XXVII/91). A long letter to her brother, Arthur Hardy, outlines why her fears about Arthur Ley are justified. Harriet explains in XXVII/48 that she believes Arthur embezzled about £700 of another trust he controlled. According to Ley's own brother, William, this knowledge may have contributed to their father's death. Both William Ley and Arthur Hardy fail to persuade Arthur Ley to give up Harriet's trust. Three versions of Harriet's intended correspondence to Arthur Hardy have been included in this group of family letters. In the first draft (XXVII/46) Harriet does not mention the problem with the trusteeship. The second draft (XXVII/48) and the third draft (XXVII/49) are substantially the same except for the passages noted in the body of the text of XXVII/48. The material added in the XXVII/49 draft directly blames Harriet's sister Caroline for manipulating Arthur. However, in XXVII/48 Harriet portrays Arthur as the primary villain.

Unfortunately, no evidence exists to indicate which of these drafts Harriet mailed to Arthur Hardy. In 1857 Harriet writes again to her brother, thanking him for his attempts to solve the trusteeship problem, and in this letter she lays blame squarely on Caroline. She writes, "Indeed Ar Ley's has long been a mere name, as he acts in all matters of business only under Caroline's direction and it was plain from her letter that she thought she should gain some advantage by refusing to resign the trust, & when once she thought that nothing would move her" (XXVII/50). Still in the next year, June 1857, the problem is not resolved, and Harriet mildly chastises Arthur Hardy for not writing more forcefully and demanding Arthur Ley's resignation (XXVII/51).

Aside from her complaints about her sister and brother-in-law, Harriet's letters to Arthur and Haji show these two family members to be her favored male relatives. In her less troubled letters to her favorite sibling, Arthur, Harriet discusses politics, eagerly sending a copy of Principles of Political Economy. *Arthur serves as Harriet's trusted brother and respected confidant. Like Arthur, her son Haji also receives Harriet's chatty correspondences (see the collection of her letters to Algernon while he traveled in Italy during 1856, including XXVII/111-XXVII/119). In his mid-twenties, Haji spends some time in Barnabite Convent in Italy. Harriet's letters to him during this period are cheerful and sympathetic. However, these messages to her son lack the emotional intensity which characterize Harriet's letters to Helen. With her son, Haji, Harriet maintains a purer and less complex affection (although probably not a very deep one) than for anyone else in her life.*

Among all those she penned, Harriet wrote only one letter to John Stuart Mill's relatives, a draft letter to George Mill, John's brother (XLVII/17). It is also the angriest letter of any written by Harriet. George Mill, on hearing of John's marriage to Harriet, wrote to her saying:

Though I have only heard at second hand, of your recent marriage with my brother, and know nothing certain except the bare fact, I will not pass over such an event in silence. My brother wrote me a letter by the mail of April 9th but not a word wrote he then, had he written before, or has not written since of what I can only conclude he must have thought me either uninterested in or undeserving to know, I don't know therefore what changes your union will make in your mode of life, if any. . . . Believe me/dear Mrs Taylor (I can't forget the old name)/

Yours affectly

Geo. G. Mill.[3]

George Mill also mentions in this same letter that JSM would probably

---

3. The entire text is presented in *CW:* XIV, 73.

not have to continue working at the India House if he hadn't made "such easy bargains with his publishers." Since Harriet helped to negotiate the publishing contracts for Principles of Political Economy, *this remark must have galled her. The obvious reference to "Mrs. Taylor" was no doubt another comment which further angered her. The general tone of the letter probably wasn't quite what this recently married woman would have expected from her new brother-in-law. Whether Harriet mailed the letter remains uncertain, but John sent his own rebuke to his brother which echoes Harriet's outrage (CW: XIV, 73–75).*

Included only to complete the collection of surviving letters, the remaining rather inconsequential letters are directed to Mr. William Fox, inviting him and his daughter to Blackheath Park, and to Mrs. Darling, asking for a recommendation about hiring a cook.

The correspondence as a whole paints a vivid picture of Harriet Taylor Mill. She was a strong woman, willing to fight for her principles as well as defend and repudiate family members when necessary. She was a fiercely protective mother who understood the potential danger associated with the mismanagement of her children's trust-fund, and she fought bitterly with her sister Caroline and Arthur Ley to keep the fund safe. In addition, Harriet championed her brother's widow, Emilia, a woman she felt her father had wronged. Harriet's keen intelligence and acute political awareness shine in letters written to friends such as William Fox and her son Haji. Meanwhile, her letters to her mother merely recount family illnesses and petty sentiments. Harriet usually didn't hide her feelings of either concern or anger. She openly fretted about those for whom she cared and chided those with whom she was frustrated.

LETTERS FROM 1840

To Miss Fox[4]

My dear Miss Fox, not having heard from L[izzie?][5] & thinking it a pity the card should lie here idle I sent it on Monday to Miss Gillies. But I

---

4. The daughter of William J. Fox. This letter is housed at King's College, Cambridge.

5. Harriet seems to be referring to Eliza Flower, William Fox's lover. Harriet is apparently explaining why she sent her ticket for the Carlyle lectures to Miss Gillies instead of to Eliza.

know Mr. Mill has one, which I do not think he will use, & which I am sure he will be very glad to send to her.

I am very glad she liked the lectures; I did not expect it; it is the highest flattery when she <u>likes</u>. I heared a <u>mot</u> of H. Mar[tineau] very charactiristic, she wrote to Mr. Carlyle approving the syllabus but reminding him that he had omitted the 'Hero' as 'Martyr' to which he replied that if he had not considered him that in every situation he should never have thought him worth talking about. Lily has begun many letters to you, so that my paper case is crowded with papers commencing 'dear Tottie' but she has never had courage or industry to complete one which she thinks 'worth sending' having a salutary horror of 'blots' and respect for your critical powers. She sends her love to you. She has often wished for you here. We have had a most lovely season & have enjoyed the sea thoroughly.

We leave this place next week to be nearer town. We shall go to Tunbridge Wells & stay there some weeks, so that we shall see you soon.

Adieu dear.

H.T.

To Emilia Hardy[6]

My dear Emilia,

I hope you will not have thought me unkind in not having replied to your letter before this time. I was in the country when it arrived & so did not receive it at once, you must therefore excuse this rather long delay.

It gave me great pleasure to hear from you. I am very happy to know that you are in good health. be sure that I am always much interested in all that concerns you & shall be very happy to correspond with you—pray write again soon & more at length.

The family at Walworth are all well. We hear but rarely from William, indeed he writes to no one but his father & that very shortly.

My mother sends her kind remembrance to you, I assure you both for her & myself we always think of you with the utmost kindness.

Since I saw you I have made a short visit to your beautiful Italy. How I envy you in being there. When you write again pray tell me your

---

6. Emilia is Harriet's brother William's wife. No postmark or watermark indicates a date, but the letter was written before William died in 1840, and Harriet was "in the country" when Emilia's letter to her arrived. Harriet was in Brighton during the summer of 1840, so this letter may have been written the fall William died. XXVII/54.

address—I shall send this to Leghorn but I do not feel at all sure of its reaching you.

M^r. Taylor begs to present his compliments & kind regards to you & Beleive me

My dear Emilia,
very affectionately yours
H. Taylor

To Thomas Hardy

Walton Thursday
Nov. 27[7]

My dear Papa,

I have this morn^g received the sad news of poor William's death which shocks & distresses me greatly. Tho' we knew of his severe illness I did not myself feel that it was likely it would kill him—he was so young & with a good constitution—I fully believed he would recover. Poor fellow! What a short life & almost all spent in struggle if not hardship—

I suppose you have received the letter from Naples of which I this morn^g have received a copy. I shall copy & enclose it in case you have not. And now dear Papa what shall you do for poor Emilia. I pray you to consider that whether 'Italian woman' or English woman, from the first hour of her connexion with ~~your~~ our family, & from the first time you have heared her name mentioned untill the last, you have never heard of her either from Willm. or any one else but to her credit. She has evidently done all in her power to make Willm. happy & has shared illness and poverty with him. She is spoken highly of on all hands—and She has no one in the world to expect help from but you. For my part if I had had any idea they were in distress for money I would have shared my last pound with them if necessary, for they have always acted in the most perfectly honourable manner with regard to money matters, & have evidently done the very best they could with their small income. You are aware that William had no otherwise overdrawn his account with John than to take his quarter in advance, a little help which John offered him. so that the amount owing to John, had this last quarter been paid, would have been but a few pounds.

I regret now extremely that I had not kept up a more frequent correspondance with William—but I did ask them in the spring to write

---

7. William died in 1840, so the letter must have been written that year. XXVII/87.

more frequently & I think the expense of postage, which is high at Naples, must have been the reason I heared so seldom. The Neapolitan bankers are very anxious to know that "her Father" will empower them to do for poor Wm Hardy—Pray dear Papa hasten to give help where it is so much wanted & so may be so justly hoped from you as in the case of the widow of your eldest son.

I hope to hear from you in a day or two & also from mama. Please direct to 3 Delaheny Street if you write at the beginning of the week, but after Wed^y here.

Lily[8] writes with me in Love. Y^r affectionate H.

Excuse the bad writing. I am not very well having a bad cold.

To Thomas Hardy[9]

John[10] tells me that he could not enclose a letter on such a subject in blank cover, & therefore desired his Uncle to write. Surely the presence of death in ones family is a fit and proper occasion and reminder to sweep away estrangements and offences great and small, & I say this because I

---

8. Helen Taylor.

9. XXVII/88. No postmark, watermark, date, or greeting appear on the letter to indicate a date or to whom it is addressed. It is probably a letter following the death of William Hardy in late 1840. The content includes the phrase "dear Papa," so it appears to have been written by HTM to her father, Thomas Hardy. John Taylor wrote to Arthur Hardy in Australia on 1 December 1840, noting: "This most melancholy event [William's death] has affected me very much. Ever since you left we have been in regular correspondence, and I have had various money transactions with him. I have invariably found him most honourable, strict and correct, never engaging to do anything that he did (not) feel sure he should have it in his power to do.

There seems to have been great poverty during his illness, and poor Emilia is obliged to seek an asylum with some friends. Her condition is represented as most desolate and deplorable. There are some most painful circumstances about this most lamented event, which I may refer to another time, if we do not succeed in prevailing upon your Father to pay poor William's debts, which are very small, and to do something for Emilia" (PRG 101, Papers of Arthur Hardy, Mortlock Library of South Australiana).

Furthermore, Edward Hardy writes his brother Arthur in 1840 to report: "The Governor [their father, Thomas Hardy] is, as John [Taylor] says, more awkward than ever, he has quarrelled with John, they have not spoken nor communicated these six months. . . ."

The quarrel between John Taylor and Thomas Hardy began before William's death (Edward says they had not spoken for six months prior to his letter in 1840) but intensified over Mr. Hardy's refusal to assist Emilia Hardy. Harriet tries to use the death of William as a means of reconciling the two men.

10. HTM's use of the first name would indicate that she is referring to her husband, John Taylor.

believe you will feel with me upon it, & because you being the chief person it is you who can at once put an end to the estrangement. For me, I cannot conceive it possible to be moved by mere temporary or angry feelings in the presence of the one only great event of life—death. I am sure John would have written the sympathy he feels if he had not fancied his doing so would offend you. Pray dear Papa write to him about this sad subject in your old way—as if nothing had occurred between you & let 'bygones be bygones.' in the case of an <u>old</u> subject of offence with one whom after all you esteem. I can assure you he would have written to you before but that he thought you would not like it.

I have here written down very hastily what I think & feel & I cannot for a moment conceive the possibility of offending you by doing so.

To Arthur Hardy[11]

Pater Noster continues in the highest dudgeon with John, forbidding them to 'name his name' in his presence and taking no manner of notice of him when they meet. Thinking all this quite unworthy either of a man of the world or a '<u>Christian</u>' I wrote a long effusion on the subject to the Padre telling him I thought it unworthy of him etc., and suggesting to him an occasion of making the matter up. But, as at the same time I showed that I thought John not in the wrong, it had no effect, Papa wrote in answer that if he received '<u>an apology!</u>' he should know how to treat it. Of course John laughs at that and so the matter ended. I shall never interfere about it again and I should not have done so then, but the thing looks so vulgar and stupid that they should not even speak when they meet at the Club and such places, and because I saw that Papa was put to great inconvenience in collecting his rents etc., by his having taken it all into his own hands. As to John it releases him from an immense deal of troublesome business, so that on my part it was mere good nature to attempt to make it up for Papa. John never heard a word from Padre about some £40 which he says you sent him through Papa, so the other day I asked Papa why he had not sent it to John, and he said that your directions were that "Mr. Taylor was to have it when he applied for it, and as he had not applied for it he had not paid it'. He seemed quite delighted to be able to turn it so.

---

11. This letter is in typewritten form among the Papers of Arthur Hardy in the Mortlock Library of South Australiana. It is not dated, although it was written before John Taylor's death in 1849. The first part of the letter is missing. PRG 101.

Edward continues at Birksgate where he seems to pass his time in smoking. Papa is in the utmost annoyance at his presence there, and says there is nothing he would not do to get rid of him, except the one thing without which he says Edward declares he will not leave, and that is to send him out 'like a gentleman'. To my thinking both the idea and the expression seems the last degree of vulgarity, if he is 'a gentleman' that fact will not be affected by the way he might go out, at all events it seems to me that the only valuable of a gentleman, his gentlemanly feelings, would be best proved by honestly setting himself to maintain himself rather than remain in a house which he has been repeatedly desired to quit, as his father told me a day or two ago. I speak to you of him severely (I never do so to his Father, nor to anyone but John) but I have but little toleration for a strong and healthy young man who prefers living upon the industry of others to his own. The whole subject of E. is unpleasant to me and I never speak of it to any one of my family except in my letters to you. Who is the Miss Newenham to whom Edward corresponds so regularly? John forwards and receives his letters for him and he thinks it must be a sister of Alfred's wife, if so has she any fortune?

I hear nothing of the Tulks[12] now, perhaps Caroline may, tho' I do not think she does. John has met Marmaduke about and sometimes sees James Tulk. James Ley is to marry Louisa, but when we do not know. Both the Leys and Tulks appear to be short of money.

Caroline is expecting to be confined in July, and Mama is coming to town on her way to Devonshire to be with her. They are just now going into their house at Bideford from the old people's place where they have passed the winter. Arthur Ley appears to be industrious and has got into a good business they say by the death of the principal attorney at Bideford. At the time of Caroline's marriage I was ill and unable to do anything in the way of choosing or buying, and after teazing myself a good deal about it, I left your present for future choice, as indeed I did principally my own. I will send it now when it will be quite as opportune.

June 15 You will see there has been a long interval since writing the foregoing. I have had a severe illness with a sort of paralysis from which I have quite lost the power of moving my right leg, and very nearly that of the other. I have indeed been very ill but am now better in health though quite unable to walk. I have just come to Leamington to take the

---

12. Charles Augustus Tulk (1786-1849) died 16 January 1849. He took part in bettering conditions of factory workers in England and founded a society for the publishing of Swedenborg's works. Marmaduke and James may be Charles' sons.

advice of a Dr. Jephson whom I think you have heard the Tulks mention and who is thought very clever in this sort of seizure. I hope to get well here and that my next letter will be from London. I do not think there is danger in my complaint. John was to send off some music which I got for you last week. It is the first and only vol. published of the Convent Music, the opera of Tancreu is for the pianoforte, and two songs. Whenever I see pretty songs I will get them and send, but they are difficult things to find. John was able to get French gloves in bond at a moderate price, but the seller refused to let him have specimens before buying, saying it was not usual, accordingly John, not thinking himself a good judge and I being unable to see them, he determined to buy but a few until you determine whether to have more or not. He has sent a few dozens. Mama has been staying with me in town a fortnight and left last week for Devonshire where she is gone to be present at Cary's accouchement. I will not write more now as I am not very strong, but I will soon write again. Lily who is the only one with me at this place sends her love and kisses, and adieu, my dear Arthur, most affectionately, H. Taylor

LETTERS FROM 1848-49

To William Fox[13]

Kent Terrace.
May 10.
1848.

Dear Mʳ Fox,

I am glad you like the book. It is, I think, full of good things—but I did not suppose you were interested in the subjects which most interest me in it, and I sent it to Miss Fox[14] because when I knew her in her early youth she appeared to interest herself strongly in the cause to which for many years my life & exertions have been devoted, justice for women. The progress of the race <u>waits</u> for the emancipation of women from their present degraded slavery to the <u>necessity</u> of marriage, or to the modes of earning their living which (with the sole exception of artists) consist only

---

13. XXVII/40.

14. Miss Fox, William J. Fox's daughter, is also referred to in letters to Helen (LII/66 and LII/77) and in a letter to Algernon Hardy (XXVII/116).

of the poorly paid & hardly worked occupations, all the proffessions, mercantile clerical legal & medical, as well as all government posts being monopolised by men. Political equality would alone place women on a level with other men in these respects. I think the interested or indifferent selfishness of the low reformers would be overmastered by the real wish for greater justice for women which prevails among the upper classes of men, if but these men had <u>ideas</u> enough to perceive that society requires the infusion of the new life of the feminine element. The great practical ability of women which is now wasted on worthless trifles or sunk in the stupidities called <u>love</u> would tell with most 'productive' effect on the business of life, while their emancipation would releive the character of men from the deadening & degrading influences of life passed in intimacy with inferiors. But <u>ideas</u> are just that needful stock in trade in which our legislators are as lamentably deficient as our chartists, who with their one idea of universal suffrage are too purblind to perceive or too poltron[15] to proclaim that half the race are excluded. I cannot but dissent from an argument you for a moment turned the light of your countenance upon, the first time, I think, you spoke in the house—to the effect that 'who would be free themselves must strike the blow' or at all events express their desire. This argument appears to me even less appropriate to the case of women than it would have been to that of the negroes by emancipating whom, from her own sense of justice alone, England has acquired the brightest glory round any nations name.

Domestic slaves cannot organise themselves—each one owns a master, & this mastery which is usually passive would assert itself if they attempted it. The condition of women is also <u>unique</u>—no other slaves have [manuscript breaks off]

To William J. Fox

May 12[16]

Dear Mr Fox,

Your note has given me a genuine & hearty sensation of pleasure. I was going to say it is delightful to find that one has done less than justice to a friend! which you should understand but which I will change into, I am delighted to find that we agree so far.

---

15. Cowardly.

16. The letter was written in 1848, shortly after *Principles of Political Economy* was published. It is housed at King's College, Cambridge.

You must not suppose that I am less interested in the other great question of our time, that of labour. The equalising among all the individuals composing the community (varied only by variation in physical capacities) the amount of labour to be performed by them during life. But this has been so well placed on the tapis by the noble spectacle of France ('spite of Pol^l Eco^y blunders) that there is no doubt of its continuing <u>the</u> great question until the hydra-headed selfishness of the idle classes is crushed by the demands of the lower. The condition of women question goes deeper into the mental and moral characteristics of the race than the other & it is <u>the race</u> for which I am interested. God knows if only the people now living or likely to follow such progenitors were what one thought of in any exertion, both common & uncommon sense would make one as utterly and as successfully selfish (for oneself and a little band of friends) as the rest. I fear that if the suffrage is gained by <u>all</u> men before <u>any</u> women possess it, the door will be closed upon equality between the sexes perhaps for centuries. It will become a <u>party</u> question in which only the highminded of the stronger party will be interested for justice. The argument is all in the general principle—and this is neither understood nor cared for by the flood of uneducated who would be let in by the male 'universal suffrage.'

I should have said that the Ded^n.[17] was confined to copies given to friends at my especial request & to the great dissapointment & regret & contrary to the wish & opinion of the author. My reason being that opinions carry more weight with the authority of his name alone.

Ever Truly Y^{rs}
H. T.

To Algernon Taylor[18]

Dear Haji

It seems to me a great pity for all your plans are so well arranged not to go to-morrow. If you could be of any use dear—I would say so—but your staying would on the contrary be quite useless therefore it will surely be better to go. Forget all that was painful this even^g and I will write if I can & tell you how I go on in any case Lily will & do you—write an account of yours.

---

17. HTM refers to the dedication of the *Principles of Political Economy* to her. John Taylor was incensed by the suggestion that it be published as part of the book. See chapter 8, page ooo above.

18. No indication of date. XXVII/100.

To Algernon Taylor

Walton
Friday[19]

My dear Haji

I mean to come to town on Monday To that about coming here on Sunday you can do as you prefer or think it worth while when you see what sort of day it is. I shall like to see you.

Ever yours,
H. T.

What a grossly selfish thing that chartist petition is—many of them w^d excuse it by saying it is not the time to injure their own chance by taking up the cause of the women—but ~~in~~ the present stir in Europe has been wholly one caused by enthusiasm for large principles & I doubt if small ones will have the same contagious effect—most certainly they don't deserve to have.

To Algernon Taylor[20]

My dear Haji

I sent you the Spectator because I thought the articles in it unusally good. Have you followed the Hampden controversy?[21] If you have you must have been amused at the extreme weakness in argument & poverty of expression of all the disputants. The letter of the Bishop of Exeter contained much temper and little talent—but even that seemed talent compared with Hampden's <u>own</u> letter, which was the weakest whining lament I ever saw in print. Indeed so vapid & pointless were the expressions that it gives some probability to the Times assertion that the Bampton Lectures[22] were not Hampden's own composition. I do not know what right the Times has to make this statement—the Bishops too show very ill on both sides. D^r

---

19. Reference to the chartist movement and the "recent stir in Europe" probably dates this letter to 1848. XXVII/101.

20. XXVII/103.

21. Renn Dickson Hampden, considered by many to be highly unorthodox, was selected by Lord John Russell for appointment to the vacant see of Hereford. There was a great deal of controversy over the selection in 1847-48.

22. In the Bampton Lectures, Hampden argued for greater authority of the scriptures over the authority of the church.

Merewether[23] is the strongest & the most valiant among the whole of the combatants. I suppose however they can carry through Hampden's election without his vote.

The Archbishop of Tuam[24] again comes out in droll contrast to the english bishops—a jolly priest militant—the english priesthood represent weak virtue the Irish strong wickedness. I should think poor Ld Arundel Surrey[25] will be shaken in his faith. We shall look for you on Saturday till then Adieu

H. T.

To Algernon Taylor[26]

My dear Haji, I shall like to see you here next Saturday if you can come & stay over Christmas day—you will have to go up on Tuesday on account of the Ellis party & I think if I am well enough I shall set off that day for France. The weather is now as gloomy as it has been fine before—but it is not cold.

Ever Y^rs Affec^ly
H. T.

To Algernon Taylor

Walton.[27] Octr 11

My dearest Haji,

Many thanks dear for your good wishes on my birthday. I send you also all manner of good & kind wishes altho' it is not yours yet.

Herby came down for Wednesday even^g. It was a very short stay, too short. I shall not be in town again for a week or two I think, as I am waiting to come when grandpapa & mama come & as yet I have not heared when that is to be.

---

23. John Merewether (1797–1850).

24. Tuam is in Country Galway, Ireland.

25. Henry Granville FitzAlan-Howard (1815–60) used his father's courtesy title of Earl of Surrey and Arundel. He was called "the most pious layman of our times."

26. The letter may have been written prior to her trip to Pau, France, which she made after Christmas 1848. XXVII/102.

27. Herbert Taylor ("Herby") was in the U.S. from April 1846 to April 1847, and again in early 1849, so this letter can probably be dated to 1847–48. XXVII/104.

I wish you to call at [Morley's][28] & say that the "Ladies Mag[e] &c" is not to be sent any more. do not forget this dear. When you write to me I wish you to use envelopes, because you fold the letters so badly. Lily is writing to you dear boy. I shall be sure to drink your health on Sunday as I always do.

Adieu love.
H. T.

To Algernon Taylor

Tuesday[29]

Dearest Haji,

I hope you will soon get rid of your cough & that you will continue to take the pills 'till it is gone. Thank you for the description. We are going to the Isle of Wight and shall stay some time if I find a house in an agreable situation and if so you must come down. If I hear of Arthur being likely to arrive I shall return for that.

The weather is now very beautiful. The place does not look like the same as on that wet Sunday.

If you direct to me or Lily Post Office Ryde we shall get it.

Ever yours
H. T.

To Algernon Taylor

Worthing[30] Nov. 13

Dear Haji I have been surprised & dissapointed for some time past at not receiving any reply to a letter I wrote to Birksgate three weeks ago. It has just occurred to me that it is possible Anne may have misunderstood my directions and have sent one to Walton. Will you make quite sure on the subject by asking her if she has sent any letter to Walton for me since I was in town? and give me her answer as soon directly?

I am anxious to hear how you are as I dreaded that long evening ride

---

28. Could read "Morphy's."

29. Harriet spent the summer of 1848 on the Isle of Wight. Arthur Hardy, her brother from Australia, arrived in London that November, so this letter can be dated 1848. XXVII/105.

30. HTM was in Worthing during the late autumn of 1848. XXVII/106. Anne is John Taylor's maid.

for your sore throat. I do hope it has not continued. The weather here to-day is as fine as it was yesterday & the sea & sky look as bright & beautiful.

You should desire Anne to finish the hemming of the little shawl, which was only partly done it seems—otherwise it will soon spoil at the edges.

Adieu dear

To Algernon Taylor

Bordeaux[31] Jan. 4
Thursday

Dearest Haji,

We arrived here on Tuesday morning at 5 o'clock, and I did not write before that I might reply if there was any letter here for me, which on enquiring this morning it appears there is not. We had a fatiguing journey here owing to the plan of the French Diligences[32] always to start in the even[g]. We left Orleans on Friday last at one & got to Tours at 4 o'clk. We left Tours on Sat[y] afternoon at 5 o'clk in the Coupé of the Diligence for Poitiers where we arrived at ½ past 3 o'clk Sunday morn[g]. We then started at ½ past 12 o'clk the same day & got to Angoulême at ½ past 11 at night. We then got a fire for it was very cold & sat up 'till one o'clk, that we might watch the exit of the old & the entrance of the new year on the stage of life, and wished you, and all who are dear to us, and to everybody a happy new year, & that it may achieve good for ourselves and others in it, tho' so eventful a year for the interests of the race as the last we cannot expect in the next. A happy and successful year to you dear and may it form a bright link in the swiftgliding chain of years—of life. Angoulême is most beautifully situated—on the summit of a steep hill from the lofty ramparts which surround the town & on the top of which are walks under trees, you seem to look down on "the kingdoms of the world & the glory thereof" so wide and boundless is the view on all sides. We left Angoulême at 5 in the afternoon of the 1st and reached this place at ½ past 5 on Tuesday morning, very much tired with so much night travelling, the fatigue of which is very much increased by their always saying that they shall start about two hours before actually do[ing] so yet insisting upon their passengers being at the Office at the time they name because as they say, sometimes, tho' rarely they do start to their time. They explain all

---

31. Written in 1849 on Harriet's journey to Pau. XXVII/108.

32. A type of stagecoach.

this by saying that it is only as the winter season that they are inexact & that it is caused by the state of the roads. The railway is in progress all the way & before long we may be able to get to this splendid place in a very few days, & then I think everybody who can should come & see it for it is by far the finest town I ever saw I sh^d think in Europe. The river is broader than the Thames & tho' it rises & falls each tide 20 feet yet the water never leaves the banks, it is so deep. A broad splendid quay with white houses like the London Club houses only higher extends three miles along one bank of the river, the opposite side being beautiful hills covered with vines & woods. There is the bridge only which had a much finer effect than so many. It is much like Waterloo bridge only about a quarter longer. The theatre is the finest modern building I ever saw. The Cathedral is fine from its look of quaint antiquity & great height. In the summer time the town must look like rows of palaces among woods, there are so many great 'places' fitted with trees. We are going to start by the Coupé of the Diligence this afternoon at 5 for Pau—the journey is to take 24 hours without stopping, but they engage to set me one out at Mont de Marsan (where there is the only inn & that a bad one on the road) if I should find I cannot go on the whole way. I shall try very much to do so, because there is no way of getting hence to Pau but their Diligence which if I get out, will only take us up again after 48 hours, & so long at a bad inn is a great infliction. The excellence of the Inns all the way we have come is what has enabled me to get thro' so much travelling with comparatively little fatigue. I am much better than when I left England the mild weather has been so fortunate for me. I am very anxious to hear how Papa is. I hope to find a letter at Pau. Give our best love to Papa. & to Herby & adieu dear—yours H. T.

To Algernon Taylor

Pau[33] March 6th

No—I have not thought you remiss as to writing dearest Haji, but on the contrary have been pleasantly surprised that you have been able to write so much, for I know what a burdensome task letter writing often is unless interest in ones correspondant conquers the disagreeable. I have not written lately—I have been out of spirits and therefore disinclined to enjoy or to write about the beautiful objects and scenery which form the staple of

---

33. Probably written when Harriet was in Pau in 1849. XXVII/109.

our quiet life here. The account I hear of George[34] and my knowledge of that insidious disease make me very much fear for him, and I most earnestly and anxiously wish that he may live. It is very important in writing to him to say very little about his health, and not to seem to think of it as anything more than a common cough, because if a person thinks themselves consumptive the effect on the spirits has the utmost possible tendency to produce or to accelerate that fatal disease. I think he would much like to hear from you and perhaps you have already written. You might give him a long letter about all sorts of impersonal objects, such as politics—your review and its articles—what you have been reading lately and your opinions thereon—our stay at this place & its scenery, Sinnett's prospects—Herbert's voyage[35] &c. All sorts of topics are amusing or interesting at a distance from home besides that the proof of interest is always agreable to those who are invalids. By the bye, in his letter to me George is very minute in his account of, and appears very anxious about postage which he says you paid in vain! for he had to pay it over again 8^d—that "letter should be sent to the brokers" or if sent by the post "they will have to be paid again" &c all of which as he takes so much interest in, no doubt you will be able to understand and arrange.

I continue to like and admire this place the more the longer I stay. The spring does not advance so quickly, as to vegetation, as I should have expected from the perfect mildness of the winter and the brightness and warmth of the sun now. The violets and spring flowers were all in bloom at the beginning of January and so they are now, but the only trees which have begun to look green are the poplars and willows. The almond trees are in blossom and the palm has been fully out for many weeks. It is a country of oak woods and vines and both these are very late trees. The turf is of a most beautiful green and the whole country so composed of meadows through which wind clear rushing mountain streams in valleys surrounded by woody hills and lofty mountains.

We drove yesterday to an old town called Lescar, the original capital of Béarn. It has a fine old church and castle crowning the summit of a hill and in the valley by the stream a large building built by Henry IV for a college & which does not look old at all. In a meadow stood a little cottage in which Henry IV was nursed. Everything here is associated with Henry the Castle of Pau is the most beautiful object with old towers and high

---

34. George Mill, JSM's brother, went to Madeira, Spain, to convalesce from tuberculosis.

35. Frederick Sinnett (1830-66), a journalist and literary critic, emigrated from England to Australia in 1849. See JSM's letter to him (*CW*: XV, 541) and well as the letter following this one. Herbert Hardy went to America in April 1846 and again early in 1849.

peaked roofs, and from its terrace which is always open there is a splendid view of the river & mountains. All the walks and drives here are beautiful because the mountains always form part of them. All the finer senses which act on the imagination are continually gratified, because every object one sees, whether animate or inanimate is either beautiful or picturesque, or both. We went a few days ago to a small town called Nay about ten miles hence, which had a very middle age air. The houses had many of them overhanging roofs and two or three rows of balconies overhanging the street Many of the houses appeared to have inscriptions over the doors as they often have in Italy. Over the door were the words "vive Jesu"[36] surrounded by a wreath of flowers.

I often wish for you when I see all this beauty and feel that if we live we will some time see it together, and that 'Ce qui est déféré n'est pas perdu',[37] as the proverb says. I am very glad to hear that Papa is better on the whole but I wish the improvement were quicker. He ought in future to pay due respect to my medical judgement as I have twice anticipated his physician's advice in the last few months! I do hope he will mend more quickly with the finer weather which may be expected in April.

Arthur's bringing Marmaduke Hart[38] to dine with Papa without his invitation was etymologically an impertinence and every way foolish. I have not read Grote's history,[39] I should think it must be interesting—tho' I think that knowing his "extreme opinions" I should think it a defect that he does not indicate them more clearly, as there is ample and easy room to do in treating of the Greek Philosophies. extreme timidity is his defect, but this is a great one indeed in a public instructor. Mr. Mill was to write a review of the book in last Sunday's Spectator, which you will like to see. And now dearest Haji, with love to Papa—Adieu.

To Mr. Sinnett

Walton[40] Oct 24

Dear Mr. Sinnett,
The little basket of Apples was very little worth sending. They belie their

---

36. "Long live Jesus."

37. "What is deferred is not lost."

38. Arthur Hardy's partner.

39. George Grote, *History of Greece.*

40. Since Sinnett emigrated from England to Australia in 1849, this letter was probably written the previous fall. XXVIII/123.

reputation this year, being scarcely half their usual size or flavour, but such as they are they have proved acceptable to many who have not gardens & I am glad if you liked them. I have never given any opinion against your Australian scheme—but the contrary. There is no one in the world less apt to pass judgment on others plans or conduct than I. I think 'the will of man is his heaven', and that no one should judge for another when the other is willing to judge for themselves. If I might depart from my usual rule of not giving advice unasked, I should say, never beleive what you hear by round about channels: Opinions rarely fail to lose or gain weight in passing through several hands even when they do not as in this case get exchanged. Whether in any particular case rashness is wise or foolish is a question which can only be solved by the individual character. I cannot tell whether your scheme is <u>rash</u> except in the sense that <u>adventure</u> must always be rash. "<u>Bold</u>, not <u>Rash</u>" I hope in this case. I admire the courage and energy you display while I tremble, not for all the success which energy can ensure, but for any one finding themselves in a new country wholly dependant on themselves.

With hearty good wishes I am
Yours very Truly,
H. Taylor

To Algernon Taylor

Pau,[41] March 20

Dearest Haji, I have not written lately because our life here is so exactly the same from day to day that there is little to tell. I intend to go to one of the Pyrenian baths about the second week in April, either Baréges or Bagnères, for two or three weeks and then to return. If you would like to meet us somewhere on the return journey I shall much like to see you, and I hope you might be spared for a week or ten days, tho' I suppose Herbert's absence makes you more wanted than usual. You might meet us at Paris, or Orleans, but this can be settled when I know if you can come, and also when I shall return. I mention the subject early that you may let me hear if you would think the pleasure of coming worth the fatigue of the journey—I know that in itself you dislike travelling and it is possible that you may not think a short stay worth so long a journey—tho' when there I am sure you would much enjoy the beautiful architecture

---

41. Probably written when HTM was in Pau in 1849. XXVII/110.

with which Paris abounds more than any city I know. I mention the <u>pros</u> & the <u>cons</u> dear that you may decide exactly as you feel—If you would rather not take the journey, then we can have another stay at the Isle of Wight in the autumn. Mr. Mill is just going to publish anonymously a pamphlet against Brougham's[42] pamphlet about the Rev^n of Feby. If was written at Worthing in November—It cuts up Brougham as he deserves— I have asked him to send you a copy. Lily's love and adieu dear

dear

LETTERS TO HARRIET HARDY, 1849-56

Monday[43] July 16

My dear Mama

Herbert had a note from Arthur on Saturday in which he said you thought of passing through London to Devonshire and that you were writing to me. As I have not heared from you I think it doubtful if you are coming, but I shall send this to the Euston Hotel, where Arthur said you meant to go, that it may meet you whenever you arrive It is with the deepest pain I tell you that my dear John has been much worse the last few days, & to-day and yesterday I fear he is sinking—we cannot leave his room either day or night—we have sat up with him in turn all night for the last five weeks. In his present state it is extremely doubtful if he can live through the next twenty-four hours. In this dreadful state you will not be surprised at my asking you to defer coming here untill the next time you come to London—I would not now leave him to see anyone and I shall much prefer having no visitor whatever, even you, at present.

I shall endeavour that Herbert shall call with this on his way tomorrow morn^g & see you if you have arrived, or if not leave it for you. The Hotel being at the station you will have no difficulty in getting on. I hope you will write & tell me that you get safely to Bideford.

Ever Affec^{ly}
H T

---

42. Henry Peter Brougham (1778-1868) served the Whigs with his prolific writing. He was associated with the Society for the Diffusion of Useful Knowledge.

43. Letter dated 16 July. The content of the letter indicates that the year was 1849, the year of John Taylor's death. This letter was sent two days before he died. XXVII/55.

Kent Terrace[44]
July 24

My dear Mama,

On the day of the Death of my dear John I was otherwise occupied than to enquire who Herbert wrote to or who he did not—nor have I yet either asked or heared.

~~That~~ I ~~should not~~ have not received one word from ~~either~~ Caroline ~~or her~~ for more than two months—nor at any time from her husband during the progress of his fatal illness nor since. ~~shows~~ This in ~~our~~ my opinion shows a ~~gross &~~ heartless want of even ordinary good feeling which would certainly prevent ~~my~~ our addressing any communication to ~~them~~ him on the subject.

Yours Affec^aly
H. Taylor

I am sorry to hear you are not well & hope to hear you are beter. I will write to you more at length at a future time.

Kent Terrace[45]
Augt 7th

My dear Mama

I could not have thought it possible that you could have written so unkind & as I think it so unjust a letter. Your subject of offence with me if I understand it rightly is that I did not write to you immediately on my dear John's death. Whether this is a sufficient ground of offence with one who has ~~behaved~~ acted this life to her mother as I have done to you I am willing to leave to the judgment of ~~any~~ every person of sense or feeling. This offence you visit by a note in which sympathy or feeling for me is mentioned only incidentally as part of the subject of your <u>and Mr Ley's[46]</u> (!) affront at ~~what~~ the omission of what I should have expected you would feel in your own case ~~an~~ a very unnecessary form at a time when my thoughts & feelings were ~~naturally~~ occupied to the exclusion of <u>forms</u>, but when if I ~~did think~~ had thought of them at all it was precisely to real friends ~~I thoug~~ that I should have thought them unnecessary. <u>You</u> who have passed your whole life in denouncing forms & saying how you never would act upon them. If one of "my children" as you ~~angrily~~ call them

---

44. The letter is dated 24 July and is written on mourning stationary. The year is 1849, the year of John Taylor's death. XXVII/56.

45. Letter is dated 7 August and is written on mourning stationary. The year is 1849, the year of John Taylor's death. XXVII/57.

46. Arthur Ley.

had said to me on that day, 'shall I write to grandmama? I should most ~~certainly~~ likely have answered 'Oh no dear she will hear ~~the sad news~~ soon enough & write or come up directly'—that Herbert, as it appears, thought it sufficient to write to Arthur who for anything I knew might be with you and who is always in ~~I beleive~~ constant correspondence with you, you call an "unparrelled insult"! You then proceed to say that you hold me accountable for what you ~~think~~ consider Herbert's omissions—I may perhaps once for all say that I have never held myself accountable for any one's actions but my own On this principle of yours I might hold you accountable for Caroline's[47] ~~total~~ neglect of me.

You say my children 'show no inclination to write to' you have they ever failed to do so when you have written to them which considering your relative ages & positions it might be supposed you would do when you wished to hear from them.

I had immediately many kind letters of sympathy & condolence from his relations & friends but none from any relation of my own except Arthur, this tho' I felt, especially on the part of Caroline to whom I acted ~~very~~ so differently when she was suffering from the loss of her child, I should not have mentioned but for your letter of blame & anger to me.

You will see by this letter that there are at least two sides to the question & that if you feel strongly in yours ~~side~~ I do so no less on mine.

I should have replied to your letter on Friday when I received it but I was oppressed with business & left town early on Saturday for the country whence I have just returned & hasten to reply immediately to I think all that your letter contains.

Beleive me Affec^{ly} Y^{rs}
H. Taylor

Brighton Jan 21.
Afternoon[48]

My dear Mama,

I am but just out of bed, having been quite ill with a very bad cold & the accompanying fever for the last two days. I meant to have gone to town to-day but it was impossible—I now intend to go to-morrow. Martha & Arthur[49] were here only from Sat^y Even^g to Monday morn^g. I understood they intended to be in London to-day from Rugby & to leave for Bideford

---

47. Caroline (Hardy) Ley.

48. The letter is written on mourning stationary, so it was probably written 21 January 1850 since Arthur Hardy had just married. XXVII/58.

49. Arthur and Martha Hardy.

on Thursday If I see them, or either of them in town, as no doubt I shall, I will tell them what you say, not to go to Bideford before Thursday, but this will not I think be any inconvenience to them as I beleive that was the day they intended.

I do not know if Martha had a servant with her here or not but I am convinced she does not need to 'learn to dispense with a maid' for she is not in the least a humbug. She said that only the one sister is going out with them now, which for her sake I am sorry for, as if this one should marry she will be very lonely. It is indeed a strange fatality that has attended Arthur's visit to England—death coming close to him in so many directions. <u>Black hideous useless</u> death! (notwithstanding its grand beauty.)

[The following two paragraphs have a line drawn down through the middle indicating they may have been crossed out.]

About the Laing's⁵⁰ affair—I think there are two things to consider

---

50. Dr. Laing had written to Harriet Hardy requesting funds to support his brother, John, and his wife (Harriet Hardy's sister). Three drafts of a reply are located in the Mill/Taylor Collection (I/16, I/17, and I/18). This letter includes all of I/17 except where noted. I/16 is dated December 1849 and reads: "Dear [   ]—I need not say that it grieves me deeply to hear such an account of my sister's & your brother's present circumstances as that you give me. But it appears that you must labour under some extraordinary delusion with regard to my pecuniary means when you ask me to contribute about an eighth of my income for their support. I think that I should be doing largely, & more than the justice of the case demands if I agree to contribute as large a per centage on my small income as you & Mrs. Webb, Mr. Geo Laing Mr. Josh Oldham & the other members of your family contribute from their large ones. I am always ready to do what is fair & just, but few things seem to me less so than the purposal that I shᵈ contribute one quarter of all that is collected for the support of your brother's family. When all the members of your family who possess larger incomes than myself have put down their names according to their means. I have little doubt I shall be able to do the same.

I must not omit to say that whatever I may contribute must not be considered an annual allowance.

(about its not being annual need not be touched upon in this stage of the business.)"

L/18 appears to be a more formal draft letter Harriet sent to her mother. It reads: "Bideford Jan. 28 1850 / My Dear Sir / Before replying to a letter I have received from Mr. John Laing, allow me to make some remarks to you connected with your application on his behalf. First when I was in London I called upon my sister Mrs. Laing who repeated to me what I had before been told by your brother that Mr. George Laing now owed his brother John a sum which if paid him would release him from all is difficulties but that it was now cut off by the statute of limitations.

Can this be possible, and if so, can he as a Christian or gentleman and moreover a brother bear to avail himself of his own wrong in suffering this to become by his own delay a debt of honour while grudgingly offering a mere dole as an act of charity.

Next I must mention that having proposed to your brother John to try to procure a situation in some house of his own trade, he replied "they are all such snobs" meaning I preume that in what you do—First, that whatever you do now you are sure to be asked to continue & that you would give far more offence by refusing to do so than you will satisfaction by anything you do now—2^{ly} by that according to Mr Laing they have enough for mere subsistence already contributed even supposing the three sums he mentions[51] to be all they have to look to.

My own opinion is that a cheque from you for £5 enclosed in a short note to Dr Laing saying that it is all you feel called on to afford, would fully meet the justice of the case.

I need not say that I do not for a moment wish you to act upon my opinion if your own would be different.[52]

I think people have no right to expect others to support them till they have done all they can to support themselves—& this Mr Laing has never done, whether from idleness, or the vulgar pride of not descending in the world I do not know but at all events those only who would be ashamed of their relations working honestly among the poor can be called on to maintain them among the rich. Mrs Laing does seem to me to be pitied, because I have always fancied that she would have greatly preferred economy & forethought. You must observe that we know nothing whatever of what they have been living on the last ten years, or why that should suddenly cease. If his business has maintained them all this while why not continue to do so. On Mr Laings part it is a mere demand of alms without

----

their vulgarity was reason enough for declining to accept from them employment that would enable him to support his family. Now when I consider that my younger and unmarried sister received from my father what would have maintained her for life and of which she has foolishly suffered herself to be utterly deprived at the instance of your brother, so that, as she has told me, she is not even able to avail herself of the shelter of an almshouse, they requiring the possession of £20 a year before admitting an inmate, I think I am justified in feeling [unjust] at the preference evinced for the charity of friends over honest earnings, however deficient the [   ] may be in refinement or good breeding. I observe, that excepting your own as usual generous assistance, none of his own nephews and nieces, some I believe very wealthy, have offered to contribute at all. To show my willingness to do what my small means enable me to offer I will enclose him five pounds which with two I gave when in London I beg may be considered as the widow's mite, but I cannot pledge myself to any annual sum. My income is sufficient for my own support but no more. Your having so kindly interested yourself in this business has caused me to trouble you with these observations for which I trust you will excuse / Dear Sir / Your very faithfully / &c. &c."

Dr. Laing responded in a gracious way (see Mill/Taylor, XXIX/244), so the note must not have been too harsh.

51. L/17 replaces "mentions" with "names."

52. L/17 added "But" to the beginning of this sentence.

any reason given for wanting it or for supposing that he intends to do anything for himself as long as he can get on without.

It is the usual spendthrift system to spend and lament instead of work & economise. <u>Real</u> <u>misfortune</u> is quite another matter.

You see Dr. Laing says nothing of any subscription from any of their nephews or neices—Jos. Oldham or Mr. Wylde &c therefore I think you had <u>much</u> better not mention your children either. Why <u>I</u> am selected by Dr. Laing to the exclusion of Arthur or Caroline I do not know, unless the whole application was caused by the idea that it would be easy to persuade the two women.

This is a very hurried & incomplete letter but I am now so tired that I must leave off—when I have written a few words to Caroline.

Adieu Ever Affec^{ly} Y^{rs}

H. T.

It is a curious part of the thing that <u>your</u> relations have not applied to you—I am too tired to write more to-day but will write to C. in a day or two.

Blackheath[53]

May 5.

1855

My dear Mama,

I received your letter last week after I had written to Caroline. You say you should have written in reply to my request that you will send me my letters but that you had been expecting to hear of me through Caroline, and you do not now give me any answer about them much to my disapointment, as I hoped you would find them and send them me before I again leave England. You mention being reading some of them, one in which Emilia is mentioned, but if you do not send them untill you have read them all through it would be long indeed, considering what long and ample letters I was in the constant habit of writing you as long as my health and strength allowed, and even longer, for I have often and often sat writing to you because I hoped to amuse you when you were dull, when if I had considered myself rather than you I should not have been able to do so. I wish you would write and tell me that you will send them by railway as I asked you, as soon as possible. I need not say that the expense of packing-case &c would be mine.

I have not any news to tell you so Adieu Affec^{ly}

H. M.

---

53. XXVII/63.

Blackheath[54]
May 30.
1855

My dear Mama

I am glad to find you say that you seriously intend to seek out and send me the letters I asked you for at your earliest convenience & hope that may prove to be not very long hence.

I hope the 'change of residence' you mention will be a pleasant one I suppose by this time it is settled and has begun to occupy you in moving. I hope Annie continues her lessons with Miss MacKenzie especially those, in history with which Miss MacKenzie it seemed that had taken some pains.

We are now preparing for our journey to meet Mr Mill tho the weather is by no means promising we shall return home with him by the end of June.

Yours Affec[ly]
H. Mill

Blackheath[55]
Aug. 19
1855

My dear Mama

I was glad to hear you have been enjoying the fine weather on the seashore as you describe. It must be a very fine beach. I have differred going to the sea owing to Haji having come home for ten days or a fortnight but we shall go next week to the Isle of Wight as Haji is going back then and we shall go directly afterwards.

Lily['s] state of health gives me serious anxiety, she is quite out of health in many ways, and the two Physicians I have consulted about her both hinting at consumption, I dread indescribably every symptom that seems like a threat of that insidious enemy—I do not myself think her symptoms consumptive but more of the sort of Haji's, tho' still very different but her continual fainting quite away as she does without any apparent cause is very trying—however she has not fainted quite since she has taken to the meat & wine diet with steel,[56] but she nearly does so at often. I know these particulars will not interest you but I have nothing more amusing to write about. I hope much from the sea air & bathing. I have had for

---

54. XXVII/65. Annie is Caroline Hardy Ley's daughter.

55. XXVII/67.

56. Iron as used medicinally.

some weeks past a return of weakness in the arm & wrist almost preventing my writing.

Yours Affec^{ly}
H. Mill

Yale Lodge
Melville Street. Ryde⁵⁷
Sep 11.

My dear Mama,

I was on the point of writing to you at Bideford this morning when I received yours from London and am sorry to hear you have been so much inconvenienced. It is unlucky that the lodgings you always liked are not unoccupied, but at this season there are so ~~very~~ many to be let that you will find no difficulty in getting others as good, and it is the cheapest season of the year.

When I wrote the sentance you mention in my last letter, "I know these particulars will not interest you but I have nothing more amusing to write about" I had no ~~idea or~~ intention of a 'sling' or that it would in the least degree annoy or offend you, or of course I should not have written it. I felt as I often do, that ~~I had written~~ it was a very dull and uninteresting letter & said so & I think I must have said the same ~~words~~ very often before for the same reason. I can most justly say that I do not deserve your accusation about Caroline—all my conduct to her has shewn the contrary & the strong desire I have always felt for her friendship.

As to whom she should consult I should be puzzled to advise—~~as~~ I have never had occasion hitherto to consult the Physicians who ~~are consulted~~ prescribe for women's complaints peculiarly and it must be those who are required.

Lily continues very unwell & causes me the greatest anxiety, the Quinine & Bark & full diet ordered for her does not agree with her & she has been obliged to leave it off, yet the continual fever & great weakness continues. She thinks she is better for the sea bathing—my own inclination is to try the water treatment. I suppose Annie is much pleased by her visit to London.

Adieu Affec^{ly}
H. M.

Mrs. Hardy at Mrs. Clemences
36 Craven Street
Strand. London

---

57. The letter is dated 11 September. The year is 1855, since HTM writes her mother a few days later from the same location on the Isle of Wight. XXVII/70.

Ryde[58]
Sep 15
1855

My dear Mama,

Now that you have got comfortable lodgings you will be able to go about and see what there is to be seen. You say they are very good and handsome but very dear, but at this season they can hardly be more than it is well worth while to pay for comfort. I suppose you see a great deal of Edward[59] as he is living in or near London which I did not know till you told me you had promised to stay with him. He will be able to go with you to whatever you wish to see. The Chrystal Palace must be from all I have heared much better worth seeing than the one in Hyde Park was. I have not seen it yet.

Have you seen Herbert or his wife? It is not a good opportunity for the sea for you. our movements are very uncertain. both I and Lily are very unwell and almost equally weak. I should like to go with her to try the water cure but do not know if we shall manage it. I have thought she has seemed better after bathing. I should think the lodgings you mentioned at Northam Burrows must be very pleasant & not dear & there would be as much quiet & repose as you can possibly wish for. If you will put up any letters you have brought for me in a sheet of brown paper & seal & direct them to Blackheath by the Parcels C° they will arrive quite safely. The weather has been delightful as yet but to-day is dull & cold & threatens a change. Affec^ly Yours, H. M.

Ryde[60]
Oct 5

My dear Mama,

When you write next will you direct to Blackheath. The weather has quite changed this last week, after having been most beautiful it is now very wet and stormy and we are thinking of returning home next week. I hope you are all the better for your short excursion. Did Caroline consult any medical man, and if so did she get any advice she thought likely to be useful? I have found them of but little use in any chronic ailment. Lily thinks she is rather better and that she shall get better with time and the medicine & regimen she is taking. The sea bathing has seemed to do her

---

58. Marked in pencil as "copy." XXVII/72.

59. Edward Hardy, HTM's brother.

60. Both the original and a copy of this letter are preserved in the Mill/Taylor collection. The letter was written in 1855. XXVII/73.

some good but her extreme weakness continues and makes me very anxious and uneasy, and she has an extreme dislike to consulting the Doctors.

Haji is certainly better which is a great comfort after twelvemonths of the water cure. I hope you saw the Chrystal Palace and some of the ~~many~~ other things worth seeing in London. Annie I suppose was delighted with her visit.

Yours Affec^{ly}
H. M.

It is not the fact that I never replied to your last but one letter at all ~~for you las~~ for your last was in reply to mine you have only written in your turn, & ~~not~~ no letter of yours has not been followed by one of mine ~~If it were true that I~~ otherwise you ~~would~~ must have written twice without one from me in the interval, which you have not done. For every letter of yours you have received one from me

Haji's address is here. Letters a pretence [note breaks off at this point][61]

Blackheath[62]
Dec. 4

My dear Mama,

I was very sorry to hear that my last [letter] had been wrong delivered, but I addressed it as I have done for many years past, thinking it was as you preferred and I was not in the least aware that any one else of the name was living in the town. I remember long ago your saying that some one from Yorkshire had come to Bideford but I supposed it was only a temporary stay. I am surprised to hear of Edward ~~being~~ living at Paris, but I never hear anything of him except from you. Some time since wanting his address, and having heared from you that you did not then know it, I wrote to Mr. Firth asking for it, but in reply he sent only that

---

61. No postmark or watermark dates the note; XXVII/76. It was probably written in the fall of 1855, since HTM had been requesting her letters be returned to her throughout the fall of that year. This note was written on the back of a note from Harriet Hardy to HTM that reads:

> I sent the large packet of letters according to your directions to Blackheath by the Parcels delivery Co. I should have been glad to have heard that they were received.
> H. H.

This note appeared without the arrival of the infamous packet of letters, however. XXVII/83, written the following winter, indicates that the Parcel Company never fails to deliver packages, and XXVII/80, written at Christmas that year, flat-out accuses her mother of never having sent the package of letters.

62. The Indian mutiny referred to in the letter happened in 1856. XXVII/83.

of his lawyer. Did he mention his address at Paris? A long time ago I received some cards of 'Mr. & Mrs. L. Edward Hardy' and one day I called at the address given, but no one was at home and I have heard nothing of them since. I do not even know whose son this is. The lady's name was on the card but I forget it. Mrs. White sent me the other day a Daguerre-otype[63] of Arthur's children with a note asking me to return it within a week as it was intended for a sister living in France but that Arthur had desired I might see it on its way. It was a very pretty picture. We have been as you may suppose very much taken up with the Indian difficulties & Mr. Mill very hard worked in consequence We ought to leave England for the winter but cannot.[*]
With my love to Louis[64] & Annie and Hajis & Lilys to you I am

Yours Affec[ly]
H. Mill

[*]any parcel sent here by the Parcels comp[y] always arrives quite safely, we receive them every day & never lost one.

Brighton[65]
Dec 25

My dear Mama

I had fully intended answering your letter of Nov 22[d] this morn[g] and I have now just received yours of last Tuesday. I have been full of occupations of all sorts which have caused the delay, not however a very long one, in replying to it.

In yours of Nov 22[d.] you repeat what you said in a former letter that my having written to you last February is a delusion. Now I hold in my hand your answer, dated March 1st 1856 which begins with these words "I received your letter of good wishes on my birthday" This you see is positive proof that I wrote & that you received a letter from me last February and that I am under no delusion about it. You will see that you have been mistaken about this. I have never knowingly neglected to answer any of your letters.

It is twenty years since you gave me that old picture which used to hang in my bedroom when I was a child and I should not like to part

---

63. Early type of photograph.

64. Louis and Anne Ley, Caroline Hardy Ley's children

65. The letter is dated 25 December. The year must be 1856, since HTM refers to a dispute about a letter from March 1856. See HTM's letter to Helen (LI/7) for more on this dispute. XXVII/80.

with it. Nor should I like to return all the letters you have ever written to me, you know you have not returned mine.[66]

I am very glad to hear you have so much satisfaction in Caroline's children & that Louis improves so much. That Annie is making not only a pleasant but an improving visit is indeed fortunate.

I do not wonder that you felt the cold even in Devonshire where I suppose it was much less severe than with us. It has been really terrible. I never knew so hard and long a winter before Christmas, It is to be hoped it will be an earlier spring. We leave this place & return home next week where we are expecting some friends to stay a week or ten days with us ~~from a very long standing invitation~~

Please to address to Blackheath & wishing you a pleasant Christmas & a happy new year. ~~Hoping to hear you are better for the mild weather.~~ I am Yours Affec^{ly} H. Mill

LETTERS CONCERNING THE TRUSTEESHIP, 1842–57

1. To Thomas Carlyle

Walton.[67] July 9

Dear Mr Carlyle,

I am going to ask you to do for me what if you consent to, I shall find to be a great favour.

It is to be trustee to a little settlement made at the time of my marriage upon me—& upon the children. of the present two trustees, one, a M^r· Travers, a brother in law of M^r· Taylor's is going to leave England to live abroad & I am anxious to have the vacancy filled so that I shall leave this portion of my young ones interests in the surest hands.

---

66. In XXVII/76, Harriet writes on the back of a note from her mother indicating that Mrs. Hardy had sent a large packet of Harriet's letters back to her; but as late as December 1856, Harriet is claiming that her mother had not returned these letters. XXVII/83 may be a clue to the mystery. In that letter Harriet adds a postscript to her mother saying that all the Parcel Company packages arrive safely and none has ever been lost. One might construe the following senario: Harriet begs her mother all fall 1855 for her letters to be sent to her. Harriet's mother writes a note saying she had sent them and demanding to know why she hasn't heard that they had arrived. Either they were sent and lost, or never sent, since on December 4 of 1856 Harriet's postscript attempts to countermand the excuse(?) given by her mother. By Christmas, Harriet is still claiming her mother had never sent the letters.

67. 1842 was the year in which the trusteeship was debated. XXVII/2.

Au reste[68] it is a very simple matter & could in no way cause any trouble or inconvenience, otherwise I should hardly feel entitled to ask it. May I hope that you will not dissapoint me in this?

Dear Mr Carlyle
Most Truly Yrs
H. Taylor

Pray present my kind regards to Mrs Carlyle. Mr. Taylor joins in this request & proposes to take an early opportunity of calling at Chelsea to make it in person.

2. To Arthur Ley

Kent Terrace[69]
Nov. 19

Dear Arthur,

From what my mother said this morn^g I understand that since I saw you yesterday you had spoken of buying something as a present to me. I suppose therefore that you did not understand me yesterday to say decidedly that I would rather not accept any present whatever. I will not defer repeating this untill I see you next, lest it might cause you inconveniences, but hasten to say ~~that~~ with all the thanks your kind intention ~~merits~~ deserves that you must excuse my acting according to my own ideas & positively declining ~~at present~~ to accept any thing.

I have thought a good deal over the various subjects of our talk yesterday in which we differed, without much change in my own opinion. No doubt I shall be able to have half an hours conversation with you again before you finally leave London.

Truly Y^{rs}
H. Taylor

3. To Arthur Hardy

I thank you for both your letters & for your offer of assistance but there is nothing at present in which I need help. I feel most deeply the loss of the

---

68. "Rest assured."

69. No date or watermark indicates the year, but the discussion of a present for Harriet may indicate that it was written the fall after her marriage at Easter 1851. XXVII/91.

truest & best & dearest friend that ever anyone had & all expressions of ~~sympathy & regret~~ sorrow for his ~~loss~~ untimely death are welcome to me.

He died without pain & without even a sigh—he had remained in the same tranquil ~~clear-minded~~ courageous gentle affectionate state to the end.

I shall be happy to see you any day after Wed^y—unless you sh^d be going out of town again immediately in which case 'we can meet when you return.

Yrs Aff^y

H Taylor[70]

4. To Arthur Hardy

Copy of half letter to Arthur.[71] March 1855

in August 1853. I shall be sorry if you did not get it as I had it bound on purpose for you and Mr Mill wrote in it. I have never much news to tell you knowing so few of the same people. Our mother is in health and strength quite as well as when you saw her last; tho' Caroline is always telling her 'that her life is very precarious' I know no one who from all appearances is more likely to live to a great age. All her characteristics have much increased with age, among others the passion for saving money—which Caroline with her intense selfishness encourages. her income is now about three hundred a year of which ~~Caroline~~ they spends a part and ~~has the rest~~ settled ~~on herself~~ the rest on Caroline. I have made it a rule to invite my mother every year—since I saw you three years I have gone to Devonshire & taken a house and she has come to me there. This last winter she spent a month with me at Torquay, & Caroline and her children came also. Caroline has grown stout and looks very well. I never see any thing of Edward. They correspond with him at Bideford & say he has let Birksgate, but no doubt they have told you about it.

I have been much concerned lately to hear that Macauley[72] is in very bad health, but you probably know more of this than I do. Mr Mill has

---

70. Pencilled on the back of a letter from Arthur Hardy, written after the death of John Taylor, July 1849. XXVII/45. This may have been a draft of a letter to JSM. See XXVIII/126 in the previous chapter.

71. This letter must have been a very early draft of the long letter she revised several times (see XXVII/47, XXVII/48, and XXVII/49). The opening refers to a box containing a copy of *Principles of Political Economy,* which she had sent him two years prior (1853) to her writing the letter (1855). XXVII/46.

72. Thomas Macauley (1800-59) wrote *History of England.* He disagreed with most of John Stuart Mill's ideas, but they remained friends.

the offer of a very nice place under government in one of the Greek islands, it being supposed the climate might suit both his and my health, but tho' much tempted I do not think we shall accept it, we both dread the heat which is said to be excessive in in [*sic*] summer. I do not know if you take much interest in the war[73]—we think there is little to choose between the two despots who are the real combatants. Lily joins in kindest love to you & with very kind regards to Martha & kisses to the dear children I am Dear Arthur always Affectionately Yours H. Mill

5. To Arthur Hardy[74]

My dear Arthur I found my letter would be too large for one envelope if I enclosed the copies, so I enclose them separately. Pray observe the implication in Caroline's last sentance that A. L, a defaulter already in one Trust, is a better guardian of my children's interest than myself. I should have said that the new Trustee we proposed is a man of the very highest character & of large fortune, living in London—therefore as Wm L.[75] said more suitable than A. Ley residing in Devonshire on this point Wm L. satisfied himself before he began to move in the affair.

Ever Affec^ly

H.M

Nothing can be more insulting to me personally than that last sentance of Carolines. I need scarcely say that Haji & Lily <u>as Caroline knows</u> desire the change as much as I do Herbert only professing indifference.

Affec^ly Yours

H M

Arthur Hardy Esq
Adelaide
South Australia

enclosing copies of mine to C of Oct 3^d. 1855 & of her answer to it Oct 10. 1855

---

73. Probably referring to the Crimean War pitting Napolean against Russia.

74. Probably written 30 October 1855, this note enclosed copies of Caroline's letter to Harriet, and reiterates a paragraph written at the end of a draft of the longer letter, XXVII/49. XXVII/47.

75. William Ley, Arthur's brother.

6. To Arthur Hardy

Blackheath Park[76]
Oct 30. 1855

(Private)

My dear Arthur,

I have not heared from you since the beginning of 1854. I hope you have not ceased to write because I have become a bad correspondent, after having been a good one. I have been so reduced in strength since my bad illness in 1853 when I broke a blood vessel in the lungs and was not expected to recover for some months, and since that I have twice undergone a surgical operation, that I have seldom had strength to write more than a few lines at a time. I wrote to you this spring to ask if you have ever received the box containing a copy of Mr Mill's Logic which we sent to you in the autumn of 1853. I fear you have not had it or you would have written. Mr Mill has enquired at the broker's but can hear nothing of it. If it turns out that you did not get it I shall send another copy & endeavour to take sufficient care, tho' we thought we had done all that was possible before. You no doubt know the name of M$^{r.}$ Gavan Duffy, he is one of the Irish members of Parliament of the young Ireland Party, & being disgusted with English Politics in their present state intends to emigrate and Mr Mill has mentioned you to him saying that in case he should go to Adelaide he feels sure you would be happy to give him any assistance or advice in your power. Information about the country would be probably what he would most value, & any use you could be of to him would much please & oblige us both. He is an old Political acquaintance of Mr Mills & was very zealous many years ago to bring Mr Mill into Parliament, which he was obliged to decline as inconsistent with his office at the India House & since then Mr Mill has seen nothing of him, but they have always continued very friendly feelings.

I wish to tell you now of an affair which is a very painful subject to me & difficult to do justice to in a short letter, but I feel that if I do not tell you the facts you may either never hear them at all, or not hear the truth.

You remember no doubt how many years ago I wrote to you telling you how uneasy I felt at Arthur Ley being a Trustee of my marriage

---

76. This is the only complete draft (although it is unclear whether it is more final than XXVII/49) of a letter she sent to Arthur about the trusteeship of Arthur Ley. I will note any differences between this draft and XXVII/49. XXVII/48.

settlement. M^r. Taylor felt the same for many years before his death & often talked of getting A. L to resign, but he did not know exactly upon what plea to make the request & so it remained undone, to his great regret. Since 1849 I have always intended to ask A. L to resign when I could find an opportunity to do so in a friendly way. Last Christmas I went to Torquay & took a house there on purpose to invite my mother & Caroline. I did all in my power (or any ones) to make them comfortable & give them pleasure, the return for which was all sorts of[77] unfriendliness so that I left after two months exertions feeling that I hoped never to pass such a time again. I invited Arthur Ley but he did not come. Among other things about him Caroline said that he was Treasurer to the Commissioners of the Turnpike Trust and that he had taken & used, or in some way made away with about £700 of the Trust money. That his brothers W^m & James were then going to communicate the fact to his father & to ask his assistance, & this[78] appears to have caused the old man's death. When Mr Mill returned from the continent in June last I consulted him about it, & he thinking it most unfit that Ar. Ley should continue a Trustee called on Wm Ley to see what he thought on the subject. W^m like an honest man said[79] that in his opinion[80] it was most ~~unfit~~ improper that A. L. should hold the Trusteeship,[81] that he felt sure he would give it up the moment he knew we wished it, & offered to write to him himself about it, which he did, & received an answer[82] saying that A. L. required that I and also Herbert should write to him making the request. This I did, but Herbert after first[83] saying he would, then made difficulties,[84] & finally (it appearing[85] that Caroline or Arthur Ley had written to him in the interval unknown to me)[86] declared that he saw no occasion to write at all, that[87]

---

77. XXVII/49 adds "petty underhanded" at this point.

78. XXVII/49 adds "communication" at this point.

79. XXVII/49 adds "at once" at this point.

80. "It was most improper that A. L. should" reads "Arthur ought not to" in XXVII/49.

81. XXVII/49 adds "and" at this point.

82. "Saying that A. L." reads "from A L—saying that he" in XXVII/49.

83. "Saying he would" reads "agreeing" in XXVII/49.

84. "& finally" does not appear in XXVII/49.

85. XXVII/49 adds "afterwards" at this point.

86. XXVII/49 adds "and at last" at this point.

87. XXVII/49 substitutes "as" for "that."

his consent is not legally ~~necessary~~ required, & that in short he would take no part in the matter.[88] I <u>had</u> <u>not</u> mentioned to him the fact of the Treasureship from delicacy to Caroline & he does not know it yet. (2)[89] It is very mean & treacherous of Caroline to make a handle of Herberts contradictory temper, as she would not have thought of it as possible if she had not duped me into writing to her confidentially about my family troubles. (1) It is true that by the terms of the settlement Herbert's consent is not required, for the children[90] have[91] no voice in the matter, but had he[92] chosen to write & give it ~~notwithstanding~~ they[93] would have had to find some other excuse for refusing. However as Wm Ley said ~~that~~ it was impossible Arthur[94] could continue to refuse if we urged it[95] I wrote again telling him his brother's opinion & again politely but more urgently requesting him to resign The Trust. To this I received no answer but Wm Ley who went to Bideford at the time told us when he returned[96] that he could make nothing of A.L.[97] at all, that he refused altogether to explain himself either about our affair or his own, & that he,[98] Wm Ley, should ~~have~~ be obliged to file a bill against him on his own account—(which he has since done) He said that he had in vain tried to get ~~him~~ A L to give

---

88. An alternate reading replaces the section beginning here and ending with (1). XXVII/49 reads: "To those who know Herbert's contradictory temper his refusal to assist in any thing which he did not himself originate is not surprising, especially as I did not mention to him the fact of A L's defalcation, not liking to have a thing which to me seems so disgraceful spread abroad—but is is [*sic*] peculiarly mean & treacherous of Caroline to make a handle of his temper against me, as she would never have known it to be possible if she had not duped me into writing confidentially to her for her own interest."

89. Harriet probably inserted the numbers 2 and 1 here and before the next sentence to remind herself to reverse these sentences when she recopied the draft.

90. "For the children" reads "they" in XXVII/49.

91. XXVII/49 adds "indeed" at this point.

92. XXVII/49 replaces "he" with "Herbert" at this point.

93. XXVII/49 replaces "they" with "Caroline" at this point.

94. XXVII/49 replaces "Arthur" with "his brother."

95. XXVII/49 replaces the phrases beginning here and ending at "at the time told us" with "& offered, as he was then going to Bideford on his own affairs, to speak to him."

96. XXVII/49 adds "he said" at this point.

97. XXVII/49 substitutes the name "Arthur."

98. "Wm Ley" is not included in XXVII/49.

any account of his stewardship[99] of their father's estate, that he had urged him to give <u>some</u> account, however imperfect, but that he refused. He said he was quite puzzled & could not at all understand his conduct. But[100] from what I ~~have seen~~ saw ~~have been~~ & heared last Christmas I can understand it. It is not A. L[101] who is acting[102] in either matter—he is a mere tool in the hands of Caroline & a clerk[103] of his named Jones who transact the whole of his affairs as well as Carolines. I knew well that Ar.[104] would neither speak nor act except under her direction—and accordingly[105] when Wm Ley went to Bideford Caroline came[106] up to town, not having given me the least hint of her intention to do so. & we were staying in the Isle of Wight at the time ~~so that~~ & I did not see her. When[107] we found Wm Ley had failed at Bideford & I had got no answer to my last[108] letters to A. L.[109] I wrote to Caroline appealing to her[110] ~~as a matter of honour and honesty~~ ~~on a matter of honour & honesty~~ to induce ~~A. L.~~ him[111] to give up the Trust. In reply I received a most base[112] & unworthy

---

99. XXVII/49 substitutes the word "management."

100. XXVII/49 replaces this sentence with the following: "for that Arthur had told him some years ago that he should be glad to be received from the Trust. But I can understand it plainly enough. at the time A L said this he had not come so entirely under Carolines dominion as he has since."

101. XXVII/49 substitutes "he."

102. XXVII/49 adds "at all."

103. Two phrases have been struck out in this section: "~~in either matter~~ ~~he is a mere tool~~" and "~~in the hands of Caroline & a clerk~~."

104. XXVII/49 substitutes "A L."

105. XXVII/49 substitutes the following for "when Wm Ley went to Bideford": "I was not surprised at William Leys want of success when I heard that on his going to Bideford."

106. XXVII/49 substitutes "had come."

107. "When we found . . . Bideford &" does not appear in XXVII/49.

108. XXVII/49 replaces "my last letters" with "a second letter."

109. XXVII/49 adds "urging him to resign, & have not to this day" at this point.

110. XXVII/49 replaces the struck out words with "sense of honour."

111. XXVII/49 substitutes "A L" at this point.

112. XXVII/49 substitutes "insolent" for "base & unworthy."

letter from her,[113] false in every particular, & made up of pretended offences to account for her determination to keep hold of the chance of future power over the Trust. ~~money.~~ If unfortunately the other Trustee (M^r. Thornton)[114] were to die A.L would be the sole Trustee. I shall enclose a copies of my letter ~~to her~~ & of her answer. ~~& of my reply to the last I have received no answer~~ reply I must wish you to know the whole case: you are pretty nearly ~~if not quite~~ the only ~~respectable~~ relation I possess & I should be ~~deeply~~ much hurt if you were to beleive Bideford culumnies & mis-representations which I ~~now guess~~ think must have been going on for years ~~were to be believed by you.~~ & which would account for many things which puzzled me in 1849 & 50.

I ~~have long seen~~ can see clearly the wish to create dislike between us. ~~Caroline~~ The personal bad feeling to me ~~shown in her letter~~ I can only attribute to my having remonstrated, tho' very gently, about ~~her~~ C's selfish conduct with regard to her mother. Nothing ~~This response?~~ can be more untrue than the accusation that I have neglected her since last Christmas—I wrote frequently to her untill she ceased to answer my letters—I have heaped kindnesses on her which she has never in any way returned even by kind feeling & the first time in my life I ask her to do any thing for me, & this a thing which ~~justice and honour would require her to do~~ she ought to have done without asking without asking [*sic*],

---

113. XXVII/49 reads quite differently from this point until the phrase "she ceased to answer my letters." The passage in XXVII/49 reads: "pretending that it is from her regard for the interests of "M^r. Taylor's children" that she refuses. I shall Pray observe &c she ~~attempting~~ attempts a half denial of what she told me about the Treasurership, & professes to be offended that I mentioned it (in my letter to herself) tho' I could get no answer to my applications to it. & she having told me often that I could write to her without reserve as A. L did not see her letters. I am persuaded that if he saw this one it was because it suited her purposes to show it to him. This is mixed up with a base jeer about how she supposes I should behave if she were poor—she knows well that I have always sought & she has always cut ~~our~~ all poor relations. Her pretence that I have ~~treated~~ neglected her ~~differently to usual~~ since she told me of A. L's conduct is utterly false, for I wrote constantly to her till she ceased to answer my letters. I beleive her reason for telling me of it was ~~the~~ an expectation that I should offer to pay ~~it,~~ the money, but considering that his father & brothers are so well off & that Caroline herself has now ample means, I did not feel at all required to do so—especially as she treated the discreditable nature of the affair with great indifference, her greed of money is so great as to prevent all delicacy. All ~~ther~~ pretended subjects of offences are to account for her deter-mination to keep hold of future power over the Trust-money. Her personal bad feeling to me I can only attribute to my having remonstrated, tho' very gently about her conduct with regard to her mother."

114. A colleague of John Stuart Mill's at India House.

she refuses, and not even with civility. Her pretending to think I ~~was or~~ was or should be less friendly ~~because I thought her if she were~~ because I thought her poor is too monstrous, being the exact reverse of all my conduct thro' life, as she well knows—besides that she is now ~~less poor~~ in fact less poor[115] than ever she was in[116] her life before. She has her own £70 per an., the entire use of her mother's £300 pr. an. &[117] at least £30 interest of her mother's savings settled on herself making considerably more than [118]400 pr an besides whatever Ar. Ley has. This is not poverty,[119] & is always increasing You are no doubt aware of the extremely bad state of the law with regard to Trustees. If A. L. were the sole trustee I feel persuaded the money would be very unlikely to be got out of their hands, and[120] I do hope ~~that~~ if I and Mr Mill were to die leaving it[121] ~~in their hands so~~ so you would watch over the interests of Haji & Lily of whom you would ~~be~~ then be the sole relation.

---

115. XXVII/49 substitutes "better off" for "in fact less poor."

116. "In her life" does not appear in XXVII/49.

117. XXVII/49 substitutes "I believe at least £50" for "at least £30."

118. XXVII/49 adds "£."

119. For the phrase "& is always increasing," XXVII/49 substitutes the much longer passage, "They say ~~he~~ AL will have about 2000 from his fathers estate. ~~I shall send you a copy of my letter & of Caroline's answer. I should say that before Wm Ley moved in the matter he ascertained that the gentleman we proposed for the new Trustee is a man of large fortune & the highest character living in London, whom Mr Mill has known all his life (a Mr Ellis) I must wish you to know the whole case. You are~~
I should say that the new Trustee we proposed (one of Mr. Mill's oldest friends, Mr Ellis) is a man of the very highest character & of large fortune residing in London, & therefore as Will Ley said, more suitable than A.L living in Devonshire I need scarcely say that Haji & Lily desire the change as much as I do—Herbert only professing indifference.
I much wish you to know the whole case: you are pretty nearly if not quite the only relation I possess & I should be much hurt if you were to beleive Bideford misrepresentations which I think must have been going on for years & which would account for many things which puzzled me in 1849-50."

120. In place of "and" XXVII/49 reads: "it would then stand in his sole name at the Bank & he (or any body else) would have only to destroy the deed to constitute it his without any legal redress but a chancery suit which might or might not succeed in proving the wrong, but which would <u>certainly</u> not get back the money, & which therefore my two children who would need it would in all probability lose along with what else they possessed if they embarked on such a hopeless affair as a Chancery suit."

121. XXVII/49 reads "the money in their hands" at this point.

Mr Mill returned from his long tour quite set up in health, but he is not strong tho' as busy as ever,[122] & I am often anxious about him.[123] Haji is much better since he has taken up his taste for farming—but I dread his attempting to farm on his own account, I think the little money he has got would soon be swallowed up—I never knew a young man succeed in farming (in this country) who was not brought up to it. Lily has been very unwell all the summer but is now recovering. She always sends very kind love to you. I also am better than I have been for several years. I am troubled much by stiffness of the right wrist[124] almost preventing my writing as you may perceive. With our united love & kind remembrance to you Martha & your little girl I am

Affec.ly Yours
H. Mill[125]

7. To Arthur Hardy

Blackheath[126] Sep 7. 1856.

My dear Arthur,

We returned only last Saturday from a two months excursion to Switzerland and I found your long letter of April 10th awaiting me here as well as one from Alfred.[127] For the kind & brotherly interest you show in my affairs accept my sincere thanks and beleive that I should act in the same manner if ever I could be of any service to you or yours. The account of your house & residence on Mount Lofty is delightful, the name is a

---

122. XXVII/49 adds "& in immense vogue, I never knew any man so highly thought of by the highest class of politicians, perhaps partly because of his studious retiring habits."

123. XXVII/49 adds: "he is so delicate, but he is in high spirits about himself, his Greek tour having succeeded so well."

124. XXVII/49 adds a footnote "*a very frequent ailment I understand of people who have been accustomed to much writing—It makes writing very difficult so that I have to a write long letter at different times" and stikes out "~~almost preventing my writing, as you may perceive~~."

125. XXVII/49 adds "I shall enclose a copy of my letter & of Caroline's answer. Pray observe the implication in her last sentence that Arthur Ley, already a defaulter in one Trust, is a better guardian of my childrens interest than myself. She attempts a half denial of what she told me about the Treasurership, & professes to be offended that I mentioned it (in my letter to herself) tho' I could get no answer to my applications to A L & she having told me often that I could write to her without reserve as A.L did not see her letters" after the closing. A version of this paragraph is found in XXVII/47.

126. XXVII/50.

127. Alfred Hardy, Harriet's brother.

poem and the place must be charming. How you contrive to get through such an immense quantity of work is to me a wonder & so far from being surprised at your not writing oftener I attribute to my own deficiences in the corresponding department the occasional long gaps in yours. do not pray think it necessary to write <u>long</u> letters for me, short ones are always welcome & pleasant when there is not subject for a long one. I am glad to hear that you still keep up your Institute, tho it has not answered all your hopes it is sure to sow good seed. we will send copies of the Political Eco^y as soon as we can get them bound. The dedication was not inserted in the 3^d edition as it was published in 1853 when it would have been no longer appropriate. Mr Mill is writing a new Philosophical book which is sure to make an immense sensation & this is to contain something of the same kind. The fourth edition of the Logic is just published—it has been translated into French Italian German & Spanish without either Mr Mill or his publisher hearing of it till it was done & published in the respective countries. This is a tribute to its utility & celebrity probably unparalled in a the case of a grave work. It is also adopted at the Universities. The sale of it is most surprizing, being so very dry a book.

I have forwarded your letter to Caroline and thank you for it. I have suffered more than you would perhaps imagine from the rupture with her & its cause. She has never answered my last letter nor has there been any further communication either with her or Ar Ley. Indeed Ar Ley's has long been a mere name, as he acts in all matters of business only under Caroline's direction and it was plain from her letter that she thought she should gain some advantage by refusing to resign the trust, & when once she thought that nothing would move her. If any thing would I imagine it would be your opinion. She has adopted with the utmost literalness our mother's incessantly repeated maxim that self interest is the only rule of life, and that all who do not make it so are either hypocrites or fools. my mother's toleration extends to allowing one to take ones choice of those two denominations. They, like many inexperienced people, fancy this opinion proves great "knowledge of the world" a thing which those who haven't it always greatly desire. It concerns me to think that I have caused you more labour in writing than I need have done, by not explaining with sufficient clearness the state of the case, but I am much obliged to you for all your suggestions. The original Trustees were our brother Thomas & Joseph Travers. Thomas was replaced by A. L. and Jos. Travers by his brother John Ingram Travers— the later proved a very careless & inefficient Trustee as I thought, & when we married we requested him to resign & a Mr Wm Thornton a colleague of Mr Mill's at the India House took his place and has been the acting Trustee ever since, & the deed of settlement is in his care. He is now I am sorry to say staying at Bournemouth for his health & I think and hope for his own sake that he will recover. In the event of his death A. Ley would be the only Trustee, & I should then have power to insist on another Trustee being appointed. any mischief A L could do would be in the interim, which circumstances (such as absence from England &c) might make of some duration. He himself might, & I have no doubt would, throw difficulties in the way of a new appointment. As to appointing a <u>third</u> Trustee now, our solicitors, [Messrs] Gregson, (Angel Court Thragmorton Street) are of opinion that we have not the power according to the terms of the deed to have more than two Trustees.

I see by the papers Mr Duffy[128] is speechifying at Melbourne as I suppose he would do wherever he might be. I do not know if Political agitation is as desirable there as it used to be in Ireland, but I think colonial <u>governors</u> must have a very troublesome & difficult post. If we hear Sir H[enr]y Youngs[129] administration spoken of we shall certainly report that we hear both his measures & motives very highly spoken of.

We have just returned from a beautiful tour in Switzerland with Haji & Lily & have benefited much in health from it. Haji has been passing the winter at Rome, he has I beleive given up his notion of farming, very wisely I am sure. Lily also is still in very poor health which is a great anxiety to me. They both send best love to their little cousins to each of whom pray give a kiss from me & with kind love & regards to yourself & Martha in which Mr. Mill begs to join. I am Yours ever Affec^{ly} H. Mill

8. To Arthur Hardy

Blackheath[130]
June 8. 1857.

My dear Arthur,

I have just received yours dated March 30th containing copies of letters from you to Herbert & Caroline about the Trusteeship. They are not likely to have had any effect. Caroline's refusal to let Ar. Ley resign was grounded on the knowledge that it would place Herbert in opposition to me on the subject. Herbert showed throughout that he cared nothing about the

---

128. Sir Charles Gavan Duffy (1816-1903), an Irish patriot who emigrated to Australia in 1855 and was elected to the Victoria House of Assembly in 1856.

129. Sir Henry Fox Young was governor of South Australia, the state where Arthur lived.

130. XXVII/51.

matter itself but would not lose the opportunity offered by Caroline of opposing me & his brother & sister.

You say he tells you he "has requested A. L not to resign unless he has the consent in writing of all interested"—This can only mean his own consent, as the only persons interested being myself Haji Lily and himself, & Haji & Lily desiring it as much as I do, it is only Herbert's consent that is in question. The sentance therefore is mere nonsense & can only have been intended to mystify. I confess I am dissapointed, since you wrote at all that you did not say that Ar. Ley ought to resign: whoever might be appointed in his place I think it must be plain to every body that he is not a fit person to hold it. However I have no wish to drag you into my affairs. We must trust to the Distringas[131] as our lawyer thinks the issue of a suit in chancery would be doubtful unless we could bring proof of A L's unfitness, which I should hardly like to do if we could, as I am convinced he wishes to ~~do so~~ resign & is only withheld by Caroline.

I hope you have quite got over the accident to your foot? I received your letter of introduction from M^{r} and Mrs Cooper & we were as polite and attentive as it was possible to be.[132] I heared a most tempting account of your house on Mount Lofty from Mrs Cooper tho' from your own account it would seem to be 'Bleak House'.[133] I have no doubt it is a delightful place. The irregularly of the mails must be very disagreable for you, I hope they will soon be put on a better footing. Your account of the election proves how highly you are esteemed where you are best known & it must be very gratifying for you. We are strongly opposed to the Ballot.[134] Please to give my love to Alfred & to Martha and kisses to the children from Yrs Affec^{ly} H. Mill

[upside down on first page]
Can you tell me if I ought not to receive something from my fathers estate? I receive each half year the 14.19.11 ~~wh~~ from your part of the estate. but ~~for some years past nothing else~~

131. The name of a writ bidding the sheriff the ability to constrain by force.

132. Harriet mentions entertaining Arthur Hardy's friends to Algernon in XXVII/117.

133. Dickens' *Bleak House* was published in London in 1853.

134. In April 1856, South Australia introduced the secret ballot. Its Constitution Act assured the vote for all men and no property restrictions for members of the assembly.

LETTERS TO ALGERNON TAYLOR 1856-58

Jany 8

Dearest Haji,[135]

Your idea of going to Italy has taken me by surprise as you may think, but I think it a very good one, it will take you through the long cold spring in a better climate, & be very amusing & interesting. It is an advantage too knowing a Catholic there as you will be able to be introduced to people & converts that otherwise you might not have heared of. Be sure dear not to let the expense be any impediment to anything you would like to do, as you know nothing would be so pleasant to me as to help you to do any thing you would like. I need not say I will send you a cheque or enclose notes whenever you tell me. I dare say you feel as I do that I should hardly like going to the Barnabite[136] Convent because they make it an exception & favour to their rule, "not to receive laymen." I think one would rather go where their rule is to receive laymen as boarders. It would be a good opportunity for you to see Rome, indeed you could hardly think of returning without. When are you thinking of going?

I enclose Mrs. Cholemely's[137] letter. She seems enchanted with the verve & gusto with which foreigners do everything—She little thinks how the same people who respond with such hearty voices to the credo in the church would respond still more heartily to a revolutionary movement & that if Victro Emanuel[138] remains King it will be because he is a reformer. Lily's love She says she thinks you will like it very much.

Ever yours
H. M.

---

135. The letter is signed H. M., so the date must be 1852 or later, since Harriet was married to John at Easter 1851. The letter was probably written in 1856. XXVII/111.

136. The Barnabites or Clerks Regular of St. Paul, a religious order devoted to the study of the letters of Paul, was founded by Saint Antonio Maria Zaccaria.

137. Mrs. Cholemely apparently helped persuade Algernon Hardy to join a Barnabite convent in Italy along with her. All that we know of her is that she was close to Algernon and that he wouldn't show his mother his letters from her. See letters to Helen LII/73, LII/105, and LIII(i)/8.

138. Victor Emmanuel II (1820-78), first king of united Italy. In November 1852 he turned the government over to Count Cavour, a statesman who helped make Victor Emmanuel II king of Italy.

Sunday March 16

My dear Haji,[139]

Lily is gone to the church so I sit down to write a little to you tho' I have but very little to tell, for all that is new and interesting is now on your side. Lily wrote to Rome a day or two ago. I suppose you are at this moment in the Sistine. I am expecting a letter every day to tell us of your safe arrival at Rome. Here the weather besides being extremely cold has been tempestuous, equinoctial gales from the north & east have shaken the house at night & I have felt uneasy at the idea that you might be at that time on the sea so that I shall be very glad to have your first letter from Rome. Did you go by the steamer and had you a good passage, and were you alone or with one of the priests? All these particulars are very interesting. We have been out but little since we came home owing to the Thuiler & Crouchers—Mr. Mill had just gone to Birmingham to pass the Holy week for the sake of the music at St. Charles, which is said to be fine in the Gregorian style.

Monday March 17

As I did not close my letter yesterday I can add to-day the news (not very interesting to us) of the birth of a son of Louis Napoleon,[140] which took place yesterday. People here seem to think the Peace quite settled. Will you buy for me at one of the Cameo shops in the Via Condotti two cameos for Broaches, the size about ½ or 2 inches, the subjects I prefer are Sybil, or a Virgin, or goddess such as Flora or Venus, or Raphael or Ceres—or in short any thing pretty & very well executed, therefore I prefer them dear & do not care about the price. But this only if you can do it quite conveniently—if troublesome never mind it dear.

Yours H.M.

April 16th

Dear dear Haji,[141]

Your last letter was dated April 2d and took eight days to come. I am anxious to hear if you have received the four letters I have sent to Rome 3 to the Convent of which one was Lilys & one of mine & I think one of Lily's to Poste Restante. There is however nothing of importance in them or which would signify if lost, but I want to hear that you do receive letters.

---

139. The letter was written in 1856, the year of Napolean III's son's birth. XXVII/112.

140. Prince Imperial, Napoleon Eugene Louis Joseph was born 16 March 1856.

141. The letter is signed H. M., so the date must be 1852 or later, since Harriet was married to John at Easter 1851. XXVII/113.

I know it is often only by dint of repeated begging & persuading that one can get the lazy officials to look over their heaps of letters thoroughly & they are very apt to mistake the letter of ones name. We have now at last some fine weather & are beginning to think of a Swiss expedition in June. I am sorry to hear that you get half starved which seems the only drawback to the interest & agreableness of your convent life. You should certainly get a good dinner most days at a Trattoria. There is a good one in the Via Condotti nearly or quite opposite Frantz's Hotel. It is of great importance to your health to have a full meat dish so I hope dear you will take it! I long to hear how you are. I am better & so is L. Adieu.

Y^r H. M.

Blackheath[142]
Monday June 9

I received your letter of May 30th dearest Haji on Saturday and I have no doubt this will be in time to find you at Genoa, where I hope you will have got without so much fatigue as you expected. You will I am sure be very much pleased if you see Florence but it seems to me that the journey from Rome to Genoa by way of Florence will be so very fatiguing that I hope you will take the steamboat instead, in spite of its unpleasantness. We have now decided, if nothing unforeseen happens to change our plan, to leave home on the 28th—and to reach Genoa in eight days. We shall go to the Ecu de Genive, but if that should be full, so that we should be obliged to go to some other Inn we should take care to leave our address there—where you would find it. We propose after staying a few days at Geneva to go to Chamonix & probably return again to Geneva afterwards, but that will remain to be decided when we get there. We expect you see dear to be at Geneva on the 6th or 7th July and there you had better send a Post Restante letter to await our arrival unless you will be there by that date. I hope however that I shall also get an answer to this before we go.

After a cold spring the weather has now cleared up & become suddenly quite summer heat & we are inpatient for the holiday. Mr Mill is better, & I too have got better again & hope to keep well till we go. Lily too continues better & tho' far from strong yet as she thinks she is better for walking I hope the Swiss expedition may do her good. She is very much interested at present in theatrical matters—She sends her love & Mr Mill his best wishes with those of Dear Haji.

Yours H. M.

---

142. The letter is signed H. M., so the date must be 1852 or later, since Harriet was married to John at Easter 1851. XXVII/114.

Blackheath[143]
Friday Nov. 23

My dear Haji,

I thought you would wonder at not hearing from me for so long. I have twice begun writing to you but have been too tired to finish it, as I wanted to write a long letter in answer to your two last, but I shall wait & answer those viva voce[144] when we meet for my wrists & hand is so weak I find it very difficult to write much at a time.

We have been occupied by having Mrs. Gibson[145] spending a week here, & before that we had the Croucher's to dinner, since which they have suddenly lost their little boy, to poor Mrs. Croucher's great distress.

I am so very sorry dear to hear that you are so very unwell. I hoped the country was doing you so much more good. Can you not think of any thing likely to be of use to you? Mr Mill has become subject to boils in the last few months for the first time—He has had three in succession, & Mr Coulson[146] prescribed something to be taken to alter the tendency to boils— but as he has taken it as ordered every day for a month & has just got a new boil come it does not seem successful, in his case at least. I think it well worth your trying however, as things agree with one & not with another.

I am so glad you like my favorite Shelley.[147] You have got the little copy I used to carry about with me. I have heared nothing lately of the refugees affairs. We subscribed to get the legal opinion—that is Mr Mill gave in our names to the Editor of the Daily News[148] to be used if he succeeds in getting others enough. I put yours for £1—which I shall pay if it comes to anything. I shall let you know anything we hear. We are now discussing the going to Bordeaux—I suffer from the cold, but as yet not very much but we think we should be ready to go now at any time. We have been talking of the 7th or 14th Dec. to go—but I feel very disinclined to go away. What do you think of doing this winter dear— Will you pass any part of it with us at Bordeaux—or do you dread the town life. I was afraid to ask you while I though you were getting better where you are, but as you are not might the change be ~~either~~ of use do you think either to health or spirits. If you would like to go with us &

---

143. Probably written in 1856, just after Lily left to join a theater troupe. XXVII/115.

144. Spoken aloud.

145. Louisa Gibson. See XXVII/41 for letter from Mrs. Gibson to HTM.

146. William Coulson (1802-77), surgeon.

147. Percy Bysshe Shelley (1792-1822), English poet.

148. Liberal newspaper.

stay as long as it seemed to agree with you I should so like to try to do you good dearest & you should have a room to yourself & all the quiet you could wish. If you do <u>not</u> do this it is time now to come up if you wish to do so before I go, as I should like to be able to leave by the 7th but I do not at all like your taking the long journey for the sake of a few days here, & unless you really wish it I should advise your not doing so. Tell me soon dear what you will do this winter. I never remember so dark & damp & wintry a November. My plan is to be away three months at the outside country going & returning

Adieu now dearest   your^s

H. M.

B. P.¹⁴⁹ Jan 17

My dear Haji,

I am glad to hear that you are riding, as exercise of any sort seems to be good for you. How I wish that it or anything could do your head any good! There is nothing new to tell you as you may suppose. There is a letter to-day for you from Genoa—one from Gilling & several railway Papers. I should have written a few words, merely for the sake of writing, before, had I not got my hand so stiff & benumbed that it is with much difficulty that I can scrawl this as indeed you may perceive. After having made two ineffectual attempts I gave up the idea of writing to Miss Fox.¹⁵⁰

Lily seems quite decided to go to Glasgow but not quite as to when. I shall hear on Monday whether she is going to Derby or not. I shall go to see her before she goes farther off, & wait to hear her wishes as to when. It is just possible that I may go to Derby next week. I shall stay with her ten days or a fortnight when I do go. If I should know anything more precise about this on Monday or even Tuesday I will write to tell you dear as even if you should have left, they can easily post it back again here. I hope the thumb is mending you do not indeed need such an addition to your pains! I hate to hear of your having a cold, I fear colds & do hope you will do all you can to get rid of it. I am pretty well. The last two days I have the comfort of being free from earache.

Adieu now dearest Haji
with love & blessings

---

149. Probably written in 1857, when Helen was contemplating a change in theaters. XXVII/116.

150. William J. Fox's daughter. Harriet sends a copy of the *Principles of Political Economy* to Miss Fox, William J. Fox's daughter (see XXVII/40 earlier in this chapter). Miss Fox is also referred to in letters to Helen (LII/66 and LII/77).

Blackheath[151]
May 20

Dearest Haji

I received your letter dated May 10 from Milan and am very sorry to hear you continue to feel so more than naturally unwell. You did an enormous days work and I wonder how you could stand it. I should think if the weather should be warm it will not be desirable to make a stay of more than a few days at Rome as I believe malaria begins there at the beginning of June. I hope you may recieve this but feel very doubtful of it. I am & have been very poorly—partly I have been overdone by the little exertion of seeing some friends of Arthurs[152] to whom he gave a letter of introduction to me & still more by the subject of L. All our plans for going out have been put a stop to by a quantity of Indian business in the House of Commons, so that after we had all but settled to go to Baden in June it now seems doubtful whether we shall go at all as Mr Mill will not get away from town before the middle of July he expects, & that is late for Baden, & besides I doubt if I shall be strong enough for such a long journey we have talked of the Lakes instead, but at present all is quite unsettled

No doubt you will get to the Camaldoli at Naples. I should think it will be very hot there in June we have had again a fortnight of hot summer weather I have written once to Naples & shall again but you must always remember that if you do not get letters it is probably the fault of the Post Office. I am always anxious to get yours the distance is so great that Genoa seemed near in comparison. Lily love with mine dear

yours   H. M.

Blackheath[153]
June 10th

Dearest Haji,

I have first received yours dated Rome June 3. I am very glad to get it as I have been anxious about your being at Rome now the malaria season there has begun. I do not feel the same at Naples as I beleive there is no malaria, only the heat must be great, and still more at Palermo. Where I should think it will be insufferable in Italy & may tho' I hope you will not need to know, that there is a very good english Physician at Naples named Dr Strange. Your physical strength seems to keep up well for you

---

151. Written in 1857, the year Arthur Hardy's friends from Australia visited. See XXVII/117.

152. Arthur Hardy, HTM's brother who lived in Australia.

153. Written in 1857, during Algernon's stay in Italy. XXVII/118.

do very hard days work. I am so very sorry to hear you are so unwell otherwise—perhaps you work too hard, especially with the eyes. We are kept from going out by the dilatory proceedings of the H. of Com^s Mr Mill is summoned for the 12th to attend the Committee on the Bank Charter act & after that ~~expects~~ which may last a week expects a number of other subjects for which he may be wanted—all this makes the time of our excursion very uncertain, I should think a month hence at the earliest, perhaps two, & it seeming now so distant we have not been able to decide where to go. I am not so strong as I was when you left and dread the long railway to Baden of late we have inclined more to the English Lakes, especially as it seems there is good botanising to be expected there. I will tell you what we think of doing each time I write. You should give me notice in time where to write after Palermo.

I hope you will be able to get us two heads for Brooches, set or unset, as large or very nearly so as a five franc piece, in pink coral if possible (or otherwise) the subject a Bacchantes head with wreath of grapes on the head & some classic head for Lily, as Raphael or Dante &c. The man under the Hotel Victoria is the best & his judgment as to beauty might probably be relied on. I expect them to cost some pounds each. I shall like to hear where you are

[upside down on top of page]
At Naples & how you manage. You should bring some bright colored views of Vesuvius as souvenirs. Lily is gone to the opera to see Alfieri's Rosamunda.[154] Adieu my dear & take care of yourself

Paris[155] Oct 15

My dear Haji,

I have just got your note of Oct 11th. I do not feel sure that this will find you at Cosmo but I shall write also to Post Restante Milan so that you will probably get one or the other. We left home on the 11th and came direct here, we do not intend to stay more than a day or two longer, we shall then go to Montpelier taking about a week on the road. Our present plan is to stay there till after Christmas, & then go perhaps to Hyères but as yet we do not decide beyond Montpelier where your next should be

---

154. Vittorio Alfieri (1749-1803) wrote *Rosmunda* between 1770 and 1780. It was produced several times in the mid nineteenth century in Europe. The Royal Opera in London burned during this year, so HTM must be referring to opera in the broad sense, including dramatic theater as well as sung opera.

155. Written two weeks before Harriet's death in 1858. XXVII/119.

addressed. You can join us when you like. I shall write to you Poste restante Genoa when we have arrived at Montpelier. I am glad you have such fine weather. It is also fine here tho' rather hot. Adieu. Affec^{ly}

H. M.

I got yours wishing me happy returns of my birthday for which many thanks. After this I will direct my <u>next</u> to Milan.

LETTER TO GEORGE MILL[156]

I do not answer your letter because you deserve it—that you certainly do not—but because tho I am quite inexperienced in the best way of receiving or replying to ~~intentional~~ an affront I think that in this as in all things, frankness and plain speaking are the best rule, & as to me they are the most natural—also it is best that every one should speak for themselves. Your letters to me & to Haji must be regarded as one, being on the same subject & sent together to us. In my opinion they show want of truth modesty & justice ~~not~~ to say little of good breeding or good nature which you appear to regard as very unnecessary qualities.

Want of justice is shown in suggesting that a person has probably acted ~~in~~ without regard to their principles which principles you say you never heared. Want of modesty in ~~their~~ passing judgment on a person thus far unknown to you—want of everything like truth in professing as you do & liking & value for a person who ~~you~~ in the same note you ~~impudently refuse to call~~ avoid calling by their name ~~& say not the fancy Dear Madam~~ ~~to~~ using an unfriendly designation after having ~~been in the habit of~~ for years addressed them in to say the least a more friendly ~~designation~~ way. In fact want of truth is apparent in the whole, as ~~personally your~~ letters overflow with anger & animosity about ~~an affair~~ a circumstance which in no way concerns you so far as anything you say shows & which if there was any truth in your profession of regard w^d be a subject of satisfaction to you. As to want of the good breeding which is the result of good feeling that appears to be a family failing ~~& must perhaps should be excused in persons who have little other family feeling to boast of.~~ The only small satisfaction your letter can give is the observation that when people desert good feeling they also are deserted by good sense—your wish to make a

156. The letter is dated 5 July 1851 and is probably a draft response to a letter from George Mill dated 20 May 1851. XLVII/17.

quarrel with your brother & myself because we have ~~assumed~~ used a right which the whole world, of whatever shade of opinion, accords to us, is ~~certainly~~ as absurd as unjust and wrong.

Harriet Mill

Richmond July 5th 1851

MISCELLANEOUS LETTERS

To William J. Fox[157]

My dear Mr Fox,

We shall like very much indeed to see you and Miss Fox tomorrow and Sunday.

The house is the last but one on the left in Blackheath Park:

I am

Ever Sincerely Yours

H. Mill

Friday

Dear Mr Fox,

We are still at home, owing to Indian Affairs, and shall be very glad to see you on Saturday & Sunday. With very kind regards to Miss Fox if she is still in town. Believe me—

Yrs Sincerely

H. Mill

July 14.

To Mrs. Darling

Mrs Mill presents her Complimets to Mrs Darling & being much indisposed & unable to have the pleasure of calling on ~~Mrs Darling~~ her to morrow requests ~~Mrs Darling she~~ M^rs D will favour her by saying if Elizabs Chalk can cook the ordinary English dishes really well—& did Mrs. Darling find her willing to alter her way of cooking any dish & to follow

---

157. The envelope is postmarked 6 J[?] 1856. Both letters to Mr. Fox on this page are housed in the library of King's College, Cambridge.

directions given her—is she strictly honest with regard to the provisions—
or is she wasteful or extravagant—does she keep the part of the house in
her care—the kitchen dining room &c thoroughly clean does Mrs D. think
her honest quiet & given to going out ~~of~~ in the evenings. ~~and~~ without
permission well mannered & generally well conducted & had she permission [at] Mrs D's to go to church which she demands from Mrs. Mill Mrs
M is [sorry] ask so many questions & will be much [obliged] to Mrs. D
if she will answer each of them as fully as possible.[158]

---

158. Written on the back of a note from Mrs. Darling (XXVII/3) which reads: "Mrs Darling
presents her compliments to Mrs Mill and begs to inform her that she will be at home tomorrow
at 3 o'clock, when she will be most happy to see Mrs Mill and give her the information she
requires respecting Elizabeth Chalks."

When forced to choose between nursing John Taylor when he suffered from an undetermined illness and caring for John Stuart Mill when he requested her aid, HTM chose JSM.

TO JOHN TAYLOR

11

Only one letter written to John Taylor survives from the period before Harriet separated from her first husband. This letter, written in July of 1828 when their first son was about ten months old and retained by John Taylor, must have been a bittersweet reminder of the loving relationship they had during the first years of their marriage, which took place in 1826. Written during Harriet's visit to the Isle of Wight, this missive reveals her passion for Taylor and the distress she feels because they are parted. Harriet wrote, "each hour that {letter from you is kept under my pillow} brings us nearer the day when we shall meet—& I think from my present feelings that I shall never again consent to our parting" (XXVIII/143). The many poems she also composed during these early years of their relationship—including Box III/189; several versions of "Written at Daybreak"; III/208; the Song (Box III/208, pages 3 and 4)—all reflect the same joy of motherhood and delight in family found in this first letter. However, by the following summer, when she is again staying in Ryde with her family and pregnant for a second time, Harriet writes a rebellious poem and note on the back of an envelope which contained a letter from John Taylor. He tells her in his letter that she had best not bathe in the sea because of her pregnancy, but Harriet replies with a poem about the sensuality of the ocean's "wild & plaintive moan" (see Mermaid poem in chapter 7).

A gap of nearly ten years separates the first letter from those which follow. In the interval, Harriet met and fell in love with John Stuart Mill. The crisis that resulted in her marriage is unrecorded in her letters to Taylor. The correspondences to Taylor resume with a completely new, businesslike tone. Harriet mentions "Mill" matter-of-factly in one of her letters from the mid-1830s (XXVIII/135), but rarely mentions him again, even when referring to affairs he is involved in, until the end of John Taylor's life, when she must explain her choice to stay in France rather than return to nurse John Taylor (XXVIII/227). When she writes to her first husband, Harriet sustains a cordial yet reserved tone reminiscent of chatty letters exchanged between friends when discussing domestic issues, travel plans, her state of health, the locales she visits, and the weather. She offers birthday greetings and always gives John Taylor her itinerary. During her trips abroad and all of her journeys throughout the south of England, Harriet consistently communicated with John Taylor.

Although she did not live with John Taylor after their separation in 1833, Harriet relied on him financially. John Taylor provided the funds which enabled Harriet to travel abroad and to live apart from him in England. He graciously provided letters of credit and secured leases for Harriet. As importantly, John Taylor served as a filter through which her communication with her family could be sustained without their awareness of her intimacy with John Stuart Mill. Taylor forwarded many letters her family sent to Harriet at John Taylor's house where they presumed, incorrectly, that she lived. Always cognizant of the harsh criticism they would reap if anyone discovered their unusual living arrangements, Harriet and John made certain that their accounts to her parents coincided and disguised the real reasons for her trips away from home.

Over half of the letters collected in this section were written sometime during 1848 and 1849. This long series provides the clearest picture of Harriet's relation to John Taylor and of her life in general during the period prior to John's death in July 1849. The letters she wrote to him in early 1848 repeatedly refer to her work on The Principles of Political Economy *(XXVIII/178, XXVIII/179, and XXVIII/170). These pieces of writing, along with her reference in XXVIII/152 to the need for John to send her some of the manuscripts she had left behind in a trunk, indicate Harriet's ongoing involvement in the work published in John Stuart Mill's name. These comments about her collaboration also reflect the openness she shared with John Taylor regarding her work with John Stuart Mill.*

After Principles of Political Economy *was published in April 1848, Harriet wandered around southern England while she looked for a new house. She was dissatisfied with the residence in Walton because John and Sarah Austin had moved close enough to the neighborhood to observe her comings and goings. Late in the fall, her brother Arthur arrived in*

England for a visit and stayed with Harriet in Worthing. Harriet was loathe to allow Arthur to observe her intimacy with John Stuart Mill, despite the fact that Arthur was her favorite sibling. About this same time, John Taylor began to complain of "stomach derangement," Harriet's father also began to show signs of illness, and Harriet herself was physically and mentally exhausted after her work on the political economy manuscript. In order to avoid further contact with Arthur, and probably to escape the invalids that surrounded her, after Christmas 1848 Harriet fled to the Basque resort town of Pau. Her letters from Pau in early 1849 are filled with cheerful descriptions of the village and with her concern over John Taylor's undefined illness. A significant letter in this group (XXVIII/227) records a decision Harriet was forced to make between her husband and her lover. At the end of March 1849, John Taylor requested that Harriet return to nurse him. (Taylor does not say, and may not have known, that he was suffering from terminal cancer.) However, John Stuart Mill had also had a miserable winter. His eyesight was so bad that the doctors ordered him to go on holiday. Harriet chose to help John Stuart Mill rather than John Taylor. In her letter to Taylor she explains:

I have arranged with Mr Mill to meet me on the 20th of April when he is to have three weeks holiday on account of his health . . . I feel it a duty to do all in my power for his health. . . . He does not tell even his own family <u>where</u> he goes for his holiday as I so hate all tittle-tattle. Therefore I do not mention it either except to you. I trouble you with all these particulars because I wish you to know that nothing but a feeling of right would prevent my returning at once.

For Harriet Taylor, to do right was to nurse John Stuart Mill.
*   But Harriet never completely abandoned John Taylor. Harriet's letters to John Stuart Mill from this period demonstrate her dedication to Taylor during the last, miserable six weeks of his life (from mid-May to the end of July). These correspondences more than prove her affection for the husband who was willing to agree to Harriet's insistence on a maximum amount of freedom while maintaining the social stability necessary for their family.*

Ryde, Thursday July 3^{rd1}

My dearest John,
    Though I know that I must not send you another letter for some days, as I only wrote yesterday, yet I cannot bear to defer the pleasure of writing,

---

1. The letter was probably written in 1828, when Herbert was ten months old. XXVIII/143.

even tho' you should not see it at present. I received your letter my dearest by Edward[2] last night—every letter you send me, the mere sight of your writing, gives me great pleasure but the happiness the delight I have received from this can scarcely be imagined—every question I asked you, all that I had said is answered in the very words I would have chosen. Do not imagine my dearest that I ever doubted that your wish for our uniting was as great as mine. I knew that my dear husband loves me, as I have loved him, with my whole heart, but I asked the question that I might receive the letter I received last night. I put it under my pillow that I might read it to our dear little one as soon as he wakes this morning, when I kissed his sweet rosy cheeks and told him that was from dear Papa, he held out his little arms towards the door with a look of expectation, and that little noise ur, ur, ur, which you know so well—I gave him some more of the kisses you sent to pacify him.

Oh my dear John each hour that paper brings us nearer the day when we shall meet—& I think from my present feelings that I shall never again consent to our parting. I fear my love that you might think from my last letter that I was not in good spirits, and I was not, untill your letter came to give me both spirits & happiness from the prospect of having repeated by your own lips all those delightful feelings which it contains.

I am now writing in my own room. I have come to read your letter and enjoy it without interruption. I am sitting by the side of the bed on which our little cherub is lying fast asleep in the most elegant attitude in the world—this is the first time he has slept in the day since you left us. I went this morning with the dogs a walk of 4 miles before breakfast as the weather is now too warm to walk far afterwards. This writing is so bad that I fear you will not be as able to make it out—but my love must attribute it to the true cause, which is that my pen will not keep pace with my feelings. ~~were~~ I shall now leave off, as my boy is waking and finish my letter, when I have received another from my love.

[written crosshatched across the first page of her letter]
Sunday Morning All the former part of this letter I wrote two days ago, as you will see, I hope you will not find it tiresome. I have now only to thank you dear one for your last kind letter—I am very happy to say that Thomas[3] seems much better than he has been, and I have now hopes that Papa['s] opinion will be realized. What I asked you to bring me from the

---

2. Edward Hardy.

3. Thomas Hardy.

closet in the dressing room is my blue cloth riding-habit, but do not bring it, if it will in the least inconvenience you. I shall be on the pier before nine every morning untill you come as I suppose that

[written crosshatched across the second page of her letter]
is the hour you would come. I need not repeat the joy I shall feel when I perceive you on the boat for I know you will feel the same. Our little one is rather poorly again, but looks well & will soon be so as his tiresome tooth does appear to be coming through at last. Adieu dearest till the happy moment comes. Adieu—

Harriet Taylor

My dear John,

I find that Usiglio's article is to be in the next number of the 'London'— Robertson it seems meets the contributors at the publisher's Hoopers Pall Mall—& Mill went in there as he passed a day or two since & found both Usiglio & Mazzini there with Robertson[4]—he had a good deal of talk with both of them & liked both very much—he has undertaken to do all the revising that is required to Usilio's article & has engaged him to write another on new Italian books & Mazzini to write one on Italian politics since 1830 at which time he was involved in them & I do not know how they are paid but I beleive at the old rate of 16 guin^s the sheet. & I do not know how soon. There seems by a letter from Greece in the Chronicle yesterday to be a man named Usilio engaged in politics there. perhaps it is a brother or relation of this man.

I hope you had a pleasant ride yesterday. I am quite well. I hope you will come again, before long. Good bye. Your affectionate

H. T.[5]

Dearest John

I have just got your letter, as I was preparing to come by the coach so I can only say one word. I am very sorry for this bad luck because I sh^d have liked to go with you & you w^d have liked, but for myself it is not much a dissapointment as I dreaded the fatigue I would come to town for this even^g only if the weather were other. but in this soaking wet day it would be a pity. I will write again to-day as now I have not time.

---

4. Angleo Usiglio (1802–75), an Italian immigrant; John Robertson, former sub-editor of the *Westminster Review* under John Stuart Mill; Giuseppe Mazzini (1808–75), an important Italian exile who helped establish a united, independent Italy.

5. Probably written in 1836 or 1837, while John Stuart Mill was editor of the *Westminster Review* and Robertson served as his sub-editor. XXVIII/135.

Will you come here on Saturday & Sunday[6]

Chalons[7] January 3rd
1839

My dear John,

We arrived here this even^g & drove, before coming to the Inn, to the Post aux Lettres in hopes of a letter from you at Boulogne: after having turned over all the poste restante lettres without finding one I suppose, either that you had not time, to write or that it has not yet arrived here, in wh case the people at the post promise to send it on to Marseilles. Lily & I were most anxious about you all the two days you must have been on the road: I do hope you are better soon, & that the journey did you no harm? We left Paris on Sunday morn^g & went that day to Fontainebleau, on Monday to Sens, Tuesday to Auxerre. I found those three days excessively fatiguing, but that was owing wholly to the extreme cold—it was quite as cold as it had been at Boulogne, so that the breath was frozen on the windows of the carriage all the day, & the inns being very much worse on this road that the other—the cold at night was terrible—on Wednesday however there was a thaw & it has been much warmer since: We came yesterday to a place called Saulieu, & to-day here, & I am very much better than I had any expectation of being—very decidedly better than when you left me at Paris, thanks to your care & kindness while you were there to which I have not any doubt I owe being able to go on at all. How very much I wish to hear from you that you have not been the worse for all the pains you took for me dear—do write but I cannot get a letter now before Pisa where I hope you have already written. We had a very comfortable carriage from Paris here. We did, the first three days 7 ½ posts[8] a day, which occupied each day about 6 hours. Yesterday we came 11 ½ posts in about 11 hours, & today 10 posts in near ten hours. We hurried in this way because we were told there was only a boat from Lyons to Avignon twice week & we feared to lose the 10th at Marseilles—but it proves there are boats every day both from here & from Lyons. We are to start to-morrow morn^g at 7 & reach Lyons at 3 oclock & next day the boat leaves Lyons at 9 & is <u>two</u> <u>days</u> in getting to Avignon, sleeping (its passengers) at a village on the banks. I have no doubt I shall get thro this pretty well & if not I shall stay as long as may be necessary, therefore do

---

6. Postmarked 1838. XXVIII/145.

7. Postmarked 9 January 1839. XXVIII/146.

8. A post, or station, was an interval for changing horses for the post chaise, a closed carriage used for long-distance travel.

not be all uneasy about me. Lily is quite well in high spirits—she talks of you very often but at this moment is fast asleep in the next room. I will write at Marseilles if anything should occur on the way or if we would be detained. if not I will write from Leghorn. I hope to be in time for the boat of the 10th, but it appears it will take at least two days from Avignon to Marseilles. This is a very egoist letter, but it is twelve oclock & you will not wonder I am stupid after the days journey. Tell Mama & Cary[9] ~~that~~ how I go on but do not give them the letter. Tell them I wish them many happiny [*sic*] new years As I wish you with all my heart many many happy new years Tell me how you get on or got off the parties? & Beleive me always yours most affectionately.

Pisa[10] January 21st

My dear John,

I received your letter dated 10th, yesterday, with very great satisfaction as I was beginning to be uneasy at hearing neither from you~~r~~ nor Mama nor Cary. I have not had any letter from either of them. Your letter gave me the greatest pleasure. Many thanks dear John for all the kind things you say in it—give my best love to the dear boys & tell them I am always thinking of them. Lily begs that you will tell them from her that "the steam-boat from Marseilles had four loaded cannon, two at the sides & two smaller ones at the stern, & also that the Mediterranean is every where quite blue" We left Marseilles on the 11th in the French Govern^t Steamer, the arrangements were like those of a ship of the line rather than a steamer, every passenger being obliged to appear at dinner & breakfast unless they were ill, & to pay for them whether they were there or not; the Capt took the head of the table. Then were placed all the women, & then the men, a most disagreable arrangement. however I & Lily staid in bed to breakfast, & I remained in bed all the time I was on board. I was not sick at all as we had a splendid passage with the sea as smooth as possible, but I had a violent head-ache all the time. Lily was on deck, with the women servant of the boat, a great deal & enjoyed it very much. We left Marseilles at 5 PM on the 11th & arrived at Leghorn at 6 AM on the 13th we however were not allowed to land untill 9 as all the passports had first to be sent on shore we then took a little boat & went on shore a distance of about a mile. The scene was most splendid. The sea & sky of the brightest blue & the mountains covered with snow glittering in the sun chine. There appears little interesting at Leghorn & we arranged to come to Pisa on

---

9. Caroline (Hardy) Ley.

10. Written in 1839 during the same trip as that of the previous letter. XXVIII/147.

Monday; before doing so, I thought it best to call on Mr Gower, as I thought you would wish me t[o] do so, & I might not have another opportunity. accordingly, I went & saw him at his counting house. he was very polite enquired about you & gave me a letter of credit for either Rome or Naples. I did not take any money, but may perhaps at Rome. On arriving here my first movement was to send a note to Emilia,[11] in return to which came a cousin with a message from her mother saying that she had left Leghorn by steamer of the 23^d November & that they had heared

[continues upside down at top of first page]
I hear from 'La Nonni'[12] that William has left the ship & has got a post to Vaccinati at Bombay—<u>whom</u> he is to Vaccinati I don't know—their descriptions here are so confused.

> Russell House[13]
> 2 Grand Junction Parade
> Monday morn^g

My dear John,

We got down comfortably on Friday & I have got pleasant apartments overlooking the sea: I am decidedly better for the change, altho' the weather is any thing but favorably—it has blown like a hurricane ever since we came down, so as to make walking almost impossible except in the streets. I hope it will be finer & brighter this week that the boys may enjoy themselves the most possible—which I have no doubt they will do. It is not at all a cold wind, only so very much too much of it, with occasional showers—but it is weather in which they can be out on the beach all day, & I am glad I came here instead of taking them to Yorkshire, for it seems to me nothing can be more healthy than this fine sea breeze & I think it is just what they want. our lodging is a few houses to the west of the Albion & has a splendid sea view.

They are not yet come. I & Lily are going to meet them, & I will not close this 'till I can tell you how they are.

I wish that you would write me a few words to-morrow. Tell me if you shall come down on Saturday? Shall I buy a book for you for Lily's birthday? & if you do not come down shall I give it her for you or bring it to town for you?

Monday Even^g. I & Lily met the boys at the coach office when they

---

11. Emilia Hardy, William Hardy's wife.

12. "La Nonna": Grandmother.

13. Postmarked 23 July 1839. XXVIII/148.

arrived at four oclock exactly—they had a pleasant ride & only a shower or two. We dined directly they came & then went on the beach, where I have left them while I came in to finish this letter. Thanks for your kind message. Lily is delighted with her [palpicorn].[14] They are delighted with their boats on the beach & I am sure nothing could do them so much good as being in this famous breeze. I think there is no such sea as this any where. I shall expect a letter on Wednesday. Mama['s] letter was to urge me to go back with Papa. I wish you would write her a few words by Papa saying how I have not strength for so long a ~~ride~~ journey at present—as I really have not.

They all send their love with mine.

Dear John Your ever affec^{ate}
H. Taylor

Friday Even^g

My dear John,[15]

We are all quite well—that is the little ones are so, & I am <u>much</u> better for this week in spite of the bad weather—which is now <u>so</u> bad that I can hardly regret that you are not coming untill to-day it has been only showery—to-day; it has been steady heavy rain all day, to the very great discomforture of the boys. They have spent all the other days in the air & I think have enjoyed themselves very much, tho' certainly not as much as they would have done if it had been fine. They are as good as possible, but they will not move or go any where without me. They have the greatest wish to go on the sea, but Herby will not go unless I go Haji wont go unless Herby goes & so they have not yet been at all, for it has been ever since I have been here much too stormy weather for me to venture. I hope to manage it however before Monday. To-morrow if it is fine I am to take them to Mr. Syke. I will give Lily your present & love to-morrow. I shall take our places to-morrow either in the 12 or the 2 o'clk coach. We shall therefore be at Wilton Place on Monday even^g about seven or nine to tea—we shall dine before starting.

Do not come home before your usual time as it may be past nine before we get there. The boys can sleep in the back bedroom & go to Manchester St. after breakfast on Tuesday. I will write to Mrs Underwood on Monday saying when the boys will be there.

Herby Haji & Lily's <u>best</u> love with that of your affectionate,

H T

---

14. This appears to be the word HTM has written, but a horned beetle seems an unusual gift.

15. Postmarked 26 July 1839. XXVIII/149.

Birksgate.[16] Sep 28

My dear John,

I am extremely glad to hear that you expect to be able to come on Friday night. They are really very kind & very desirous of seeing you & of <u>trying</u> to give you pleasure. They refer upon every subject to "what Mr Taylor will like" &c & in short are as zealous & friendly as possible. <u>He</u> tho' of course, always himself, is seen to much better advantage at home than anywhere else, & tho' you may feel somewhat overdone with attentions yet as you will see them to be well meant I hope you will not find the two days disagreable. The place is lovely.

The mail train leaves London at 9 PM and gets to Sheffeild at 4.15. There is a train from Sheffeild to Penistone at 7.15 reaching Penistone at 8—and another from Sheffeild at 9 reaching Penistone at ½ past 9. The carriage will meet you at Penistone at ½ past 9 if you will come by this train.

The Inn at Sheffeild they say is called the Tontine. Adieu with love to Herby & Haji—who should send a kind remembrance to their Grandpapa & Mama because they are very anxious to see them here & Herbert has been & is very neglectful not to remember them. Ever yrs. H T.

Birksgate.[17] Oct^b 2^d

My dear John

I could not write yesterday as I said I would as Papa went off to Huddersfield the moment after breakfast & there was no other mode of sending to the post. We had a beautiful day on Sunday—we got to Birmingham at two, where they staid an hour, & to Manchester about half past seven. We went to the Albion & left at nine on Monday morn^g. We reached Huddersfield at twelve & found Papa waiting for us. Mama looks very well & was delighted to see me, Carry too is very well. The place is most beautiful, far more so than we had been told—indeed it is the very loveliest situation I ever saw. The house is larger than I expected, very plain outside, of stone, & altogether in very good taste, the arrangements within are very nice—it is a much better home than you would expect & the furniture extremely pretty. I should like you to come & see it—it is so lovely—both Papa & Mama want you to come very much but I tell them you will not be able to come this journey—Mama tells me to say that you <u>must</u> come if it is only for one night.

I will tell you all about it when I see you: I have a head-ache & cannot

---

16. Probably written during Harriet's first visit to Birksgate in 1839. XXVIII/166.

17. Postmarked 3 October 1839. XXVIII/150.

write much this morning, but in other respects I am better than I was in London, it is a brisk sharp air which always agrees with me, when, as is the case here the house itself is warm—& this is the warmest house I ever was in—it has thick double walls, & all the rooms are so beautifully carpeted & curtained, with, in all Mama's splendid large fires, that I have never felt the least cold. That bill of £120 that you had the other day, was for part of the spare room furniture. Altogether it is a delightful place. Papa busies himself in the garden & reading & Mama is as usual all warmth & kindness—Carry too is very well tho' she complains a little but that is only owing to the ennui of Ley's absence. Papa has some messages He says when you write, to us I hope you will to-morrow or next day, will you say when another £100 is likely to be wanted from Mr Book for the bank—& secondly he "will be particularly obliged if you will urge on Perkins[18] to settle Bullers[19] business" that means of course make desire Perkins to communicate with Papa. he says he has not heared a word from him. I shall leave here the end of next week as I intended—but I will write again in a day or two. Pray give me an account of your day at Gravesend? When did you go? Was it fine? It was fine all day on the railroad route.

Lily's best love & kisses.

Kiss the darling boys on Sunday for me & for Lily. She does look so blooming the little creature. Grandmama's love to boys & she wants to see them very much she has a nice little room on purpose for them & next spring they must come. Grandpa has a beautiful horse & three others are coming home on Saturday, so they will be able to ride.

[written upside down on first page]
Carry's and Mama's love to you.

Birksgate[20] October 9th

My dear John

It seems very fortunate that you did not come into Yorkshire with me, as I suppose you have had ample occupation & bother in the city. Mama sends her love to you & hopes to see you whenever you can come, & I promise you a great treat whenever it is—for certainly it is the very prettiest place I ever staid in & of course for a mere visit no one who think

---

18. Perhaps Henry Perkins (1778-1855), a book collector and founder of a library in Springfield, Surrey.

19. Perhaps Charles Buller (1806-48), a liberal politician taught by Thomas Carlyle.

20. Postmarked 10 October 1839. XXVIII/151.

a place <u>dull</u> so very pretty—but for Mama especially it is most dreadfully dull & even when the carriage arrives I think it will be so, the neighbours are such a very dowdy old world set. The better class of neighbours such as Lord Dartmouth whose house is next to theirs & Sir Joseph Radcliffe[21] &c are all absentees. They have now four horses, two for the carriage & Papa's & Carry's for riding—still I think it will be very dull for Mama in the winter—she says so & says that her friends are bound to come & see her.

I am glad you had a pleasant day at Gravesend—I of course have no news & only write to say I shall leave on Saturday & be in town on Sunday night about nine oclock. I shall therefore not see the dear boys on Sunday.

Love to Herby & Haji & tell them to come & see us the first fine afternoon they are able.

Were you not very much surprised at the apparition of 'el signor Padre?' You must tell him you do not dine at home when I am not there & so defer having him till I come. Otherwise there will be so much plague for you.

Lily's love Carry's & mine
H. T.

Thursday[22]

Dear John,

We got home very comfortably & very tired—& I dare say you were the same.

Lily sends her love & kisses—& my reason for writing is that having been kept awake half the night by violent indigestion which I attribute to eating one of those half ripe peaches, I recommend to you to do <u>otherwise</u>. I am sure they are the most unwholesome things in the world.

I have got another letter from poor little Cary, who seems in a peck of troubles—but only about domestic arrangements—the Padre proving restive about the bills[23] I have told her not to tear herself & so on—she wants me to come sooner as she thinks I can do more with this Governor[24]—but I can't—at least I won't—which comes to the same thing.

---

21. William 4th Earl of Dartmouth, 1788-1848; Sir Joseph Radcliff, 1799-1868.

22. Postmarked 3 September [no year]. Probably written just before her visit to Birksgate in 1840. Caroline had just married and the letter mentions buying silverware, presumably as a wedding gift. XXVIII/153.

23. The word could be "hills," but the context seems to indicate "bills" as a more logical reading.

24. Probably a slang term to indicate Harriet's father, Thomas Hardy, since she and Arthur Hardy refer to him in other letters by the same term.

I shall only go the 15 or 16—Ley is to be there the 23. I have written to order from Lamb a butter knife in addition to the Sugar Tongs. thinking it better so.

Good bye dear. I have nothing new.
Ever affect^{ly}
H T.

Saturday[25]

Dear John,

I have just got a half hour alone in the excessive bustle & confusion to say a word or two. I am already feeling quite knocked up. I envy you beyond measure being quietly at home & both I & Lily pine to be back in town & shall come back the end of next week when I will tell you all about it. Here my head-aches so incessantly & violently that I am unfit for writing or anything else.

Edward's account of his father's treatment of him was most untrue for in fact he & Cary have made a league together & completely rule every body & every thing here—& the sort of management you can imagine. I would give the world to get away but I suppose I must stay over the day which continues to be the 23^d. I dare say I shall get Lamb's parcel,[26] but it does not matter if I do not it will do just as well in town & indeed would have just as well been omitted—for any thing she seems to notice or to care for any of her friends. Indeed the sort of things she says are quite repulsive, but perhaps she may cool down into a reasonable creature some day. I have plenty to tell you about it all but I will not write any more now.

I will write again & tell you when I come home. Kiss the dear boys for me. Lily sends her love.

Yr affec^{ate}
H T.

Tuesday 3 o'clk[27]

My dear John,

I have just got your note & I will be in Delahay Street at six or most likely before. We came to the little cottage yesterday. it is a very droll little place

---

25. Postmarked 3 September [no year]. Probably written the same year (1840) as the previous letter. XXVIII/154.

26. Harriet mentions ordering a butter knife and sugar tongs from Lamb, apparently a silversmith, in the previous letter.

27. The paper is watermarked 1840. XXVIII/156.

because it is really what it pretends to be—a <u>poor</u> <u>person's</u> cottage. It is very pleasant—the garden very pretty—& the walk from Richmond Hill most lovely. I walked here from the Castle—which is no trifle in this weather for it must be quite three miles—Lily will come also to-morrow.

Adieu now—

Aff^{ly} H T.

Walton Friday[28]

My dear John,

I entirely agree with you as to that application—to return no answer, of course, & if a further application is made to say no. Your letter went to the other Mrs Taylor this morning & was returned opened, which is not agreable, tho' in this instance it happened to be of no moment. You see it is necessary to put <u>some</u> distinctive mark upon the letters. Yesterday I opened a letter of hers about an annuity which I sent to her & which I dare say she did not like.

I enclose the prescriptions which if you can send either tomorrow or Monday I shall be very glad. If the box is made up at the Counting House & you could make them put in for a shilling of Leman's mixed biscuits it would be pleasant.

I continue better. I have a long letter from Pater[29] asking my advice on the lawsuit & saying that Mr Laing[30] is chosen as the medium of communicating to him the plaintiff's proposal[31] to pay the costs & advance £300 on which condition he will give up the suit I have told him that if I were he I would go on at whatever cost—but that if he cannot help fretting he had better give in to the extortion. If he gives in now he will

---

28. Paper is watermarked 1840. XXVIII/157. Harriet moved to Walton in the fall of 1839, so this must have been early enough in 1840 that the postman is still unfamiliar with her. The last paragraph indicates a lawsuit was pending between Harriet's father and (perhaps?) Arthur Ley. John Taylor may have been blamed in some way for the trouble, since from the early 1840s on, his father-in-law, Thomas Hardy, refused to speak to him even in public. The problem between the men was exacerbated by Thomas's refusal to aid Emilia Hardy after William's death at the end of 1840.

29. Father.

30. Mr. Laing was the husband of Mrs. Marianne Laing, who, according to Mineka and Lindley, is a relative of Harriet's (*CW:* XIV, 136) and a cousin of Helen's (*CW:* XV, 668).

31. It is unclear who the plaintiff is. It could be Arthur Ley. Arthur had married Caroline the previous year, but shortly thereafter there was a "peck of troubles" concerning Arthur (see XXVIII/153, above). However, Thomas Hardy was also having a row with his son Edward, who left in 1840 with a married Birksgate maid for New Zealand, where they lived together.

probably have it all to do over again when it is spent—besides it is an unprincipled extortion, he has no claim nor right to it, & it is all but sure not to be used honestly if it is got. I do think you should not let him have any money if he applies again. he does not even profess now to intend to go abroad if he gets it—& what is the use of £300 here?

Adieu Affec^{ately}
H T.

Monday[32]

My dear John,

I have just received letters from Herby & Haji! & such nice & long letters. I am so sorry to find Haji has not lost his cold. How did you think they looked? Lily is perfectly well. I am better than I was on Saturday & I hope to get better this week again. but the fact is the slightest thing that goes wrong with me is sure to bring back one or other of the troubles which I seem for a time to have conquered. however patience must be my motto.

Mama & Car. want me to go there, but it is too early in the year & too long a journey at present—besides that I could not stand the fatigues which are sure to be met with, of the spirits if not of the body. I am sorry to find you speak of annoyances—I hope they were only slight—& that they are past. If you should have a few moments to spare some even^{g} will you take a little trouble for me about which I must otherwise go to town myself—I have left ~~in~~ some ~~of~~ where, I do not precisely remember where a long bundle of manuscript tied with red tape—I have some notion that having left it out of one of my own packages, I put it in the hurry of packing into that large iron-bound chest of yours. will you just look if it is there & if it is, it is quite loose, not done up in paper or any thing but merely tied—you will see it directly if it is—& if so will you be kind enough to enclose it & send it me by post? If it is not there I must get some of my boxes sent down here, as I am very busy writing for the printers & want to get some scraps out of that.

Do not be at much trouble about this, for if it is in that ~~box~~ chest it will be to be seen immediately. I hope your mother is better pray tell her I send my best wishes for her speedy restoration to health.

Ever affec^{ty}
H. T.

32. Probably written in 1842, since Harriet asks about John Taylor's mother's health. John's mother died in 1842. XXVIII/152.

Walton[33]
July 27

My dear John,

It is impossible to feel more grieved than I do on account of this most sad illness of your mother. I grieve for her for you, the children & on all accounts. If her mind could be set at rest she would recover, but I suppose you find it impossible to succeed in that. Eliza[34] should <u>pacify</u> her mind, even if she changed her own mind afterwards.

Have you tried the effect of reminding her that she is necessary to you to her grandchildren & to all her family & that she <u>ought as a duty</u> to <u>exert</u> herself to cast off from her mind & thoughts the affair which distresses her & <u>which after all</u> is <u>not</u> of the importance that her life is—& by being patient she will find it go[es] better than she expects—that it does not distress you in any thing like the degree she feels it & that it is <u>wrong</u> to injure all her family by giving way to a state of nerves which may kill her & that on account of any one member of it doing a foolish thing. You have probably said all this as well as every thing else you can think of to say—but I suggest what I can—& I know how much the idea of its being a <u>duty</u> to conquer her feelings for the sake of others is calculated to affect her if said at once <u>strongly</u> & tenderly. Tell her that every one has their own sorrows & afflictions & that you beleive those do rightest who bear them bravely if they cannot conquer them. <u>Above</u> <u>all</u> that her death would be a thousand times worse for all, than any going or staying of Eliza. It is her <u>excessively exaggerated</u> notion of the importance of this later movement which has got so strong hold of her nervous system.

I cannot think of any thing else to suggest. Give my best love to her & do tell her that I should certainly come to nurse her & converse with her if I could move.

Lilys love & kisses to you & you must kiss her poor grandmama for her & say how she thanks her for her kind thought of her. I have half a mind to send her over to Highbury to see her—sometimes a small thing changes the current of a painfully excited state.

I am sorry that we cannot see you to-day, but we must keep dear Lily's birthday again next week. If Herby could be of any use I will send him over, but shall not without hearing from you. I shall be very anxious for to-morrows letter.

Adieu dear. Ever affec^{ly}
H T.

---

33. The letter was written in 1842, the year of John Taylor's mother's death. XXVIII/158.

34. Eliza Taylor, John Taylor's sister.

My dear John,

I hear that Peter Taylor called on Mr Mill yesterday wanting him to undertake Miss Flowers[35] affairs conjointly with himself (P Taylor) & you. P. Taylor had not apparently any suggestion to make from himself, but quoted you for every thing he said. He said that you told him to apply to Mr Mill to interest himself with Novello[36] that you suggested making a subscription to be kept a secret from Miss Flower while it is to be pretended that the money is the produce of her music! I feel quite sure that you never suggested or thought of such a scheme.

He never mentioned Mr Fox's[37] name no more than if he did not exist. I have no doubt Mr Fox is at the bottom of the plan for raising the wind & so escaping his own share. Did he not have Miss Flower's money & ought he not to return either the principal or the interest. P Taylor said that Miss Flowers has about £80 a year from mines & that Novello offered £10 a year for her copyright. This seems quite as much as could be expected for music which does not sell. He said he thought not, but he evidently has not a word to say except what is prompted by some one else. He said you wanted Novello to give more at once instead of annually—do you not see Mr Fox in that? always grasping for more & for the present. Surely whatever is done should be annually & above all no secret from Miss Flowers. No one but Mr Fox would have impudence enough to suggest that a sub^n sh^d be made by ~~friends~~ acquaintance upon whom she has no claim for a person having £80 pr an. & that secretiv. What is Mr Fox about? Why is not he the principal & lead of the subscription? Why is he not to be 'at the meeting?' The friends appear to be intended to consist of M^r P Taylor you & Mr Mill? I should certainly dislike being made a tool of by Mr Fox's maneuvres— There ought to be a list openly made of names of those willing to subscribe before saying the sum, that the sum likely to be raised may be seen & the two or three willing willing ones not be made to pay for all. There ought also to be a treasurer not like P Taylor a mere cat's paw in Mr Fox's hands who w^d be quite capable of paying it over to him. You or Sallie ought to receive the money raised & to pass it openly & avowedly to Miss Flower as a friendly subscription, for her use. I strongly advise you to pay no money but into the hands of Miss Flower or those of Sallie. I should propose that

35. Peter Taylor may be Peter Alfred Taylor (1819–91). See John's letters, *CW*: XV, 823, 942; XVII, 1604-5, 1607-8; XXXII, 196-97. Eliza Flower ("Miss Flower") died in 1847, so the letter was written between 1843 and 1847. The paper is watermarked 1843. "Sallie," below, is Sarah Flower Adams, Eliza's sister. XXVIII/136.

36. Vincent Novello (1781-1861), English composer, conductor, and music publisher.

37. William Fox.

a list of names of subscribers sh^d be got to gether by P Taylor (at the head of which I suppose would be Mr Fox's) & that you sh^d be treasurer if possible or if not Mrs Adams.

This is what occurs to me & I write it at once so it may help you if you are going, as P T said to meet him to morrow.

It is dark & I can scarcely see to write. Adieu aff^y H T.

No one sh^d state their sum till Mr Fox has put his down I think. It is evidently Mr Fox's plan that you & Mr Mill sh^d be the Subscribers, Mr P. Taylor the treasurer, & Mr Fox the recipient.

Wednesday[38]

My dear John,

I cannot prove the return of the ring—it is so long since that it is forgotten. The only person I could bring to prove anything about either the seal or ring is <u>Turner</u>, the present occupier of the shop, for who was then shopman & who I am certain would remember the fact of both ring and seal being returned.—whether he would choose to say so is another question—yet as I still deal with him I should think he would. This could only be ascertained by your calling on him & asking him. If it is inconvenient to you to do so, I suppose there will be nothing to do but to pay the demand—perhaps both ring & seal are at this moment in Turner's shops. It was of him. I bought the seal & ordered the ring & to him they certainly were returned—but I cannot swear to anything about them.

I am sorry to give you so much trouble. We are quite well.

Ever y^r affec^ate
H T.

of the bill

I owe, silver clasp— 12 -
    clean^g Watch— 7.6
Rep^g Pencil case 2.
        1.1.6
Not owing
      ring— 2.14
      Seal— 1.10
    Stone— 10
  Engraving— 7.6
      5.1.6

38. There is no indication when this letter was written. XXVIII/137.

11 April[39]

My dear John,

I am really very far from well & as I see no immediate reason for hurrying, I will fix <u>Thursday</u> to come to town. I shall be very glad to hear from Herby again. I will write to Craven St on Tuesday.

Adieu Affec^y
H T.

My dear John,

We got down very well but I had a tremendous cough & cold on Friday even^g. I had a large fire kept up in the bedroom at night, & yesterday I was better & to-day it is evidently going.

I will come up on Wednesday and as I suppose I must call at that place on my way, if you have not invited them before I will do so—please therefore write on Tuesday saying if you have—& if not shall I say Thursday or Friday? If you dine at home on Wednesday I will dine late also. If you don't do not order anything for me.

The weather is warme but too wet for the garden. The trees here have got on amazingly in the last fortnight. The Pears & Cherry trees in full blossom.

Lily's love & kisses. The Maize[40] shall be put under glass—It cannot thrive better than that we produced here in 1841.

Adieu affec^ly
H T.[41]

Friday morn^g

My dear John[42]—we left Brighton yesterday morning & had a very pretty ride here. We were just four hours coming. What a remarkably pretty place Lewes is? do you know it? I thought it almost as pretty as Malvern & in the same 'genre'.

I got here about three o'clock then Lily & I walked about the place & took a lodging. We then went back to the Inn & dined & came to the lodging in the even^g. We have got the prettiest situation by far in the place but it is a <u>wood cottage</u> & I think the rooms will be very cold—besides that the weather is so much colder & damper than at Brighton,

39. There is no indication of the year. XXVIII/139.

40. Corn.

41. Written between 1842 and 1849. XXVIII/165.

42. No indication of date. XXVIII/141.

w[h]ere it had not ceased to be bright & warm. It has not yet rained here, but looks threatening, & if it does it will be very cold. I have taken these rooms only for a week—& I mean to look out for others. They call this <u>cottage</u> 'Mount Edgcombe House'. Lily likes this place very much. The sheep with their tinkling bells feed quite up to the door.

Please tell the dear boys to direct to me 'Post Office' untill I write to them, which I will do on Monday or Tuesday.

Lilys love & kisses to you & to them & mine. I must come to town for a day soon.

Adieu now. Affec^{ly} Yrs. H T.

Mount Edgcombe House[43]
May 27

My dear John,

Thanks for your long amusing letter. I had a letter from each of the 'gars'[44] this morning: They seem to have been much pleased with this Saturday's excursion. Lilkin[45] has been writing to you, but she likes scrambling over the common & the rocks much better than sitting down to anything so her letters is not a model, either as to style or writing. She is so well & rosy it is delightful to see. This place is really very pretty, far prettier than I expected it to be; but then I should not think it so perhaps if we had not the best situation in the place: we are at the farthest extremity of Mount Ephraim next the open country & on the very top of the hill—The cold here this last week has been extreme & since Sunday it has rained incessantly untill to-day. It has cleared up this afternoon & is very fine, but also very cold.

I mean to leave this place next week as I do not like it enough to wish to stay over Mid Summer & I wish to come nearer town to pursue my house hunting. I have seen a place advertised at East Deen which may do for a time. If not I think of going to Richmond & taking apartments there for the present. When I am on the spot I shall soon find a furnished house somewhere in the neighborhood of Richmond.

I hear Mama has been ill & wants to see me. If she continues to wish it I must go down to her for a week.

Adieu dear Affec^{ly} H T.

---

43. Written on the same trip to Lewes as the previous letter. XXVIII/142.

44. Probably "garçons," her sons.

45. Helen Taylor.

Friday[46]
Sept. 23

My dear John,

I write to wish you many happy returns of to-morrow—which I do with all my heart. We agreed to keep the birthdays next Wednesday. shall you come on that day, or the evening before & stay over the day? The boys we agreed were to come on Tuesday evening did you not say they should stay 'till Friday morn^g. Lily is very well & I as usual.

Adieu affectio^{ly}
H. T.

My dear John,

Many thanks for your kind wishes on my birthday,[47] which for a wonder turns out a bright sunny day; the air here is as warm & moist as that of a vapour bath, & I imagine it very far from healthy. We sat yesterday with the window open all day the consequence of which was a violent fit of face-ache in the evening, which was releived but not cured by some hot brandy & water. I am very glad indeed to hear you say you are better. I think you should take every means, however inconvenient, to get rid of your disorder—I should think Brighton quite the best place for it, and with strict attention to diet—I hope to hear that you have profited greatly by the visit.

I think it very desirable for us to go to the sea again for some weeks and I mean to look for a house either at Brighton or Herne Bay. I shall not go to Brighton till I have seen Herne Bay, as if I can find a pleasant house there I shall take it at once. I intend at present (unless anything happens to prevent it) to go to Herne Bay next Saturday.

I shall not in any case go to Brighton before next week.

I suppose you go to the Bellford.

Ever yr affec^{ate}
H T.

Sunday.

Thursday even^g

My dear John,[48]

We got down most easily and pleasantly, and certainly I never came to

---

46. There is no indication what year these birthday greetings were sent. XXVIII/138.

47. October 8. There is no indication what year this thank-you for birthday greetings was sent. XXVIII/171.

48. Written after their stay in the same cottage in 1839 (see XXVIII/148, above). The letter may have been written during their stay in Brighton in 1842 or 1843. XXVIII/159.

Brighton in my life with so little fatigue, and this is saying much considering how I dreaded the journey but a week or two ago. The weather was delightful—the sun came out brilliantly just before we arrived & we have had a beautiful afternoon. Haji & Lily have been out for more than two hours on the beach at Kemp town. We are in the same house where we have been once before, 2 Junction Parade, so we have the fine sea view, and I never saw the sea more beautiful. The ease & even pleasure of the ride has put me quite in charity with railroads, but in none of those I have been on before have the arrangements for peoples convenience been nearly so good. They offered to take charge of the luggage for any length of time; but finding the <u>fly man</u> very willing to carry it as well as us in his fly & I took it with us & drove to these houses where I engaged the first rooms I saw. so that we were settled & at home at three oclock. They got us some dinner very quickly, after which Haji & Lily started with great zeal for their walk. Since they came in we have had tea, & are now all feeling sleepy & tired & so I will end my note. I hope there is a prospect of the weather brightening up again & that if you go out on Sat^y you will have as fine a day & as pleasant as we have had. If you have I am sure the air will do Herby good, as I think a week here would be of great use to him. Adieu with my Haji & Lily's love to you both,

Yr ever affec^ate
H. T.

Caen^49 June 24th

My dear John,

You will be surprised to find that I have got so far as this place, but I find myself so much better for moving about that I have been able to see all the places on the Seine which appeared worth going to, with very little fatigue. I received your letter, as well as Herbert's & Haji's, sent on from Dieppe. Your description of the overfilled steamers would almost apply to the steamers on the Seine, those from Rouen to Havre tho' very large boats were so full as to be most disagreable. We however only went in it from Rouen to Canteleu, a small town on the bank, thence we went in a small boat to Maillerage, a very pretty place indeed, and w[h]ere the 'living' was most capital & every thing as cheap as at Rouen every thing was exorbitantly dear. we then had a splendid ride through thick forests to a lovely place called Pont Audemer & thence another exceedingly lovely ride to Honfleur.

I wished for you & the boys very much at Honfleur as I think you would

---

49. Written during the trip to France in 1844. XXVIII/140.

very much like it. It is the prettiest & nicest & most amusing place by far that I have seen in France, & very cheap there could not be a nicer little excursion from England. The wooded valleys all around are most lovely walks & drives. The views from the Chapel of Notre dame de Grace are splendid. The Harbour too is amusing as the steamers from Havre come & go incessantly, the fare is I believe half a franc. From Honfleur we went to Trouville, a watering place on the coast. Thence to this place last Thursday, from here we have been to two watering places on the coast, and to-day we leave here for Falaise.

This is a very nice town but the country is flat. The fine country of the Bocages begins at Falaise & we shall go by Vire, Mortain, Granville, Avranches to St. Malo, & thence to Dinan, w[h]ere there are mineral waters & w[h]ere I hope to stay for a week or two. will you therefore direct to <u>Dinan</u> <u>Côtes du Nord</u>. I expect to be at St. Malo next Sunday and at Dinan, a day or two after. The weather is splendid only too hot, I hope you have the same. I dare say Uncle D is very disagreable when he is not in his best humour, for he is always rude—but I think you should make it a great object not to have any difference with him, & the more because I do not at all beleive he means to be annoying & I do think he would be both kind and considerate when there was occasion to be so. I dislike the idea of Herbert going to Birksgate, because there would be no end to questionings & wonderments at every thing I do. I mean to return from Britanny to Dieppe (unless we should prefer Havre) & after staying there a short time, return to Brighton. I think you would be surprised at my good looks both the travelling & climate suit me so well. I still walk with the utmost difficulty, but still I do manage to walk very short distances.

Lily is writing all her gossip to Haji. She sends her love we are both very glad you are looking so well & young again.

Adieu dear affec^{tely} H T.

[written around the sides of the letter]
Lily is very well indeed. She enjoys the churches, dinners & Diligences[50] immensely, but grumbles excessively whenever we come in contact with people, as in the crowded steamboat. She has all the intolerance of a young person for anything strange, & could not find words strong enough to express her dislike of the French on the steamboat because they talk so much & so fast. indeed their tongues seem never to weary, & the great heat, which makes the little girl cross, seems only to make them more lively.

---

50. French stagecoaches.

May [2]9

My dear John,[51]

I send a letter for Herby, but fancy it will be too large to enclose in yours. If so it must go separate.

What really fine weather we have now. I hope you will get out to enjoy on the Saturdays in June—that is your free month is it not—and I really think short excursions of a few days only do as much generally for health and spirits as long ones.

You must have had an amusing & pleasant party & it is always pleasant to know those people; I have heared of L^y Palmerston[52] being a very agreable woman—and among that class a woman's being old is never thought a reason for not finding her agreable, but the contrary as indeed is natural, for to those who know life & the world the most amusing society is not by any means that of the young.

I shall be glad if you <u>will</u> send the Examiner to Mama as I know she wishes it, & as she asked it[.] it may as well be done if you do not mind.

Politics, after years of dullness begin to be amusing again. The sudden 'conversion' that take place in the opinions of people who never had nor ever will have anything that ought to be dignified with the name of opinions. The next ten years will probably show great changes & yet can hardly produce greater than the last have done. Ld John[53] longs to be in, but I greatly prefer Peel,[54] a man with no decided opinions is so much more convinc[e]able than one, like Ld John, with decidedly narrow opinions.

Lily's love & mine,

Ever affec^ly
H T.

Walton.[55] June 2.

My dear John, I have written a few words for Herby tho' I had nothing new to say, which you will perhaps enclose in one of yours. I send his last. He is quite delighted apparently with all he meets.

---

51. Paper is watermarked 1845. Probably written in 1846, just after Herbert left for the United States. XXVIII/161.

52. Wife of Henry John Temple Palmerston (1784-65). Lord Palmerston served as Secretary of War from 1809-1828 and returned to the Foreign Office under Russell from 1846-51.

53. Lord John Russell (1792-1878) served as Prime Minister from 1846 to 1852. He advocated parliamentary reform.

54. Sir Robert Peel (1788-1850).

55. Probably written in 1846, after Herbert had sailed for the United States. XXVII/162.

This weather is very pleasant. It suits me well—but I am in a very low state with increasing cough and stomach derangement.

Lily is quite well.

Adieu affec^{ly}
H T.

I have had a cake made for Haji which shall be sent to-morrow.

Walton⁵⁶ March 19

My dear John,

I have not had a letter from Herby. He will be very late in returning, but if his stay is of advantage it is all well—& he evidently enjoys it.

It is quite summer weather. I and Lily had a drive yesterday round Claremont, which was very pretty & pleasant. It was the first time I had been out of the house since November.

I had Mrs. Adams⁵⁷ on Tuesday. She looks <u>most</u> wretchedly—but this seems chiefly because she gives herself up to passionate fits of crying—ten minutes, five minutes, after she will laugh quite merrily. She is in no way altered in character during the eight or ten years I have lost sight of her—she is even more what she calls "impulsive"—what I call horribly sentimental. It is a way of taking life most disagreable & "antipathique" to me. Her account of all that old set is most disagreable—as far as you can call it <u>an account</u>, which consists of scattered words & expressions very hard to form any intelligible notion of facts from. Of Mr Fox⁵⁸ in particular it is the most extraordinary & absurd account. Among a dozen other stories, she says that the day after the funeral service for Lizzie⁵⁹ she (Mrs Adams) received a letter from Mr Fox enclosing a list of property of his which had been in L's possession, made out in his own handwriting consisting of such items as this[:] "1 bedsheet, 1 Reading easel—" &c &c—& requesting its return!—She says this was soon followed by an application from him for £300 "from Miss Flower's estate" which he said was due to him, partly for rent for Charlotte St. for which he alleges she agreed to pay part of the rent, £20 pr annum, partly for advances years ago to Miss Flower! This Mrs Adams says she shall pay. I told her I thought

<hr>

56. Written in 1847, after Eliza Flower's death and not long before Sarah Flower Adams herself died. XXVIII/163.

57. Sarah Flower Adams.

58. William Fox.

59. Eliza Flower.

she was quite uncalled upon to do so. Then she received a letter from him, saying that he had heared she (Mrs Adams) had said he was indebted to Miss Flower for money she had lent for the 'True Sun'[60] that he denied that he was so, but still he should pay it as she had said so—& that this letter contained an immense number of bills of acceptance of Mr Fox's to the amount of £200! That she enclosed or returned them directly.

She told a hundred other things tho' none perhaps so intense as this. I was very much tired by her—as I do not agree in her way of viewing any question. For instance she seriously wanted me to share her intense pity for poor Mr Horne, because after being always understood to be <u>Mary</u> Gilles lover he had offered to <u>Margaret</u> and on her persisting in refusing, is now on the point of marrying Miss Faggo! And she was quite hurt that I laughed at the whole story & at her "poor Mr Horne"! One cannot get on with such people. She describes that Mr Adams "<u>was ruined</u>" (her favorite expression) in Decr but that now they are very grand. She is a great boaster, & very curious, & a bit of a gossip, but she means well—but her company is to me not at all agreable. You will begin to tire of <u>my</u> gossip—so adieu dear. Lily's love & kisses.

affec^ly

H T.

6 April[61]

My dear John

The weather has been so cold that I thought he would hardly venture to leave Birksgate. But it is now growing milder every day so I suppose they will come. Please when he asks after me (or without if he does'nt!) to say that "I mean to come to town as soon as I hear they are arrived & that you will write & tell me they are come"

I do not know if it would be more satisfactory to have Herby come home by the steamers? That is as safe as any thing can be, while about sailing there is always some risk. What do you think?

If you have got Hahn Hahn's Turkey[62] from a library will you keep it for me.

---

60. A newspaper for which Fox was the lead writer and editor. The paper closed in 1837 after Fox had increased the circulation significantly.

61. Written in 1847, as Herbert in preparing to sail home from the United States. XXVIII/164.

62. Gräfin Hahn Hahn, a German writer who was very much in vogue during this period, visited England in 1846. Harriet is making a pun on her name which means "little turkey" when she refers to her book as "Hahn Hahn's turkey."

I have had it down at the three librarys which I keep in contribution & have not yet got it.

I hope Haji's cold is better. It seemed very bad on Sunday Even^g & he must avoid being out at night.

Lily's love. & Adieu affec^{ly}

H T.

What a long letter you have written me I must answer it all when I come.

Thursday^{63}

My dear John,

Herbert arrived on Tuesday, having had a very pleasant ride. I hope he will look better for his visit here, he is I think looking very thin—but he says himself that he has gained a pound in weight in the last two months, so I hope he is not really thinner. He came down with M$^{[rs]}$ Laing^{64} from whom we had a visit yesterday. I shall not see any more of her, as I would rather avoid their acquaintance here. She and Augusta are staying with their Uncle for a fortnight. I think it would be very bad for Herby to remain at this place at all after I leave it, & he himself is most strongly of the same feeling, in fact he cannot bear the idea of it. He absolutely requires that everything depressing to the spirits should be avoided, and nothing is half so depressing to a young person as being left alone when others go. He will therefore return on Saturday even^g by the last train, which is half past six from here.

I have been thinking that if you want an excursion on Sunday it might be a good plan to go to some place on the Brighton line & so meet Herby as thus his fare would be saved. but if you do, pray take Haji with you. There is Croydon or Redhill, where there is a good inn. or Godstone which is very pretty. Let us know if you should like either of these. The weather has seems likely to change & be wet. It is raining this morning. If the weather should be very stormy on Saturday, I shall not go—& if I do not go till Monday Herbert will stay till Monday; unless I hear from you that he is to meet you anywhere on the railway line. Adieu with Lilys & Herberts love. Your affec^{ate} H T.

[on top of front page]
4 o'clk It has now cleared up & seems likely to be fine. Adieu

---

63. Written in 1847, just after Herbert's return from the United States. XXVIII/160.

64. Mrs. Marianne Laing, a relative of Harriet's.

Birksgate.[65] Oct 1

My dear John

I am exceedingly concerned at this news of Shewells failure. Of course your coming here was impossible—I never saw a man so annoyed as he was when told you could not come yet on hearing the reason he saw the impossibility.

I only hope there may be no run on the bank—in any case you must have a most anxious time. I shall return on Monday as I intended & I suppose be at Kent Terrace about eight or nine o'clock in the evening.

Do not please order anything for us but tea & eggs. Poor Mama is very unhappy at not seeing you as she has been making preparations to do you all sorts of honours all the week.

Adieu very Affec[ly]
H T.

I must tell you how much she regrets &c &c

Walton - Friday[66]

My dear John,

Marianne Laing has been here all the week which has prevented my writing before as I intended. I hope she will talk of leaving to-morrow as so long a visit is very wearysome. She seems very well & just as usual.

I do not wonder you are anxious—you must have a most unpleasant & fatiguing time of it in the city—how long is it supposed this sort of crisis will last. I wish I could help you. Is Herby come home? I was surprised at that passage of Arthur's letter, as you say you were, but supposed it must refer to some accounts between you & him of which you had not told me.

It was I thought a strange sort of letter in more than one respect. Perhaps he thought "The least said soonest mended" about Alf's Son.

I will write again soon

Adieu Affec[ly] H. T

---

65. Probably written during Harriet's visit to Birksgate in 1847. England suffered a financial crisis that year. XXVIII/167.

66. Probably written in 1847, before Arthur Hardy's trip to England in 1848 and after Alfred Hardy's return to Australia from England in 1846. XXVIII/168.

Sunday[67]

My dear John,

I do not wonder at your feeling fatigued & overdone—business at the present time must be both anxious & perplexing—it must be difficult to know whom to trust—I wish I could help you.

The Birksgate letter is only remarkable for its extremely friendly tone. The boys should do any thing they can, in the way of "making out the account" (tho I am sure I do not know what that is) if their doing so will be any pleasure to him. Arthur's letter strikes me, as did that late letter to his father, as displaying very obviously in its <u>tone</u> the effect of Alfred's[68] descriptions, and I am sorry to see it, because not only will every thing Alfred says be contrary to what we think is true, but what I think a great deal more of, it seems to show Arthur to be very inferior in judgment and good sense to what I hoped for from him if he has not yet discovered Alfred's incompetence foolishness & untrustworthiness.

However it cannot be helped—if he comes over with his mind prejudiced, if he has good sense he will soon find out his mistake—& if he has not, the provoking & dissapointing it cannot be helped.

The passage "I am amused at the airs some of the English mercantile people give themselves in impressing upon the colonists the ~~advantage~~ importance of punctuality" is so evidently <u>verbatim</u> what Alf^d has reported to him about your sayings to Alfred—& is in itself so very silly a sentence—that I strongly recommend your sending the letter to Birksgate that that sentence may be seen, because it so completely gives you the right of it—to a person of any brains what could there be <u>amusing</u> in advising <u>punctuality</u>! or what "<u>airs</u>"! It is Alfred's stupid vulgar pique caught up by him—which dissapoints me in him.

Yours very Affec^ly
H T.

Brighton. Thursday[69]

My dear John,

We left Walton on Tuesday morning at ten & got here at two. It was so bright and beautiful a day that the country & every thing looked and felt like summer. After we got here we drove on the cliff for an hour and a half

---

67. Probably written in 1847 or early 1848, prior to Arthur Hardy's arrival in England. XXVIII/169.

68. Arthur Hardy and Alfred Hardy.

69. Written in fall 1847. XXVIII/173.

in an open carriage and did not find it cold. I never saw so many people at this place in winter. On Tuesday & to-day owing to the extreme brightness of the days every body in the place seem to have come out & there are as many carriages as at any season. Yesterday, I wrote to you but it was so thoroughly wet that we could not go to the Post office to take it.

It is fortunate for us that the weather is so much less cold. We should soon be forced to decamp if it turned cold again for lodging rooms are complete caves of Eolus.[70] at each blast of wind the carpet rises up in emulation of the waves without. I have been occupied all this morning in going over furnished houses & the result is that I quite give up the plan of taking one. Such places do very well in the summer when open windows & out of door life make one overlook defects, but in very cold weather when the comfort of home is most needed I see that I could not endure the squalid appointments & shabby furniture & great bare rooms of these lodging houses. There are plenty to let & at moderate rents.

I shall return to Walton on Tuesday next & come here or somewhere else occasionally during the winter.

Lily has quite lost the cold she had on Sunday. I had a return of face ache yesterday but to-day it is gone off nearly.

I think that letter of Swetenham's showed only the unpunctuality you have before remarked. I do not myself think that unpunctuality proves poverty—but where that is the habit one cannot but doubt the fortune being made untill one knows that it is realised. I do not however doubt that he has made money & think that he will arrive here in the spring or summer. Lily's love.

Ever Your Affec^{ate}
H T.

Jan 18.

My dear John,[71]

I enclose the new agreement which Manners[72] has sent, signed as you see. I do not know why he has said 'witness' when there is no witness to his signature, nor, as he has signed it can there now be. I sh^d think therefore there sh^d be none to yours—but whether without witness it is a legal document I do not know. If a witness is necessary he must be made to draw it up & sign it again?

I am very unwell the face-ache never having left & the continued taking

---

70. Aeolus, Greek god of the wind.

71. Written in 1848. XXVIII/174.

72. Manners owned the house Harriet rented at Walton.

laudanum[73] has besides making me feel poorly made me so liable to take cold that I have both cold & a troublesome cough. Lily's cold tho' now but slight is not yet gone quite. The letter from Birksgate contained that of Alfred's I had sent. He[74] it seems is full of satisfaction at having at last got on the bench, where he took his seat for the first time last week with the Earl of Effingham Hon. Howard[75] &c &c

my mother fears this will keep him & therefore her more fixed to Birksgate—& for a time I dare say it will. They say nothing of coming to town.

Mr Mill has just had an overture from Sir J. Easthope[76] wishing him to share the proprietorship of the Morn^g Chronicle. It seems Easthope has had a quarrel with his son in law Doyle & which he says it is impossible can be made up—nor can they go on in the same concern. The quarrel however is not about the Chroni^l but about a will made by Easthope's eldest son, who has lately become a lunatic & Easthope and Doyle mutually accuse the other of having made away with or retained this will! Easthope is in a terrible rage—I have not heared anything of Doyle's version, as all this is Easthope's. Easthope says that 100,000 have been divided among the proprietors since he took it. He has 7. 8^ths & Duncan the bookseller 1.8^th. He offers 3 or 4. 8th at 1700 each. He says the Daily News has made an offer to be sold to the Chronicle but they want too much. The To[r]y's are very eager to get it. Mr Mill does not mean to take it as he thinks part proprietorship would not ensure the opinions he would take it solely with the object of advocating—but he is very anxious to save it from the Tories. It seems Alderman Farebrother[77] has made offers for it.

Shares enough to constitute a majority would amount to a large sum. Sir J. Easthope said that <u>La^y</u> Easthope had one share which she would not give up. Easthope said the present sale is 3200 & that it has been done up so far by the Daily News. yet that paper seems on its last legs. I shall be very sorry if the "rascally Times" is to become the sole representative of english liberalism!

You had no great loss I imagine in not seeing Brooke. He is a mere yachting dandy & his 'Rajah'ship a complete farce.

I do not know at all how far the schism in the M. Chol is talked about yet.

---

73. Alcoholic extract of opium used frequently in the Victorian period.

74. Thomas Hardy, Harriet's father.

75. Henry Howard, 2nd Earl of Effingham (1806-89) sat as an M.P. for Shaftesbury.

76. Sir John Easthope (1784-1865) bought the *Morning Chronicle* in 1834.

77. According to Hayek (297), "probably Charles Farebrother, a member of the Vintner's Company and Alderman from 1826 until his death in 1858."

There is a good article in the last Quarterly on overspeculation & panics by a man named Newmarch[78] a clever man who was a country banker & a Quaker is now I beleive a manager of a joint Stock Bank <u>somewhere</u>: I dont know where but I dare say you do.

I have a strong opinion that I ought to leave England for the spring & sh^d certainly do so at once if I did not dislike leaving you all the trouble of their long spring visit.

Excuse the very illegible writing, but having the head-ache I hasten to finish. Lily's love. Ever affec^ly

H T.

~~I enclose both Manner's papers that you may see the mode of his signing to which I refer.~~

a mistake

Walton. Sunday.[79]

My dear John,

Thank you for your letter. I return that from Birksgate. I have had no return of the face ache since last week—but am now, I am sorry to say seriously alarmed about paralysis again. On Friday I felt the sudden cold extremely & on rising to go to bed at night I found great difficulty in moving the left leg—yesterday the stiffness seemed all but gone, but last night I could not walk without assistance & instead of going off with the night's rest, to-day I cannot move without help & it is also very painful. This last symptom of <u>pain</u> makes me hope it may prove <u>rheumatic</u> & curable—as when I lost the use of it before I never had any pain. I am very anxious about it & regret much that I did not go to the south of Europe a month ago while I was still able.

The Chronicle affairs are still pending.[80] I fancy the Parker[81] who is concerned about the paper is the Parker of the poor Law Commission who

---

78. Probably William Newmarch (1820-82), an economist who co-authored volumes 5 and 6 of *A History of Prices*. See *CW*: XV, 551-52 for a letter from JSM to Newmarch.

79. Written just after the previous letter, in early 1848. XXVIII/172.

80. See XXVIII/174, above.

81. Mr. H. W. Parker was the Assistant Poor Law Commissioner assigned to hold an inquiry into allegations of inadequate food of some workhouses and the cruelty of one particular master. Parker was invited to resign his post due to the manner of the inquiry, but was probably a scapegoat for the commissioners as a group. A more general dispute about the Commission itself ensued, resulting in a change in the constitution of the Commission in 1847.

has been acting as accountant or something of that sort. I hope the Whigs will take it as no one better seems disposed. Lily is quite well again.

I with her love & mine

I am Ever Yours Affec^{ate}

H T.

Walton. Tuesday[82]

My dear John,

I sent Arthur's letter to Birksgate on Sunday, requesting them to return it to you immediately. I was unable to write on Friday & Sat^y was not a post day hence. I have not been well for the last fortnight: indeed I have been very <u>unwell</u>—& that has made me rather out of spirits & disinclined to write. The sudden change to warm weather both made me feel ill & languid & also brought on, (along with the damp I suppose) the rheumatic pain in the left leg, amounting too to [*sic*] complete lameness. Then the change & cold on Sat^y gave me cold & cough. I am better to-day—but I have quite lost the feeling of being unusually well which I had before.

I have not heared from any one. What a wretched piece of cowardice on the part of the ministers this fast will be! It is quite disgraceful. I hope you & Haji have both lost your colds.

Adieu Affec^{ly}

H T

Walton.[83] March 24.

My dear John,

I am much concerned to hear that Haji has not lost the cough. I would not suggest his coming here because I think he increases his cold here, when he has one; not <u>necessarily</u>, but because he systematically refuses to pay any attention to my advice on that subject—as on any other.

To see <u>any one</u> voluntarily risking their life, for no earthly purpose is annoying, but when the person is ones son it is depressing.

I think it very proper that he should know my strong opinion, which is that he is in great danger of becoming consumptive, owing to his contempt for all recommendations or precautions. He needs to be told most decidedly that in his case a long continued cough will prove mortal. Of this I feel sure. And, <u>if</u>, having been told this by you as well as by me, he still persists in neglecting to ~~cure it~~ use the means pointed out to him of curing it—I can only feel that I have done my utmost for him & that

---

82. Probably written prior to Arthur Hardy's visit in 1848. XXVIII/175.

83. Written in 1848, this is the first indication of John Taylor's failing health. XXVIII/176.

he has a "right" to do as he pleases with himself. I pointed this out to him the last time I saw him, as indeed I have done 'till I can do it no more.

It may be as well to let him read this note, not that I expect he will take any notice of it. but if he should happen to see, before it is too late, that his own interest is concerned, that may have an effect upon him which no wishes of mine have.

I suppose the Birksgates[84] will come for their usual long stay. I fully enter into your feeling on the occasion. Had I better come to town when they do, do you think? I only wish to do what will make the infliction least to you. What do you think of my coming to K. T. for a week or ten days (God knows I do not think I can stand it longer) and then going to Brighton, when you could come down on a Sunday or two, it being your month of freedom, & I might invite them once? I really can think of nothing else, except running away altogether, & that is not fair to you. But that "dangling after" people whose whole ways are contrary to one is too annoying. The place I wish to go to, when I can—is Cauterets in the Pyrenees—it is a mineral watering place & much recommended by Clarke[85] & others for my state.

It is perhaps about midway between Toulouse & Pau. about 50 miles beyond Bayonne.

I am sorry you have been unwell. I think the very sudden change to almost summer weather is exceedingly trying. I have not felt well since the warm weather began—weaker than usual even, languid & loss of appetite.

Lily has a bad cold. she has had it a week past severely—but I hear of Influenza on all sides.

I ~~have~~ hear that Longmans have determined to bring the Edinburgh to London & that Empson who is editing it temporarily is to give it up to Merivale[86] of Oxford. This is what I wished & is my only bit of news.
Adieu Affec^ly
H T.

---

84. HTM is referring to her parents.

85. Probably James Clark (1788-1870), who wrote treatises on consumption and was an important physician during this period. See JSM's letter to HTM concerning Clark's treatise and various other doctors (*CW*: XIV, 198-99).

86. Longmans Publishing Company; *The Edinburgh Review*, a prestigious Scottish magazine published from 1802-29. William Empson (1791-1852) was editor of *The Edinburgh Review*, 1847-52. See *CW*: XXVII, 67 for a letter from JSM to Empson. Herman Merivale (1806-74) wrote frequently for *The Edinburgh Review*. See *CW*: XIII, 701; XV, 766, 966 for letters from JSM to Merivale.

Walton. Friday.[87]

My dear John

The leg has improved <u>really</u> this week and it is now all but well. Yesterday I and Lily took a rather long drive tempted by the beauty of the day, we were out more than two hours, going across Esher commons toward Letherhead—it is a most beautiful drive and we enjoyed it much. I paid for it by having the cramp all night at intervals, but am none the worse to-day. I do certainly look more like a ghost {than} a living person, but I dare say shall soon recover some better looks when we get to Brighton. I think I shall not be able to go before the end of next week being just now much occupied with the book. Thanks for the Birksgate letter which I return. I did not know they were going to Devonshire as she had never mentioned it to me. We shall much like to see you at Brighton.

Lily's love & Adieu Affec[ly]

H. T.

Walton. Wednesday.[88]

My dear John,

I told Haji to tell you I was very much obliged to you for the Tinct of Bark.[89] I have taken a spoon full every night & certainly think it does good. I am sure it is a narcotic—it makes me sleep almost like laudanum.

Thank you also for the parcel of clothes which will be a great treasure to John Russell, who having been out of work all the winter has his coat in a most dilapidated condition.

I have a letter from Sidmouth where they arrived last Thursday. She says he dislikes the place as it is so dull. I was sure he would. She says as they were a week later in going than they intended they shant have to stay 'so long' but she says nothing of <u>how long</u> they intend. She wishes me to go there to them—& I do not know but I might as well take lodgings there for a few weeks & so break the length of their visit to town.

Ever Affec[ly]

H T.

---

87. Written in March 1848, just before *Principles of Political Economy* appeared. XXVIII/170.

88. Paper is watermarked 1847. Probably written in March 1848, since Harriet's parents are in Sidmouth. XXVIII/177.

89. Cinchona, a medicinal bark, closely related to quinine.

Walton. Friday.[90]

My dear John,

The second note from Sidmouth said that they do not like the place & that he had settled to leave it (for London I suppose) on the 6th. Caroline was with them. I wrote to repeat that I could not go there before next week & that as they stay no longer I should only arrive as they were leaving—I therefore decided not to go.

If they had staid a week longer I should have gone for I should not have disliked, but the contrary, to have stayed some weeks after them. but I could not go before the 6th & it is absurd to go, <u>because</u> they are <u>there</u>, on the day they leave.

The book on The Principles of Political Economy which has been the work of all this winter is now nearly ready & will be published in ten days. I am somewhat undecided whether to accept its being dedicated to me or not—dedications are not unusual even of grave books, to women, and I think it calculated to do good if short & judicious—I have a large volume on Political Economy in my hands now dedicated to Madame de Sismondi[91]—yet I cannot quite make up my mind—what do you advise— on the whole I am inclined to think it desirable.

Ever Yr affec^ate
H T.

Monday 3 April 1848

My dear Harriet,[92]

I was so much surprised on Saturday when I received your note & found you to be inclined to have the Book dedicated to you that I could not reply until I I had a little time to reflect upon the question, & this I had during a walk to Pall Mall from whence I wrote my letter.—Consideration made me decidedly think, as I did at the first moment of reading your letter, that all dedications are in bad taste, & that under our circumstances the proposed one would evince on both author's parts, as well as the lady to whom the book is to be dedicated, a want of taste & tact which I could not have believed possible.—Two days have since passed & my conviction remains the same notwithstanding your letter of yesterday.

It is not only "a few common people" who will make vulgar remarks, but all who know any of us—The dedication will revive recollections now forgotten & will create observations and talk that cannot but be extremely unpleasant to me.

---

90. Written in March, 1848 just before *Principles of Political Economy* was published. XXVIII/179.

91. Auguste Comte's lover.

92. XXVIII/180.

I am very sorry you should be much vexed at my decided opinion. You asked me, "what do you advise" —and feeling & thinking as I do, that the proposed dedication would be most improper, I felt bound to give you my opinion in decided terms, & such as could not be mistaken. I much regret, as I always do, differing in opinions with you. But as you asked me what I advised; I have not hesitated to give my opinion.

No one would more rejoice than I should at any justice & honour done to you —and if I thought my feelings and wishes alone stood in the way of your receiving both, it would be a source of great sorrow to me. But I do not believe that either would result from anything in such bad taste as the proposed dedication would, in my opinion, shew. I can assure you that this subject has given me much anxiety & trouble these last two days, —it is never pleasant to differ with you— most of all upon questions such as this.

Yours affy
J. T.

Friday.[93]

My dear John

My face is better tho' still very troublesome & I fear will continue so untill I go to the Dentist.

It <u>is</u> a droll note from Sidmouth—one would think coals were not to be bought. I was sure he would not like that or any other watering place especially a small one. Perhaps you will say about me that I have been talking of going to Sidmouth, but that if it is such ~~an uninteresting~~ a cold and forlorn place you should think some other place would be fitter for me. I think I had better be in town part of the time they are in London & part at the Isle of Wight. They could come to see me there if they chose. I have written yesterday to Sidmouth saying that I could not go there before the first week in April & asking her to write & say if there is a good choice of lodgings as of course I should take lodgings. I shall perhaps hear by return how long they mean to stay.

If she still urges my going I think the best plan will be to go & ~~remain~~ pass on from there to Ryde or Weymouth.

If I <u>dont</u> go to them I had better come to town when they do. I am so taken up with the Book[94] which is near the last & has constantly something

---

93. Paper is watermarked 1847. Written in March, 1848 just before *Principles of Political Economy.* XXVIII/178.

94. *The Principles of Political Economy.*

to be seen to about binding &c that ~~I have not time just now~~ I could not leave town before the beginning of April If even then.

Ever Yr Affec^{ate}

H T.

Walton.[95] June 16

My dear John,

I have seen so many advertisements lately of houses to let that I cannot help sending you some, in hopes you will go and see them. It seems a pity to take or lease again a house without a garden if as good a one in the same neighborhood could be had at no higher rent, but at all events it would surely be worth <u>looking</u> <u>at</u> some of these—an afternoon or evening would probably suffice to see them all.

How very warm the weather is: as much so here as in town I should think for there is more shade in town probably.

I hope to hear from Herby to-morrow.

Adieu,

H T.

Walton. Sunday.[96]

My dear John,

I am glad you are going to the sea this splendid day—the change I hope will do you good. I could not now be at Ryde in time for your coming to be on Wednesday next. If you can be there on Wednesday the 11th that would suit me perfectly—in that case I shall go next Saturday. If you cannot come till the 19th I do not think I shall go this week. either will suit me tho' I prefer the earlier time.

Please reply to this as soon as you can.

The letter from Birksgate was rather indefinite. as she said that <u>he</u> had asked his niece Deborah for a week, to begin last Tuesday. That after this the Laings[97] were coming, after which she hoped to see me—or, if I liked to come while the Laings were there, she would manage to accommodate me—now as they have but one spare bed room I should not think of this last proposition. I write therefore to say that as they had so many visitors to get through I would defer my visit till September & that we were going for August to the Isle of Wight.

---

95. Written in 1848. XXVIII/181.

96. Paper is watermarked 1846. It appears to have been written just after the previous letter in June 1848. XXVIII/182.

97. Relatives of Harriet.

He has never sent any message on this or any other subject, not even his love, & I doubt whether any thing would have been said by either on the subject of my going if I had not mentioned it. It would therefore be quite out of place for you to mention the subject at all unless he first mentions it to you.

Lilys love and Adieu Affec^{ly}
H T.

Ryde.⁹⁸ Wed^y
My dear John,
I wrote to Herby yesterday telling him to tell you how bad my face has been. It is better but I am far from well. The weather gets worse every day. It is very wet & cold If it does not soon change I shall not stay here. I have not had any letter from Birksgate If one arrives please forward it.

I am much shocked to-day by the note I enclose. another quiet death from a broken heart.

Haji & Lily's love

Ever affec_{LY}
H T.

I wrote to a house agent at About a house advertised at West Wickham near Keston. He will I suppose reply to Kent Terrace.

If he encloses a card will you forward it here?

Ryde.⁹⁹ Augt 21.
My dear John,
Herby sent me an extract from the Birksgate letter in which he seems to complain much of his health—in a letter I had from her last week she says he is contemplating "a southern trip". His own letter you see says the contrary—but I should rather expect, putting the two accounts together I should that he will perhaps come to London in October. In reply to questions about me it would be best to say that I am unusually out of health owing partly no doubt to the continued wet & cold weather and that you think I had better defer going there till I have gained a little more health & strength.

The weather[,] which seemed as bad as possible last week[,] is even worse this—It was gloomy & showery, and now it appears to have set in

---

98. Written in 1848. XXVIII/187.

99. Written in 1848. XXVIII/188.

confirmed heavy rain. There is no use in Haji staying in this weather, as we are quite confined to the house—he shall therefore return to Kent Terrace on Wednesday evening. I fear you had but a dull excursion unless the weather was better at Brighton than here.

Haji & Lilys love with that of your affec^ate

H. T.

I mentioned in a letter to Birksgate that Herby had been ill.

Ryde.[100] Aug 24.

My dear John,

I hope Haji arrived safe & well last evening. I do not wonder you found your last Sunday's excursion dull. The weather makes every place dull. I intend to leave this place and return to Walton in a day or two. I shall be glad therefore if you will let no more letters or papers be sent here after the receipt of this note.

I will write as soon as we are at Walton. I shall perhaps go back by way of <u>Southampton</u>, but not by any other route.

Walton.[101] Augt 31.

My dear John,

I returned here with the intention of going to the sea side again in a week or ten days if the weather cleared up at all. I should have returned even if the weather has been finer, for a short stay as I do not like being more than a few weeks away without returning. I think I shall go to Dover next week for about a fortnight. If you write to Birksgate there is no occasion to mention me. I suppose you will do so to communicate this news of Arthur. If he had not left Sidney on the 29th of May he can scarcely be expected here before the end of September I suppose?

I am going to look at a house at Leddington & one at Weybridge but I do not think either will do. The first I fancy will be too large, & the second too small. It is the most difficult thing possible to hear of anything at all good which is not too large or encumbered with a quantity of land. This pretty place is now quite spoiled in front by a row of poor peoples little houses. The weather is fine, but it has quite the autumn chill & blue mists rise in the even^g over the houses.

---

100. Written in 1848. XXVIII/189.

101. Written in 1848. XXVIII/190.

Ever Affec^{ly} Yrs—H T

Walton. Sunday.[102]

My dear John,

Thanks for your exertions in the cause of the house & the long account you give me of those you saw. and all the trouble you must have taken about it. Brighton must be very full. I think of going both there and also to Worthing about the middle of this week when I shall look at all the houses you mention and also at lodgings and take which of the two I think most reasonable & best combined. Thirteen guineas a week, the price of the best you saw seems too much to give for the accomodation I want— because what I want is the best in point of quality, but few rooms. However I shall choose between the three places Brighton[,] Worthing & Hastings, & as I do not care whether it is a house or lodgings, I dare say I shall find something. We got down to Herne Bay very comfortably & found the Inn just as you described it, very comfortable. The place pleased me too very much. I thought both the Sea Pier and surrounding country very pretty—but it blew a gale, & was terribly cold and bleak—we saw several houses, but each had some fatal objection to my mind. The chief being bad smelling drains. I was much pleased with the excursion & should like the place for fine summer weather, but did not decide to take any of the places we saw. We got back here at six oclock on Thursday not at all over fatigued.

I hope to hear that you are still improving—after months of stomach derangement[103] you cannot hope to be quite free from it, but in process of time—I hope you will take the greatest care about <u>diet</u>—& that the uneasiness will soon leave you altogether. You rather feared not having company enough in the coffee room at the Bedford, but it seems that you must have had rather more than less than enough. I am glad you saw the P. Taylors they are rather good sort of people I think and might be pleasant acquaintance for Herby being easy friendly people & not without a taste for literature & Politics.

I felt very poorly <u>indeed</u> in the railway on Wednesday going down. The uneasiness & burning about the stomach increased, so that I feared I was to have an illness but at Ashford Lily got out & got a captains biscuit & a sandwich part of which set me to rights & at the Pier Hotel they gave us some very good ox tail soup which was a great comfort, & tho' I have had some return of the same pain each day, it has been not so violent & I

---

102. Paper is watermarked 1847. Written in early September 1848 while she was in Walton briefly before leaving for Dover. XXVIII/191.

103. An indication of the cancer that will kill John Taylor within a year of this letter.

expect will quite go off now the weather has ceased to be so relaxing &
unwholesome.

I find that wine increases the uneasiness & the less I take the better I
am—I do not know whether it might be good for you to try very little
wine for a week, as an experiment?

Adieu Ever Affec^{ly}
H T.

Walton. Wednesday.[104]

My dear John,

The weather seems to have cleared up & I hope for a little fine weather
again.

I shall go to Dover on Friday, but as we shall perhaps make a little
round, & it is doubtful whether I shall find good lodgings at Dover, I may
have to try Folkstone, Sandgate or even other places—for it is now the
fullest season at watering places. I wish therefore that you would not write
before Monday or untill you hear from me. If you write before I do, please
direct <u>Post</u> <u>Office</u> Dover. I would prefer having the newspaper sent <u>here</u>
all the time we are out, as Lily is anxious to keep it, & it is apt to get lost
at the watering places, and we can easily have one sent, by the day, while
we are staying out.

The letter from Birksgate contains no thing new.

Adieu in haste
Ever Affec^{ly}
H T.

Love to the boys.

Dover. Sep 11th
Ship Hotel.[105]

My dear John,

We have been quite unable to find any lodgings at all agreable here.
Indeed they are worse here than at any place I know. It is an <u>old-fashioned</u>
place, and old fashioned as I dare say you have long ago found out is
equivalent to everything that is mean & disagreable. To-morrow I think of
going to Herne Bay & seeing if there is any thing better there. I will if
possible write again to-morrow. I suppose there is no news as I find no letter
for me at the Post Office here. I shall enquire again at it to-morrow, but I

---

104. Written in early September 1848, after returning from Ryde and before departing for
Dover. XXVIII/192.

105. Written in 1848. XXVIII/194.

did not expect one unless there was something new to write about. I am very tired of lodging hunting and so will now say Adieu with Lily's love

Ever Yrs Affe^{ly}

H.T.

4 Wellesley Terrace
Dovor[106]

My dear John,

I succeeded this morning in finding good lodgings at this place and so did not go on to Herne Bay as I yesterday thought we must do.

As I do not find any letter from you at the Post Office I take it for grantid that there is no further news about Arthur.

We have tolerable weather, that is we have no rain and very little sunshine but as the rooms are very large and handsomely furnished they are cheerful. They are also close to the beach & the warm baths so that I can walk to both without fatigue, and I expect a week or ten days will be of service to the health which certainly needs something.

Lily has taken a bad cold & sore throat she does not know how, but I think it shows signs of going off with care. I will write to both Herby and Haji tomorrow[,] to-day I am tired. My love & Lily's to them & to you. Ever Yrs H T.

Dover.[107] Sep 15.

My dear John,

I received your letter yesterday with its enclosures. This place is not at all attractive after the better places — it is thoroughly cockney in every sense, & not very pretty to compensate for the sort of company. I shall return to Walton on Monday or Tuesday next & perhaps if I feel well enough for the exertion, go to Herne Bay on Sunday & to town thence on Monday. Therefore it will be best not to write here again unless there is anything that requires it, and in that case not later than to-morrow. If you write tomorrow, I should get it on Sunday before starting, but it will as I said be safest not to write unless there is any particular reason. Lily is progressing, but she has been confined to the house, warm shawls &c, since Tuesday, she is now decidedly much better & proposes going out again to-morrow. She has had no other ailment than a bad cold in the head, but that is always a tiresome thing.

There is really nothing to see in this stupid place but the steam boats

---

106. Written in September 1848. XXVIII/ 195.

107. Written in 1848. XXVIII/197.

going & coming incessantly so I have nothing to tell of. I fancy from your account Herne Bay must be much better.

Ever Affec^{ly} Yrs
H T.

Walton. Tuesday.[108]

My dear John,

We came here yesterday & are quite well, but the wet & gloomy weather makes the place look its worst. I shall not stay here long at this season, & I am anxious to find another house, as they have now quite spoiled this with a vulgar row of poor people's houses in front. I wrote to a house agent for the particulars of a house at West Wickham desiring him to send them to Kent Terrace (that is to say addressing the note from K. T.) but as you have not mentioned it I suppose he has not done so.

I suppose your month of excursion is now in its eclipse.

Lily's love. Ever Affec^{ly}
H T.

Walton[109]
Sepr 20th

My dear John,

When the day came I did not feel well enough to undertake the excursion to Herne Bay and we therefore remained quietly at Dover till yesterday, when we came up and got here without very much fatigue at six oclock. I am pretty well, but very weak. I have not profited by this summer as usual, owing to the absence of the continental excursion & am not nearly so well as I usually am at this time of the year. Lily's cold seemed all but gone several days ago, it remains however as a slight cold much the same. She is very well otherwise. I shall like to come to keep the birthdays at Kent Terrace—but I cannot well come before Monday— we will if you like keep them together on that day.

I liked Dover better at the end of our stay than at first. The place is even pretty—and altho' the people one sees there are decidedly vulgar, one is much less mixed up with them than at Ryde or Brighton because there is no particular promenade or promenade hour. The lodgings also being quite the best I have ever seen any where made things feel handsome & agreable.

_____

108. Probably written 19 September 1848, on her return to Walton after a visit to Dover. See the following letter. XXVIII/198.

109. Written in 1848. XXVIII/199.

I must occupy myself seriously in house hunting, as we certainly must give up this nice little house the sooner perhaps the better, for they have spoiled the appearance of it now from the outside by poor people's little places opposite,—and what is another great nuisance I hear that the Austin's[110] have taken a furnished house at Weybridge & like the place so much that they are looking out for a cottage there. I have no doubt this is to be near Claremont, & for her to make a circle of French people, the Guizots[111] &c as an attraction to the english already I hear of numbers of people going by the railway to call there—and I neither wish to renew the acquaintance nor to seem to avoid it.

Ever Affec^{ly} H T.

Walton.[112] Oct 22.

My dear John,

I was very much pleased by your note of Friday to find that you are better instead of worse as I had feared. I am quite aware that the sort of complaint you have been suffering from will only go off by degrees and with care, & I hope that you will take care and that the colder & more seasonable weather will be beneficial to it.

I have had some things to do which have made me delay going to Worthing a few days—I now think of going next Wednesday or Thursday. I will write and say the day before I go.

I do not myself see that there will be any differences or discussions with Birksgate I think 'the Govr'[113] is much less disposed to interfere & more friendly, especially with you, than he used to be—& as Arthur[114] seems of a quiet turn I hope we shall go on smoothly.

I wonder Arthur has not written to you.

Adieu Affec^{ly}
H T.

Please give my love to Haji & tell him I shall write to him in a day or two.

---

110. John and Sarah Austin.

111. François Pierre Guillaume Guizot (1787-1874).

112. Paper is watermarked 1847. Written in 1848. XXVIII/201.

113. Harriet's father, Thomas Hardy.

114. It is not clear whether Harriet is referring to Arthur Hardy, who is newly arrived from Australia, or Arthur Ley, about whom John Taylor had a dispute with Thomas Hardy.

Worthing. Oct 29.
2 Camden Terrace[115]

My dear John,

We had as you would see a very wet morning on Friday for our expedition—but as Lily and I had fortunately a carriage to ourselves we were able to keep the windows closed and so were very comfortable. We left London at 12 and got here at ½ past 2. At Brighton the sun shone brightly & it continued to do so all the remainder of the day. I found but small choice of apartments facing the sea, there being but two sets—one of which we have, they are very nice rooms and very comfortable. The situation is I suppose within a few houses of where [Leotrino] must be, or have been, we have not seen anything of him however. We have the drawing room floor and the windows being to the floor we see the sea across the esplanade very prettily. I like the place, as far as I can judge yet, it seems both quiet cheerful and pretty. It is however to be hoped that the wind does not always blow such a gale as it has done these two days—the house quite rocks under it—we have had two fine April days, alternate showers & sunshine. I have not been out since Friday as I am so very weak that after every exertion a long rest is necessary. The pain I was suffering from has on the whole been rather less. I hope to hear that you are improving in health. Lily is quite well & writes with me in best love.

Ever Yr Affec^ate
H T.

Worthing[116] Nov 10.

My dear John,

I hope the colder weather will have a good effect on your health and that I shall hear you are better. I cannot say much for my own state of health, which is certainly very bad—the pain from which I suffered is much better as it returns now only at intervals of several days, but the stomach derangement is very great, and the night cough too troublesome. I am excessively feeble and the leg has become since the weather set in colder very stiff.

I do not think I should get through the winter, & I think it will be most desirable to go the South of France for the winter months, but as we are extremely comfortable here as to lodgings etc. I think of staying here a few weeks longer.

I have not heared a word from any body since I have been here, tho' I

---

115. Written in 1848. XXVIII/202.

116. Written in 1848. XXVIII/204.

wrote a fortnight ago to Birksgate asking for an answer. Lily is well, tho' she is also troubled by derangement of the stomach and bowels—the complaint seems universal. I shall like to see Haji for a few days & hope he can stay till Tuesday. My love to Herby.

Ever Yr affec^te

H T.

Worthing[117] Nov 15.

My dear John,

I am glad to hear that your Doctor has changed his medicines & I hope that combined with the more healthy weather they will soon make much change for the better in your health. That sort of ailment is so very tedious—it is always returning again after a few days interval of improvement.

I am glad it proves that the people Arthur is introduced to turn out civil, as they appear to consist of the kind of people he likes, & so he will be able to amuse himself without giving you so much trouble as I feared he might do. How did he manage his Club dinner party. I have heared nothing from him & suppose I shall not till he has got through his present stock of invitations. This is however quite as well as I am at present hardly well enough to entertain him. I am much surprised at not hearing from Birksgate, as I wrote three weeks since asking her to answer at once. If no letter has arrived for me at K. T. I suppose she considers this note of his as sufficient reply. Will you tell Anne to forward by the same day's post any letter that may come for me.

The weather is now beautiful & this place is very full—the shopkeepers say they never knew so full a season—but I am so weak that I do not get out much, the stomach derangement is not gone tho' better, & my leg is so stiff I can hardly walk.

Lily is well again she walks about a great deal.

I think of coming up for a day or two next week or the week after while Lily goes to Walton to fetch some things. Give my love to Herbert.

Your ever Affec^ate

H T.

Worthing.[118] Nov 19.

My dear John,

I return your Birksgate letter: from his writing such long notes in his own hand I think he must be pretty well. I will write before I come to

---

117. Written in 1848. XXVIII/207.

118. Written in 1848. XXVIII/209.

town, which I do not think will be this week unless quite at the end. I had a note from Arthur yesterday, & I have written to invite him to come here for a few days on Tuesday or Wednesday next. I suppose he will write in reply. He dates his note 105 Pall Mall—is that the number of the club? I have replied to that address.

I had not heared of Sam[l] Sharwood's[119] illness—it will be a great trial for his father I fear if he dies. I saw the death of Quintilia Kennedy in the paper this last week. If your sisters are at Brighton I suppose they will be interested in this. My stomach derangement is better, but the leg has been very bad all the week. It follows in a remarkable manner the changes of the temperature. When the day is colder it is stiffer & the reverse. Some days I cannot walk a step without holding by something, nor without great pain & it is so very painful in bed as to spoil the night's rest & this makes me sleepy in the day. altogether I am in a very low bad state of health and I see no prospect of not growing worse except by spending all the cold months in a warm climate. I am therefore seriously planning going to Pau for the winter—to which Lily is constantly urging me, as she thinks I shall be killed by the winter here. If I go in December, could you accompany me as far as Paris or Tours?

Ever Yr affec[ate]
H T.

Worthing[120] Nov 21

My dear John,

I am very sorry to hear that you are not so much better as I hoped you were. Surely you ought to take some tonic for the purpose of <u>confining</u> the bowels—all the Doctors say that you must pass through a period of confined bowels before they will act healthily after stomach derangement. I am much better of the stomach complaint—I took for a week a Tea spoon full of Tinct of Bark twice a day, & since this I have taken half a Teaspoonful of Tinct of Hops[121] twice a day, an hour before breakfast & an hour before dinner, & I thought it very useful. I do not know if it would suit your case, but some tonic you must surely need & this is a very innocent one.

a very simple thing but I think likely to be very useful in your case is a dessert spoonful of Arrow root raw in a wine glass of <u>cold</u> water. There could be no harm in trying it—ask your doctor if there would.

It is out of the question your going on the continent at present for the

119. See his letter to Eliza Taylor, John Taylor's sister, Mill/Taylor Collection, XXVIII/125.

120. Written in 1848. XXVIII/211.

121. Medicine made from the hops that also serve in the production of beer.

reasons you state. I do not however the least need an escort, being so old a Traveller and quite accustomed to going about alone & to all the business of of [*sic*] Continental travelling. It was for the pleasure of your company & also thinking it might be a useful change that I asked you—I see however that it would not do in your present state of health.

I had a note from Arthur saying he would come here to-morrow—probably by the 2 o'clk train—so I suppose he will.

Lily's love—Yr ever Affec^{ate}

H T.

Worthing¹²² Nov. 24th

My dear John,

I hope to hear to-morrow how you are. The few last days have been very warm here, & my leg has been getting better. Ar^r made his¹²³ appearance here on Wed^y at half past four and is still here—he does not say when he shall go,—tho' I should think he must be dull enough as I find it too much exertion to go out for drives, and of walking a very little suffices him. There is but <u>one</u> train from here to town on Sunday, which leaves here at 5 in the evening getting to town about 9. I should like to come up by this if I find myself able to do so, but to <u>leave it rather uncertain</u> whether I come or not. This would not probably be any inconveneince, as if we come we shall of course dine first.

It does not matter whether Anne prepares the bedroom or not, as it does not take long to do, & if ready will remain till we do come. I mean to come unless Arthur says nothing at all about going in which case I suppose I must stay here till he does.

Lily's love & mine.

Yrs ever Affec^{te}
H T.

Worthing¹²⁴ Dec 6.

My dear John,

I want to hear if you are any better—I cannot say I have the least improved since I returned here for I have a complete return of the stomach derangement & feel thoroughly low & unwell. I have sent for the whole

122. Written in 1848. XXVIII/212.

123. Arthur Hardy.

124. Written in 1848. XXVIII/213.

of Tuson's[125] Iodine course of medicine & mean to begin it completely to-day. You will say this is not the thing for stomach complaint & it would not be but that I think the stomach depends in a great measure on not being able to take any exercise, & this I cannot do on account of the leg which has been very painful & quite unable to be used ever since that day I came down. I expect the Iodine to cure the leg, so long as the weather is not cold, & then I may have a chance of getting better otherwise and of being able to go to the continent.

I had a note from Arthur yesterday & have written to him telling him that I must give up all idea of going to Birksgate this Christmas & the more as you are really not well enough to venture from home. I said that I should go next summer—if I live. I think it would be very desirable, at all events to me, not to have him at K. T. on a Sunday untill after Christmas. There are but two Sundays more to come before he will be in Yorkshire.

Lily has rather a bad cold & sore throat for which she is wrapt up—she sends her love & a kiss—with that of

Yr ever affec^{ate}

H. T.

Worthing Monday[126]

My dear John,

I am very much pleased to hear that you are really better—I hope the improvement will last and then by being careful of yourself for the remainder of the winter the habit may be corrected altogether.

I took to the full course of Iodine rather too suddenly for my present weak state, so that tho' it has certainly improved the leg I have had to leave it off the last two days. The pills being in combination with mercury produced much pain at the back of the head, palpitation, and general excitement—besides loosening the teeth. I have only to-day recovered from these symptoms & now mean to continue the Iodine in small quantities. The stomach is also rather improved. Yesterday & Saturday have been more like summer than winter. The sunshines into the room & makes it quite warm & beautiful. Lily's cold & sore throat has been very bad & it has shown little improvement untill today. She thinks of venturing out again a little today & I hope it will soon be quite well. I do not fancy <u>ale</u>,

---

125. Dr. Edward William Tuson (1802-65). See letters from JSM to HTM referring to Dr. Tuson in *CW: XIV*, 223, 226, 231, 233, and 305. Tuson's Iodine course was a typical treatment for tertiary syphilis during this period.

126. Written in December 1848. XXVIII/214.

even tho' the-pale bottled kind, would suit you for long. I suppose when you take it you take no wine. The mixture of beer & wine is always so unwholesome. Have you heared how Sam Sharwood goes on.

I wrote to Birksgate saying that I am too weak & out of health to go there this Christmas & that even if I could you were really unfit to be away from home & that as you could not possibly on account of your health go also, I would defer my visit till the summer. I mention this that we may agree in the reasons given—as Arthur may ask if you cannot go. I had a note from him on Saturday in very good spirits.

Lily's love

Yours affec^{ly}
H T.

Worthing.
Friday.[127]

My dear John,

I suppose you saw the letter you enclosed me from Birksgate. In it she said that he[128] had been suffering very much lately from a cold he had taken a fortnight ago. But as she added that <u>she</u> had gone to Chapel last Sunday at his request, & I know she hates going, I thought that he could not be feeling very ill or he would not have wished to be left alone. This morning I have a note from Arthur saying that his father wishes him to go down at once & that he is going on Sat^y morning. When Arthur was here he showed me a letter from his father saying that he should not sign his will till A went down at Christmas & I imagine this to be the reason of his hurrying him down. He does not say any thing about this however, but if I had not seen that sentence about the will in his letter I should have thought he must be really feeling very bad to send for Arthur a week before he would otherwise have gone, but as it is I have no doubt that is only one of his usual attacks. I have written to say that if I can be of any use I will go down immediately. If he thinks himself seriously ill he will I am sure accept my offer and if not, not.

I suppose Arthur will write on Sunday to me. If he directs to Kent Terrace will you <u>open</u> the note before forwarding it, if you stay to breakfast—but if not desire Anne to forward it here the same day?

I hope to hear from you tomorrow that you are still improving. I have been decidedly better the last two days.

---

127. Written in December 1848. XXVIII/215.

128. Harriet regularly refers to her parents simply as "she" and "he." Thomas Hardy is probably suffering from whatever illness that leads to his death in May of the following year.

Lily's cold has gone as suddenly & completely as it came.

Ever Affec^{ly} Yours

H T.

Worthing¹²⁹ Dec 17.

My dear John,

I received both your notes & I suppose we shall hear from Arthur on Tuesday. I offered to go to Birksgate if I could be of use, which was not a very wise thing, as I am totally incapable of doing any thing there. But I feel entirely persuaded that it is only a cold which has naturally made his breathing uneasy, & I do not therefore expect that they can think it necessary for me to go down. If I am not asked to go there I think I had much best go off to Pau before severe weather sets in, as I think on every account it is best that I should leave England for the spring months. I now think of staying at this place over Christmas day & going immediately after it. Would it be inconvenient to you to pay into Coutt's Bank £100 on my account & to take their circular notes for the same in my name. There is no signature required I beleive untill I use the notes at Pau. Lily will be in town one day this week, Wednesday I beleive, & she could bring me back Coutt's Book.

I shall hope to see Haji for Christmas day here. Herby I suppose will go with you. Give my love to him. I hope you continue to mend. I am better, tho' easily upset, & I have to-day so violent a headache that you must excuse this scrawl.

Ever Affec^{ly} Yrs

H T.

Jenkins' bill is right.

Worthing¹³⁰ Dec 19

My dear John,

I am very sorry to find you say <u>you are sorry</u> I am going to Pau. I can assure you I do not do it for my pleasure, but exceedingly the contrary, & only after the <u>most anxious</u> thought. Indeed I am half killed by <u>intense anxiety</u>. The near relationship to persons of the most opposite principles to my own produces excessive embarrasments. —and this spring it must be <u>far</u>

---

129. The letter is dated 17 December. The year is 1848, since she is contemplating going to Pau and Arthur Hardy is in London; both events occurred in 1848. XXVIII/216.

130. Letter is dated 19 December. The year is 1848, since HTM is preparing to go to Pau for the winter just prior to John Taylor's final illness the following summer. XXVIII/217.

worse than usual owing to the constant presence in London of it,[131] whom I must either neglect (which is very disagreable to me) or admit into a degree of intimacy which must inevitably lead to an interference on the part of Birksgate and either a rupture with them or to discussions & dissensions which I have not strength to bear. I feel scarcely any doubt that A[132] will not stay in England another winter & I therefore think that my going away for the next four months would <u>cut</u> the difficulties I feel about this spring, while I should return at a season (May) & in health to exert myself during the summer months—having got through ~~the~~ by leaving England the otherwise insurmountable difficulties of ~~getting through~~ those months with A. I think if you turn over in your mind my circumstances you will see how completely my going is a matter of expediency ~~necessity~~. It is the alternative of a rupture with them which may thus be avoided—& it is always so undesirable to make family quarrels if it is possible to avoid them.

I fixed the day after Christmas day to set off that I might have the opportunity of seeing Haji on that day, otherwise I should have fixed Sunday next. I need not say I sh^d like to see Herby, I have told him so so often. but as I said in my last note to you I do not <u>positively</u> fix till I get the next answer from Birksgate. Lily will I beleive come up to K. T and sleep there to-morrow and return here on Thursday. Your saying that you are sorry I am going has given me ever since I read your note so <u>intense</u> a head-ache, that I can scarcely see to write. However it is only one of the vexations I have to bear & perhaps every body has. Just as I got so far a letter from A. has come in by the day mail—which I think exonerates me from staying in England on ~~the~~ my father's account.

Ever Affec^ly Yrs
<u>H T</u>.

I am sure ~~the~~ I shall get better directly I get on the continent owing to the release from the constant dread of Birksgate, &c—Excuse haste & untidiness.

Worthing[133] Dec 21.

My dear John,

I think it would be very imprudent for you to go to Newington on Xmas-day in your present state of health. The probability is that it will

---

131. Harriet is uneasy because her brother Arthur, visiting from Australia, could discover her relationship with JSM, and might reveal this information to her parents (at Birksgate).

132. Arthur Hardy.

133. Written in 1848. XXVIII/218.

be a most severe night, & for you to turn out of a warm room at midnight or near it, to face frost or snow or a temperature at freezing point, even tho' you ride, is not I think at all prudent. I will if you like come up on Sunday even^g and spend time Xmas day with you at K.T. Please let me know by return of post if you will like this. I shall thus get your answer on Saturday morning. I still think of leaving for Pau next Tuesday, not for any pleasure to myself but because I think it necessary. If I see you on Monday I can enter more fully into my pros & cons.

There are two most decided mistakes in your letter which I wish to explain as they are liable to cause misunderstanding. You say I have told the Birksgates that I am—too unwell to travel to them. Now I always most carefully express that it is not the travelling that I ever dread in any & always say that I never fear, but on the contrary am the better for journeys. I am obliged to leave very indefinite what it is that I dread in going to Yorkshire, because I cannot say or hint the truth, which, is their ways. But as I never say anything but the truth, I told them the fact that I require regular early hours & simple diet. Two things which of all things on earth they both most abominate. Accordingly I see they neither want me to come at this season.

The other thing which is a mistake is that it does not suit me to see Herbert on a Sunday. On the contrary he knows as I have told him a dozen times, every day & always it is equally convenient & desirable to me to see either him you or Haji.

As for any body else but the five members of my own family a very little society is most agreable to me.

Ever Affec^ly
H T.

P.S. Please say nothing to Herby of anything I write about him. We go on very well, & I am quite satisfied if he is left to do as he likes.

If I come for Xmas day do not order anything more on my account than you would otherwise as you [know] nothing is too simple for me.

Orleans[134] Dec 29.

My dear John,

We had as I dare say you perceived a very fine day on Wednesday, and the sea was as smooth as I ever knew it in the summer, so that we were

---

134. The letter is dated 29 December. The year is 1848, since Harriet has just left England in route for Pau, where she spends the last winter before John Taylor's death. XXVIII/219.

not at all ill—our only fellow passengers were Sir Fitzroy[,][135] Kitty &
his wife & sister. We got here only last night, for tho we arrived at Paris
at half past three yesterday & drove strait to the Orleans railway terminus,
there was no train for Orleans untill half past six, so we had nearly three
hours to sit in the waiting room, which was very tiresome. They keep time
on these railways to a minute nearly, & we got here at a quarter past ten.
None of these railways have more than three trains a day apparently, which
makes it often impossible to get on by two of them on the same day. Their
hours of starting are early in the morning, middle of the day & evening.
We shall go on at one o'clk to-day to Tours & I hope to be able to get
either the cafe or the Malle Port to Poirtiers to-morrow & <u>perhaps</u> get as
far as Bordeaux on Sunday—but if that should prove too fatiguing we
shall go to Angouleine on Sunday & Bordeaux on Monday. I will write
from Bordeaux again. I have borne the journey very well, <u>considering</u> tho'
I have a rather bad cough. Lily is quite well & strong. I was terribly tired
when I got into the train last even^g & hardly know how I should have
endured the four hours, but that there was no one in the carriage with us
but a nice old priest in one corner & the carriages being all of the broad
gauge & no division between the seats, I was able to lie on the one seat
as on a sofa & so slept the whole journey.

It is most fortunate for us that the weather is only wet & not at all cold.
If it had been like last week, I should never have borne it.

I am very anxious to know how you are. I do not expect to leave
Bordeaux before Thursday afternoon at soonest, I think therefore there is
little doubt that if you write on Monday I should receive it there. If not
please direct Poste Restante Pau—where I have no doubt we shall be by
Saturday night. Love to Herby & Haji and Lily's love to you

& Adieu very affectionately H.T.

Pau.[136] Sun^y 9th

My dear John,

We left Bordeaux on Thursday last & reached here on Friday afternoon
after having been twenty three hours in the Diligence, with the exception
of one quarter hour for breakfast. This was fatiguing, but as little so as
any mode of conveyance, the Coupé of the great Diligences is the easiest
carriage I know, and Lily & I having it to ourselves I was able to lie on
the seat & slept a good deal. I was very much pleased with Bordeaux, but

---

135. Sir Charles Fitzroy (1796-1858).

136. The month and year is January 1849. HTM is in Pau during the winter before John
Taylor's death. XXVIII/220.

rather dissapointed with this place, altho' the view of the Pyrenees is very
fine from all the walks and drives, yet as we do not see it from the streets
of the town I can only enjoy it when we drive out. I have not yet succeeded
in getting apartments & it is a very difficult matter, as at all the best they
refuse to let for a shorter time than a year or as a favour for six months.
There are also very few which command a view but I have seen one on
the same 'place 'Royale' as the Hotel de France where we are staying,
which I think I shall be able to take by the month which condition I make
a sine qua non. I shall be very glad when I get a letter from you. I have
been to the Post aux Lettres every day but as yet there is none. It seems
quite necessary to put <u>Poste Restante</u> on every thing, as in their excessively
careless way they will otherwise probably send it to the wife of the Dr
(Taylor) who lives in this place. I want so very much to hear that you are
better. I shall like to hear what sort of weather you have, to compare it
with this. Here it is very much like April in England but the sun shines
for such short times at once, that altho it has shone occasionally for a few
minutes every day we have only once seen a small part of the Pyrenees for
about ten minutes; when it does shine it is very beautiful & the sky of the
brightest blue, & they say here that in Feby the trees will come into leaf
& the weather be very fine. As yet the best thing here is the warmth — we
have not once felt cold since we arrived at Bordeaux. I am much better
than usual & Lily quite well. I am very anxious to hear from you. Please
tell me what you pay for letters from & to, this place. Lily's love and with
mine to Herby & Haji. I am Ever affe^{ly} Yrs H T

Pau.[137] Jan 12th

My dear John,

I received your letter dated the 6th (& containing the Birksgate letter) on
the 10th to my very great releif as I had grown extremely anxious to hear
that you were better. It is the only letter I have received from you. I left
Bordeaux on the 4th having enquired each of the days I was there for letters
& being told there were none. I wrote to Haji just before leaving & just
after the enquiry. If you wrote to Bordeaux tell me, & I will write there
desiring it to be sent on. I am most glad to hear that Power[138] thinks you
are really getting over your complaint — his opinion is likely to be correct —
you must remember that the number of <u>glasses</u> he allows means of the

---

137. The year is 1849, since HTM is in Pau during the winter before John Taylor's death.
XXVIII/221.

138. John Taylor's doctor throughout his terminal illness.

<u>ordinary</u> size. Each day when we dine I wish I could send you some of the very nice fresh Bordeaux wine they give without charge with the dinner. We took possession of our lodgings yesterday & shall now have to buy wine, it costs I beleive about ½ a franc a bottle. We staid at the Hotel till yesterday seeking apartments every day, & the continual going up & down stairs has made my leg stiff & painful, otherwise I am decidedly better. The diet is to me so very wholesome. The Hotel de France is celebrated for its cuisine & gave us large & fine dinners every day which was tiresome. They undertake to send to our apartments a good dinner for four francs a day—that is 2 francs each. This is not dear but I beleive it can be much cheaper cooked at home, & as our servant here seems annoyed at our not trying her I am going to do so. We have very nice rooms in the best situation, on the Place Royale whence there is a magnificent view of the Pyrénées. It is one of the chief promenades & the military band plays here. It is planted with large trees under which are benches commanding the view, so that I can sit there without having to walk any distance. I do not know whether this is a more than usually favorable season. It has not since we have been here been cold or chilly in the smallest degree. It is as warm as May in England & I do not think we should feel the want of a fire if we had not one. January is said to be the worst month here as it rains almost every day, but it also is bright & beautiful in the middle of the day almost always. The climate therefore does even more than kept its promise & the scenery is very beautiful. The town is very ill supplied with shops, in which it is a great contrast to Bordeaux. In fact it has none worth calling so except for eatables. It is the only French town I was ever at where there is not a good bookseller's shop. This is a great want as it makes me wholly dependant on the english newspaper I may receive for I cannot as yet discover any newspaper office here.

I hope to hear that Haji's cold is quite gone—when I take this to the post I hope to find a letter from him. The rise in the price of the Daily News[139] I should expect to ruin the sale & knock it up—which would be no loss if another liberal paper sprung up in consequence. I suppose Herby is now fully engaged with theatricals—give my love to him. I have not yet received the Times[140]—if it comes it will be a great amusement in the absence of books. I shall perhaps find it at the Post office to-day. I enclose my address which I wish you would put as otherwise my letters may go to the D^{rs} wife. Ever Yrs affec^{ly}

H T

---

139. London newspaper.

140. London *Times*.

Pau.[141] Jan.y 23.

My dear John,

I received your letter of the 15th as I have done all yours except that to Bordeaux which you will have perceived was no fault of mine but that of the Post Office there—in fact there is no dependance to be placed upon French Post offices delivering at the right time—<u>sooner</u> or <u>later</u> one gets every thing, but the inexactness is extreme. There they undertake to deliver the letters at the house, & they do so generally, but now & then a letter comes a day too late because the Post man had nothing else in this direction that day & so left it till he was passing—or some other excuse. The Times is a great amusement, altho' it always arrives two numbers at once, which makes it less so than it would otherwise be. I am much releived to hear that you still think your health mending, but I am well aware, as indeed by my own example I may well be, that when a complaint once gets into the chronic or constitutional state it is a work of time, often of years to get rid of. I hope yours may not prove to have taken so strong a hold, nor require so long a time to cure as mine has. I am obliged to be content to feel <u>better</u> from the change to this place without much expectation of <u>decided</u> improvement. indeed I feel quite sure the latter will not be—the habit of congestion would take as long a time in favourable circumstances, to cure as it has taken to form itself. I am glad to find that you have not a very severe winter. It is quite spring here & the place is very pretty, but I pity the unfortunate englishmen who have made it their winter quarters, they walk up & down the Place with their hands behind them looking ennui itself. There is in fact nothing whatever but the pretty scenery as amusement—like all foreign towns I have known which are much frequented by the English, they lose their foreign free cheerfulness & gaiety, which the english always discountenance & get nothing but english dullness in exchange. There is a theatre, but it is not patronised & seldom open. Whatever there is going on we see from our windows— last Sunday there was a review of the Garde Nationale of the Department in the Place which lasted from 11 till 2 o'clk. The band played airs from Norma[142] &c and the officers galloped up & down & it was very pretty. About one o'clk the English people began to arrive & promenade solemnly with their prayer books in their hands. There was one evening a grand exhibition of fire works in the Place which we saw also from the windows. We have as I think I told you very comfortable rooms in the house of an

---

141. Postmarked 27 January 1849. XXVIII/222.

142. *Norma*, an opera by Vincenzo Bellini (1801–35), was first performed in Milan at LaScala 26 December 1831. It was a big hit when it came to London in 1833.

old gentleman named Faneher who amuses us by his efforts to be polite to "les Dames". I had been paying a franc a bottle for wine, but he sent to tell me that if I would excuse his interference he thought his wine was better than ours & that it cost only 15 sous.

You see I have no news or I should not tell you these trifles. I continue well, but my leg does not recover from the stiffness it acquired in the process of lodging seeking. I have now begun the Iodine course again in hopes it will have its usual good effect. I have just seen the paper[,] Mr. Tulk's death.[143] This must have been sudden. I thought he was an older man. I suppose the Daily News has now raised its price, if it is bought by this Financial Reform Association they may perhaps get enough subscribers to make it pay—but it is not likely. The Times is as unprincipled & more impudent than ever. I am going to write to Arthur to-day tho' I have not much to say. Your letters are always amusing (as well as interesting) as at this distance every bit of news is so. Tell me how you are and if Haji has quite lost his cough—and with love from us both I am

Yours very Affec^{ly}

H T.

The enclosed is from Lily to Haji.

I do not know if I mentioned that the Post Office people say there are six families at Pau named Taylor & therefore without the address Place Royale N° 5 they cannot distinguish them.

Pau.[144] January 30th

My dear John,

Lily received your long letter on Saturday & sends her love & thanks. I am sorry to find that your health does not improve more decidedly: The mild weather you speak of must be very unfavorable for the sort of complaint, and therefore you should be the more careful and cautious to abstain from everything which by experience you find has an ill effect as well as to do all your Doctor recommends. What a capricious thing the english climate is—after several mild winters we had every reason to expect a severe one this year—yet it appears that after the week or ten days about Christmas you have had very little cold since, so that I need not have come so far[,] as far as warmth was the object. Here it is scarcely to be called winter, altho' the last week has been cooler than the preceding

---

143. Charles Augustus Tulk (1786–1849) died 16 January 1849. He took part in bettering conditions of factory workers in England and founded a society for the publishing of Swedenborg's works.

144. The year is 1849. XXVIII/223.

ones, it is much like both in appearance & temperature an english April—alternate showers & sunshine & feeling a <u>little</u> fresh in the mornings & evenings. Lily said yesterday "How odd it will seem next winter in England. I have forgotten what cold is like"! I cannot help thinking in spite of the people here saying the contrary that it must be an unusual season here, & I can well conceive the climate would be felt unpleasantly relaxing by people in robust health. I am well, tho' somewhat under the influence of the Iodine I am taking in hopes of improving the leg, which is still very stiff and quite lame—there is I think a slight improvement in it in the last day or two. I hope we shall not have such winds here as you describe at Lisbon in March—the same piercing cold winds prevail at that season at Marseilles & all along the South of Italy, but this place is said to be quite free from them. It quite justifies its reputation for stillness—I believe a candle would burn all night in the middle of the place as steadily as in the room. The number of English people makes a great drawback to the pleasantness of the place to those who like a French town & French ways—the tradespeople & servants attempt to copy english ways which generally produces something neither French nor English nor as good as either. They are however an excessively quite clever people & do most things they attempt well. The 'Times' is a great amusement altho' it comes very irregularly & always two numbers together—but it would be quite useless & impossible to complain. The very suggestion of complaining about anything done by 'L'Autorité' makes the French look aghast at ones boldness. However I asked how it was that two numbers arrive together & they said that sometimes the Journals arrive in the even^g & sometimes in the morn^g & so they are delivered together. They certainly need revolutions for they have no political freedom of any kind apparently, & they do not know what freedom is for they have never tried it. Many thanks for your offer to send me weekly papers, but the 'Times' is enough & keeps me au courant[145] of the <u>news</u>, which is the interesting thing here, so that I do not care to see any other paper. I have not found any english Library here worth the name but there is a tolerable French circulating Library with a good stock of old books, tho' no new ones, so with these & writing and drives in the neighborhood which is very pretty we do not find the time long. We are well placed in the principal place for seeing whatever there is going on, but this is pretty nearly confined to the occasional practicising & twice a week the band, of the Garde Nationale which plays waltzes & other dance music. This letter is not very well worth sending, but you may be sure I have no news except what I see in the Times! In

---

145. Up to date.

which I saw the death of poor Mr Tulk—& also, to my amaze, the marriage "at St George's Hanover Square"! [of] Florance the son of W. S. Fox. M.P! This is the deaf & dumb one, of whom the last we heared was that some one had consented to take him into their printing office with the charitable wish to enable it to be tried if he could do anything for himself! I suppose you saw the announcement "to the daughter of something Caufeild Esq" I suppose there will soon be a letter for me at K. T. from Birksgate which perhaps Haji will copy or you enclose for me. With Lily's & my love to you, Herby and Haji I am Yours ever Affec^{ly}

H T.

I do not know why they always charge 32 sous (one & four pence english) for every letter however small that I send. Also they charge 2 sous for every letter & Newspaper I receive—I paid 9 francs for postage last week. And as you pay but 1 frc. this charge I think cannot be right—but it is no use asking them—they merely reply It is all right. Perhaps the French postage is more than the English.

Monday Feby 5

My dear John,[146]

Your last letter was quite a budget of news and I was much amused by it—your description of Arthur is so like him, yet he seems to be well contented with the life he is leading, as he wishes to arrange his affairs so as to live in England altogether. I cannot imagine however that he can ever raise any money on an estate at that distance. By way of loan I mean—he wants to realise his Australian property he will find it necessary to go there to do so. I thought I should have had a letter from him as I wrote to him a fortnight ago but I have not. Do not however mention the subject to him as I would not have him write unless he feels inclined of himself, for I am rather overdone with writing & correspondence. The account J. Ley & Hart give you is a very queer one, & I fancy if their account were a true one they would not feel the want of the support of other's opinion, making them relate their private affairs. I wish it was true that each of Mr Tulks children has a clear 600 pr ann. from his estate as ~~they~~ J. Ley would then cease to drain dry old Ley perhaps, as they say at Birksgate he does. However one never knows what to beleive of all their inconsistent stories. I was afraid poor Arthur's supplies would fall short when left to be administered by Alfred—but no doubt his father will be willing to lend him what he wants. Since I wrote last I have succeeded in getting the French papers sent to me every day from the Café Nationale

---

146. The year is 1849, the winter before John Taylor's death. XXVIII/224.

They send all the Paris papers of any note & they are a a [*sic*] great amusement. We have always received the Times & many thanks for it.

I am well in health, all but the lameness, which mends very slowly. Otherwise I am in very much better health than I ever am in England except in the middle of the summer. I am always very anxious to hear how you are—I hope that dinner at the Club did you no harm—It was not very prudent of your D^r to exercise his <u>power</u> in that way—by making you assist at a Club dinner. Have you tried the effect of French wine since you have been unwell. I find the change to it from the stronger Spanish wines has so <u>alterative</u> an effect that it is just possible you might find the same. If taken it ought to be without any mixture of other kinds of wines, as I think its wholesomeness depends in a great degree on this. I think the ordinaire[147] quite as wholesome or more so than the higher priced kinds—& it is to be got, as you know, very good at Hedges & Butler's. All French wines contain an astringent quality which acts more on the stomach than the bowels. I merely suggest this as it might be worth asking Power[148] about. I received Haji's letter this morn^g & shall answer it soon. The weather continues very mild & pleasant, but I fear it is in London too mild for you. The letter from Birksgate which Haji enclosed contained nothing particular, it said that my father continued but very poorly. Love to Herby & Haji from Yours ever Affec^{ly}

H T.

Pau.[149] Feby 27th

My dear John,

I received yours of the 20th on Saturday as I did also the former letter telling me that you had deferred changing the servants for the present. I need therefore say no more about them as I sent you all the particulars necessary if you should want to do so. Anne had told me in reply to my questions every time I was in town that Cook did not 'drink' <u>at all</u>. That "whatever defects she might have she had not <u>that</u> one" were Anne's words—showing how entirely unworthy of credit any of her asseverations[150] are. I knew that Cook took spirits occasionally as they almost all do—but as Anne said this I thought it was only in a permissible quantity. Now that she is aware that she is observed, I hope she will not <u>exceed</u>.

I am glad that you think (<u>my prescription</u>) the Ordinaire likely to be

---

147. Ordinary table wine.

148. John Taylor's doctor.

149. Postmarked 27 February 1849. XXVIII/225.

150. Solemn oaths.

useful—I do think it will be so even if you should not continue it very long, because I am convinced it has a very alterative effect. It is excellent here at a very low price but I suppose the duty is too high to make it worth importing. It has agreed with me excellently, but no one knows better than I how difficult it is to change permanently any chronic derangement of health. I do not [know] how they should have the notion at Birksgate that you are not better as I told my mother that you were better. I imagine his saying so was only to have a reason for inviting you. I told her also that Herbert's going to America was a rather sudden resolution, as I did not know of it untill a short time ago. I did not however say what is the fact that had I known of it before leaving England I should not have come here. I said you had been thinking of it for some time but had only just resolved on it finally. I hope Herbert will give the same account—it being just the true one. Give my love to Herby & tell him I have been always expecting a letter from him as he promised to write. I hope he will find time to write before he goes. Will you please send notice to Manners[151] at Walton of your intention to give up his house on the 25th of September next. Six months is the notice required but as he asked permission to send his work people to do outside repairs in the spring I think the sooner he receives notice of our leaving the better as he may not then do his repairs till after.

Do you suppose this Californian discovery[152] will make any change in the value of money for some time to come? If it continues I suppose it will lower the value of fixed incomes, but I suppose benefit trade? If I were a young man I would go there very quickly. The most probable chance is that the gold will not continue below the surface meanwhile there must be fine opportunities of placing goods, & especially drugs, in the placiemento.[153] are you going to send out quinine.

Since the beginning of February the weather has become very warm and always dry, & the consequence is the place has quite changed its appearance, the streets & promenades are thronged & the place fully equals in gaiety Brighton in its fullest season. There are many visitors from Paris—& many Spaniards as well as English. None of the shopkeepers servants &c here speak French except to the visitors. Their language is Basque, a dialect of Spanish. They are very like Spaniards & one does not hear a word of French spoken in the streets.

---

151. Manners owned the house Harriet rented at Walton.

152. California gold rush.

153. Harriet may be referring to Placerville, California, the place of an important discovery of gold in 1848.

I have begun writing to you every morning of the last three but I have had such a bad headache that I have been forced to give it up. Love to Haji to whom I shall write in a short time.
Ever Your Affec^ate H. T.

Pau.^154 March 20.

My dear John,

I received your letter of the 10 and also Herbert's. in the lat[t]er he says that he expects to be in England again about the same time that I am—this must be a mistake, as I have no intention of being later than the middle or end of May. I had a letter from Arthur dated Birksgate when Herbert was there, it says little beyond the fact that his father had been ill and was now better. I suppose that whenever the weather is cold he will be liable to Asthmatic attacks which must be very distressing while they last. Arthur says he has had nearly enough of London life and does not care how soon he returns to Adelaide—also that Caroline had received a letter from Edward condoling with her on the loss of her infant, so that it appears that she & E. correspond regularly which I did not know before. I wish your account of your health was more decidedly good. I do hope the summer season, with the various changes in causes in the health and constitution will enable you to conquer the obstinate derangement that it has been—you need not wonder that it is hard to cure, for all stomach derangements & all connected with the digestive functions is so very tedious & ennuyeux^155 when it once gets wrong. I know this well for now I am scarcely more than a week or ten days without some ailment of the kind. I am not surprised that the Ordinaire did not answer well in cold weather. When the weather becomes warm you must try it again, but I fear there are still many weeks to wait for warmth in England. Here the temperature is that of summer but the vegetation is scarcely at all advanced since January owing I suppose to the total absence of rain or damp. I hope you will be able to spare Haji to meet me on our return if he w^d like it—If but a short time it w^d do him good no doubt: where & when exactly I shall be better able to say a month hence.

How does the new servant go on?^156 Lily's & my best love to you both,
Ever very Affec^ly Yrs.
H. T.

---

154. The year is 1849. XXVIII/226.

155. Boring.

156. Harriet inquires about references for a new servant in L/37, above.

Pau.[157] March 30.
Friday.

My dear John,

I had just received your letter of the 20th and am more concerned than I can express to hear so poor an account of your progress. I however reassure myself by thinking that the month of March is always peculiarly injurious to invalids and that better weather is now to be expected. Even here the last ten days have been like a different climate, and last Sunday there was a slight fall of snow and on Tuesday again a pretty considerable one—and tho' it did not remain on the ground more than a few hours it showed the air to be cold, and the whole week has been chilly & cloudy. I entirely agree in the wisdom of going to Brighton for change of air. I have from experience great faith in change of air, which I have known have a most <u>alterative</u> effect. You should have a private sitting room and it might be better to be at one of the quieter hotels, such as the Albion or York or Norfolk. If I only consulted my own inclination I should come back to England immediately on the receipt of your letter in hopes of being able to be of use to you. The reason I cannot do this is that I have arranged with M[r] Mill to meet me on the 20th of April when he is to have three weeks holiday on account of his health which has been the whole winter in a very precarious state, for the last two months he has been almost unable to read or write & has had to engage a man to read to him & to write from his dictation & both Clarke[158] & Alexander the oculist say that a complete change & cessation from all work is absolutely necessary to save his sight—he has had blisters & irritating applications innumerable without any effect & is indeed about half blind. They say that giving up using the eyes & mild weather will cure them as they attribute all the bad symptoms to extreme debility. I shall therefore return with him as far as Paris & I shall get back the earliest that I possibly can in hopes of being of use to you. I have not been quite well lately having had some return of my stomach derangement, but I am getting better again & the traveling will be sure to do my health good. I feel it a duty to do all in my power for his health & it is unfortunate that he is so much required at the change of direction on the 11th April that he cannot leave London before that. He does not tell even his own family <u>where</u> he goes for his holiday as I so hate all tittle-tattle. Therefore I do not mention it either except to you. I

---

157. The year is 1849. XXVIII/227.

158. Probably James Clark (1788-1870), who wrote treatises on consumption and was an important physician during this period. See JSM's letter to HTM concerning Clark's treatise and various other doctors (*CW*: XIV, 198-99).

trouble you with all these particulars because I wish you to know that nothing but a feeling of right would prevent my returning at once.

As to dear Haji he must have a holiday in the autumn with me as he had last year, & adjourn a foreign excursion till another opportunity, of which if we live there will be many.

I am very glad to hear Herby is to return soon as it will leave you at liberty to take some weeks change, & which I do hope & think, combined with fine weather may be made of such use as to conquer your obstinate complaint.

I really pity poor Arthur—he thinks so much of all that money will procure that I am sure he must be quite mortified at his "financial condition"! We thought his chance of <u>remittences</u> with Alfred for facto term w^d be very small. I am quite surprised at his account of Birksgate. I thought every thing there was suspended untill Arthur's arrival for his advice & assistance. Please tell him I have not written to him again because there is really nothing for me to tell but description of scenery but I must make up for it when I get back. Give my love to him & Lilys but three months here will expire on the 10th April and I mean to leave somewhere about the 15th. It will be necessary therefore to stop sending the newspaper after the <u>10th</u> April. also no letter should be posted after that date. Those posted <u>on</u> that day we shall receive here the 14th.

I wish no newspapers sent after 10th, But if you write to me on the 14th directed 'Poste restante Bagnéres de Bigorres, Hautes Pyrénées' I shall be sure to get it, & I hope you will do so as I shall feel uneasy if I do not hear how you are. Lily's best love & mine. Ever Affec^{ly} yours H T.

Pau.[159] April 6.

My dear John,

I got your letter dated Brighton this morning, and was you may be sure much surprised at the contents. The conduct of his[160] father in demanding back his money of Arthur without any notice, and knowing as he did that <u>he</u> had no money to pay with, was most unjustifiable. He counted you see upon Arthur getting it from you—or by your help, in which I am sorry to find he was not dissapointed.

I cannot help wishing that Arthur had taken it more coolly, and had simply written his "Dear Papa" a short note saying, that as he knew he had no money in England, he must tho' with regret, keep him waiting till he had. This would have been perfectly fair—as his father's conduct

---

159. The year is 1849. XXVIII/228.

160. Arthur Hardy and Harriet's father.

in demanding payment instantly was not fair, and I am very sorry his manuevre to make sure of his money before Arthur leaves England, which of course was his feeling, has succeeded so far. Do you think it sure he will honour the bill? If he does not, you are not bound to, are you?

I think all you said to Arthur was quite natural, true, and right, but I wish it had happened that you had adopted my plan towards Arthur and made no remark whatever on any of his proceedings, because he is a person whose whole mode of action is as opposed to your ideas as to mine. I wish you had simply tho' good humouredly declined to lend any more money. He would then have been forced upon his own resources, which is the only means of bringing these colonials to their senses, and still more I should have really enjoyed dissapointing the trick of the Governor.[161] I do not beleive his father will advance Arthur a shilling again. But your only plan if asked is to tell him he must force his father to lend him what he wants.

I hope it will not be a quarrel or even a coolness between you and Arthur—but indeed I cannot think so ill of him as to suppose that he will not see you were right when he cools. How very flat Arthur must be to think he should ever get money through Alfred's hands! It reminds one of the proverb about 'getting butter out of a dog's mouth.' I hope exceedingly that Brighton will have done you good. We have had wet & dull weather here since the 25th of March. I shall go to Bagnères about the 15th and shall make a short stay and take the baths either there or at Cauterets. When I asked you to write on the 14th to Bagneres, I only meant if you wished to write, I do not want you to write there particularly, only not to write here after the 10th nor to Bagnères after the 14th. I will write to you from the next place I stay at, but as I shall not stay at one for any length of time it will be best not to address to me again untill I can give a certain address. I shall be at Paris by the 8th or 10th of May.

I shall receive your reply to this here if you write the day you get it. and I wish you would, as I want to hear both how you are and if there is any thing new about Arthur. I enclose a word for Haji—Lilys sends her love with that of yr ever Affecte

H. T.

If Arthur should talk of writing to me please tell him I am at a watering place, Bagnères, but that as I shall leave & return to England very shortly he had better not write.

---

161. HTM's father.

Toulouse.[162] April 29.

My dear John,

We left Pau on the 17th having differed our journey a little in hopes of finer weather. We had a pleasant drive to Bagnères but the next day a heavy fall of snow kept us prisoners for several days. Since the end of March we have had almost incessant rain, and the people hearabouts say that they have had the finest winter & the wettest spring known in the south of France for twenty years. They are unable to sow the maize in consequence of the rain & fear the crop, which ripens late, will fail. The wheat and rye are looking very fine, the later in full ear. The incessant rain adds much to the fatigue and lessens the pleasure of a journey — it is however not at all cold. From Bagnères we went to Cauterets, a beautiful bathing place in the high Pyrenees, but the snow lay deep everywhere, so I gave up seeing any more of the Pyrenees & commenced the journey back by Montauban Limoges and Chateauroux. This enables us to see a new line of country and is not longer from Bagnéres than the Bordeaux line. We shall join the railway at Chateauroux. I expect to reach Paris about the 9th of May. (and stay there about a week.) If you write to me on that day I shall no doubt get it, but it is necessary to say nothing in Poste restante letters which you care about getting into wrong hands, because there are so many 'Taylors' in France, and even a Poste restante letter is sure to be taken to any Mrs J. T. who may reside in the town. I shall be very desirous to hear how you and Haji are. I am well tho' beginning rather to knock up with travelling. I know no conveyance so easy a[s] the Diligence when one has got the coupè — but as we depend wholly on the two great Diligences from Toulouse to Paris via Limoges, we shall have at each stopping place only the chance of places next day, or night, as we cannot ensure places even from here to Cahors the first days journey of twelve hours untill the last moment. From here to Chateauroux is 50 hours by Diligence, which we must divide as well as we can. Lily is quite well. She is gone to the Cathedral. This is a fine old place, quite like another Paris for bustle & noise. From Bagneres we hired a voiture[163] which brought us here in four long days. With best love to you & Haji,

Ever Your Affec^{ate}

H T.

---

162. The year is 1849. XXVIII/229.

163. Carriage.

Harriet's nearly daily correspondence with Helen, who was attempting to become an actress, records the psychological and physical turmoil in her life.

TO HELEN TAYLOR

12

*The letters Harriet Taylor Mill wrote to her daughter, Helen, affection-
ately known as Lily, present the most sustained look into Harriet's life.
Harriet penned two sets of letters to Lily, separated by a period of eighteen months. The first set, composed between 21 November 1856 and 17
February 1857, records Helen's first departure from her home. Helen, her
mother's constant companion throughout childhood, decided to work as a
professional actress. She had always been an avid fan of the theater, and
at the age of twenty-five, she wanted to practice and perform among
professionals.*

*The letters written during the first months of their separation will echo
in the heart of every parent who has witnessed such an event. How does
one encourage independence without appearing to be pushing the person
away? How does one express one's sadness and loneliness without appearing to be heaping guilt on the person who has departed? Harriet struggles
to learn to express opinions while acknowledging that her daughter must
make difficult decisions for herself. Accepting her daughter as a responsible adult who is working and living away from home is particularly
hard for Harriet, whose own relationship with her mother was anything
but a model (see Harriet's letters to her mother in chapter 10). These letters disclose that Harriet is consciously afraid that this separation from
her daughter might lead to the same kind of alienation she felt from Mrs.
Hardy, "The sentence in your letter 'let us keep a firm alliance & we
will not care for them or anybody' does me the greatest good—it is the
doubt of that your feeling so which has been so dreadful" (LI/14). Because Harriet derived so much happiness and security from her close ties to*

Helen, she requires reassurance that Helen's feelings for her have not changed despite the miles which separate them.

In the first group of letters, Harriet and Helen negotiate Helen's career options, discuss what she should wear on the stage, where she should go for Christmas holiday, examine how she spends money, and debate how often she should write to her mother. In short, all the usual points of contention that arise when a child leaves home for the first time become topics in these missives. Although choosing what to wear may not appear to be a critical issue, most women have experienced the delicate act of asking their mother what they should wear for a job interview or a special occasion. The kind of advice offered by mothers and the manner in which it is received accurately measure the emotional state of a mother–daughter relationship. Helen had a particular reason to be unsure about her wardrobe, since she had to supply her own costumes when performing in the theater. Mother and daughter manage to survive the slight hurts, assertions of independence and dependence, and the emotional turmoil that always accompanies a separation from the family. Helen even endures Harriet's visit, including her mother's desire for separate housing which contained a decent toilet (LII/83 and LII/107).

In order to fully understand the dynamics of the intense mother-daughter bond depicted within the lines of these letters, two dimensions of Harriet Taylor Mill's emotional state deserve special attention. Harriet displayed a personality prone to "nervous" depression and passive-aggressive tendencies. HTM reports bouts of depression after the second separation from Helen, Christmas 1856. Harriet explains to Helen that she went to London with Algernon "feeling the black melancholy into which I has {sic} fallen must be in some way lessened." She also writes about feeling "nervous & bored lately" (LII/73) and "nervous" (LII/113). Harriet further complains, "I have got out of spirits about everything, but as I do my utmost to argue myself into better in time I shall succeed" (LII/82). At intervals in her life, the depression overwhelms Harriet. For example, she states, "I cannot write this even^g at all—but it is only a sudden intense nervousness which I shall get over by to-morrow" (LII/117). When this sadness overtakes her, Harriet is determined to improve her outlook, and usually succeeds.

The record of her depression begins after Helen returned to the theater after a Christmas holiday together. Harriet warned her daughter before Christmas that a second separation would be more difficult than the initial one (LI/33), since a second parting would reinforce the permanent nature of their divided lives. They also disagreed during the time together, probably about money; they settle their differences, but the hurt they inflict *on one another lingers. This rift may have added to Harriet's depression. In addition, Harriet's son Algernon left for Italy during this period and Harriet suffers from the considerable cold (the thermometer located in her bedroom read 38°). Finally, many of the drugs HTM took for her chronic illness were powerful depressants and may have contributed singly or in combination to her "nervousness" and melancholy.*

Harriet does not consciously use her reports of depression to inflict guilt on Helen or to motivate her to return home. However, she is not above some passive-aggressive whining. Twice Harriet complains about an intense headache & feverishness, and she writes, "I must not be ill in your absence dear if I can help it" (LII/71). Harriet also composes a long opening paragraph in one letter describing her poor health and disparaging the lack of care she is getting from the servants. She believes that she "got my present cold & earache by standing ringing her bell" (LII/74).

This grumbling may be the innocent expressions of a woman who suffers from chronic illness, but it is not inconceivable that the grousing was meant to make Helen feel guilty. This young woman's function for many years included assuring that her mother's servants were prompt and that she was well-tended in her illnesses. Lily must have recognized that her absence in her mother's life was perhaps the greatest gift Harriet could give her daughter. On the other hand, dwelling too much on the possibility of Harriet's using descriptions of her illness as a means of manipulation is unfair, since Harriet was actually quite ill during this period. She suffered a severe illness, probably a lung hemorrhage, when she was visiting Helen in February 1856. She died in November 1858, at the end of the second series of letters. Harriet had been suffering from what was probably tuberculosis as well as another chronic condition, possibly syphilis, for a number of years, which could account for the depression and for a fair amount of honest complaint. Being the daughter of a physician and having had two elder brothers die of tuberculosis in their youth, Harriet had more knowledge, personally and professionally, of this disease than most people living in the mid-nineteenth century. The regular reports that she includes in her letters must be evaluated in light of her real state of health in a period without aspirin or decongestants, much less antibiotics.

Despite Harriet's medical problems, she serves as a source of advice to Helen on purchasing clothing, on negotiations with managers, and on relations with her daughter's new friends. Above all else, Harriet wants the best for her daughter. In a bleak moment of rejection in Helen's career, Harriet writes to her daughter:

Keep up your spirits my darling for my sake, you cannot yourself be more interested in succeeding than I am for you. There is <u>nothing</u> I would not do to help you, my spirits rise and fall exactly as you are pleased or the contrary. We must remember that we should not have heared so much about the disagreables of the profession even from those in it, if there were not all sorts of dissapointments & annoyances to be expected & these in life never come where one could best bear them, they always hit one on the tenderest parts. Good bye now my precious take all the care you can of your dear self for my sake. (LII/122)

Harriet's reminder that obstacles are inevitable in the professional theater must have helped cheer Helen. There is no hint of finger-wagging or I-told-you-so's. Harriet wants to give her daughter the strength to bear life's trials with grace.

The second and much shorter series of letters exchanged between Harriet and Helen begins 12 October 1858 and ends in November of the same year, when Harriet dies. As the second group opens, Helen is about to assume a position in the theater in Aberdeen while Harriet prepares to leave on a trip to Europe. Helen had apparently left the theater in February 1857 because of her own illness (LIV/20). After what Fanny Stirling calls a "long rest at home," Helen begins to think about returning to the stage in fall of 1858 (LIV/28). Mrs. Stirling suggests a fortnight's practice in the provinces (XXIII/629), and that must have been the purpose of Helen's trip to Aberdeen just before her mother's death.

This correspondence records the sad decline of Harriet's health, beginning in Paris and continuing through the final two weeks of her life as she limps south and finally dies in Avignon, France. These letters are especially poignant because they are <u>not</u> more alarming than any of Harriet's other complaints about her health. Helen must have had no idea that her mother's death loomed just ahead. Harriet's health had long been so precarious that her last attack did not at first seem any more alarming than the many she had survived. Both her acknowledgment of her illness and her down-playing of its seriousness in her final two weeks substantiate the significance of Harriet's earlier reports of health problems. Helen had every reason to note every murmuring about a cough or fever that her mother included in her letters. More than anyone, Helen may have recognized the potential hazard inherent in such seemingly trivial announcements.

Perhaps even more striking than Harriet's constant references to her medical problems in these letters is Harriet's desire for privacy. Helen Taylor worked in the theater under the name "Miss Trevor." The practice of using stage names survives today, but in the Victorian theater, the desire for anonymity went beyond the desire for a more noteworthy marquee.

Proper Victorian young women were not appearing regularly in profes-
sional theater productions. In order to maintain Helen's anonymity,
Harriet directed her to mail letters at post offices not near her residence
and to direct some letters to John Stuart Mill at India House. Algernon,
who had been staying with Helen, arouses his mother's anger when he re-
turns home with his suitcases displaying the travel stamps that would in-
dicate to servants and other observers where he had been (LI/45). Before
Harriet visits Helen, her letters discuss what Helen should tell the theater
manager (LII/115) and what to tell the landlady (LII/118) about her
mother's identity. Not only are these measures designed to protect Helen's
reputation, but they are also intended to keep the Hardy and Mill family
members from learning of Helen's work in the theater.

In the second set of letters, Harriet worries more about her own privacy
and John's reputation. As a precaution in case the correspondence falls
into the wrong hands, Harriet regularly refers to John Stuart Mill as
"he" or at most "Mr. M." On their trip to France, Harriet goes even fur-
ther when trying to protect herself and John from gossip when she asks
Helen to check for press coverage of their journey (LIII(i)/1) and invents
excuses to avoid traveling with governmental officials who know John
(LIII(i)/4). HTM even objects to writing the French "Angleterre" as
part of the address in her letter to Helen because "it makes it perhaps
more observable" (LIII(i)/13). Although she says in the same letter, "I
avoided the Merivales quite as much because it was a bore to get among a
large party of staring women, as on account of any thing they might
think," she wrote on the inside of the envelope flap, "I think it would be
better to address from Scotland the name without the initials." Further-
more, Harriet assures Helen in the next letter that "no one has seen or
heared one word of any of your letters, nor will" and in a final note ei-
ther to Helen or John records her hiding place of the key that unlocks the
box of her letters (LIII(i)/30). Whether her illness during the last two
weeks of her life had caused this paranoia or exacerbated it is unknown.

Around the edges of her letters to Helen, we can glimpse yet another
side of Harriet's personality and gain some insight into her relationship
with John. Writing to her daughter, Harriet groused that John had for-
gotten to mail a couple of letters to Helen—letters which sustained a sort
of emotional lifeline for Harriet. Also, Harriet's careful collection of writ-
ing, probably used as a source for their coauthored work, is evidenced
when telling Helen, "I am very vexed to find that that scrapbook you re-
member of mine must be lost . . . Will you tell me dear up to what date
you have got Notes & Queries that I may take care to have them all
right" (LII/74). Furthermore, as they leave on their final trip to France,

Harriet complains that John has directed the Inn to post their names "& one cannot tell where else in consequence! It might easily get into the paper from this & show that we were along—you may imagine how vexed I am at this—he said they asked him & he did not know I cared!" (LIII(i)/1). Despite knowing Harriet for more than a quarter of a century, John is still unaware of her driving desire for privacy. John is sadly lacking in the art of daily living. JSM appears to lack the necessary skills to ease the difficult problems associated with Harriet's ability to travel in the last week of her life. As Harriet drags herself from Dijon to Lyons she candidly writes to Helen:

the fact is we always get the last seats in the railway carriages, as I can not run on quick, & if he goes on he never succeeds, I always find him running up & down & looking lost in astonishment. So I have given up trying to get any seats but those that are left & those are always of course the sunny ones, & the sunshine is terribly hot (LIII(i)/12).

Only to her twenty-seven-year-old daughter does Harriet reveal anything of the inside of her life with John. After Harriet's death, Helen returned to her step-father and never resumed her career in the theater. These letters from her mother may have been good preparation for Helen's longest running role: the same kind of intellectual sparring partner, confidante, and practical caretaker of JSM that her mother played.

Friday[1] Even[g].

You may guess dearest girl how glad I was to see your little note which Mr. M brought me. It was so very sweet and thoughtful to write it in the cab—but it was worth the trouble for it is a great comfort to know that you would get the train. By this time (10 oclk) I hope your long weary journey is all but over. How very tired you both must be!

When the tea things come there was the sign of your sweet care in the pretty dish of pears—& I was sorry to see a great number of <u>gingerbreads</u> which I hoped had accompanied you. I shall hardly expect to hear how you are off in all respects by Monday—for you will not have had time to get fixed—but do not mind sending a single line just to say you are all right & I can hear more when you have time.

I fear you will knock yourself up with too much hard work and running about. It will be some days yet before I shall expect you will have leisure to tell me all about the people there. Adieu & good night now my dearest girl—& the same to Haji.

---

1. No postmark or watermark. LI/4.

Saturday Even^g

I will write only a word or two now dear to say address here, the usual B-P-K-.²

Tomorrow I shall hear how you have got on so far—it will be a little way only tho' for Saturday would be too full of things to do to get much settled—I[t] will very likely be some days before you will know anything definite.

I have been very ill but I hope now to recover. I had one of my most violent fits of fever yesterday & last night & I thought I was going to be delirious, but was not, & after staying in bed till the afternoon I am now free from this attack.

Adieu now dear I shall have more to write about when I get your next. I was very much pleased to get your second nice note last eveng. It was very kind indeed of you to find means to write and post twice on the long fatiguing journey.

Monday Eveng.³

I will answer all your questions dearest girl as well as I can: but at this distance it is not always easy to judge about <u>details</u>. I do not see why Mrs. S.⁴ is always for putting off seeing the man. I should have judged as you did that in any case it was best to see him at once.

With regard to the wardrobe woman you can best judge if she has helped you about an attendant—if you think so I suppose 2/6 would be the sum—tho' I am surprised that any thing should seem required to be given at the very beginning of your having any thing to do with her, one would expect that nothing w^d be customarily given till the end, of or till something more than the mere recommendation of a woman (certainly not a thing usually paid for)—but you might give 2/6 perhaps without being thought strangely ready to pay—I do not know—the idea is so different to what I should have guessed to be customary & I cannot judge about it. With regard to the servant I would engage her sooner or later according as you find you want her. so with regard to her sleeping in the same house, from your account it seems a thoroughly safe respectable place & it might be quite as convenient or perhaps more so that she should sleep at her own place (after seeing you home of course) as thus you could have

---

2. The initials probably stand for Harriet and John's home, Blackheath Park, Kent. No postmark or watermark. LI/5.

3. Postmarked 25 November 1856. LI/7.

4. Well-known actress Fanny Stirling (born Mary Anne Kehl, 1813-95) was Helen's mentor.

no annoyances about her diet &c ~~which she would~~ as you would make a simple bargain for her services she finding herself.

I sh^d think a pattern which fits well is necessary for the stockings & as to both those and the muslins I would do as you say, ask Mrs. S to send them when you want them. If you get Miss N's bill in time might you not get Haji to pay it for you & so settle the post office question—but I only suggest this, if there is any objection to it you might send it thro' the post office in your own name as you will have no other personal intercourse with it. Another plan w^d be to send it to Mrs. S. perhaps this is 2^d best. I have you see dear gone thro' your letter answering each question as well as I can but I feel the writing very badly. I do not wish to say anything about my feelings or state because I wish you to be wholly uninfluenced by me in all your future proceedings. I would rather die than go through again your reproaches for spoiling your life. Whatever happens let your mode of life be your own free choice henceforth. With my usual (of late years) unfortunate ill luck there came on Saturday morning one of the vicious Devonshire letters,[5] which he exactly described on reading it by saying "every sentence is intended to wound except those intended to boast" It begins by saying that I am "under a delusion in saying I wrote to her last Feb. as no such letter ever reached her" (Her letter with its date Mar 3^d, 1856 is by me thanking for mine of Feb 26.) then after great boasting of the grand acquaintance, they have made a baronet who entertained the Prince of Wales &c, it goes on to talk of Herberts great kindness in inviting Annie to spend her Christmas holidays 'with his sweet little boy who took just a fancy to her &c['] which she is going to do. ending by desiring that I will send her back all the letters she ever wrote to me. This is <u>cool</u> I think after promising & then refusing to send me mine.

I wish the thing had not come just now as I feel entirely incapable of sitting down to answer it, & it must stand over.

In reply to your question dear I now dine in the dining room at 3. the first day I was too ill & he stayed at home late and came back very early, since, he has come home early each even^g and I am beginning to emerge out of darkness. Write to me <u>here</u> dear twice a week, when you write oftener let it be directed to him (he does not open yours) I sent a word or two twice to Haji at Post Office. I have not yet been into your room or anywhere, but I shall soon. Give my love to Haji

[written on the side of the last page:]
and take my best yourself.

---

5. A letter from Harriet's mother, who was staying with Harriet's sister, Caroline Hardy Ley.

Tuesday Eveng[6]

I was going to write a few words this eveng dearest to thank you for all the sweet & loving things you said in Sundays letter, which I had not done in that I wrote last night for I was too tired to say more than just what was wanted. I feel all that you say so kindly & lovingly exceedingly and I have now also got yours of Monday for which again thank you dearest. I am better to-day, I shall calm down by degrees — & we both perhaps need more & much longer experience to know what we shall feel in these new & strange circumstances. But I feel clearly this dearest girl that deeply as I feel & thank you for the offer of sacrifice you make your happiness only must be considered & if you are happy I shall I hope become so in time. I must be with you sometimes, I hope often, but generally or always as you propose that I could not do — I could not leave alone my one generous firm unchanging friend and that when his health is not strong, for any other motive than your health, & that thank god does not require it.

I shall be better in time. & we shall see in time what is best to do on this point.

I am so glad to hear that you will be able to keep warm dear, you are fortunate I should think in the lodgings. I think Mr D[avis][7] quite justifies Mrs. S's[8] description of him — evidently professing less value & care for what you can do than he feels, or he w^d not consent to rehearse a part he has said he did not want now. however it is too soon to judge him. I sh^d think Constance would suit you from Mr M[ill]'s account of it. I am very glad the servant is pleasant, I did not expect it.

I hope you will put in the letters you address <u>here</u> at Gateshead those to him do at Newcastle & now darling adieu for to night with many many kisses.

Wednesday Eveng[9]

I have got you[r] letter dear but am vexed that it was not directed here as my receiving no letter from you for so long must necessarily appear to the people here to show either concealment or neglect of me. At first I could not think of anything, but I know I asked you to write here in mine of <u>Monday</u>, & so expected one here this morning. I do not wonder that you have little time — I rather wonder how you find time for so much both of learning and working.

---

6. Postmarked 1856, probably November 26. LI/9.

7. Mr. Davis was the theater manager in Newcastle.

8. Fanny Stirling, Helen's mentor.

9. Postmarked 27 November 1856. LI/11.

About the trimming for the white merino does it not seem that <u>white</u> will not do, neither lace nor pearls would show on the white—perhaps a <u>narrow</u> rim of gold down the fronts & either round the bottom or not as you think—yet I do not quite like the idea of gold on white merino—how would puffs of white Tulle interspersed with bows of blue & silver (or gold) ribbon? You will be better able to judge when you see how <u>carefully</u> or the reverse other people dress there—if they are careless in Helena Faucit[10] style, or indeed in any case, the gold <u>would do</u>, tho' it does not seem recherché.[11] If you put the narrow rim of gold without Tulle you might add 2 or 3 bows on each side of blue and gold or silver ribbons. I do not think the body need be trimmed with Tulle, it is so very difficult to manage well—the lace perhaps would answer for that. About what you say about coming home dearest girl it does not seem desirable to run home just for a short time and leave again directly—it would be better to come when you can stay a good time.

The only way I can share in your enjoyment as you say dear is to wish you all possible happiness which I do ~~from~~ with all my heart and to be pleased to hear of your pleasure. I have not thanked you enough dearest for all the loving things you say, they have done me much good & now adieu my dearest girl & keep warm for which you will need all your good fires if it is as cold as it is here

[written along the side of the page]
we had a heavy face of snow last night

Can you tell me dear if there exists any Cayenne in the store room and where?

Thursday morng[12]

I have just got your letter dearest the first I have received in a morning. How I wish I could find my answer instantly, for I cannot bear that you should be made unhappy by anything I say. I thought I had avoided painful subjects & cannot recall what there was in my Tuesdays letter. But now my dearest girl a thousand thanks for this precious beautiful letter of yours, it is the first thing that has done me any good since that dreadful night which took all hope & energy out of me. because I did not think that you loved me then at all. Do not talk of the sacrifice of your happiness for me, that would never make me happy—no, you must have your own

---

10. Helena Faucit (1817-98) made her debut in 1836. She was a leading actress until 1871.

11. Elaborate.

12. Postmarked 28 November 1856. LI/14.

course and I must fit myself to it in the best way I can for both & for all. What the best way will be finally it is impossible to judge untill we know more of what sort of life, I mean of how much of your time will be engaged. I suppose it will be some months before you will begin to see what your mode of going on will be? At least I have no exact idea as there seem several contingincies, such as whether you will get engagements & for how long at a time you will be likely to stay at one place—& especially whether, if you do about it all exactly as you would prefer irrespective of me, you should in that case intend ever to have or stay at a home at all? or be always ~~en route~~ travelling with more or less length of stay at each place? This last question must necessarily have much to do in determining my plans.

You say that I & he were willing to be separated for six months for his health & would I now do the same for your happiness—yes dearest certainly, but this is not stating the question, as what you propose is that I should be always travelling with you. The thing which is certain dear is that you are to have your whole wish in the matter and that I must arrange to suit that. Therefore do not my precious be again unhappy or pained about me—we love each other most dearly & together can be independant of all enemies. The sentence in your letter "let <u>us</u> keep a firm alliance & we will not care for them or anybody" does me the greatest good—it is the doubt of ~~that~~ your feeling so which has been so dreadful. But now dearest let all unhappiness be past, let us live to make each other happy. Mr Mill is as always all kindness & will agree to & help in every thing I wish. Let me hear darling that you are well & cheerful again that I may be so. To hear of your crying about what I write is so painful, but still I would far rather you tell me when it is so, but I am determined not to cause it. Tell me that you are happy & cheerful & enjoying your rehearsals.

Do not refrain from asking me about details because I said I was tired one night—I said so to account for so short & ~~hurried~~ empty a letter. as I know you do not wish me to overfatigue myself when I find it so I will write shortly, & generally answers to questions need not be long. From what you say I sh^d think it w^d be best to give the wardrobe woman a present as she said she was giving up the woman for you—perhaps 5/ perhaps 10/ I cannot judge—in giving to subordinates ~~all~~ so much depends on the sort of person. I did not answer what you said in one letter about money dear—I always feel that all we have is in common—& you are to have & use whatever you like—we have always been perfectly one about that darling. you will tell me when you want it sent. Do not fear that details will be tiresome to me as I take the greatest interest in all that interests you and need not answer them when I am tired. Is your idea of the circumstances you would most desire that we should have a fixed home at all? you speak of six months but this six months would only be the beginning as you mean the life to be permanent.

Thursday Eveng

I am better dear than I have been before since you went. Your letter has done me much good by showing how much you love me. I think I have answered all but one principal point. you speak as if the only alternative were between your sacrificing your happiness or my leaving home to join you. But there remains that of my remaining at home while you try your experimental life, & as far as I can judge at present this seems to me the best. I do not see what use there could be in my sitting in a lodging while all your hope and aim would be to be away almost all the mornings & evenings. However since I feel most that we shall be able to judge better about the future when you have had some months trial of the sort of life—as for me I am better, & shall be able to be well again if you are happy. Think of me as well & cheerful & to keep me so let me hear that you are so. And now good night darling with love & kisses.

[along side margin]
I hope you have never less than nine hours in bed?

Friday eveng[13]

I will only write a word to-night dear as otherwise you will not get one from me untill Tuesday, as there is no post doubtless on Monday. I have yours of yesterday—It seems plain Mr. Davis[14] wants to make you useful, & as you say perhaps that will answer your purpose. Mr. Davis excuse about L^y Macbeth that he wanted a part where the cheif woman had not all the interest in her part was peculiarly inappropriate for for pieces [*sic*][15] have the interest more divided—Lady Macbeth is by no means the only essential part of the play. But it is plain from the first he did not wish Macbeth. I am glad to hear he is aggreeable. I am amused & interested in all your details & picture it all to myself.

It is very cold now on Wednesday the whole country was deep in snow, but it shined all day & melted it.

Adieu now dear.

---

13. Postmarked 30 November 1856. LI/16.

14. Mr. Davis was the theater manager in Newcastle where Helen was attempting to find work.

15. The correct spelling is "forepiece," which is a curtain raiser.

Love to Haji who I hope is better—of the illness you spoke of.

I think, but am not quite sure that I made a great blunder in the words I sent for Mrs Knill's note. It ought to begin "Miss T presents her compliments & regret, &c" What do you think? <u>This</u> is no doubt very formal, yet as I sent it, it seems almost rude for want of this form. I think it should go with the compliments & therefore that you will have the trouble of writing & sending me another note as soon as you can dear. Dont you think so. Can you tell me what sort of green it is that Mary has just begun cutting, saying they want cutting—It is a very nice solid heart of a light colour, with the outer leaves much curled. I sh^d guess it to be savoy[16] by the heart but the leaves being curly I do not know. What did you wear to dine at the Glover's—The black silk?[17]

No. 9   Monday[18]
I have got yours here to-day darling so alls right about that. I shall have to hurry over my writing for the cold is so intense that I shake with cold at any distance from the fire & have to get up every moment to go close to it. Everything is hard frozen—the thermometer in my room with a fine fire at 9 this morn^g was 38. The last two evengs we have had tea & stayed in the dining room after his dinner, it is much warmer than here—indeed I could not have stayed in this room.

About your questions dear I quite agree with you that it would be an advantage to try your power of being heared & facing an audience there— & having taken all the trouble of going & getting settled it seems better to make it of as much use as you can—Davis can hardly fail to give you something to do which you could make suit your purpose either there or at Sunderland—would he not be ~~the~~ a better person to recommend you somewhere else than that Bow Street place, which seems such a low sort of proceeding. It seems to me not a good plan to come home & leave again in a week or two. If you mean to be out all the winter it seems better to continue than to come in & out as it where [*sic*], which must excite so much curiosity. I enclosed a letter for Haji this morn^g. Does he manage not to give his name? I think having got such comfortable lodgings it would be much better not to ~~leave~~ change them. ~~for others.~~ It strikes me that if you mean to apply to Butler[19] you could do that by letter from

16. A variety of common cabbage with compact head and crinkled leaves.

17. Postmarked 2 December 1856. LI/18.

18. Postmarked 2 December 1856. LI/19.

19. In Helen's letter, LI/17, she describes Butler as "the Theatrical agent in Bow Street."

where you are as well or better than from here? Would not Mrs. Stirling find you some other place—I should think she would—& hers is a much better introduction than [Butlers][20] I sh^d think.

I think the landlady must cheat you, yet you are such a good house-keeper I wonder at it, but 1.3.0 is much more than provisions for you & Haji can cost for a week. The lodging too you said were 15/ a week & with the addition you mention of 4/6 for Haji would not make 1.2.6. I will pay the 6/ for Haji. You will see dear that I do not think at all a good plan to come home to seek another engagement, It would be to be out all day as before ending by the same painful leaving. It must be far easier to do it where you are free to take all necessary steps on the spot. If I do not get a letter as usual I shall know you are

[written along the side of the last page]
gone to Sunderland as you say dear. & now good bye darling

Wednesday[21]

I will begin by answering all the details in yours of this morning dear. and first I am sorry you were vexed at what I said about not writing here sooner. I said twice a week here, because I thought you found it trouble-some to put them in at Gateshead, but I like you to write here as often as you like, & if you find it really troublesome to put them in there then put them at Newcastle. I prefer Gateshead, but still not would not make a sine qua non of it. About Miss N.[22] I agree with you but think that where there is curiosity shown that constitutes a reason not to gratify it as there is probably in that case some object in it—but whether so or not, I think it w^d be better not to give Miss N. the name & address but to ask Mrs S. to have the things sent to her & to pay the bill. Of course you sign to Mrs S. in your own name.

About the numbers of your letters, I marked outside the N^o. of each as I receive it—It is a most excellent plan because you thus see in a moment if all are there—I keep them in an India rubber band. The one that came to-day is N° 11. and so I sh^d like you to mark them. The want of a few

---

20. The spelling appears close to "Bullens" here, but Harriet must be referring to the same person mentioned in the previous sentence.

21. Postmarked 6 December 1856. LI/23.

22. Miss North, a seamstress in London, is first mentioned in Helen's letter, LI/6. Helen worries about whether Miss North should know her current address in order to send the dresses she had ordered or to have the dress sent to Mrs. Fanny Stirling.

such systemation[23]—is the cause of so much labour if one keeps letters, as otherwise there is no referring to a back letter without opening all &c &c. The weather here has been & still is most wretched, tho' this morning there is a thaw it seems very little less cold, but if the thaw lasts it will become so. There has been skating every where, crowds on the pond on the heath—but I think I never felt it so cold. yesterday I seriously c^d not think what to do. I suffered so from the constant stooping over the fire in the quite vain effort to get warm, since Sunday I have remained always in the dining room which is certainly as you always said much warmer.

I should not I think have suffered so much if it had been fine bright weather, but it has been the most dark & dismal I ever knew so that I c^d hardly see to read ever before 3. Mr Mill had candles at his office. To-day is less dark because tho there is as much fog it is white instead of yellow. The rain is now changing to snow & it will probably be another heavy fall. It is now the hardest winter, but I think when it sets in so easily it does not last altogether more than when it begins later & if so it is only a change of when we have the severe part. Mr Mill had a long friendly letter from Dr Ruge[24] yesterday by which we suppose he is prepared to accept an invitation for some part of Christmas holidays. If at all it will be perhaps best. to make it for Christmas week—however we shall see—something must depend on weather for I could not have sat through dinners &c with strangers this last-week & in any case it is a formidable undertaking to entertain people all day long.

I have not had my return of the illness I felt the first days & since then my hands do not swell at night & I sleep well. If it were not for the extreme cold I should be as well. To-morrow he has got to open the discussion as usual at the P. E. club[25]—he undertook to do so in the summer & so cannot be off it, which he would gladly be.

In all you say about parts & practise I agree. what I cannot judge of is what, if anything, would lessen the prestige of a London appearance—very likely nothing—as in no case would you be likely to appear with a great flourish & flare up beforehand—if you did it would be because some manager thought it worth while to make it, & then I do not suppose theatrical antecedents would signify. They might make a difference in a

---

23. This word does not appear in the Oxford English Dictionary. She may mean "system-ization".

24. Dr. Arnold Ruge (1802-80), emigrated to England after the German revolution of 1848. He wrote on politics and philosophy. JSM wrote to Theodor Gomperz in September 1856 asking about Dr. Ruge's arrival in Brighton (CW: XXXII, 91).

25. Political Economy club.

London or first class country managers first idea of your value, but I think it most probable as you do, that they are accustomed to expect that actresses, even with pretensions have done all sorts of parts when they began. Thus you see I agree in all your opinion on that part of the question. I thought <u>before</u> that you had determined never to play anything but Tragedy, and reminded you of this lest you were being drawn in by Davis to do what you did not really wish. I do not see that you could have a better stage for practise, as it being so considerable a one in all ways (size, numbers, activity) (& a decent family conducting it) must make it infinitely better practise than a smaller place. ~~With yor feelings on the matter~~ There is no doubt you will have gained your object from Davis if you can make him give you a part qulqoncque.[26] ~~You know how~~ I agree that you are ignorant of the mechanical things. I have always thought & said, to your disgust that I say "if an experienced actress c^d show me as a mother shows, not as a mere stranger, how to dress." I have been ever since you were a child telling & showing you as far as you would allow me, my ideas of dress, which you always rejected—they did not agree with yours—~~but~~ I know no way in which I could have done more.

As far as I have seen, Mrs S. has never given any advice—she evidently feels that she cannot judge for you but will help you in any way you ask her. As I agree in all you say in your letter dear I need not repeat it, as you will remember it all. for ex: "hard and obscure work the only thorough preparation for the stage" I have no doubt this is so.

Evening.
I am sorry I said what struck me about the change for provisions as it probably was not all the woman's expenditure & I have no doubt you manage as well as you can. You know I wish you to have every comfort in that line.

And now adieu & good night my dearest girl—I hope you keep warm—you are pretty sure to be warmer there than here but you must try not to get a bad cold. Will you take your Blk silk (the corded) with you ? If others wear silk at rehearsal &c that looks extremely well & makes more effects much than the green tartan. but this of course is a mere suggestion.

Thursday Morn^g
I think it will be necessary to tell Mrs. S. that you are vexed—or that you particularly wish Miss N paid—or she wont probably think it worth

26. Harriet may have meant the French word "quelconque " meaning "any, some, commonplace."

while to take the trouble—as her notions are no doubt that keeping those people waiting won't matter—or that you shall be particularly obliged to—This morning the whole country lies under snow & is as cold as ever again

Thursday night
12 oclk[27]

My dearest Lily

Imagine how vexed I am on his coming in half an hour ago & telling me he had forgotten to put my letter in the post! So you will get none till Saturday. I am so sorry—& he is much vexed too. It is always very long between my writing & your getting the letters owing to not sending them to the post here, & now this additional delay is very annoying. & now I have just read your Tuesday (N° 12) I am so glad to hear dear that the change for provisions was all right & not any cheating on the part of the woman but "because you eat so much" go on & do so dear, you know that is just what I wish—& for nine days it is very little—I supposed & do not talk of mangling[28] & be sure you manage exactly the same otherwise about it—The charge for Haji is all right so stay where you are dear altogether all the time you are there & go on just the same. Mr. Davis seems desirous to show he is not in need of you—but that is only what you might expect If he or his son can be made to give you the opportunity for practise you wish all that does not matter. You will see by the letter I wrote yesterday that I agree with you on this. It seems a remarkably respectable Theatre. I am writing on the little table by the fire in my bedroom—it is between 12 & 1 oclk so I shall not say much more dearest as I believe I have answered all you asked me. The weather tho still very cold & the ground covered with snow seems quite mild today after the last week. I do hope it is also improved with you for I so fear you will suffer & perhaps get a bad cold if it ~~gets~~ keeps so cold. The Times must have some correspondent at Newcastle, for they have every day a paragraph describing the weather there. And now adieu darling you will only get this on Sat. & then you cannot get another from me before Tuesday. stay in the same lodging & be sure you eat & drink all you can. for my health.

Y^rs H

27. Postmarked 5 December 1856 and addressed to Miss Trevor / 34 Blackill Street / Newcastle on Tyne. LI/25.

28. Being spoiled.

12   Friday night[29]

O my dearest girl you cannot think how vexed I am about that letter not
going yesterday, all day I have been so uncomfortable thinking that you
would be uneasy at not getting it. And the day it happened was just as
unlucky as possible as you will be so busy & hardly able to see to getting
it to-morrow, however I can only hope you will get the two together.

Do not dear have any tense or trouble about my letters — if they or any
of them should be lost there is no harm done beyond the immediate
inconvenience and as to yours to me put them in <u>anywhere</u>. Sunderland
too is just as good as Gateshead, but I do not mind any, so let that source
of trouble cease. I think it very likely you may get on better with the son
than with Davis himself, who seems an intangible sort of person. but
perhaps not — I don't know. But I feel quite sorry that you have to leave
the comfortable rooms you had got for less comfortable ones, I feel exactly
as if I was leaving them myself from what you say I suppose those you
have taken do not take in Haji too? If so what will he do for a room. Do
not answer my questions when you are busy dear as they will always wait.
I t̶h̶i̶n̶k̶ have already said t̶h̶a̶t̶ ̶t̶h̶e̶ ̶o̶f̶t̶e̶n̶e̶r̶ ̶y̶o̶u̶ write here as often as you
like, I said twice a week only to save you trouble.

With blk velvet dress & Blk satin shoes I sh^d say white stockings, as I
think the stockings sh^d be white always except when mourning is intended. I sh^d have thought for Jane Shore[30] <u>white</u> satin shoes — but I do
not <u>know</u> what is usual.

This is the only question you have asked me dear. I hope if the lodgings
do not prove comfortable you will try to get others — I cannot bear to
think of you as in an uncomfortable place. I sh^d have thought Haji had
better be with you as the difference in the expense is too trifling to be
worth considering — but you will h̶a̶v̶e̶ ̶j̶u̶d̶g̶e̶d̶ I hope do as you like best.

How I wish I c^d <u>learn</u> some of that great task for you! I cannot see how
you will find time to do it before Monday. Tell me darling if I shall
continue to direct to this same address and good night my darling

                                                          Friday night

Oh my dearest girl when I hear the wind roaring as it does to-night I
wonder if my sweet Lily is warm & comfortable it makes me quite
wretched to think that perhaps you are not. Tell me darling if you keep
up your good appetite & have <u>everything</u> you like. Tell me that you have

---

29. Postmarked 6 December 1856. LI/27.

30. *Jane Shore,* a tragedy written by Nicholas Rowe, was first performed at the Theatre-Royal
in Drury Lane, 1776.

cakes for tea—& good ale & plenty of meat? Mind if you would do as I wish you will have everything you like to eat.

Saturday Morn^g
This morn^g dear the ther^r is at 50 (from 36 & 38 which it has been for nearly a week) yet stranger this morn^g for the first time my cough has been most painfully violent, more so than I ever had it. I suppose it is the sudden change & that it will go off.

About Christmas dear, I suppose you will be quite as much occupied that week as any other therefore I propose to come and spend it with you. He would come with me & leave me & I could stay at an Inn or in lodgings as you like best. That is to say if you like the plan at all. In this case of course Haji would stay with you till I come at all events. It w^d be unnecessary to mention my coming to the Davises. & now adieu darling as he waits. I do hope you will get this

13   Sunday[31]
I will only write a word or two to-day dear just to say that I am well. I have been most uneasy thinking of your annoyance at not getting any letter on Friday—but I hope I can feel sure you would get the two on Saturday explaining how it happened. Also one to-day.

I need hardly say again[,] put yours in for me here at any Post office The only one I ever had any objection to is Newcastle—that I would rather not—but even that rather than plague to you. Sunderland is in all respects as good as Gateshead, & I do not mind variety at all. It hardly does to tell you every little thing about health lest I make you uneasy before I can give another report. That bad fit of coughing I had just before I wrote the other morn^g went off & I had no more. The weather is now too mild, for the change is too sudden & gives one the headaches. The ther^r in my room after being for near a week at 38 <u>with</u> a fire, is now 58 without a fire. I hope you have the same change. I am impatient for my next letter I so fear you are not comfortable as to lodgings, and be sure you have all comforts as to food dear—unless you tell me this I shall be very uncomfortable & afraid to make any observation ~~without~~ as it comes into my head.

I am well & have not a single thing to tell as I have seen no one & done nothing but sit by the fire & read thro' all this cold. If the weather continues fine I mean to go out Tuesday and call on Mr. Fox.[32]

Give my love to Haji & Adieu dearest. Yours HM

---

31. Postmarked 8 December 1856. LI/29.

32. William Fox.

14   Monday,[33] Dec. 8

To-day I have your two letters dear & I am so glad to hear you are comfortably off as to lodgings. If there should be any failure of a letter when you expect one again you will know it is from some such cause, for if I were ill or there should be any thing unusual I would write or get him to do so all the more.

What you say in your last about your prospects there, does not seem to me to agree exactly with what you said before—you say if Mr Davis[34] keeps you dangling uncertain you had better leave—but are you not sure to have a great deal of dangling uncertain wherever you go, & if you can get practise where you are is it not a better stage for it than most you could try? It is at once a large complete stage, yet not a great publicity attending it. & so long as he will give you opportunity for practise, changing to another place seems to have no advantage, whatever, but much disadvantage. If you sh^d be writting to Mrs. Stirling you can tell her that I am going out of town for Christmas but shall much like to see her at a future time. The fact is I sh^d much prefer her coming here when you are at home as I do not suppose she speaks french fluently & all our talk would be overheared. Besides I w^d rather defer her having that name & address as it is plain she has no idea of 'keeping' ones 'counsel' however strong she was on the subject of "keeping your own counsel" as she said. I like her & shall like to see her very much, but not just yet, especially as I think her proposing it now after rejecting it before is from curiosity to have the name. You will not agree in this I dare say but still I think so.[35]

I do not think there is any thing else to answer in yours dear. I shall be impatient for Wednesday's letter to tell me how the great night went off—I can hardly help setting off to be present. I have very little doubt of its being quite successful. Adieu darling

I hope you do not suffer as we & according to Mr Mill's account everybody seems to suffer from the sudden change from great cold to a peculiar kind of heat. The damp is frightful & extraordinary & one feels as if going to have a fever. I dare say it is not so much felt in a town as in the country.

15   Monday[36]

I shall not hear till Wed^y how you have got on dear, I have no doubt well,

---

33. Postmarked 9 December 1856. LI/32.

34. Theater manager in Newcastle.

35. HTM and Fanny Sterling had become intimate friends by 1858. See LIV/24, below.

36. Postmarked December 1856, probably the 11th. LI/33.

& if not a striking success that will not dissapoint you as it can hardly be looked for so soon. I shall be very impatient to hear how it all went off. I so fear Mrs Davidson might not make her appearance in time & so you be inconvenienced about dresses.

I do not see any reason to come to town about dresses as a good sized country town is quite as good a place both for materials & dressmaking as London. It would be only coming to go away again and that would be very painful to me. I have no doubt everything is to be bought at Newcastle. I do not mind what sort of place it is I come to to [sic] see you at Christmas, Sunderland will do just as well as any other. I think Haji had better stay till I come as otherwise he would be left here alone.

You say "the non success of Dred[37] had left them without anything particular to do & ready to try experiments" Is not this exactly the circumstance you wished for? Just that which will induce him to give you the opportunities of practise you wish, especially when he finds you are willing to do it without pay? I do not see where you could expect to get better. And as to coming home for a few weeks between two engagements, it would be just that <u>second</u> leaving home, not the first, which would be strange & unaccountable to the people here. So long as, & however long, it is <u>once</u> it passes as a long visit, but the repetition of it could not.

Wednesday morn[g] I left this space to fill this morn[g] dear & now I have my hands swollen & am not of spirits & so have nothing to say but I shall write again to-day when I have got your letter. I do shall be well enough when I get up so do not think anything of this dear—It is nothing

[along the side]
adieu with a thousand loves

Wednesday[38]

I thought you would succeed dear one and it seems to have been quite a thorough success and I am so glad you were able to get it all managed so comfortably I was full of fears lest Mrs. Davidson should not keep her engagement, the dresses not do, &c but all seems to have answered perfectly & I am sure you must have looked most beautiful. It will be a pleasure too to be able to like this Miss Markham.[39] That notion they all have that you must of course be frightened shows what a low class they

---

37. *Dred* played in Sunderland on December 8-10, 1856.

38. Postmarked 12 December 1856. LI/37.

39. Miss Markham, another actor whom Helen describes as "a very nice 'girl' (in theatrical parlance) open, hearty, goodnatured, and thoroughly friendly to me" in LI/34.

generally are connected with Theatres, as no well bred young lady would show any, or feel much trepidation on such an occasion & I was sure you would not. There was the same want of savoir vivre[40] in asking you the question continually, as if anything w^d make a person timid it w^d be doing so as you say.

About the blue silk I should think it w^d be very useful and if you prefer Miss North's making to trying the Newcastle dressmaker you can do as you say. I sh^d suppose there were first rate shops for the sort of thing at Newcastle & dressmakers too, but do as you like best dear.

I sh^d have thought the silk good enough for a dress, if not indeed any <u>silk</u> w^d be inappropriate with the rough Swiss jacket w^d not light blue merino petticoat with many rows of Blk velvet (made rather long) do better.

As to lining the white I see the same objection to part of the way as you do & it needs to consult Miss Markham or Mrs. Stirling about it. I have been poorly to-day & my side is very painful with writing and I must now leave off

Thursday morn^g

I will only say good bye my dear. I am very poorly with pain in the chest as I was yesterday. It is caused by the constant sitting, without change 10 hours a day—I must try to go out.

Adieu till to-morrow

Thursday[41]

I think dearest that Davis shows himself just what Mrs. Stirling said he was—It is not behaving well to keep you waiting near a month & then ~~to~~ give but one appearance. As for his talk about your being more fit for comedy & so on, that is merely ~~to say~~ a way of ~~saying~~ depreciating what he knows you wish to do. I take it, by the playbill you send (& which I meant to ask for) that he has an ad libitum[42] stock of ladies ready & able to play any thing, as well as he wants it played. I do not know if you have offered to play for no remuneration for the sake of practise—but even if you have he very likely prefers his own troop of ladies. The newspaper critic is evidently anything but friendly to Davis or to his Theatre—he finds fault with all more or less therefore no wonder he does with you.

---

40. Good manners or tact.

41. Postmarked 13 December 1856. LI/39.

42. At pleasure.

I do not know if you offered to play any parts & without pay? That is I think what you would like to do. If so you had better make him the offer if you have not already done so.

In any case I mean to come and spend Christmas week with you. If you have before then quite decided to leave that part of the country we can meet any where you like best, Newcastle, York, Scarborough, or any where you like best and after that few days or week we will come home together If you do leave could not Davis recommend you what other place to try? he must know all about all the country places one w^d think. Ask Mrs Stirling to look out if you like dear. Of the satins the cheap ones are much brighter blue than the less cheap one (they are all very cheap) the difference of price should not be considered the better one is also lighter & whiter looking—it is <u>more</u> than the difference of price better, quite another thing indeed but whether one w^d choose for colour or quality I do not know how to decide. I rather think I should vote for the cheaper, ~~if~~ the much inferior in quality, as being more advantageous to the complexion

Friday morn^g

I went out yesterday and called on Mr. Fox[43] and there were all the stairs to mount & tho it seemed to have done some good yet the pain in the chest continues & this morn^g the chest & side is very painful & contracted in the old way you know. I can hardly move the right arm. In the night I lay awake for hours anxious & dispirited from thinking you are perhaps so dearest. I shall be glad to see you at Christmas, my headache is so very bad that I know not how to write now what to say—he says blisters, but last time that did no good & I shall try lying in bed to-day tho' very inconvenient. I have not done so since you left. ~~If~~ This bad ~~chest~~ fit is caused by the monotonous sedentariness. I shall write again to-morrow so do not think of being anxious dear one as you will hear each day & I hope to be better to-morrow all this will excuse any omissions in my letter—but I think I have answered each point darling.

18   Friday[44]

It appears as if he had an ample stock of actresses, probably at very low salaries (do you think he pays them at all?) Perhaps they are all persons of that county, and even of that town, who make their business of the Theatre, and whom he does not wish to turn out. Perhaps the only ones whom he pays or whom he wants besides them are a star from London

---

43. William Fox.

44. Postmarked 13 December 1856. LI/41.

occasionally to give an impetus. If they won't give the amount of occupation you want, and I do not think they will, then come home dear and get all your things. If you do not mean to stay there it seems scarcely worthwhile for me to come so far (if you would leave the place directly after) and in this case we might as well meet at a nearer easier place for Christmas if you would like it as well. I should say Brighton, on account of the easy journey. We would then return home together If Haji comes back before Christmas he will be left here alone for Christmas week—but leave him to do as he pleases. The objection to his returning before you is that it gives necessarily here the idea of complicated circumstances, while if he remains with you till all return together, up to that time the circumstances seem simple and ordinary. But as he is so excessively disagreeable he must be left to do as he likes: only if you decide to quit the North before Christmas and to meet us at Brighton, it would be better that he should know before leaving you where we are going, because if he returns, it will be better that he should remain here during our absence. I should not like that he should return here and go out again with us. It is not necessary for you to say any of this to him, and I only tell you that you may know what I think of the subject. Tell him anything or none of all this just as you find convenient. The only thing it would be better he should know is that we go to Brighton, if we do so, and you can decide if it would be to Newcastle or Brighton that we go. I wrote to him yesterday saying that if he returned he would have to remain here Christmas week alone. I suppose he wants to return to pass Christmas week near the church, and it is possible (but I do not know if it is so) that if he knows we are going to Brighton he would prefer to go there, while I think that if once he returns he had better stay. I think dear that I explained yesterday that if you do not think it worth while to stay at Newcastle you can as well leave Christmas week as a week or two after. In that case you will write as you say to Mrs S.[45] and leave Newcastle on the 22nd to meet me. About the dress I answered yesterday dear. I have not got up today because I was so unwell this morning. The day of rest has done good and now the chest and side though very week have ceased aching.

Saturday morn^g

I am rather better this morn^g & shall get up tho' I dread very much that Mr. Fox is coming to spend to-day & to-morrow. But I shall take care of myself dear that I may be able to come to you. I think you might well

---

45. Fanny Stirling, Helen's mentor.

say to Mr. Davis that Jane Shore is a very bad part for a debut because it is wearisome & monotonous & the interest too personal. If he were to see your l^y Macbeth he might think more of your tragedy. That is a far more suitable part because the interest is in <u>facts</u>, not in mere personal sorrows.

I shall not like to write again untill I hear again what address—but if anything occurs to me that I want to say I will address again to the Post Office and now adieu darling for another ten days & then I shall kiss my sweet <u>fair</u> girl again

19   Sunday night[46]
It is eleven o'clk dear & this is the first moment I have had alone since yesterday & after a most fatiguing & also a ~~vexab~~ vexing day I am so tired that I will but write one word. There is not anything in yours of yesterday dear one that requires answering as I had written on each various point in it before.

I fully meant to enclose a note in mine yesterday but being ill & very hurried forgot it. I shall enclose one in this & when I hear that is received safe I will send another You have been quite right about the money dear all along.

Good night my darling

20   Monday,[47] Dec 15
It is now so near Christmas dear that it is necessary to decide ~~our~~ what we do. It is next Monday that I propose leaving home. I have explained in my last my feeling—I do not like to judge for you whether you had better stay there longer or not. I wish you do as you like best as then at least somebody does as they like. I think whenever you come to town you must come home—and I think it would be foolish for us to come to you (anywhere) for a week & then you to return home <u>in a week or two afterwards</u>. Therefore if you would in any case prefer to come to town in two or three weeks, it would be better to come home with us after Christmas.

Decide as you like best dear & let me know & I will now ~~arrange~~ say how we will arrange in either case & you will tell me which you decide for. If you prefer staying at Newcastle I shall come down at the beginning of next week & there is no <u>plan</u> to make; but if you decide to leave, & spend a week with me at Brighton before returning home, we must arrange our plan as ~~it~~ there are so few trains. In this case you should leave

---

46. Postmarked 15 December 1856. LI/42.

47. Postmarked 17 December 1856. LI/45.

Newcastle <u>next</u> Monday at 8 in the morning arriving at King's cross[48] at 7 Then go by the 8 o'clk <u>P.M.</u> to Brighton & he would meet you at the station there. If by any mischance you were too late for the 8 o'clk from London Bridge there is another train at 10.20 arriving at Brighton at 12 — & of course if you did not come by the first he w^d meet that. I will now reply to your other questions dear — you must not wonder that I write stupidly for I am so tired from nervous vexation, & it is past twelve.

You say you are so glad to find by my note to Haji that I do not [mind] his returning. I am sorry you c^d think this as it seems to justify his doing so, while on the contrary I dislike it most exceedingly, as I sh^d have thought both my note to him & to you showed — I said he sh^d do as he liked thinking that when he saw what I wished he w^d do it & not wishing to say more & be refused. However that is done he came in about nine & was I suppose very cross as he did not speak I agree that you had better fix with Mrs. Davidson[49] to write for her when you want her. Her idea of writing to Glasgow seems a good one. I suppose you will have your answer addressed to Mrs. S.[50] must you ask her permission. I do not wish you not to ask her to apply to Butler[51] dear I have but one feeling since we cannot both be pleased about all this at least let one be — therefore do in all as you wish dear. I find that the expense w^d be just the same of our going to Newcastle or your going to Brighton, so that need not be considered.

Tuesday morning

I was so utterly done up last night dear that I hardly knew what I said or thought. It strikes me that we can decide about your next movement when we meet & the only point to settle now is where that shall be. I am anxious about this because there is so little time for replies I fear we may be wandering about & not meeting! A third plan equally feasible would be to meet at York (at the principal Inn) in case you like to stay longer at Newcastle. in this case I should not come till Wednesday. whichever place we meet at you will be equally free to return thence to either Newcastle, London, or home, or anywhere else you like.

I suppose Haji's luggage is covered with all the tickets — so that all the care about Postmarks is thrown away by that. I think my dear girl I have answered every question you asked me. If not do not fear to ask again or any number and I will answer the best I can.

---

48. Railway station in London.

49. Mrs. Davidson is Helen's seamstress.

50. Fanny Stirling.

51. In Helen's letter, LI/17, she describes Butler as "the Theatrical agent in Bow Street."

It is again this morn^g exceptionally cold—I fear we are going to have it all back again.

I have got over the attack of the chest which I did not expect to do so soon. I shall feel better in spirits as the time for seeing you comes nearer.

21   Tuesday Eveng^{52}

I have got your sweet letter my darling girl it will indeed be happy to meet. If you got my yesterday letter all right I shall soon hear from you, saying that you agree in & understand how we are to meet. If it is to be Brighton we will go to the Albion, but if by any most improbably chance the Albion were full, we would next go to the Queens (after that par impossible the old ship) I repeat all these details dear that I may be sure to hear from you that our plan is fixed & understood.

I sent a note in mine of yesterday & I shall enclose one in this, before waiting to hear that the first is received, because the time is so short. It is only five days to that when we shall meet next Monday the 22?

I have answered all your questions in mine of yesterday dear. It is difficult to judge what the proper pay of a person like Davi[d]son should be If I had to do it, before I decided I should ask for what she had been accustomed to have—I sh^d not think it necessary of course to give what she said—that would depend on whether I thought it too high. of course she must be paid so as to be contented & even pleased—but some of them talk in such a bragging way about their expectations.

Fourteen shillings a week & to board herself might be right—but it may be too little or too much it depends so entirely on the custom of such cases It can hardly however be too much more like too little, but a needle woman thinks it handsome.

good night darling.

Wednesday^{53}

Yes you should certainly ask him that question dear whether it c^d have been a worse house with Macbeth on any standard price.

I suppose it is now decided for Brighton and I shall hear to-morrow that our plan for meeting is quite plain. I hope no mischance can happen but in case it did & that you did not meet him at the train station at Brighton at 10 o'clk on Monday we shall be at the Albion or (in the impossible case of there not being rooms) to be heared of there. You had better tell Mrs. S. that you are going ~~to join~~ with me ~~at~~ to Brighton & ~~to~~

---

52. Postmarked 18 December 1856. LI/47.

53. Postmarked 18 December 1856. LI/48.

~~write to Post Office there~~ that you will send her the address ~~when you in a day or~~ when you get there. She will of course address to Miss Taylor.

The reason I w^d not say <u>Post</u> <u>Office</u> is that I think I remember they said they w^d not receive letters so addressed.

It has become again painfully cold but he says it is going to thaw. I was ill last night & this morn^g with severe pain in the chest, but this evening it has gone. This has been caused by the union of the great cold & of some very nervous circumstances which however I will not write about as they will wait to tell when we meet & I am very much afraid of writing.

Adio carissima mia figlia Bendetta mia![54]

23   Thursday,[55] Dec. 18

I should hope dear that there is a chance of your being in time for the 8 o'clk train from London Bridge because Haji came by it—but I know it is doubtful—but there is no other plan possible than that I mentioned except if you prefer sleeping in town & coming down next morning.

It will be a very long fatiguing day and you must judge if <u>too</u> fatiguing to come down by the 10.20 in case of losing the 8 o'clk. If you think this will be too much the only other plan w^d be for me to stay in town ~~that~~ Monday night & we meet there, & this I will do if I hear from you that you prefer it? In this case Mr. M[ill] w^d meet you at the arrival of the train, or perhaps better, you join us at the Brunswick Hotel Jermyn Street which you decide of these plans shall be done to me they [are] pretty equal.

I mentioned Butler in mine of Monday dear saying that I had no objection—do as you like about him.

It is most painfully cold here tho' they say it promises a change I have been but poorly this week. Perhaps the change of air & seeing you may do good. I look forward to it with impatience. Adieu now dearest girl.

Your HM

[written inside the envelop flap]
au revoir mon ange chère[56]

Friday morn^g

This morn^g I am better for the first time this week. I have been very unwell—but feel now as tho' I shall again recover

---

54. "Goodbye dearest daughter My Blessed / My Beloved."

55. No indication of the year. LI/51.

56. "Goodbye my precious angel."

24   Wednesday night[57]
                                                                   Dec 31

My dearest girl I have been reproaching myself all the even[g] for not having
made you promise to have a good meal with meat when you arrive. I fear
you will be over tired—it is still so cold I think it will have been—a very
hard day for you. As it is now ten o'clk I hope you have got through it
and are going to bed. Adieu this last day of the year and a happy waking
to you my darling on the New Year morning.

    There is nothing yet to tell and I only write for the sake of writing.

[The following was written on a small piece of paper which was added to
the letter.]

I hope you will never walk home without a sufficient person with you.
How far is it? & is through a lane? or lonely?

25   Jan 1st
A happy new year to my dearest Lily[58]—how many years and how happy
ours I cannot say—you may think too my dear one how I have been
wishing you a happy day to-day or at least not a dissapointing one. how
it has gone I shall not hear till to-morrow or scarcely so soon. I have been
to town with Haji to-day, he wanted me to help him to buy a Port
Manteau[59] & other things of the travelling sort, so I went suddenly this
morning feeling the black melancholy into which I has fallen must be in
some way lessened, & all the bustle of a day in town & the exercise &
fatigue in some measure disperses inward feelings for a time—with time
I shall get better especially when I have written to you something of what
I feel most—but this must be another day—when one is very tired it is
not easy to choose expressions, a thing never easy to me to those I really
love. It is natural to me to say what I feel without reserves, & when I
feel liable to be misunderstood—I immediately express myself ill from
constraint.

    However I did not mean to write a word of this sort, so let it be as if
unwritten—all I wish to say is all the love & interest with which I look
for my dearest girls letter.

---

57. Postmarked 2 January 1857. LI/55.

58. Postmarked 2 January 1857. LI/57.

59. A type of suitcase.

Friday morn^g Jan 2

I do not like to send this as I hate to say any thing which could make you less cheerful—& you are perhaps as busy as possible I must now send this or none & I shall write better this even^g

adieu darling

You must not mind the hasty <u>composition</u> of my letters as I know you w^d rather I write so than tire myself by writing either more or better

---

P.S. Can you tell me if there is loaf sugar in the store room as I have sought about with Mary & could not find any—what a queer woman she is when you speak more than a few words to her—more like some sort of half savage. one sees those glimmerings of perception which make the galleries go with the right but also the excessive [leaderbleness]⁶⁰ of the half reclaimed human animal. certainly the [sheep?] are more moral naturally than the [herd?]

26   Friday,⁶¹ Jan. 2

I have got your dear letter and you need not speak of writing a better one for it is impossible to write more sweetly but I am pained at your having taken a lodging at such a low price, as judging by the prices at ~~the~~ Newcastle I think it cannot be good enough and it seems to show that you separate yourself from me in that matter in a way I never thought possible & which you could never do if you judged rightly or by yourself. It makes me extremely out of spirits that you have taken wrongly what I said about money. I have always said & shown that I feel that all that we have is in common, you my sweet girl have always felt so & so entirely do I that I would not have any unless you shared equally with me. If I had but a shilling in the world you should have eleven pence of it, you have always acted so & I am sure I have & I shall not be happy till you tell me you are feeling this again & acting upon it as you did before. What I said at Brighton was not about money but about a feeling which hurt me because I thought it & still think it unjust—but this is another subject. About making use of money you & ~~are~~ I are always[,] have been[,] & must continue to be <u>one</u> if I am to ~~be~~ have any happiness from & with you. If you judge me by yourself on this subject you will feel that it is so & never separate us in either thought or fact.

---

60. Perhaps HTM meant "leaderlessness."

61. Postmarked 3 January 1857. LI/59.

I have now written what has been depressing me these last days & if I do not write at greater length it is because my hand tires so that I always say everything in the fewest words that will do. The effort to write shortly sometimes ends in making ~~the~~ what is meant not so plain as it might be.

You cannot yet judge how Mr Chester[62] will turn out, but I hope from the commencement he will be pleasant to deal with at all events, & you will not mind the smallness of the house if you can get good practise, but about that we shall know more presently. It is quite mild here too now & even fine. Haji sends his love & wishes you a happy new year & Adieu & good night now my darling

from your
HM

Be sure not to write when you are tired—& when you have written not to take it to the Post when inconvenient.

Write home dear two or three times a week—others to him.

Sunday,[63] Jan. 4

I am very melancholy & unhappy. I think that you are not living with the comfort of any sort that you had at Newcastle. There I had the comfort of thinking you were comfortable, now I feel that you have changed & have determined to finish me for ever speaking freely by living in a way you know is painful to me. I cannot have or enjoy any pleasure if I know that you are not having all I can give you—Therefore you must either revert to feeling & living as you did at Newcastle or you will purposely lessen altogether my happiness in and from you. At Newcastle I saw & felt that you wrote freely, and lived as you would if I were with you, & had whatever you liked in the way of assistance and dress and every thing else & I enjoyed every thing you spent—now this source of pleasure has ceased. Have you ceased to wish to share all that gives you pleasure with me? And what pleasure can I have but in sharing yours? When I cannot be with you all my interest is in you, in what you are doing, and my pleasure in thinking that I can help you, if in no other way, by giving you or rather sharing with you ample means to do all you wish.

There is another thing which has hurt me very much—you said that what I said was because I was dissapointed that I could not disgust you with your taste & induce you to give it up—this would show a complete

---

62. Mr. Chester was the theater manager at Doncaster. See Helen's letter, LI/56.

63. Postmarked 7 January 1857. LII/61.

inability to understand me (if you really meant it & it was not a hasty expression) The whole idea is so absolutely foreign to, & contrary to, my character that no one who knows me could think it. I never for one instant did or could suppose that anything that could be said by anybody would disgust you with it & so make you give it up—such a thought never entered my head & you might have known & felt that <u>that</u> never was & never could be my mode of acting—if I wanted to induce you to give up your own wishes to mine I should never <u>try</u> anything, above all things it would not be through pain to you that I should wish to gain any object—I should ask it of you, from your love, not try to force it from annoyance. I never in my whole life did an underhand or mean thing of any kind, great or small or towards anybody. It is not in me, & I had not the remotest idea of the kind. I spoke the vexation I felt but I had no manner of object—as indeed I never have.

Monday.

I have now got your sweet & beautiful letter of Sunday my darling and it has taken away all the distressed & pained feelings I have been writing about, and I now feel quite happy & in spirits seeing that you (as I hope) feel just as you did & just as I wish you—That is perfectly one with me. I will write this evening an answer to the rest of yr letter

Monday Even^g.

I am made at ease by this mornings letter dearest about your comfort & safety—It was a fortunate chance that lodging, being both clean & civil and so near. Of course if anything happened to make you wish it you could change, but as yet it seems all right. I am amused at your account of Saturday—It is experience at all events & I should think you are right about preferring to stay where you are rather than changing except for a <u>positive</u> engagement. It is very likely there will be the same sort of going on at any of the very small country places—at all events it seems no use leaving one for another equally indefinite engagement But even about this you are a better judge than I, being in it all you can see the pros & cons I suppose you tell Mrs S that what you want is the opportunity to study with practise the first rate parts of your own kind & you would not mind <u>appearing</u> but seldom if you c^d practise well among good performers? Perhaps however this w^d not do what you want, which may be more quantity than quality of practise? I have no doubt you will judge well what is best for you to do for your object.

Adieu now dearest girl—I always think of you at night & hope you are safe & well. Be well & happy & take care of yourself above all things for me.

Monday[64] morn[g]

I began writing to you dearest yesterday but was interrupted in the middle of my letter & in the even[g] was too tired to finish it, & as I was telling you what distresses me I think I had better finish it to-day rather than send it half said—so this is but a word or two written in bed.

Yours of Sat did not contain any questions It seemed not quite sure if you would get practice, but I am glad to see that the people seem pleasant. You will tell me more in your next. Tomorrow as I cannot send it you[.] You must buy a 5/ cake (sugared) for me for your tea or any other time be sure you do & tell me you did.

Adieu now my darling till tomorrow

Wednesday[65] Jan[y]

I was not able to write my dearest girl anything last even[g] & was very tired—cheifly owing to the return of cold weather and also I had written to Arthur[66] Now I have overslept myself & he is standing waiting while I say, do not be dissapointed dearest if sometimes I do not write. I only send this lest you should be dissapointed & even so I fear the direction may startle you but do not mind as I am in bed & so he will do it for me.

In haste,
Adieu

Wednesday,[67] Jan[y]

I did not write to you yesterday dear one, partly I was very tired, partly the cold makes it hard to sit from the fire. my fingers now are so cold as you may see by the writing. You may be sure my darling I shall not write when it would hurt me, (which it hardly ever would to write in this careless way) I fear dear you are overexerting yourself, I am always expecting to hear of a bad cold—the places must be very cold & the change of dress too—when you have a cold you must take care to nurse yourself well on all accounts. If you are laid up I shall come & nurse you. I wish you w[d] get someone to help you with needlework—you can have a woman by the day or week—or give it out to be done—but in some way you must need assistance & I hope you will have it. There must be good dressmakers

---

64. Postmarked 5 January 1857. LII/62.

65. Postmarked 8 January 1857. LII/65.

66. During this period Harriet was writing Arthur Hardy about the trustee dispute with Arthur Ley.

67. Postmarked 9 January 1857. LII/66.

in the town. You seem likely now to have rather too much than too little to do, but it seems all successful.

We have had no answer from the Ruge, so Mr M[ill] has written to-day to him.

Haji says he is going to Malvern on Monday he thinks for a day or two to fetch away some baths & hampers of things he has left there. He talks about going to Italy, but does not say when. In answer to a remark of mine he said he should have no objection to escort Miss Fox[68]—this he said as if he should like it. I hardly know whether to propose it to her—I have so constantly found interfering, with the intention of doing a pleasure to other people turn out ill—& in this case I feel ~~as the~~ one ~~was~~ is almost sure to burn ones fingers in interfering where Haji is concerned. So I do not know whether to propose it to them or not: Of course either he will not, or else do it in some way they will not like—or some mess made of it.

Adieu now dearest as it is past eleven—I am afraid I cannot think you are in bed! So I will say Adieu & good night darling. We are sitting in the dining room & I shall do so in the evenings while it is so very cold.

Thursday[69] even[g]

You are so busy dearest that it is impossible you can comfortably write every day & do not do so dear when you are so busy as you are just now, for I fear you will find yourself too hard worked, & the addition of a letter to write even if not such nice long ones as yours always are is too much do not fear I shall be dissapointed dear as I shall much rather wait two or even three days for a letter than have you obliged to write when you need every moment of your time. I have suffered so much often from the feeling of being obliged to write for fear of dissapointing that I am very anxious you should not feel so. if you write seldomen [*sic*] when you are busy, you will write often when you have little to do—write when you have really a vacant hour, but never feel it any necessity—be sure I shall never mistake you dear as you will not me. Have you put in your box the name & address[70] here, as we decided you should? if not do dear, if you have a box or place you keep locked. It is quite a comfort to me to hear of the land lady & her daughter being so friendly. Is there nothing which I could do

---

68. Perhaps William J. Fox's daughter. Harriet sends a copy of the *Principles of Political Economy* to Miss Fox (see 27/40 in letters to the family and friends, above). Miss Fox is also referred to in another letter to Helen (LII/77) and in a letter to Algernon Hardy (27/116). Eliza and her father came to visit Harriet, and John at least twice in 1856. See Chapter 10.

69. Postmarked 10 January 1857. LII/68.

70. The word "mine" is inserted between "address" and "here."

for you dear? I would so gladly do anything. I am sure you must have looked very beautiful in the white muslin. I sh^d have thought the gold lace & stones rather too old for a mere girl like Juliet, but you can judge best on the spot—a white satin un-adorned w^d be most suitable. you should have a good white satin you would look so lovely in it. you do not tell me you have got someone to do needlework? I hope you have.

good night & bless you my precious.

Friday,[71] Jan. 9
I thought of you all yesterday evening dearest, of how busy you were and how pretty you would look. I shall hear perhaps to-morrow how it went off. I am anxious about your cold—I do hope I shall hear it is better, otherwise you should lay up in time. The weather here is most unpleasant, very cold wet & stormy & dark. I have the earache & am feverish & poorly to-day, but hope it will go off with a nights rest. Haji talks of going to Malvern on Monday for (I suppose) some days or a week. He is making preparations for going to Italy but does not say when he means to go. It was to Arthur I had been writing dear, not Annie[72] as you had it. I sh^d not have done that without telling you of it.

Mr Mill has a letter from Dr. Ruge in which he does not mention our invitation—I do not know whether to repeat it, for I am feeling most unfit for so very onerous an undertaking. I feel the weight & drag of housekeeping & the tie caused by servants excessively—directly I am tired or ill & wanting change that is a stumbling block.

However there is nothing new in this: & it is useless to write what you so well know—but I have such a bad head-ache that I can write about nothing. Haji says gives his love & say he wants to hear about Juliet.

Saturday morn^g
The intense headache & feverishness with which I went to bed last night is better this morning dear & I think will go by keeping very quiet to-day—I was to have gone to town to-day but I feel I cannot venture to attempt that. I must not be ill in your absence dear if I can help it—nor must you in mine my precious—be sure you let me know how you are truly & exactly. I am already wanting to come & see you but I suppose I must wait a little longer.

Adieu my darling—a resting Sunday to her to-morrow

---

71. Postmarked 11 January 1857. LII/71.

72. Annie Ley, Harriet's niece.

Sunday[73]

To think of my dear little girl being accused of rudeness! when I know there was hardly anything she would not have done for them for the sake of the whole subject—I hope she saw the injustice next morning. What could she have been thinking of to make such a blunder as if on purpose for from your account she insisted on placing herself just in the wrong place. Is she generally good humoured & agreable? I am sure you must be so entirely innocuous besides being so full of zeal. Shall you be able to expostulate with Mr. Chester[74] on the want of regularity in rehearsals &c. Perhaps it will be better when he comes back.

I wish I could write any letters worth having—which mine are not except because they are letters & that I know is much. I have been nervous & bored lately—& the last two days, to-day especially, I have a bad earache. I shall poultice the ear to-night as it is swelled & very painful. I am afraid you have some difficulty in reading mine. They are sad scrawls. Haji is going to Malvern to-morrow, he does not tell me for how long, so I guess for not long. I suppose he is going to Italy by his having gone to town yesterday to buy gloves & ordering new summer coat but he does not seem to like to be asked. He had a long letter from Mrs. Cholmeley[75] a few days ago, after reading which he said he thought he should go to Genoa before Rome This is all he has said to me about it.

Mr Mill had a note from Dr. Ruge telling about his writing projects but saying not a word in reply to our former invitation. Of course we do not know what this means—but I guess it is extra delicacy & waiting to be more asked. Whether to do anything more on the subject we have not yet decided with the present state of the weather making going out even in a carriage almost out of the question, & my being quite alone in the house all day I do not see how I could make it at all pleasant to them, or less than killing to me. I had almost a bad attack on Friday from a very short nervous incident combined with the cold. To-day it is mild but a perfect storm of wind & rain. Good night my darling

Monday morng

I poulticed the ear last night dear & hope it will be better to-day. For the

---

73. Postmarked 13 January 1857. LII/73.

74. Mr. Chester was the theater manager at Doncaster.

75. Mrs. Cholmeley apparently helped persuade Algernon Hardy to join a Barnabite convent in Italy along with her. All that we know of her is that she was close to Algernon and that he wouldn't show his mother his letters from her. See letters to Helen LII/105 and LIII(i)/8 and Harriet's letter to Algernon 27/111.

first time since you went there is a bright sun this morn^g, but also there is again a hard frost. I am well dearest & shall be better I dare say.

bless you!

Monday,[76] Jan. 12

I hope you will do all that is possible dear to cure your cold. It frightens me to think of your having a cold occupied as you are for I cannot see how you are to get rid of it. Do not be uneasy about me dearest as tho' but weakly I am certainly better than I usually am during the worst part of the winter, & especially considering how much less I am tended & taken care of than when you were at home. Davis is a most unfit servant for me or for anyone who wants an attendant. Her pretensions hid for a long while the fact that she is fit for nothing but a drudging house servant, & I suppose it is best one finds this out that she avoids in every way she can coming near me, so that I have difficulty in getting to see her during the whole week. She tries to tire me out of ringing for her by all sorts of excuses for not answering her bell. I believe she hopes to avoid needlework. I got my present cold & earache by standing ringing her bell. But even when she does come she is not fit for a maid to any lady she is so vulgar in feeling. I shall however let her stay as long as she likes, & should not bore you with the subject, which is an old one but that I write about what is going on at the time. I sat last night leaning my head on my hand, & it has been benumbed (my hand) ever since, so that I really find it difficult to write.

No doubt dear Glasgow is more tempting than Derby, but on the other side you seem sure of an engagement & to do a good deal of what you like at Derby, while Glasgow being going on trial, may fail altogether. Would it not be wisest to accept the Derby deferring going to Glasgow if you have the option. But I feel always that you are the best judge of this.

Mrs. Courtenay's[77] enmity does not affect Mr. Chester you see, since he continues to wish you to take the ~~same~~ best parts—& if he does continue to do so she must get over it. Perhaps she would not be so angry at Lady Macbeth or any more serious parts—it is the juveniles they all want to be. The blue satin should be trim^d with lace, berthe[78]

---

76. Postmarked 14 January 1857. LII/74.

77. In LII/70 and LII/72, Helen describes her first appearance as Juliet in *Romeo and Juliet*. Mrs. Courtenay was apparently playing Romeo and chose to die on the part of the stage on which the curtain fell. Mrs. Courtenay blamed Helen for not pulling her out of this awkward position before Juliet herself died. Mrs. Courteney was also jealous of Helen's getting the part of Juliet.

78. A deep falling collar attached to top of a low-necked dress.

fashion, at the ~~throat~~ neck & sleeves (turned up over the sleeve that is) either white or blk lace—white is prettier. In modern dress there might be a wreath of white roses or a single white camelia in the hair. To make it very smart w^d require two lace flounces deep & high or puffs of blue tulle with bows of satin ribbon down each side. A white muslin low body looks very well—it requires to fit well & should be a little full round the top the narrower possible edging, standing up of an open pattern or else very scalloped.

You want a white satin—nothing tells more among other dresses & the skirt quite plain looks best. The blue satin skirt too will look very well quite plain sometime[s] but of course you require constant change White satin should not be poor <u>Nothing</u> w^d suit you better than pink satin—it suits dark hair at night. Juliet ought certainly to wear both white muslin & white satin. Desdemona white satin.

It is not nearly so cold as it was but it is never two days alike. Haji is gone to Malvern. He said he meant to go to Italy early in February.

I am very vexed to find that that scrapbook you remember of mine must be lost—I suppose stolen—as it is nowhere to be found—it contained so many good extracts & I had had it so long. I know I had it in this house. It is not likely that I took it to the Torquay is it? Well you tell me dear up to what date you have got Notes & Queries that I may take care to have them all right.

[along side of front page]
I fear his head is very bad. Adieu now my darling from your HM

Wednesday[79]

I so sorry dear that you will get no letter from me to-morrow—I fear you may be dissapointed or uneasy. I stayed in bed all yesterday on account of my earache & I had with it a good deal of fever, which is however all gone to-day. The earache is rather better, but I have no doubt will go away in a day or two—being up seems better for it than in bed—it was worse there much.

I do not know when I can best arrange to come to you,—tho' I want to do so very much. I told you Haji said he sh^d go early in Feb. unless Miss Fox would like to go, when he w^d defer it to suit her time, & seemed to wish me to write & ask her. I suppose he will be back from Malvern at the beginning of next week at latest. This only leaves a fortnight till the beginning of Feb^y & no doubt he w^d not think it kind

---

79. Postmarked 16 January 1857. LII/77.

for me to leave for that fortnight—yet this defers my seeing you for these weeks at least.

I suppose you will go to Derby next week. I hope you will take good & comfortable lodgings.

I cannot help thinking that Tragedy would more likely to attract audiences than such plays as Romeo & Juliet—that is than sentimental subjects. much must depend on the sort of audiences. If a working class audience are to be considered I think Tragedy & farce are the things they can understand & I think they always prefer real Tragedy. It seems as if managers are made to run upon the soft sentimental subjects by the actresses who all want to play love scenes. I w^d try to persuade Mr Chester to give Macbeth. It is altogether a mistake that you look too young for Tragedy, the moment great tragic feelings are expressed age disappears— this it does in your case You look very young as Juliet, but not so as Lady Macbeth.

You are exactly fitted to look Juliet (in white satin) I have no doubt you would soon do light comic well. Perhaps as few do those well as do Tragedy well, but the difference between pretty well & very well is not near so great or so easily distinguished in comedy as in Tragedy Comedy would be much more troublesome to dress, as in in your appearance should excite applause & pleasure before beginning to speak, while in Tragedy nobody who is interested notices or cares about the dress. Might you not persuade him to alternate Macbeth Othello Shylock & Juliet

Does it not seem better to go on where you can have the best parts constantly & so most practise, so long as this continues, supposing that you can go to the Glovers[80] afterwards? and now good night my darling— I wish I could think you were going to bed. I am quite anxious about your cold & hoarseness.

Thursday,[81] Jan 15

One can scarcely think that this offer will hold[.] it is such an engagement in the dark on the part of Mr Glover that, combined with the perfect freedom allowed as to time of beginning, it must mean I think that he feels himself just as free to put an end to the engagement as to begin it. But at all events it is just what you wished for and therefore I am so glad of it. You see Mrs. Stirling seems to suggest as best your going to Derby. What does she mean I wonder by his being sure not to

---

80. Mr. Glover was the theater manager in Glasgow (see Helen's letter, LII/60).

81. Postmarked 17 January 1857. LII/79.

be there long? As Mr. Chester has given you the best parts he could (has he not) it seems rather unhandsome to leave him in the lurch when he is counting on you for his opening. I do not know but hardly think this is the reason why Mrs. S says "it becomes a question whether ~~to go~~ or would be better to go to Derby for the sake of practise["]—It seems as tho' she recommends your doing so. I should be for going to Derby first, but still would have you judge independently of me. You might manage to get a few lessons from Mrs. S. before going to Glasgow I should think I will send you the letter back again dear as you may want to see it again. I think you should make a great point of not leaving with any unfriendly feeling in the minds of the different managers towards you. So that you could ask any service or friendly turn of them at any time, & this is the least reason for doing so it is so much pleasanter to be on friendly terms with them as I have no doubt you are for they both seem extremely well conducted & gentlemanly, so much more so than one fancied they would prove. Mr Chester is the best of the two. How you are hurried & I am afraid overworked—How I wish I could help you with all that needlwork—you <u>must</u> get it done for such as can be done for you. However much you are helped there is always enough to do in trying on & directing &c. Do dear get a woman to work. Adieu now my darling with a hundred kisses

Good night

The enclosed thing has come for you to-day I think you had better write the reply as I have sketched it on the other side (if you agree) on a sheet of good paper, without date or address & direct the envelope Mrs. [K—The G—B—] and I will send it by post. This seems the only thing to do as far as I can see. You sh^d send it off to me on Friday that there may be as little delay as possible. Haji is to return from Malvern to-morrow.

And now my dearest girl adieu with all possible love & blessings, Be pleased, Be happy & love me always as I love you, as you so often & sweetly tell me to love my darling Lily.

––––––––––––

Miss Taylor regrets that a previous engagement will prevent her having the pleasure of joining M^rs K's party on Tuesday the 3rd of February

(I can see nothing possible but this after much thinking) I enclose an envelope for you to address & return along with the note folded square unless on a smaller sheet

Friday,[82] Jan 16

I suppose you will be as busy & hurried till after Monday dear. I shall hear soon how you have decided about Derby. I am impatient to come to see you as soon as possible. you will tell me when you think best. I am pretty well, the ear is nearly well again I have got out of spirits about everything, but as I ~~am~~ do my utmost to argue myself into better in time I shall succeed. I have written to a woman, a servant, if she comes perhaps I shall try her, as it is the same thing as having no body in the house, this Davis[83] — her evident wish is to live in the kitchen & do the bedrooms & never see me if she can help it — This must naturally deter one from having the inclination to have the services done one needs. But on the other hand in one respect it might <u>suit</u> our present circumstances as I do not feel called on to say a word of when or where any of us go out, nor anything about it, which is quiet — & comfortable & it is a consideration — so that I only feel inclined to take another if very promising. I am delighted for you dear about the Glasgow offer & anxious to hear what you decide & if I can help you. I suppose you will get this on Sunday, & that you do not in any case leave before Tuesday, so that I can write on Monday but I will write so that it will not matter [if] it should be left behind

[manuscript has been cut at this point]

Saturday,[84] January 17

Your letter of today dearest put things in a different light to me, as I thought Mr Chester had given you the first part instead of to Mrs C. & that he would continue to do so. I suppose also he had or would pay what he promised. Have you ~~not~~ asked him for your money. You are fully entitled to tell him that you <u>must</u> <u>have</u> "you feel you are entitled to" either ~~practise~~ the <u>first</u> <u>parts</u> or <u>the</u> <u>salary</u> he promised (of course you are freed from any obligation toward him by his not keeping his engagement to you.) You will be able to judge when you hear from Mrs. Stirling how soon Mr. Glover wishes you to go, whether to go to Derby or not — but even if you do go you are not bound to stay all the six weeks. I conceive that you are quite free to leave any day with a day or two notice & quite free not to go to Derby if you don't like it. I will come & see you dearest

82. Postmarked 18 January 1857. LII/81.

83. Harriet's maid.

84. Postmarked 20 January 1857. On the envelope of Helen's letter LII/82, Harriet wrote, "not give the alternative / but insist on / Haji being there / can be left." LII/83.

whenever you think it a convenient time. If you go to Derby I will come there as soon as you like. If you go to Glasgow at once should you come to London first? Mrs. S evidently wishes you not, but I sh^d not care for that if you think it w^d be of use as she is very good natured — but she does not see in what she c^d be of use nor do I but that is of no consequence. If you go direct to Glasgow you will cross from the line of rail you are now on to the North Western line & I should think there is not a much nearer way than through Derby. Perhaps however it w^d be nearer to go to Sheffeild & thence to Manchester. Glasgow would be too far for me to venture alone, & too far for Mr M[ill] to be able to go with me unless when taking a holiday. In any case I hope to manage to see you before you go there. I shall hear from you about this when you know about Glasgow. It does not seem that Mr. Glover hurries you to go. But this is what Mrs. S is to tell you. I question all these particulars to help[.] you would not be going out of your way, or not much, in going to Derby, & I could easily come there at once. If you should not go there we must think of where to meet. I will not write again to Doncaster unless you tell me to (on 2^d thoughts I will write to Doncaster on Tuesday, but such a note as will not at all matter if left behind.)

I fully agree with you that you sh^d insist on L^y Macbeth. In case you are puzzled how to decide you might go to Derby telling him that you shan't stay if you don't have the parts you want.

When you have decided about Glasgow you had better write & engage.[85] I think 12/ a week & to find herself w^d be as much as she ever has got or expected, dont you?

I should think there is a very good chance of matching the satin — have you tried? As Mr Chester is so very cool, using you up with no return for it, I do not see why you should work so hard as two parts each evening — but you on the spot are the best judge about it. It seems all work & no play. If you go to Derby had you not better take lodgings which would do for me too? If you do I need not go to the Inn when I come. You know I always feel a tolerably good water closet a sine qua non — but I know it is very probable it can't be had, especially in the country, it is hard enough to get it at the watering places. Still it might be tried for. However, I hardly expect you could find it.

Shall I try to match the satin if you send me a pattern I will. Or if you prefer it you might get the same sent by post from where you bought it, I suppose by returning a Post office order or stamps for the amount.

---

85. Harriet may be referring to Davidson, the seamstress Helen used earlier.

Sunday Even^g.

I have been lying all the eveng on <u>your</u> sofa, that one which you so sweetly
& laboriously covered for me yourself. I have never looked at it without
thanking & loving & blessing you for it from the bottom of my heart. It
was so truly loving of you my dearest girl & now she is away I lie on it
& rest & think of her. I have had it brought down into the dining room.
Adieu now darling, I shall hear from you in the morning.

The weather is milder & my ear ache is gone.

Tuesday,[86] Jan 20

I felt more hurt than I can express by your letter of Sunday (received
yesterday) Indeed it has made me quite ill. I do not know what I can
write without the chance of offending you if that sentence in my last
about Mr. Chester so nearly did so. I thought I was saying precisely what
you would agree in that bit of general reflection on the subject of managers. I did not think it at all <u>necessary</u> to say it, nor mean it as any
information or lesson to you—The only objection I should have thought
you could have found to it would be that it was self-evident, but when
one writes freely one as often says things knowing that we agree about
them, as for the opposite reason & this was the case with that very
unfortunate remark of mine ~~about~~. I who have nothing to <u>tell</u> in my
letters should find it difficult to write constantly if I need to take care to
say only what is well worth saying.

My next letter after that one was altogether looking at the other side
of the question, I do not know if you would feel annoyed at that also, but
you might & should see that in both cases I was as I thought feeling with
you on the subject & expressing what I fancied you were feeling. Your one
letter gave me the impression that he was not behaving well to you, your
next gave the contrary impression, in both cases I felt & wrote in consequence. I must be more careful how I write.

This Glasgow expedition seems to promise all that you desire—may it
keep its promise dearest! I fear you will arrive terribly tired out—after
being up so late on Tuesday night to start before seven on Wednesday for
a 10 or 11 hour journey! I hope at least you will get a good nights rest
after arriving. I know nothing to suggest about Mr. Glover from all Mrs.
S says I suppose it will be quite a different thing from what you have had
hitherto—I should hope also much less laborious as well altogether different. I shall be very anxious to know how it turns out. It is a sad distance

86. No indication of year. LII/86.

to me, I seem to lose you doubly so far away, but if you are better off, that is less overworked & more as you like, that will make amends to me.

I fancy even if I could get so far as Glasgow it would not be the easy thing for me that going to either of the other places would have been. as Mr. Glover & his family would have to be regarded as acquaintance. I was extremely sorry for poor Mr. Chester it made <u>my</u> heart ache to hear of his misfortune. I surely need not say that of course you could not take his money. & By the bye you must want money but I will not enclose it till I get the address, as this will go only to the Post office. I shall get no letter from my dear girl on Thursday! & do not ever write the first day you are there if as I expect you will be very tired & excessively busy. I know so well what harassing work looking for lodgings is & made work by the thought that one <u>must</u> write after it. Do not feel this dear, for much as I love your letters I would rather wait than have one at that cost to you. Adieu now my dearest girl with a thousand loves & kisses.

[upside down]

P. S.
Please dear do not direct here this week but to the I. H. Your letter of Monday numbered <u>15</u> sh^d have been 16.[87]

The weather is warmer tho gloomy (& very wet). but my ear which seemed well has again grown painful. & torments me. But of course it will not last long.

Wednesday[88]

I have thought of you all day & of where you are on your journey so hoping that you are well & will not be too tired. It makes me very unhappy to think that you will get an unhappy letter of mine to-morrow but I could not have written otherwise if I wrote at all your letter had[,] besides that about being annoyed at what I said about Mr Chester[,] an unkind tone as also has this last about money, showing that you have not seen & felt as you should have done all that I have said & shown & wrote to you not long ago about it. You feel indeed differently to what I wish you when you think it necessary to put in "your" in this sentence "at my expense (that is yours)" and you must have done so in that letter because you were

---

87. Harriet and Helen numbered their letters to each other, presumably so that they would know if one were lost in the post.

88. Postmarked 23 January 1857. LII/88.

angry with me. Then your refusal to have Davi[d]son[89] after my so continually wishing you to have her, & to have had someone at Doncaster. I
scarcely wrote a letter in which I did not say so. then the unkind formality
of talking always of "if Mr M will be so kind" which "if" refers in this
case to what he does every day of his life namely bring & take letters
between us. I feel these unkindnesses (the last is a trifle) in your otherwise
so sweet & dear letters & I say what I feel in hopes that you also will wish
that there we should feel one in all that is possible, but especially on the
about money & I shall not be happy or think you love me as I thought
you did unless you tell me that you feel as I do, that is that we all I &
you have is absolutely in common, between us, & that you will use it as
if it was only yours. This is what I want you to do what I shall feel very
much deserted by your love if you do not.

[inserted portion]

I must add there another sentence because I feel it so much. How am I to
continue to feel that sweet confidence in your love you gave me years ago
when you said do not care for the future I would work for us both & we
shall always be able to do together—& the same tho' on a different subject
you said in one of your first letters from Newcastle, & it has been the great
source of my cheerfulness ever since. Remember if you do not prove that
you feel so now, how could I act so at any future time.

And now dear to answer yours—when I got Mrs. S's letter I took for
granted that you would go at once as you did, there could be no doubt
about it.

I did not write to Doncastle yesterday because I know that you would
leave to-day. It was only when I was uncertain that I meant to do so. You
say "do not think me selfish for writing letters full of nothing but myself
& asking your dear help" you know darling that is just what I wish & like
best & what shows your love & confidence in mine. Write exactly as you
have written dear one for your letters are all that I love with that one
exception.

I hope you will write for Davidson as soon as convenient. I fear you
may have mistaken (tho' it is strange you sh[d]) my saying give her 12/
instead of 14/ & have thought it was to save the money—this it was not,
but because I thought (I am very likely wrong) that it was not desirable
for your own object to give the impression of being indifferent to cost. As

---

89. Mrs. Davidson, Helen's seamstress. See Helen's letters, LII/87 and LII/92, for more on the
controversy over whether or not Mrs. Davidson's services were too expensive for Helen to afford.

far as my feeling is concerned I would rather that you never took any salary at all but had everything you like & want, as an amateur would do. It has made me very much less happy since you took poorer lodgings. If you really care for my comfort you will show it by letting me be able to feel that you have as much comfort as if you were at home as far as that is possible.

I should certainly mention Mr Chester's wish to Mr. Glover & write to tell to express regret if unfavorable. I should be glad to hear Mr. Glover could employ him. I hope you have not much difficulty in reading my scrawl my hand is so stiff & benumbed that I cannot write better for more than a few words at a time.

Thursday,[90] Jan. 22

A day without a letter from my dearest Lily feels quite strange & dull. How I hope my dear one you are well and have succeeded in to-days arduous work. Perhaps I shall have a letter to-morrow to tell me how you got through the long cold journey, but I can hardly wish to have it because I think you will have been so hurried & harassed to-day. It is very cold here again, Haji has just arrived & found it intensely cold travelling, & I so dread you may have done so in that 11 hours! It is a long way to have you from me & I am so anxious for you. You will not be able to tell me much just yet I dare say — it will perhaps be some days before it is settled what you are to do — but tell me anything & everything you do my darling as I am most interested in all, great & small, only never think it necessary to write when you are tired or hurried.

I have had a return of the pain in the ear the last few days which I thought had quite gone, & this gives me the headache so that I am fit for nothing.

Adieu now my dearest — she will give me an address soon, but meanwhile I write to the Post office which, I hope is not far off. I fear the Post hours will be earlier at that great distance & therefore not so convenient for you. be sure you consider your comfort before anything for that is the way to cause mine. Adieu darling.

P.S. I have meant to say several times before that no one reads your letters but myself. This makes always some difference in the way one writes. Yours are never seen except by me, unless perhaps one in a dozen I have shown to Haji when I thought it suitable & interesting to him.

Friday morning

You may see dear by the sort of letter or rather no letters that I end that

---

90. Postmarked 24 January 1857. LII/90.

I am good for nothing. The headache continues & also the pain in the eyes which makes me almost unable to read. I am dreadfully out of spirits & so nervous I suppose I can write nothing worth sending I hope I shall get better. Haji looks dreadfully ill as tho' his excursion had done him more harm than good. I thought he seemed glad of being home. Mr. M. too is poorly. The beginning of my present state, was crying on Monday, then thinking never-mind all these tristesse[91] dear one. I will be better to-morrow, if you are well

Friday night,[92] Jan. 23

I cannot tell you the good your letter of Thursday (& Wednesday) has done me. I have been ever since Monday quite ill with anxiety, & growing worse & worse each day. I have feared you would be lonely & badly off there—that you might be pained by my letter & either unable to answer it from hurry or else doing so at the cost of overhurry & fatigue. Now I have got it & I feel excessively relieved knowing that you are safe & the people kind. I have written three times to the Post Office dear—the third letter would be no loss, as I was too poorly last night to write more than a few words. I did not know how much anxiety about you & fear that my letters might pain you had to do with my illness till I got this of yours—now I begin to breath[e] freely again.

I shall still be anxious to hear how you got on with the people there, if you are comfortable, & all you do—but not that fear & indefinite anxiety—I felt before I got your letter. I thought you judged best to go at once after Mrs S's letter & am so sorry you felt uncomfortable about not hearing from me before deciding. It was indeed a terrible journey infinitely worse than I expected tho' that was bad enough, & I wonder how you could bear it without knocking up. I think you must surely have looked very tired & poorly as the first impression for the Glovers—however perhaps not, you seem to bear up thro' any amount of fatigue. But sleepless nights should be avoided. I cant [sic] bear to think of you all alone at the Inn on Wednesday night after such a day. If I had known it at the time I should have been obliged to set off & come to you I think. You write so well that I see exactly all you do my darling. You say just what I wish about that painful expression dearest—I did think it possible that it was a careless expression, & not meant seriously that you could be offended at me. No more need be said about that for you say all in these words "How utterly impossible any <u>real</u> offence or annoyance is"

---

91. Sadness or melancholy.

92. Postmarked 25 January 1857. LII/91.

And now I must say Adieu and she will get no more—from me before Tuesday bless her continue to direct to I.H.[93] for the present dearest & Adieu & good night—some few <u>good</u> nights I hope at all events you will get before recommencing the late ones

    my dearest girl!

Sunday,[94] Jan 25

My own dearest girl your letter has done me all possible good, but it makes me long intensely that this could go to you directly to pray you on no account to be out of spirits or to think of it more. All you say is so true & so perfectly natural—how I sympathize in your putting in words in haste, without waiting to choose in order not to seem grandiose & consequential, & how I love her for wishing not to seem so, as well as for always writing so much & so fully without waiting to choose ~~the best~~ expressions (the <u>best</u> are just what you always use the simplest & truest[)]. I know so well that feeling of writing consequential expressions for I have found I have done it very much in my letters to you, as it is a consequence of writing in haste—those expressions are often easiest & shortest & so come ~~of themselves~~ instead of longer & better sentences I think it is because being indefinite they fill the gap when it w^d take time to express oneself precisely.

My precious do not say you do not know how to speak & write as I like & so make mistakes in your effort to do so—you shall find that you always speak & write exactly as I like as you do in this sweet letter. I see now exactly how it all happened & shall never mistake again any thing you write.

You say 'it w^d be a happiness if you could add to my comfort & not diminish it by spending so much' but dearest—will you beleive me as I beleive you when I say that the only comfort I wish for or pleasure I enjoy in the spending money is when it is some way anyway connected with you—and now that you are away I more & more feel all my interest & pleasure concentrated in what you are doing, in your happiness & pleasure. The only way I wish to spend money is on you, in whatever way best pleases you, & knowing now what that is, that is how I wish to spend. If you would but know how true it is that the greatest good you can do me after your letters is to use the money quite freely. If you do not you will see I shall not, & then nobody will have any pleasure from it. I am sure Glasgow will be very expensive for you on account of the greater pretensions both social & theatrical of Mr. Glover & his family, The large town,

---

93. India House, where JSM worked.

94. Postmarked 2[?] January 1857. LII/94.

& of course larger theatre &c. I hope to hear that you have or will write for Davidson, as soon as you know what he decides & if you are likely to get on well with him. I am very anxious for you my darling. I feel as if you are more alone & more separated than when you were so much nearer. Tell me just what you feel about my coming, as I will come off any day if you wish it & as soon as you wish. I fear you may sometimes want my advice when I am not there to give it—but you have always judged as I sh^d in the particular case.

I cannot tell you how earnestly I wish that the Glasgow engagement may prove all that you hoped & expected. Ah if it depended on me you should succeed to your heart's content. Do know me better my darling than to think I could possibly wish you not to succeed for my good. I make myself so entirely one with you that what you wish I wish without any reserve, or would do all possible to help. How I wish I could but shield you from every dissapointment. But do not dear one be discouraged if all does not turn out as you hoped—I so hope it will, but the sudden engagement seemed almost too good to be true. I shall ~~hear~~ be very anxious to hear what sort of person Mr Glover seems to be. How can I write dear to make you know how much I love you. I will never mistake your meaning again so be at ease in writing—all I wish is that you will write just as you have done. with the exception of that one line all your letters have been perfect to my mind—instead of as you say seeming unkind, from hurry, they are all I can desire. Do not say you were extravagant, you never have been, & if you love me you will spend much more & be really comfortable, as well as buy not only all you ~~either~~ want but all you would like.

I fear the Post office will be troublesome—more distant, & earlier hours. Do not let it be too much so, but if necessary write seldomer. I fear too your lodgings are not good enough—should you not have two rooms?

I hope you will have got my Sat^y letter on Sunday & so send another note for that tiresome woman the compliments seem quite indispensable & how I could have omitted them I do not know.

It must be Miss T presents her compliments & regrets &c Saturday's letter was addressed <u>street</u> instead of <u>Road.</u>

Adieu darling adieu

Monday,[95] Jan 26

I have got your long letter of yesterday dearest girl but it pains me to think that I have caused you so much labour & taken up so much time.

---

95. Postmarked 28 January 1857. LII/96.

You want rest now while you have a short time of respite from hard work, & you must not let writing to me tire you. You have said every thing possible on the subject of that letter dear & there is but one thing I would say about it & this is that you mistake the words I spoke of they were "I was half inclined to be annoyed by what you said about Mr. C[hester]"[96] but as soon as you mention the haste & hurry, how you feel "now if I can get on quickly enough I shall be able to say something about this & this—" I know all that so well &—it is so exactly true & it is so impossible to write much or freely if one chooses expressions[;] all I wish is that you will write anyhow, just as you can, & if anything seems to me to need it I will just ask you in my next what it means—so let us think no more of that pain.

About Davidson dear one I did not think her unnecessary at Newcastle, I pressed you to get somebody both before you went & before you got her. I think if you do much at Glasgow you will need her more & more dress[es] of all kinds, as it is a place & circumstance of much more pretension—all the others will no doubt be people of much more both knowledge & pretension & you will care more about their opinion. If you will only have her directly [when] you feel any want of her, or if it would give you pleasure to have her, I shall be satisfied. I wish you were not so far from the Theatre. I think you will find it better to move nearer if you can. The fleas must be in the bedding or closet most likely or room, for you could not get them on the journey, one or two is likely but not many & lasting. Have you told the landlady of it. I enclose sketches of the 2 notes you asked me but you must judge if they are the right sort of thing—If not I will think of something different. I do not like your having to take the letters to the Post Office every day it is a terrible burden—what can be done? does a Postman come round? How far is it. I think if you go to the Glovers again I would wear the little black silk & malachite brooche. I am so happy to find you say you are stronger—have you any of the bad symptoms you used to have? Your letters are the great event & pleasure of my day, indeed I care for nothing else. I think I am very well indeed for the season—better than usual in a cold winter. The earache is all but gone, but the stiff hand will no doubt last long, I got it by leaning my ear on my hand with the elbow on the table. This sort of benumbing always lasts long. Haji says he always has it from holding his arm up. He looks very ill but seems in better spirits. He says he is going on the 4 Feb Was it not a stupid mistake of mine about that womans note. I hope to

96. See Helen's letter LII/93 for more on the misunderstanding about Mr. Chester, the theater manager at Doncaster.

get another copy to-morrow? I must say Adieu now my sweet girl & write more to-morrow—

[first additional sheet]

Miss T. requests Mrs. D[avidson] will send her the[97]   which she (say how to be sent)

   Miss T does not at present require Mrs. D. (or require assistance) but will write again if having more to do she should need her services (or her assistance) or simply, need her.

This is something of the sort but you who know the woman can best judge of the right tone of your note.

[second additional sheet]

Dear Sir,
   According to your request I mentioned to Mr. Glover your wish to assist him at Glasgow but I regret to say without result. I am Dear Sir
                                                            Yours Truly
                                                                HT

(This of course is supposing that Mr G. shows a decided negative to the proposition)

                                                    Tuesday Eveng[98]
I have now got yours enclosing the Knill note[99] & after all the former one must go—for it is impossible to send this, with compliments to M^{rs} K[nill]—This makes the note positively rude—the former one is curt & im-polite perhaps—but this mentioning her twice, seems purposely to omit him.
   I am sorry for it as it will be supposed perhaps that we are somewhat affronted, either by her not calling or not asking us, & I wished to avoid any appearance of that sort. I meant & (I think said) it to be. Miss T[aylor] presents her compliments & regrets &c—
   However as one <u>must</u> go now it is no use saying all this about it.

---

97. Harriet leaves blanks for Helen to fill in.

98. Postmarked 29 January 1857. LII/99.

99. Harriet and Helen are still deliberating about the correct response to a party invitation from the Knills which arrived shortly after the new year. See Helen's letter, LII/97.

I must only write a few words this evening dear as I have been out to town with Haji buying his things for his journey & having been very cold & dined late. I am sleepy & tired & so must wait to reply to the questions about dress matters till to-morrow I hope dearest I shall not dissapoint you when, like to-day, my letters are short & empty. In part I think the real reason I cannot write to-night is more a discussion which Haji set up on the subject of note writing & manners in general, which as of course he took the opposite side of every thing I said (tho all I said was in the effort to say only what he would I thought agree in) has made me a little nervous, as any discussion with Haji is sure to do.

Wednesday morning and a most severe frost & excessive cold. Adieu my darling I hope I shall write more & better this eveng.

Wednesday,[100] Jan 28

I have got your sweet long letter dearest & a thousand thanks for it—I do not know how you contrive to find time to write so much. I feel it making hay while the sun shines knowing that any day you may be set to work so as to be unable to give me such nice long letters. I am amused by your descriptions of all the people, I seem to know them all—How curious that is (which I have always found just as you say) that people who won't talk about any large or serious subject will not either talk <u>simply</u> about common ones. You are quite right in saying that if you talk on educated subjects i[t] is likely to seem pretentious, but not I think that to talk on common subjects <u>simply</u> would seem vulgar. It is only the best bred english who even ~~say~~ talk in the company of strangers as they would alone. They feel no interest in any but domestic subjects & they do not speak out about those because they want to appear more than the truth. I shall be glad if you find Miss Keeley[101] or any of them at all agreable acquaintances. I think a girl must have had either some education or some breeding for you to like her. I should think there must be many with the last. I ~~must~~ will try now dear to answer some of your questions about dress—Yes I agree that you may as well wait for the white satin till you want it as you think so. I feared you must be inconvenienced for want of it, it is a thing so generally useful. The grey may suit some persons better, I do not think it w^d you. As to wearing Berthe[102] always—the various trimmings you call so are generally not called berthe—every way of trimming is

---

100. Postmarked 30 January 1857. LII/100.

101. Helen first mentions Miss Keeley, an actress, in LII/98, but her most vivid description of the gossip and Helen's defence of her is in LII/104 and LII/114.

102. A deep falling collar.

berthe according to you. I w^d not wear always the same sometimes perhaps nothing then there is a piece of lace palling[103] over of different widths—the way you speak of covering the short sleeves is very pretty, but it does not do to get known by one only style, tho' you can wear the same often. The flat folds of gauze or other light materials forming a point in front & on each shoulder is pretty, but needs very good dressmaking to set quite flat for it [is] ugly if ill made. One row of old lace round the neck with the same turned up at the edge of the short sleeve. I know of no other ways—perhaps 2 little very narrow edgings run together in the middle round the top so as to be scarcely visible, to take of a bare look when nothing else is worn.

Yes I think both white net to loop up & also worked white net with bows w^d make a pretty change. You will always look well in muslin if in nice order (a most essential condition) & I think pink would suit you at night better than blue—but not a _pale_ pink it should be a bright full pink.

The Swiss dress, blue merino petticoat with rows 4 or 5 of blk velvet, the lowest broadest & so each a _little_ narrower upward—the length very nearly to the ancles, as long as you think will do. The tuckes of the most transparent Swiss muslin. This dress will require I _should_ _think_ a bit of red some where, perhaps a red bow on the head, or a red rose at the breast or red velvet at the throat. The plain style will always suit you best, but avoiding bareness.

Thanks dearest for what you say about getting something for me. The only kind I should use would be sleeves of a very open gay pattern something of the bright effect of those of M Laings.[104] no collar suits me which is not capable of being made up like a frill—so that it ought to be a pair of sleeves & the same pattern worked on a strip of muslin about 5/8 lhs[105] long. This probably cannot be got—& then as I must certainly come & see you before long we can talk of it then. If there were a fire could you easily get out? see & tell me. I will look out & send you some Prescriptions you have not got you know of course that if there were a sufficient reason you could send a letter to the Post.

I think it will be best to tease him _moderately_, not to seem content to do nothing, but to show plainly that if you are not employed it is not for want of wishing it. I dare say you find it troublesome to read this writing but my hand is both benumbed & also so weak it will hardly hold

---

103. Palling is fine cloth spread over something.

104. Mrs. Marianne Laing, a relative of Harriet's.

105. Lengths.

anything I dare say it is somehow nervous & will go off in time. Tho' I
have got through the winter wonderfully well so far, yet the being almost
constantly in the position of bending over the fire & always reading causes
many temporary feelings of ailment—but I am quite surprised how I have
got thro' so very cold & long a winter so well. There is no doubt too that
writing causes the benumbed hand & shall I fear have often to write but
a few words. When I do so you must know that the only reason is the
fatigue of writing. I had a note from M[arianne] L[aing] the other day
asking how I was & so on—and asking me to come over & see them, by
which I suppose she means a sort of spending the day or part of it. This
at some future time when the weather is better I will do & perhaps ask
her to spend a day here first but in either case it is almost necessary to
explain where & why you are absent. I do not know if there is any objection
to do this—I have always thought M.L. friendly on the whole, & I have
always found her honorable, so that if I said dont publish a thing abroad
I beleive she would not. It is trying to seem to make a secret of anything
which people ask & I would rather avoid seeing people than have to do
it, as that is a shorter plan. I am so vexed I ever said anything to Mr.
Fox[106] now I see what a gossip he is & among a theatrical set too; so that
what he told would be known to any body directly. Not that I care, but
still it is surely better not. Dont you think so? Good night darling.

Thursday Eveng[107]

I think it would be better for you to write direct to Davidson, & to have
the berthe sent to you. I do not think it matters that you are at Glasgow
as the last sentence shows that it is not want of good will that hinders
your having her. I will enclose a sketch. Haji went to-day to Newington
they were out but came in soon having been to call on the elders Annie[108]
& they seemed he thought curious (as far as they ever choose to seem so)
about the younger Annie[109] who is still there they said & whom she
praised much. Haji brought a little basket sealed up, & with a paper saying
a rem[ce] from Aunt Sarah[110]—you had better send me a note to forward in
return. I will enclose what I think. It strikes me that the postage of the

---

106. William Fox.

107. Postmarked 31 January 1857. On the back of the envelope of Helen's letter LII/102,
Harriet wrote, "consolation / Sunday / Texts / I affirm / open both ears."

108. Probably referring to Harriet's aunt, Anne Hardy Richardson.

109. Annie Ley was Caroline Hardy Ley's daughter.

110. Harriet's aunt, Sarah Hardy Gloyn.

Berthe & sleeves will be ~~very~~ large if not pre-paid ~~beforehand~~ I do not know how you mean to arrange about paying Davidson, as I suppose you owe her something for it, if you will have a payment to send her, of course the postage can be then included, but I notice you say nothing in your note about either postage or paying her. I cannot make the sketch I send run neatly from not knowing those particulars Aunt Sarah's note must be in a directed envelope 4 Adeu Terrace Stoke Newington.

If Mr Chester's note is not gone it might be made much less short by what you mention now, that M^r C had spoken of a Mr Turner & that Mr Glover[111] said that Mr T. being still with him he does not require any one for that class of parts. When you ask me what to say in a note you do not give me those particulars which would enable me to write one. I beat my brains to think of any thing possible to say to make poor Mr Chester's note more gentle while entirely keeping up your dignity. I was obliged to take for granted a simple and curt negative on Mr Glovers part—but having this good & palliative reason to give it should on all accounts have been given. Of course Chester will think that Turner is gone, & therefore will not know of having the chance of applying for the place whenever he does go.

I can send you the box you packed up when you want it The little brown silk is perhaps the next best after that blk silk to go to the Glovers in next to that the black silk. I so hope to hear that you have lost the cold It is a very hard frost here for the last two days & seems likely to last My hand is worse & I could not write except in this careless way. It will go off with time no doubt. I manage to keep warm by never leaving the dining room. Haji has seemed better than when he came back. Good bye now my darling I w^d write more but for my hand.

[written on the side of the page]
The ear is well at last.

[new page]
Friday Morn^g It is colder than ever. The ther at 36 in my room before the fire. How will you keep warm dear & I hate to think of you going out to the Post with your cold. I think you must send the landlady with the letter. But a letter put in on Sunday will reach me as soon as Saturday. I

---

111. Mr. Chester was the theater manager at Doncaster. In Helen's letter, LI/101, she refers to Mr. Turner as "the actor of Mr. Chester's class of parts who Mr. Chester thought was gone. Mr. Glover was the theater manager in Glasgow.

feel puzzled whether to put "Blackheath" to Aunts letter. If you think best not put only "Sunday morn^g" as date. This no doubt <u>suggest</u>[s] the idea of absence wh as yet they have not got, but it does not <u>prove</u> it—but the long time between now & yr writing is likely to suggest it combined with no date or place. If you really dislike putting Blackheath why dont send if possible the Aunts note by return of post.

[separate draft by HTM of potential reply]
My dear Aunt,

Accept my best thanks for your kindness in thinking of me <u>and</u> for the pretty basket Haji brought me from you. We were very glad to hear so good an account of your <u>and</u> my Aunts health <u>and</u> that you have not suffered from the long continued cold weather. Mama joins in wishing you many happy new years with my dear Aunt

Your always affectionate
Lily

Blackheath
Sunday

[separate draft by HTM of note to seamstress]
Miss T requests M^{rs} D[avidson] will send her the lace Berthe and sleeves by Post directed   please to pre-pay the parcel & send by post an account of what   & including the postage & it shall be sent by Post Office order Miss T does not at present require Mrs D. but will write again if having more to do she should need her assistance.

Friday[112]
I am so vexed that I have not sent you the newspaper before as I fully meant to do. I do not wonder I never remembered it, the days & evenings have been so cut up, & I have felt so out of my regular circumstances that I have forgot every thing. It has again become very cold. The last three days have been hard frosts & looking as tho it had set in for a six weeks frost but Mr Mill has been out this even^g & brings word that he thinks there are signs of the frost going. If only it would prove so! I have begun to suffer as I find now I always do after a few days of extremely cold weather from pain of the back—this is caused by always <u>sitting</u>, & that always in the same position. There is I see no help for this except in a change of weather. I manage to keep warm & to keep the cough in

---

112. Postmarked 1 February 1857. LII/105.

moderation by sitting all day in the dining room which is really warm—
but constant sitting never does suit me even in warm weather—in fact if
one observes I never do sit long together—the habit of passing so much
of ones time in ones bed room as I do in fine weather prevents long sitting
as you know. But if this frost goes I shall get better of this, & otherwise
I am unusually well. I am always making plans for coming to see you,
which I must do before very long, after the little bustle made by Haji's
departure is over. He is full of interest in all the preparations & I have one
day to choose a number of waistcoats, another coats, twice to town to buy
travelling cap, umbrella Portmanteau,[113] Bag &c. To-day I have been
superintending a lot of pommade[114] making. He has all sorts of commis-
sions to take out for Mrs. Cholmeley[115] He is to take her silver salt spoons
& a bracelet, which objects do not seem exactly in accordance with her
professed great choice to enter a convent. She writes very often very long
letters to Haji which he says take him some days to read, but he never
shows them to me nor mentions their contents. But I only write this gossip
by way of a talk with you. Mr Thornton[116] has suddenly been attacked
with a head complaint something like Haji's apparently & has got a leave
of six months & is off to Italy. Mr. Mill has had this last week some new
kind of head complaint which w^d oblige him to leave off work if it
continued, but I hope it will not as I think it w^d be very dull for him to
be unable to write.

The pattern of satin looks very pretty & will do very well for the front,
tho' that is a style I do not like, yet among others it will make a change.
You sh^d certainly try to match the blue. I should think you would be able
to match it at Glasgow as it is an easy colour to match. Continue at present
to address as you do—& now Good bye & good night my dearest dear girl

Sunday,[117] Feb 1

I hope you have got the Exa[118] and Times dear. It w^d be as well to order
the Exa of a news man near you as no doubt it is regularly received there
by railway & so you w^d get it earlier.

---

113. French type of suitcase.

114. Ointment for skin and lips.

115. Mrs. Cholmeley apparently helped persuade Algernon Hardy to join a Barnabite convent
in Italy along with her.

116. Probably William Thomas Thornton (1813–80), a co-worker of JSM at the India House.

117. Postmarked 3 February 1857. LII/107.

118. *Examiner.*

How disgusting the conduct of those two girls towards Miss Keeley.[119]
Of course you made her see how differently you felt—but you do not tell
me enough about it. I cannot help thinking that you will buy much better
at shops where Mrs Glover[120] does not deal. For 5/ a yard you ought to
get—a very good satin—Mrs Stirling would say too good, & if she gave
that for her niece I should guess the shopman has his own reasons for
changing it. I do not think it too much for you to give, as you know I
told you before I think you had better have a good one as it makes so
much more effect, but I should advise seeing what they have at other
shops, the best shops, before buying. You may perhaps feel it necessary as
a matter of policy to buy as Mrs. G. recommends—I cannot of course
judge of that—if you see that it is so of course that is best, as not to offend
her is of more importance than the dress, & she may very likely be offended
if you do not take her advice. The pattern you sent and which I returned
was a remarkably poor thin satin (tho a pretty colour & very fit for the
purpose you meant) but I supposed it must be very cheap, I think we
should get better much for the money in London. Perhaps silks are dear
in the North—we know that muslins are their specialty. If you should
find that they will work a cape of ones own pattern I will send or bring
a pattern of mine.

How do you think we should do about lodging when I come? I propose
to come with Mr. M[ill] to York on a Sat^y and he would see me off to
Glasgow on the Sunday, but perhaps it would not do to arrive there on a
Sunday Even^g if all we hear about shutting up places in Scotland on
Sundays is true. It w^d perhaps be necessary to stay at York till Monday &
then come on. Which is the best Inn at Glasgow? I should propose to
return on the Sat^y (fortnight) so as to meet him at York on that day. This
twelve days stay would be long to stay at an Inn—If it is the way of the
place to let lodgings for short times & there are any good ones to be got,
that would be best. Is there a Water closet to yours on the same floor?

I am anxious about your cold. I do not know how you are to get rid of
a cold with such continual going out. It makes me very uneasy when I
hear of your having one. a neglected cold may so easily lead to serious
mischief. How I wish I could persuade you of this truth. And it is a sort
of danger against which youth is no protection, rather the contrary. It was
a 10 not 5? I sent you dear but no doubt it arrived safe & you had not
looked at it.

While we were at dinner to-day a lovely hare came & sat on the snow

---

119. An actress, about whom Helen had been relating gossip to HTM.

120. The wife of the theater manager in Glasgow.

on the edge of the lawn just before the window, then the pretty creature skipt away across the lawns & into the shrubbery. The whole country is covered with deep snow for the last two days & a hard frost. I hope it will not last.

[written on sides of pages]

I do not think I should think the blue too scanty & I am sure I should think it prettier all blue than with the white front—unless for a change
Good night my dearest girl be sure you tell me how the cold is?

Monday,[121] Feb. 2
I have got all her little notes and shall send the choicest to-morrow—They are all so neat.

It seems to me very strange about the pay—that he should pay people whom he gives nothing to do seems incredible—we shall see what happens next week Meanwhile I hope you will not be wanted till your cold is gone, but I fear going out to take letters to the post is the worst thing you can do for it, & so I hope (much as I shall miss them) that you will not write till you are well again dear. If I do not get a letter for a day or two I shall know the reason.

If there should come any hitch about the pay, you would probably rather stay & act with Mr. Glover's company without pay than elsewhere with, & it is the use of not requiring pay that you can take your choice freely. It would be mere form to care about pay if you can get what you want better without it. You say you shd be glad of it (the pay) if you were sure I do not dislike it—but I do not dislike it dear, about that part of the matter I am indifferent. You speak of blue & white patterns dear, but none came, probably you were prevented.

As the Glovers seem going to make the engagement bona fide you had best I shd think do anything Mrs. G. seems to wish in the way of buying with her &c. I told you I do not think 5/ a yard too much for a white satin. I am sure you quite exaggerate what you call your incapacity for being pleasant with those people—only take the lead yourself sometimes, as when there is a gap in their talk, & talk of artistic subjects—the dresses in old pictures for instance, Holbein Vandyke, Watteau—discussing them with an eye to the taste of the company. The more you talk the more ~~better~~ they will think of you, & on all accounts this must be an object where you are so connected with people. I scratched thro' _better_—you would see

121. Postmarked 4 February 1857. LII/108.

why. The sort of women like Miss Bland as far as they like any body, which nearly not at all, like those whom they see inspire consideration & certainly Mr. G must prefer a girl of educated mind & taste if only as an assistance in the choice of ~~subject~~ plays? At all events I return to my opinion that the more you talk the better for all parties as they say.

I gave Haji your message & I saw he took the little book up with him. I dare say he will send a message to-morrow. He has been reading it every even^g so it must be an opportune present.

My ear has got quite well dear & the cough is very slight, but I am beginning to suffer from the consequences of the lasting excessive cold. Each day we hope there are signs of a change but as yet only hope.

I do not think my hand will get better till warm weather comes, or not cold at least—I think it is partly caused by the same which causes the ~~aching~~ pains of the back—the constant one uneasy sitting position. This sort of numbness is common from constrained positions I think we may expect this frost to go soon, it has been such a long cold winter, we can hardly have a long frost still to come. Good night now my darling girl.

Do not ever put more than one stamp dear. <u>three</u> are always useless—2 or 4 go with the weights

She has got her numbering one in advance[122]

Tuesday,[123] Feb 3

I have no letter to-day but I make up my mind it is because you have done as I wished dear & not gone out while you are so poorly. I shall be anxious to hear that you are better but still I would rather be without hearing than you should go out in the cold. I may feel sure, may I not? that if you were ill you would send off a letter for me directly, of course directed here and I should set off instantly.

It continues very cold & the snow remains on the ground, but I do not think it <u>so</u> cold, & therefore I expect a change of weather. Haji is occupied with his packing as he goes to-morrow I suppose he will write to thank you for your present. I enclose the railway cheque, if you sign it at the back (where it is marked <u>signature</u>) he will pay it to your account at [Prescott's] when you return it.

I wish you good night my dearest girl with such anxious wishes that it is & will be a good night for you. It is a great comfort to know that your room is warm, & it will be the greatest comfort to hear that you are

---

122. Harriet is telling Helen that the numbering on her letters is out of order.

123. Postmarked 5 February 1857. LII/110.

better & will soon be well again. Adieu now darling with a thousand loves & kisses.

Wednesday night[124]
I have now dear got your letters of Monday & Tuesday together, so my not having one yesterday was probably some post office reason. I almost wish I had not got either, for I can see how very unfit you were to go on with them or even to write. How I wish you had left me without a letter for a couple of days as I should have known the reason, & it distresses me to think of you ill & feverish yet writing & then going out. I shall be anxious till I hear you are not worse for it. I am afraid dearest I cannot manage to come next Saturday. How I wish I knew if you will be dissapointed by my saying this, for if I thought you were expecting me then I should come at any cost. If I hear nothing to make me think that you will be so, I shall wait till Saturday week It is not absolutely necessary to have taken a lodging for me before I come as it could be done afterwards. Tho it would of course be a convenience I would not have you plague yourself about it. If you can easily take one do, but not otherwise. I suppose there is none in the house with you—The next best would be to have it as near yours as possible—a bed room & a sitting room. I never for a moment thought of your giving up yours (unless of course you wanted to change wh. I believe you do not) I do not think it necessary for you to meet me at Edinburgh dear, it would be a pity to give you all that trouble & besides you could not do so I suppose without sleeping out which w^d be better not, as you might just be sent for then. I suppose I shall come on from York by the train at 9 am on the Monday morn^g. but if that takes 8 hours! I do not think I should bear that. Tomorrow I will get time tables & see what other plan seems possible. To night I am so <u>very</u> tired & knocked up (from feeling nervous owing to Hajis day of preparations & going) that I can hardly think enough to write so do not mind the defects in this The satins seem very nearly the same colour the long strip is perhaps a shade darker but I should think they would go quite well together. I will look at them again in the morning before closing this.
Good night my darling.

Thursday morng
It is colder than ever instead of the thaw we have been hoping for of late my leg has been troubling me & this morn^g it is particularly painful in

---

124. Postmarked 6 February 1857. LII/113.

moving. You remember dear one that it always becomes so when the great cold (a[nd] consequent constant sitting) lasts long I feel rather low this morn^g & dread the length of the journey from York but I shall know more about it when he brings me the railways time table this even^g.

Adieu now dearest till this even^g when I shall write again

Thursday Eveng.[125]

I hope you will not have vexed yourself dear at the miscarriage of your letter as it arrived next day & I was not alarmed. As I think by yours of to-day that you will not be dissapointed by my not coming this week I will come next. I have been looking at the time table & it seems very difficult to arrange the journey. The best plan I have been able to see is for me to go to York on Friday even^g (the 13th) and on to either Glasgow or Edinburg on Saturday—leaving York at 2.40 arriving at Glasgow at 10.45. It is possible that I may find I cannot go on so many hours at once & so have to stay at Edinburg at 8.20 but of course. I should try to do the whole—all the more that there seem no trains at all between Edinburgh & Glasgow on Sunday either way.

In this case as I shall not go to the lodgings before Monday as I suppose it will be too late at night when I come? & if you think so it will be time enough to take them at the end of the week.

I write about these particulars so soon because if we do not it gets too late for answers before one is aware.

I am so sorry to hear of your going out when you were so evidently unfit to do. You should have left me without a letter for a day or two.

The white satin seems to me <u>very</u> good and not at all dear for what it is. I do not think a better could be got. I wonder they use them so good for the stage. You might as well buy it even if you do not have it made up till you want it, as it will keep easily & without injuring so long as it is in the piece. I would certainly have the full quantity. I would have the one of which you sent me the pattern & which I re-enclose.

About any question by the Glovers I am sure they will not as indeed they cannot ask any which cannot be answered easily & simply enough I should not answer either as I spoke of for Newcastle (that is half joking & evidently evading) nor should I say 'I do not wish to say'—the first way would be out of place, the last childish. I can see no possible question which you cannot answer easily & politely. They will not be <u>rude</u>, & if ever people are really rude that exonerates one from answering. But they will not be so—& otherwise I can conceive no question which you cannot

---

125. Postmarked 7 February 1857. LII/115.

answer by saying as little as you like. For instance, Do your relations or does your mother live in the country—or where does she live in—the country not far from London. They cannot press for more than that. Then you may feel quite at your ease as I feel sure you will not be tried, or find any difficulty & I shall not mind what you say. I would rather the name[126] were not mentioned, but it is not likely to be asked by them and besides they would take it for granted it was the same as yours. Mrs Stirling does not know it yet & she should be the first to I agree in what you say about your engagement there. It seems quite the thing you want if he gives you enough to do & it is not likely he would pay if he did not mean to do so.

Do not talk of sending more tidy letters, yours are all that is possible in that way. I am very anxious to hear that you are well again, I dread the effect of going out when you were so unfit for it. I am told it is a thaw, I have not yet perceived any difference but hope it will prove so. The ear is quite well & the hand better and I think the back will soon be better now. Good bye now darling girl, be well & happy dearest It seems very very long to wait till next week to see you & I do not at all like it, but as he can only go part of the way with me on a Saturday & would be dissapointed if he did not I must wait till then.

I have been trying & I cannot think of any questions which you could not answer quite freely. The only two I can think of are where you live & (par impossible) my name. To the first you can say a short distance from town in Kent. If asked further you can say. As to the name they must suppose it to be the same as yours, if asked you might say, shall I tell you when I have the pleasure of introducing you to her as I hope to do. If the young woman asks this when alone I should say smiling, or why ~~not~~ do you not suppose it is not likely to be the same as mine. Adieu dearest. It really seems going to be a thaw at last. I must ask in time if I am to bring the box you packed up? & which is it? anything else?

Friday[127]

I am afraid my dear girl you are likely to be as much overworked as before you were the contrary. Only take care of yourself. Do not attempt to write long letters when you are busy—write just a word or two, or none at all whenever you are hurried as I cannot bear you to have to go out when you are already too busy. I cannot write this even^g at all—but it is only

---

126. Harriet is probably referring to the name "Mill."

127. Postmarked 8 February 1857. LII/117.

a sudden intense nervousness which I shall get over by to-morrow. Mr Mill had a sudden fit of inability to see, at his work to-day, his head has been bad & his sight also lately & this I suppose is part of the same as the head I have sat talking instead of as usual reading all the evening because he cannot read & what with the absence of the calming effect of resting & the remain of the nervous state I was in the last days before Haji left—altogether I have a racking head ache & can neither write nor think. I do hope your cold was gone before all this new work came—it is very lucky to have such a change in the weather just when you have to go out & face it. I take it for granted you have the same change to a mild thaw.

I have forgotten to ask if you get letters on Sundays? You see I can hardly manage to write at all so Adieu for this even^g dearest.

Saturday

My head is quite well this morn^g dear and I am quite well again. I long to hear how your hard work has gone. I suppose you will not get this till Monday

goodbye dearest

Sunday,[128] Feb. 8

How inopportunely things are apt to go! now when you are full of business and when therefore I shall perhaps be more plague than profit I am coming Mr Mill had another fit of loss of sight on Friday and yesterday the Chairman told him to take a few days after next Wednesday so he will take the three last days of this week and go with me to Edinburgh. We shall go to York on Thursday—and to Edinburgh on Friday and I shall come on to you on Saturday. It does not seem by the time table as tho' I shall be able to get to Glasgow untill ½ past 5. Do not plague yourself dear about lodgings as I must stay at the Inn (the Queen's you say) untill Monday & then look out for them somehow as it is out of the question your doing anything in it occupied as you are now. You will not thus you see dear write to me after Tuesday, as we leave home on Thursday. I suppose you will say nothing to your landlady about my coming till after I have come—or if you should say only <u>a friend</u>, or <u>a lady.</u>

I heard from Haji on Friday from Paris—all well. He told me to give his love and thanks for your present, which he has taken with him.

Be sure to tell me dear if I am to bring the Box you packed up? Is the

---

128. Postmarked 9 February 1857. LII/118.

key in it and do you think it (the Box) strong enough to stand the journey? I think it is probable that there are other trains between Edinburgh & Glasgow than those marked in my time table & therefore that I may get there earlier on Sat. I do not know the name of the Inns at Edinburgh nor therefore where we shall go—but I shall come on to Glasgow as early as I can on Saturday & send off a note to you as soon as I g[e]t to the Inn (unless I hear anything to the contrary from you.)

On second thought dear one do not expect me before the afternoon on Saturday because I know I shall not be able to leave early after the two long days. If you say anything in your letter which I shall get on Wednesday to make me alter in any respect my plan I shall do so & write to you on Thursday from York, which I suppose would reach you on Friday. Adieu now my darling. I feel anxious for your letter to-morrow and quite excited at the thought of seeing you so soon.

Monday[129] Feb 9

Do not be out of spirits dearest girl—you are tired and overdone—and if you are I shall be, but do not be dear one, and we shall meet on Saturday & I hope get a few hours talk on Sunday. I shall send a note to you as soon as I arrive, but I shall not be surprised if you are out. I wish Sat^y were come—I am almost done up with the excitement of expecting it.

Perhaps Mrs Glover expects you to call on her to thank her for her invitation or to say why you could not ~~accept the~~ go. I should think you had best call the first Sunday you have time & are able. I do not think it follows that Davidson[130] is untrue about that—very likely she was away, you must write again—would it be well or not to enclose it to Mr Davis[131] for her. Never mind about lodgings dearest as I think you cannot possibly have time to look for them. If you should (which I do not expect) you know what is wanted—a bedroom & sitting room. I shall of course be at Glasgow at latest by ½ past 5 on Sat^y

I shall not hear from you after you get this—as Tuesday is the latest for you to write. I cannot write at all this evening. The idea that you are not comfortable makes me so out of spirits—but I shall determine not to be so & you must not either. I am so glad we are to meet so soon. I wish

---

129. No postmark, but letter is dated 9 February [1857]. On the back of the last page of Helen's letter LII/119, Harriet has written, "spirits out of / lodgings / no matter / M^{rs} G call / Davidson." LII/120.

130. Helen had insinuated in her letter LII/119 that Mrs. Davidson, her seamstress, may have absconded with the money Helen had sent her as an advance.

131. Mr. Davis was the theater manager in Newcastle.

it were sooner. Good night my darling, how I wish I could make it be a good night.

Perhaps you did thank Mrs Glover 'for her kindness' if not you must the first time you see her. Adieu my dear one I am miserable till I see you.

Tuesday,[132] Feb 10

I have been terribly out of spirits all day dearest because I have thought you were so—I would give any thing that you should not be dissapointed there. It makes me perfectly miserable to think of it, you so counted on Glasgow and the Glovers—but do not feel dissapointed dear one—you are tired and overdone It will take a turn & go better before long no doubt, things always do in such cases, and it is so natural to feel disheartened when one has been excited with expectation. Mrs Glover too will come round when she sees how simple & sincere you are. You must tell her about your purchases as she has shown an interest in them she will think it uncomplementary if you do not. It is not now now so very long (tho' a great deal too long) untill we shall meet. Perhaps I may get there by Friday night but I do not expect it, for I so dread the long days journeys, the first especially that I cannot fancy I shall ever get through them. But I hope it will not prove so formidable as it looks to me now.

Thursday to York will be just 8 hours from home & if I bear that well I may be able to leave York at ½ past 9 next morning arriving at Glasgow at ½ past five on Friday. I hope to do this but it is very doubtful. Do not take any steps to meet me dearest as it is so very uncertain when I arrive. All day I have kept repeating oh my dearest girl you must not you shall not be dissapointed. We will have a nice long talk on Sunday when my darling will have an hour or two not quite full of work. Do not give up hope of Davidson as most likely she was away some where when your letter went. It is most unlikely that she would purloin the things you must write again next week.

I have no letter to-day which I much fear means that you are overdone with work. I shall have one to-morrow no doubt & then no more till we meet. Keep up your spirits my darling for my sake, you cannot yourself be more interested in succeeding than I am for you. There is nothing I would not do to help you, my spirits rise and fall exactly as you are pleased or the contrary. We must remember that we should not have heared so much about the disagreables of the profession even from those in it, if

132. Postmarked 12 February 1857. LII/122.

there were not all sorts of dissapointments & annoyances to be expected & these in life never come where one could best bear them, they always hit one on the tenderest parts. Good bye now my precious take all the care you can of your dear self for my sake.

P.S.

I would say nothing to your land lady about me till I am there. I am getting ill with impatience & so fear you are being knocked up with overwork.

Wednesday[133] Even^g

I have got your letter dearest and shall bring the box &c. We are to leave at nine to-morrow morning & I will put this in the post as we pass, not that there is any thing worth sending but that she may have a word from me on Friday.

As far as I can judge I expect to come on Sat^y morn^g by the train which leaves Edinburgh at 12.15 reaching Glasgow at 2.25 — then if I do not see my dear girl at the station which I shall not expect, I shall send to her.

Thanks for the time table dear. I am quite nervous with impatience to hear all you have to say & also a little from dread of the length of the days journeys, but still I think the feeling of getting nearer at each hour will keep me going. When you get this I shall be between York & Edinburgh.

Adieu now dearest — I must go early to bed that I may get up so early — I have been always so very late at nights.

York[134]
Saturday ev^g

My dearest love, if I do not write tonight you will not hear from me till Tuesday, so I write though it is but to say that I have got here comfortably. I had a pleasant hour & a half ramble in that beautiful train. & the journey was very pleasant as long as there was light, though I could not succeed in getting a foot warmer till Newcastle. There was a stoppage of seventy minutes at Berwick which I availed myself of for a bit of dinner which disagred with me. However, I have done very well, and have just time to write this scrawl before it will be too late for the post. I enjoy excessively the feeling of these three days and shall enjoy the remembrance of them & be very happy till you come & a great deal happier afterwards.

---

133. Postmarked 13 February 1857. LII/123.

134. Postmarked 16 February 1857. LII/125.

so be cheerful darling & keep loving me as you so sweetly do. bless you my own only darling love.

I am at the George & alone in the coffee room by a flaming fire.

cher ange, Il faut porter la même robe que hier. je le <u>préfère</u> dans tous les cas. aussi il faut venir dans un fiacre. n'oubliez pas les petits envelopes. chere chere fille.¹³⁵

To Fanny Stirling¹³⁶

I only mean that we look at things from different points of view. You seem to have a great taste for the ordinary English 'strong calvinistic bias (while I strictly speaking do not even believe in the idea of <u>sin</u>. This you will allow is a wide difference

[on separate page]
I thought Ld Bali{   }¹³⁷ delicious but was outvoted by Mr Mill & Lily. when voted I stupid I delighted in the elegant young page, wished I c^d get him, then the bride sitting in a chaise & the bride's mama & the coming on fast & going back altogether I delight it is full of realfun

tho why I agreed sh^d the Turk lady not be a Jewess? It reminded me of the ballad of little Bernard in The¹³⁸ ages religeus{e} —where her Lord having found his lady & little Bernard making a faux pas incontinently killed them, orders his servants to bury them together but adds, "but lay my lady on the upper hand, for she comes of the better race" having quenched his honour by killing them there is a touch of natural sentiment in burying them together mitigated however by pride in my lady & 'our' superiority—

135. No postmark or watermark. The note was probably written on the 17 February 1857, the day Harriet arrived in Glasgow to meet Helen. The text of the letter, translated, is "Dear angel, you must wear the same dress as yesterday. I like it better than all your others. Also, I will come in a hackney carriage. Don't forget the little envelopes. Dear, dear daughter." LII/126.

136. This note from HTM to Fanny Stirling is enclosed in LIV/24, a letter to Mrs. J. Mill from Fanny Stirling, postmarked 20 May 1858. Apparently Mrs. Stirling was returning the note to HTM.

137. The handwriting looks like Balieran, Balienun, or Balunan. HTM is referring either to an actor or to a character in a play.

138. The Child ballad "Little Musgrave and Lady Barnard" is quoted in Beaumont and Fletcher's *Knight of the Burning Pestle* (c. 1611). The ballad continues to be sung by traditional musicians today. The essential story is as reported here by HTM. She added "The" after writing "Per" without crossing out "Per."

* * * * *

(Private)   Folkstone 10 o'clk[139]
First I cannot seal with the crest because the luggage is left at the station,
so I have not got it.

I cannot express the pang I felt when the train moved off and I [was]
unable to see you my sweetest and this by my foolishly saying 'dont
stay'—The reason, as you I think know, why I said so was the wish to save
you the trying nervous moment that it is to stand waiting & looking adieu
for a long while. I thought to save you this & so lost the last look & nod.
I saw you look back & say adieu once at a distance & then the building
came in the way against which I very nearly knocked my head off so that
the point man waved me back in my anxiety to catch a last glimpse. I
hope you did know the reason of my saying dont stay—I did not remember, in the feeling of bustle & nervousness, that being express it w^d go off
so quick—still I should have seen you again but for the poste which
projected. It upset me quite & I burst into tears which lasted a long while.
I just lost that very last look which I so much value & love. However I
have all your sweetness & kindness to think of & think of you my treasure
as you were all day so pretty sweet & kind.

You are now in the midst of that play—a complete success I hope it
is—and soon I shall think you are going to bed & recovering a little from
the fatigue of these last days.

I could not rest till I had told you how I felt—and that I never meant
to deny you or myself the comfort of waving a last adieu as the thing
went off—I particularly counted upon it. However we had a nice parting
just before I got in & I saw the dear bonnet walking away as I had said,
& because I had said so, dearest girl. Will you post my note which he
forgot to do & it is sadly crushed. Tell her I congratulate her beforehand,
till I hear particulars from you at Paris. If you can will you scan thro the
Times every day to see if there is anything about him leaving England?
Imagine in my absence his giving them the names so that we shall be
posted up in the entrance of this Inn & one cannot tell where else in
consequence! It might easily get into the paper from this & show who
the party consisted of that we were alone—you may imagine how vexed
I am at this—he said they asked him & he did not know I cared! Adieu
& bless you

---

139. Postmarked London, 12 October 1858, to Miss Taylor at Mrs. [Fanny] Stirling's. LIII(i)/1.

Folkstone

Tuesday[140]

{pencilled in at top}

Have gone over this in pencil to save it from obliteration

I just wrote one word dearest before going to the boat to day I have seen the Times but do not ~~then~~ know if its account is to be trusted at all events it recognizes that she did wonders with the part.[141] It is the second piece this even^g. I see it is probably too serious for the olympic[142]

I shall hear[143] all about it from you at Paris

{upside own on back}

It is a beautiful Morn^g & quite calm

Boulogne
Tuesday
Hotel d'Angleterre[144]

I sent you two poor little words dear from Folkstone & am impatient to hear from you at Paris how it all went.

You will be surprised to see that we have stayed here instead of going on at once & I am much surprised myself, but it happened in this way—It was a beautiful morn^g & we determined to go straight on & so took <u>through</u> tickets and had the luggage registered to Paris so as to avoid the Custom house here. We had a very good crossing—I had engaged a place to lie down & of course remained there till we had stopped in the harbour—as soon as it had stopped Mr Mill came down & said that Merivale (under Secretary for the Colonies) and all his women were on deck and had just asked him if his family were on board & if he was going on by the train to Paris to-night as he was? Mr Mill said yes & came down to tell me. I saw it would not be well for his family to make their appearance in the shape of <u>one</u> only, so said at once, to his great astonishment 'Oh I

---

140. The paper is watermarked 1857. The letter was written just before her last departure from England in October 1858. LIII(i)/2.

141. Helen was staying with Fanny Stirling, who had just opened in a new play.

142. Olympic Theater.

143. Harriet seems to have corrected her own mistake when she rewrote the penciled note by writing "hear" over her original "have."

144. Postmarked 12 October 1858. LIII(i)/4.

am too ill to think of going on to night'—He forgot all about the
Merivales in his sadness at my sudden illness, till I put him out of harm
by telling him it was not very bad—so we drove to this pleasant old
houses, where the smiling waiter & chamber-woman met us with Bonjour
Mons. et Mad. as if we had only left yesterday, tho I believe we have not
been here since 1853—I think we have always been at the Nord lately.
Mʳ Mill went to the Railway & got them to exchange our tickets for
tomorrow so we avoided the enemy for the second time already in these
two days!—& got instead a splendid little diner a la francaise as the old
waiter promised the only fault of which to me was that I could not have
by a ~~wish~~ the little party from Brook Street to share it & all the pleasant
things here. You will sympathise in my satisfaction at having so successfully avoided that disagreable rencontre.¹⁴⁵ The consequence is we are
landed here without even our carpet bags but the femme de chambre¹⁴⁶
promises to supply all wants.

I should not write you all this history but because I know you will like
to hear all our doings. A[s] it happens it is as well for I am very tired &
glad of the rest I did not sleep last night for thinking of our parting &
all that rest & lay turning over Aberdeen in my mind—the idea of which
is pleasant except for the very long journey which without a break I fear
will be too much for you. I long to hear how you are? & How Mrs Stirling
is? Give my true & kind love to her & Adieu darling now in haste.

Paris¹⁴⁷ Thursday, 14ᵗʰ
Hotel Clarendon

I got your two dear letters sweetest girl this mornᵍ and they were the
greatest comfort & pleasure to me. I am so glad to hear you are not
overworking yourself. I feel anxious about your journey to Aberdeen it is
so long, I do hope you will take it in the easiest way you can I hope you
will divide it into two or three day journeys—I should think the Carlisle
line would be the best but you will get the Bradshaw & see by that. Be
sure to put me in a word whenever you stop for the night to say you have
got on so far well as I shall be very anxious. I think of you always my
darling night & morning, & even thro' the hubbub of the day. We came
on from Boulogne yesterday, a very tiresome fatiguing day—The people
at the Hotel Castiglione, finding we did not arrive Tuesday night as we

---

145. Meeting someone or something unpleasant.

146. Chambermaid.

147. Postmarked 15 October 1858. LIII(i)/6.

had said, had given our rooms to other people & then taken rooms for us here—nearly next door, between Hotel Castiglione & the corner of Rue Rivoli They are comfortable little hotels, about as big as a bird cage the three, but making up for the smallness by the prettiness of the <u>décors</u>. We have been out driving about all day—Mr Mill had not seen the Bois de Boulogne since the alteration & was delighted with it—it looked excessively pretty & all the ladies dressed out in their modes & so on—we then dined at the Frères Provencaux, from which I gained a new dish. Oysters stemed with Parmesan—very good if you had been there to share it & now dearest girl I have told you all our little doings, except indeed that we could not get our luggage last night till eleven o'clk which made the second short night & the third day without dinner, so that we earned our little dinner to-day. Yesterday was a very very tiresome tiring day seven mortal hours in the train & no luggage at the end! You know all the <u>wear</u> of that sort of thing. However now I feel quite well again but must hear often from you or I shall come back again to see after you.

I saw the Times account of the piece at Folkstone.[148] I do not [give] the Olympic audience the credit to suppose it was the want of character in the thing they disliked—I take it[,] it was the <u>subject</u> I imagine it is an audience who do not want to hear of death in any shape. Wilkie Collins[149] should take his wares to the Surrey or even the Haymarket. I am sure Mrs Stirling would be beautiful in it, but she alone could not do all, & evidently Robson[150] did not do as well as he might—Certainly the the subject if well executed is not fit for the atmosphere of the Olympic—& Wilkie Collins has no conception of character—only of <u>situations</u>, good melodrame, but not the drama. I hope Mrs Stirling won't plague herself about it, <u>she</u> comes off with flying colours in it. If it takes down the conceit of the author it ~~will~~ would have done good—The man might do something good if he frequented better society for he has a good idea of the mise en scéne.[151] english people have forgotten that there is such a thing as real <u>character</u>, real <u>emotion</u>—the most any of them think of, is what shall they pretend to feel. So one rather likes the cynical refusal of the audience to pretend to feel at all—as the truth, however bad, is nearer good than lies. I have written in a great hurry as he is waiting to take this

148. Referring to the play Fanny Stirling had recently opened in London. See Helen's letter LIII/3 for her impression of the opening night.

149. William (Wilkie) Collins (1824-89) is best known for introducing the mystery-story genre to Britain, but he was also an actor.

150. Thomas Frederick Robson (whose real name was Thomas Robson Brownhill) (1822-64).

151. Stage setting.

and it is a good way to go. So adieu now dearest—give my very kind love to Mrs. Stirling and tell me how she is?

Paris[152]

Friday, 15

I have no letter from my dearest girl this morning which is made up for by thinking that she has not had the trouble of writing. You must remember my sweetest that I have nothing to do but to write & no trouble in sending to the post, therefore you must not think it necessary to write as often as I do, nor think I shall be surprised now.

When I do not receive one from her—they are the greatest possible pleasure when I do get them, but I w^d on no account that you sh^d tire or trouble yourself with writing & taking to the Post—only write when you feel able easily, then if i[t] is but two words, two lines, it is most delightful to get them. I would so much rather have a few words often than a long letter seldom, but my chief fear is the fatigue for you of taking them to the Post. After you get this dearest address once Lyons France after that Montpelier, Herault. I hope we may get away from this to-morrow, for I feel that I shall be ill if I stay here. They are nice little rooms, enough but the smell of cooking from nine o'clk in the morn^g till night is so excessive that they are perfectly uninhabitable while the heat & want of air is suffocating & I am sure most unwholesome & as we neither have the smallest wish to stay, but on the contrary, & I have an ardent desire to get out of it, I hope to get away to-morrow (that is if Mr Mill can get back his watch which he gave to mend yesterday).

I had a note from Haji saying as usual nothing[153]—but that Mrs Cholmeley has just decided to go to England & that he shall stay some little time at Milan Genoa & Nice & then can join us.

I suffer so much from the strong smell of cooking & the total want of a breath of fresh air that I have all the sensations of congestion, & bad headache & even some diarheea.

I cannot therefore write any more to-day to my dearest dearest girl, I shall ask again for letters to-day & tomorrow

[written on the envelope]
I shall perhaps write—a word to Post Office Aberdeen on my journey but it shall contain nothing which would signify if it is lost.

---

152. Postmarked 15 October 1858. LIII(i)/8.

153. Harriet's reply to Algernon is XXVII/119 (in chapter 10, above). The difference between the letter to Haji and this one, to Lily, are instructive.

Saturday[154] morn[g]

After an unspeakably dreadful day & night <u>Black yesterday</u> is past. I can just add good day dear to last nights scrap, tho my hands are so swollen I can scarcely write.

The only comfort I can have is to hear that you are well & happy— Monday evening will I hope bring that

Dijon Saturday

We have just got here dearest & are in the old rooms at the Cloche which you know so well How they remind me of you darling! We have had a most fatiguing day from Paris—we left at 11 and got here at six—The heat & sun all day have been really terrible, there were seven men in the carriage and myself and they all were quite knocked up owing to the fierce heat of the sunshine all day. It has been a day like a hot & cloudless July, & now at 8 o'clk all the windows stand open & the people promenading like a summer even[g], as it feels. I never was more delighted to leave Paris, the close heat of the small rooms having made me quite ill—tho' otherwise they were pleasant—it is a very good hotel indeed, but you know how one suffers from that smell of cooking. I scrawl these few words ~~that~~ because I cant bear you not to know where I am & what doing—if you write to me Post restante Lyons on Monday I have no doubt I shall get it, as I do not mean to go on quick—I shall write once more to Brook St but only a few words, so that if you do not get it it will not matter—after that I shall write to Aberdeen but do not be uneasy if you should lose it as I shall not write any thing that matters till I know exactly where to write to. I saw the moon shining on the beautiful hills & woods just before getting here & thought how my dearest girl had admired the same scene some years ago. Bless you my darling, as I say to myself always, day & night & now sweet one, Adieu as I am very tired, but all the better for writing these few words to her.

Dijon Oct. 18.
Monday.[155]

I do not know if this will find you still in town my dearest but in any case I like to write—when two days have passed without writing it feels dreadfully long to me—I am always thinking of you. We got here on Saturday and as I was extremely tired determined to stay over Sunday and now I am refreshed again we are now getting on to Lyons, which as it is

---

154. Postmarked 17 October 1858. LIII(i)/9.

155. Postmarked 18 October 1858. LIII(i)/12.

only four hours ought not to be so very fatiguing, but the fact is we always get the last seats in the railway carriages, as I can not run on quick, & if he goes on he never succeeds, I always find him running up & down & looking lost in astonishment. So I have given up trying to get any seats but those that are left & those are always of course the sunny ones, & the sunshine is terribly hot. However there are only moderate days journeys now left. I shall stay at Lyons till I get a letter from you, & then go on either to Geneva or Montpelier but I think the latter. Geneva is only about four hours by railway from Lyons, but I think it is very desirable to get to Montpelier in fine weather, otherwise one does not get a good impression of the place—& tho the sun is hot in a railway carriage it is only just pleasant in the house.

I passed all yesterday thinking of you & of what you were probably doing—preparing for your long journey no doubt. How I hope you will remember how anxious I am that you should take care of yourself during it. It will be at Montpelier that I shall get your letters telling me about it—& how you succeed about lodgings—& how you like Mrs Pollack[156]— How I hope she will prove kind & serviceable! There was such a splendid moon last night—I thought of my dear girl travelling & thinking of me as she looks at it, as I do of her. I am only anxious about that long journey, when there, as it is I suppose a quiet place I hope you will be able to get lodgings without more than the usual difficulties—Mrs. P must know all about them & I should hope will be of some assistance.

We saw in the Galignami[157] that Mrs. S had what they called quite an ovation after playing that piece, but it did not say which night it meant. I fear she has teared herself about it & so made the eye bad. Tell me dear how many <u>acts</u> & <u>scenes</u> there are in the pieces she usually plays—masks & faces, & sheep in Wolfs clothing for instance? and how long are they? It would not I should think be very difficult to write that sort of vaudeville. Give my love & remembrance to Mrs. S.

and adieu for the present my dearest

[written inside the envelope flap]

I think it would be better to address from Scotland the name without the initials. I shall write ~~every~~ tomorrow again, & most days, if not all

---

156. The theater manager in Aberdeen. See Helen's letters LIII/16 and LIII/19.

157. A newspaper.

Lyons Oct. 19
Tuesday[158]

I got your Saturdays my dearest this morning—I have not yet got the one of Thursday you mention but have no doubt of having it as they took the directions down on a printed form.

You will see that I could not help leaving Paris quickly it was so unendurable. We got to Dijon on Saturday & I did not know <u>how</u> tired I was till afterwards—that terrible heat & bad air is what now I cannot endure without much suffering & bad effects. We staid very comfortably at Dijon till yesterday (Monday) & then came here by the express in rather more than 4 hours. There were six huge frenchmen with great cloaks &c in the carriage besides ourselves, & the sun came in dreadfully hot & they would keep one window closed, so that it was a very bad journey—being in a perspiration & heated terribly all the way—we have both got very bad colds & I stayed in bed till 2 o'clk he was very kind, getting me a lemon & making some lemonade in your way—for I tried to do just what you would have done—Now I am up I am much better than I expected & I dare say tomorrow shall be quite well—Do not dearest be surprised if you do not get a letter when you are expecting one as I do really think they some times miscarry. I shall write "Angleterre" on this because he thinks it quite necessary, otherwise I should not as it makes it perhaps more observable. In answer to your question darling write about theatricals & <u>everything</u>—I do not care in the slightest degree if any body sees it—I avoided the Merivales[159] quite as much because it was a bore to get among a large party of staring women, as on account of any thing they might think. Tell me all you think feel & do dear—the more the better except not to feel obliged to write when you have time, long, when not, & that will be generally a few lines saying only "I am well but busy"

I am thinking of you all day on the railway, may it only prove a good inn at the end. And how I hope the same at Aberdeen, that you will go to the best Inn & refresh well before beginning business. How very glad I shall be when I hear you have arrived safe & well I shall feel fidgetted till I do but that will only be at Montpelier & I do not think we shall be there before Sunday on account of my not being well, we must go on slowly & we shall <u>certainly</u> not leave here tomorrow I feel. It is near five & he is to take this to the post before <u>he</u> dines w/ the Hôte.[160]

---

158. Postmarked 19 October 1858. LIII(i)/13.

159. Merivale was the undersecretary for the Colonies that Harriet had avoided seeing after the crossing to France; see LIII(i)/4, above.

160. Innkeeper or landlord.

[written on the edge of the first page]

I shall write to Mrs. S. when I am better. Adieu & bless my <u>darling</u>.

Lyons Wednesday[161]

I have just got your Sundays letter dearest—you are <u>so</u> mistaken in think-ing the delay at Boulogne &c was bad for me. I have no doubt it saved me a severe illness at Paris. It was the only bit of comfort on this journey & I only wish I had stayed there. I took a thorough disgust to Paris air coming here the ~~heat~~ closeness with the men in the railway was suffocat-ing. We had here a great height to mount wh. knocked me up also. Today my violent cold is better—if I c^d have stayed in bed yesterday I sh^d have got well, but the woman declared those rooms were let & we had to <u>discend</u> a floor—I managed it but was very feverish—Now I am quietly lying in bed & taking Travis[162] fever mixtures—I am better & expect to be nearly quite well to-morrow but shall not think of leaving here for several days at least, because I am determined to take the greatest possible care of myself & do <u>just</u> what you w^d recommend if you were here & I know so well by sweet experience what my sweet girl would say & do. The worst I have now is an excessive bad headache, so I will not write more but ask him to direct this for me. I forgot to say dearest that no one has seen or heared one word of any of your letters, nor will.

Lyons[163] Oct. 21

Dear Lily

Mama is decidedly better today, and has no doubt that she shall be quite well with two or three days more rest. Her head is a great deal better than yesterday, but still it aches with the least exertion, and therefore she asks me to write for her. It has been one of the usual attacks of fever. She has taken the fever mixture and some pills, and it is now over. She is very weak, and does not mean to get up till tomorrow when she has ordered a warm bath in the bedroom which she says will quite get her up. This is

161. Postmarked 20 October 1858. LIII(i)/15.

162. Probably medicine made by Dr. Travis, a doctor living in Nice, who had treated John in 1854. See *CW*: XIV, 160, 170.

163. Postmarked 21 October 1858. LIII(i)/17. Written for HTM by JSM. This and all sub-sequent letters from Harriet probably did not arrive in Aberdeen until after Harriet's death. Fanny Stirling writes about receiving the mail from Mr. Mill, forwarded from Aberdeen to her, as Helen's guardian after Harriet's death (XXIII/633). Harriet receives no further com-munication from her daughter after this date. The letters written by Helen were all sent to the wrong post offices since Harriet misjudged the speed of their journey south.

the exact state of the case, therefore be sure there is nothing to be uneasy about. As it is doubtful if they deliver letters on Sunday she will not write again till Saturday. If this reaches you in time to write a word to Avignon on Saturday, it will be sure to be in time, we shall go so slowly or you might even write on Sunday with scarcely a chance of not being in time: besides that at the worst it would be sent on. And now, Mama says adieu dear—as do I.

Yours

JSM

Lyons

Saturday[164]

I must write but a few words dearest because I am very weak tho getting better very slowly—I had a warm bath yesterday which did me good & I got up in the afternoon & I have got up again this afternoon—I am still so very weak—I suppose I must expect to take longer to recover my strength—meanwhile you may be quite sure I do exactly everything that you w^d say & all I can think of which is best—I have got my Quinine[165] mixture to-day & I dare say it will soon take effect—but it is impossible to help taking bad colds—I did so again yesterday—but I am nursing it away. I have no idea when we shall go away from here—the only quick train is at ½ past 6 in the morning or ½ past 10 at night. I have had two of your dear letters here & am most impatient to get on to get others. It will not be safe to write here again as we may have left. I write as I lie wh accounts for the scrawl. In another day or two I shall write quite another thing but I know you would rather have this than nothing—o how I hope to hear you are comfortable I have everything I want & it is only a little <u>time</u> will give me some strength again. This is a wretched note—but it is instead of none & to morrow shall be better. I think of you always & do all you would do my darling!

Lyons

Sunday[166]

O my dearest girl I really am better to-day. I cannot express my impatience to get your letters & that will only be at Avignon. For the first time

---

164. Postmarked 23 October 1858. LIII(i)18.

165. Medicine usually prescribed for malaria.

166. Postmarked 24 October 1858. LIII(i)/20.

I feel as if I may be able to get there, but in the ordinary way by railway not for a very long time—so he is gone to try to arrange for a caleche[167] to go on the railway by which means I shall be saved the long walk & detention & we shall be alone—in this way I think I can venture, & if I feel the same in the even^g. shall order it for to-morrow (Monday) morning. I hope you have not made yourself unwell by anxiety about me dearest— you must not—you see how often I write tho' it is but little I can write yet. I have been dreadfully low-spirited these two last days, but am better to-day. There seems a total want of air in these deep sunk gloomy rooms in these streets, I seem unable to breathe, I hope to succeed in getting to Montepelier, & then if it does not suit me better I must go on round to Bordeaux or that neighbourhood. You may be sure I will take all possible care. Do not wonder when there is a day without a letter as on a travelling day it often cant be done. If we do go on to-morrow perhaps I may not be able to write. I am so anxious to get yours that I can aim at nothing else.

Ever since I left home except the one pleasant day at Boulogne it has always been in close hot <u>airless</u> rooms in dark streets & the noise night & day head-splitting—the whole so opposite to what I am used to that I can scarcely endure on. You know that feeling too well. We have to wait, to hear each other speak between the clang of two omnibusses.

This is not fit to send, but I can not sit up longer at a time, & I am very tired. Do not mind my lowness—I shall be better when I get your letter. —I think of you all day & night my darling & cry a great deal, but next time I write I shall be a great deal better I hope. <u>bless you</u>

Valence Tuesday[168]
26th

If you are as glad to get this from this place as I am to write it my dearest girl you will indeed be pleased. We were obliged to give up leaving Lyons yesterday & it was with fear & trembling it was attempted this morn^g. but now it is done I am in great hope—I shall by degrees get over this attack. There is no train possible by which to leave Lyons later than ½ past seven in the morn^g. not for <u>anywhere</u>, & then not till ½ past 10 at night. If there had been we sh^d have gone by it wherever it was—to Geneva was still earlier & besides a 4 ½ hours journey which I could not take—we came here in 2 hours which was the outside of what I c^d do—I was carried on a chair to the train, or c^d not have come, I am <u>so</u> weak.—but I have eaten nothing for a week past & never sh^d have done at Lyons—all

---

167. "Calèche," a light carriage.

168. Postmarked 26 October 1858. LIII(i)/23.

the things are greasy or unsuitable in some way & the air was so close & the noise kept the head bad—now in time I hope to pick up again especially when I got your letters at Avignon as I hope to-morrow. <u>That</u> will give me animation again. However I ought to say that I was as comfortable at Lyons as one could be in an Inn ill—the landlady was very civil & left me in peace & quiet all day—He got me several medecines made up by telling a pharmacien[169] what I wanted. The last two days I have taken Quinine & Sulf Acid[170] which has done good I think. I hope by great care to avoid any relapse but what will really do me good will be hearing from you. If all goes well I hope we may be at Montpelier by Friday perhaps—after that we shall judge about staying in this part of France.

Now I will not write more dearest tho' in fact I have said nothing worth saying—but it is a choice between this nothing or a great no. of small details wh. are not worth writing. Adieu darling mine.

Avignon Wednesday.[171]

27

At last we have got to this place dearest as I have so ardently longed to do—the first object you may be very sure was the Post office, but no letter has yet come. I thought it possible both that you might not get mine on Saturday & that if you answered it on that day it might not yet have come so I was not so much dissapointed as I sh^d have been. Now I expect it to-morrow morn^g—& Oh how glad I shall be to see that you have not been overanxious, & how you are in all respects. It is now so very long since I had a letter—it seems weeks—it is just one week—& such a week to me! but now I hope it is all over & I shall have more cheerful letters to write. Valence proved a terrible stopping place, the bed was impossible for me to sleep in & I sat up nearly all the night—it was necessary to come on but the being able to do so after such a night shows that there was a change for the better in my state—I was very knocked up and can scarcely crawl about, but I am better & this dear quiet inn will do me good. Montpelier is only 3 hours by railway from this so this journey is nearly over for the present at least. I know not what might have happened to me yesterday at Valence but for the rest of your chair, & the same here now. I think of it as yours each time I sit in it—He gets it out for me & puts it up so well & kindly indeed for ten days past he has been

---

169. Pharmacist or druggist.

170. Sulfuric acid or oil of vitriol, a typical treatment for syphilis during this period.

171. Postmarked 27 October 1858. LIII(i)/25.

entirely devoted to nursing & has been unable to sleep at night for anxiety—but now all will I hope be soon in the more usual way. I shall write more at length about everything when I am stronger—These notes are but to keep you dearest aware of how each day goes on on the whole—particulars must be for a future time. So now my darling adieu for a little time till I have a precious note to answer.

Will you dear remember this memorandum—If I sh^d be some night taken so ill as to be unable to speak or even worse to die suddenly you know I cannot bear that the servants sh^d get to my papers &c I shall therefore from to-night always leave all places locked & put my keys on the hook behind the window curtain thus they would not be found until you came. The cold is very bad & makes me feel altogether most ailing. We shall talk over all things when we meet. <u>Bless you</u> dear one.[172]

---

172. There is no postmark or watermark on this small piece of paper. This is Harriet's last note before her death on 3 November 1858. It may have been directed to John Stuart Mill, Helen, or both, but the penultimate sentence seems to direct the note to Helen. LIII(i)/30.

Hardy Family Tree[1]

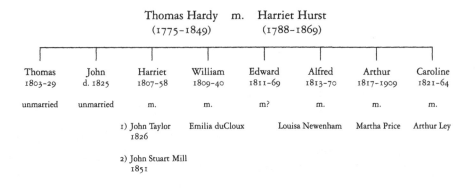

Thomas Hardy   m.   Harriet Hurst
(1775-1849)   (1788-1869)

Thomas	John	Harriet	William	Edward	Alfred	Arthur	Caroline
1803-29	d. 1825	1807-58	1809-40	1811-69	1813-70	1817-1909	1821-64
unmarried	unmarried	m.	m.	m?	m.	m.	m.
		1) John Taylor 1826	Emilia duCloux		Louisa Newenham	Martha Price	Arthur Ley
		2) John Stuart Mill 1851					

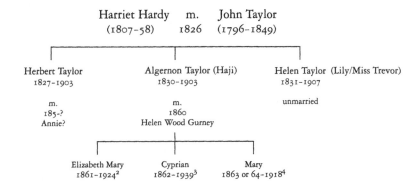

Harriet Hardy   m.   John Taylor
(1807-58)   1826   (1796-1849)

Herbert Taylor   Algernon Taylor (Haji)   Helen Taylor (Lily/Miss Trevor)
1827-1903   1830-1903   1831-1907

m.   m.   unmarried
185-?   1860
Annie?   Helen Wood Gurney

Elizabeth Mary	Cyprian	Mary
1861-1924[2]	1862-1939[3]	1863 or 64-1918[4]

---

1. From information contained in Mabel Hardy, "The History of the Hardy Family" (1959), unpublished.

2. A family tree found in the Mill/Taylor Collection comments: "paralyzed but sane."

3. Family tree comments: "suffer[ed] for forty years from religious mania of Folie circulaire. was removed in 1899 from Totnes Union Workhouse to Asylum, had before been Midshipman in Navy."

4. Family tree comments: "at Northumberland House after having been certified."

References

Anderson, Patricia. 1995. *When passion reigned: Sex and the victorians.* New York: Basic Books.

Ashworth, M. 1916. The marriage of John Stuart Mill. *Englishwoman* 30:159–72.

Atwood, Margaret. 1989. Biographobia: Some personal reflections on the act of biography. In *Nineteenth-century lives: Essays presented to Jerome Hamilton Buckley,* ed. Lawrence S. Lockridge, John Maynard, and Donald D. Stone. Cambridge: Cambridge University Press.

August, Eugene. 1975. *John Stuart Mill: A mind at large.* New York: Charles Scribner's Sons.

Bain, Alexander. 1882. *John Stuart Mill: A criticism with personal recollections.* London: Longmans, Green & Co.

Buret, F. 1891. *Syphilis.* London: F. A. Davis.

Borchard, Ruth. 1957. *John Stuart Mill: The man.* London: Watts.

Bourne, Henry Richard Fox. 1873. John Stuart Mill: A sketch of his life. *Examiner* 17:582–86.

Courtney, William. 1889. *The life of John Stuart Mill.* London: Walter Scott.

Cranston, Maurice. 1959. Mr. and Mrs. Mill on liberty. *The Listener* 62:385–86.

Diffenbaugh, Guy Linton. 1923. Mrs. Taylor seen through other eyes than Mill's. *Sewanee Review* 31:198–204.

Ede, Lisa, and Andrea Lunsford. 1990. *Singular texts/plural authors: Perspectives on collaborative writing.* Carbondale: Southern Illinois University Press.

Ellery, John B. 1964. *John Stuart Mill.* New York: Twayne.

Elliot, Hugh S. R., ed. 1910. *The letters of John Stuart Mill.* Vol. 1. New York: Longmans, Green and Co.

Garnett, Richard. 1910. *The life of W. J. Fox.* London: John Lane at Bodley Head.

Glassman, Peter. 1985. *J. S. Mill: The evolution of a genius.* Gainsville: University of Florida Press.

Gomperz, Theodor. 1936. *Briefe und aufzeichnungen assgewählt, erläutert und zu einer darstellung seines lebens verknüpft.* Wien: Gerold & Co.

REFERENCES

Hagberg, Knut. 1930. *Personalities and powers.* Translated by Elizabeth Sprigge and Claude Napier. London: John Lane at Bodley Head.

Hamburger, Joseph. 1965. *Intellectuals in politics: John Stuart Mill and the philosophic radicals.* New Haven: Yale University Press.

———. and Hamburger, Lotte. 1991. *Contemplating adultery: The secret life of a victorian woman.* New York: Fawcett Columbine.

Hamilton, Mary Agnes. n. d. (1932?). *Sidney and Beatrice Webb: A study in contemporary biography.* London: Sampson Low, Marston.

Hayek, F. A. 1951. *John Stuart Mill and Harriet Taylor: Their friendship and subsequent marriage.* New York: Augustus M. Kelley.

———. 1963. Introduction. *The earlier letters of John Stuart Mill.* In *Collected works of John Stuart Mill.* Vol. XII. Toronto: University of Toronto Press.

Hayter, Alethea. 1965. *A sultry month: Scenes of London literary life in 1846.* London: Faber and Faber Ltd.

Held, Virginia. 1971. Justice and Harriet Taylor. *The Nation* (October 25): 405-6.

Henshaw, S. E. 1874. John Stuart Mill and Mrs. Taylor. *Overland Monthly* 13:516-23.

Himmelfarb, Gertrude. 1965. The two Mills. *The New Leader* 10 (May):26, 28-29.

———. 1974. *On liberty and liberalism: The case of John Stuart Mill.* New York: Alfred A. Knopf.

Jacobs, Jo Ellen. 1995. 'The Lot of Gifted Ladies is Hard': A study of Harriet Taylor Mill criticism. In *Hypatia's Daughters: 1500 Years of Women Philosophers.* Ed. Linda Lopez McAlister. Bloomington: Indiana University Press. Also published in *Hypatia* 9, #3 (Summer 1994): 132-162.

Kamm, Josephine. 1977. *John Stuart Mill in love.* London: Gordon & Cremonesi.

Le Dœuff, Michèle. 1987. Women and Philosophy. In *French feminist thought.* Ed. Toril Moi. Oxford: Basil Blackwell.

———. 1991. *Hipparchia's choice: An essay concerning women, philosophy, etc.* Translated by Trista Selous. Oxford: Basil Blackwell.

Mason, Michael. 1995. *The making of victorian sexuality.* Oxford: Oxford University Press.

Marston, Mansfield. 1873. *The life of John Stuart Mill: Politician and philosopher, critic and metaphysician.* London: F. Farrah.

Mayo, Herbert. 1840. *A treatise on siphilis.* London: Henry Renshaw.

Mazlish, Bruce. 1975. *James and John Stuart Mill: Father and son in the nineteenth century.* New York: Basic Books.

Mineka, Francis E. 1944. *The dissidence of dissent: "The Monthly Repository," 1806-1838.* Chapel Hill, NC: University of North Carolina Press.

———. 1963. The *Autobiography* and the lady. *University of Toronto Quarterly* 32:301-6.

———. and Lindley, Dwight N., editors. 1972. *The later letters of John Stuart Mill.* In *Collected works of John Start Mill.* Vols. XIV and XV. Toronto: University of Toronto Press.

Packe, Michael St. John. 1954. *The life of John Stuart Mill.* New York: Macmillan.

Pappe, H. O. 1960. *John Stuart Mill and the Harriet Taylor myth.* Melbourne: Melbourne University Press.

Parker, Langston. 1839. *Modern treatment of syphilitic diseases.* London: John Churchill.

Pool, Daniel. 1993. *What Jane Austen ate and Charles Dickens knew: From fox hunting to whist—the facts of daily life in nineteenth-century England.* New York: Simon & Schuster.

Robbins, L. 1957. Packe on Mill. *Economics* 24 (August): 250–59. Also published in *John Stuart Mill: Critical assessments.* Vol. 4, ed. John Cunningham Wood. London: Routledge, 1988.

Robson, John. 1966. Harriet Taylor and John Stuart Mill: Artist and scientist. *Queen's Quarterly* 73:167–86.

Rose, Phyllis. 1984. *Parallel lives: Five victorian marriages.* New York: Vintage.

Rossi, Alice S., ed. 1970. *Essays on sex equality,* by John Stuart Mill and Harriet Taylor Mill, Chicago: University of Chicago Press.

Russell, Bertrand, and Russell, Patricia, editors. *The Amberley papers: Bertrand Russell's family background.* Vol. 1. 1937. New York: Simon and Schuster.

Ryan, Alan. 1970. *John Stuart Mill.* New York: Pantheon.

————. 1991. Sense and sensibility in Mill's political thought. In *A cultivated mind: Essays on J. S. Mill presented to John M. Robson,* ed. Michael Laine. Toronto: University of Toronto Press.

Stillinger, Jack, ed. 1961. *The early draft of John Stuart Mill's "Autobiography."* Urbana: University of Illinois Press.

Strachey, Ray. 1928. *The cause: A short history of the women's movement in Great Britain.* Portway: Cedric Chivers.

Tatalovich, A. 1973. John Stuart Mill: *The Subjection of Women*: An analysis. *Southern Quarterly* 12 (1):87–105. Also published in *John Stuart Mill: Critical assessments.* Vol. 4, ed. John Cunningham Wood. London: Routledge, 1988.

Taylor, Mary. 1912. Mrs. John Stuart Mill: A vindication by her granddaughter. *Nineteenth Century and After* 71:357–63.

Trilling, Diana. 1952. Mill's intellectual beacon. *Partisan Review* 19:115–16, 118–20.

Tulloch, Gail. 1989. *Mill and sexual equality.* Boulder, Colo.: Lynne Rienner.

General Index

Adams, Sarah Flower, 330n, 461-62
Anderson, Hans Christian, 224, 232
Arts and architecture, xiv, xxxiii, 160, 165-68, 336, 337, 400
    literary critique, 232
    poetry, 209-21, 229
    theater critique, 574, 578
    theory, 165, 168-70
    travel journal, 170-75
Atheism. *See* Religion
Austin, John and Sarah, 166, 180, 368, 438, 481

Bain, Alexander, xi
Borchard, Ruth, xi
Brougham, Henry Peter, 401. *See also* Society for the Diffusion of Useful Knowledge

California gold rush, 499
Carlyle, Jane, 368
Carlyle, Thomas, xi, xviii, 224, 225, 228, 235n, 237, 359, 368, 379, 382, 385, 412-13
    HTM's anger at, 235-36
Carry, Cary, Cat. *See* Ley, Caroline Hardy
Catholicism. *See* Religion
Caxton, William, 237, 273-91
Charlatanism. *See* Religion
Chartist. *See* Mill, Harriet Taylor: anger at Chartist
Children, 213-15
    and marriage, 23
    custody, 75, 85-88, 91-94
Christianity. *See* Religion
Class consciousness, 9-10, 24-25, 31, 35-36, 40, 63, 87, 121, 137, 147, 161, 224, 229-31, 232, 235, 291-92, 305, 368, 479-80, 527-28, 558. *See also* Equality, class
    children's education, 112-14
    education of laboring classes, 296-97
    in judicial treatment, 119
    JSM's views on, 338
    paternalism vs. self-dependence, 293-98
Cobbe, Francis Power, xxxiv
Coleridge, Samuel, 150n, 169n, 208n
    with JSM, xiii-xvii, xxxiv-xxxv, 17, 27, 29, 33, 35, 43-46, 48, 50, 75, 77, 126, 135, 137, 157-58, 291-98, 321-22, 340-43, 349-50, 359, 364, 369, 374-75, 438-39, 544
    in conversation, xvii, 333, 336, 341, 365, 368
    with John Taylor, 237
Collins, Wilkie, 578
Comte, Auguste, 31, 224, 235, 337, 338, 374n
    HTM's anger at, 235-36
    sexism of, xiv
Crowe, Eire, 339

Daily News, 95, 98, 339n, 341, 342, 342n, 368, 429, 467, 493, 495
Desainteville, 323
Dickens, Charles, 224, 232
Disraeli, Benjamin, 176n
    The Wondrous Tale of Alroy, 166, 176-78
Domestic violence, xvi, xvii, xx, 3, 56, 75-76, 95, 101-104
    and children, xxxiv, 76, 88-90, 100-104, 116, 119-22

and servants, 76, 98-100, 104-108
and women, xi, xiv, xxxiv, 17, 29, 85,
    87-88, 116, 122-26, 224, 233-34
Fitzroy's Bill pamphlet, xiii
punishment for, 118-19, 121-22, 125-31
Duffy, Gavan, 416, 424

Edinburgh Review, 368, 374n, 470n
Education, women's, xiv, 3-13, 22, 29-30,
    46, 52, 65-66, 181-82. *See also*
    Motherhood, education
and equality, 45
Ellis, Mrs., 32
Emerson, Ralph Waldo, xxviii, 141n, 145n
Empson, William, 470
Enfranchisement, 28-30, 37-43, 46, 48
"Enfranchisement of Women," xiii, 27, 29,
    30, 51-73, 76, 321
suffrage, xiv, 4, 28-30, 39, 43, 48-49,
    52-54, 299n, 342, 392
English
    views on, 68, 235, 337, 340, 343, 394,
        481, 494
Equality, xiv. *See also* Class consciousness;
    Power; Sexuality
    class, 17, 24-25, 299-301, 305
    women's, 5, 12, 17, 22-25, 36-48, 52-
        73, 153, 299, 390-92
    and religion, 157, 161
    and sexuality/sensuality, 16
    and women's rights, xvi, 24-25, 27-73,
        85-88, 91-94
    in marriage, 16, 40
    in work, 298-99, 390-91
    nature vs. nurture, 31-33, 45
    political, 47, 391
Ethics. *See* Morality
Examiner, 369, 460, 563

Fitzroy's Bill, 76, 126-131
Fitzroy, Charles Sir, 491
Flower, Eliza, 224, 328, 330n, 379, 384-
    85, 461-62
Flower, Sarah. *See* Adams, Sarah Flower
Fox, Eliza (W. J. Fox's daughter), 390, 430,
    434, 540, 544
Fox, William J., xxxviii, 4, 12n, 166, 224,
    233, 336, 337, 384, 461-62, 525,
    529-30, 560
HTM's anger at, 233, 339, 341, 453-54,
    461-62
HTM's letters to, 328-29, 390-92, 434
French
    views on 337, 340, 343, 494-96

Galignami, 581
Gilles, Margaret and Mary, 462
Goethe, J. W. von, 180, 192n
Grote, George, 368, 399
Guizot, François, 203, 481

Hagberg, Knut, xv, 157
Hahn Hahn, Gräfin, 224, 232, 462
Haji. *See* Taylor, Algernon
Hampden controversy, 393-94
Hampden, John, 185-92
Hardy, Alfred (brother), 422, 425, 464-65,
    467, 497, 502, 503
Hardy, Arthur (brother), xx, xxi, xxiii, xxx,
    335, 371, 379-80, 382-83, 399n,
    403-404, 411, 431, 438, 464-65,
    469, 476, 479, 481-89, 495, 497,
    500, 502, 503, 539, 541
HTM's anger at, 425
HTM's letters to, 386-90, 413-25
Hardy, Edward (brother), xx, 379, 387n,
    409-11, 440, 449, 500
HTM's anger at, 389
Hardy, Emilia (sister-in-law), 379-80, 387,
    406, 444
HTM's letters to, 385-86
Hardy, Harriet (mother), xii, xxi, xxii, 333,
    335, 379-80, 389-90, 417, 423,
    443, 445-48, 451, 456, 464, 467,
    471-74, 483, 487, 514
HTM's anger at, 381-82, 402-3, 408,
    410, 411
HTM's letters to, 401-12
Hardy, Thomas (father), xx-xxii, xxix, 379-
    80, 389, 399, 440, 445-50, 462-64,
    467, 471-75, 481, 483, 487, 500, 502
HTM's anger at, 388
HTM's letters to, 386-88
Hardy, William (brother), xxi, 379, 385,
    386, 444
Hayek, F. A., xxi, xviii, xxx, xxxviii, 339n,
    341n, 343n
Henshaw, S. E., xi, 157
Herby. *See* Taylor, Herbert
Himmelfarb, Gertrude, xv
Holyoake, George, 157, 158n, 340, 343,
    359
HTM's anger at, 340, 349-50
Human nature, 338

Irish
    views on, 342, 343, 352, 394, 416
Italians
    views on, 224, 234-35, 441

Jameson, Anna Browell, 32

Labor. *See also* Class consciousness; Power; Socialism
  charitable, 112-15
  in prison, 114-15
  social production, 300-301, 310-13
Laconicisms. *See* Morality, moral rules
Laing affair, 404-406
Laing, Marianne, 450n, 463-64, 474, 559-60
Legal system, 150-51. *See also* Domestic violence; Violence
  juries, 77-79, 109-11
  legislation, 115-22
  punishment, 76, 77-79, 95-98, 109, 111
Ley, Arthur (brother-in-law), XX, 224, 379, 382-83, 389, 402-403, 415, 417-21, 423-25, 447, 449. *See also* Trusteeship
  HTM's anger at, 422n
Ley, Caroline Hardy (sister), xx, xxiii, xxxvii, 224, 333, 379, 381, 383, 389-90, 402-403, 406, 408-409, 412, 443, 446-49, 451, 472, 500. *See also* Trusteeship
  HTM's anger at, 414, 415, 417-22, 423-25
Liberty, 342. *See also* Domestic violence
  and oppression, xv, 28, 30, 44-45, 185-92, 298, 301
  in America, 183
  personal, xiv, 29-30, 37-43, 49, 50, 54-73, 215-16, 221
Lily. *See* Taylor, Helen
Loesberg, Jonathan, xv
Louis Napoleon, 427

Marriage, xiv, 15-25, 390
  and affection, 68
  and companionship, 66, 68-69
  and divorce, 15, 17, 22-25
  and law, xii, 15-16, 18-19, 20-21, 22, 52
  as ownership, 15, 16, 19, 62, 76, 115-16
  as prostitution, 4, 9, 12-13
  freedom of opinion, 49
Martineau, Harriet, 385
Mazlish, Bruce, xxx
Mazzini, Giuseppe, 441
Medicine. *See also* Mill, Harriet Taylor; Mill, John Stuart; Taylor, John
  hydropathy, 79-82
Merivale, Herman, 470, 511, 576-77, 582

Mermaid poem, 215-16, 437
Mill, George (JSM's brother), 344-45, 398
  HTM's anger at, 346-47, 383, 433-34
Mill, Harriet Taylor. *See also* Collaboration
  anger about child abuse, 121-22
  anger about conformity, 155
  anger about custody judgments, 87-88, 94
  anger about domestic violence, 89-90, 97, 100-101, 103, 105, 118, 126
  anger about French Revolution, 342
  anger about legal system, 96, 106-108, 110-11, 121
  anger about marriage institution, 13, 18-23, 225
  anger about religious institutions, 160-63, 225-26
  anger about women's issues, 6, 9, 24, 152-53, 380
  anger at Chartist, 54, 380, 391, 393
  anger at *Daily News*, 342
  anger at doctors, 346, 356
  anger at Joseph Hume, 341
  anger at women writers, 32-34
  depression, 508-9, 535, 537, 542, 547, 553, 567-68, 570-72
  desire for privacy, 322, 371-73, 406, 409, 411, 476, 488, 498, 510-12, 515, 519, 520, 524-25, 532, 540, 547, 550, 552, 554, 568-69, 570, 573, 575-77, 581-82, 587
  family life, xix-xxi, 437
  health, xxix-xxx, 321, 334, 336, 389-90, 429, 431, 442, 443, 445-49, 455, 457, 461, 466-69, 471, 473, 475, 477, 480-86, 489, 490, 493-94, 497, 499, 508-10, 513, 518, 521, 525, 527-31, 533-34, 541-44, 547, 552-53, 556, 559-62, 566-67, 569, 570, 579-87
  outlook on life, 228
  personal notebooks, 225-37
  relationship with JSM, xii-xiii, xvii-xix, xxi, xxxiii, 292, 319-23, 339-40, 355, 361, 365, 381, 438-39, 511-12, 517
  relationship with John Taylor, xii, xiii, xxviii, xxxi, xxxii, 168, 359, 360, 413-14, 437, 439-41
Mill, James, 237
Mill, John Stuart (second husband), xi, xii, xiv, xxi, xxvii, xxviii-xxix, xxx, xxxii, xxxiii, xxxvi, xxxviii, xxxix-xlii, 15, 31, 33n, 34n, 35n, 76, 77, 79, 82, 85, 88, 91, 95, 100-101,

104-105, 108-109, 112, 115, 119, 122, 126, 136, 150, 157, 166, 224, 235n, 236, 238, 383-85, 399, 401, 407, 411, 414, 416, 417, 421-24, 427, 429, 431, 441, 439, 453-54, 467, 501, 514-15, 521, 526, 529, 534, 539-42, 548, 551, 562, 564, 566, 576, 578, 582-83, 586-87n. *See also* Collaboration; Mill, Harriet Taylor: relationship with JSM
Autobiography, xiii, xvii, 291, 375
health, 373, 544, 553, 563, 570
HTM's anger at, xvii, xix, 31, 228, 235-36, 325-27, 330-33, 337, 360, 511, 523-24, 575, 581
HTM's letters to, 318-77
Logic, 416, 423
Utilitarianism, 17, 137, 374
Mineka, Francis E., xv, xxxviii, 450n
Mirabeau, 192-96
Miss Trevor. *See* Taylor, Helen
Money, 226, 236-37. *See also* Taylor, Helen
Monthly Repository, xiii, xxxviii, 4, 12n, 165, 166, 167, 168, 178, 179, 180, 185, 192, 196, 204, 218, 219, 320
Morality, xv, 19-21, 50, 78, 136, 140-41, 142-43, 145-46, 338
blame, 136-37, 155
civil disobedience, 136-37, 150-52
duty, 138
education, 130-31
knowledge, xv, 136, 149-50
moral rules, 136, 143-48, 149-50, 152, 223
self-interest, 136-37, 152-53
utility, 137, 153-154
virtue and enjoyment, 136, 154-55, 224
Morning Chronicle, 77, 79, 82, 85, 88, 91, 100, 104, 108, 115, 122, 441, 467-68
Motherhood, 10, 59. *See also* Education
education, 7-8
rights of, 85-88, 91-94

Nature, 209-13, 216-21
seasons, 204-8
New York Daily Tribune, 51
Novello, Vincent, 453

On Liberty, xiii, xiv, xv, xvii, xxxiv, 17, 28, 77, 135, 231n, 232n, 374n

Palmerston, Lady, 460
Pappe, H. O., xv, xviii

Parker, H. W., 468
Peel, Robert, 460
Pleasure/happiness, xxxiv, 325, 329, 335. *See also* Morality
men's vs. women's, 4
Political Economy Club, 521
Population control, 225, 292, 298-300
Poverty, 225. *See also* Class consciousness
Power. *See also* Class consciousness; Women
capitalist over laborer, 313-15
fathers over children, 86-87, 120
husband over wife/family, 4, 11, 24, 63-64, 87-88, 90-91, 116, 301
master over servant, 108
master over slave, 44, 68, 391
men over women, 5, 6, 15, 30, 44, 49, 67-69, 136, 147
mother over child, 4, 10-11
officer over enlisted men, 82-85
upper classes over lower classes, 294-96
women over men, 6, 22, 68
Principles of Political Economy, xiii, xvi, 75, 321, 380, 383-84, 390, 392n, 438. *See also* Collaboration
dedication controversy, 291-92, 371, 392, 472-73
Protestantism. *See* Religion
Proverbs. *See* Morality, moral rules

Quarterly Review, 32, 193, 368, 468

Reasoner, 157, 158n, 159, 340
Religion, xxxiv, 24, 69, 92-94, 147, 157-63, 167, 187, 195-96, 223, 225-26, 296, 337, 370, 374, 393-94, 426, 574
atheism, xiv, xvii, 158-60, 340, 341, 358
charlatanism, 158, 162-63
Christian morality, 157-58, 160, 161-62
in America, 184
salaries of clergy, 194
Robertson, John, 441
Romilly, John, 368
Ruge, Arnold, 521, 540-42
Russell, Lord John, 460
HTM's anger at, 341

Sand, George, xiii, 27, 33-34, 224, 232, 233
Schiller, 169n, 192n
Sexuality, xiv, xviii, xxxii, 23, 223, 226, 235. *See also* Equality
Shelley, 8, 170, 173, 429
Sinnett, Frederick, 398-400

Socialism, xxxiv, 292, 313-15, 341, 392.
   See also Labor
   examples of, 302-13
Society for the Diffusion of Useful Knowl-
   edge, xiii, 6, 223, 237, 297n, 401.
   See also Brougham, Henry Peter
Spectator, 393
Sterling, John, 359, 368
   letters concerning, 362n, 363, 364, 367
Stillinger, Jack, xv
   Stirling, Fanny, 368, 513-15, 520, 522,
      526, 528, 532-533, 538, 545-49,
      551, 553, 564, 575n, 577, 578-79,
      581. *See also* Taylor, Helen
HTM's letter to, 374
Suffrage. *See* Enfranchisement

Taylor, Algernon (son), xii, xiii, xxv, xxviii,
   xxxvii, 335, 349, 366, 373, 375,
   379, 380, 383, 407, 415, 421, 424-
   25, 444-49, 451, 456-59, 461,
   465, 471, 475, 478, 479, 481-83,
   488-91, 495, 497, 498, 500-502,
   503-504
   health, 395-96, 410, 463, 492-94
   HTM's anger at, 351, 469-70, 532, 558
   HTM's letters to, 392-99, 400-401,
      426-33
   trip to Italy, 426-33, 535, 537, 540-42,
      544, 552-53, 556, 560-61, 563,
      566-67, 570, 579
   with Helen during acting, 512, 514, 519,
      520, 523-25, 527, 530, 534
Taylor, Helen (daughter), xiii, xxii, xxviii,
   xxix, xxx, xxxii, xxxvi, xxxvii, 224,
   229, 232, 320, 322, 366, 373, 383,
   385, 415, 421, 427, 430, 443, 444,
   445, 447-49, 450-52, 455-60,
   462-63, 467, 469, 475, 477-78,
   480, 482-85, 487, 489, 495, 500,
   502
   career, 375-76, 508, 518-23, 526-29, 531,
      533, 537-38, 543, 545-49, 552, 559,
      561, 572-73
   clothing, 230, 231, 508, 514, 516, 519,
      522, 524, 527-28, 541, 543-44, 548,
      556, 558-61, 563-68
   friends, 527-28, 558, 564-66
   health, 407-409, 424, 428, 466, 470,
      479, 486, 488, 541, 543, 561, 564,
      566-67
   holidays, 508, 525, 529-34, 547-48, 555,
      564, 567-68, 570-73
   HTM's affection for, 507, 510, 515, 517-
      18, 531, 534-35, 538, 549, 551, 555,
      566-67, 575
   HTM's anger at, 536-38, 549-51, 554,
      556-57
   HTM's letters to, 506-87
   independence, 507, 515-18, 520, 527,
      531-32, 535, 537-41, 543, 546, 550,
      553, 555, 562, 572-73
   money, 508, 513, 517, 520, 522-25,
      532-33, 536-38, 546-48, 550-52,
      554-55, 562, 565
Taylor, Herbert (son), xii, xiii, xxviii,
   xxxvii, 335, 349, 356, 372, 373,
   379, 382, 394, 397, 398, 400, 401-
   403, 409, 417-18, 424-25, 444-
   49, 451-52, 455-58, 460-65,
   474-75, 477-78, 483, 488-93,
   496, 497-99, 502, 514
   HTM's anger at, 424
Taylor, John (first husband), xii, xvi, xxiv,
   xxix, xxx, xxxvii, 224n, 238, 291,
   379, 387-89, 397, 412-13, 417. *See
   also* Collaboration; Mill, Harriet Taylor: relationship with John Taylor
   death, xiii, xix, xxi, 76, 370-73, 402,
      413-14
   financial arrangements with HTM, 444,
      454, 466, 474-76, 480, 488, 499,
      503
   health, 321, 344-70, 401, 439, 470, 477,
      480, 482, 484, 487, 492-93, 495, 498,
      500-501, 503
   HTM's anger at, 215n, 489, 490
   HTM's letters to, 436-504
Times (London), 77, 78, 82, 85, 91, 109,
   112, 114, 119, 377, 393, 467, 493-
   96, 498, 523, 563, 575-76, 578
Tocqueville, Alexis de, 368
Tolerance, xxxiv, 135, 137-42, 144, 184-
   85, 226-27. *See also* Morality
   conformity, 135, 137, 138, 141-42, 145,
      326
   conscience, 145-46
   eccentricity, xxxiv, 135, 138
   self-reliance, 135, 138, 142
Travel journal, xiv, 165, 170-75
Trilling, Diana, xi
Trusteeship, 382-83, 412-25. *See also* Ley,
   Arthur; Ley, Caroline Hardy
Truth, xv, xxxiv, 139-42, 143-45, 224,
   232
   and language, 135

Usiglio, Angleo, 441

Victor Emmanuel II, 426
Violence, 75-76. *See also* Domestic violence
    animal abuse, 88-90
    corporal punishment, 76, 368-69
Virtue, 148
    chastity, 226
Vote. *See* Enfranchisement

Westminster Review, xiii, 30, 51, 76, 441
Women. *See also* Domestic violence, and
       women; Enfranchisement; Equality,

women's; Human nature; Marriage;
    Mermaid poem; Mill, Harriet Tay-
    lor; Power
and love, 225
as economic threat, 60-62
as slaves, 6, 20, 47-48, 390-91
domestic life, 28
Women's rights. *See* Equality, women's

Young, Henry Fox, 424

Index of Documents

LETTERS

The number on the left is the number assigned in the Mill/Taylor Collection of the British Library of the London School of Political and Economic Sciences. The number on the right of each column is the location of the text in this volume.

Box II/63	170–75	Box III/128	226–27
Box III/77	17–20	Box III/138	236
Box III/78	137–42	Box III/144	160–61
Box III/79	20–24	Box III/145	155
Box III/80	8–9	Box III/147	236
Box III/81	7–8	Box III/150	236–37
Box III/82	10–11	Box III/154	237
Box III/83	176–78	Box III/155	324
Box III/84	150–52	Box III/157	162
Box III/85	9–10	Box III/186	220
Box III/86	143–50, 154–55	Box III/188	221
Box III/87	5–7	Box III/189	209
Box III/90	162–63	Box III/203	220
Box III/91	24	Box III/204	209
Box III/92	152–53	Box III/205	209–10
Box III/97	9 ft., 12–13	Box III/206	211–12
Box III/98	137	Box III/207	210–11
Box III/99	142–43	Box III/208	212–15
Box III/100	32–33	Box III/212	216–18
Box III/101	228–35	II/300	323
Box III/102	168–70	II/313	336
Box III/103	31–32, 337–38	II/314	334–35
Box III/104	24–25	II/315	338–39
Box III/105	170	II/316	325
Box III/106	235–36	II/317	323–24
Box III/107	225–26	II/318	334
Box III/113	284 ft.	II/319	334
Box III/127	153–54	II/320	324

II/321	326	XXVIII/126	370
II/322	342-43	XXVIII/135	441
II/323	325-26	XXVIII/136	453-54
II/324	324-25	XXVIII/137	454
II/325	336-37	XXVIII/138	457
II/327	337-8	XXVIII/139	455
II/330	335	XXVIII/140	458-59
XXVII/2	412-13	XXVIII/141	455-56
XXVII/3	434-35	XXVIII/142	456
XXVII/40	390-91	XXVIII/143	439-41
XXVII/45	413-14	XXVIII/144	215-16
XXVII/46	414-15	XXVIII/145	441-42
XXVII/47	415	XXVIII/146	442-43
XXVII/48	416-22	XXVIII/147	443-44
XXVII/49	416-22 ft.	XXVIII/148	444-45
XXVII/50	422-24	XXVIII/149	445
XXVII/51	424-25	XXVIII/150	446-47
XXVII/54	385-86	XXVIII/151	447-48
XXVII/55	401	XXVIII/152	451
XXVII/56	402	XXVIII/153	448-49
XXVII/57	402-3	XXVIII/154	449
XXVII/58	403-6	XXVIII/156	449-50
XXVII/63	406	XXVIII/157	450-51
XXVII/65	407	XXVIII/158	452
XXVII/67	407-8	XXVIII/159	457-58
XXVII/70	408	XXVIII/160	463
XXVII/72	409	XXVIII/161	460
XXVII/73	409-10	XXVIII/162	460-61
XXVII/76	410	XXVIII/163	461-62
XXVII/80	411-12	XXVIII/164	462-63
XXVII/83	410-11	XXVIII/165	455
XXVII/87	386-87	XXVIII/166	446
XXVII/88	387-88	XXVIII/167	464
XXVII/91	413	XXVIII/168	469
XXVII/100	392	XXVIII/169	465
XXVII/101	393	XXVIII/170	471
XXVII/102	394	XXVIII/171	457
XXVII/103	393-94	XXVIII/172	468-69
XXVII/104	394-95	XXVIII/173	465-66
XXVII/105	395	XXVIII/174	466-67
XXVII/106	395-96	XXVIII/175	469
XXVII/108	396-97	XXVIII/176	469-70
XXVII/109	397-99	XXVIII/177	471
XXVII/110	400-401	XXVIII/178	473-74
XXVII/111	426	XXVIII/179	472
XXVII/112	427	XXVIII/180	472-73
XXVII/113	427-28	XXVIII/181	474
XXVII/114	428	XXVIII/182	474-75
XXVII/115	429-30	XXVIII/187	475
XXVII/116	430	XXVIII/188	475-76
XXVII/117	431	XXVIII/189	476
XXVII/118	431-32	XXVIII/190	477-78
XXVII/119	432-33	XXVIII/191	476-77
XXVIII/123	399-400	XXVIII/192	478

XXVIII/194	478-79		L/15	352-53
XXVIII/195	479		L/16	358-59
XXVIII/197	479-80		L/17	359-60
XXVIII/198	480		L/18	350
XXVIII/199	480-81		L/19	355-57
XXVIII/201	481		L/20	347-49
XXVIII/202	482		L/21	357-58
XXVIII/204	482-83		L/22	361-62
XXVIII/207	483		L/23	360-61
XXVIII/209	483-84		L/25	364
XXVIII/211	484-85		L/26	353-55
XXVIII/212	485		L/27	362-64
XXVIII/213	485-86		L/28	364-66
XXVIII/214	486-87		L/29	366-67
XXVIII/215	487-88		L/30	368
XXVIII/216	488		L/31	368-69
XXVIII/217	488-89		L/32	369-70
XXVIII/218	489-90		L/33	370
XXVIII/219	490-91		L/34	370-71
XXVIII/220	491-92		L/35	372
XXVIII/221	492-93		L/36	371-72
XXVIII/222	494-95		L/37	372-73
XXVIII/223	495-97		L(ii)/40	373-75
XXVIII/224	497-98		LI/4	512
XXVIII/225	498-500		LI/5	513
XXVIII/226	500		LI/7	513-14
XXVIII/227	501-502		LI/9	515
XXVIII/228	502-503		LI/11	515-16
XXVIII/229	504		LI/14	516-18
XXVIII/233	335-36		LI/16	518-19
XXVIII/234	334-35		LI/18	519
XXVIII/235	330		LI/19	519-20
XXVIII/236	376-77		LI/23	520-23
XXVIII/237	377		LI/25	523
XXVIII/238	333		LI/27	524-25
XXVIII/239	336		LI/29	525
XXVIII/240	376		LI/32	526
XXVIII/241	360		LI/33	526-27
XXVIII/242	375-76		LI/37	527-28
XL/4	158-60		LI/39	528-29
XL/2	33-50, 161-62		LI/41	529-31
XLVII/17	433-34		LI/42	531
L/3	323		LI/45	531-33
L/4	326-28		LI/47	533
L/5	329		LI/48	533-34
L/6	332-33		LI/51	534
L/7	330-32		LI/55	535
L/8	339-42		LI/57	535-36
L/9	343-44		LI/59	536-37
L/10	344-45		LII/61	537-38
L/11	346-47		LII/62	539
L/12	349-50		LII/65	539
L/13	345-46		LII/66	539-40
L/14	350-52		LII/68	540-41

LII/71	541	LII/125	573-74
LII/73	542-43	LII/126	574
LII/74	543-44	LIII(i)/1	575
LII/77	544-45	LIII(i)/2	576
LII/79	545-46	LIII(i)/4	576-77
LII/81	547	LIII(i)/6	577-79
LII/83	547-49	LIII(i)/8	579
LII/86	549-50	LIII(i)/9	580
LII/88	550-52	LIII(i)/12	580-81
LII/90	552-53	LIII(i)/13	582-83
LII/91	553-54	LIII(i)/15	583
LII/94	554-55	LIII(i)/17	583-84
LII/96	555-57	LIII(i)/18	584
LII/99	557-58	LIII(i)/20	584-85
LII/100	558-60	LIII(i)/23	585-86
LII/103	560-62	LIII(i)/25	586-87
LII/105	562-63	LIII(i)/30	587
LII/107	563-65	LIV/24	574
LII/108	565-66	Yale University	
LII/110	566-67	Library letters	328-29
LII/113	567-68	PRG 101	
LII/115	568-69	(Library of	
LII/117	569-70	South	
LII/118	570-71	Australiana	
LII/120	571-72	letter)	388-90
LII/122	572-73	King's College	
LII/123	573	Library letters	384-85, 391-92, 434

Published Works

"Enfranchisement of Women" in *Westminster Review*	51-73
Newspaper articles in *Morning Chronicle, Daily News*, and *Sunday Times*	75-126
"Remarks on Mr. Fitzroy's Bill for the More Effectual Prevention of Assaults on Women and Children"	126-131
Book Reviews in *Monthly Repository*	178-204
"The Seasons" in *Monthly Repository*	204-208
Poems in *Monthly Repository*	218-219
"Life of William Caxton" in *Lives of Eminent Persons*	237-291
"On the Probable Futurity of the Labouring Classes" in *Principles of Political Economy*	293-315

Jo Ellen Jacobs is Griswold Distinguished Professor of Philosophy at Millikin University. She is the author of "'The Lot of Gifted Ladies Is Hard': A Study of Harriet Taylor Mill Criticism," in *Hypatia's Daughters: 1500 Years of Women Philosophers* (1995), as well as articles on aesthetics.

Paula Harms Payne teaches at Georgia College and State University.

CPSIA information can be obtained at www.ICGtesting.com
Printed in the USA
BVOW06*1636181115

427638BV00014B/93/P

Above: *Bibury church at the east end of the village.*

The western boundary of the Cotswol[d] is formed by a steep escarpment which runs in an unbroken line for 50 miles (81 km) from Chipping Campden in th[e] north to Bath in the south. East of the Edge, as this escarpment is known, the Cotswolds slope gently away, drained [by] a series of placid rivers whose waters a[re] eventually find their way to the Thames. The main ones are the Evenlode, the Windrush, the Leach, th[e] Coln and the Churn, all good trout streams and remarkable for the purity of their waters. Exploring their beautif[ul] valleys is certainly one of the best way[s] of getting to know the Cotswold countryside more intimately.

The Coln rises high on the western plateau in the fields between Brockhampton and Charlton Abbots. After flowing through Chedworth Woods, where the National Trust look[s] after the best-preserved remains of a Roman villa in the Cotswolds, it reache[s] Ablington and then, at the end of an idyllic little valley, it enters Bibury, perhaps the most famous of all the Cotswold villages since it received its stamp of approval from William Morri[s] about a century ago.

Unlike most Cotswold villages, Bibu[ry]

Old weavers' cottages in Arlington Row, Bibury.

Above: *Fairford's great 'wool' church.*

a hive of activity. Its main attraction is rlington Row, a picturesque terrace of ny cottages converted from a medieval ool store in the early seventeenth ntury for the use of weavers at the earby Arlington Mill. Arlington Mill self is now a folk museum with a llection of furniture and implements well as working mill machinery. The d mill race feeds a trout farm which is en to the public.

From Bibury, the Coln meanders on Fairford, one of the many historic arket towns in the Cotswolds which rived on the medieval wool trade. airford's church is one of the finest otswold 'wool' churches – that is a urch built (or rather rebuilt, since ost Cotswold churches have Norman igins) in the fifteenth century, usually the expense of hugely wealthy local ool merchants. In Fairford's case the enefactors were John Tame and his on, Sir Edmund. Amazingly, the onderful stained glass they ommissioned sometime around 1500 rvived both the Reformation and estruction by Puritans in the Civil War nd is now the only complete set of edieval stained glass existing in the hole of the British Isles.

Medieval stained glass depicting the Last Judgement in Fairford church.

3

Above: *The River Leach glides past Eastleach Martin church.*

Cottages face the First World War memorial on the green at Guiting Power.

After Fairford, the Coln flows on to join the Thames at Lechlade. The Leach, from which Lechlade takes its name, also meets the Thames near here.

North of the Coln and the Leach are the valleys of the Windrush and Evenlode. The Windrush valley in particular embraces more of the history, beauty and traditions of the Cotswolds than any of the other river valleys, and more than fulfills all that its evocative name seems to promise.

The river rises at Cutsdean near one of the steepest sections of the western scarpment. The first villages it comes to are the Guitings: Temple Guiting, once the property of the Knights Templar, and Guiting Power, a classic Cotswold stone village which is also the home of the Cotswold Farm Park and its Rare Breeds Survival Centre. Of outstanding local interest at the Centre are the Cotswold sheep which brought fame and wealth to the Cotswolds in the Middle Ages when their wool was the most sought-after in Europe.

After the Guitings, the Windrush flows through the village of Naunton, with its fifteenth-century pigeon house, and so on to Bourton-on-the-Water. Here it is joined by the Dikler which links it with two famous villages a mile or so to the north, Upper Slaughter and Lower Slaughter. Upper Slaughter is the more interesting of the two, particularly its superb Cotswold manor house visible from the road, but Lower Slaughter attracts all the visitors, being both more accessible and within comfortable walking distance of Bourton-on-the-Water.

Both Lower Slaughter and Bourton share the unusual feature of a river, crossed by low bridges, running down their main streets. In Lower Slaughter's case, the river is the Eye, a tributary of the Dikler. Once it powered the mill, whose brick chimney, so unexceptional in most other parts of the country, stands out like a sore thumb in the Cotswolds where everything from a pigsty to a mansion is built with the local golden stone.

Above: *Naunton nestles in the Windrush valley.*

Above: *A hazy day at Upper Slaughter.*

Cottages at Lower Slaughter reflected in the River Eye.

Bourton-on-the-Water is one of the largest villages in the Cotswolds and also one of its most popular attractions. It has plenty of shops, tea rooms, pubs and accommodation and, like Bibury, no shortage of things to keep visitors occupied, including a motor museum, a trout farm, a perfumery and exhibitions of butterflies and model railways. Its most famous sights are the model village built out of Cotswold stone in the garden of the Old New Inn – a ⅑ size replica of Bourton itself – and Birdland, with its collection of penguins and other exotic birds.

From Bourton the Windrush flows down to Burford, passing the Barringtons and Taynton on the way. These villages were once an important quarrying centre, producing some of the best stone ever dug in the Cotswolds. The Cotswold limestone is an excellent building material because it is easy to work when freshly quarried yet becomes very hard when exposed to the weather. It is also found in a range of lovely colours, from a rich tan to pale cream or grey. Taynton stone has been used in Oxford since the Middle Ages and Sir Christopher Wren shipped large quantities of it to London for the rebuilding of St Paul's and the city churches after the Great Fire. He brought masons from the Cotswolds as well, including Thomas Strong, a native of Little Barrington. Strong performed the historic task of laying the foundation stone of St Paul's.

Above: *A tiny cottage at Great Barrington.*

The River Windrush flows down the main street of Bourton-on-the-Wa

Above: Bourton-on-the-Water's model village.

Above: A traditional ploughing match at Swinbrook.

...ven a toddler dwarfs the model village.

Burford was also famous for its quarries, but wool was the main source of its wealth in the Middle Ages. In fact, the first wool merchants' guild in England was established here soon after the Norman Conquest. Many houses dating from the heyday of the wool trade still survive in the long main street running up the hill from the river at the bottom. There is also a fine fifteenth-century 'wool' church with some interesting Civil War associations. Burford is now a busy market town. Its old Tudor market house contains a museum, and nearby at Bradwell Grove the Cotswold Wildlife Park has a collection of animals and birds from all over the world in 200 acres (494 ha) of gardens and woodland, one of several nature reserves in the Cotswolds.

By the time the Windrush reaches the Witney area it is approaching the Cotswolds' eastern border. Evidence of this is provided by the odd thatched roof to be found in the nearby village of Minster Lovell. Thatch is a very rare sight in the Cotswolds, most roofs being made of Cotswold stone tiles. Quiet though it now is, Minster Lovell was once the seat of a powerful aristocratic family, the Barons Lovell. The ruins of their old medieval hall still stand in the old part of the village on the banks of the river.

After Witney, the Windrush turns south and meets the Thames at last at Newbridge near Standlake. The Thames itself also rises in the Cotswolds, in a field a few miles south-west of Cirencester. The reclining figure of Old Father Thames grasping a shovel which used to mark the source has now been moved to St John's Lock, downstream at Lechlade.

Above: *An old threshing machine at the Cogges Farm Museum near Witney.*

Stone roofs give way to thatch at Minster Lovell.

Above: *The Thames at Ashton Keynes, not far from its source.*

Old Father Thames at St John's Lock, Lechlade.

Above: *The sun sets as sheep feed near Stow-on-the-Wold.*

The prehistoric Rollright Stones.

Climbing out of the river valleys you soon come to the wolds and the familiar Cotswold landscape of arable land, woods and farmsteads. Before the fields were enclosed with their superb dry-stone walls, however, the wolds looked very different indeed. Vast open pastures stretched from one end to the other with few features to relieve the bleakness of the scene. Here grazed the great flocks of Cotswold sheep whose wool, and later the cloth produced from it in the valleys around Stroud, dominated the Cotswold economy from the Middle Ages to the Industrial Revolution. And thousands of years before that, prehistoric man left his mark on the landscape. Long barrows and hill forts are scattered all over the area, and near Great Rollright there is a mysterious stone circle of about the same date as Stonehenge. Two long barrows particularly worth seeing are Hetty Pegler's Tump, near Stroud, and Belas Knap, near Winchcombe, and there is a fine hill fort in Crickley Hill Country Park.

The market towns of the Cotswolds were once among the wealthiest in the country. One of the loveliest is Winchcombe, which serviced the wool trade in the north-west. The town used to be dominated by its abbey, but so thoroughly was it knocked down at its dissolution in the sixteenth century that every trace of the actual building has been obliterated. A link survives in the George Inn, however, which used to be a guest house for pilgrims to the abbey and still has the initials of Richard Kidderminster, Abbot of Winchcombe around 1500, carved on a doorway. The town's simple fifteenth-century 'wool' church was built partly with the assistance of a local magnate, Sir Ralph Boteler. He was also responsible for building nearby Sudeley Castle where Henry VIII's sixth wife, Katherine Parr, spent her last days.

Above: *One of the 40 or more gargoyles on Winchcombe church.*

Above: *Charlbury church tower in winter.*

Harvest starts in the Cotswolds near Shipton-under-Wychwood.

Overleaf: *The Cotswold Hunt meets near Cheltenham.*

Cirencester, at the hub of a network of major Roman roads (the Foss Way, Ermin Way and Akeman Street) was *the* centre of the wool trade. Fittingly, its church, rebuilt in the fifteenth century, is also the greatest of the Cotswold 'wool' churches. The parish built the church itself, while the local abbey provided the three-storey south porch as an office for the transaction of its secular business. The size and richness of this, the most magnificent church porch in England, indicates how great that business must have been and how wealthy in consequence was the abbey.

Cirencester is still a busy town today and the unofficial capital of the Cotswolds, but it has nothing like the status it enjoyed in the past. In Roman times, for example, it was the largest city in Britain after London. Some evidence of this is provided by the collection of Roman artefacts in the Corinium Museum, one of the best collections of Roman antiquities in the country.

The Foss Way leaves Cirencester to the south-west and north-east in the shape of the A433 and the A429 respectively. The A433 soon diverges to link Tetbury with Cirencester. This is another lovely old market town with an unusual painted seventeenth-century market house on pillars. North of Cirencester, the Foss Way passes close by Northleach, whose 'wool' church is one of the finest in the Cotswolds. Inside, local wool merchants of 500 years ago are commemorated in a unique collection of memorial brasses. Just outside the town on the other side of the old Foss Way is the Countryside Collection, an award-winning museum of rural life and agricultural history housed in an eighteenth-century 'house of correction'.

Opposite: Cirencester Park on the edge of the town.

Above: *A polo player on a Cirencester pub sign.*

Sudeley Castle glimpsed through the trees.

Tetbury's unusual painted market hall.

After Northleach, the old Roman road called the Foss Way comes to Stow-on-the-Wold, at nearly 800 feet (243 metres) the highest town in the Cotswolds and the focal point for seven roads. Its market square – large, unspoilt and almost completely enclosed with sixteenth and seventeenth-century houses, mostly built in the traditional style – is the finest market square in the Cotswolds. Two fairs are held here in May and October when hundreds of horses are sold. Stow-on-the-Wold has few special tourist attractions, but it is well known for its antique shops.

North of Stow-on-the-Wold, though not on the Foss Way, Chipping Campden was another major centre of the Cotswold wool trade. In fact the Woolstaplers' Hall still survives as does the house of William Grevel, whose memorial brass in the fine 'wool' church describes him as the flower of the wool merchants of all England. Grevel died in 1401. His house, built about 20 years before, is only one of a number of early buildings in the High Street, which must be the most beautiful in England. The almshouses (1612) and the market hall (1627) were built by Sir Baptist Hicks, a great benefactor of the town in the early seventeenth century.

Some experts think that Hicks's Chipping Campden almshouses are the finest example there is of the Cotswold style of architecture. This unique style evolved during the sixteenth and seventeenth centuries when the cloth trade was booming and much new building was going on. Its main features are the stone-tiled roof, steeply pitched to allow water to run quickly off the porous limestone tiles, large gables and dormer windows, mullioned windows, and fine architectural details such as drip-stones above the windows and finials on the roof.

Above: *A corner of Stow-on-the-Wold's large market square.*

Sunshine streams through the arches of the market hall at Chipping Campde

Above: *Rich golden Cotswold stone at Adlestrop.*

Above: *A roofer lays Cotswold stone tiles at Charlbury.*

The curving village street at Adlestrop.

17

A sheltered corner of the lovely garden at Snowshill Manor.

Above: *Chastleton House and church.*

Many manor houses in the Cotswolds show off this classically English style to perfection. Chastleton House near Moreton-in-Marsh was built about the time of the Gunpowder Plot by Walter Jones, a Witney wool merchant who had bought the estate in 1603 from Robert Catesby, one of the Gunpowder plotters.

The house is unusual in having hardly changed since it was built, apart from the addition of some panelling to one room in the eighteenth century! It also has a secret room where a seventeenth-century owner of the house, a Royalist refugee from the Battle of Worcester, took refuge while Cromwellian soldiers slept in the bedroom next door. Fortunately his quick-thinking wife had taken the precaution of lacing the soldiers' drink with a strong dose of laudunum so he was able to tiptoe quietly out and escape.

At Stanway there is a particularly magnificent group of Cotswold buildings. The house, now the residence of Lord Neidpath, is open to the public in the summer. The remarkable gatehouse is one of the last great gatehouses to be built in this country. Hereafter lodge houses became more the fashion for country mansions.

Perhaps the most interesting building at Stanway, however, is the thirteenth-century tithe barn. The Cotswolds are famous for these barns, often as big as churches and mostly built in the Middle Ages by the great monasteries to store their tithes of wool and corn. In those days the abbeys were enormously wealthy and owned as much as three-fifths of all the land in the Cotswolds.

In the last century the Cotswold style, still the rule by and large for cottages, was revived for a number of large houses. Batsford Park near Moreton-in-Marsh, was designed on an Elizabethan 'E'-shaped plan for Lord Redesdale in 1884. Magnificently sited on the side of a hill overlooking the vale of the Evenlode, Batsford is famous for its arboretum. Covering 50 acres (124 ha), it contains over 1000 different trees and shrubs and is ornamented with oriental features such as buddhas and a Chinese temple. Another Cotswold arboretum, Westonbirt, run by the Forestry Commission, is the largest in the country.

Stanway's superb gatehouse.

Above: *Livestock in the park at Chastleton.*

Towards the end of the seventeenth century new classical styles began to be adopted by the country house builders in preference to the traditional Cotswold style. Snowshill near Stanway is a beautiful hybrid of old and new. The original manor house, long, narrow and gabled, was built about 1600 or earlier. A century or so later, a new wing was added, but with a classical façade.

In more recent times the estate was owned by a rich eccentric called Charles Paget Wade. He lived in a primitive cottage in the grounds while the house was gradually filled up with an extraordinary magpie collection of objects, including musical instruments, clocks, toys, bicycles, weavers' and spinners' tools, and Japanese armour. The house and collection are now in the possession of the National Trust.

Glorious colours in the arboretum at Batsford Park.

19

One of the earliest classical houses in the Cotswolds is Cirencester Park, situated, unusually, on the very edge of the town and separated from it by a high wall and an enormous semi-circular yew hedge. The house was built by Lord Bathurst in 1714–18. It is not open to the public but the enormous 3000-acre park is. This was planned by Lord Bathurst himself with a bit of help from friends like Alexander Pope, the poet. Pope's Seat, a feature of the park, is near the Broad Ride, a 150-foot (46-metre) wide avenue stretching from the house to the village of Sapperton five miles (8 km) away.

Three other Cotswold houses are famous for their lovely gardens. Barnsley House, near Cirencester, was built at the end of the seventeenth century. The garden was laid out about 80 years later and most of the trees planted in 1840. In 1960 it was replanned by Rosemary Verey, a well-known gardening writer and lecturer, and now features spring bulbs, a laburnum avenue, a lime walk, herbaceous and shrub borders and a beautiful knot garden.

In the north Cotswolds, next to the famous National Trust gardens at Hidcote, is Kiftsgate Court. The garden here was made by Mrs J.B.Muir between 1920 and 1950 and is now carried on by her daughter. There are many unusual shrubs and plants, as well as the Rose Filipes Kiftsgate, claimed to be the largest rose in England.

These gardens are relatively intimate and personal compared to that at Sezincote, near Batsford Park. Designed by Humphrey Repton and Thomas Daniell with oriental thoughts in mind, this is more of a picturesque landscape than formal country-house garden. It clothes the side of a fairly steep hill, and surrounds the early nineteenth-century house, whose onion-shaped copper dome also suggests strong oriental influence. This is not surprising since Daniell, the leading expert of his day on Indian architecture, also had a hand in the design of the house, while his client was Sir Charles Cockerell, who had recently returned from India with a fortune made in the service of the East India Company. It is said that the walls, a rich orange colour, were actually stained with dye to enhance the 'Indian' effect. It is also said that the house inspired the Prince Regent to build the Brighton Pavilion after he visited Sezincote in 1807.

20

Above: *The gateway and tall yew hedge separating Cirencester Park from the town.*

A profusion of flowers, shrubs and trees envelopes Kiftsgate Court.

Above: Grey-stoned Barnsley House amidst its spacious gardens.

Sezincote House is dominated by its onion-shaped copper dome.

Above: *Tunnel entrance on the Thames and Severn Canal at Coates.*

Part of the arboretum at Westonbirt.

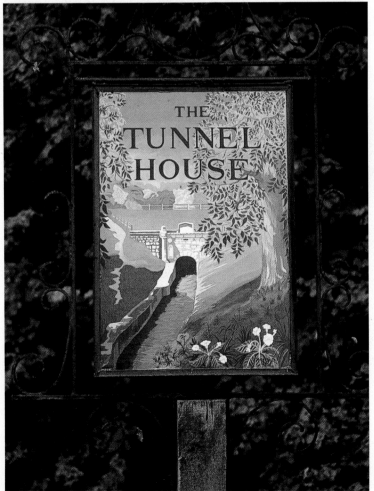

Craftsmanship in building is one of the strongest and certainly one of the most visible traditions in the Cotswolds. William Morris discovered this in the nineteenth century when looking for a holiday retreat from London. The house he found at Kelmscot near Lechlade is a beautiful example of simple, strong Cotswold building with stone roof and gables.

But good building was only one of a number of crafts that survived in the Cotswolds when elsewhere they were slowly being killed off by the Industrial Revolution. Some of Morris's followers in the Arts and Crafts revival sought to make use of the skills of local craftsmen by actually moving their workshops to the Cotswolds. In doing so they put new life back into local crafts. Now all over the Cotswolds there are workshops, some open to the public like the Cotswold Woollen Weavers at Filkins near Lechlade and the Campden Pottery at Chipping Campden, keeping alive the old traditions of craftsmanship which through the centuries have made the Cotswolds what they are today – an example of man and nature working together in complete harmony.

Left: *A pub sign near the tunnel entrance at Coates.*

Above: Morris dancers performing in Charlbury.

The craft of dry-stone walling is still practised in the Cotswolds.

Above: *A relic of the Industrial Revolution: the Bliss tweed mill at Chipping Norton*

Sunlight bathes the manor house at Kelmscot where William Morris lived.